Wilhelm Scherer, Friedrich Max Müller

A Short History of German Literature

Volume 2

Wilhelm Scherer, Friedrich Max Müller

A Short History of German Literature
Volume 2

ISBN/EAN: 9783337205362

Printed in Europe, USA, Canada, Australia, Japan

Cover: Foto ©Thomas Meinert / pixelio.de

More available books at **www.hansebooks.com**

A HISTORY

OF

GERMAN LITERATURE

SCHERER

2

London

HENRY FROWDE

OXFORD UNIVERSITY PRESS WAREHOUSE

AMEN CORNER, E.C.

A HISTORY

OF

GERMAN LITERATURE

BY

W. SCHERER

TRANSLATED FROM THE THIRD GERMAN EDITION

BY

MRS. F. C. CONYBEARE

EDITED BY

F. MAX MÜLLER

VOLUME II.

𝔒𝔵𝔣𝔬𝔯𝔡

AT THE CLARENDON PRESS

1886

CONTENTS OF VOL. II.

CHAPTER XI.

CHAPTER XI.

THE AGE OF FREDERICK THE GREAT.

FREDERICK THE GREAT reigned from 1740 to 1786. When he began to reign Gottsched was the leading German writer; when he died Goethe was preparing for his Italian journey, and was just completing his 'Iphigenie.' This interval of forty-six years is a period of unparalleled literary and æsthetic progress, and though personally the king rather held aloof from the movement, yet his home and foreign policy contributed powerfully to its advancement. Everywhere we find traces of his influence; everywhere men's eyes *Literary progress in Frederick's reign, 1740-1786.* were fixed upon one, who could so stir their minds and stimulate their zeal, who could incite other rulers to follow his example, and awaken even the admiration of his enemies.

The rise of modern German literature is connected with the Seven Years' War, just as the rise of Middle High-German chivalrous poetry was connected with the first Italian campaigns of Frederick Barbarossa. Poets were to be found among the officers of the Prussian king just as among the knightly followers of the old emperor. And though Frederick the Great gathered French writers around him, and had no great confidence in the literary powers of his own people, yet the very annoyance which this caused them was but a new *Frederick's French tastes.* incitement to exert their powers to the utmost, and prove to the King that he was mistaken in his judgment.

A small group of Saxon poets alone remained unaffected either directly or indirectly by Frederick's influence; but these very poets were in point of taste most akin to him, for their culture, like his, was chiefly derived from the French; it owed its characteristic features to that phase of German taste which had been inaugurated under Frederick's grandfather, and which had subsequently diffused

The Leipzig poets.

itself more and more. It was in Prussia that French Classicism first found a sympathetic reception, and Prussians like Wernicke and Gottsched were its most devoted apostles; but it was in Leipzig that it established its head-quarters.

LEIPZIG.

During the Seven Years' War Frederick the Great paid repeated visits to Leipzig, and did not neglect the opportunity of acquainting himself a little with the state of contemporaneous German poetry. He sent for the two Professors, Gottsched and Gellert; the former he received on October 15, 1757, the latter on December 18, 1760.

Relations of Frederick with Gottsched and Gellert.

Gottsched he frequently saw after this; Gellert too received a friendly invitation to come again, but never availed himself of it. Gottsched read him his translation of Racine's 'Iphigénie,' but the king was not much impressed by it. Gellert was made to recite one of his fables, and this gained the Royal favour. 'That is beautiful,' he said to Gellert, 'very beautiful; there is such a lilt about it ('*so was Coulantes*'), I can understand all that; but there was Gottsched now, who read me his translation of " Iphigénie," and though I had the French in my hand at the same time, I could not understand a word. They also brought another poet to me, one Pietsch, but I dismissed him.' 'Your majesty,' answered Gellert, 'him I also dismiss.' We remember that Gottsched declared this very Pietsch, his teacher, to be the greatest poet of the eighteenth century.

When Gellert was gone, Frederick remarked, 'That is quite a different man from Gottsched.' And the next day at table he called him the most sensible among all the German scholars.

Three years before this, the king had written a French poem to Gottsched, in which he eulogized him as the Saxon swan, and assigned to him the task of founding the literary reputation of Germany. Gottsched hastened to have these verses published and translated into several European languages. But when they appeared among the king's collected works, they bore the inscription: '*Au Sieur Gellert.*' The author had meanwhile altered the address.

The German public agreed with their great king in thinking Gellert quite a different man from Gottsched. Even before the end of his life Gottsched was looked upon as a fallen hero, while Gellert is esteemed even in our days. Gottsched aimed at making an impression in high circles, but he only succeeded in making his way into a few small German courts; Gellert sought his readers in the middle-classes, and found them in all ranks of society. Gottsched was only acquainted with the outward tricks of poetry; Gellert was a true poet, though in a narrow sphere.

Gellert preferred to Gottsched.

Gottsched wished to make Leipzig the centre of German literature, and the place could not have been better chosen. Leipzig united the features of a large town with those of a flourishing University. It was the most important commercial emporium of the Saxon-Polish Empire, and the centre of the trade between the Romanic West and the Slavic East. In the eighteenth century it became the centre of the book-trade, ousting Frankfort from the leading position which it had hitherto occupied. Its fairs were the scene of most varied life, collecting, as they did, men of all nationalities, and bringing long caravans of merchants from a great distance. The best troops of actors in Germany always went to the 'Leipziger Messe.' Everyone liked going to 'gallant' Leipzig, as it was called, to Little Paris on the Pleisse, where the whole world was to be found in miniature. As early as the fifteenth century Leipzig was famed for its politeness, and even its students acquired something of its refinement. The rude manners of the smaller University towns were tabooed there, and young aristocrats studied by preference in Leipzig. The town had no court, no local aristocracy, no garrison; but its burghers strove after moral and intellectual culture, and Leipzig was considered the most educated town in Germany. The University, with its hereditary oligarchy of Professors, orthodox and conservative, proud of their vast knowledge, which they were perhaps more intent on transmitting than on increasing, was yet alive to the general interests of culture.

Advantages of Leipzig as a literary centre.

The book-trade drew into its service scholars, both old and young, and was of great advantage to authors on the spot. Nowhere did literary journalism flourish as in Leipzig, and nowhere else was it so easy to become an author as there.

Gottsched knew how to make the best of such a favourable situation, and put forth all his great personal energy and his wonderful power of organization, in order to carry out his own aims. He noticed that French literature was centralised, subjected to fixed rules, and protected, as it were, by an Academy ; this Academy kept guard over the purity of the language, and saw that the rules were followed; it produced a grammar and a dictionary, it taught the right use of synonymous terms, it distributed honours, and decided what was beautiful. Gottsched wished to make Leipzig, in a literary aspect, the German Paris, and to raise the Leipzig ' German Society' to the rank of an *Académie Allemande*; he himself, its senior member, wished to have been the president of the Academy, and to have stood at the head o the German world of letters. Ambition and patriotism pointed to the same goal, and he taxed his energies to the utmost to gain for German literature what the French already possessed.

Gottsched's literary aspirations.

His German Academy.

He was, as we know, a disciple of Wolff. His ' World-Wisdom ' (1734) is a text-book of the Wolffian philosophy. Clearness and intelligibility, the ideals of the Wolffian philosophy and the special attributes of the French mind, were by Gottsched transferred to German language and style. He wrote a German grammar, or ' Art of language,' a book which had the widest influence, and which in many points fixed the rules of language as they have remained to our day. He furnished some teaching on the use of synonyms, and planned a dictionary such as Adelung afterwards carried out; the latter was a scholar of great versatility, but of limited æsthetic culture, like Gottsched himself, and succeeded him as legislator in language..

His ' Welt- weisheit,' and his Grammar.

But good taste and correct style were regarded as even more important than a fixed grammar. Gottsched wrote an ' Art of Rhetoric' and a ' Critical Art of Poetry,' based on classical and French models. Horace and Boileau were to him what Scaliger and Ronsard had been to Opitz. He compiled a small dictionary of *belles-lettres* and liberal arts, a book full of useful information. He wrote many papers and essays on literary history; he tried to survey the whole field of German literature, and till the present century, **His 'Redekunst' and 'Kritische Dichtkunst.'**

till Jacob Grimm and his associates, no one showed such an extensive knowledge of early German literature as Gottsched. He gave his attention both to Old High-German and Middle High-German poetry and prose, wrote papers on Veldecke's Æneid and on Old-German **His study of early German literature.**

morals, and translated 'Reinecke Fuchs' into modern German prose. He devoted some of the articles in his small dictionary to Walther von der Vogelweide and other Minnesingers; he intended to write a history of the German drama, and he gathered together the materials for it and arranged them chronologically. In all these endeavours he was actuated by the same motives of national pride and patriotic emulation which had animated the scholars of the sixteenth and seventeenth centuries; he held up all the treasures of a past literature before the eyes of those who despised the Germans, to show them what his country could achieve.

Gottsched exercised a practical influence by his example and by his teaching; the more so as he was not too proud to take a warm, indeed a supreme interest in contemporary literature. He thought it no dishonour to his professorial chair to try his hand at writing German poems, or for the advancement of German poetry to associate with actors and give them his advice. He succeeded in persuading the Leipzig actors to adopt an improved form of stage, after the French model, and by his own activity, by inciting others to help him, and by **His dramatic reforms.**

numerous translations, he enriched their *répertoire* of plays. He made tragedy his speciality, and only wrote one somewhat clumsy pastoral-play; comedy he left to the lighter talent of his wife, the much-extolled 'clever friend,' Luise Adelgunde Victoria, *née* Kulmus. Other original German writers were not altogether wanting at this time, but their works were almost all indifferent or bad.

Corneille, Racine, and Voltaire now became the presiding geniuses of German tragedy; Molière, Dufresny, and Destouches supplied the audience with merriment, and even the coarser farces of the Danish writer, Holberg, were welcomed on the German stage, since they were the productions of a celebrated scholar.

Gottsched was also an assiduous journalist, and this enabled him to bring all his various literary interests before the world. During thirty-four years of his life he published newspapers, which he skilfully edited, and for the most part wrote himself. His position at the University enabled him to gather young men around him, or to employ them as collaborators. He had numerous translations made, and in so doing he rendered a service not only to literature, but to the cause of general enlightenment. The most important English weekly papers, Bayle's Dictionary, Leibniz's 'Théodicée,' the works of Fontenelle, were through his labours, and through those of his wife and other fellow-workers, rendered accessible to German readers. If we pass in review his work in this direction, his contributions to the history of literature, his strong interest in the Drama, his union of theory and history, of poetical and journalistic activity, and of original work and translation, and if we ask who was his successor in all these respects, as Adelung was in his linguistic labours, the answer cannot be doubtful. Lessing was Gottsched's heir, Lessing, the greatest literary and art critic, the greatest translator, dramatist and dramaturgist in Germany in the period following Gottsched. But Lessing was not only Gottsched's heir, but Gottsched's destroyer. He felt that Gottsched's influence fettered and hindered him, and in order to free himself from it, no means seemed to him too strong, no words too bitter, no judgment too harsh.

His journalism.

Down to the last years of his life Gottsched continued to render real services to the German language and to the history of German literature. But step by step the nation had deserted him, and the authors who would have nothing to do with him became more and more numerous. As a creative poet he had never accomplished anything worthy of notice; his poems are absurd; his dramas are either not original or else quite useless, a miserable patchwork of

Gottsched's decline begins about 1740.

borrowed ideas badly cobbled together, and far removed from that correctness which he was always advocating as all-important. His labours as a literary and art critic lost more and more in importance as German literature grew strong enough to dispense with the French leading-strings, and passed from imitation to original production. His stand-point was the same as that which had been adopted by Canitz, Besser, Neukirch, and Pietsch, and he wished to impose this stand-point permanently on the whole nation. He attacked the Lohensteinian taste as Wernicke had done, and he scented Lohenstein wherever he met with a loftier flight of fancy, a more exalted style of diction, or an unusual figure of speech. His influence was at its height between the years 1730 and 1740, but after that it gradually declined; he still sought to play the dictator, but no one obeyed him except a few insignificant people, who, along with himself, excited general contempt. In the year 1739 he quarrelled with his Academy, the German Society in Leipzig. In the year 1740 his celebrated dispute began with the Zürich scholars, Bodmer and Breitinger, and their adherents. In 1741 the Neuber 'troupe' caricatured him on the Leipzig stage under the name *Gottsched's dispute with Bodmer and Breitinger.*

of 'Fault-finder' ('*Tadler*'). This action was much applauded from Dresden, where Gottsched had never gained any firm footing, and Rost, a former pupil of the dictator's, celebrated the event in a satirical epic. In the year 1744 the most talented Leipzig poets, Gellert, Rabener, and Zachariä, ceased to contribute as hitherto to the 'Belustigungen des Verstandes und Witzes,' a paper conducted by Magister Schwabe, a disciple of Gottsched's, agreeably to his master's views and in the interest of his party, and started on their own account a paper entitled the 'Bremen Contributions.' In 1748 appeared Klopstock's 'Messias,' and the violent attack which Gottsched made on *The 'Bremer Beiträge' started in opposition to Gottsched, 1744.*

him only proved detrimental to his own reputation. In the year 1752 Koch, a theatre-manager at Leipzig, produced on his stage an operetta of English origin, 'Der Teufel ist los.' Gottsched could not tolerate this apparent revival of the German opera, which he hated, and *Gottsched's quarrel with Klopstock and others.*

accordingly he attacked it himself and persuaded others to attack it in pamphlets. Koch answered, speaking from his own stage, and had the laughers on his side. A long literary war now began ; Rost was at once ready with his pen, and wrote in doggrel verses a witty Epistle from the Devil to Gottsched; this he caused to be distributed gratuitously, and also arranged that Gottsched himself, who was just then on a journey to the Palatinate, should have a sealed packet, containing several copies, handed to him at every post-station on his route. Gottsched made a personal complaint to the Minister Brühl, whose secretary Rost was, but the minister had the cruelty to pretend he knew nothing about it; Gottsched had himself to read out the lampoon in Rost's presence, and was then only told, by way of good advice, that it was surely better simply to ignore such practical jokes altogether. After that he took no further active interest in the German stage, and in 1769 Lessing denied that the stage owed anything to his efforts. Six years later, at the time when young Goethe was studying in Leipzig, he could thus report of the quondam dictator, who had just given new offence by a second marriage with a very young girl : ' All Leipzig despises him ; no one associates with him.' Goethe himself, however, paid him a visit, of which, in later years, he gave a most amusing description. The former and the future leader of German literature, whose lives together embrace the years from 1700 to 1832, did thus once meet and converse together.

At the time when Goethe was in Leipzig, Gellert set the literary tone in the University, where he was professor extra-ordinarius. Though he was of sickly appearance and lectured in a hollow and whining tone, still he gathered a large circle of listeners around him, whom he exhorted alike to purity of morals and purity of style. His authority was great both in Protestant and in Catholic Germany, and he had correspondents, male and female, both among the aristocracy and the middle-classes. The soldiers of Frederick the Great, as well as their Austrian opponents, did him homage. As Melanchthon may be said to have founded the German school-system, so Gellert may be said to have fashioned German taste. Men came to him for literary as for moral advice; he was consulted about tutors and governesses, and

Gellert's influence.

his advice was sought in the choice of wives or husbands. 'To believe in Gellert,' said a later critic, 'is among our people almost the same thing as believing in virtue and religion.' But the general confidence which he enjoyed as a man and a teacher was due really to his extraordinary popularity as a writer.

Gellert tried his hand in many branches of literature. He wrote pastoral plays, well meant but crude in style, comedies, awkwardly composed, yet giving a faithful reflection of German middle-class life, and a novel which rambles through distant lands, and piles up extraordinary phenomena of the moral world in a somewhat repulsive manner. All these *His plays and lectures.* works had a certain success; his manual of epistolary style too was well received by the public, and his 'Moral Lectures,' published after his death, seem to have found readers to appreciate them, in spite of what we should consider their commonplaces. But his fame really rested on his poetic fables and tales, which appeared in a collected edition in the years 1746 and 1748, almost at the same time as the first cantos of Klopstock's 'Messias,' and his religious odes and hymns, which were published in 1757.

Gellert's poetic fables and tales belong to the same school as the writings of Hagedorn and his models. They set out with the purpose of 'telling the truth in a figure to those who have not much understanding.' They were meant accordingly to be popular and didactic, simple *Gellert's Fables, 1746 and 1748.* and useful. 'Where hast thou learnt to write thus?' said Frederick the Great to Gellert. 'In the school of Nature,' answered the poet. 'Thou hast imitated Lafontaine?' 'No, your Majesty, I am an original writer.' Still, we cannot speak of Gellert without being reminded of Lafontaine, though at the same time we cannot give to the German poet the unqualified praise lavished by French critics on their great fable-writer. The bourgeois-literature of the sixteenth century was continued in Gellert, and he formed a just and appreciative judgment of the older German fable-poetry. He himself wrote more tales than genuine fables; his heroes are more often men than animals, and the types of character which he brings before us have no symbolical and general value, but are only true in their particular context. They are not types of humanity as it

exists in all ages, but are the men of that particular age, described
by a poet who formed his style on Lafontaine, and who tells, in a
natural and artistic manner, stories full of the charm of innocence
and cheerfulness. His versification is free and flowing, and his
rhymes so unaffected that they seem almost to come in by chance.
His easy and flexible style seems to be but an idealised form of the
conversational language of every-day life; sometimes,
His style. however, he is almost too simple and transparent, and
draws in coarse outlines as though for childish minds, while in
genuine descriptive power he falls far short of Lafontaine. As it
happened, Gellert's readers were really as childish as he reckoned
on their being: they delighted in having everything clearly brought
before them, they expected to find in poetry a better world than that
in which they lived, and were well pleased to see the good rewarded,
the bad punished, and the hypocrite unmasked and disgraced.
One thing Gellert learnt from the French and introduced once
more into German art, namely grace, the most subtle secret of
poetic charm. Gellert, like Hagedorn, devoted himself mainly to
satirical pictures of contemporary manners, and derived much of his
material from the English weekly papers. In his lectures he would
sketch out moral characters in the style of Labruyère and Theophrastus, in whose sketches all the leading characteristics of the same
type are accumulated in a single individual. He does not always
borrow his materials from real life, but often from literary tradition.
Thus he described women in the true spirit of the older satire, as
fond of dress, quarrelsome, prudish and yet voluptuous, inconstant,
gossipy, and somewhat selfish, fond of feigning to swoon and of all
kinds of artifices. But what were formerly called vices are now
only weaknesses. Gellert does not despise women, he only teases
them; and with him, these frail, worldly, and imperfect creatures are
almost always pretty and charming; they have grace and that subtle
wit for which the Saxon women were specially famed, and they know
how to converse with roguish *abandon* and charming freedom on
all the tender experiences of the heart.

Gellert's paternal home was a Saxon parsonage, and he had
begun by studying theology. He remained all his life a strictly
religious and scrupulously conscientious man. Still this self-

examining bachelor did his best to be a liberal man of the world, and
to entertain tolerant views of life ; and pious moralist   Gellert's
as he was, was still a disciple of the ' enlightenment '   character.
movement. With all his humility, gentleness, and love of peace, he
was yet ready to do battle for the cause of reason and humanity.
It was part of his creed to make men happy, and not to interfere
with their harmless pleasures.   He declared the flatterer of great
people to be more dangerous than the free-thinker.   He fought
against hypocrisy and intolerance, against religious and class
prejudices; but he only fought with the weapons of temperate
warning, and in his hands men grew up docile and amenable to
reason.   It was not his way to rail at vice directly, but to enlist
men's sympathies and admiration on the side of virtue; and
this he did by depicting the good as beautiful, expedient, and
conducive to happiness, thus winning to the side of a not too
rigorous morality the æsthetic as well as the egoistic impulses of
men.   As utterances in song of the spirit of liberal   Gellert's
religion, Gellert's hymns rank as classics.   Human   hymns.
and general interests preponderate in them.   Their most sacred
aim is to glorify virtue and to inculcate the duties of practical
Christianity.   They are divided by the author himself into didactic
odes, and odes for the heart.   The former are intended to furnish
instruction and food for the understanding, while the latter are meant
to bring home to our feelings all that is sublime and touching in
religion.   But predominance is given throughout to teaching and
reflection, and the heart is appealed to through the intellect.
Gellert had the warmest admiration for the old church-hymns, and
he speaks with reverence of the inimitable language of the Bible,
its divine sublimity and ravishing simplicity.   But he himself had
not the language of the Bible at his command, nor did he profess
that strength of conviction and emotion which alone lends power
to the word.   He took extreme pains to elaborate the form of his
sacred songs, availing himself even of the help of his friends in the
work, but he permitted things notorious for their bad taste to remain in them.   Still, his hymns must not be rejected as a
whole on account of a fault here and there.   No one can listen
without the deepest emotion to those six hymns of his which have

been set to powerful music by Beethoven; and it was Gellert's words which inspired that music.

Gellert died in 1769, at the age of 54; he did not live to see the great literary awakening which took place during the next ten years. Round him clustered a circle of able lite- rary men, some of whom were really distinguished: Gärtner, Rabener, Konrad Arnold Schmid of Lüneburg, the three Schlegels, Cramer, Ebert, Giseke, and Zachariä. Klop- stock too, though less in sympathy with Gellert, belonged to the same group, and in 1747 he celebrated these poets in an ode, entitled 'An meine Freunde,' which he later on changed to 'Wingolf.' The members of this circle were mostly natives of Upper Saxony, or of some part of central Germany, and had received a thorough classical training at the Saxon princely schools; they all studied in Leipzig, and mostly devoted them- selves to the clerical or the teaching profession. Their literary organ for four years (1744–48) was the 'Neue Beiträge zum Vergnügen des Verstandes und Witzes,' the so-called 'Bremer Beiträge.' The contributors to this paper mostly followed in Hagedorn's steps; they polished their writings industriously, and attained to great smoothness and correctness in form. They declared from the first that they meant to be cheerful, and to try to afford both pleasing and profitable reading for the boudoir. Thus, besides serious and moral subjects, they sang and told of love and friendship, drinking and dancing, roses and zephyrs. They published religious odes, and Klopstock's 'Messias' first saw the light in their columns; but they also imitated Horace and Anacreon. They tried to draw tender pictures of the feelings, and asserted that 'to enjoy life was the command of Nature.' They hoped that an Athens or at least a Paris would arise in Germany, where good taste in literature would purify the tone of society, and where men would learn to speak and jest more elegantly, and con- verse in a livelier way upon serious topics. Meanwhile their imagination peopled Leipzig with shepherds and shepherdesses full of coquettish *naïveté* and grace; these masques of the Renaissance had not even yet lost their charm, and were adopted as a matter of course in love-poems and love-dramas. The small china figures of

Gellert's disciples.

The 'Bremer Beiträge.'

people in pastoral costume, well-dressed and powdered, richly be-
laced and be-ribboned, and advancing in stately minuet steps, bring
before our eyes, even at this distance of time, the 'painted doll-
ideals,' as Goethe called them, of this class of poetry.

None of the writers in the 'Bremen Contributions' can be compared in fame and influence to Gellert and Klopstock, and but few
of them have any striking individuality.   The learned   Cramer and
Cramer wrote numerous hymns, and sermons full of   Ebert.
solemn rhetoric.   Ebert composed cheerful songs of love and wine,
and translated much from English.   Rabener distinguished himself
in satire, Zachariä in the burlesque epic, Elias Schlegel in the drama,
and these three men exerted a marked influence, although the style
and kind of writing to which they adhered has been superseded in
the maturer poetry of a later epoch.

Rabener was a revenue officer in Leipzig and Dresden. He died
in 1771, at the age of fifty-seven. In choosing the sub-   Rabener,
jects of his satire he found himself limited on every   1714–1771.
side ; public affairs were forbidden by the strict Saxon   His satires.
censorship, and derision of private characters excited the resent-
ment of those who felt themselves hit.   Rabener made a virtue of
necessity.   He declared that a true satirist shrank from the very
thought of offending religion or princes, and protested that the
characters of his fools had no personal application, but only a
general one, for there was not one amongst them which did not
apply indifferently to a dozen actual fools.   Rabener's private
letters contain many remarks on the state of affairs in Saxony,
full of patriotic wrath and asperity.   But there is nothing of this in
his satires ; there he seeks out harmless fools, and arranges a whole
gallery of them, as Sebastian Brand and Thomas Murner, and later
on Johann Lauremberg and Christian Weise had done before him.
Gellert brought the fable of the sixteenth century to a classic perfection, and Rabener, although he always uses prose, seems to
continue the work of the older masters of satire, and is the last
representative of that line of writers. He surpasses the older satirists
in elegance and variety, but he does not come up to them in force.
He was indebted to the English weekly papers and to the writings
of Swift, and is a kindred spirit to Lucian, Cervantes, and the Danish

Holberg. He is inexhaustible in new forms of writing; now
he gives us ironical eulogies, such as the Humanists loved, now he
relates a fairy-story or a dream, now he communicates to us a bit of
a chronicle, a death-list, or a will. Sometimes he chooses the form
of a treatise, sometimes that of a dictionary. Sometimes he uses
parody as his instrument, sometimes he clothes his satire in the
epistolary form, as had been done by the authors of the ' Epistolæ
Obscurorum Virorum.' The modern reader would soon be weary
of him ; his writings, with their mild jokes, were specially calculated for the domestic German middle-classes of his day, and
between them and us a wide chasm intervenes. The art of
delineating individual character does not reach a high level in his
writings, if we measure them by the great models, but it is there,
nevertheless, and Rabener's poems helped beyond a doubt to render
the psychological and moral insight of his contemporaries more
subtle and acute.

In close connection with the satire stands the mock-heroic
The mock- poem, which first appeared under the form of the
heroic poem. animal-epic, then in the fifteenth century chose
peasants as its characters, and finally in the seventeenth century
received its modern form at the hands of Italian writers, who
found imitators in Boileau, Pope, and the German Zachariä. Unimportant events were treated of in the style of the Iliad ; dreams,
oracles, and omens were introduced, and the diffuse narrative was
adorned by long drawn-out similes; human beings were surrounded
by a legion of imaginary gods, protecting spirits and demons, who
fight their battles for them, guide their resolutions, and decide their
fortunes. The contrast between the insignificance of the object
and the grandeur of the apparatus for bringing it about affords
great amusement, while the requisite epic breadth of treatment
leads to detailed descriptions of the interests and manners of daily
Zachariä's life under all circumstances. Zachariä wrote a series
' Renom- of these poems, among which his earliest, ' Der
mist.' Renommist,' is most worthy of notice, for in this
case the youthful poet was intimately acquainted with the sphere
of life which he described, and followed in a path which had
been successfully trodden by various writers since the sixteenth

century. His hero is an old Jena student, Raufbold by name, who comes to Leipzig, where he revels and brawls with old Jena comrades, and even gives the constables a flogging; but he falls so deeply in love with a Leipzig beauty, that for her sake he puts on a more civilised appearance, and has his head treated by a French hairdresser; but he only earns thereby his lady's ridicule, and after a duel with her favourite, a gallant student of Leipzig, in which he is himself worsted, he retires abashed to Halle. The contrast which actually existed, between the roughness of the Jena and Halle men and the refined manners of the Leipzig students, has been very happily turned to account. Gallantry, Fashion, and similar allegorical figures people the necessary Olympus. A few scenes are quite excellent, but the author too often falls back upon mere description. He holds the scale impartially between the gallant and the boor, giving the preference to neither; in fact he contemns and ridicules both, and is as hostile to the French fashion as any satirist of the seventeenth century. We are reminded of Moscherosch as we read of the people 'who are never to be relied on, who forget their promises in treaties as in marriage, and look down with pity on German faithfulness.' In a similar strain, Gottsched's wife, in one of her comedies, wrote against French governesses and the demoralisation which they introduced into German homes. The Gottschedians and the writers for the 'Bremer Beiträge' rivalled each other in patriotic feeling, and, like the novel-writers Lohenstein and Bucholtz before them, they sought for congenial subjects in early German times. Arminius, the liberator from the Romans, and Henry the Fowler, the subduer of the Hungarians, became favourite heroes. They have been celebrated by Elias Schlegel, Cramer, Klopstock, the Gottschedian von Schönaich and others, in epics, dramas, and Pindaric odes.

Among all the Leipzig poets, Elias Schlegel was perhaps the one who excited the greatest expectations, and in many respects he may be considered the forerunner of Lessing. He wrote tragedies and comedies, and passed from imitation of the French to imitation of the Greeks; he compared Shakspeare with Gryphius, and came to the conclusion that the rules of Aristotle were sometimes better observed in English

Elias Schlegel, died 1749.

than in French tragedy. He aimed more and more at establishing
a national literature, and abandoned classical myths for subjects
chosen from German and Northern history. But he died in
Denmark at an early age, in 1749. The advances which he made
in theory did not exercise any direct influence on German literature,
and his literary achievements hardly rose above the level of the
productions of the strict Gottschedians. His comedies are only
French comedies in the German language; in his tragedies the
French *technique* is always apparent, and both his tragedies and
His dramas. his comedies hardly come up to the second-rate
works of French writers. They are utterly de-
ficient in life and in hold upon reality. Their author has never
realised in his own inner experience the characters he seeks to
pourtray. The contrast which he draws in his play entitled
'Hermann.' 'Hermann,' between Germany as the home of virtue,
and Rome as the home of vice, is frigid in the
extreme, as is also his division of the characters into good and
bad, patriotic and unpatriotic.

Elias Schlegel's first dramas were published under Gottsched's
patronage. A few years after their appearance, in January, 1748,
Caroline Neuber, manageress of a Leipzig theatre, Gottsched's
former ally, but now his enemy, produced on her stage a small
Lessing's comedy, entitled 'Der Junge Gelehrte:' it was the
'Junger work of a student, called Lessing, who was then in
Gelehrte,' his third term at Leipzig. The piece received the
first acted applause which it merited, but its author was destined
in 1748. to surpass by far all the hopes which this youthful
effort excited. He soon left Leipzig, and never returned thither,
except for passing visits.

Leipzig still remained for a long time a favourable soil for
the development of dramatic talent. In Leipzig a certain Herr
von Cronegk, an enthusiastic disciple of Gellert's, wrote tragedies,
Christian inculcating the lesson of self-sacrifice, while another
Felix young nobleman, von Brawe, came at the same time
Weisse, under the influence both of Gellert and of Lessing.
1726-1804. Both unfortunately died young. In Leipzig, too,
Christian Felix Weisse laboured with great perseverance, and in

various ways, for the benefit of the stage. He lived from
1726–1804, and was a revenue-officer, like Rabener. He was
a friend of Lessing's, and received a powerful impetus from
Lessing's early writings, but afterwards he remained far behind the great critic, and represents the later Leipzig, when it
had considerably sunk in literary importance. He was a voluminous writer, but destitute of taste and originality, and he never
succeeded in forming a characteristic style of his own. Still he
enjoyed a kind of reputation as a lyric and dramatic poet, a writer
of children's books, and a journalist. From 1759   His
he was editor of the ' Bibliothek der schönen Wissen- journalism.
schaften und freien Künste,' and of its successor, the 'Neue Biblio-
theke,' two very highly esteemed German periodicals. From 1775
to 1782 he published his 'Kinderfreund,' a weekly paper for children, ·
more didactic than imaginative, but outwardly more successful than
any other of the current publications for the young. His dramatic
activity belongs to an earlier period of his life. In tragedy he had
passed through various fashions, while in comedy he had never got
beyond the tastes of about the year 1740. He had   His
achieved his best in operetta; Weisse was the author   dramas
of the text of the operetta, ' The Devil is loose,' which   and
caused Gottsched so much grief (see vol. ii. p. 7).   operettas.

The operetta (*Singspiel*) came over to Germany together with
Shakspeare. In 1741, Herr von Borck, Prussian Am-   The
bassador in London, afterwards a Minister and one Operetta in
of the curators of the Berlin Academy, translated   Germany.
Shakspeare's ' Julius Cæsar,' and in 1743, the English operetta
' The Devil to Pay,' by Coffey. The latter was first performed in
Germany with the English music, under the title ' Der Teufel ist
los;' then, in 1752, it was produced in Weisse's version, with partly
new music by Staudfuss; and finally, in 1766, it was altered, improved and set to new music by Johann Adam Hiller. For about
ten years after this, the Operetta dominated the German stage,
and the most celebrated German operettas of this Operettas
period, such as ' Lottchen am Hofe,' ' Die Liebe auf by Weisse
dem Lande,' ' Die Jagd,' and ' Der Dorfbalbier,' were and Hiller.
the joint work of Weisse and Hiller. Once again Leipzig asserted

her position as a centre of dramatic activity in Germany. Many young Leipzig poets followed Weisse's example, and others in other places vied in copying him. Directors were everywhere eager to get these light pieces, and the public were not tired of paying for them. Weisse mostly turned French operettas into German, freely altering them to suit a German public, and rendering them, on the whole, somewhat coarser. From the French he borrowed his chief theme, namely, rural innocence and simplicity putting to shame the corruption of the upper classes. But the best intentions and the best models were of no good if the music was a failure ; the chief thing in the operetta was the blending of both arts. Weisse was not worth much as a poet, nor Hiller as a musician, but the two together mark an important advance in poetry and music.

The German opera had perished, and German popular song had taken refuge with the lowest classes of the people ; the Italian opera and the Italian *aria* reigned supreme. With Hagedorn's light poetry, however, and the numerous imitations which it called forth, the German song in stanzas rose again into importance as a form of music, and the old connection between poetry and song asserted itself once more. But it was Hiller and Weisse who really founded popular song anew in Germany ; they started those ' songs in the popular tone,' a few of which became real 'people's songs.' Weisse's operettas were prose comedies with songs inserted in them, and these songs soon gained a wide-spread popularity. Weisse was able to hit on the simple and natural style suitable for ballads and slight poems of sentiment and reflec-tion, and these, when set to flowing melodies, found ready acceptance in all classes of society. The cheerful style of poetry, started by Hagedorn, achieved its greatest triumphs in these simple popular songs of Weisse's. The popular tendency, which Opitz had adopted from the old social songs, and which, since the middle of the seventeenth century, had gained so much ground among the scholar-poets, now, thanks to Weisse and the composers who aided him, found its way into secular lyric song, and recom-mended itself to the people in poetry of deeper import and greater artistic value. The Leipzig drama, which had begun with classical

Revival by Weisse and Hiller of German popular song.

tragedies in Alexandrine metre, thus ended by assuming an entirely
popular form; and long after the operetta had lost the great influence which it possessed about 1770, Weisse's harmless songs, often
taken from his operettas, continued to be sung in wide circles.

Gellert's fables, comedies, and pastoral plays, Rabener's satires,
Zachariä's mock-heroic poems, and Weisse's operettas
all belong to the same family, which we may consider   Advance of
Lessing
to have been founded in the seventeenth century by   upon
Christian Weise, Rector of the Gymnasium at Zittau.   Christian
Weise's
All these Saxon poets have a leaning towards satire,   School.
and excel most in innocent and somewhat tame
humour. Middle-class life with its humorous figures on the one
hand, and ideal shepherds or ideal rustics on the other, form the
staple of their poetry. They treat their subjects with an easy
diffuseness, and in a thoroughly natural and commonplace manner.
Goethe speaks of the great water-floods which had gathered round
the German Parnassus, and in the history of German literature
Christian Weise and his school are remembered under the name of
' Water-poets.' In spite of a certain want of historical fairness about
it, this nickname, it must be admitted, is very appropriate to the
general state of literature at the time of Lessing's appearance. Lessing was almost the only writer who emerged from the flood, and
set up in himself a new ideal for his fellow-countrymen to pursue.
Like Pufendorf and Thomasius he left his native Saxon land, and
found in Prussia a more favourable sphere for his efforts, a more
promising basis to build upon. Even there he quickly superseded
his teachers, and found that in the literary traditions there prevalent
there was much to fight against and overthrow, many inveterate
and time-honoured prejudices to root up, in order to pave the way
for the final triumph of a self-dependent German literature.

ZURICH AND BERLIN.

We have already noticed the opposed characteristics of Haller's
and Hagedorn's poetry (see vol. i. pp. 376 seq.). There   Schools of
was no personal opposition between them, and   Haller and
their differences did not exclude mutual appreciation.   Hagedorn.
Haller himself has drawn a just comparison between himself and

Hagedorn, and Hagedorn was undoubtedly influenced by Haller's poetry.   In the same way an author might be, as a rule, subject to Gottsched's or Hagedorn's influence, without being therefore necessarily blind to Haller's merits.   The Saxon, Kästner, who had been educated under Gottsched's influence, tried his skill in didactic poetry after Haller's style, and bore eloquent witness to Haller's greatness. This Kästner was a Professor in Leipzig, and afterwards in Göttingen, a mathematician and an astronomer, known to German literature chiefly as a writer of epigrams.   Gellert too used frequently to adorn his moral lectures with quotations from Haller, and even Frau Gottsched cited him in private letters as her favourite poet.

Nevertheless, Haller and Hagedorn did represent two important and naturally opposed tendencies in poetry and philosophy, views which, not only in the time of these writers, but subsequently, separated whole groups of German poets.   Hamburg and Switzerland were the centres of two different circles of culture, which were gradually extended, now meeting, now intersecting, now hostile to each other, now mingling together, till at last they were both obliterated by new disturbing forces.

Hagedorn's school of poetry had spread to Leipzig, and it was he

Hagedorn's, or the Leipzig school.

who moulded the literature of Lower and Upper Saxony. Haller's literary canons on the other hand were adopted by the Zurich scholars, who developed them theoretically, and through their Prussian colleagues transplanted them to Prussia, to Halle, and to Berlin, while in the South

Haller's, or the Swiss and Berlin school.

they held sway over the whole Allemannic district, that is to say, over Switzerland, Alsace, Swabia, and the Upper Rhine.

Characteristics of the literature of South Germany and Switzerland.

The Allemannic Upper Rhine, the cradle of the Hohenstaufen, had in the twelfth century led German progress, while the Saxons had remained conservative.   Now, in the eighteenth century, we find the Saxons inclined to progress, and the people of the Allemannic districts conservative.   At that earlier period the centre of German intellectual life lay in the South-West; now it had been transferred to the North. But when those Southern provinces, with their traditions of ancient culture, began once more to take an active interest in literature, they presented, in contrast with the international polish of the North, a stronger originality, a greater power of language and a surer instinct for developing the distinctively Germanic tendencies of the modern spirit.

The literature of Hamburg and Leipzig was based on a mingling of English, French, and popular elements; it was thoroughly modern, progressive and open to the latest influences. The Swiss, too, were thoroughly imbued with French culture, and their upper classes were at one time more at home in French than in literary High German; but when they threw off the fetters of French influence, and in their search for freedom turned their glance on England, their attention first fell, as though by elective affinity, on Shakspeare and Milton, who embodied in a supreme degree Germanic power and art.

Contrast between the Leipzig and the Swiss schools.

Gottsched had a thorough acquaintance with the older German literature, but his chief interest was the modern drama in the French style. The South-Germans and Swiss concerned themselves little about an artistic form of drama ; but in Strassburg Schilter, Scherz, and Oberlin rendered great services to the study of the old German literature and language, while, thanks to Swiss scholars, the Minnesang, the Nibelungenlied, and the chivalrous epics were recommended anew to the attention of the public.

In Hamburg and Leipzig the religious life and the æsthetic were carefully separated. Gellert purged his comedies of all allusion to divine things, and biblical phrases, such as the young Goethe brought with him from Frankfort, were tabooed in polite conversation. But with the Leipzig poets, as with Hagedorn, a vein of blithe love-poetry and drinking-songs ran peacefully side by side with religious hymns and prayers in verse. A cheerful view of the world was quite compatible with sincere religion, if each was strictly confined to its own sphere. No doubt Gellert did give offence to some pious souls by his comedy, ' Die Betschwester' (The female devotee), but on the whole, religion and the Church had now lost their undivided sway over men's minds. In the Allemannic

Liberal views of Leipzig, and Puritanism of Switzerland.

provinces, on the contrary, this dominion was as powerful as in the time of the Reformation. The ·University of Strassburg was a stronghold of Prussian orthodoxy ; in Würtemberg, pietism had struck deep root ; the magistrates of Swiss towns exercised a rigid censorship in religious matters, and imposed, whenever they could, the yoke of theology upon science. No doubt, superstition was often mistaken for faith, and honoured as such ; still, great stress was laid on upright living, austere morals, and Puritanic bearing. Wieland declared that the idea of a ball was enough to alarm all the patriots of Zurich, and to call forth, even from the mouths of babes and sucklings, prophecies of the destruction of such a second Nineveh.

Bodmer and Breitinger of Zurich. This spirit of seriousness and often of gloom in matters of religion and morality pervades Haller's poetry, and offers a striking contrast to.the cheerfulness of the Leipzig school. The same spirit animated the literary champions of Zurich, Bodmer, and Breitinger, and led them to consider the religious epic as the highest possible form of poetry.

Bodmer and Breitinger were much of the same age as Gottsched ; Bodmer was born in 1698, Breitinger in 1701. The former was a busy, ambitious, and contentious literary propagandist ; .the latter was a modest, thorough, and original thinker. The former was a historian, a translator, a poet of little talent, but a very voluminous writer, inclined to satire, and continually finding fault with other writers ; the latter was a theologian and a philologist, a scholar of great learning, who exercised important local influence. These two writers were accustomed to have their work and interests in common, and combined to publish a weekly paper ; they also worked together at the development of a scientific theory of art. They both defended the merits of Haller and Milton, and fought against Gottsched's dictatorship in literary taste ; and, like Haller, they both advocated comparative freedom in religion, in opposition to

Bodmer translates Milton's ' Paradise Lost,' 1732. the narrow ecclesiasticism of the Swiss. In the same year in which Gottsched's ' Cato ' and Haller's poems were published, in 1732, there appeared a German prose version by Bodmer of Milton's ' Paradise Lost.' In the preface the translator refers to Addison, to whom was due the credit of having revived the appreciation of Milton in the eighteenth century. He also speaks with reverence of Shak-speare, calling him the English Sophocles, who introduced the metre of Milton, namely, blank verse, into England, and was Milton's model in point of language. Bodmer had from the first the greatest distaste for rhyme, which he considered as a remnant of 'the barbarous poetry of our forefathers.' In this point, as in all others, he thinks Milton's poem a masterpiece of poetic genius, the leading work of modern times, as the Bible was the leading work of ancient times. All his criticisms and æsthetic writings, as also those of his colleague, Breitinger, are inspired by a study of Milton. The most important of these æsthetic papers appeared in 1740: Bodmer's Treatise on the Marvel-lous in Poetry, and Breitinger's Treatise on Similes, and Critical Art of Poetry. Two editions of Gott-sched's 'Kritische Dichtkunst' had been published by that time, in 1730 and 1737, and in this work Gottsched often referred with approval to Bodmer's labours. Nor, indeed, were the stand-points of the two writers so essentially different as one might suppose. Neither attached much value to rhyme, and both attached a very great deal to imaginative power in poetry. But Gottsched studied to attain great clear-ness, and also, as far as his means would allow him, a certain elegance in writing; he made poetry an art to be acquired by systematic instruction, and appealed to the rules of the Greeks as authoritative canons in matters of taste. The Zurich writers, on the con-trary, were more clumsy in form, but showed greater depth of thought; their theory was less systematic, and their aim was not to make a receipt-book for the various classes of poetry, but to discover the fountain-heads of poetic beauty. They did not succeed in their object, and their thoughts may be found also in Gottsched's writings, only more incidentally introduced and not so thoroughly worked out. Both parties were agreed in this: that poetry was an 'imitation,' or, as we should rather say, 'representa-tion,' of nature; that what was new and above the ordinary was alone beautiful and worthy of representation, and that the highest function of poetry was to depict the marvellous. In depicting

(marginal notes:)
Bodmer and Breitinger's critical works.

Points of agreement and difference between the Leipzig and Zurich schools.

the marvellous, however, the poet must not transcend the bounds of probability, and accordingly we find the adherents of the two rival schools divided upon the question of how far the marvellous may be allowed to be probable, and therefore permissible in poetry; whether, for instance, Homer's walking tripods and Milton's devils were admissible or not. Gottsched was inclined to narrow the scope of the imagination; he brought up again the threadbare objections to Homer; he impugned, with Boileau and Voltaire, the æsthetic propriety of the devil, and protested in the name of enlightenment against the supernatural creations of Milton. On such points the Zurich school sharply set him to rights, and hence the feud between them. The quarrel turned chiefly on the merits of Homer and Milton, though many other questions were involved in it; and since in this matter the Swiss scholars represented the more universal taste, since they defended the cause of beauty against narrow dogmatism and pedantry, the victory remained theirs.

Feud between Gottsched and the Zurich writers.

They found their best allies in Halle and Berlin, and in Klopstock Prussia furnished them with the German Milton whose advent they so ardently desired. While the spirit of Enlightenment was reigning supreme, there arose a pure poetic soul, moulded by the sentiments of pietism, who carried away with him the noblest of the nation, and roused the highest religious and poetic enthusiasm for that very Messiah whom Frederick the Great had termed only a Jewish carpenter's son. Frederick the Great granted liberty of conscience and freedom of the press within certain limits. In his reign, church influence lost its power, and philosophy was left comparatively free to carry out its speculations to their logical conclusion. The king was thoroughly in sympathy with the scientific and religious movements of the age. Wolff, the leader of German rationalism, had the greatest influence on his mental development. The disciples of the Wolffian philosophy had already in the last years of Frederick William I begun to gain new ground in Prussia. The Provost Reinbeck in Berlin was a Wolffian. Halle counted among its teachers the two brothers Baumgarten;

Halle and Berlin under Frederick the Great.

of these the elder, Siegmund, was a liberal theologian, who had started with Wolffian views, but was now in complete sympathy with English science, while the younger, Alexander, later on Professor at Frankfort-on-the-Oder, first developed more fully the theory of sensuous perception, and of beauty as perfect sensuous perception, within the system of the Wolffian philosophy, and gave to this theory the name of *Æsthetic*. Under Frederick the Great the philosopher Wolff himself was recalled to his old chair, from which he had been so shamefully banished. Wolff left Marburg and returned to Halle, and his philosophy now promised to dominate the Universities even more than before; but it had to divide its influence with other forces. Among the spirits to whom Frederick rendered enthusiastic homage were Locke, whose views Leibniz had attacked; Newton, Leibniz's rival; the English free-thinkers and deists, who left of Christianity hardly anything but bare generalities; the moral philosopher Shaftesbury, who, as a disciple of the Greeks, taught the identity of the good and the beautiful, of virtue and happiness; the sceptic Bayle, who, in his celebrated Dictionnaire, led the revolt of reason against revealed faith; and, above all, the arch-sceptic, Voltaire, who carried on the work of Bayle, with redoubled force, with inimitable freshness and precision of language, with all the weapons of relentless mockery, and all the cheerful assurance of an imperturbable conviction—Voltaire, who popularised the ideas of Newton, Locke, and Shaftesbury, who taught that God is only known through Nature, and who founded morality on belief in God, at the same time that he assailed all positive religion. It was these spirits who threw the Prussian Wolff, Frederick's early teacher, into the shade, and who for a long time exercised a potent influence on the best minds of the nation. Berlin clergymen of high position, such as Sack and Spalding, sought to modernise Christianity, to explain away the dogmas, to remove, as far as possible, all that could give offence to reason, and to lay chief stress on virtuous conduct. These liberal tendencies were focussed in the Berlin Academy, which had been re-organized by Frederick,

Revival of Wolffian influence.

The brothers Baumgarten.

Liberal tendencies of thought in Frederick's reign.

The Berlin Academy.

and which gathered together distinguished French and German
scholars and men of the world. This Academy counted among
its members natural historians like Maupertuis, mathematicians
like Euler and Lagrange, statisticians like Süssmilch, philosophers
like Merian, Sulzer, Wegelin, Lambert, Prémontval. But the liberal
tendencies which it represented were not pushed so far as to
become subversive of religion; for, in truth, mere scoffing has
always been alien to the German intellect, and has never been
more than a passing fashion, even the bitterest enemies of faith
assailing it seriously and with reverence.

Though many Germans were members of the Berlin Academy,
yet it contributed nothing directly to German literature. Its trans-
actions appeared in French, the language which the king wrote in,
and which was still for the German nobility and for the German
courts the language of the highest culture. 'From my youth up, I
have not read a German book,' said Frederick to Gottsched, 'and
je parle comme un cocher; but now I am an old fellow of forty-six,
Frederick and have no longer time for such things.' Frederick
the Great must be reckoned among the most original and bril-
as a writer. liant writers of the Germany of his day. His poems
and letters are a living picture of a remarkable individuality;
His 'Anti- in his 'Anti-Machiavelli' he set up a new ideal of
Machiavelli,' a prince, full of moral elevation; his historical works
and take a high rank in the historical writings of all
historical nations in all ages. Seldom has such a compre-
works. hensive knowledge of facts in all departments of
politics and government been united with such unflinching love
of truth, with such philosophic grasp, and with a style equally
fascinating, whether he is unfolding the condition of affairs,
appraising men's characters, or relating measures taken in peace or
war. No king ever judged his ancestors so impartially; no statesman ever revealed his motives of action so openly, or acknowledged
His poetry. his faults so freely. As a poet, he most resembles
Horace, and among the Germans, Hagedorn might
be compared with him; but the king is more profound in his reflections than Hagedorn, as we should expect of one who had
wrestled seriously with the great problems of existence, and had led

a life full of responsibilities, successes, and dangers.   When he is
encompassed with perils, as at the beginning of the Seven Years'
War, he imagines himself succumbing to misfortune, and utters the
gloomiest forebodings.   His poems and letters bear witness that
he felt and underwent much that no other man of that   **His**
age did.   He liked calling himself a disciple of Epi- **character.**
curus, but in reality, it was the Stoic view of life which moulded his
character. ' The shield of Zeno,' he would say, ' is for misfortunes;
the wreaths from the garden of Epicurus are for happiness.' It was
from the doctrines of the Stoa that he derived his high sense of
duty and his firm resolution not to survive the misery of his Fatherland.   It was Marcus Aurelius, the Stoic Emperor of Rome, whom
he revered and made his example, and, like him, he was penetrated by the enthusiasm of humanity.   The elevated sentiments of
a genial ruler, of a faithful friend, of a distinguished man who
devoted his best powers to the common weal, the anger and scorn
of the satirist who looked down with contempt from his own
pinnacle of wisdom and lofty resolution on the weaker creatures
below him, who attacked stupidity and egoism, and was least of all
indulgent to his princely colleagues—all these found expression
in Frederick's writings, and caused the nation which produced
him to be held in honour throughout the whole civilised world.
The Germans had a classic in their great King, but unfortunately, a
classic in the French language.   He did not address
himself to his people, but to the nobility and the courts **His writings**
of Europe ; he strove to gain the approval of French　　**all in**
French.
writers, and especially of that Voltaire, whom he
wished to retain at his Court, and who really did remain for a
time, till his vices made it impossible to keep him there any
longer.   But though Frederick's writings cannot be   **Literary**
reckoned as belonging to German literature, except **influence**
through translations, yet the spirit which they breathed **of Frederick**
had a favourable effect on German literature.   As   **the Great.**
Frederick introduced greater latitude in religious matters, so in the
poetry of his reign the secular spirit became more and more predominant ; cheerfulness, unquestioning enjoyment of life, worship
of friendship, and the Horatian delight in rustic life became more

and more strongly marked features in the Prussian poetry of this period. The pride of belonging to such a State and such an army also found poetic expression, and the great warlike achievements of the king soon furnished poetry with a most worthy theme.

Two groups of poets which sprang up among the students of
Schools of Halle show us most clearly the change in the spirit of
poetry the times. Both were opposed to Gottsched and on
in Halle. the side of the two Zurich friends; but while the elder group, formed about 1735, and consisting mainly of Jacob Immanuel Pyra and Samuel Gotthold Lange, was still subject to the influence of Pietism, the younger poets, Gleim, Uz, and Götz, who joined together in Halle about 1740, clearly evidence the liberal tendencies of a new period.

Pyra, who died young, was a worshipper of Milton, and planned
a Biblical epic and Biblical tragedies; he also trans-
The
Pietistic lated the first book of the Æneid, wished to retain the
school. ancient chorus in the drama, and was a strenuous
Pyra and advocate of rhymeless verse. Lange, whose father
Lange. was a Halle Professor, and the chief opponent of
Wolff, was a lyric poet, and chose Horace as his model; still his poems breathe religious fervour, and were meant to imitate the style of the Psalms. Pyra and Lange were the first representatives of that school of poetry in which Klopstock gained such renown; they wished to give a classical setting to Biblical subjects.

Gleim and his friends also adopted a classical form, but for the
most part only the easy, four-footed trochaic verse of
The
Anacreontic Anacreon; and in this metre they, like their Greek
school, prototype, wrote songs of love and wine. The reli-
Gleim, Uz, gious seriousness disappeared in their verse, and the
and Götz. spirit of Epicurus triumphed. Whereas Pyra and Lange approach in the tone of their poetry to Haller, these followers of Anacreon must be classed with Hagedorn and the most cheerful of the Leipzig poets. Their poetry was not burdened with many thoughts; love, wine, and roses are their only themes, and rather narrow ones; still their increasing reiteration led the imagination of these poets to be fertile in small details, and what had originally been simple outpourings of student merriment became

most elegant poetical creations, full of a tender regard for the taste
of the ladies, and emulating the most graceful productions of the
Alexandrian age.   The members of this brotherhood of Anacreontic
poets in Halle were in later life scattered somewhat far apart from
each other.   Gleim became a canon in Halberstadt, and for many
years devoted his energies to helping on young poets ;   **Uz's 'Früh-**
Uz attained to the rank of privy councillor in the   **ling,' 1742 ;**
principality of Ansbach, and Götz ended his days as   **Gleim's**
a ' Superintendent ' in the Palatinate.   Uz's ' Spring '   **'Versuch in**
scherzhaften
appeared in 1742; Gleim's 'Essays in Humorous   **Liedern,'**
Poetry' in 1744, and the translation of Anacreon by   **1744.**
Translation
Uz and Götz in 1746.   These works first brought this   **of Anacreon**
group of poets before the general public.   Gleim was   **by Uz and**
then in Berlin and Potsdam, and was rejoicing to see   **Götz, 1746.**
that the Prussian capital was gradually becoming a rendezvous for
German poets and authors.   Pyra came there as a schoolmaster ; one
of the King's officers, Christian Ewald Kleist, was   **Poets in**
destined to be the classic poet of spring ; Karl Wilhelm   **Berlin.**
Ramler, a teacher at the Cadet-School, evinced a rare sense of outward form in poetry; Professor Sulzer, a true apostle of Bodmer,
defended the æsthetic views of the Zurich scholars ; Swiss youths
like Solomon Gessner and Kaspar Hirzel the physician stayed for
a time in the Prussian capital, and the Court preacher, Sack, took
all aspiring poets under his wing.

Serious endeavours were made to interest the king in German
literature.   Canitz, it is true, had pleased his taste, and   **Frederick's**
he had called him the German Pope ; it seemed as   **contempt**
though it might be possible to convince him that im-   **for German**
portant advances had been made since Canitz, and   **writers.**
that the literary glory, which he too desired for his country, was
really beginning.   Sulzer lost no opportunity in this respect, and
sent conscientious reports on the result of his efforts to Zurich.   But
in 1747 he could not say more than that at least the ladies at court
were beginning to read German works.   It was in vain that Pastor
Lange sang the battles of the second Silesian war, and laid himself
out to gain applause at court; it was in vain that the king's attention was called to Haller's poems ; he refused to read them, though

he thought very highly of Haller as a scholar, and repeatedly tried to win him, first for Berlin and then for Halle.   It was useless even for Sulzer to pay homage to the omnipotent French, in order through them to influence the king.   The Swiss longed to bring under Frederick's notice the gifted young poet Klopstock, author of the 'Messias,' the creator of Biblical epic poetry, who was a true disciple of their own, and at the same time a subject of the great king.   But it was folly to turn to Maupertuis and Voltaire in hopes of achieving this object.   A French translation of the 'Messias' only brought Sulzer into thorough contempt with Maupertuis, and Voltaire roundly declared that a new 'Messias' was quite unnecessary, since no one even read the old one.

Friedrich Gottlieb Klopstock was twenty-four years old, when in

Klopstock, 1724–1803. First three cantos of his 'Messias' published, 1748. 'Messias' finished, 1773. 1748 he published the three first cantos of the 'Messias' in the fourth volume of the 'Bremer Beiträge.'   It was not till 1773 that he brought the great work to an end with the twentieth canto.   Klopstock was born in 1724, and died in 1803; though he thus lived nearly eighty years, yet by his twenty-fourth year he had reached, if not the height of his fame, yet the height of his poetic achievement.   Subsequently he wrote many odes and religious poems, Biblical and national tragedies, propounded an extraordinary system of poetics, and absorbed himself in metrical, grammatical, and orthographical speculations, but in all these later efforts he rarely or never transcended the first three cantos of his 'Messias.'

Klopstock came from Quedlinburg, the scene of Christian

Klopstock's life and character. Scriver's (see vol. i. p. 345) last years of labour, the place where Gottfried Arnold (vol. i. p. 347) had completed his Church history, and where Pietists and Separatists had found a home.   Religious fervour was traditional in his family, as in his birth-place.   His father, a man of strong and courageous character, finding himself once in a company of religious scoffers, is said to have struck his hand on his sword, and exclaimed: 'Gentlemen, if anyone says anything against the good God, I take it as an insult to myself, and challenge him.'   The son inherited the strong self-reliant spirit of his father, and if we compare this spirit with the hesitating and timorous manner of Gellert, we see at once the difference between the Prussian and the Saxon character. Young Klopstock grew up in the country, where he was able to take the hard bodily exercise which his athletic nature demanded. The liberty which he enjoyed in his early youth had great influence in forming his character. He had no special inclination to develop his mind on all sides ; his emotions were very strong, and the most striking feature in his life is the energetic concentration of his powers on one narrow sphere, on one purpose which he conceived in early years, and afterwards unwaveringly adhered to. He remained for ever young, and could never quite get rid of a certain unripeness in his judgments of the world.   He was at school for six years at Pforta, one of the princely institutions in Saxony; thence he went to study at Jena, and afterwards at Leipzig, but could not bring himself to choose any special branch of study. Neither theology nor philosophy had sufficient attractions for him ; he wished merely to be a poet, and Providence happily granted his wish. The King of Denmark, and later on the Margrave of Baden, provided for his outward needs, so that poetry gained him not only the glory he had desired, but also such patrons as he had wished for.

While he was still at school, Breitinger's ' Critical Art of Poetry ' formed his canons of taste, and he became a poet after the notions of the Swiss critics.   Bodmer had written a kind of German literary history in Alexandrines, in which he foretold the advent of the future epic poet of Germany. Klopstock made up his mind to fulfil the prophecy in himself.   When he left school in 1745, he had already conceived the plan of the ' Messias,' **His 'Messias' planned as early as 1745.** and in his farewell speech on the nature and office of the epic poet, he distinctly alludes to the great work which he contemplated. The most sublime theme, and the dearest to a religious mind, the centre of the Christian faith, the sufferings and death, the resurrection and ascension of the Saviour—this was to be the subject of his poem. The epic attempts of the early Christian and of the humanistic poets, the Messiads of the ninth century, the religious plays of the fifteenth and sixteenth centuries, the epic, lyric, and prose treatises of the seventeenth, and the oratorios of the eighteenth century, had prepared the way for him; it was the most popular subject that he could choose, and as yet no poet had exhausted it or brought it once and for all into definite shape, as Milton had the history of the Fall, to the exclusion of all possible rivals on the same ground.   It was the vision of Milton that floated

Klopstock's 'Messias,' suggested by Milton. before the poet's eyes, and indeed he could not have had a better model, for Milton had achieved the highest that could be done for the Biblical tradition. Milton's 'Paradise Lost' stood unrivalled in grandeur of conception and effective development of the theme.   Amid Klopstock's many debts to Milton, the following may be mentioned: the detailed description of hell, the council of the devils, the differences of opinion amongst them, their punishment by metamorphosis, the paths through the universe along which devils and angels wander and fly, and the vision of the Last Judgment at the close of the poem.   But Klopstock did not profit half enough by Milton's

Klopstock's inferiority to Milton. example.   While Milton leads us from hell into paradise, and thus relieves a gloomy scene by a bright one, Klopstock, on the contrary, begins with the glories of heaven, and then keeps us in his irksome limbo of disembodied spirits till we long for a change out of very weariness. Milton exerts himself to the utmost not to let the interest flag, and pays particular attention to unity of composition, steady unfolding of the plot, and graphic narration; Klopstock, on the other hand, lets the thread of his narrative decidedly drag, and accompanies each step of the gradual *dénouement* with the sentiments of all the spectators.   His chief interest lies in the spiritual life of the Messiah, and in the sentiments which that life awakens in the souls of the spectators in heaven, earth, and hell; and since these sentiments would necessarily range over a somewhat narrow scale, Klopstock had to resort to endless repetition of the same few ideas.   The emotional speeches are drawn out to a tedious length, and, instead of letting the characters reveal themselves in action, the author naively sets himself to tell us about them in a way altogether out of keeping with the best traditions of epic poetry.   He relates incidents in such a confused manner that we often do not know what has happened.   The constant resort

to supernatural regions causes a constant change of scene, and angels are constantly appearing to disturb the natural course of events. Such an incident as the scourging is not made nearly so impressive as it might be, because the poet himself is too much overpowered, and can only sing 'with a weeping tone' just where he ought to pourtray with a firm hand; in the critical moment he declares that he is unable to sing all the sufferings of the Eternal Son. When he tries to rise to the sublime, Klopstock becomes stilted and unnatural; his poetry is full of the very faults which Milton condemned, and, however   **Defects of the poem.**
much Milton may have been his model, yet his 'Messias' is more closely related to the religious oratorios than to 'Paradise Lost.' The life of Jesus had touched the hearts and stimulated the reflection of earlier poets than Klopstock, of Otfried and Father Cochem for example. But these earlier poets took care in their works on the subject to keep pure narrative distinct from such alien elements as their own prayers or moral teaching. Even in the Passion-oratorios the epic element was duly kept apart from sentiment and reflection; in Klopstock, on the contrary, narrative and reflection are hopelessly mixed up together to the great prejudice of the former. Klopstock is really a lyric poet, masquerading as a writer of epic. It is a pity that he did not remain a lyric poet, and, like Angelus Silesius, for example, confine himself to a sympathetic commentary upon the sufferings of Christ. As it is, even Father Cochem stands, as a narrator, above Klopstock, for he has done what Klopstock neglected; he has filled in the details of the Saviour's life where the traditional records leave a blank, and has really tried to give his readers a clear idea of places, and a graphic picture of events. Klopstock ought to have tried to realise the state of Palestine as it was in the time of Christ; he ought at least to have read the descriptions of modern travellers; he ought to have studied the people around him in order to pick up some traits wherewith to characterize the Jewish populace of old. But he did not think of anything of the kind. He painted without making any preliminary studies either from life or from books, and evolved everything out of his own unassisted consciousness. For this very reason, however, his poem has certain redeeming

qualities, for he invests his characters with his own nobility of soul, and dignity of language and action; he sends a ray of sympathy even into hell itself, and thus, like the sacred poets of the twelfth century, divests the religious sentiment of its gloomy severity. He lingers over the tender and poetic scenes, and his work in many parts has rather the tone of lyric than of epic poetry.

Klopstock's rhymeless religious odes and also his rhymed hymns
Klopstock's hymns and religious odes. are spoilt by the same excess of sentiment which mars his 'Messias.' His hymns, although set to old and well-known melodies, were written in a style utterly different from that of the old and approved Protestant hymns. Klopstock was bold enough to lay his hands on these, and try to re-write them to suit his own one-sided taste, thus setting an example which was generally followed, of improving these sterling old religious songs. This so-called improvement consisted in banishing terse, picturesque, and popular phrases, and in substituting empty and conventional ones.

Klopstock rendered great services to the development of the
Klopstock's improvements in metre and poetic style. German language and prosody. His own verses he balanced, polished, and elaborated with unwearying care. He was the first to gain a clear idea of the difference in accent between the various syllables in German words, on which difference all imitation of classical metres is based. Following in the steps of Haller, he immensely enriched the poetic vocabulary, but his style was far from popular. The hexameters even of the 'Messias,' the elegiac metre,
Defects of his style. the Horatian or original stanzas, and free rhythms of his odes repelled a public accustomed to Gellert or to Christian Felix Weisse; moreover, in the odes as well as in the 'Messias,' there is a want of solid subject-matter, and everything is vague and impalpable. Klopstock was seldom able to discern the poetry latent in real life; he was under the necessity of first transferring reality to an unreal region, of imagining living men as dead, and those before him as being far away, of transforming the present into a visionary future, before he could begin poetic creation. In his odes, which are imitations of Horace, he sought to carry out the rules of the theorists, who insisted in this class of poetry

upon a headlong style, a wild beauty, intense feeling, striking metaphors, and startling turns and digressions. But this artificial passion and irregularity led to all kinds of obscurity and confusion, and it was quite impossible that such a style should attract the simple reader, who did not bring to it a mind imbued with classical culture. Complete control could not be at once acquired over the unwonted form and the novel diction, so that many stiff and awkward phrases naturally crept in, and few of Klopstock's odes can be enjoyed throughout as pure, finished works of art. Yet they are full of beautiful details, many of which were now introduced into German poetry for the first time, and moreover they consummate that revival of the serious form of lyric poetry which had been begun by Haller and carried on by Pyra and Lange, in marked contrast to the light and popular lyrics produced by Hagedorn and the Anacreontic School (see p. 28).

Klopstock's poetry gave the first impulse to that remarkable outbreak of sentimentality to which modern German literature owes all its fire and inspiration. Klopstock's particular art lies in his power of calling forth emotion. He seeks to express the unutterable feelings *Emotional character of his poetry.* which shake the very foundations of our being, and he succeeds to a certain extent. He not unfrequently introduces physical designations of emotion such as 'shaking,' 'trembling;' he says that his heart beats loud, and that a soft shudder runs through his whole frame. Spiritual conceptions are brought together in wonderfully affecting combinations, and a descriptive rhythm heightens the effect of the whole, which is almost like that produced by music. Still more affecting are often the very words which Klopstock uses; he knew that the mere word by the very charm of its sound will often throw all arts of paraphrase into the shade. Yet he is far from despising paraphrase, and is very happy in his choice of descriptive epithets. The opening lines of some of his odes move us deeply, though the sequel is often disappointing. He can with a few strokes draw the most impressive natural scenes. In these descriptions of nature some particular scene floats before his eyes, and keeps him from wandering into vague and indefinite regions. Among his love-odes too, those are most successful in which he not only wishes to express feeling, but also to describe a situation, an action. Two or three of them are addressed to his lady sleeping, a very favourite motive in the poetry of that time. He is fond of introducing the conventional roses of lyric poetry ; at one time he throws dewy rose-buds into his lady's curls to awaken her, at another he binds her brow with a wreath of roses; in the latter case he writes in a simple style and produces a very charming poem.

We cannot help regretting that Klopstock so seldom touched the **Want of reality in his poetry.** earth in his poetry, and thus threw away his best chances of success. There was one form of writing by which he might have appealed to wider and more popular circles, namely, patriotic songs. In his youth he had been animated by a strong patriotism which, like his religious spirit, he derived from his father, who was enthusiastically devoted to Frederick the Great. The patriotism of young Klopstock found expression in an **Klopstock's 'Kriegslied,' 1749.** excellent 'War Song' written in 1749, in honour of Frederick the Great. This song is full of real life and fire, and is written in the bold metre of the ballad of Chevy Chase, which Klopstock knew through Addison's two essays in the 'Spectator.' It speaks of the Prussian king in terms of enthusiastic admiration. But this enthusiasm was not to last. The **His want of sympathy with his own age.** ardour and ambition of the poet in Klopstock suppressed the patriotism of the citizen. Because Frederick disappointed the hopes which were set on him, because he failed to patronise German poets, and favoured French free-thinkers instead, Klopstock felt himself called upon **His devotion to old German history and mythology.** to avenge German poetry of her king, and religion of her scorner. He accordingly set himself to draw his patriotic inspiration not from the living present, but from the dead past. The 'War-Song' was dedicated afresh, this time to Henry the Fowler, and Arminius, chief of the Cheruski, was celebrated in odes and dramas. By such methods the German Muse was to be schooled to independence. Nor was this all. Imitation of the ancient writers was to cease ; the Northern gods, whom no one knew, whose names Klopstock himself was only just learning to pronounce, and which he had to explain to his reader in notes, were to take the place of the well-known figures of ancient mythology. The battle-cry of the old Teutons, the *barditus* mentioned by Tacitus, was supposed by Klopstock to refer to battle-songs sung by bards; he knew of such bards from Celtic poetry, and supposed that they were also to be found among the early Germans. Accordingly, he gave to his dramas, founded on early German history, the sounding title of 'Bardiete.' The Ode 'Her- Klopstock's mann und Thusnelda,' written in 1752, is one of 'Bardiete.' his happiest inspirations, showing, as it does, powerful situations and action revealed in the speeches; the whole is a kind of ballad in dialogue-form, full of incident and character-drawing. But his three *Bardiete*, 'Hermann's Schlacht,' 'Hermann und die Prinzen,' and 'Hermann's Tod,' completed in 1769, 1784, and 1787 respectively, were quite useless as plays for acting, and the first of them alone contained a few really poetic incidents.

Though many of Klopstock's literary experiments may seem to us very strange, yet they all give expression to some Klopstock's wide-spread tendency of the age, and in most of them influence he found imitators. In his worship of Hermann he on other was the connecting link between the friends of his writers. youth at Leipzig, and the poets of the war of Liberation. His classical Odes found imitators in Giseke, Ramler, Götz, and many of his younger contemporaries. Goethe learnt from him the use of free unrhymed rhythms. His biblical epic found successors chiefly in Zurich, where the idea had really originated.

The Swiss critics and their partisans greeted Klopstock with enthusiasm, and quickly made him famous. Bodmer Klopstock had some time before published the outline for an and Bodmer. epic on 'Noah,' and he now set to work to develop it; he also turned several other Bible stories in rapid succession into bad hexameters. In the summer of 1750, Klopstock, at Bodmer's invitation, came to Zurich. A short time before he had made the acquaintance of the Anacreontic poet Gleim, who had rejoiced to find in him not a Homer with a prophet's mien, but a man 'like one of us.' Bodmer, on the contrary, expected at least a divine youth, who would think of nothing but his great work, and who in intercourse with worthy men would strive to become more and more worthy of his task. But Klopstock kept with the young people, went much into society, drank and smoked, kissed girls and women whom he saw for the first time, worked very little at the 'Messias,' and took no interest in 'Noah.' Klopstock was just fresh from the gallantry of Leipzig and the pleasures of student-life; he was no stranger to the Anacreontic mood; he sang the praises of wine, and declared in one of his Odes that a single glance, a sigh, an inspiring kiss was worth more than a hundred cantos with all their long immortality. Such a frank determination to enjoy life was all very well in North Germany and among poets of the Hagedorn school, but it shocked the Swiss puritans, even when exhibited by the poet of the 'Messias.' Bodmer was soon awakened from his illusion, and a rupture between him and Klopstock was only just avoided. Klopstock went to Kopenhagen, and other poets took up their abode by the Lake of Zurich, about which he had written so many beautiful lines.

In the summer of 1752 Ewald von Kleist, the poet of spring, came to Zurich as Prussian recruiting-officer; Solomon Gessner published there his first literary efforts; and Bodmer soon thought he had found in young Wieland all that he had missed in Klopstock.

Other poets at Zurich. Kleist, Gessner, Wieland.

Kleist's 'Spring' had appeared in 1749, a year after the first cantos of the 'Messias;' it describes, through the medium of a country walk, field, wood, lake, island, cultivated shores, rain, and sun, and the labour and homes of the peasants. It extends over four hundred and sixty hexameters, each hexameter having an extra syllable at the beginning. The description is rather too detailed; still it is not dull, but written throughout in an exalted style, and combined with much praise of the Deity. Kleist's 'Frühling' was one of the poems which this period of the dawn of modern literary glory was most proud of. It was a new variation of that old yearning of the townsman for simpler conditions of life, to which Horace, and, following in his steps, Fischart and Opitz had given expression. It was a new essay in the way of a poetic description of Nature, less in the diffuse style of Brockes than in the more concise manner of Haller. It was cer-

Kleist's 'Frühling,' 1749.

tainly influenced by Thomson's celebrated poem on the ' Seasons,' which was then being translated by Brockes, and which ;still lives on in Germany in the selection of it set to music by Haydn.

Kleist's descriptive poetry was entirely after the heart of the Zurich critics, and the idyllic elements of his poem *Influence of Swiss* could nowhere reckon on a warmer welcome than in *of Swiss* Switzerland. Haller had found pure, uncorrupted *scenery on* nature in the shepherds of the Alps. Bodmer, charmed *Kleist and others.* by the idyllic beauty of Milton's ' Paradise,' had sought the same in the patriarchs of the Old Testament, and some of the characters in his biblical epics were esteemed very highly by his friends for their unaffected simplicity. Solomon Gessner, of Zurich, a bookseller, poet, and landscape-painter, acquired the art of poetic landscape-painting in part from his friend Kleist, and gained Europpean renown as an elegant imitator of Theocritus by *Gessner's* his prose-idylls, published in 1756. Gessner's shep- *idylls, 1756.* herds are honest rustics with Greek names, such as appeared in the pastoral-plays performed at Leipzig; in small carefully finished pictures he described a golden age of generosity, virtue, and innocence, and his primitive sons of Nature are remarkable for their tender sentiment and elegance of speech. It is true that we find in these idylls few touches of true unadulterated Swiss scenery; still we may suppose that love of it, and feeling for its striking contrasts, helped to mould the taste of both Haller and Gessner. For was not Rousseau also a Swiss, and did not he also call upon men to abandon the fictions of civilisation, of arts and sciences, and to return to Nature? In his ' Devin de Village,' a dramatised villagestory, Rousseau gave an idyllic turn to the French operetta, and in his ' Nouvelle Héloise' he described the grandeur of the Alps in impressive language, that reminds us strongly of Haller.

In France, as in Germany, the Swiss nature showed itself to be emotional and enthusiastic, and was in conse- *Opposition* quence opposed to the cold logic of modern ration- *between the* alism. The intellectual opposition which was so *rationalistic and the* marked between Voltaire and Rousseau, was antici- *sentimental* pated in Germany, where it afterwards exercised *school.* such a strong influence. Haller, Bodmer, and Klopstock, took up a hostile attitude towards Voltaire, while Gottsched translated him, flattered him, and sought to make use of him for his own purposes. And though it did not at first follow that the enemies of Voltaire were necessarily friends of Rousseau, though an orthodox Bernese aristocrat like Haller could only see in the Theist democrat of Geneva a madman or a criminal, yet the sentimental school both in Switzerland and in Germany soon attracted to itself younger men, who did not recoil from Rousseau's levelling conclusions.

Pietism and rationalism, enthusiasm and frivolity, the straitlaced and the pleasure-seeking life, Haller and Hagedorn, Klopstock and Voltaire, strove together for mastery over the soul of a young

Christoph Martin Wieland, 1733–1813.
Swabian in this period—Christoph Martin Wieland. Wieland learnt to write in a brilliant and imaginative way in the school of dreamy enthusiasm, but he finally threw himself into the arms of enlightenment and became one of the greatest German epic poets. He was nine years younger than Klopstock, and was the son of a clergyman in the Swabian village of Oberholzheim, four hours from the town of Biberach. His father, a Pietist of the Halle school, was his instructor from his third year, and sent him in 1747 to Kloster-bergen, a college near Magdeburg, in which rigid Pietism was the rule. There his emotional nature was subjected to the prescribed course of contemplation, repentance, and ecstacy, not, however,

Pietistic and sentimental phase in his youth.
without experiencing an early and vehement attack of doubt. As early as his fifteenth year he was tossed about between the opposing views of the age. In his seventeenth year his newly-awakened religious enthusiasm found an earthly object to concentrate itself upon, in Sophie Gutermann, a young relative, whom he translated to the region of the Klopstockian angels, and glorified in prose and verse. While he was still at the University, his marvellous ease in writing began to show itself, as well as his extraordinary capacity for absorbing knowledge and his facility in reproducing it under a new form. Wieland was both a didactic and an epic poet; precept and narrative, philosophizing and story-telling, were what his literary talent was inclined to throughout his life. Like Haller or Hagedorn, he sang of a perfect world; he joined with Kleist and

Thomson in the praise of Spring, and Hermann and Thusnelda were destined to be his heroes as well as Klopstock's. A hymn of praise to Love, moralizing letters, and an 'Anti-Ovid' were committed in rapid succession to paper by young Wieland, and he also produced short tales in blank verse, such His early writings. as Bodmer copied from Thomson. The subjects for some of these tales were borrowed from the English weekly papers, such as the 'Spectator' and the 'Guardian;' their style reminds us of Gellert, while their great sentimentality, their psychological analysis and sympathetic description betray the influence of Thomson and Klopstock. Wieland delighted in the idyllic form of poetry, and considered innocence the subject most worthy of poetic treatment. The lofty idealism of his poems reminds us of Klopstock, but Wieland's writing is free from the harshness, obscurities, and exaggerations which disfigure Klopstock's poetry.

In August, 1751, Wieland sent his heroic poem 'Hermann' anonymously to Bodmer, to receive his judgment on it; this gave rise to a correspondence which led to an Wieland at Zurich. invitation to Zurich. There he at first lived with Bodmer, and wrote at the same table with him; he satisfied Bodmer's passion for biblical epics by the production of a poem on the trial of Abraham; he openly attacked the Anacreontic poets, denouncing them as corruptors of morals; he found great delight in holding intercourse with Breitinger and other old gentlemen, he drank water and did not smoke like Klopstock, and, in short, lived for a time thoroughly after Bodmer's own heart. Then he accepted an appointment as private tutor, and, being removed from the direct influence of his Mentor, he became gradually more and more estranged from him, so that the honest Bodmer had at last to lament a new and much more bitter disillusioning than he had suffered a short time before in the case of Klopstock. Nor was our young poet without his sorrows; his Sophie, who had inspired his earliest poetic efforts, whom he had sung of as Doris and pourtrayed as Thusnelda, jilted him and gave her hand to a certain Herr von La Roche. But Wieland's impressionable mind soon recovered its equanimity; he declared that his love for her had always been a Platonic love, that her marriage need not make the slightest difference in his affection, and thus the thread of old acquaintance was not snapt. But his poetry now assumed more and more the tone of extravagant Christian enthusi-

Religious enthusiasm in his writings. asm. His letters from the dead to friends left behind, the idea of which he borrowed from an English writer, show clearly to what an extent Heaven must draw upon the delights of earth in order to become beautiful and attractive. Simple, spiritual religion is as much lacking here as in Klopstock's religious poems; but Wieland could describe in a more graphic and picturesque manner than Klopstock, and in his wealth and colour of diction he is hardly surpassed by any other German poet. We seem to hear the voice of Goethe in some of his verses—for instance, in the following: 'Thou weavest deftly a halo of truth around thy cherished error.' Wieland could not dispense with the society of women, and even in puritanical Zurich there were a few fair souls in whom his religious enthusiasm awakened an answering chord, and whom he transfigured in several of his religious writings. But by the year 1754 he had begun to run his thoughts and

Influence of Greek on Wieland's writings. fancies into Greek moulds. Shaftesbury directed him to Plato and Xenophon; this gave rise to a Socratic dialogue, and he also commenced discourses on beauty and love. Greek influence combined with the great historical events of the age and with the entanglements of his susceptible heart to bring him back to earth. One of his Platonic friendships carried him too far; the tender-hearted enthusiast suddenly felt himself a human lover, and had to be checked and rebuffed. 'Araspes and Panthea,' an episode taken from Xenophon's

His 'Araspes und Panthea.' Cyrus-Romance, is the poetic memorial of this affair, and the idea which here appears for the first time runs through the whole of Wieland's subsequent literary activity: the transition from spiritual enthusiasm to earthly passion. Xenophon's hero was also to become his own. When at the beginning of the Seven Years' War all eyes were directed towards the King of Prussia, Wieland began an epic

His 'Cyrus.' entitled 'Cyrus;' Cyrus was only Frederick the Great in Persian disguise, and the epic was undertaken in the hopes that it would bring him some appointment in Prussia, either a place in the Academy or the Directorship of some school. Bodmer corresponded with Sulzer on the subject, but Wieland's hope in this direction was destined to be disappointed, like many others.

In June, 1759, Wieland went to Berne, where he was fortunate enough to fall into varied and stimulating society, and where he gained the undeserved love of a noble and highly intellectual girl, Julia Bondeli by name. At the end of May, 1760, he returned to his native Biberach, where he was given a small legal appointment, and hastened to break his faith with the excellent Bernese girl, and to fall into the meshes of a common coquette. He compromised his honour in one more love-affair after that, and then brought the history of his loves to a close by marrying the daughter of an Augsburg tradesman, a worthy but insignificant girl. The weak, fantastic, susceptible, and fickle youth became henceforth a model husband and father.

Wieland goes to Berne, 1759.

Meanwhile, as a writer, he had entirely freed himself from the old fit of extravagant enthusiasm, and passed into the opposite extreme, into frivolity. 'Don Sylvio von Rosalva' (1764) and the 'Humorous Tales' (1766) bear eloquent witness to this change. The castle of Warthausen, distant an hour from Biberach, had since 1761 been the residence of Count Stadion, an old man of much culture, and with a thorough knowledge of the world; he was the patron of Herr von La Roche and his wife, Wieland's youthful love, who both lived with him. Nothing was more natural than that Wieland should have frequent intercourse with them, and that the tone of the cultivated world, which, under French influence, and especially since the Regency, had taken a perceptibly frivolous turn, should affect him too, and according to his usual tendency incite him at once to literary production. Wieland, who in his youth had so vehemently attacked the Anacreontic school, now became himself an Epicurean; he, who had been a disciple of Bodmer, began to follow in the footsteps of Voltaire and the younger Crébillon, and gave himself up to the poetry of humour and innuendo. But in so doing he won over to the cause of national literature the German aristocracy, who found

Wieland gives up sentimentalism. 'Don Sylvio von Rosalva,' 1764; 'Komische Erzäh- lungen,' 1766.

a further attraction in his flexible, eloquent, and finished style
of writing, which had much to offer beyond the jests and mockery
of the French style.   This transition from extravagant enthusiasm
to nature, also turned his attention to Shakspeare, the master of

His translation of Shakspeare, 1762-1766. naturalness and truth of delineation.   Between the
years 1762 and 1766 he translated either the whole or
parts of twenty-two of the plays.   The golden age of
Athens, the epoch of Socrates, Pericles, Xenophon, and
Plato, became henceforth the ideal region which took
the place in his imagination of those paradisaic fields of the blessed,
where his muse had wandered in his earlier years.   Now he
sought, instead of an imaginary innocence, plain, unvarnished
human nature, men such as he himself was, full of kindness, and
with susceptible hearts.   Around these he wove the history of his

Wieland's novels. 'Agathon,' 1766-67. own experiences in love and life, and the 'Story of
Agathon' (1766-67) is really the story of himself.   In
this book he conducts us to Delphi, Athens, Smyrna,
Syracuse, and Tarentum; the 'Ion' of Euripides supplied a few incidents for the history of the hero's youth; we follow
his inward development from childhood to mature manhood, and
trace in his love-experiences and in his public career a gradual
reaction from the extravagant enthusiasm and Quixotism of his
early youth.   While he was in Zurich Wieland had been a rapturous
admirer of Richardson's novels; he joined with Gellert and many
others in admiring the faultless heroes set before the world by this
novelist, Pamela and Clarissa and Grandison, and he even took the
materials for a drama from one of these stories.   But in England
Fielding had headed a reaction against heroic untruth, while in
Germany Musäus had written a parody on Grandison; and
Wieland now became a follower of Fielding and fell in with the
principles of Shaftesbury, who declared perfect characters in the
epic and the drama to be simply monstrous.   Still Wieland's characters are not of the solid motley texture that belongs to real men,
but are thin impersonations of the opposed stages of morality
through which Wieland had himself passed.   These one-sided
ideals are set forth by his heroes in long dialogues, so that his novels
became at the same time philosophical disquisitions.   Even in the

charming poetic narrative 'Musarion,' where a misanthropic Athe-
nian philosopher is converted to pleasure and unre-   'Musarion.'
strained enjoyment of life, we notice a didactic *arrière-*
pensée, and the very title of the book recommends it as a philosophy of
the graces.   In another book, half novel, half history, he chose the
cynic Diogenes as his hero, and most inappropriately grafted an
Anacreontic element on the stern old philosopher.   'Die
The 'Abderites,' on the contrary, begun in 1774,   Abderiten.'
must be reckoned among the best things that he ever wrote ; it is a
satirical romance, in which contemporary German events and incidents from Wieland's own life are pourtrayed and ridiculed,
under a Greek mask.   In the light and playful   'Die
'Graces,' in which, as in the old pastoral romance and   Grazien.'
in many modern French epistles, verse alternates with prose,
Wieland directed his steps back to the Arcadian regions which
he had forsaken, but it was only because the happy mood of the
idyll, the rosy dream of innocence and simplicity seemed the
proper medium in which to set delicate mythological beings such
as the Graces. Wieland, we see, rose from Greek men to the
eternally fair ideals of Greek art, to the gods and heroes.   And
though in his youth he had made a miserable failure in Christian
tragedies, such as 'Lady Jane Grey' and 'Clementine von Poretta,'
yet he now determined to try his hand once more at dramatic
writing.   This time he resolved to choose some pre-Christian
legend and to employ the fashionable form of the operetta.
Accordingly in 1773 he entered the lists against   Operettas of
Euripides with another 'Alcestis,' and in 'The   'Alcestis'
Choice of Hercules' gave a rhythmical version in a   and
few scenes of Xenophon's well-known story. Though   'Hercules.'
these pieces had no lasting success, and though the former of
them excited the angry scorn of young Goethe, yet they were
not without effect on the further development of German poetry,
and on Goethe in particular, for the 'Alcestis' suggested his
'Iphigenie,' while his 'Faust' seems to echo some of the tones
struck in the 'Hercules.'

Wieland's versatility is apparent in every epoch of his life, till age
began to lay its fetters on him.   Parallel with his Greek current

there runs a strong romantic one in 'Idris' (1768), and 'The New

'Idris'
(1768),
and 'Der
neue
Amadis'
(1771).

Amadis' (1771), for which Ariosto and Hamilton supplied him with models. His remarkable epic talent
was not content with prose or with the easy versification of Gellert, or with original metres; he wished to
try his skill in all forms, and therefore adopted the
Italian stanza in order to add the charm of its inter-
laced rhymes to his highly coloured and sensuous style of description.
And again, with his popular philosophic propensities Wieland could
not resist the temptation of turning his attention to political
questions; already in 'Agathon' he had introduced his hero into
the field of political activity, and he himself had a share in the
administration of a small state, extremely small it is true, with its
little intrigues and rivalries, and its storms in a tea-cup. No sooner
had Haller in his novel 'Usong' made use of an oriental garb in

'Der Goldene
Spiegel'
(1772), and
'Der
Danishmend'
(1775).

which to clothe political thoughts, than Wieland
followed his example in 'The Golden Mirror' (1772)
and its sequel 'The Danishmend' (1775). In these
works the idea which had inspired his 'Cyrus' revived
again; as in the earlier work Frederick the Great was
to be his hero, so now the enlightened despotism of
the eighteenth century floated before his eyes as the best possible
constitution, and Frederick's imitator, Joseph II, as its most happy
representative. But this time his high conception of the princely
calling really brought him into contact with a princely house; after

Wieland
called
to Weimar.

having been made in 1769 Professor of philosophy and
literature at Erfurt, he was called in 1772 to Weimar
as Hofrath and tutor to the young prince Karl August.
There he was soon allowed to devote himself again exclusively to
literary activity, and he lived in comfortable circumstances till his
death in 1813. At the very commencement of this Weimar period

The
'Teutsche
Merkur,'
started by
Wieland.

he started a quarterly magazine, which for many
years secured him great influence; this was the
'Teutsche Merkur,' in which he used his powers to
promote the cause of enlightenment and pure taste,
and gave expression to that moderate optimism which
had gradually become his view of life. If he did not always find

favour with the younger generation, which in the last quarter of the century began to strike out powerfully in all directions, yet the best of these hot-headed youths soon rallied round him, and he on his part was always ready to welcome true genius with enthusiasm. But his ripest works were still to come (see p. 131); they were not produced until new impulses had awakened in France and Germany a new love for the Middle Ages, so that Wieland could rely on public sympathy and appreciation for his own romantic tendencies.

Wieland had gradually freed himself from the bonds of literary partisanship which had trammeled him as a youth at Zurich. He had entirely outgrown the opposition between Gottsched and Bodmer, between the Leipzig and the Swiss school, and though he was now good friends with the Anacreontic writers, the tender and delicate ladies' poets, yet, as an epic writer, his horizon necessarily extended further than this, while, as an editor, his interests forbade his becoming one-sided in his tendencies. He at- *Wieland* tained somewhat later to that independent standpoint *and* which Lessing took up from the first. Lessing began *Lessing.* as an enemy of Gottsched's, but was not therefore a partisan of Bodmer's ; on the contrary, he proved himself from the first to be an independent critic. He carefully watched Wieland's development, ridiculed his dreamy extravagance, refuted his polemics, annihilated his dramatic efforts, praised his 'Agathon,' and shared his enthusiasm for the Periclean age ; and in German literature he did for the drama what Wieland had done for the epic, he raised it from mere good intentions to real merit.

LESSING.

Gotthold Ephraim Lessing was five years younger than Klop- stock, and four years older than Wieland; he was *Lessing,* born on the 22nd of January, 1729, at Kamenz, in *1729–1781.* Upper-Lusatia. He, too, came of a clergyman's *His early* family, and was brought up in the Lutheran faith; *life.* but he never had anything in common with pietism, and in his poetic language we miss the magic solemnity, the sensuous charm,

the imaginative fire which Klopstock and Wieland acquired in the
school of emotional religion. Lessing received his public-school
training at the princely college of Meissen, matriculated at Leipzig
in the autumn of 1746, at the age of seventeen, and as early as
1747 first came before the public with some short poems and a
comedy. In January, 1748, another comedy of his, the 'Young

His Comedy Scholar,' was, as we already know, brought out on the
'**Der junge** Leipzig stage, where it met with great approval.
Gelehrte,' Unlike the 'eternal youth' Klopstock, Lessing quickly
performed grew to ripe manhood; while Klopstock hardly de-
1748. veloped at all, but obstinately adhered to his first

standpoint, Lessing's life was one of steady progress, and his
Lessing's labours, which were many-sided without being diffuse,
progressive- continually revealed ever fresh capabilities of his rich
ness. nature. He has few points of contact with the writers
for the 'Bremer Beiträge,' of whom Klopstock was one.   These
Saxon poets were, as we have seen, thoroughly moralised writers,
good-natured, self-satisfied, and as correct in their style as in their
religious and political opinions; they lived as peaceable citizens,
without struggles, without conflicts, happy in their mediocrity, and
like quiet settlers cultivated their small field with industry and
understanding.   Lessing, on the contrary, was full of the spirit
of enterprise and, far from being a peaceable nature, was inclined
to assail mediocrity and give no quarter.   It is, therefore, all the
more to his honour that he was never revolutionary in his proceed-
ings; he always started from the existing state of things, took
account of present facts, and with the genuine zeal of reform
aimed only at introducing gradual improvements.   Neither in
poetry nor in science was he a radical innovator; he never lost his
inner balance, nor that rare tact for distinguishing the possible and
the useful, in which a fiery poet's nature is so often deficient.   The
impulse to go forward, however, drove him from place to place, and
he was not comfortably settled till late in life; though adverse circumstances may have had much to do with this, yet it was mainly
the result of his temperament.   He did not like to bind himself, he
easily entered into relations and quickly broke them off, and was
fond of seeking new surroundings and new interests.   He passed

through many varied experiences, many illusions and disappointments, and was like a roaming seafarer, gathering treasures from all
countries, but finding no fixed habitation anywhere.

Lessing's rapid development began early; even the 'Young
Scholar' is a step in his emancipation, for the very   Lessing's
pedantry which he ridicules therein was his own. As   early
a boy he had loved books, quickly ransacking their   emancipa-
contents, and school-life at first strengthened his pro- tion.
pensity towards unprofitable learning. But nature had endowed him
with a cheerful and lively disposition, and with a fund of healthy
mother-wit, which made him turn his pedantic teachers to ridicule,
and soon· revealed to him his own pedantic tendencies.   With
him too the spirit of modern enlightenment breathed life into the
dry bones of scholarship, while mathematics, natural science and
Anacreontic poetry all helped to emancipate him.   The great
city, whose University he entered, widened his horizon and gave
him the wish to become above all a true man, and to learn how
to live his life best.   He aimed at attaining bodily and mental
proficiency, followed his poetic leanings, and sought to develop
himself into a German Molière.   He associated with actors, which
gave great offence to his parents, and finally he left Leipzig to try
his fortunes in Berlin.   The opposition between pedantry and
human feeling plays the same part in his character as the opposition between extravagant sentiment and nature did in Wieland's;
but while Wieland never got beyond this one problem of his life, in
Lessing it was a youthful episode and he soon triumphed over it.

He went to Berlin against the will of his parents, and while they
were fearing the worst for his religion and morals, he   Lessing
was earning a scanty but honourable livelihood by his   goes to
pen, writing reviews, making translations and publish-   Berlin.
ing original works, poems and dramas.   But the apprehensions of
his parents were, it must be confessed, not without foundation; his
orthodoxy was put to the test and succumbed.   In   Becomes
November, 1748, he had come to Berlin, and in 1750,   acquainted
shortly after Voltaire's arrival, he made acquaintance   with
with the great philosopher.   Voltaire employed him   Voltaire.
in making translations, and for a time is said to have invited him

daily to dinner. It was, of course, an enormous advantage for a young beginner like Lessing to be the guest of the greatest writer in Europe, and of the King of Prussia's friend. It opened out to him prospects of instruction, advancement, and patronage, and of course, in the opinion of his parents, of spiritual harm. If Lessing had summed up his views and plans at that time, they would probably have borne a great resemblance to Voltaire's. He wished to become a free author, not to influence literature from the professorial chair, but to be independent of the academic tradition, and, like Voltaire, to rely on the intrinsic power of his pen. Voltaire had written some counsels for a journalist, in which he recommended impartiality in all things; in philosophy he advised respect for greater thinkers, in history he called men's attention to the various grades of civilisation, and laid special stress on the modern periods; in dramatic criticism he required faithful analysis, moderation in judgment, and a comparison with other extant pieces on the same subject. In æsthetic criticism in general he insisted on the method of comparison, a method as valuable, he declared, in such departments of knowledge as in anatomy.

Lessing's method of criticism derived from Voltaire. Lessing conducted his journalism in accordance with these counsels; he did not adhere to any particular party; in philosophy he attached himself, like Voltaire, to the greater of his predecessors, and he scrupulously followed the inductive and comparative method in æsthetic criticism. The interest which he then took in history in general was not continued later, but literary history proved a subject of permanent attraction to him. Lessing did not remain faithful to the physical sciences which Voltaire popularised, and neither tried his skill in the epic nor in the novel; but he shared Voltaire's pre-eminent delight in the drama, and, like Voltaire, proceeded cautiously in the reform of the stage. In their disinclination to positive religion and in their demand for religious toleration they were both of one mind; and Lessing's clear unadorned prose, which fits and follows every *nuance* of thought, might have been acquired from Voltaire, had it not been natural to himself.

For good or evil, Lessing's relation to Voltaire was an important element in his life. Personally he afterwards broke with him

altogether. Lessing received a copy of Voltaire's 'Siècle de
Louis XIV' before publication, and did not keep it   Lessing's
carefully enough from strange eyes; Voltaire suspected quarrel with
him of dishonourable motives in this, and a breach   Voltaire.
ensued, which was productive of much harm to Lessing in later years.
But even without this breach, it was not in Lessing's nature to
resign himself to a foreign influence; mere scoffing at religion exercised no power over his soul, and the weak points in Voltaire were
too apparent to escape such a clever observer as he was. Voltaire
was to him only a lever by which to raise himself to independence.
If Voltaire had learnt from the ancients, Lessing might read them
also; if Voltaire had learnt from the English, Lessing could follow
suit there, and draw from the same source as Haller, Hagedorn,
and Klopstock had done. In Berlin Lessing became not dependent
but free; and, what is more important, he brought about the
literary emancipation of Berlin from Swiss influence. Lessing's
He struck out a new line of criticism, and gathered   influence
round him young writers such as the Jewish merchant   in Berlin.
Moses Mendelssohn, and the bookseller Nicolai, who were his
literary disciples and, like himself, adhered neither to the Swiss
school nor to the Gottschedians, neither raved for Klopstock nor
for Schönaich, and always reserved their own right of judgment.
When, in 1755, he published a collected edition of his works, he
was already a celebrated man, a dreaded critic and an admired
poet. His little Anacreontic poems found great favour as songs,
and the powerful drinking-song where Death appears before him
and he succeeds in deceiving Death, has lived on among German
students to this day. In his poetic fables he imitated the easy,
conversational tone of Gellert. His epigrams borrowed much
from foreign sources, but were seldom without the true epigrammatic ring. In certain fragments of didactic poems he has
the conciseness of Haller without his obscurity. His 'Briefe'
and 'Rettungen' are works of a scholar, in which he uses
his multifarious knowledge to correct old-established errors, to
censure contemporary mediocrity, and defend calumniated worthies of the past, all in a clear and flexible style. But it was
above all as a dramatist that Lessing took the first rank among

his colleagues even early in life. His little comedies were more
Lessing's French than those of Gellert; but by his closer ad-
Dramas. herence to a foreign technique, he became a master of
technique in general. His plays are written with a sure and correct
hand; the purpose in view is always attained, and the plot is
clearly developed and never drags; his scenes are well contrived,
his jokes are good, and his characters, in spite of a lingering con-
ventionality, well drawn. But he did not remain content with light
pieces for the amusement of the public; his idea was to use the
stage as a moral influence, and to prove to his father that he was
not giving up his life to empty aims. In 'Der Freigeist'
'Der
Freigeist,' he places a noble theologian and an honourable free-
'Die thinker side by side, and shows how the latter was
Juden,' and cured of his prejudice against the clergy. In 'Die
'Der
Schatz.' Juden' he attacks the Christian prejudice against these
unhappy people, who were just beginning to breathe
freely under the blessing of Frederick's tolerance, and whose
noblest representatives in Berlin Lessing had learnt to honour and
love. His extensive historical knowledge of the drama among other
nations was of benefit to his own productions; in 'Der Schatz'
(The Treasure) we have a modernised version of a comedy of
'Miss Plautus, and his endeavour to modernise the Greek
Sara legend of Medea resulted in the production of his
Samson.' first tragedy, 'Miss Sara Samson.' This piece brings
before us a fickle lover, who has become unfaithful to his first lady,
and elopes with a second, but does not mean to marry her; his
former mistress pursues him, upbraids him, threatens to kill her
child, and really does kill her rival. These contemptible and
horrible characters are put into English masks, and the play is
written after the model of English plays like Lillo's 'Merchant
of London;' the dialogue is in prose, full of gushing sentiment
which often becomes offensive. This play was the beginning of
middle-class tragedy in Germany, of that *tragédie bourgeoise* against
which Voltaire had raised a warning voice. Under Lessing's
influence it now at once came into fashion, supplanted the Alexandrine tragedy, and began to drive out every other kind of play.
Various causes co-operated to call this new style of drama into life,

such as the wish felt by authors to be true to nature, their conviction that characters drawn from modern middle-class or aristocratic society would appeal more strongly to the hearts of play-
goers than the fates of ancient kings and princes, or the desire to
break with the remote idealism of French classical tragedy, a desire
which in France had already led to the introduction of a ' *comédie
larmoyante*,' i. e. a tragedy with characters drawn from private life
and with a happy ending. But unfortunately these middle-class
plays often degenerate into sensationalism on the one hand, or into
the depths of commonplace on the other.

 ' Miss Sara Samson ' closed an epoch in Lessing's life and in
his poetic activity ; while the plaudits of the public still rang in his
ears he was already filled with higher aspirations. In order to put
himself *en rapport* with a higher style of drama, Lessing
Lessing returned to Leipzig in the autumn of 1755. returns to
There an opportunity offered itself of making a tour Leipzig,
through North Germany to Holland and England in 1755.
company with a young man of property, Winkler by name. But
this tour was soon interrupted by the outbreak of the Seven Years'
War ; Lessing returned in October, 1756, to Leipzig, and at once
became a centre of literary interests there. His old friend Christian
Felix Weisse sought to benefit by his teaching as before ; the young
Von Brawe chose him as his model ; Ewald von Kleist, now
Major, and ordered to Leipzig with his regiment, became his
intimate friend. By Lessing's advice Kleist gave up descriptive
poetry and took to epic or dramatic poetry, as containing
more life and action ; his tragedy ' Seneca,' idylls like Kleist's
his excellent ' Irin,' full of feeling and rich in thought, 'Seneca,'
and a heroic poem from the Greek world entitled ' Cissides
' Cissides and Paches,' bear witness to this change. and Paches.'
The war now fired all hearts ; men felt that a national interest was
at stake, and the conflict with the French and the victory of
Rossbach excited an indescribable enthusiasm. Poets all of a
sudden found great subjects close at hand, and no longer needed to
seek their heroes in a remote past ; and though it was hard on
Bodmer, Sulzer, Lessing, and others, that the hard-pressed king
should at this very time have given a man like Gottsched an

opportunity of publicly glorying in the praise formerly bestowed
on him by Frederick, yet this did not hinder them
Effect of the Seven Years' War on literature. from doing their part in that rise of German literature for which Frederick's deeds were the signal.
Lessing, though a Saxon by birth, was in his heart
on Frederick's side. Another Saxon, Kästner (see p. 20), then
Kästner, Kleist, and Ramler. Professor at Göttingen, glorified the Battle of Rossbach in German and Latin epigrams. Many were
of opinion that Frederick was greater than Cæsar.
Kleist sang the praises of his king and of the Prussian army,
and the patriotic death which he had desired for himself fell to
his lot at the battle of Kunersdorf (1759). Ramler produced
solemn and artistic odes in honour of the glorious war, and
deserved the name of the 'Prussian Horace.' Johann Gottlieb
Willamow attempted to glorify in heavy dithyrambs 'Frederick,
Willamow and Anna Karschin. the hero, the prince, the sage,' and aspired to be
the Prussian Pindar. A Prussian Sappho, too,
according to the exaggerated praises of that time,
appeared in the person of Anna Louisa Karschin, who, owing
to meagre culture and too great indulgence on the part of her
admirers, never got beyond mere rhyming. Many other writers
besides these, cultured and uncultured, a few with a vocation for
poetry, many with none, made their voices loudly heard. Amongst
these Gleim made a decidedly happy hit in his 'Prussian War-
songs by a Grenadier,' which first appeared in 1757 and 1758 in
flying sheets, and were published in a collected form in 1758, with
a preface by Lessing; these poems really mark a new departure in
popular lyric verse.

Lighter poetry had never quite lost touch with the popular song
Gleim's 'Grenadier Songs.' from which it had sprung. In Hagedorn we see the
relation clearly, and Gleim, who belongs to Hagedorn's
school, had in his earlier years written humorous
romances in ballad-form; the Spanish Gongora and the French
Moncrif were his models in these poems, which he really wished to
be disseminated through ballad-singers. Klopstock, in his song on
Frederick the Great, had struck a powerful and popular tone, and
had made use of a celebrated English ballad-metre. It was this

very metre, with lines only rhyming alternately, that Gleim now chose for the descriptions of battle which he put into the mouth of a grenadier, and these War-songs of his were quite as spirited, manly, and rich in action as Klopstock's poem. The artificial obscurity of the classical ode was laid aside, and all digressions and sudden transitions were done away with ; the grenadier-poet renounced all pomp, tinsel, and even decorative epithets, and simply called things by their real names. Though he sometimes becomes too diffuse, and though we meet with harsh and awkward forms of expression in his songs, yet on the whole he gives us happy ideas and striking scenes. Gleim is most successful in his fusion of epic and lyric elements ; he introduces God, or the king, or Frederick's generals as speaking; his tone is now grand, now naive, now comic, and he never forgets that he must speak as being himself a fighter in the battles which he relates. Lessing might well assign a high special literary place to the grenadier-poet, and expressly reckon him as one of the 'people' who were always at least half a century behind modern refinements of language, and therefore opposed to French canons of criticism. The grenadier, Lessing says, reminds us rather of the German 'bards,' the character of whose poems we can divine from those of the old Northern Skalds ; nor does Lessing forget to mention the younger bards of the age of Hohenstaufen, and to cite their style as a parallel to Gleim's. He thus shows his appreciation not only of the value of national and popular poetry, but also of the great epochs of German literature.

With these and such-like reflections, Lessing introduced the Grenadier-Songs to the public, and the impulse thus given was partly beneficial, partly injurious; we soon seem to trace its influence when we see the old Northern poetry and the Minnesingers coming into favour again, and the longing after the Germanic bards feeding itself on the Celtic Ossian. The general applause called forth by Gleim's war-lyrics led to many imitations, expressive rather of local patriotism than of national feeling. The Saxon Anacreontic poet, Christian Felix Weisse, who had no glorious deeds to celebrate, wrote in 1760 his 'Amazon-songs,' without reference to particular battles or to any particular war; by

Imitations of Gleim. Weisse's 'Amazonen-lieder.'

'Amazon' he means a girl who has a soldier-lover, and he thus showed that such popularity as lay within his reach could only be attained by poetry which appealed not to national but merely to private sentiment, a fact which he later on still further attested by the songs of his operettas. The Schleswig-Holstein Anacreontic poet, Heinrich Wilhelm Gerstenberg, published in 1762 'War-songs of a Royal Danish Grenadier.' The Zurich theologian Lavater, a disciple of Bodmer and Breitinger, produced a great but not a lasting effect by his 'Swiss-songs.' And in 1770 an Austrian Cuirassier, in 1778 a Saxon Dragoon followed with limping gait in the steps of the Prussian Grenadier.

Gersten-berg's 'Kriegs-lieder,' and Lavater's 'Schweizer-lieder.'

But these Grenadier-songs also produced another and much wider result. This new form of popular poetry inspired the Germans with a higher esteem for popular poetry in general; Hagedorn and Hoffmanswaldau had already taken an interest, half scholarly, half poetical, in the lyric poetry of foreign nations, and especially in the poetry of uncivilised nations. This interest was kept up in Lessing's circle, as is attested by Kleist's 'Song of a Laplander.' Lessing himself published a couple of beautiful Lithuanian 'Dainos'; he was averse to the very word barbarian, and was glad to prove that there are poets born under every sky, and that strong emotion is not a privilege only of civilized nations. Addison had already directed attention to the English ballad-poetry, and Klopstock, Gleim and others had profited by his example. Bishop Percy's collection of English ballads was, therefore, received with general rapture in Germany, and the sentimental heroic poetry of Celtic origin, which Macpherson sent forth under the name of Ossian, was greeted with enthusiastic applause by a race of poets full of sentiment and warlike sympathies. About the same time part of the Edda was rendered easily accessible in Mallet's 'History of Denmark' and its German translation; and in 1766 Gerstenberg, by his 'Gedicht eines Skalden,' introduced the Northern mythology into German poetry. Klopstock, who had long designated him-

German interest in foreign popular poetry.

English ballads and Macpherson's Ossian.

Scandina-vian poetry.

self and his friends as 'Bards,' followed Gerstenberg's lead, and
began to produce his 'Bardiete.' The Viennese Jesuit Denis,
an admirer of Klopstock, translated Ossian into hexameters, and
wrote some poetry in imitation of him; he and Klopstock were
imitated in their turn, and thus there arose—long after the Seven
Years' War was over, and when there was, in fact, no war going on
anywhere—that vague kind of battle-poetry of which Weisse had
set the example, and which has become so notorious under the
name of the 'Roaring of the Bards' (*Bardengebrüll*).

Lessing looked somewhat coldly on this whole warlike fit which
he himself had helped to induce; at the same time
he had long paid much attention to popular poetry,
and had asked himself whether it would not be possible to atone for Gottsched's sins, and restore the
connection, which Gottsched in his conceit had so wantonly
destroyed, between the regular stage and the old forms of drama
represented by the wandering comedians. He was acquainted with
the popular play of Dr. Faustus, and proposed to make the
magical Doctor a character for the regular stage. He meant to
endow him with a passionate love of truth, but finally to save
him from hell; an angel was to declare at the end of the play:
'God has not given to man the noblest of impulses in order
to make him eternally unhappy.' Lessing began to work out this
plan in his mind about the same time as that of 'Miss Sara
Samson,' and it occupied his attention for a long time; he even
thought of two ways of treating the subject, one of which was
to retain the traditional devil, while the other was to manage without him. In neither direction did he get beyond the mere sketch;
for the time being, the present, the Seven Years' War, laid hold on
his imagination, as it also gave new impulses to his life.

His odes in prose, addressed to Gleim and Kleist, were disguised
eulogies of the Prussian king, with here and there a sarcasm upon
the condition of Saxony. A Spartan war-song, laconic and pruned
of all superfluous ideas, marks a new departure in
Lessing's taste. In the little drama 'Philotas' he draws
in the same laconic way the character of a king's son, who kills
himself for the weal of his fatherland rather than fall as a valuable

Lessing's projected play of Faust.

'Philotas.'

hostage into the hands of the enemy. The same laconic style is
noticeable in the prose-fables which he now published.
Gellert and Gleim had written fables of epic length ;
the Prussian Lichtwer had made the fable the vehicle of his peculiar
humour, and the Swiss Meyer von Knonau had embodied in it close
observation of nature. Lessing's fables displayed none of these
characteristics ; they have just the epigrammatic brevity which pro-
perly belongs to so trifling a branch of didactic poetry. In Lessing's
hands the fable was curtailed of the exaggerated importance which
it had acquired in an age of literary sterility. But Lessing was
able to convey very profound matter in his fables in spite of their
concise style and meagre form ; we catch in them quiet echoes of
the strong emotions of a fiery soul. In these contrasts of true with
false greatness, of real with fictitious merit, in the onslaught made
on pretence, hypocrisy, and fanaticism, we have a reflection of the
views of life, and probably of the life-experiences, of their proud
and self-reliant author; and this is what raises these poems to the
rank of classical masterpieces in their modest sphere. These fables,
and still more an essay attacking the established view of the fable,
are sufficient evidence that Lessing was dissatisfied with current
literary ideals, and filled with the presentiment of a new age and
a new art. But the future of poetry seemed to him to be menaced
by the stirring political events and interests of the time, which
nearly monopolised men's minds and incapacitated them for steady
literary work. Accordingly, in various literary essays, he set himself to divert men's attention to the cause of letters by discouraging
bunglers, by setting those who had talent to work on worthy subjects, and by rendering men's artistic perceptions more acute.
But such an undertaking could at that time be worked from
Berlin alone. Lessing had returned to Berlin in 1758,
and there his 'Literary Letters' began to appear in
1759. Lessing adopted in them the tone of conversational and witty letter-writing ; he wrote with reckless
candour and veracity, calling a bad thing bad without
circumlocution. At an earlier period he had, perhaps with unnecessary vehemence, held up to ridicule an unsuccessful translation of
Horace, and ruined for ever in public opinion the unhappy author,

Side notes: Lessing's Fables. — Lessing at Berlin, 1758. — His 'Litteratur-Briefe.'

Pastor Lange of the older Halle school (see vol. i. p. 429), a *protégé*
of the Swiss school, and a fore-runner of Klopstock. He now set
himself to chastise, though with less severity, the bad taste of a
wider circle of scribblers. He delivered his most cruel   His
judgment on Gottsched, and had a sharp word for   **literary**
French tragedy; he made short work with the bad   **criticisms.**
translators and the prolific literary hacks; he found fault with
Klopstock's odes for being so full of feeling that in reading them
one is not touched at all; he attacked the 'Nordischer Aufseher'
(Northern Observer), a periodical which was issued by the Klopstockian circle in Kopenhagen, and which had asserted that no one
could be an upright man without religion; he sharply rebuked
Wieland for his fanciful extravagance. Yet we must not suppose
that his criticisms were wholly negative; there was no want of
positive suggestions in them. After the first flush of his reforming
ardour had passed off, Lessing, satisfied with the success which had
rewarded his efforts, retired from the field and handed over the
publication to his friends, Mendelssohn and Nicolai, who were soon
joined by Thomas Abbt, a young Swabian by birth, but enthusiastically Prussian in his sentiments; Abbt had received his education
in Halle and at Frankfort-on-the-Oder, and, fired with rapturous
admiration for Frederick and his generals, had written an essay on
'Death for the Fatherland.' The 'Literary Letters' continued to
be published till 1765; meanwhile Lessing had been since 1760 in
Breslau, as secretary of General Tauentzien, whose acquaintance he
had made through Kleist. In Breslau, Lessing gave himself up to
various diversions, and even to the passion of gambling; at the
same time he was carrying on important studies, and was preparing himself for two of his greatest achievements, 'Laokoon'
and 'Minna von Barnhelm,' which he published in 1766 and 1767,
during a third sojourn in Berlin. The one reveals his Hellenic
tendencies, while the other gives expression to his national sentiments. The former is connected with general European culture,
while the latter is founded on the special interests of the German
nation, and marks the culminating point of the influence of the
Seven Years' War upon German letters.

 'Minna von Barnhelm' was the first really national drama

dealing with contemporary events, and in it the Prussian soldier
whom Gleim had introduced into lyric poetry, made a
glorious *début* upon the comic stage. The scene is laid
in Berlin, immediately after the war; the characters
are no longer burdened with Greek or English names,
and are not typical masks, but living people with individual traits
drawn from the author's own experience, and in sympathy with his
own character. There is, first of all, the Prussian Major Tellheim,
a retired and impoverished officer, generous, noble, and sensitive
even to excess; the military element is further represented by the
sergeant, Paul Werner, and the Major's servant, Just, whom his
master has imbued with his own noble nature. The female characters are: the widow of one of Tellheim's fellow-officers, who
finds a friend and benefactor in the Major; his *fiancée*, Minna, of
whom he no longer thinks himself worthy, and who, therefore, has
to woo and wed him in despite of himself; lastly, Minna's maid
Francisca, an improved edition of those Lisettes whom the poet
had introduced as *intrigantes* in his earlier comedies, written after
French models. All these characters are excellent, loveable and
thoroughly German people. The play is a homage to German
women, and a glorification of the Prussian army, in whose midst
Lessing had lived for four years; it is, furthermore, a eulogy of the
great king who looms in the background as the administrator of
that justice which restores to the Major his lost pride, vindicates
his injured honour, and brings everything to a happy conclusion.
By way of contrast and as a salve to wounded national feeling,
Lessing places by the side of the honest German, a French ad-
venturer, a contemptible character, who excites the laughter of the
audience by his broken German. All this is very happily embodied
in scenes, partly mirthful, partly affecting. 'Minna von Barnhelm'
was the first of a whole succession of soldier-plays, in which this
hobby was driven to death, and finally, in time of peace, became as
wearisome as the ' Roaring of the Bards.'

Lessing, inspired by the great war, and as a voluntary partisan
of Prussia, had thus nationalised the German drama, and had
made it really popular without the least sacrifice of artistic form.
Before long, much the same thing was attempted for the novel,

(marginal note:) Lessing's Minna von Barnhelm, 1767.

though by an extremely inferior writer, namely, the theologian Johann Timotheus Hermes. This author, who was a The German Prussian by birth, rescued the novel from those remote Novel. regions which had been alone thought appropriate to it, and made it a story of current events in Germany, as Grimmelshausen had done before him. As Lessing had laid the scene of his play ' Miss Sara Samson' in England, and thus acknowledged his indebtedness to the English, so Hermes, who was an imitator partly of Richardson and partly of Fielding, first came before Hermes's the public in 1766 with a novel entitled ' Miss Fanny ' Miss Wilkes;' subsequently, however, he took to trivial and Fanny Wilkes,' common-place representation of German life in ' So- and phien's Reise von Memel nach Sachsen' (1769–1773), 'Sophien's a many-volumed and disconnected medley of adven- Reise.' ture, moralisings, and sentiment. Hermes soon found a successor in Lessing's friend Nicolai, whose novel ' Sebaldus Nothanker' (1773) was a continuation of another novel written some time before, Moriz August von Thümmel's ' Wilhelmine,' a burlesque epic in prose, which gained the esteem of Lessing. Lessing had given a prose form to tragedy, the fable, and the ode, and now, too, the mock-heroic poem was transformed into prose; it was thus assimilated to the novel and the romance, and helped to bring these two forms of literature down to the interests of Thümmel's every-day life. Thümmel's ' Wilhelmine,' which ap- ' Wilhel- peared in 1764, was an attack on the depravity of the mine,' German courts. The heroine is a chambermaid in a 1764. reigning prince's household, and marries the good village-clergyman, Sebaldus. After the appearance of Oliver Gold- Nicolai's smith's 'Vicar of Wakefield' in 1766, Nicolai endowed ' Sebaldus this same Sebaldus with some qualities derived from Nothanker,' the English country-clergyman, and related his further 1773. fortunes after his marriage. Sebaldus comes in contact with orthodox people, pietists and free-thinkers, with noblemen and Prussian soldiers; he suffers much on account of his opinions, is persecuted and driven from place to place, but is finally more or less consoled by winning a prize in a lottery. In this book Nicolai supplied the public with a patriotic work, dealing with middle-class life, and setting forth enlightened views ; and in spite of its incessant theological discussions, in spite of the traditional apparatus of robbers, shipwrecks, and slave-merchants, and of many other defects, the book proved not unpalatable reading to those who were not over-critical, for it was full of interesting information about religious conditions in Berlin, it contained a couple of happily-conceived characters, and teemed with protests against aristocratic arrogance, Gallomania, intolerance, and hypocrisy.

But at the same time that German poetry was establishing itself more and more firmly on German soil, the love of classical antiquity was also increasing.   The humanistic element of modern culture gained redoubled force from the general spirit of creative activity which animated the age, and from the increased energy of æsthetic and scientific aspirations.

Revival of classical influence.

While the war lasted the German nation had shown a Spartan endurance and valour, and had rivalled the ancients in its deeds ; now that peace was restored the greatness of Athens seemed a worthy object of emulation.   In January, 1771, shortly after the German comedy and the German novel had tendered a solution of the problems of national life, Frederick the Great entrusted the superintendence of Prussian instruction to Baron Zedlitz, who first made the Prussian gymnasium what it is, or what it was in its 'best times.   Zedlitz doubled and trebled the number of hours to be devoted to Greek instruction, substituted for the New Testament the great writers of antiquity, and thus transformed the Gymnasium of the Reformation period into the modern classical school.   As a parallel to this we find Lessing, before he completed his ' Minna von Barnhelm,' publishing his ' Laokoon,' a work in which he ranged himself by the side of Winckelmann, and of those writers who not only gave an intellectual justification of the prevalent tendency to return to the pure Greek forms, but also educated and developed the taste for classical antiquity.

The course of Winckelmann's life was exactly the reverse of Lessing's. Lessing was drawn from Saxony to Prussia, there to have his genius moulded by Prussian influences ; the Prussian Winckelmann, on the contrary, left his native province to go to Dresden, and there, in the classic

Winckelmann's Classicism.

abode of German *Rococo*, found satisfaction for his æsthetic
nature in the treasures of modern and ancient art.   His
There, in intercourse with the Austrian Oeser, a   'Gedanken
many-sided artist and stimulating character, he learnt   über die
to worship that ideal of noble simplicity and quiet   Nachah-
grandeur which he revealed to the world in 1755   Griechischen
in his 'Thoughts on the imitation of the Greeks   Werke in
                                                    der Malerei
in painting and sculpture.' But his stay at Dresden   und Bild-
was only preparatory to his life at Rome, whither   hauerkunst,'
his conversion to the Catholic Church naturally led   1755.
him.   There, in the midst of the grand ruins of the ancient world,
he enjoyed unparalleled personal liberty, and in 1764   His
gave to the world his 'History of Ancient Art,' the   'Geschichte
first historical work of art in the German language;   der Kunst
                                                        des Alter-
in it he adopted that philosophic and generalising   thums,'
treatment of history which had been initiated by   1764.
Montesquieu, and combined with it a vast experience and knowledge of facts at first hand, along with a marvellous divination of
the characteristics of the purest Hellenic style, although no monuments of that style had at that time been recovered.   Nor should
we omit to notice the remarkable sharpness of perception and enthusiasm in observation which the book attests, nor the graphic
language peculiar to Winckelmann, rich and sensuous in its description of works of art, and often rising to poetic sublimity, nor
lastly the glorious principle with which the work culminates, that
art flourishes where liberty reigns.

Winckelmann gave an æsthetic turn to classical studies by re-
cognising as he did the importance of a knowledge of   Revived
Greek art and by advocating the study of monuments   study of
in connection with ancient literature. But Winckel-   Greek Art
                                                        and
mann was only the most important representative of   Literature.
a wide-spread tendency of the age.   Three years before the appearance of the 'Thoughts on the imitation of the
Greeks,' a certain Abbé Laugier had made a pitiless attack on
the highly ornate style of architecture then in vogue, and had
condemned all styles except the three orders of Greek architecture.
Practical architecture had entered on the same path, and simplicity,

self-restraint, and close imitation of the ancients had become its watchwords. German Professors like Ernesti in Leipzig, and Gesner in Leipzig and Göttingen, had begun to pay greater regard to the Greeks. Christ, also a Leipzig man, and Lessing's chief teacher, had bidden his pupils study ancient art, and Gesner's Greek 'Chrestomathie' had established itself in the schools by the side of the New Testament. In Halle Professor Schulze was wont in his lectures expressly to compare the Greeks and Romans, and to adjudge pre-eminence to the former; Berlin possessed such a school-master as Rector Damm, of whom Winckelmann learned Greek; the Saxon princely schools were beginning to put the Greek classics in the hands of their scholars. German poetry reaped decided advantage from this Hellenising tendency; though the serious Greek lyric poetry was still chiefly represented to the Germans by Horace, the disciple of the Greeks, yet Anacreon had already exercised a strong influence on German poets. Thanks to Breitinger's efforts the name of Homer began to be mentioned with more and more reverence, and Wieland and others derived from Plato and Xenophon an ideal picture of Socrates, with which they mingled their own moral ideals. The same Wieland, by the magic of his imagination, transported his readers to the Greek shore of the Mediterranean Sea, and made them quite at home among the contemporaries of Pericles; his Greeks may sometimes have rather resembled Frenchmen of the eighteenth century A. D. than Hellenes of the fifth century B.C., but this resemblance really only bears witness to a sympathetic conception of ancient times, and the neo-Greeks of Wieland's creation made it all the easier for the Germans to become acquainted with the genuine old Hellenes. The need of discarding French models in favour of original Greek ones began to be more and more strongly felt. Elias Schlegel returned to Sophocles, though without discarding the French Alexandrine tragedy. Pyra, as we know, wished to revive the ancient chorus. Klopstock introduced Greek metres into German poetry. Lessing early learnt from the characters of Theophrastus much that was of use to him in his comedies; in the fable he returned to Aesop; he meant to write a life of Sophocles, to treat the subject of Philoctetes, and to attempt a Nemesis-tragedy based on classical models. Winckelmann's first work incited Lessing to devote his attention to the study of ancient art, and the feeling that a review of æsthetic criticism up to that time was much needed led him to make the important researches embodied in ' Laocoon.'

The work was intended to fill three volumes, of which, however, only one appeared. Lessing could as little compete **Lessing's** with Winckelmann in the advancement of the history **'Laocoon.'** of ancient art, as he could in his acquaintance with the monuments. Neither from the ' Laocoon,' nor from the controversial literature which it called forth, did archæology directly reap any great advantage ; only the beautiful little treatise—' How the ancients depicted death,' first established a fact now well known to all, and restored the genius with the reversed torch on many of our graves. In defending ' beauty' as the supreme law of ancient art, and of sculpture and painting in general, in esteeming beauty of form higher than that of colour, in desiring that expression should be toned down and subordinated to beauty—in all this Lessing stood in essential agreement with Winckelmann, and he and Winckelmann together established grandeur and repose as the ideal of Hellenic sculpture and painting, and as the principle which should govern modern artists. But when Winckelmann went further and derived the distinctive character of the Greek masterpieces from a certain Stoical composure of soul, and tried to discover the same spirit in the Greek poets, Lessing could not agree with him. Heroic stoicism, which only excites cold admiration, was not at all to his mind ; and it was easy to show that it was also contrary to the spirit of the Greeks. In the development of this controversy with **Lessing's** Winckelmann, Lessing has given us signal proof of his **controversy** ability to think out a thing in the abstract, and at the **with** same time to accurately observe and appreciate facts. **Winckel-** He pointed out how differently the death of Laocoon **mann.** had been treated by Virgil on the one hand, and by the Greek sculptor on the other, and how in this they had only followed the different laws regulating poetry and plastic art ; he sought to remove the confusion between the two, and above all to abolish that kind of word-painting in poetry, which had come into vogue in Germany, particularly through Breitinger's influence. He sought to deduce the limits of the two arts from the nature of the means with which each must work, and argued that good writing only describes things and persons indirectly through their actions, and that Homer in particular only depicts by narrating.   He thus furnished most valuable contributions to the theory of the epic, put an end to mere word-painting, and fixed the method of Wieland and of his successors in this branch of poetry.   He set forth his views in a kind of impromptu style, without attempting systematic deduction of them; his work has all the liveliness of oral exposition, and yet it really rests throughout on the basis of a consistent system.

It seems that for Lessing an important personal hope was bound up with this work; he hoped by it to attract the King's attention, and to obtain the appointment of Director of the Royal Library in Berlin, a post for which both his name and Winckelmann's had been mentioned favourably to the King.   But both Winckelmann and Lessing were destined to be disappointed in their hopes.   The **Lessing and** King's impression of Lessing had been formed by the **Frederick** description which the enraged Voltaire had given him **the Great.** of the young author who had offended him; Frederick, therefore, utterly refused to appoint Lessing to the post.   Winckelmann's appointment also fell through owing to a dispute about the salary, Frederick declaring that the proposed two thousand Thalers (£300) was too much for a German, and that he would only give him half that amount.   In the end an utterly incompetent Frenchman was appointed over the heads of Lessing and Winckelmann.   If Frederick could only have recognised it, no German author was really so akin to his inmost character as Lessing.   Both had the same vivacity and ambition, the same youthful thirst for glory which led them recklessly to humiliate their enemies, the same severity towards what was bad; both felt strongly the need of friendship, while both were but slightly susceptible to the love of women; in both enjoyment of life was combined with a strong sense of duty; both had the same liberal views, and tolerance, the same clear, ready, and rational style.   Lessing demanded of a historian that he should relate contemporary events, a demand which Frederick fulfilled..   Lessing introduced strict rule in literature, as Frederick did in the field and in home-government.   Lessing, like

the great king, defended the national cause against the foreigner.
There were never two men more created for each other than Lessing
and Frederick the Great, and Frederick could not have found anywhere a subject who would have served him with greater faithfulness
and a more worthy aim, or a writer who would have so fully compen-
sated him for the loss of what attracted him in his beloved French.
But the unproved and unjust accusation made years before by a
Frenchman, whom the king despised much as he admired him,
was sufficient reason for striking out the name of this German poet
and scholar for ever from the list of those who might serve him.

Lessing shook the dust of Brandenburg from his feet, and went
in April 1767 to Hamburg, where a new disappoint- Lessing and
ment awaited him. A permanent German national the Hamburg
Theatre was about to be founded in the town which theatre.
had been the home of the early German opera, the 1767.
birth-place of Brockes and Hagedorn, and which was then the place
of residence of so many old and young scholars and poets. The art
of acting had been raised to a much higher level since the first start
had been given it by the efforts of Caroline Neuber, already mentioned in connection with Gottsched. The Schönemann, Koch,
and Ackermann companies had become quite celebrated, and their
best actors were beginning to give up imitating the French, and to
aim at a less affected style of acting. Many excellent actors and
actresses in Hamburg were ready to support Lessing in his new
dramatic schemes. Lessing was to be the reporter, The
was to train the actors by his free criticisms, and to 'Hamburg-
educate the public taste. From the first of May 1767 ische
his 'Hamburgische Dramaturgie' appeared twice a Drama-
week; it was a paper written entirely by himself, and turgie.'
exclusively devoted to the interests of the National Theatre. But
the actors, as usual, did not care to be found fault with, but only to
be praised; the public did not show any very great sympathy with
the undertaking, and the means soon began to fail. The scheme
was abandoned after two years, and the 'Dramaturgie,' which had
for some time given up criticising the representations regularly, and
had introduced general discussions of the drama instead, did
not get further than two volumes. But these two volumes are of

inexhaustible value ; they are rich in information about the plays of the time, rich in penetrating criticism of dramatic art and dramatic poetry in general. They form a continuation to the theatrical periodicals which Lessing had published in his youth, a continuation to his earlier polemical writings on the weaknesses of the French school, and a sequel to his 'Laocoon.'

In subsequent volumes the 'Laocoon' was to have culmi-

Lessing's theory of the drama. nated in a glorification of the drama as the highest form of poetry. All art, Lessing declared, must aim at the direct representation of nature ; and poetry, which can only describe and represent indirectly and by means of words, rises in the drama to the full level of a first-hand representation, a real imitation of life. We can judge from this how deeply interested Lessing must have been in coming into direct contact with an excellent theatre. He had already discussed the theory of the fable, and in 'Laocoon' had furnished contributions to the theory of the epic, and it must have seemed to him of far greater importance to lay a theoretical basis for his favourite branch of poetry, the drama. As in the fable he had held up Æsop, and in the epic Homer, as infallible models, so now in the drama the Greeks of the best period were his guiding-stars, Aristotle for theory and Sophocles for practice. As in 'Laocoon' he had sought after true poetry and true painting, so now he sought out the way, which he had already indicated in his 'Literary Letters,' towards the true drama. In common with the French school he laid the greatest weight on the authority of Aristotle ; in common with

Aristotle, Sophocles, and Shakspeare, his authorities. the Wolffian philosophy, in which he too had been educated, he attached the greatest, nay, too great importance to correct definition as the basis of all theory. In Aristotle's definition of tragedy, or at least in his own interpretation of it, Lessing thought he laid his finger on the true essence of the drama, and with this definition he found the dramas of Sophocles to be in full agreement ; but, strange as it may seem, the dramas of Shakspeare seemed to him to be also in full agreement with the demands of Aristotle, and this judgment of his shows how strong was the hold upon him of the literature of a kindred nation, and how surely he penetrated through the semblance to the substance, and was able to discern true genius under different forms.   Such tragic elements as were common to Sophocles and to Shakspeare seemed to him to constitute the essence of tragedy, which, as he thought, should excite not amazement but sympathy, by representing overpowering events as inevitable consequences flowing from the character of the agents. From this standpoint he criticised the achievements of German tragedy up to his own time, and the tragedies of his old friend Weisse did not come off much better under his treatment than the comedies of Frau Gottsched.   Then he attacked the false tragedy of Corneille, Racine, and Voltaire, the false interpretation and arbitrary perversion of the Aristotelian doctrines by the French, and pointed out how entirely Voltaire had failed in his attempts to rival Shakspeare in depicting passion or in introducing supernatural elements into the drama.   It was at Voltaire that Lessing's hardest blows were levelled, for in him he was attacking a living man, a personal enemy who had done him grave injury; and besides, was he not indirectly avenging the cause of German literature against Frederick the Great, by lowering the reputation of a poet whom the king esteemed as the highest genius? Still, Lessing was no indiscriminate hater of the French.   In earlier life it was Diderot who had nerved him to attack the French stage, and who had directed his attention to the special limitations of the various arts; they both agreed in preferring the tragedy of middle-class life.   Lessing had translated Diderot's plays, and always gratefully acknowledged the influence which this worthy philosopher had exercised upon him.

Lessing broke off his 'Dramaturgie' in a fit of indignation, and resuming those archæological studies which he had dropped in displeasure some years before, proceeded to fling his 'Antiquarian Letters' at the head of Professor Klotz of Halle.   Klotz was *Lessing's controversy with Klotz. The 'Antiquarische Briefe.'* an elegant Latin scholar, who had come into a good appointment early in life, and had skilfully organized a clique of his own with its own periodicals.   He now set his clique and his papers to bait Lessing.   Lessing struck all such opponents to the ground in the person of their chief, and gibbeted once and for all the mean intrigues of this miserable pedant. Lessing dropped this controversy also in disgust; he longed to get away from Hamburg, away from Germany, and to go straight to Rome. On the 8th of June, 1768, Winckelmann had been assassinated in Trieste. His place in Rome was vacant, and Lessing thought he might fill it; but not in the literal sense, as his German enemies supposed, who were only too anxious that he should incur the odium of changing his religion[1]. What Lessing wanted was to succeed to the position in which Winckelmann had done so much for the archæological interests of Europe, and to live with the monuments of ancient art close at hand in the city where the best of them were preserved. For he felt, like Winckelmann, that to make these monuments known, to interpret them, to classify them historically, and to subject them to æsthetic criticism was a task demanding a man's full powers, and worthy of his undivided attention.

But the journey was deferred, evidently because Lessing could not find the necessary money, and it was finally given up when he was offered an appointment in Germany, that of Librarian at Wolfenbüttel. The post was small, it is true, but it was worthy of his acceptance, and suited to his tastes.

He becomes Librarian at Wolfenbüttel, 1770.

In Brunswick the Abbot Jerusalem, a clergyman of enlightened views, endeavoured to the utmost of his power to help on German poets, in the same way as we have noticed the court chaplain Sack did in Berlin. Jerusalem's advice was of great influence in the appointment of the teachers at the Brunswick 'Carolinum,' an institution founded by Duke Charles on the model of the English public schools. Some of the writers in the 'Bremen Contributions,' Gärtner, Ebert, Zachariä, and Schmid, had received masterships there, and Klopstock was just about to join them when the call to Kopenhagen opened more agreeable prospects to him. In this circle and from these teachers the hereditary prince of Brunswick derived his culture; and it was at his demand, reinforced by Ebert's strong approval, that the librarianship at Wolfenbüttel was offered to Lessing. He accepted the offer, and entered on the duties of his office in the spring of 1770.

[1] Winckelmann had turned Roman Catholic.

Lessing's writings now assumed for the most part a bibliographical character.   He made many a happy find in   Lessing's
the treasures of the library confided to his care ; and   bibliogra-
whenever he lighted on a valuable and unknown work,   phical pub-
he always furnished the learned public with a full re-   lications.
port of his discoveries.   Yet the impressions wrought on him by
the Hamburg stage were still active in his mind.   His important
advances in the recognition of the principles on which the drama
rested were yet to bear some tangible fruit.   He wished to put his
theory to a practical proof, and did so in his ' Emilia   His
Galotti,' which appeared in 1772.   The piece had   ' Emilia
been planned long ago ; it was meant at first to have   Galotti,'
been founded on the story of Virginia, and, like   1772.
other tragedies which Lessing sketched in the fire of youth, was to
have extolled an uprising in the cause of liberty ; later on, however,
he gave up the idea of dramatising public affairs, and transferred
the scene to a small modern Italian principality.   The play gives
us a terrible picture of a princely egoist, who, in the satisfaction of
his riotous desires, sets the life of his subjects at nought ; he hurries
from one *amour* to another, drives one woman almost mad by de-
serting her, then murders a bridegroom in order to possess his
bride ; the girl herself longs for death, and at her request her father
plunges a dagger into her heart and thus saves her from dishonour.
The characters are all excellently drawn ; Emilia's worthy old
father, rough and recklessly impetuous, yet at the same time afraid
of his own impetuosity ; the weak, imprudent, somewhat down-
trodden mother ; the honest, straightforward, manly bridegroom ;
the girl herself, charming, modest, the most timid yet the most
resolute of her sex ; the refined, princely profligate, who can converse cleverly with a painter about art, and whose mind is open to
all higher interests, but who knows no restraint to his wishes, because he thinks himself above all laws ; his first victim, the half-
crazy Orsina ; his pliant courtier Marinelli, the servant of his lusts,
in whom every feeling of morality and honour has been destroyed
by associating with the despot—all these characters, and even the
bandits hired by Marinelli are graphically presented to us, and the
course of action springs, as the ' Dramaturgie ' demanded, from the

nature of the characters. Though the plot may have been settled beforehand, and the characters only drawn out afterwards to fit in with it, though the father may be blamed, and has been, for stabbing his daughter and not the despot—yet all must own that the plot is developed without any awkward halts or gaps, and the difficulties involved in its presentation on the stage got over with wonderful ease. Lessing proved himself in this piece a master of tragedy as in his ' Minna ' he had shown himself a master of comedy. As the author of ' Emilia Galotti ' he became the real teacher of a younger generation of dramatists.

But Lessing's dramatic activity was not to end with this play.

'Nathan der Weise,' 1779. He had it in him to rise to a yet higher level. The form of the prose drama, which he had introduced by his ' Sara,' and to which he had, notwithstanding earlier intentions to the contrary, remained faithful in his ' Emilia,' was yet to be abandoned for the drama in verse, in order that he might clothe a most ideal subject in a worthy form, and add the grace and charm of rhythm to a noble hymn of all-embracing human love. ' Emilia Galotti ' was followed unexpectedly, after seven years, by ' Nathan the Wise.' Theological controversies induced him to write this, just as contact with a real stage had induced him to write ' Emilia.'

He seemed to be absorbed in his duties as librarian, and actively engaged in various departments of harmless science, when in 1773 he began his ' Contributions to history and literature drawn from the treasures of the Wolfenbüttel library.' But in the next year

The 'Fragmente eines Wolfenbütteler Ungenannten,' edited by Lessing, 1774. the question of toleration came up incidentally in connection with some point of literary history, and there appeared, without exciting much notice, the first instalment of a publication purporting to be extracts from the papers of an ' anonymous Wolfenbütteler,' which was followed by further instalments in 1777 and 1778. These papers contained the sharpest attacks on Christianity; the writer denounced the ' crying-down of reason from the pulpits,' questioned the possibility of a Revelation, and denied the character of a Revelation to the Old Testament on special grounds; in the New Testament the story of the Resurrection

in particular was sharply criticised, and highly irreverent views
were put forth as to the aims of Christ and his disciples.

In truth, this new work, which Lessing disguised as a humble
bibliographical publication, precipitated a crisis in the history of
Protestant theology and of the Protestant Church. The whole
theological world was soon in uproar, though it had seemed fully
prepared for the strongest criticism. The general development of
the Church and of religious doctrine had been in a decidedly liberal
direction ; orthodoxy was retreating, and most of the influential
Church appointments were filled by the Liberals.   Liberal
The influence of the English Freethinkers was mak- theological
ing itself more and more felt, and their views were criticism in
secretly accepted by many, and openly avowed by   Germany.
a few. The society of Freemasons, which had spread from England about the time of the accession of Frederick the Great, undermined the esteem hitherto cherished for positive religion, and
Voltaire's malicious criticisms on Christianity were eagerly read in
Germany, as in the whole of Europe. An increasing indifference
to dogma was everywhere apparent, and theological writings were
becoming more elegant in style, more secular in tone. As in the
time of the Humanists, so now, the general advances in history
and philology were, after German fashion, at once turned to the
account of theology in particular, and this could only result in an
increasing independence of thought and criticism,   Ernesti,
and a corresponding diminution of faith. The cele- Michaelis,
brated scholar, Ernesti of Leipzig, was the first to and Semler.
begin an unbiassed and strictly learned interpretation of the Bible,
in opposition to dogmatic prepossessions. He was followed in
this by Michaelis and Semler, both of whom studied at Halle.
Semler became the father of modern historical criticism from
original sources; he was the first to distinguish between contemporary and second-hand evidence, original and indirect authorities,
and treated the writings of the New Testament as monuments of
literary history, trying to discover the purpose with which they were
written, and the occasions which called them forth. He wished to
separate what was of permanent value in them from what was
merely local and temporary. But the boldness of Semler and

of every other scholar was far surpassed by the one-sided and
sweeping criticism put forth by the Hamburg philosopher and professor, Hermann Samuel Reimarus,
in a work which was submitted to Lessing in manuscript form, and by him published, as we have seen, a
few years after the author's death, under the title of the
'Papers of an Anonymous Wolfenbütteler.' Reimarus
could perceive in the origin of Christianity nothing but
the worldly aims of its Founder, and the false pretensions of his
disciples. This was too much, not only for the orthodox, but for
the Liberal party. Among the former the disputatious Melchior
Goeze of Hamburg, and among the latter Semler and many others
rose up and challenged these views.

Reimarus' views published by Lessing in his 'Fragmente eines Ungenannten.'

All of them made Lessing responsible for the opinions set forth,
and he had to answer all attacks. He had been prepared for this,
and knew what a storm he was conjuring up. But the frame of
mind in which he had published those first cutting fragments was
very different from that in which he now set about undertaking the
defence of the anonymous Wolfenbütteler. Then, peace and happiness had just begun to dawn for him. Alone, and often in struggle
with want and debts, he had lived on till his forty-eighth year; at
length fortune seemed to smile upon him, for his outward circumstances had improved, and a clear-headed and energetic woman,
Eva König, the widow of a Hamburg friend, had become his wife
in October, 1776. She had the best influence upon him, and made
him quieter, steadier, and less hasty. But on Christmas Eve, 1777,
she gave birth to a son, who died in twenty-four hours,
and on the 10th of January, 1778, she died herself.
Lessing wrote heart-rending letters, letters breathing
the bitter misanthropic mockery of his Tellheim or his Orsina, letters
full of unfathomable misery, and such as no one had ever before
written, except Frederick the Great in his most desponding
moments. 'My wife is dead,' he writes, 'so this experience, too, I
have now made. I am thankful there cannot be still reserved to
me many such experiences, and am quite easy.'

Death of Lessing's wife.

It was in this frame of mind that Lessing had to begin to answer
the polemics against the anonymous author and his publisher.

He wrote his 'Testament of John,' his 'Duplik,' his 'Parables,' his 'Axiomata,' and that whole series of scathing polemics to which he gave the title of 'Anti-Goeze.' He applied all his marvellous powers of language and keen argument to the task before him; meta- **Lessing's theological controversy, 1778.** phors and similes suggested themselves in abundance at his call, and yet he appeals less to the imagination than to the **His 'Anti-** understanding. His quick transitions of thought keep **Goeze.'** us continually on the alert; we seem to be listening to a dis- cussion carried on in flying haste, and where the objections of the opponent are left to our conjecture. The dramatic vivacity of the Lutheran pamphlets is revived here in the hands of a true dramatist. Now Lessing adopts the form of the dialogue, now of the epistle. At one time he propounds a parable, at another he brings forward a chain of theses.; here we have calm evidence and statements, there a storm of query and invective. He has a special style for every separate opponent. Goeze gets the hardest blows, being stamped as a disloyal persecutor and bigot, an intolerant hypo- crite and slanderer. Every weak point which he betrays Lessing at once spies out with eagle eye, and mercilessly assails. But his object is rather defence than attack, and he triumphantly answers the onslaught made upon him for publishing the 'Fragments.' Free enquiry, he says, is the right of all Protestants. Luther's spirit demands that no man should be hindered in seeking after truth according to his lights, for the final purpose of Christianity is not that we should be saved in any manner, but that we should be saved through the truth illumining our souls. And the letter is not the spirit, the Bible is not religion; consequently attacks on the Bible are not necessarily attacks on religion.

As a matter of fact Lessing by no means agreed with all the opinions set forth in the 'Fragments.' He wished to distinguish the religion of existing Christian Churches from the religion of Jesus, the 'divine friend of man,' the religion which **Lessing's** his beloved disciple summed up in the words—' Little **real** children, love one another.' He was prepared to follow **religious** Semler's example, and vigorously promote the study **views.** of the Gospels as monuments of literary history, and, by a

more intimate acquaintance with primitive Christianity, to bring
about that emancipation from a slavish adherence to the letter,
which he saw to be so necessary. He would have treated Christianity as Winckelmann had treated Greek art, and would have
shown how different climates produced different wants and satis-
factions, different manners and customs, different ethics and different religions. He considered religions as the products of a
necessary but purely human development, and said that their chief
importance lay in the moral effect they produced. This was why he
regarded as proof against any refutation the pious feeling which is
happy in its faith, and why he so earnestly longed for a new and
permanent Gospel, which should recommend virtue for its own sake,
and not for the sake of a future happiness. The noblest flower of
virtue seemed to him to be that love which unites men and lifts
them above the earthly limits of nationalities, states, and religions.

Lessing did not find time to set forth all his thoughts on religious
subjects. His controversy with Goeze was only a preliminary
skirmish; the real battle was to come. He was not a man who
would build up a system in too great haste. His strength lay
in discriminating, examining, refuting; in one word, in criticism.
But above the particulars which he subjected to a strict in-

Lessing's 'Ernst und Falk, Gespräche für Frei- maurer,' 1778, and 'Erziehung des Mens- chenge- schlechts,' 1780. vestigation, his mind rose in anticipation to a view
of the whole. He had formed for himself concep-
tions of God, the world, and the human soul, in
accordance with those of Leibniz and not altogether
unlike the views held by Spinoza. He gave the
frankest utterance to what he deemed essentials in his
'Freemason dialogues' of 1778 (he had joined the order
in Hamburg), and he set forth the same convictions
more covertly, not in his own name, but as an interpretation of Christian dogmas, in his 'Education of the
Human Race,' published in 1780. These convictions form a quiet
background to the stormy activity of his controversial writings.

Lessing's most violent controversy took place in 1778. Then
silence was suddenly imposed on him by a command from Brunswick, and the right of free publication was withdrawn from him.
He had to lay down the weapons of theological warfare, and

resorted instead to his old poetical weapons, which were still untarnished and had never been wielded in a nobler cause, for the question was not the triumph of one opinion over another, but the victory of tolerance over intolerance.

In this very year, 1778, Voltaire had died, and Lessing had written this epitaph on him :

> ' Here lieth one, who, if ye truly prate,
> Ye pious 'folk, here lieth all too late.
> Forgive his Henriade, O God of mercies,
> Forgive his tragedies and little verses;
> ·I will not ask forgiveness for the rest
> Of what he wrote, for that was much the best.'

In the year 1762 Voltaire had published extracts from the Anti-Christian Testament of Pastor Meslier, and in 1763 had written his 'Traité de la Tolérance.' Lessing published the 'Fragments by an Anonymous Wolfenbütteler' from 1774 to 1777, and in 1779 wrote 'Nathan the Wise.' In this drama he returned to a subject which had suggested itself to *· Nathan der Weise,' 1779.* him at the time of his intercourse with Voltaire, and for which Voltaire had even furnished a few ideas. In his comedy of ' The Jews,' Lessing himself had taken a few features from the same story, which in its main outlines was derived from Boccaccio, the great story-teller of the middle ages. The following is a short outline of the story.

Sultan Saladin is in need of money. He sends for a rich Jew, and, in order to entrap him, puts the question to him, which of the three religions he holds to be the true one—the Jewish, the Mohammedan, or the *The Story of the Three Rings.* Christian. The Jew, who is prudent as well as rich, asks leave to relate a story, and tells of a ring which was in the possession of a noble family, and was handed down from father to son, always exalting the son who had it above the other sons; this ring came at last into the hands of a father who had three sons, all of whom he loved equally well, so that he did not wish one to be better off than the other two. He therefore had two other rings made, which he himself could hardly distinguish from the original one, and gave a ring to each of his sons. After his death they all raised the same claims, which no one could settle, since no one could find out the true ring. The Jew applies the story to the case of the three different religions; Saladin recognises the truth of the parable, acknowledges his need, receives what he wants, and treats the Jew henceforth as his friend.

This is a short outline of Boccaccio's story, and a similar story was told of a Spanish king of the eleventh century. In Spain all three religions were represented, and flourished peacefully side by side. The Greek culture which had been revived there by the Arabs had dissipated many of the religious prejudices which separate men. The story of the three rings became in Spain a customary parabolic expression of tolerant views. The story spread over Europe, and the bigots gave it a different termination, according to which the true heir is found out by reason of the true ring working miracles. Sometimes the rings are omitted, and we have only a story of three brothers. In the seventeenth century the brothers went among Lutherans by the names of Peter, Martin, and John, and Martin was of course the true heir. In the eighteenth century Swift availed himself of .the story in his 'Tale of a Tub' in order to mock at all three sects. The poet Gellert followed the same idea in his story of the hat, which was always assuming new shapes, and yet always turned out to be the same old hat; he was not scoffing at religion, however, but at philosophy with its varying systems.

From this allegory of the three rings, Lessing now, in the eighteenth century, set himself to draw the same moral of toleration as had already been drawn in the eleventh. But he availed himself of the old tale not merely as a weapon against intolerance, but also in order to inculcate the gospel of love. He attributes a miraculous power to the ring, and makes the father declare that that power lies in the gift which the ring has of bringing favour with God and man to him who wears it in this assurance; and the judge gives the following counsel to the three brothers who crave justice at his hands: 'Test the power of your rival rings by emulating one another in gentleness, concord, benevolence, and zeal in the service of God.'

The plot of ' Nathan der Weise.' But Boccaccio only furnished Lessing with a few scenes, whereas he required a plot of five acts, and, if possible, a crisis in which the character of the Jew should be put to the test and come out triumphant. Lessing's Jew

was to be a wise and good Jew, like Moses Mendelssohn. By way
of making Nathan yet more interesting, Lessing represents him as a
much persecuted man of sorrows, whose wife and seven sons have
been all slain in one day by the Christians. Nevertheless, Nathan
conforms to the hardest of Christian precepts : he loves his enemies
and adopts a Christian child as his own, and Recha, this adopted
daughter, turns out to be the Sultan's niece and the sister of a
Knight-Templar. Christians and Mohammedans are thus united
by a family tie, as had already been described by Wolfram von
Eschenbach in his 'Parzival' and 'Willehalm,' and a Jew is received
into their circle, not by a dispensation of nature, but owing to the
power of his noble character.

In this play, as in ' Emilia,' the action issues naturally from the
characters, which are life-like, individual figures, such as Lessing
knew well how to draw from his faithful observation of human
nature in himself and in those around him. Nathan is   Character
a merchant and philosopher like Moses Mendelssohn ;   of
he is a man who has been sanctified by sorrow and   Nathan.
self-denial, an ideal character, who calls forth the highest admiration, and yet is never idealised into vagueness, but, on the contrary,
leaves on the mind the impression of a portrait. Widely-travelled
and wise, rich and unselfish, he is invaluable as a guide, philosopher,
and friend. In his attitude towards the great ones of this world he
is fearless though cautious, and in dealing with noble natures, he has
learnt that it is the best policy to appeal to the noblest moral feelings.
He extends his tolerance to all except the vicious. He   Other
has educated his adopted daughter Recha to be simple   characters
and sincere, and has fortified with his enlightened   of the play.
teaching the natural purity of her heart. Child-like in her innocence,
she knows nothing of love, and the appeals of a lover awake no
echo in her heart; all the affection of her enthusiastic nature is
centred on Nathan, whom she believes to be her real father. Then
while Nathan is away there comes a moment of peril, and she is
saved by the Templar. She is so infatuated that she regards her
deliverer as an angel, until Nathan returns and undeceives her.
The Templar is an upright man, and fair-minded, except for a
certain arrogance towards the Jew, which, however, vanishes as

soon as he comes to know him.   He is carried away by his youthful passion to take a thoughtless step, which imperils Nathan and
plunges himself in the bitterest remorse.   Saladin is a hearty,
impulsive man, as soldiers and men of action often are ; he is easily
roused and as easily forgets.   He is enthusiastic in his devotion
to his brother and sister, and in practical affairs, for which he has
no talent, he lets himself be guided by his clear-minded and prudent
sister, as Lessing probably was guided by his wife.   But her influence
is not always for good, and the line of conduct which she suggests
should be adopted towards the Jew, turns out to her own and to
Saladin's discredit.   Nathan's friend the Dervish, ' the wild, good,
noble man,' the beggar whom Nathan declares to be the true king,
has put himself as the Sultan's treasurer into a very false position,
from which he finally escapes by simply running away ; this creation
of Lessing's humour owed its origin to a Jewish mathematician of
Mendelssohn's circle.   The groom, who had long ago brought the
little Christian child to Nathan, finds himself in a similar false
position ; he has afterwards to prove his simple piety in the service
of an unscrupulous, but happily also stupid Church dignitary.
He, like the rest, becomes Nathan's friend, and exclaims, in admiration of him : ' By God, you are a Christian ; there never was a
better Christian than you.'

   All these characters share more or less consciously in the
views which Nathan, as the wisest among them, is the best able
to put into words.   These views, Lessing tells us, had been his
own from his earliest years, or, to speak more accurately, since
Theological the time of his first sojourn in Berlin.   The lead-
views in   ing characters of the play are all opposed to the
' Nathan.'   pretensions of positive religion ; they are all of
one mind in seeking beyond the differences of creed and nationality the common basis of humanity, and in considering good
action to be man's aim in life ; but they also all hold fast to
Theism, to a general belief in God, and in His government of the
world, though not by means of supernatural interference.   This
faith is their guiding principle.   They all, with the exception of the
one hero, fall away once, either from noble or ignoble motives,
from the way which they consider right, and the chief complica-

tions in the play arise from these aberrations. As a contrast to these characters, we have the Patriarch of Jerusalem and Recha's nurse Daja ; these pretend to know the only true way to God, and the Patriarch, a caricature of Melchior Goeze, is quite prepared to drive the whole world by fire and sword into conformity with his own views.

In 'Nathan,' differing nationalities and creeds are united by bonds of harmony and peace, a dream which had floated before Lessing's eyes as a Free-mason. But the spirit of peace which breathes throughout this play is also a cheerful spirit. Cheerful characters and incidents alternate, as in 'Minna von Barnhelm,' with serious and affecting ones, and this mingling of light and shade brings the play down to the level of real life, instead of keeping it in a purely ideal region of noble sentiment and generous deeds.

In one of his pamphlets against Goeze, Lessing casts a retrospective glance on his stormy period of impetuous ardour, and says he feels himself now driven by softer winds towards the harbour where he hopes to land as happily as his opponent. Three years after he had written this, two years after he had published 'Nathan,' and in the sentiments of the wise Jew had given a reflection of his own convictions, Lessing died, on the   Lessing 15th of February, 1781. His step-daughter, Malchen   dies, 1781. König (the original, as we may suppose, of Nathan's Recha), attended him faithfully on his death-bed.

Lessing was a true and resolute man in an effeminate age. He was capable of tender feelings himself, and of love and   His sympathy for others, but he had no desire to let the   character. world look into his heart. Not sentiment, nor subtle reasoning, but action seemed to him to be the true end of man ; virtuous action was to him the only touchstone of true religion, and the mature man, who does his duty without regard to reward or distinction, was his moral ideal. He considered action to be the highest theme of poetry, and the drama, which represents action most graphically, the highest form of poetry.

When we reflect on his impetuous activity, his restlessness, his delight in animated conversation, his readiness to engage in controversy, his Protestant zeal for truth, and then remember that he was also a classical scholar, a patriot, an enemy of tyrants, who refused patronage and worked on in the present, careless of the future,—it seems to us as though Ulrich von Hutten had appeared again in him, only under a more gentle and agreeable aspect.

HERDER AND GOETHE.

In May, 1773, six years after the publication of 'Minna von Barnhelm,' a small, badly printed, anonymous book appeared, entitled ' On German style and art, a few fly-sheets.' It contained essays by three different writers; Justus Möser, counsel to the governing body of the cathedral foundation of Osnabrück, contributed a highly original sketch of German history, in which he upheld the liberty of the ancient Germans as a vanished ideal; Johann Gottfried Herder, counsel of the Consistory of Bückeburg, celebrated the merits of popular song, advocated a collection of the German 'Volkslieder,' extolled the greatness of Shakspeare and prophesied the advent of a German Shakspeare; Johann Wolfgang Goethe, a lawyer at Frankfort-on-the-Main, who was destined to be the long-expected German Shakspeare, and whose name was then in everyone's mouth as the author of ' Götz von Berlichingen,' gave utterance in the same volume to his delight with the Strassburg Cathedral, and attacked the Abbé Laugier, who would recognise nothing but ancient columns as good architecture. Goethe praised the Gothic style as the national German style of architecture, and asserted that art, to be true, must be characteristic. Möser was at this time fifty-three years old, Herder twenty-nine, and Goethe twenty-four. Herder and Goethe had made each other's acquaintance in the autumn of 1770, at Strassburg. Möser's essay was taken from the preface to his ' History of Osnabrück,' and was probably incorporated at Herder's instigation in these ' Fly-Sheets.'

Möser was a man of the older generation, a lawyer and an official, who had long before evinced a sympathy with the patriotic tendencies of German literature. The two younger authors, who took part with him in this publication, were not fanatical partisans of the movement in favour of restoring the old German style of

(marginal notes:) 'Von deutscher Art und Kunst,' 1773. Möser, Herder and Goethe.

writing, and of keeping up the popular art of by-gone times;
nevertheless they did for a while lend it their strong support, and by
doing so conclusively showed that the strong current of national
feeling, which had set in after the Seven Years' War, still retained
its force.   These patriotic tendencies had continued to go hand in
hand with hostility to France and with à friendly
attitude towards England.   They now waxed stronger   Literary
and more impetuous, till they acquired the character   revolution
preluded
not of a mere reforming but of a revolutionary force,   by the
intensifying and exaggerating the spirit which had 'Fly-sheets'
and Goethe's
characterised Klopstock and Lessing, and carrying   'Götz.'
along with it all young and enthusiastic minds.

National and popular in its tendencies, this great movement was
in fact a revulsion from the spirit of Voltaire to that of Rousseau,
from the artificiality of society to the simplicity of nature, from
doubt and rationalism to feeling and faith, from *a priori*
notions to history, from hard and fast æsthetic rules to the freedom
of genius.   Goethe's ' Götz ' was the first revolutionary symptom
which really attracted much attention, but the ' Fly-sheets on
German style and art' preceded the publication of ' Götz,' as a kind
of programme or manifesto.

Möser was born in 1720, at Osnabrück, in the very heart of old
Saxony; he lived there till 1794 and was much   Möser's
esteemed.   He had no interest in questions of inter-   life and
national politics, for in the district of North Germany   character.
where his home lay, there were no large cities where such questions
would be discussed.   But the neighbourhood offered him great
facilities for making himself acquainted with the every-day life of the
peasants, with its narrow interests and trivial details. Consequently it
was the social and economic differences, the traditional laws and
customs that were brought within the range of his observation and
occupied his attention, much more than the natural equality and
rights of man.   He devoted himself entirely to the study of his
immediate surroundings, and adopted as his literary model the
essays on manners in the moralizing weekly papers. He apparently
wished to write only for his countrymen, to report their experience,
and to teach them; but he did this in such a thorough and in

teresting manner, and with so much humour and irony, and, following in the steps of Montesquieu and Voltaire, he adopted such a high historical standard, that his small essays, collected in His 'Patrio- 1774 under the title of 'Patriotic Fantasies,' furnish tische Phan- a perfect treasure of observation, wit, and reflection, tasien,' 1774. of practical, historical, and theoretical wisdom.   In these essays he succeeded in generalizing and, as it were, idealizing His 'Osna- the local interests in his immediate neighbourhood; brückische and in the same manner his 'History of Osnabrück,' Geschichte,' which began to appear in 1768, opened out by its 1768. bold conjectures a wide outlook into early German times, and originated views of German constitutional history, whose influence lasted on far into our own century. Möser's name is mentioned with equal respect by German lawyers, historians, and His Con- political economists.   But his conservative attitude, his servatism. respect for existing institutions, and his strong veneration of the past put him in opposition to the general tendencies of the eighteenth century.   He was an enemy of centralising and levelling tendencies, of enlightened despotism with its meddlesome bureaucracy.   He was also incidentally an opponent of philanthropic sentiment, and delighted to utter paradoxical praises of club-law and serfdom.   On the other hand he demanded the institution of trial by jury, and foretold the advent of national armaments.   England, which he knew from direct experience, seemed to him in many respects a model worthy to be copied.   He looked up to the English aristocracy with the same admiration with which Lessing. and Herder looked up to Shakspeare, and he sang the praises of early German times with as much enthusiasm as Klopstock.

Herder, too, was in opposition to the spirit of his age.   He was Herder, inclined to look at things historically, and the sum and b. 1744. substance of all his speculation and writing was, in a word, the history of the human spirit.   He was the son of a schoolmaster, and was born on August 25, 1744 at Mohrungen in East Prussia, in the dominions of Frederick the Great.   Taught during his earlier years by a pedant, then mentally enslaved by a priest, it was not till he went to the University that he won intellectual freedom.   Of a very excitable temperament, he early nursed ambitious dreams ; as a member of the clerical profession, he looked forward to influencing the great and raising the common people. As a student in Königsberg, he soon showed a talent for teaching and a decided tendency to intellectual independence. The philosopher Kant opened to him the wealth of his own knowledge, and led him to suspect the soundness of the fashionable ' enlight-   Hamann's ened' philosophy. But more than any other, Hamann   influence attracted him into his strange sphere of thought.   on him.

Johann Georg Hamann, the ' Magus of the North,' as he was called, was a fantastically original man, and a writer of mystical works ; he was a great reader, had a thorough knowledge of the Greek writers and of Shakspeare, and introduced Herder to the study of the latter. He was born in 1730, and after many wanderings at length found rest in his native town of Königsberg. From 1759, he published a succession of fragmentary writings, full of allusions and with strange titles, ' Sibylline leaves ' people called them. They were disconnected papers, now oracular, now humorous, never fully worked out or deductively proving anything, but in their merely aphoristic and ardent style rather suggestive than convincing. An enemy of mere analysis and abstraction, he sought to understand man and his faculties as a whole. Nature, he said, works upon us through the senses and the passions, which in turn can neither appreciate nor utter themselves in anything but images ; therefore poetry is the original language of the human race. The passions are the driving force of human nature and the life of all thought and imagination.

Hamann adopted a hostile attitude towards the theology and philosophy of the so-called 'Illuminati' or rationalists.   Hamann's During a sojourn in London, in a time of great   hostility to inward and outward difficulty, he began to read   the the Bible, and this made a turning-point in his life ;   'Illumi-nati.' orthodoxy gained a new prophet, who everywhere defended faith against reason, and asserted the insufficiency of the latter for the recognition of the deepest truths. And as on the one hand he mistrusted logical argument, so on the other he attacked æsthetic rules ; as he championed revelation, so he also did homage to unfettered genius in poet and artist. Whereas the Illuminati strove to attain an ordered system of knowledge, he revelled in disconnected assertions. Whereas they tried to shut up everything in sweeping general formulæ, he laid stress on the radical unlikeness of everything to everything else. While they sought to be clear and reasonable in their literary style, Hamann scorned to be merely logical in what he wrote, and preferred exceptions to rules, imagination to understanding, poetry to prose, the particular to the general. Though any systematic progress in knowledge would be impossible on these lines, yet Hamann's teaching might render it easier for a true poet of original talent and liberal culture to break from the fetters of finite thought, might strengthen his faith in his own powers, and quicken in him the impulse to poetic creation. The seeds of Hamann's teaching germinated in Herder, and through him bore fruit for Goethe.

Warmly recommended by Hamann, Herder, in November, 1764, left Königsberg for Riga, where he soon en-chanted everyone as a teacher and preacher; but this did not suit him as a permanence, and after four years of work he suddenly gave up his office. He was not yet twenty-five, and he wished to see the world. A journey to France confirmed him in his aversion to the French. He was next to go with a German prince to Italy; but on his way thither he engaged himself to a lady in Darmstadt, and during his stay in Strassburg he received a call to Bückeburg, which he accepted. For five years, from 1771 to 1776, he remained chained to this little Westphalian town, where in 1773 he made a home for himself and his bride.

Herder at Riga, 1764-68.

Thomas Abbt, author of the writings entitled, 'Of death for one's country,' and 'Of Merit,' had been Privy Councillor and friend of Count Wilhelm of Lippe-Schaumburg, and had died in Bückeburg at an early age, in 1766. Herder, who had a great respect for him, had praised his popular philosophy and his historical gifts in one of his works. This directed Count Wilhelm's attention to him, and he hoped to find in him one who would make up to him for the loss of Thomas Abbt. But the two did not agree well together and the relation between them remained a cool one. The Countess, whose beautiful character

Herder at Bückeburg, 1771-76.

strongly attracted her clerical friend, died in the summer of 1776, and Herder, who had long felt himself an exile at Bückeburg, was called in the autumn of the same year to Weimar, as Court chaplain and 'Superintendent' of the Church district of Weimar. There amid varying circumstances he worked till 1803. In his sensitive nature there lay a tendency to discontent; he did not develop freely, boldly, victoriously, but found hindrances everywhere, which were in part due to his own character. He kept silence from sensitiveness where he ought to have spoken, and then he suffered greatly from awkward situations, which he might have avoided by timely frankness. He attacked his enemies violently, and was surprised when they answered in like manner. His literary production began with great ardour, but easily flagged, and not one of his original great works was carried to completion.

Herder at Weimar, 1776–1803.

His first important works, which he published in Riga, were the 'Fragmente über die neuere deutsche Literatur' (1767), and the 'Kritische Wälder' (1769). The former were meant to be a continuation of Lessing's 'Literaturbriefe,' while the latter stood in close connection with his 'Laokoon.' In the former Herder wrote like Hamann, in the latter he sometimes reminds us of Lessing. He showed himself throughout to be a careful, enthusiastic, but at the same time critical reader of Lessing, for whom he cherished all through life the greatest reverence. He continued to follow in Lessing's steps when he praised Shakspeare, Homer, and the popular songs. He showed Lessing's spirit too in the tolerance and wide human sympathies which prompted him to rescue barbarian nationalities, so-called dark ages, despised branches of poetry and forgotten poets from oblivion, and to give them their due honour. He sought to determine the boundaries of poetry and plastic art in a different manner from Lessing, and he went beyond Lessing in his endeavours to define the difference between plastic art and painting. He most successfully corrected and amended Lessing's theory of fables and epigrams, but he required, quite in Lessing's spirit, that lyric poetry as well as other kinds should above all be full of movement, progress, and action. But whereas Lessing was in the first place an

Herder's 'Fragmente' and 'Kritische Wälder.'

Herder and Lessing.

art-critic, and only secondarily a historian of literature, of Herder the
reverse was true : he was first and foremost a historian of literature,
and only incidentally an art-critic. Lessing had recourse to his rich
literary knowledge in order to find rules of composition and bases
Herder's
sympathy
with foreign
literatures. of criticism, but Herder · studied the literature of all
nations and periods for its own sake, and with en-
thusiastic appreciation. He tried to transport himself
into the local and temporary conditions under which
literary works had been produced, and to adopt the point of view
then prevalent ; he sought to be a Hebrew with the Hebrews, an
Arab with the Arabs, a Skald with the Skalds, a Bard with the
Bards ; and in these endeavours, which were strengthened by kindred
efforts among English writers of the same time, he proved himself a
true pupil of Montesquieu and Winckelmann ; their power of
appreciating the past lived on in him, and bore new fruit in
literature.

Herder showed his sympathetic appreciation of foreign poetry
not only as a historian of literature, but also as a translator. His
His powers
as a trans-
lator. original poems, which evince a characteristic tendency
towards didactic narrative, towards allegory, parable,
and sacred legend, do not rise to any great merit, but
his translations must be reckoned among the classical achievements
of German literature. From Opitz down to Klopstock and Lessing,
foreign influence exerted its sway over German literature ; Herder
founded the universal culture of modern Germany on the remains
of this foreign dominion, and taught his successors that lesson
of open-hearted surrender to the influences of foreign races or
of the remote past, which, far from enslaving the learner, really confirms his independence, while it enriches and strengthens his mind.

Herder's art, as a translator, was based on his deep insight into
His theory
of poetry. language and poetry in general, their origin, their
development, and their relation to each other. In
this especially he showed himself to be a disciple of Hamann.
' Poetry is the mother-tongue of the human race,' Hamann had said ;
a whole world of truth is indeed locked up in the pregnant word, and
Herder was the man to make it yield up its secret. Poetry is
older than prose ; poetry lives in language, lives in myth, and greets

us at the threshold of history. Primitive poetry, the poetry of
Nature, in which all Nature acts and speaks, being personified by
man, who is all feeling and passion, poetry such as breathes in the
songs of barbaric peoples—this, said Herder, is true poetry. The
paradise of the Scriptures and Rousseau's ideal natural man meet
us purified and transfigured in Herder's thought. He too is convinced that a return to Nature alone will regain us our original and
ideal perfection. In his 'Literary Fragments,' Herder sang the
praises of his mother-tongue, its freedom and native force, and it
was then already clear to him that the history of the human soul
can only be deciphered from its language. His treatise on the
' Origin of Language ' cast the deepest glances into primitive times.
His ' Spirit of Hebraic Poetry ' contained his ripest   His 'Geist
thoughts on the connection between language and   der Hebräi-
poetry. His general views as a historian of litera- schen Poesie.'
ture were revealed in his prize essay on ' The causes of the lowering
of taste amongst various nations once distinguished for it.' His
fame as a man of universal sympathies, and as a versatile translator,
was established by his collection of ' Popular Songs,' published in
the years 1778 and 1779. Later publishers gave to   His ' Stim-
the work the affected title of ' Voices of the Nations   men der
in Song.' It comprised not only popular songs   Völker in
by unknown authors, but characteristic poems drawn   Liedern.'
from the literature of all nations alike. All forms of lyric
poetry were here represented, and the only principle of classifica-
tion which Herder allowed of in this collection was an æsthetic one,
namely, community of subject and sentiment. It is marvellous how
Herder was able to appreciate the spirit of these songs, to strike the
right note in his translations and retain it throughout, to reproduce
exactly not only the feelings, but even the peculiar metre and style
of each poem. The whole collection is a series of gems of poetry,
all written in exquisite German, and free from the barrenness which
meets us in most anthologies.

Herder's scientific work is marked by the same breadth of view
and catholic sympathy as his poetry. Many of his thoughts had
been uttered before, and few of them are thoroughly worked out ;
he furnished more suggestions than results, more questions than

answers, bold hypotheses, but little argument. But we can well excuse

Herder as a philosopher of History.

in science the imperfection which is confined to details, and which is but the condition of rising to a wide view of the whole.   It may be true that Herder looked at things only from a distance, where the eye deceives and forms melt into one another.   Yet his point of view was so well chosen, that he could direct many people to their goals, and indicate the paths which are followed, even in the present day.   He took in at a glance the limits and interrelation of the various sciences; and whoever advances to the highest problems in any of the sciences of the human mind, whoever studies history, or the science of language, mythology, or ethnology, whoever collects popular traditions or explores German or Hebrew antiquity, or would trace the development of national peculiarities in all spheres of life, and understand the formative influence of nature upon man—each one of these must reverence Herder as a seer of extraordinary powers.   His work teaches on all sides the value which the union of separate departments of science has for the progress of knowledge.   And more than this; if the example of Lessing proves how much criticism and poetic activity may advance each other, when combined in one man, the influence of Herder on Goethe shows how much benefit a clear-sighted young poet, thirsting for knowledge, may derive from an equally clear-sighted critic, who has all the resources of history and theory at his command.

Herder's mental development.

Herder's mind seems to have developed with wonderful consistency.   His earliest works contain all the later ones in germ.   Nevertheless, he did pass through momentous changes in mental attitude.   In his early youth he was an orthodox Pietist; in Riga his religion took a freethinking direction; in Bückeburg he became a Biblical Christian, and in Weimar he returned to liberal views.   When at the zenith of his influence in Riga, as we have already said, he suddenly gave up his office there; after this, the new impressions gained from a long sea-journey, and also from life in France, among a foreign people and in new circumstances, had a powerful effect on the development of his mind, and set all his ideas in ferment.   In a diary which he kept at this period, we find plan after plan proposed.   He dreams alternately of distinction as a teacher or as a statesman, of becoming the Calvin of Riga or the Lycurgus of Russia, but, in spite of himself, the instinct to be a man of learning triumphs, and all his schemes revert in the end to the books he would like to write. Energy enough to divert the world from its course, ambition, thirst for action, vagueness about details, but certainty about the whole—such 'storm and stress' (*Sturm und Drang*) of wit and intelligence as we notice still seething at this period in Herder's mind, characterized the German literary Revolution. Herder's ardent impulse towards literary creation had as yet found no satisfaction, when in Strassburg he made the acquaintance of Goethe, and won him as a pupil.

Goethe came from Frankfort, from the Rhine and Main district, where the popular poetry of the fourteenth century had blossomed. The Franconian race to which Hutten and Hans Sachs belonged, and the republican city which had formerly been the centre of the German book-trade, had the honour of producing Germany's greatest poet, and some of Goethe's leading characteristics may have been in part called forth by the scenes of his early life. The conservative city in which the German emperors were crowned, was quite free from that artificial æsthetic and social culture which reigned, for instance, in Leipzig; it looked not to the future but to the past, in which its greatness lay.

Goethe's birthplace, Frankfort on the Main.

Goethe's family on the paternal side was one which had risen rapidly in the social scale; his great-grandfather was a farrier, his grandfather a sailor, his father a lawyer and a man of independent means, who lived for self-culture; the great event of his life was a journey to Italy, which he wrote an account of, and was always referring to; he was a collector and kind of Mæcenas, a man of many-sided interests, literary, scientific, and artistic, with a love of order and regularity amounting almost to pedantry, stern, serious, true to his convictions, a good patriot, an enemy of the French and a worshipper of Frederick the Great. The mother, on the other hand, came of one of the leading families of the town; she was twenty-one years younger than her husband, and had a singularly easy and cheerful nature,

His parentage.

pliant and averse to all care; she bore with cheerful resignation a marriage which had little of happiness, and consoled herself by adorning her life with the charms of imagination, and lavishing the rich treasures of her heart and mind on her children and especially on the eldest, Wolfgang. Restraint and freedom, seriousness and cheerfulness, fear and love all helped to educate the boy; they complemented each other, and so gave him breadth of mind and character, great desires, yet also the necessary discipline to keep his passions in check and direct his extraordinary gifts to a worthy object. From his father he inherited method and the scientific spirit, and it was also his father who turned his thoughts to Italy, and inspired him with zeal for learning and dilettante interests. His poetic talent, his gift of figurative speech, his fiery nature, and his sweeping fancy descended to him from his mother. She herself was gifted with a straightforward, cheerful eloquence; every unimportant note that she wrote breathes the charm of naturalness and originality; she was an incomparable teller of fairy-tales, and by telling the boy but half a story and letting him guess the rest, she early trained him to poetic invention. His education was somewhat irregularly pursued, but was such as would promote rapid development towards intellectual freedom, and the most important productions of contemporary literature were at an early age put in the boy's hands. Goethe

Goethe, b. 1749. His early education.
was born on the 28th of August, 1749, when Gellert, Gleim, Klopstock, and Lessing had already begun to write. His father favoured the rhyming poets, and a friend of the family introduced the 'Messias.' The beauty of the Old Testament called forth a willing admiration in the boy, and laid the foundation of those naive, idyllic elements which he soon handled in such a masterly manner. A pantomime to which he was taken gave him the first impulse to dramatic writing, and a translation of Tasso's 'Gerusalemme Liberata' seems to have furnished him with the first chivalric-heroic subject. Precocious and ambitious as a boy, he had, by the time he was sixteen, tried his hand in all branches of poetic composition, and had learned everything there was to be learned in the Imperial city; he had witnessed an Imperial coronation, had mixed with all sorts and

conditions of men, had looked more than was good for him into social evils, and had loved often and known the disappointments of love. At sixteen, following his father's wish and suppressing his own leaning towards philology, he went to the University of Leipzig, with the avowed purpose of studying law; but in fact he dabbled in all sciences, and received a really deep and lasting impression only from his intercourse with an artist, *He goes to Leipzig University, 1765.* that same Oeser who at an earlier period had influenced Winckelmann in Dresden. He returned after three years, out of health and depressed in spirits, to his paternal home ; but during his time in Leipzig he had made great advances in taste and in poetic power. A couple of unrhymed odes written at this period are full of happy imagery, and in a number of rhymed poems he combined the half-jocose, half-didactic, operetta-like tone of the Leipzig school with a keen appreciation of nature, and thus brought the graceful, frivolous, Anacreontic poetry to its highest perfection. In a pastoral play entitled 'The Humour of the Lover,' he succeeded in giving quite a new rendering to an old theme, well known in Leipzig; the interest of the old plot is enhanced by the life-like way in which he *'Die Laune des Verliebten.'* draws the characters, and the whole play is a true and unique work of art, written in the charming but usually somewhat trivial style of the dramatic idyll. Older Frankfort associations of Goethe's are reflected in the disagreeable, but powerful comedy of 'The Accomplices.' In all these productions it is evident that Goethe had not only imbibed the Leipzig literary *'Die Mitschuldigen.'* spirit from Gellert and Weisse, but that Lessing's newly published 'Minna' had greatly benefited his dramatic technique. It is clear also that Klopstock and Wieland had enriched his poetic language and ideas, and that Oeser's teaching had not been thrown away upon him. We may further notice that in all these poems he does what, as a writer of lyrics, he continued to do for many decades,—he treats almost exclusively of matters drawn from his own personal experience, and seeks to alleviate his inward distress by uttering it in verse.

His ideal at this time was innocence and he preferred the

cheerful and naive to the exaggerated heroism and stupendous
virtue which Wieland had already attacked. But beyond this,
Lessing's 'Minna' had directed him to great national subjects;
he was also familiar with Shakspeare, and at Strassburg, whither

Goethe and Herder in Strassburg, 1770. he went in the spring of 1770 to complete his legal
studies, he made the acquaintance of Herder, with
whom he spent the winter of 1770–71. He occasionally felt himself somewhat roughly treated and
cruelly mocked at by his master, but this stern discipline was whole-
some for him. Herder's gods became his gods; the pupil of Wieland
was taken into the school of nature, and his lyric poetry at once
underwent a thorough transformation. To see the difference, one
need only compare the Leipzig poem: 'Nun verlass' ich diese
Hütte' in which he describes himself coming out from the
cottage of his beloved into the lonely wood and the moon-light,
with the celebrated Strassburg poem: 'Es schlug mein Herz,
geschwind zu Pferde.' The former does indeed contain one beautiful
metaphor :—

> 'Und die Birken streun mit Neigen
> Ihr den süssten Weihrauch auf'—

the first instance of Goethe's incomparable art of finding a
poetical meaning in the appearance of plants. In other respects, however, this poem is full of affectation, such as the
pastoral fancy and the introduction of ancient mythology;
description takes the place of action and the poem winds up
with a very ordinary lover's jest. Very different is the poem
written at Strassburg, describing how the lover sets out to see his
beloved, his welcome and his farewell. Here, four stanzas give
us a succession of dramatic scenes in the fewest words, and the
whole is penetrated by the glowing breath of passion. All fits
in exactly with Herder's theory of the song, a theory which he
founded on the primitive nature of language, and which may be
summed up in the sequence: 'verb, life, action, passion.' There
is no dragging in of dead mythology here, but actual creating
of it anew, as if it had never existed before. While in Strassburg
Herder had thus described the genesis of mythology : 'the savage
saw the lofty tree towering in its majesty, and he marvelled thereat ;

the tree-top rustled, and he heard the godhead weaving; the savage fell on his knees and prayed. There you have the history of man as a sensuous being.' Goethe had learnt to look on nature as a savage. He had listened to Herder's advice and thereby made immeasurable progress. He had as it were drunk from the original source whence poetry first sprang, and now he was fortified for every task.

But in this Strassburg song Goethe had not created according to abstract rules alone ; he had also drawn from real life. The beloved one really existed of whom he sang. In Alsace, in the country parsonage of Sesenheim, he had met Friederike Brion. She was a quiet, bright, naive, faithful girl, and was soon devoted with her whole heart to the merry student; in her Goethe found his long-sought ideal. The pastor's family at Sesenheim seemed to him the Vicar of Wakefield and his family in real life ; here was an idyll without affectation, without any false halo; here was pure, beautiful family-life, with all its kindliness and gentle charm, the simple country occupations, the happy atmosphere which good people diffuse around them. Reality, imagination, and love combined to make Friederike the real embodiment of his ideal ; thus Herder's pupil learnt to base his poetical creations upon reality. It was at Sesenheim that he made his preliminary studies for Gretchen and Clärchen, for 'Werther' and for his 'Hermann and Dorothea.'

Goethe and Friederike Brion.

But Alsace gave Goethe more than Herder and Friederike. The Strassburg Minster made him an admirer of Gothic architecture. The national enmities apparent in his immediate vicinity, the general tendency of German feeling after the Seven Years' War, the religious phase he was then passing through, and in this case too, Herder's example, excited in him an aversion to France and French literature. He and several young and turbulent companions vied with each other in passionate patriotic sentiments, and in doing homage to the spirit of Shakspeare. Leipzig gallantry began to be supplanted by free-and-easy, student-like manners, joined with plain speech and coarse jokes, and this spirit even penetrated into

Influences of Goethe's Strassburg period.

poetry. Julius Cæsar and other great historical characters captivated the fancy of the youthful Goethe, whose self-confidence soon
soared beyond all limits; Mahomet and Socrates floated before
his mind, while Lessing and the marionette-plays had already directed
his attention to the figure of Faust. But chance threw another
hero in his way, who for the time being attracted him more than
these, and who could more easily be made the centre of a drama—
Götz von Berlichingen.

The historical Götz, a robber-knight and a leader in the
'Götz von peasant-wars of the sixteenth century, had employed
Berlich- the enforced leisure of his later days in writing an
ingen,' 1771. autobiography in defence of his life and conduct. He
represented himself as an honest but much misunderstood and
slandered person, a man who had always followed right and justice,
and had never fought but in defence of the weak. His record of himself was printed, and falling into Goethe's hands, was completely
believed by him. He took the old knight just as he had described
himself, and determined to rescue him from oblivion, just as
Lessing was so fond of doing to forgotten worthies. It was the
more natural that Goethe should choose such a subject because
at that time chivalry was being revived in literature, especially
in France. Goethe's early acquaintance with Tasso and with
popular romances such as the 'Haimonskinder' had laid a good
foundation in this direction, and the subject of Götz attracted
his glance to the most important period of the Reformation, as
well as to those old imperial relations and conditions which
had from old time been fraught with special interest for the
imperial town of Frankfort. Protestant sympathies are reflected
in the piece, and the poet draws a by no means flattering picture
of a clerical court, and gives a lamentable description of the
condition of the Empire at that period; no one can find justice,
each must shift for himself, and the blame of this disorder lies
with the independent princes, against whom even the Emperor can
do nothing. Götz is a good Imperialist, but he hates bad sovereigns,
Goethe's and though he should succumb in the struggle, still
Liberalism. with his dying breath he will invoke success for the
cause of Liberty. In this play Goethe championed the cause

of freedom against the tyrants of Germany, and contrasted the honest, patriotic, chivalrous life of his hero, with the corrupt life of the courts. Haller's newly published novel 'Usong' and the criticism of the courts in Thümmel's and Weisse's works were not without influence on Goethe in writing this piece; but at the same time he was also under the power of a local and family tradition, which urged upon him a certain liberalism in politics. His father was in the habit of warning him against becoming a mere courtier. Herr von Loen, a relative of the Goethe family, had described in a didactic novel the difficulties which an honest man has to overcome at court; and Frederick Karl von Moser, one of the most eminent German statesmen of the last century, had published at Frankfort in 1759 a book, called 'Der Herr und der Diener,' which in bold and passionate language ruthlessly criticised the sovereigns of the smaller German states.

Goethe was back in Frankfort, when about the end of 1771 he wrote down the first sketch of his 'Götz.' On the 28th of August in that year he had been called to the bar. His old interests and connections were taken up again, and new ones were added to them; yet he was not happy, for he was oppressed by a sense of having injured an innocent person; Friederike Brion had given him her heart, and though perhaps no formal vows had been exchanged, they seemed to belong to each other, and she might well have expected a declaration from him after his return home; instead, there came a letter taking leave of her altogether. The young lawyer did not dare to introduce the Alsatian clergyman's daughter into the Frankfort patrician family. He reproached himself for his conduct, and could not forgive himself for it, but he did not repent and return to his deserted love. He did not see her again till eight years afterwards, when he was Minister at Weimar; the meeting between them was calm and affectionate, and set him at rest with himself. His poems written during the intervening years testified that he anyhow deeply felt his guilt in the matter; we find him creating, as a foil to his honest Götz, the character of Weislingen, the unfaithful lover of Götz's gentle sister. Weislingen is a portrait of Goethe himself, and a portrait more honest than

Goethe's desertion of Friederike.

Characters in 'Götz.'

flattering. He is an elegant and seductive young gallant, of weak character, and spoilt by court-life ; he wavers between two very different women, but is finally drawn away from the gentle and good one by a lovely but fiendish rival.

Lessing's ' Sara ' was the only important German tragedy which

'Götz'
written in
imitation of
Shakspeare.

offered itself to the young poet as a model in writing this play, and it was no wonder that so imperfect a work compared unfavourably with Shak- speare. Shakspeare's name was the standard under which Goethe resolved to win. Addison and Bodmer, Lessing and Herder, Wieland and Gerstenberg, had proclaimed the great dramatist's merits. Christian Felix Weisse's ' Richard III,' though meritorious, could not hold its own by the side of Shakspeare's, and his 'Romeo and Juliet' only awakened a longing for the Shakspearian original. Gerstenberg sought to approach nearer to the real Shak- speare in his 'Ugolino,' but it was impossible to feel any enthu- siasm for a play in which hunger reigned through all five acts. The Strassburg brethren would hear no more of dilutions of Shakspeare ; they wanted to transplant the real Shakspeare into German literature, and with this object Goethe treated his ' Götz ' in the manner of a Shakspearian historical drama. In this first version of the play unity of time and place is utterly disregarded, and change of scene occurs for a monologue of three lines or a dialogue of six. The unity of action is spoilt by the introduction of Weislingen, who thrusts himself in as a second hero. Men of all ranks, citizens, soldiers, ser- vants, and peasants are dragged in ; the variety of character and sentiment is carried to excess, tragedy and comedy being inter- mingled, and a Shakspearian clown and jester set down in the midst of a society of courtiers. Small songs are introduced, and there is much strong language and coarseness, along with far-fetched similes and exaggeration, reminding one of Lohenstein and the old ' chief- actions and State-actions ' (cf. vol. i. p. 398), while at the same time many Shakspearian reminiscences occur throughout the play. Over- joyed with this work, which he had accomplished so quickly and easily, Goethe sent it to Herder. But Herder, who was an inexorable opponent of all imitation, summed up his judgment in the following words: 'Shakspeare has quite spoilt you.' Lessing's ' Emilia Galotti,' which made its appearance about the same time, showed how different a conception the master of German drama had formed of the manner in which Shakspeare should be followed. Goethe at once felt that 'Emilia' was an original work, while his 'Götz' was only an imitation. Without being discouraged he set to work afresh. He could not now alter the essential features of the piece, but he could weld it into greater unity, and could remove as far as possible all forms of expression which he was conscious of having borrowed from Shakspeare. He could at the same time aim higher than Lessing, for he despised all artificial restraints, all affectation, and high-sounding language in the dialogue generally, while he retained the ornate language and formal expressions proper to the conversation of courtiers. He often used words merely to indicate actions, and altogether succeeded in imparting to his dialogue the tone of natural conversation. 'Götz von Berlichingen' appeared before the public in this new and improved form in the summer of 1773. It presented a picture

Improved version of 'Götz,' 1773.

drawn from the past history of the nation; the characters were purely German, such as had never hitherto been seen in German tragedy, and of which Lessing's 'Minna' offered the only examples in the sphere of comedy. The play is full of life, action, and truth. The noble character of its hero, powerless to stem the wickedness of the world, is most pathetic, and the interest of the play is enhanced by all the display of a romantic chivalry, and by the quick succession of exciting incidents.

Goethe's 'Götz' was the signal for a perfect Shakspeare-mania in Germany, though it marked the end of this same mania in its author. By writing 'Götz' Goethe freed himself from the servile imitation of Shakspeare, and learnt from him original and independent dramatic art. Only two of his other plays, 'Faust' and 'Egmont,' both planned simultaneously with or shortly after 'Götz,' show the same rapid change of scene, which is so incompatible with our theatrical arrangements. Goethe sought henceforth to put himself in sympathy with the living stage, and Lessing's technique, which differed little from that of the French, was adopted by him as authori-

Smaller dramas.

tative. By operettas such as 'Erwin und Elmire' and 'Claudine

von Villabella,' he sought to win the favour of the average theatre-
goer by cultivating the fashionable dramatic form of the day.
In his ' Clavigo,' a tragedy dealing with middle-class life, and
in his ' Stella,' he countenanced change of scene but once at
the utmost within an act, and maintained unity of time also to a
certain degree. But he did not yield himself up entirely to modern
subjects and modern treatment. The historical mood in which he
had begun this literary Revolution had by no means passed off with
the appearance of 'Götz,' and though ' Faust ' and ' Egmont' took
shape more slowly, yet their author's whole heart was in them.
The sixteenth century with its free and active spirit of enquiry and
its valiant struggle against intellectual slavery, seemed to him the
ideal epoch of history. There he found characters such as he
wanted, thoughts and deeds, the study of which might elevate and
brace up a more effeminate age, and in addition to these a style of
art full of characteristic truth and simple nature. The fame
of Hans Sachs began to be revived about this time. In 1765
he was made the subject of a monograph; then Kästner put
in a good word for him, and the local patriotism of Nürnberg,
thus encouraged, burst forth into warm eulogies. Goethe himself
Influence of considered the poetic shoemaker of Nürnberg of suffi-
Hans Sachs cient importance to make his style worth reviving.
on Goethe. Goethe's study of Shakspeare enabled him to take up
the threads of literature at the point where the Thirty Years' War
had suddenly stopped the development of the German drama.
Hans Sachs gave him the clue to what Opitz and his school had
missed in the seventeenth century; and while his own refined
sense of form and beauty purified the old shoemaker's easy doggrel
verse and realistic style, the influence which Hans Sachs exercised
over Goethe is traceable in his satirical dramas, such as ' Das Jahr-
marktsfest zu Plundersweilen,' or ' Satyros,' or the Carnival play,
' Pater Brey;' in little didactic plays, such as ' Künstler's Erden-
wallen ' (The artist's earthly wanderings), and 'Künstler's Vergöt-
terung' (The artist's apotheosis), in his poem written in praise of
the old master himself, and above all in ' Faust.'

But while Goethe was following these national aspirations he
was at the same time absorbed in the study of classical antiquity,

just as Lessing had produced almost simultaneously his ' Minna '
and his 'Laokoon,' and Goethe himself, when in   Classical
Leipzig, had been equally influenced by the Dutch tendencies
genre-painters and by Oeser's classic grace. At   in Goethe.
Strassburg, in Herder's company, he began to read Homer, and
after he had, under the strong influence of Shakspeare, written
down the first sketch for 'Götz,' he devoted himself to Theocritus and Pindar. ' Götz ' had hardly appeared when he ventured
to rival Æschylus with a ' Prometheus.' Teutonic and Hellenic
elements of culture, with their two opposite styles, gained power
over him simultaneously, and each benefited the other. Beside
the doggrel verses he employed rhymeless, free rhythms, with
beautiful, sonorous epithets. He produced odes, scenes, and fables
modelled upon the Greek type, and at the same time rhyming proverbs
and sarcasms about correct style directed against the critics of the
day. He united Hans Sachs' method of description with Homer's epic
breadth, and was able, as we have seen in the Strassburg song mentioned above, to clothe pathetic descriptions of travel and wandering,
set in the midst of nature's ever-shifting scenes, in the powerful and
exalted style of the Pindaric odes. His poem called ' Der Wan-
'Der Wanderer,' in part suggested by Oliver Gold-   derer.'
smith's ' Traveller,' deals with motives and incidents of rustic life,
full of human interest ; here he followed Theocritus' example, and
employed the form of a dialogue in order to suggest a walk presenting change of scene and varying objects of nature and art, and
to give the reader a glimpse of the conditions of domestic life in the
country. In this poem too we can everywhere trace Herder's literary
and historical many-sidedness bearing fruit in Goethe, and developing dormant powers in the mind of the young poet. He had now
got far beyond the rhymed prettinesses of Wieland's Hellenism,
which he had so admired in Leipzig, and he strongly attacked them
in his plain-spoken prose farce, entitled ' Götter,   'Götter,
Helden und Wieland,' in which the Greeks are made to Helden und
                                                       Wieland,'
behave in a rude, bragging, and student-like manner. and 'Prome-
But his ' Prometheus,' which he began in 1773   theus.'
as a drama in blank verse, and which he afterwards cut down
to a single monologue, remained free from such extravagances,

and is throughout grand and elevated. Prometheus is a creative artist, who loves his creatures and breathes life into them. He looks to Heaven for nothing, but relies entirely upon his own power; in this respect he expresses one side of Goethe's own religious convictions.

The inner life of the poet had already passed through various phases. Though from early years, as we have seen, the Bible enriched the store of his poetic imagination, yet a superficial religious teaching and unedifying sermons loosened even in school-years the ties binding him to the Church. At the University of Leipzig biblical and dogmatic criticism gave to his mind a thoroughly liberal tendency. But an illness and a pious friend were the means of bringing him again nearer to the Gospel; and on his return home, a friend of his mother's, Fräulein von Klettenberg, won him as a convert to the Pietism of the Moravians. Mystical ideas struck root in him, and he began to give vent to passionate yearnings after deliverance from earthly fetters, and union with God. But this pious mood, which at the beginning of his Strassburg career was still strong upon him, did not last long. We learn that in the summer of 1772 Goethe no longer went to church or to the Sacrament and seldom prayed. He was loth to disturb others in their views, being thoroughly tolerant in religion and morals; sympathy for human weakness appeared to him the true theology. But in the very next year this toleration forsook him, and we find him attacking those with whom he had so recently been in close sympathy. He not only ridiculed the vulgar rationalism represented by Doctor Bahrdt, who gave much offence by extreme teaching and frivolous living, but he also scoffed at sentimental religiosity and the pietistic worship of the Lamb, at separatism and missionary zeal. He conceived the plan of devoting a religious satirical epic in doggrel to the character of the Wandering Jew. The shoemaker of Jerusalem, who, according to the mediæval legend, jeered at Christ bearing the cross, and was in consequence condemned to wander until Christ's second coming, was transformed by Goethe into a Moravian and Separatist; but Goethe makes Christ return, not as the judge of all mankind, but as the ruler of the millennium.

Goethe's religious development.

The moment when deeply moved he beholds the earth once more is one of the grandest things that Goethe's imagination ever produced. With the *naïveté* of a Hans Sachs, and with an unconcerned humanising of divine things, he succeeds in revealing to us wonderful depths of the soul, so that our hearts are touched to the very core. Unfortunately the work never got further than a few fragmentary beginnings, which were not made public till after Goethe's death.

When he wrote these fragments Goethe had quite broken with the belief in a Providence arbitrarily interfering with human fate, and retained nothing but the universal Deity of Goethe's Spinoza. His experience seemed to have taught him Spinozism. that in the moments of our life when help is most needed we are thrown upon our own resources. He had discovered, he thought, like Frederick the Great in the exigencies of the Seven Years' War, that God is deaf to our entreaties. His creative talent seemed to him the only thing on which he could now rely. Faith in his artistic power alone did not deceive him, and Beauty was his Goddess. His Prometheus rejects the demands of the Gods like the Prometheus of Æschylus, and like the Cyclops of Euripides is devoted to earthly possessions. He knows that nothing is his but the sphere of his activity and influence, 'nothing below that and nothing above.' He says with Spinoza: 'Thus I am eternal, for I exist,' and he deems himself on a level with the Gods. But the defiant words which he launches against them were probably not meant to be his last; if Goethe had finished the drama, he would probably have shown that men do stand in need of the Gods; the arrogance of the artist would have been humbled, and the result would have been the joy of which his brother suggests the prospect, the bliss when the Gods, Prometheus, his creatures, and the world and heaven shall all feel themselves to be parts of a harmonious whole. Although Goethe no longer looked to Heaven for help, yet he had not wholly lost his reverence for the Deity. That mystic union with God which he had learned from the Moravians, he found echoed in Spinoza's teaching. Goethe too felt himself to be a part of the all-embracing, all-sustaining spirit of the universe, and in ineffable emotion he celebrated his recognition of the Deity. The monologue of Prometheus was completed by a monologue of Ganymede, in which Love of Nature becomes love of God.

Our salvation, our happiness, our liberty, consist, according to Spinoza, in constant and eternal love of God, which is nothing else than a part of that infinite love with which God loves himself. But though Goethe grasped this idea, and recognised in Spinoza himself the free man, who rises above the sea of passion and in happy serenity bids the storms be still, yet he him-

His restless and turbu-lent life. self was all the time tossing on the wild sea of turbulent emotions; he could only long for, not win the calm of the wise man, and he was on the way to become what he himself designated later on 'a problematic nature,' a man whom no sphere of life would satisfy, and who was not good enough for any sphere of life.

His barrister's work made no great claims upon him; he had but few briefs and even in those his father helped him. There were frequent intermissions in his work; he was often in Darmstadt where he had a valued friend in Merck, a member of the War Ministry, with whom he shared literary, artistic, and personal interests. During the year 1772 Merck had the editing of the Frankfort 'Gelehrte Anzeigen,' a critical review to which Herder and Goethe contributed, and in which were heard the first distant notes of the German literary revolution. In the summer of 1772 Goethe passed four months in Wetzlar in order to become acquainted with the procedure of the Imperial Chancery (Reichskammergericht). In the summer of 1774 he travelled down the Rhine to Düsseldorf, and in the summer of 1775 he went to Switzerland. It became more and more manifest that Frankfort was not the right sphere for him. The many distinguished strangers who came to see him there could not compensate him for what he missed at home. He felt himself confined and fettered on every side. The legal profession did not satisfy him, and he could not devote himself exclusively to a poetical career. In addition to this,

His love-affairs. love-entanglements of various kinds had brought him into equivocal and difficult positions. In Wetzlar he fell violently in love with Lotte Buff, the affianced bride of his good friend Kestner; but in this case the firm character of the girl,

Goethe's friendship for her betrothed, and finally separation and departure all worked together to quell the passion. In Frankfort, however, he fascinated girls and women, awakened feelings which he could not share, and excited wishes which he might not satisfy. Now it was an excellent, simple girl to whom he seemed so much attached that his parents fully expected an engagement, which however never came to pass ; at another time it was the brilliant vision of Lili Schönemann which irresistibly attracted him, and in spite of many objections an engagement took place, but neither did that end in marriage. Then again, side by side with Lili, another figure appears, a girl whom, according to the expression of his diary, he wore like a spring flower upon his heart. In short, the lovingness and loveableness of his nature were constantly carrying him away and almost turning him into a Don Juan; but all this disturbed his daily life, darkened his pleasures, troubled his conscience, and filled him with the most painful emotions. He was right when, in the October of 1775, he called the months which had just passed the most distracted and confused, the fullest and most empty, the strongest and most foolish epoch of his life. This life of inward and outward unrest Goethe goes was happily cut short in November 1775 by his to Weimar, accepting an invitation to the court at Weimar, where 1775. he was henceforth to make his home.

But however prejudicial these four stormy years of barrister-life at Frankfort may have been to Goethe's moral de- Goethe's velopment, they have left indelible traces in his poetry. lyrics, up to In Strassburg his lyric poetry was only just begin- 1775. ning to free itself from the fetters of the Leipzig style ; simultaneously with the passionate poem, 'Es schlug mein Herz,' he wrote the charming song, ' Mit einem gemalten Bande,' the flower of German Anacreontic poetry. The poems to Friederike are true lyrics and breathe the pure and peaceful happiness which he found in loving her. But the poems to Lili are more dramatic in their effect ('Neue Liebe, neues Leben,' ' An Belinden,' ' Lili's Park'); we detect in them discord and struggle; now he wishes to tear himself away, now he gives up resistance, but the feelings which she excites are always of a mixed nature. We see what enthrals him here—the youthful freshness, the lovely form, the look full of faithfulness and kindness, the voice, the song. We also discover what vexes him : the frivolous, social life, the unbearable people who surround her, the whole menagerie of her worshippers, the childish coquettries indiscriminately showered around, and which he is to share with the rest. And whether he sets before us the whole painful situation in an elaborate allegory, or whether a single despairing sigh escapes from his breast, still it is always a moment of inner conflict, intense and irreconcileable, which his song reveals. In his poems to Lili Goethe characterizes the object of his passion, but not himself; for the latter purpose he employed other forms, epic and dramatic, in which he continued the personal confession which he had begun in the character of Weislingen. In his next play this character becomes the hero himself, under the title of Clavigo, a man of modern times, an author, tossed hither and thither by ambition and love, till he is finally stabbed at the bier of his beloved one, by her brother. Crugantino, the scapegrace in ' Claudine von

His
' Clavigo,'
' Claudine
von Villa-
bella,' and
' Stella.'

Villabella,' a Don Juan and a restless wanderer, fairly reflects Goethe's own character at the time. Fernando too, in 'Stella,' has traits taken from Goethe himself. Fernando has left his wife Cecilia and has then seduced Stella; now he would like to return to his duty, yet at the same time shrinks from making Stella unhappy; in the depths of despair he is saved by the proposal of Cecilia, that they should all three remain together. Goethe has never carried his indulgence towards human weakness, and his sympathy with a loving, suffering heart to such lengths as in this piece, to which however he subsequently gave a tragic termination by the death of Fernando and Stella. It is worth noticing how disinclined he seems to make use of German surroundings in the modern drama. In both ' Clavigo' and ' Claudine ' the scene is laid in Spain. Even the farce of ' Pater Brey' contains a captain Balandrino ; and even in ' Stella,' which is otherwise German, the vacillating, aristocratic lover must needs have the sounding name of Fernando. But we are altogether transported to native soil and to the present, namely, to the time of Goethe's youth, in the fullest and most faithful confession which he made at that time, his ' Werther.'

'The Sorrows of young Werther' appeared in 1774, and though thoroughly German in character, the book was known in a short time over the whole civilised world.   It was translated into all civilised languages, and found imitators in many literatures.   Unlike 'Götz' it did not presuppose in the reader an interest in the past history of the German nation, but appealed to every warm-hearted man of whatever race. Goethe ventured in this novel to reproduce in an artistic form his experiences at Wetzlar.   He introduced Lotte Buff into it with her Christian name unaltered, he placed beside her as bridegroom and husband, under the name of Albert, a person who might suggest Kestner, and he drew the character of the hero half from himself, half from a youth called Jerusalem, the son of the Brunswick clergyman (see p. 70), who shot himself in Wetzlar on the 29th of October, 1772.   Jerusalem, like himself, had been in love with the wife of another man, and his death decided Goethe to write the book.   By drawing on his own experience, by representing a similar situation in which he had found himself in the same town, Goethe sought to discover what could be the cause of a man's committing suicide. He wished to make the catastrophe result from the character, as Lessing had taught him to do in his 'Dramaturgie.'   His purpose was to combine consistent and exact development of character with the breadth of treatment which the novel allows of more than the drama.   He therefore accentuated to his utmost the character of the hero.

'Die Leiden des jungen Werther,' 1774.

Werther is a conscientious, good man, who even as a child loved to indulge in dreams and fancies.   School and restraints of every kind were hateful to him.   He lost his father young, and we are led to suppose that his mother neither educated him with a strong hand, nor understood him enough to gain his love and confidence.   He is not obliged to work for his living, but he has been educated for the bar ; his understanding and talents have been much praised, but he does not care to use them for the public benefit by entering the public service, and still less does he wish to lead a scholar's life.   His one idea is to revel in the most refined spiritual pleasures, reading sympathetic poets, listening to good music, drawing, enjoying nature, holding inter-

Werther's character.

course with simple, good people, and revealing his inmost soul, and all his joys and sorrows to a single friend. He writes an ardent and passionate style, reflects on what he observes, and in talking about it easily grows excited. He respects religion, but derives no support therefrom. He thinks of God as a loving, pitiful Father, and he is full of love for his fellow-men, provided they do not repel him. He has a deep sense of the evil in the world, and he wishes that men would not arbitrarily poison the pleasures which are granted them. His over-sensitive nature is easily wounded, and feeling himself to be misunderstood by those around him, he seeks solitude, or associates with children and people of the lower classes. He follows every dictate of his heart, has no self-control and no energy, lives a life not of action but of feeling, and like a true child of his age, prides himself on his wealth of sentiment. With all these qualities he has a peculiar attraction for people, and has excited the love of women without returning it ; now it is his fate to be in love himself, but without any prospect of possession, for he loves a woman who is first bride then wife of another. This is the rock on which he is wrecked ; his passion consumes him, and as it is the strongest force in his nature, and he is impotent to fight against his feelings, he chooses to commit suicide rather than endure a life of enforced renunciation.

Goethe has introduced a conversation between Werther and

Werther's suicide. Albert on the subject of suicide. Werther considers it as merely the result of an incurable disease, and in this he expresses Goethe's own view of the matter. In this book Goethe gives us the whole pathology of the disease ; we are meant to observe the inner disposition, the causes and the symptoms, and

Gradual development of the catastrophe. to follow their course to the end. The change which takes place in Werther's mind, the slow development of his madness is carefully traced by Goethe, and the catastrophe is prepared for with great skill, the excitement being gradually worked up and the tension increased. Throughout the book Goethe not only traces the natural growth of the disease, but notes the outward circumstances which contributed to its development. He tells us that Werther's attempt to employ himself in an official capacity failed, owing to an unpleasant superior, and to the offensive and slighting treatment which he experienced at the hands of the aristocracy. He supposes that Albert and Lotte have been married in Werther's absence ; Lotte is unhappy in her marriage, and feels herself more strongly drawn to Werther than before. Werther perceives her unhappiness, and is inclined to break through the reserve he has hitherto maintained towards her. By reading aloud to her long passages of the mystical poetry of Ossian he raises himself and her to an unnatural pitch of excitement; this clouds his reason and goads his feelings, till he loses that delicate reserve which has hitherto characterised all his relations with Lotte; he embraces her, and she tears herself away and refuses to see him again; the next day he shoots himself. Goethe assumes that Werther remains to the end the same moral man, that he reproaches himself bitterly for having disturbed a marriage, and hopes by his death to reconcile husband and wife to each other again.

The description of Werther's end, as well as the experiences of his short period of active life, is exactly borrowed **Realism of** from the fate of young Jerusalem. This close ad- **'Werther.'** herence to reality was a guarantee of high poetical truth and probability. But this is not the only respect in which Goethe does his utmost to strengthen the impression that we are here dealing with a story taken from fact. Till near the end he does not speak himself, but lets Werther speak. He makes a pretence of publishing Werther's long journal, written by way of letters to an intimate friend ; occasionally he adds a remark, or pretends that he is suppressing something, and only takes up the narrative himself where we must suppose that Werther's letters to his friend cease. But even then he apparently has access to Werther's last memoranda, and the remainder he pretends to have learnt from the mouth of Lotte, Albert, and others. Goethe treats the somewhat exaggerated and over-strained sentiment with the firm and skilful hand of an artist, and by his clear arrangement of the story helps us to take it in at a glance. It is not very long in itself, and falls naturally into two periods, the one prior, the other subsequent to Werther's abortive career as a public official. In each of the two divisions into which the story thus falls we may easily distinguish three stages : first we meet Werther alone, then Lotte comes upon the scene, and then Albert ; in the second part Werther is absent at the beginning, then he returns, and finally, when the story is approaching its end, narrative takes the place of the letters. Every letter bears its date, and the story lasts exactly from the 4th of May 1771 to Christmas 1772.

Novels in epistolary form had been written before Goethe's time, **Novels in epistolary form.** in particular by Richardson and Rousseau. But whereas till then authors had preferred to make a number of people correspond, Goethe on the contrary only lets the hero speak. By this means our attention is engaged more strongly, and focussed on the hero, and in one respect the task was thus rendered easier, since the letters could' all be written in the same style, whereas the older form required as many styles as there were writers ; but in another respect the difficulty was increased, inasmuch as the out-pourings of one mind are much more liable to become monotonous than the utterances of many. Goethe surmounted this difficulty with the greatest ease, and by his ' Werther' introduced a new style of letter-writing into German literature.

We possess German letters dating as early as the thirteenth cen- **German Letter-writing.** tury. Ulrich von Lichtenstein's memoirs contain a note addressed to him by the lady of his heart, a mere dry report of events. In the fourteenth century we may find the correspondence between a pious nun and her father-confessor, who interchange presents and spiritual experiences, marked occasionally by sentimental outbursts. At a later epoch we find sterility of imagination helping itself out by external assistance ; for instance, in a love-letter, if a tender phrase was not at command, a drawing of a heart pierced by an arrow might serve as a substitute. Model letter-writers in the early years of printing suggest forms of address such as : ' Sweet, subtle, benevolent, well-conducted, most dear lady.' We find Luther writing to his ' dear **Luther's Letters.** Sonikin, Hänsichen,' or to his wife as his ' kind, dear master, Frau Katherine von Bora.' In his letters to his boy he describes Heaven in childish fashion as a beautiful fairy garden, and he greets his wife with all kinds of chaff, and gives her a very amusing account of his travelling adventures, expressing everything in quaint and original language, but without a trace of artificiality. In fact, Luther fills his letters with his own heartiness, vigour and cheery humour, and this popular and original epistolary style started by him was never quite lost; the tradition was reserved down to the Duchess Elisabeth Charlotte of Orleans (see vol. i, p. 374) and to Goethe's mother, though side by side with it the intolerable bombast and foreign affectations of the seventeenth century were fostered by polite letter-writers, and through their influence ultimately became the ruling fashion. In the eighteenth century, on the contrary, efforts were made to attain a natural and yet cultivated style. Madame de Sévigné was considered the great model in letter-writing. Frau Gottsched's letters show a roguish grace which her comedies would not have led one to expect from her. Gellert reduced the new ideal of letter-writing to a theory, and instructed his fellow-countrymen most thoroughly as to how they were to set about it in order to appear as natural as possible; they were to follow their own disposition, to strive after variety of style, to seek their matter near at hand, to make reference to the small circumstances under which they were writing, and so on. He found in young Goethe a willing pupil, who at once grasped the matter with a Goethe's Letters. boldness which far exceeded the good Gellert's intentions. His first student's letter from Leipzig rises to a dramatic level in its lively and graphic representation of what is passing at the moment he writes. This dramatic enhancement of reality, these true reflections of his passing moods characterize all his youthful letters, and form the basis on which he Style of 'Werther.' worked with conscious art in 'Werther,' arranging and leading up to definite effects. But he took care not to entertain his readers solely with the feelings of his hero. A number of people appear in the book, who are all briefly characterized. Pictures of nature and of human life are faithfully executed, and everything is made to bear upon the hero, and reveal to us his views, tastes, and character. Goethe informs us what Werther read; the Old Testament, Homer, Goldsmith, Klopstock, Ossian, are his favourite reading, as they were also Goethe's. Shakspeare does not seem to have

attracted him, for Shakspeare would break in too rudely upon the
world of such a sentimentalist.   But these other writers with their
idyllic and emotional elements determine Werther's own views and
interests, such as we find them reflected in his letters.   He would
like to establish patriarchal and Homeric conditions of life around
him; nature and natural characters he describes in terms of deep
affection, finding in them inexhaustible variety.   But he does not
show us idylls only ; his embittered heart can spur him on to satire,
and he can also recognise the poetic side of the prose of everyday
life.   He describes Lotte knitting a stocking, or cutting bread for
her younger brothers and sisters, and himself playing with the
children or helping Lotte to gather fruit. He gives us a picture of a
rustic ball and its break-up by a storm.   He works in ordinary, uninteresting conversations, and introduces us into various households ;
and all his experience is drawn from the sphere of middle-class life,
the sphere in which Gellert's comedies generally move, and which,
one would think, could not possibly offer any elements of romance.

By his 'Werther' Goethe introduced a new phase into German
sentiment; this kind of sentiment had been fostered by
pietism and by the pastoral poetry of the seventeenth
century, and already in Philipp von Zesen we find an
attempt to impart a sentimental colouring to middle-
class life; but Goethe was the first to succeed in an endeavour which a
hundred and thirty years before seemed a half comic, half pathetic
enterprise.   He had first to divest Klopstock's characters of their
saintly halo, and Gessner's shepherds and Weisse's rustics of their
unreality. He succeeded in making his descriptions of nature more
animated and varied than those of Haller, Kleist, and Klopstock, and
his bourgeois characters and bourgeois sentiments more interesting
than those of Gellert or Rabener, by exhibiting them as they appeared in the mind of an ardent youth, who had acquired the power
of faithful delineation in the school of plastic art. Werther's exalted
sentiment and ever-ready reflections are combined with genre-
pictures and landscapes in the style of the Dutch school.   The
whole gives the impression of a realistic sentimentality, whose ideal
is to be found in the housewifely Lotte, cheerful and active in her
homely life, and yet capable of elevated thoughts and feelings.

Influence of Werther on German Sentiment.

Though Rousseau is not mentioned among Werther's favourite authors, perhaps owing to Goethe's hostility to French literature at that time, or to deeper causes, yet Rousseau's influence really exercised great power over the production of ' Werther.'   No book then published was so akin to 'Werther' as Rousseau's 'Nouvelle Héloise ;' the French romance presents a similar hero, similar ideas and incidents, similar language, and only far inferior art.   In 'Werther,' too, as in all Rousseau's writings, there breathes a truly revolutionary spirit. Goethe's novel is a protest against a state of society which cannot make worthy use of the brilliant talents of an ardent youth, against inequality of classes and the haughtiness of the nobility, as contrasted with Werther's sympathy with the people, against the ruling code of morals, which looked on suicide far otherwise than with mere pity ; it is a protest against conventional pedantry of style and strict æsthetic rules, though Goethe himself does not break any established rule in the work, and, finally, it is a protest against the dominant mode of expression, for the author expresses himself not only with freedom but with arbitrary licence. By his drama of ' Götz ' Goethe had already questioned the existing stage arrangements, but now even the established grammar was not safe.   The unity of the literary language, won by toilsome effort, was imperilled ; the grace and perfection of form, which had been attained thirty years before in the ' Bremer Beiträge,' now gave place to personal caprice, provincialisms, phrases forcible but colloquial, an elliptical style, and a novel mode of spelling.

[sidenote: 'Werther' and Rousseau.]

[sidenote: Revolutionary tendencies and arbitrary style in 'Werther.']

Once more a revolution disturbed the quiet and steady development of German æsthetic culture, in the same way as the Reformation had interfered with the Renaissance movement, in the same way as Opitz had unnecessarily broken with the past and Gottsched had despised the connection with the popular drama.   It was Goethe this time who denied all reverence for established rules, and carried with him all young and impetuous spirits.   But this movement differed essentially from the older revolutionary convulsions.   The interruption did not last so long this time, and the return was not so

[sidenote: Influence of 'Werther' and 'Götz' on German literature.]

difficult. The leader of the revolution himself returned almost immediately to the old lines of development, and subsequently went far in reaction, but he could not quite efface the traces of his youthful performances. 'Werther' could, indeed, be easily purged of its faults and transformed into a perfect work of art, but it was impossible to do the same with 'Götz;' with all its beauties and with all its depth of feeling it remained what it was, a work of caprice and a bad example to posterity, a standing encouragement to all young poets who thought themselves geniuses, but disdained the trouble of learning.

THE LITERARY REVOLUTION AND THE ILLUMINATI.

'Storm and stress! The period of genius! The original geniuses!'—These are the terms which are used in praise or in

The literary and religious revolution. mockery to designate the German literary revolution and its chief leaders. The movement was a poetic and religious one. The literary revolution demanded emancipation from rules, and was, in its political aspect, a movement of opposition to established authorities ; the religious revolution was directed against the so-called enlightened school, and was in this respect conservative. Both movements apparently failed. The poets were obliged to submit themselves again to the sway of rules, and their political declamations had not the slightest direct effect ; on the other hand, the Illuminati only became bolder and more radical in their advances, and won back to their side a few of their most decided opponents. Yet the chief effect of the revolution was, after all, an extraordinary increase of poetic and scientific power, and the wide extension of literary interests throughout Germany; many of the tendencies, too, which could not assert themselves for the present, remained dormant and awoke to fresh life in Romanticism.

Lessing had only just produced his masterpiece in tragedy, his 'Emilia Galotti,' when Goethe's 'Götz' appeared, and though unable entirely to supplant Lessing's piece, yet considerably thwarted its influence. 'Götz' and 'Emilia' reigned side by side, and we have many opportunities of observing how the young dramatists of this period formed their style on both; but 'Götz' exercised the greater influence of the two; chivalrous dramas became all the fashion, and Shakspeare was copied with untiring zeal. The extravagance of 'Stella' also attracted imitators, while the less outrageous 'Clavigo' was more or less left out of account. German provinces which had as yet played little part in modern literature now sent forth their representatives, and some of the violent Shakspearians, such as Lenz, Klinger, and Wagner, belonged to the circle of Goethe's acquaintance in Strassburg and Frankfort. Lenz, a German Russian, who ended his days in madness, often reveals in his short songs   Lenz. and tales a strain of pure and pathetic poetry; in his dramas he allowed himself the most outrageous extravagances, but even in them we here and there light on a cleverly-drawn character, a simple and innocent girl, a pedant or a kind-hearted reveller. Klinger, a Frankfort man of low origin, began with confused and faulty productions, dramas full of bombastic declama-   Klinger. tion, coarse language, ravings against tyrants, and such naturalism as we meet with in Rousseau. Subsequently he abandoned these revolutionary extravagances, and having grown up into a composed and rational man, profited by experience, and ended as a high Russian dignitary. Heinrich   H. L. Leopold Wagner of Strassburg drew scenes and   Wagner. characters from middle-class life with a rude but effective realism. Friedrich Müller of Kreuznach, poet and painter, and   Friedrich hence designated 'Painter Müller,' turned his attention   Müller. to classical and to popular subjects, to Genovefa, Faust and Niobe. He carried realistic treatment into his idylls, which are some of them faithful descriptions of the life of the common people in the Palatinate. Count Törring, of Munich,   Törring. by his 'Agnes Bernauerin,' prepared the way for the chivalrous drama in Bavaria; and in Swabia there arose a political dramatist, who carried on the revolutionary tendencies of 'Götz' and 'Emilia Galotti' with still greater energy: Friedrich Schiller (see Chap. XII. § 3).

Political interests had struck deep root in Swabia. The worthy John Jacob Moser, counsel to the Würtemberg Parliament, boldly-opposed princely despotism, and his son, Friedrich Carl von Moser, exerted his influence as a minister and writer in favour of enlight-

Political writers.

The two Mosers.

ened systems of government, upholding the interests of the state as against the selfishness of kings. We have already noticed the works of Wieland and Abbt dealing with political subjects. Among journalists, Wilhelm Ludwig Weckherlin ridiculed the constitution of the Imperial towns. The journalist, poet, and musician, Christian

Christian Schubart.

Schubart, a true Bohemian in disposition, but also an ardent worshipper of Frederick the Great and of Klopstock, was at once a German and Swabian patriot; he greeted with enthusiasm all the productions of the 'Storm and Stress' party, and sang their praises in newspaper articles. His best wrok is to be found in his popular songs. His poem entitled 'Fürstengruft' (The Grave of Princes), was an attack on tyrants, reproaching them with their crimes against humanity.

Friedrich Schiller.

Friedrich Schiller, at that time a military surgeon in Stuttgart, became a disciple of his; on the title-page of his first play, 'The Robbers,' he had placed the figure of a lion rampant, with the motto, 'In Tyrannos,' and he put the following words in the mouth of the hero of the piece : 'Put me at the head of a troop of such fellows as myself, and Germany shall be turned into a republic, in contrast with which Sparta and Rome shall seem like nunneries.' These people of Würtemberg could speak of the rule of tyrants from personal acquaintance; the elder Moser had been shut up for five years in the fortress of Hohentwiel, Schubart for ten years in that of Asperg, both unjustly and without trial, only because it was the duke's pleasure. Schiller might well expect the same fate, and therefore took refuge in flight. The iron despotism which weighed upon his country and upon himself personally, would necessarily instil revolutionary sentiments into the mind of this disciple of Rousseau, who was panting for nature and liberty. Adopting a motto derived from Hippocrates, he recommended blood and iron as the best remedies for a corrupt

Schiller's 'Räuber.'

world. The hero of his first drama, the enthusiastic young robber, Moor, like Goethe's Götz, has recourse to force on his own responsibility. He has all the

- 2

feelings of a Werther, and, like Werther, he falls foul of society. Werther turns the destroying weapon against himself, but Moor directs it against society. He is a rebel, like the Satan of Milton and Klopstock, and a vagabond, like Goethe's Crugantino, but while love and reconciliation lead Crugantino back to the bosom of his family, the shameful intrigues of an unnatural brother turn Moor into a robber and a murderer. Hostile brothers had already been depicted by Fielding in romance, and by Leisewitz and Klinger in tragedy; the two latter had introduced fratricide upon the stage itself, and Gessner had written a patriarchal romance based on the story of Cain and Abel; but Schiller far surpasses these writers in power in the grand scene where the criminal, in fear of the avengers of his crime, pronounces and carries out his own sentence. The poet shows, on the whole, dramatic talent of the first order. It is true that he lays on the colours too thick, that he fills the dialogue with bombastic exaggeration, that in trying to be forcible he occasionally lapses into coarseness, that he fails to make the connection between action and character sufficiently apparent, that he consistently violates the laws of probability, and lastly, that the plot is clumsy and the only woman's part a failure;—still, in spite of all these defects, he manages to retain the attention of his audience from beginning to end; contrast, which can alone animate dialogue, is never wanting, nor conflict, the essence of dramatic action. The action almost always progresses rapidly and impetuously, and the power of single scenes affects readers and spectators as much to-day as when the play first appeared. Schiller's contemporaries not only applauded the tragic talent and the entrancing interest of the play, but adopted the robber Moor, as they had done young Werther, as a kind of ideal. There was no occasion for Schiller to appeal in self-defence to the authority of Rousseau, who commended Plutarch for having chosen grand criminals as the subjects of his literary portraits; there was no need for him to cite the example of the noble robber Roque in 'Don Quixote.' His audience was quite ready, without any such authorities, to accord a sympathetic reception to the attractive robber Moor. The public had learnt with Goethe to excuse a suicide and to forgive a Don Juan, with Heinrich Leopold Wagner, to bestow pity on a child-

murderess; Lessing had taught them to reverence noble humanity
in Jews and Mohammedans; it was no wonder, therefore, that they
should now be so ready to recognise the same humanity even in
a robber.

Schiller's play appeared in 1781, eight years after 'Götz,' two
years after Lessing's 'Nathan.' Two other tragedies soon followed,
'Fiesco' in 1783, 'Kabale und Liebe' in 1784.   The scene of the

Schiller's
'Fiesco,'
1783.
former is laid in Genoa, of the latter in modern Germany.   In 'Fiesco' we have a revolution which fails
in the moment of success through the death of the
leader. The play brings before us the brutal tyranny of Gianettino
Doria, the clever dissembling and marvellous fascination of Fiesco,
the rude Republicanism of Verrina, the base motives of the lower
conspirators; it is a play of intrigue and crime, of plots and
counter-plots, such as the poet had no personal knowledge of, so that
he had to draw upon tradition and his own imagination in representing them.   The central figure is an ambitious politician, to
whom the author attributes fits of devotion to the public welfare in
order to make him more attractive, although he thereby violates
the consistency of his character.

In 'Intrigue and Love' the interest centres round a pair of

Schiller's
'Kabale
und
Liebe.'
lovers who are ruined by class-prejudice; it pictures
the well-known misery of the smaller German states
at that time, the Sultan-like prince, the all-powerful
favourite, the miserable court, the scoundrelly minister
and his rascally tools, the immorality of the nobles and their haughty
scorn of the bourgeois class, the extortion practised towards
the people, the shameful selling of soldiers to foreign rulers, the
arbitrariness of justice—all features drawn from sad reality, which
the poet could either observe in his own country or learn of
from reliable sources.   The obvious purpose of the play was to
strengthen the hatred against oppressors and excite pity for the
poor and innocent victims.   It was no wonder that 'Intrigue and
Love' met with a far warmer reception than 'Fiesco.'   As regards
artistic merit, the two pieces are barely on a level with the
'Robbers.'   The ideas, however, which had been first mooted in
'Emilia Galotti' and 'Götz' had ripened to maturity in these

two plays, which embody the very essence of the poetry of the 'Storm and Stress' epoch.   The revolutionary party in literature were, as we have already remarked, the party of opposition in politics. They no longer kept up the pretence of attacking Italian princes when they really meant to attack German ones, but boldly knocked at the castle-gates of the petty German sovereigns.   On the eve of the French Revolution, and while North America was fighting for its freedom, the old Roman ideals of Republican glory stirred in the hearts of German youths.   Gottsched had at an earlier time praised the stoical suicide of Cato, and now Brutus, the assassin of Cæsar, became the hero of these ardent spirits, and was held up as a worthy example.

Schiller's revolutionary tendencies.

In Göttingen, political connection with England[1] naturally suggested comparisons between the two countries, and sharpened men's judgment ; there, from the year 1776 onward, Professor Schlözer published his 'Correspondence,' subsequently known as the 'Staatsanzeigen,' a political paper which brought existing abuses to light, and soon became the terror of petty German tyrants.   In 1772 a few enthusiastic Göttingen students formed a poetic brotherhood, which they called the 'Hain' and from which they anticipated extraordinary results. They assumed each the name of some ancient bard, swore eternal friendship to one another, glorified God, the Fatherland and virtue and venerated Klopstock almost as a deity. They hated the French nation, French poetry, and the Frenchified school of German poets, with its chief representative—the 'murderer of innocence' as they termed him—Wieland.   They prattled of liberty, despised the slaves and parasites of courts, and set up the Swiss hero Tell by the side of Brutus, Arminius, and Klopstock.   In their drinking-songs they enumerated the crimes of sovereigns and pictured future battles in which they would be avenged on them, or imagined the hour of triumph when tyrants should have been

Göttingen.

The 'Hain.'

Klopstock heads the Göttingen brotherhood.

---

[1] Göttingen belongs to the Duchy of Hannover, which, by the accession of George I, was united with England.   The University of Göttingen was founded in 1733 by George II.

swept from the earth. Klopstock gave his blessing to the movement. He had a short time before made a collection of his Odes and completed his 'Messiah,' and he thought the time had now come for him to set himself upon the throne of German poetry. The members of the 'Hain' were to disperse themselves through Germany, and to be his lieutenants. The Statute-Book of his new kingdom was to be his own foolish Art of Poetry, published in 1774 under the title of 'Gelehrtenrepublik,' in which he treated most contemptuously the hitherto prevalent theory of poetry. But sensible men, who had not yet quite died out in Germany, laughed at the whole thing; the new Klopstock kingdom had no duration, and the Göttingen Brotherhood, as such, exercised no influence on the further development of German poetry; it was only through the medium of a few able writers among its members that it produced any effect at all.

Heinrich Christian Boie was the oldest, maturest, and most

Boie. moderate member of the society; he produced little himself, but indirectly, as an editor, he rendered good services to the literary life of Germany. In 1769 he started the 'Musenalmanach' as a magazine for lyric poetry, and in 1776 the 'Deutsches Museum,' an excellent monthly paper.

Martin Miller, of Ulm, began as a lyric poet, but soon took to

Martin Miller. novel-writing, and by his 'Siegwart, a Convent-story,' he drew many tears from the eyes of sentimentalists.

The consumptive and short-lived Hölty, in his lyrics full of

Hölty. gentle contemplation of nature and life, reminds us of Kleist, the author of 'Spring' and of 'Irin.'

The two Counts Stolberg are always mentioned together, and

The two Stolbergs. also published their works jointly; but the younger brother, Fritz, the translator of the Iliad, of Æschylus and Ossian, alone attained to any great distinction. He was an aristocrat through and through, in his extravagances no less than in his conversion to the Catholic faith, in his stormy, blood-thirsty odes against tyrants as well as in his high-sounding but occasionally awkward hexameters. From his youth upwards he felt a profound need of worshipping something above himself, be it Homer or Nature, the heroism of his ancestors or the majestic grandeur of the

sea. But this imaginative and emotional spirit, who needed outward symbols and sought for a firm support upon which to lean,
could in the end only find the rest which he longed for and the
ideal society which he loved in the Roman Catholic Church and
her saints.

Johann Heinrich Voss, Boie's brother-in-law, was the best of
the many who vied with one another in creating
a German Homer. He, like Klopstock, recognised **Voss.**
the value of German syllables for metrical and rhythmic purposes. Of his manifold and in part mechanical translations
from the ancients, none come up to his Homer. The Odyssey
appeared in 1781, the Iliad, with a revised version **His**
of the Odyssey, in 1793, but unfortunately this **Homer.**
revision was not an improvement. Frequent attempts had already
been made at translating Homer, and in the eighteenth century
the German versions of the two great Greek epics became more
numerous than ever. Bodmer had produced an uncouth translation, Fritz Stolberg a more successful one, but Voss surpassed all
his predecessors in this field. His version is natural and straightforward, neither too exalted nor too commonplace in tone, and reproduces to a reasonable extent the style of the original ; the Homeric
formulas and epithets are successfully preserved, and the whole
work is one of devoted industry and serious study, resting throughout on a clear appreciation of old Greek conditions of life. Voss
had thoroughly satisfied his countrymen, but not himself; he
wanted to improve his work still more. Accordingly, he carried
his faithfulness to the original too far, and thus spoilt the Iliad
from the first and the Odyssey in the later versions. Voss was a
Mecklenburger of plebeian origin, the grandson of an emancipated
serf; he had seen with his own eyes the evils of serf- **His**
dom, and his poems against tyrants, exaggerated though **original**
they may seem, rest on deeply-rooted convictions. **poems.**
His whole life long he was in politics and religion an uncompromising Liberal. His idylls, written partly in Low-German,
tell of the sufferings of the people ; they have nothing to do with
Arcadian shepherds or with Gessner's drawing-room dolls, but
picture the German peasant as he was, but yet not with the crude

naturalism of the painter-poet Müller; Voss was saved from that by his classical culture, and by the classical hexametric form in which he wrote. Voss drew materials for his idylls and songs not only from rustic but from German middle-class life, the sphere in which he himself lived, and in whose domestic interests and simple pleasures he took such delight. Voss, like Goethe, united delight in the Homeric world with the German love of domesticity; but he did not always succeed in raising the every-day prosaic life which he chose as his theme into the sphere of pure poetry, and more beautiful idylls than he ever wrote are to be found in his wife Ernestine's records of his and her life, of their intercourse with Fritz Stolberg, of the time of Voss's first schoolmastership, and of their poor little *ménage*.

All the band of Göttingen friends found a common sphere of labour in lyric poetry, and in their hands German lyric poetry acquired new forces. Though all the members of the Göttingen brotherhood tried their hand at classical rhymeless odes after Klopstock's model, yet their strength lay really in rhymed popular songs, and their most successful productions of this kind, when set to simple attractive melodies, spread quickly through the length and breadth of Germany. The bards of the 'Hain' continued the work of Christian Felix Weisse, while in South Germany Schubart, and to a certain extent Maler Müller, laboured in the same direction. But their lyric poetry was mostly of the quiet kind, describing not action, but passive emotion of some kind; the more stirring and dramatic poetry such as Herder demanded and Goethe created was only represented in any real excellence in one of the poets of the Göttingen brotherhood, in Gottfried August Bürger. In him alone Herder's suggestions really bore fruit. The English Ballads were to him what Shakspeare was to the Strassburg poets, and he became a most enthusiastic admirer and imitator of these ballads as well as of the old German songs and legends. The half-romantic, half-burlesque ballad-form which Gleim had essayed, and which Bürger himself cultivated at first, became later on in his hands a serious and powerful picture of character and emotion. Terror, mystery, and gloom had special attractions for him, and he conjured

The Göttingen poets all lyrical.

Bürger's ballads.

up ghosts and spirits in the midst of that enlightened age. His 'Leonore' is perhaps his best production in this respect, with its powerful picture of the furious, ghostly ride to the grave, in the course of which it gradually becomes clear to us that the anxiously expected lover, the soldier who comes and wakes his sweetheart, is none other than death. This poem leaves on us to some degree the impression of an unsolved mystery; all the details are clear, but at the end we have to ask ourselves what has really happened; was it a dream of the girl, a dream in which she died, or did the ghost really appear and carry her away? Any incidents causing anxious suspense Bürger was able to portray with masterly skill, for instance, a noble deed done in the face of danger, or secret enjoyment with sorrow lurking behind. He describes with great power the conflict between love and caste-prejudice, faithfulness, unfaithfulness, treachery, the dissolute egotism of the higher classes and the despairing rebellion of the lower, while he is also a master of humorous narrative, as is seen in his poems, 'Frau Schnips' and 'Kaiser und Abt.' In his love-poems he strives after action and striking situations, but his imagination failed him in the world of tender feeling, and he tried to replace the want of poetic motives by high-sounding words and empty jingle, which spoils many a stanza of his best ballads. He ruined his life by profligacy, and the severe form in which he sometimes clothes passionate feeling, the melody of his sonnets and smooth polish of his verses, could not take the place of inward nobility of feeling.

Character of his poetry.

The thought of a genuine revival of the historical and literary past of Germany animated young Goethe during his Strassburg days, and the same spirit stirred in the Göttingen poets and through the whole of North Germany. As early as 1748 Bodmer had published specimens from the Minnesingers, in 1757 he had brought out a part of the Nibelungenlied, in 1758 and 1759 a more complete collection of the Minnesingers, and till 1781, till just before his death, he continued to produce editions of the Middle High-German poems. Another Swiss writer, Christian Heinrich Myller, a pupil

Revival of early German poetry.

of Bodmer's, who had an appointment in Berlin, published in 1784
and 1785 the whole of the Nibelungenlied and the most important
of the chivalrous epics.   Lessing, in his preface to Gleim's War-
songs, called attention to the Middle High-German poets, of whom
he continued to be throughout his life an ardent admirer.   Justus
Möser took great interest in the Minnesingers.   About the time
when 'Götz' appeared, this enthusiasm for early German poetry
was at its strongest, and Bürger, Voss, Miller, and Hölty wrote
Minnesongs, in which they imitated the old German lyric poets.
In 1773 Gleim published 'Poems after the Minnesingers,' and
in 1779 'Poems after Walther von der Vogelweide.'   Some enthusiasts had already hailed the Nibelungenlied as the German Iliad,
and Bürger, who vied hard with the rest, but without much success,
in turning Homer into German, insisted on dressing up the Greek
heroes a little in the Nibelungen style.   He and a few other
poets loved to give their ballads a chivalrous character.   Fritz
Stolberg wrote the beautiful song of a German boy, beginning—
'Mein Arm wird stark und gross mein Muth, gib, Vater, mir
ein Schwert;' and the song of the old Swabian knight—'Sohn,
da hast du meinen Speer; meinem Arm wird er zu schwer.'
Lessing's 'Nathan,' too, appealed to this enthusiasm for the times of
chivalry, and must have strengthened the feeling.   An historian
like the Swiss, Johannes Müller (see Chap. XIII. § 1), began to show
the Middle Ages in a fairer light, and even to ascribe great merits to
the Papacy.   But in doing so, Johannes Müller was only following
Herder's Me- in Herder's steps.   Herder, while at Bückeburg, had
diævalism. written against the self-conceit of his age, its pride in
its enlightenment and achievements.   He found in the Middle Ages
the realization of his æsthetic ideas, namely, strong emotion, stirring
life and action, everything guided by feeling and instinct, not by
morbid thought, religious ardour and chivalrous honour, boldness
His in love and strong patriotic feeling.   This appreciation
religious of mediæval times went with Herder hand in hand
revival. with a stricter form of religion.   He gave up his freethinking views; when he stood in the pulpit, and still more when he
was writing, his feelings were those of a mystic enthusiast.   Now,
for the first time, the full fervour of his soul poured itself forth.   It

was only in uncompromising opposition to the so-called enlighten-ment of the age that he could find satisfaction. His share in the literary revolution was not only to call attention to the popular sources of art, not only to sing the praises of Shakspeare and Ossian in the 'Letters on German Style and Art,' not only to influence Goethe and Bürger, but, above all, to try and reanimate religion by proclaiming, in prophetic and enthusiastic tones, the worth of the Bible and the dignity of the priestly office. His style then became dithyrambic and highly original, full of words arbi-trarily coined, and of phrases fashioned simply for force and effect. His old researches on the origin of mythology and of the Hebraic legends now assumed a new colour. Was not this primitive poetry so much primitive revelation obscured, and was it not his mission to interpret it? Faith founded on Biblical Revelation is the funda-mental basis of preaching. Away with the slanders of the Illu-minati, who dared to hint that the priests of those ancient nations were often liars and deceivers! The position of the priests should become once more such as Möser had described it among the old Germans.

Herder embodied these thoughts in three works produced in the year 1774, viz. the 'Oldest Record of Man,' 'Pro-vincial Leaflets for Clergymen,' and the pamphlet entitled 'Another Philosophy of History with reference to the development of the human race.' In these works he does not by any means pose as an orthodox be-liever of any particular confession. Slight differences of opinion were not now so strictly regarded; the orthodox party and the pietists had both been thrust into the back-ground; the dominating views were those of the enlightened school, and a common aversion to them drew together nearly all finely-touched souls. The result was a general reinforcement of faith and pious feeling, which was further promoted by the increasing worship of Klopstock. Hamann, Lavater, Jung, Claudius, Jacobi, were all religious in spirit; the Catholics were not behind the rest, and though the Jesuit order had been suppressed in 1773, yet this very loss of material power may have stimulated the Catholics to redoubled intellectual activity.

Herder's 'Aelteste Urkunde der Mensch-heit,' and 'Provinzial-blätter für Prediger,' 1774.

Lavater of Zürich, a preacher and a Swiss patriot, lived wholly in the Christian faith and in love of Christ. He travelled through Germany, and charmed all who became acquainted with him; even Goethe, from his totally different world, extended a friendly hand to him. By his attempt to read the character of men from their faces, and by his 'Physiognomical Fragments,' in which he gave an account of his science of physiognomy, and published, with Goethe's co-operation, numerous portraits of contemporaries and of deceased persons, with an interpretation of their characters, he greatly strengthened the feeling for individuality, and stimulated poets to rivalry in the art of characterization; but he himself, with all his great literary activity, did not succeed in producing a single artistic work of lasting merit. His feeling for individuality and his loving nature and gentle manners must have given him the power of winning hearts; but his zeal for proselytizing broke down, and his faith degenerated into superstition. He was always hoping for new miracles, and allowed himself to be imposed upon by false miracle-workers, by swindlers and rogues such as Cagliostro and Christoph Kaufmann. Thus we see that it was not in poetry alone that ghosts were reinstated in their former honour; in real life too they were accredited afresh, and proved a profitable speculation.

Lavater.

His 'Physiognomische Fragmente.'

Jung-Stilling's faith in ghosts was a more innocent one. He was a friend of Goethe's youth, the acquaintance dating from his Strassburg period. He was first a doctor, then a political economist, and he wrote a narrative of his own life, which breathes throughout a simple and religious spirit. He was imbued with a touching faith in a special Providence, which had smoothed his way in difficulties and watched over him with fatherly care. But the purest spirit, the most truly childlike heart, was that of the gentle Claudius, the 'boy of innocence,' as Herder called him, 'full of moonlight, and with the lily-scent of immortality in his soul.' One must first get over the tone of affected popularity in which his newspaper, the 'Wandsbecker Bote,' is written, in order to enjoy the really beautiful things which it contains. Peculiar forms of writing still play

Jung-Stilling.

Claudius.

a great part in it as in Rabener, Möser, and the older weekly newspapers; but we cannot help liking this naive humourist, and we read his fables and proverbs with pleasure, and lend a friendly ear to the sentiments expressed in his songs. His evening song, 'Der Mond ist aufge- **His poems.** gangen,' is written in the spirit of Paul Gerhardt, but with that higher appreciation of nature which this later age had acquired. His poem at the grave of his father is remarkable for the love and deep sorrow which it expresses. The poem entitled 'Der Tod und das Mädchen' gives us a most powerful picture of the terrified maiden and the consoler, Death. Merriment reigns supreme in the story of the giant Goliath and in the narrative of the travels of Master Urian. Claudius shows the nearest affinity to the poets of the Göttingen brotherhood; like them, he wants to be popular, and sometimes affects a rustic style, and his songs, like theirs, are meant rather for singing than for reading. With him, as with them, we sometimes feel ourselves reminded of the Middle High-German lyric poets, by the absence of all rhetorical ornament, and by the union of natural freshness, humour and piety with a simple and patriotic heart. Like Voss and his wife Ernestine, Claudius, too, sometimes allows us a glimpse of his modest household and his married bliss. Voss and Claudius both found their highest satisfaction in the poetry of domestic life, sanctified by religion, only religion, which was the support of both, assumed a somewhat different colour with each.

While Claudius was writing from Hamburg as an independent author, and contributing to the new religious revival, **Fritz Jacobi** Fritz Jacobi rallied around him the faithful on the **in Düssel-** lower Rhine at Düsseldorf. He considered Spinozism **dorf.** to be the most consistent philosophy; but Spinoza's Pantheism seemed to him mere Atheism, and he restored the God whom reason deprived him of, through the means of direct perception, feeling, presentiment, and faith. Jacobi was a kindred spirit to Hamann. Later on his chief sphere of influence lay in Munich, and he drew his philosophical disciples mostly from the ranks of the Roman Catholics.   In Bavaria the religious revival was led by the ex-Jesuit Michael Sailer, while the North German Catholics gathered round the Princess Galitzin of Münster, the 'Christian Aspasia,' as they called her, who was also intimate with devout Protestants. Hamann died in her house in 1788, and it was through her means that Fritz Stolberg was won over to the Roman Church in 1800.

Jacobi occupied a peculiar middle position. He was intimate with Wieland, and was a friend of Goethe's, who had met him with enthusiastic affection on his Rhine journey in **Jacobi's** 1774. He made two weak attempts at novel-writing, **novels.** in both of which the heroes are a mixture of Goethe and of himself. His was a tender nature, all feeling and sentiment. **Georg** His elder brother Georg, a gentle and loving character, **Jacobi.** and an intimate friend of Gleim's, wrote lyrics and prose works, and knew well how to polish his language, and how to ingratiate himself with the ladies. From 1774 he published a monthly magazine, the 'Iris,' to which Goethe also contributed, and under Goethe's influence his poems gained in truth and reality. **Heinse.** Wilhelm Heinse, who was co-editor with Georg Jacobi, likewise belonged to the school of Wieland and Gleim, and the wine- and love-songs of the Anacreontic school assumed in his romances a wild and passionate character. Not but what he interwove the highest pleasures with lower forms of enjoyment, and gloried in enthusiastic conversations on sculpture and music quite as much as in the description of luxurious feasts. As Goethe loved the Dutch genre-painters, and praised Dürer and Gothic architecture, so Heinse rebelled against the one-sidedness of Winckelmann and Lessing's ideal, and loved to extol the art of Rubens and of the modern landscape-painters as against the taste which did not extend beyond ancient statuary. In this respect, as well as in his poetic extravagances, he too reflects the so-called 'Storm and Stress' spirit. But while the new literary movement **Opposition** spread to such an extent in Wieland's immediate neigh-**to Wieland.** bourhood, and even carried away his own disciples, how did it fare with the master himself? He was one of the potentates of the older literature, one of those against whom the Revolution was directed. He was looked upon as the opposite pole to Klopstock, and the Göttingen brotherhood burnt him in effigy, while Goethe ridiculed him in his farce entitled: 'Gods, heroes, and Wieland.'

In the face of all this opposition Wieland acted with consummate skill. His 'Teutscher Merkur' had just begun to appear in the very year of the literary revolution, 1773, and he felt that he must lose no time in defining his position. He accordingly threw out feelers in the shape of the articles written by his contributors, refusing to acknowledge their views as his own, whenever it suited him so to do. At the same time he could censure writers whom he disapproved of by simply passing them over in silence. He made short work of Hamann's obscurities; he distinguished with great discrimination what was valuable and what was merely exaggerated in Herder; he criticised Goethe's 'Götz,' this 'beautiful monster,' as the most important phenomenon of modern German poetry, freely acknowledged the uncommon talent shown in it, and was altogether so just in both praise and blame that Goethe was obliged to exclaim in amazement, 'No one understands me better than Wieland;' he also reviewed with much dispassionateness Goethe's farce directed against himself, and recommended it to his readers as a masterpiece of *persiflage.* Goethe said, 'Now I must let him go for ever. Wieland is gaining as much in the public estimation by the line he takes as I am losing. I am just put to shame.' Such being the attitude on each side, we are not surprised to hear that the meeting in Weimar at once smoothed all differences, and that Wieland's enthusiastic good-nature succumbed to the fascination of Goethe's personality.

Wieland's attitude.

The 'Teutscher Merkur,' 1773.

Wieland at Weimar, 1777.

A poem of Goethe's headed the first number of the 'Merkur' for the year 1776, and Herder, too, soon appeared among its contributors. The 'Merkur' became the recognised organ of the Weimar band of authors, and experienced many transformations in consequence, for Wieland, too, now became another man, and reached the summit of his powers only under Goethe's influence. He ventured on an expedition into the old world of romance, into the bright fields of the Middle Ages, of chivalry, and of fairy-tale. His early

His taste for mediæval and chivalrous literature.

taste for Ariosto and even for 'Don Quixote' had revealed a tendency in that direction, and if he ridiculed fairy-tales in the person
of Don Sylvio, it was only that he might himself win access into
their magic gardens.   It was just becoming the fashion in France
to write about the age of chivalry, and many mediæval stories were
now rendered more accessible to modern readers.   In 1775 Count
Tressan began the publication of a Library of Romance, including
abstracts of many old chivalrous romances ;   these formed a mine
of wealth for the epic poet, from which Wieland did not fail to
draw.   At the same time Goethe taught him to admire Hans Sachs
and the humorous-popular literature of the fifteenth and sixteenth
centuries, which in consequence suddenly became an absorbing
topic in the 'Merkur;' portraits of Sebastian Brand, Geiler von
Kaisersberg and others were published in it, with accompanying
essays on each.   Wieland himself praised Hans Sachs in prose,
while Goethe eulogised him in doggrel verse.   Herder wrote an
essay on Ulrich von Hutten.   But Wieland went further than this;
he studied single mediæval poems, and turned all these studies to
account in his own poetic productions.   Following the example of
Haller and the Zurich school, Goethe, Bürger, Voss, and others had
adopted old words and dialectal expressions, and despised the correct
diction of the Saxon school and the precepts of a Gottsched or an
Adelung;   and now Wieland too began to enrich his vocabulary
from Old German sources.   As Goethe had revived Hans Sachs'
doggrel verses in an improved form, so Wieland now tried his hand at
tales of greater or less length in the Hans Sachsian manner; but he
soon gave up copying Sachs' external peculiarities, and by dint of re-
modelling the easy colloquial style which he had learnt from Gellert in
accordance with his Old German examples, he sometimes attained in
various metres to a style which bore the strongest resemblance to
the chivalrous epic poetry of Hartmann von Aue.   He narrated the
battle of the Titans, and derived many of his materials from oriental

**His 'Gan-
dalin' and
'Geron der
Adeliche.'**   or other fairy-tales and from tales of chivalry; his
'Gandalin' and 'Geron the noble,' stories derived
from the Arthur-romances, are specially worthy of
notice.   'Geron' is Wieland's most serious poem,
and the self-restraint shown in it, the quiet tone, the absence of

mannerism, the æsthetic and moral tendency make it perhaps his most perfect work. After such preparatory studies, he was well fitted to write a comprehensive, well-planned epic, full of colour and contrast. Such is his poem of 'Oberon,' the His materials for which he found in the French Library 'Oberon.' of Romance, in Shakspeare and in Chaucer. Three separate elements are thus combined in this epic of Wieland's:—the elves of the 'Midsummer Night's Dream,' the fantastic deeds and adventures of the Knight Huon of Bordeaux, and a story of noble love and passionate devotion. The poem rolls on in free stanzas, and for graphic narrative, splendour of outward incident, and truthful delineation of character, it can count but few equals in the whole range of modern literature. We are carried on from scene to scene without the interest flagging for a single moment. The poem is almost throughout truly epic in tone. Wieland's own personality is more concealed than in any of his youthful romances, his jesting and irony have become more discreet, and more moderation and proportion are observed in description and analysis of feelings. 'Oberon' is a variation on his old theme of human weakness, but in this poem he visits such weakness with hard punishment and heavy expiation, purifying two noble souls and qualifying them for the highest happiness.

'Oberon' appeared in 1780. Goethe was delighted with it, and Lessing spoke of the work with admiration. But Wieland's epic power had exhausted itself; 'Clelia and Sinbald,' a legend of the twelfth century which followed on 'Oberon,' is dull and diffuse, and manifestly inferior. He achieved more success in his His translations masterly free translations of Horace's 'Satires' and lations of 'Epistles,' which appeared from 1782 to 1786. In the classics. addition to these, there appeared from his pen in 1788 and 1789 a complete German Lucian and later on Cicero's Letters, a few works of Xenophon, and some plays of Aristophanes and Euripides; but in fresh attempts at novels drawn from the Greek world he never again attained to the excellence of 'Agathon.'

The young Goethe had learnt from Klopstock, Wieland, and Lessing, but he had quickly outgrown all three of them, and was superior to them all in original creative power. Although in his

sympathies Klopstock was most akin to the revolutionary German
Goethe's youths of this period, yet he could never bring him-
critics. self to frankly recognise Goethe's power, and in this
respect he contrasts unfavourably with Wieland. Even Lessing,
in whose mind both ' Götz ' and ' Werther ' must necessarily have
excited mixed feelings, did not shut his eyes to their merits ; he
contented himself with publishing a few philosophical essays of
young Jerusalem's, thus comparing the real Werther with the
Werther of fiction, and at the same time using the opportunity to
utter a few golden words on the use of æsthetic rules. The new
revolutionary literature as a whole had its many weak sides to show,
and an excellent satirist like Professor Lichtenberg could hit on these
with unerring judgment, when he ridiculed Lavater's science of
physiognomy and zealous proselytism, and made fun of the moonshine romanticism and extravagant enthusiasm generally. But it is
surprising that a man like Friedrich Nicolai should have dared to
parody ' Werther ' and the taste for popular songs, and so clumsily
and stupidly as he did. Anyhow, this foolish attack only reacted on
its perpetrator, by depriving him for ever of his credit as a critic.

In spite of its errors, Frederick the Great's late-awakened
Frederick sympathy with German literature contrasts favourably
the Great's with such dulness. About the end of 1780 he sud-
' De la Litté- denly, in a work entitled ' De la Littérature allemande,'
rature Alle- uttered himself on a subject which people had hitherto
mande,' 1780. supposed to be quite indifferent to him. But we have
noticed his conversations with Gottsched and Gellert at an earlier
period in his life. It was of course impossible for him to acquire
late in life a real knowledge of German literature, and his boldness
was great in attempting, notwithstanding, to write about it. He
would hear nothing of Lessing, and he really knew nothing of
Klopstock and Wieland. But he spoke of Gellert, and gave full
recognition to his merits, as he had done years before ; he mentioned Gessner and a few other names of peculiar selection which
happened to have come under his notice. He attacked the bad
taste of an earlier period ; of the literature of the present and of
the immediate past only Goethe's ' Götz ' had come within his
horizon, and, as was to be expected from the disciple of Voltaire,

he expended the full vials of his wrath on this miserable imitation of the miserable plays of Shakspeare. His criticism was after-date, for Goethe himself had by this time quite forsaken the Shakspearian manner, and had a short time before planned his 'Iphigenie' after those very rules and examples of the ancients which the king wished to be held in esteem. Frederick's opinion that the German language must be improved before it could be adapted to poetry, and his suggestions, hardly seriously meant however, for the said improvement, can only be read with a smile; but this display of warm patriotic zeal combined with such utter ignorance of facts and with such naive proposals, this wish for preparations, arrangements, rules, which were already extant and had already borne fruit, is very pathetic and full of irony, symbolising as it does the division of the nation and the separation of the higher classes from the intellectual life of the people.

This work of Frederick's made a great sensation. Many pens were at once ready to undertake the defence of German literature, and much weak stuff appeared with this intent. The best that was written on the subject came from Justus Möser. Goethe purposed a reply, but never carried out his resolution. The answer most calculated to make an impression on the king himself came from a Danzig Jew, Gomperz by name, and his work elicited a friendly acknowledgement from Frederick. The king was now really better informed as to the actual condition of German literature, and when he received Gleim in Potsdam on Dec. 22, 1785, he asked whether Wieland or Klopstock were the greater writer.

Berlin had made great progress under Frederick's government. It had become large enough to be the centre of Berlin under attraction for all classes throughout Prussia; at the Frederick's same time it had remained small enough to facilitate government. personal relations between people who agreed in their tastes, and to favour the formation of a cultured society composed of aristocratic and middle-class elements. Berlin possessed a public opinion which, just because it could not assert itself in political matters, acted all the more powerfully in matters of religion and literature. Moreover, at Berlin people were pretty much agreed in matters of taste, thanks to Lessing's journalistic activity. In fact there was

in the Prussian capital a public to appeal to, and if we think
for a moment what a difference it would have made if Berlin
had retained Lessing and given appointments to Klopstock and
Wieland, what a powerful attraction the city would then have
exercised on a young author like Goethe, and how it might
thus have become the intellectual metropolis of Germany, we can
the better understand how fatal the king's exclusively French culture was to the literary development of his people.   Such a
metropolis would have steadied German taste and given it a
single predominant tendency.   It was the want of this which led
to that extraordinary variety of style which we meet with in Goethe's
writings, and which resulted in the production of works so utterly .
different from each other as 'Götz' and 'Die Natürliche Tochter,'
but which also, through the medium of Goethe's example, occa-
sioned in the case of beginners so much tentativeness and vacil-
lation, revolutionary experiments, and a very Babel of criticism and
production.

The literary endowment of the Prussian capital was very inferior.
Literature The Academy was indeed fortunate enough to call
in Berlin. forth through its prize-essays a few excellent works of
Herder's ; but the German world of letters was only represented
there by second-class writers, who might be very valuable in the
following of great men, but could not compensate for the absence
of first-class authors.   Sulzer, Ramler, Engel, Gedike, Biester were
Nicolai's   not much to boast of.   In the year 1765, Friedrich
'Allgemeine Nicolai started the 'General German Library' as a
Deutsche   kind of continuation and extension of the 'Litteratur-
Bibliothek.' Briefe' started by Lessing; it was a critical review
which embraced all the various provinces of literature, and continued
to exist till the year 1806; it did not contribute much to the æsthetic
culture of Germany, but it was a great power in the sphere of philosophy and religion, attacking with unwearying energy and far-reaching
effect all theological tutelage, all religious exaggeration and superstition.   Nicolai's description of a journey through Germany threw
light into many a dark corner, and this work was seconded by the
'Berlinische Monatschrift,' a publication which he started in the
year 1783.   In ecclesiastical offices, Spalding and Teller helped to

further the cause of religious enlightenment. Outside Prussia an enlightened theologian like Basedow initiated reforms in school-teaching by combining the rationalistic demand for a rapid, easy, unimaginative method of ac- quiring knowledge with Rousseau's principles for a more natural form of education; and his innovations, in so far as they contained any elements of real progress, now forced their way into Prussia too. Every measure of public benefit, every proposal of general utility, every humanising idea was joyfully greeted and quickly fol- lowed out in Frederick the Great's dominion. As soon as Lessing's 'Nathan' appeared, Dohm wrote on the improvement of the political position of the Jews; Moses Mendelssohn also uttered himself on the subject, recalling to mind the old accusations against the Jews and the refutation of them, rebutting charges made in modern times against Jews, and finally, in his work 'Jerusalem,' raising a demand for the total separation of church and state (1784). But he not only struggled to gain a better position for his fellow- believers, but sought to render them more and more worthy of such a position by elevating and improving them. And for these efforts in particular he deserves the greatest praise, for, with all his modesty, he was a great liberator in this sphere, and contributed more than any other man to make the Jews in Germany into Germans. He exerted an influence on the wider German public by his psychological researches, by his 'Phaedo' (1767) and his 'Morning Hours' (1785), works written to prove the immortality of the soul and the existence of God. He showed himself throughout to be a clear writer, but not a thinker of striking originality.

After the appearance of Lessing's 'Laokoon' and 'Minna von Barnhelm,' Berlin did not give birth to any leading æsthetic or scientific ideas under the government of Frederick the Great. The focus of German enlightenment lay not in Berlin, but in Königs- berg and Wolfenbüttel, and its leading representatives were not Mendelssohn and Nicolai, but Lessing and Kant. Lessing, in the last four years of his life, gave a new impulse to theology, and in the year of Lessing's death Kant brought about a revolution in philosophy.

Marginal notes:
Basedow's educational reforms.

Moses Men- delssohn's writings in favour of the Jews.

His 'Phaedo' and 'Mor- genstunden.'

In the year 1784 Kant wrote a small essay entitled, 'What is Enlightenment?' He answered the question thus:—
Kant's views on Enlightenment. Enlightenment is intellectual majority; its motto is: Have the courage to use thine own understanding! He enquired further: Are we now living in an enlightened age? and answered, No, but in an age of enlightenment; the greater number of men have not yet attained their majority, and are not yet capable of dispensing with the guidance of another in matters of religion; but they are on the way to dispense with it. And therefore ' this age is the age of enlightenment or the century of Frederick,' for Frederick the Great granted that liberty which enlightenment demands, liberty to make open use of reason in all matters. How Kant himself made use of this liberty may be seen **His three Critiques.** in his philosophical works, above all in his three epoch-making Critiques, which appeared at the close of the age of Frederick as the most valuable scientific bequests of German Enlightenment: the Critique of Pure Reason in 1781, the Critique of Practical Reason in 1788, and the Critique of the Power of Judgement in 1790. Kant was as old as Klopstock, and five years older than Lessing; when he published the Critique of Pure Reason he was already fifty-seven years of age. He seemed to develop quickly, but in reality he held back his speculations till they were quite matured. In early years he made great **His scientific works.** discoveries in the realm of cosmic physics. Going even beyond Newton, he propounded in 1755 a hypothesis on the origin and development of the cosmic system, which has been recognised as correct by the most modern researches in natural science. He sought, at the same time, to work on the imagination of his readers; he drew a grand picture of a burning sun, one of those priceless flames which Nature has lighted as torches to the universe; he spoke of the inhabitants of distant planets and of the possibility that our souls might find new homes in distant heavens. Finally, he says, that if we fill our minds with such reflections, then the aspect of the starry heavens on a clear night affords a pleasure which only noble souls can feel; in the general calm of nature and with the senses at rest, the hidden intuitive powers of

the immortal spirit speak an ineffable language. The 'Reflections on the sense of the Beautiful and the Sublime' (1764), almost entirely conceal the philosopher, and show us only the experienced man of the world, who gives vent to observations, often very acute, on the characters of races and nations, and, as a side-remark, utters the maxim so characteristic of himself, that in order to *His 'Beobachtungen über das Gefühl des Schönen und Erhabenen.'* attain to truth one must not be bold but careful. In the 'Dreams of a Ghost-seer' (1766), he shows a most delicious vein of humour. He gave regular lectures on anthropology and physical geography, through which he *His 'Träume eines Geistersehers.'* hoped to exercise an influence on real life. In fact, he had struck deep roots in the culture of his time; his learning sometimes bears an artistic colouring, and he wrote at first a clear and often energetic, though not exactly flowing style. In *His style.* his chief works, however, the language is difficult and often obscure, and moves awkwardly in long, involved sentences. This, from the first, prevented his books from exercising any direct influence on the cultivated public; the unpleasing race of commentators and popularisers had to lend their services, and among philosophical authors by profession, who affected originality, the opinion gained ground that clearness was incompatible with depth. *His philosophical works.* But the thoughts which Kant set forth in so uncouth a manner were the ripest fruit of the whole philosophical movement since Leibniz; only that here, too, perfection meant finality. In many respects Kant belongs rather to the party of his countryman Hamann than to the earlier school of Enlightenment. Hamann delighted in quoting the maxim of Hume, that mere reason is not sufficient to convince us of the truth of the Christian religion, and Kant too had received a strong impulse from Hume. Though much of his system is in direct opposition to Hume, yet he was agreed with him in the main *His religious attitude.* point, in his hostility to so-called natural religion, that is, to that popular enlightened philosophy which arrogated to itself the power of proving the most important truths of religion by the light of reason. Mendelssohn's 'Morning Hours' had been refuted before they appeared. Kant's 'Critique

of Pure Reason' sought to demonstrate that all the usual arguments
for the immortality of the soul, the freedom of the human will and
the existence of God, were insufficient and even impossible.   And,
furthermore, he appealed, not like Hamann, to revelation, but, like
the same Hamann, to faith.   He destroyed the visionary harmony
of knowledge and faith; but he wished, as he said, to uproot knowledge in order to keep a place for faith, and that other world which
he destroyed in the sphere of knowledge he built up again in the
sphere of morality.   From the voice of reason, which says to man
'Thou shalt,' from that moral ideal which lives in him, Kant
thought he might infer liberty, immortality and God, and make
this the substance of faith; and he even went so far as to undertake that philosophical interpretation of Christian dogmas, which
Lessing, in his 'Education of the Human Race,' had put into the
mouth of a fictitious author.   But throughout he held fast to the
moral point of view; he rejected all other worship of God than
such as consists in a moral attitude in thought and action; he only
recognised positive religion in so far as it could be interpreted in
the spirit of a religion of morality, and he looked forward, like
Lessing, to a time when all ecclesiastical religion would become
unnecessary.   In their high conception of a morality which acts
only from duty, which does good only for the sake of good, and in
which no motive of temporal or eternal advantage tarnishes the
purity of the will, in their noble worship of the dignity of the moral
man, Lessing and Kant were quite at one, and by their faith they
gave to their nation a moral fervour which stood them in good
stead in days of trial.

But Lessing and Kant were not the only men who, at the end
of the age of Frederick, attained to a purer and deeper form of
philosophy; Herder also must be added to them.   Not only Wolf-
Herder and enbüttel and Königsberg, but Weimar too was one of
Goethe's the classical homes of German Enlightenment.   Herder
later reli- and Goethe adopted a theory of the universe in har-
gious views. mony with the views of Spinoza.   Together they built
their temple on a height from which Goethe had already, at an
earlier period, cast a far-reaching glance into infinite distance.   They
now separated themselves completely from men like Lavater, Jacobi,

and Claudius. Herder discarded his ardent prophetic manner, and
wrote a clearer and more regular, though still at times somewhat
unctuous and rhetorical style; a style in which we seem to trace
Goethe's influence. He gave up his exalted faith, bestowed his
respect again on such men as Spalding and Michaelis, whom he
had attacked in Bückeburg, and in an enthusistic necrologue he
eulogised Lessing as the true seeker, discoverer, and defender of
truth, the courageous enemy of all hypocrisy and half- Herder's
truths. In his ' Letters concerning the study of theo- theological
logy' he advanced a proposal for reading the Bible works.
' from a human point of view,' and laid down the maxim that
' theology is a liberal study, and requires no slavishness of soul.'
In a succession of theological writings he proved himself to be a
gentle disciple of Christ, and in a special volume, entitled ' God,'
published in 1787, he set forth his view of Spinoza's doctrine,
which is rather a re-modelling of Spinozism for his own use than a
faithful reproduction of the same. In the four volumes
of his ' Ideas on the Philosophy of the History of man' His 'Ideen
(1784 to 1791), he unfolded a grand picture of nature sophie der
and humanity, fulfilled with the thought of an all-per- Geschichte
vading law. He begins with the position of the earth der Mensch-
in the universe, ' a star among stars,' then passes from heit.'
the constitution of our planet on to inorganic and organic nature,
and rises from minerals, plants, and animals to man; he dwells
upon man's organization and significance, his dependence on surrounding nature and the beginnings of his culture, and describes
the development of this culture among various nations, in Eastern
and Western Asia, and along the coast of the Mediterranean, in
antiquity and in the Middle Ages. He has arranged a wealth of
material into an articulate system, with infinite skill and true talent
and taste, and has interwoven throughout noble moral reflections.
Humanity is the leading and determining thought which runs
through the whole; the history of the nations is represented as
a school of probation for the attainment of the fairest crown of
human dignity. Reason and wisdom alone last, while senseless-
ness and folly destroy themselves, and bring ruin on the earth.
Humanity is Herder's last word in history, humanity is his last

word in religion.   His thoughts have much in common with Lessing's; but the two views which Lessing carefully distinguishes, the view of a divine education of the human
race, which he himself could not wholly accept, and the
other view of a purely natural development of all culture, including religious culture, are often confounded
in Herder.   In contrast to Lessing's views, as expressed through
the mouth of the fictitious author of the 'Education of the human
race,' Herder does not accord a place of honour to the Hebrews
as a nation, but reserves his warmest admiration and esteem for
the Greeks.   Still he has much reverence for Jesus, and expresses
it in a few solemn sentences.   Christ is to him a man, a teacher of
humanity; 'as a spiritual Saviour of his race he wished to form
divine men, who, under whatever laws it might be, should advance
the welfare of others from pure principles of right, and willing
themselves to suffer, should reign as kings in the realm of truth
and benevolence.'   But, like Lessing, he distinguishes the religion
of Christ from the Christian religion; and while he gives an exalted
position to the former, his attitude towards the latter is cold and
even hostile.   At this stage of his development Herder had lost his
earlier sympathy with the Middle Ages.   His work breaks off at
the end of the Middle Ages; the fifth book was never
accomplished, and the disconnected 'Letters for the
advancement of Humanity' (1793 to 1797) were no
real compensation for it.   In these letters Herder
connects his old ideals of Reason, Tolerance, and Benevolence
with great historical figures of the last centuries, and pays, for instance, his tribute of reverence to Frederick the Great, in whose
State he was born.   'When Frederick died,' he remarks, 'a lofty
genius seemed to have left the earth; both the friends and enemies
of his glory were affected at his death; it was as though even in his
garb of mortality he might have been immortal.'

Kant had reviewed the first and second volume
of Herder's 'Ideas,' and had in so doing showed his
superiority as a philosopher and critic to his countryman and pupil, in a somewhat irritating though not
violent manner.   The East-Prussian character embraces strong con-

Side notes:

Comparison
between
Herder's
and Lessing's
views.

His 'Briefe
zur Beförde-
rung der
Humanität.'

Opposing
types of
the East-
Prussian
character.

trasts; it has a gentle and imaginative and a hard and rational type. The Königsberg poets of the seventeenth century, Simon Dach and his friends were of the former, Gottsched of the latter type. Herder, excitable and full of enthusiasm, belongs to the former ; Kant, full of reflection, self-restraint, and calmness of mind, to the latter. In such a character as Hamann these opposite qualities are mingled in the same nature, so that reason is kept in check by imagination, and imagination by reason, and now one and now the other gains the upper hand.

As Kant gave a somewhat cold reception to Herder's ' Ideas,' so Herder was from the first prejudiced against the new Kantian doctrine, and at last was so far carried away by his anger at the growing authority of the critical philosophy, as to make a violent attack upon *Opposition between Herder and Kant.* it in his ' Metakritik ' and his ' Kalligone.' But though these differences in intellectual temperament led to outspoken hostility between the two parties concerned, they appeared to outsiders and to posterity to be rather supplementary each of the other. Kant forced his readers into the grey calm regions of abstraction, pure thought, and metaphysics ; Herder, on the other hand, transported them into the midst of the glories of nature and the activities of history. Kant kept them strictly and seriously on the other side of the senses, where pure reason has her abode, and utters her commands ; Herder opened to their wondering eyes the fair world of sensuous experience, as it reflected itself in his marvellous imagination.

While these contrasts were developing themselves, while Kant on the one hand, and Spinoza and Herder on the other, were gaining disciples and followers, and the foundation was thus being laid for the science of to-day, the greatest German poets were also creating *Foundation of modern science and literature.* their best works. The heroes of the ' Storm and Stress ' epoch of poetry, the revolutionisers of the drama, became disciples of the Greeks and the representatives of refined classical poetry. They too, like Herder, passed through a refining process, and Lessing's ' Nathan ' pointed them the way to greater purity of form. A year after the death of Frederick the Great appeared Goethe's ' Iphigenie ' and Schiller's ' Don Carlos.'

CHAPTER XII.

WEIMAR.

'YOUR son Goethe sits in the Wartburg, like Dr. Luther a
century and a half ago, and is enjoying himself thoroughly, I think, among the ghosts of chivalry, who
have their home in this noble castle.' Thus Wieland
writes to Goethe's mother on the last of September,
1777, and he adds, after a complaint about his friend's silence:
'Still he is and remains, with all his peculiarities, one of the best,
noblest, and most splendid creatures on God's earth.'

Goethe was in truth thoroughly enjoying himself in the Wartburg,
'that pure, calm height in the midst of the rushing autumn winds.'
His Darmstadt friend Merck visited him there; the Duke of
Weimar, the lord of the castle and his own master, was in the
neighbourhood. The poet was trying by his sketches to impress
the surrounding landscape on his mind, and he wrote to his most
intimate lady-friend: 'This is the most delightful dwelling I have
ever known, so high and so cheerful that one could only bear
to be here on a passing visit, otherwise one would be overpowered
by its elevation and cheerfulness.'

The Wartburg has several times before this figured in our history
of German literature. It was on the Wartburg that Landgrave
Hermann of Thuringia, in the thirteenth century,
received Wolfram von Eschenbach and Walther von
der Vogelweide; it was there that in the fourteenth
century one of the earliest German dramas was performed in the presence of another Thuringian prince; there Luther
translated the Bible in the sixteenth century; the ruling princes of

Weimar, who were his patrons, took a prominènt part in the labours of the 'Fruit-bringing Society' in the seventeenth century, and in the eighteenth century acquired the renown of having brought more fruit to German literature than any other princely patrons.

German writers had hoped in vain for encouragement from Frederick the Great. In vain had Klopstock and others looked forward to the accession of Joseph II. Occasional, but never constant, encouragement had been given to literature in Brunswick, Bückeburg, Eutin, Karlsruhe, Dessau and Gotha, but the Weimar princes alone succeeded in permanently attaching to their court a succession of the most distinguished men. The Duchess Anna Amalia, a Guelph princess from Brunswick, who was early left a widow and burdened with the care of the little state, called Wieland into her service as a tutor to her son Karl August. This young prince, who assumed the reins of government in 1775, at the age of eighteen, supported the national policy of Frederick the Great, and proved himself throughout his life one of the most patriotic and liberal-minded of German princes; he followed in the steps of his mother in securing the presence at his court of Goethe, Herder, and Schiller. In the last years of his great-uncle's life, and till 1788, he prosecuted with burning zeal a reform of the German Imperial constitution, in close connection with Prussia. The revival of a truly national policy and the brilliant union of the noblest spirits of the German nation were both the work of this noble-minded ruler. The University of Jena, founded in the Reformation period, when Wittenberg was lost to the successors of Frederick the Wise, passed through its most brilliant era under the patronage of Karl August. Herder left the stamp of his genius on the ecclesiastical and educational system of the Duchy. Side by side with the great poets and scholars, lesser men also contributed to that wonderful literary activity which now began to develop itself in the little duchy of Weimar. Among the classical scholars there were writers such as the busy journalist and archæologist Böttiger, and at an earlier period Musäus; the latter was a story-

The Weimar princes as literary patrons.

Duke Karl August, 1775.

Men of letters at Weimar.

teller of the Wieland type, and his ironical rendering of old German legends, 'Popular Fairy-tales of the Germans,' as he called them, long enjoyed great favour. From 1778 onward Bode lived in independent circumstances in Weimar. He was a friend of Lessing's from his Hamburg days, and had a high reputation as a Freemason; he made excellent translations of Montaigne and the English humorists, Sterne, Smollett, Goldsmith, and Fielding. At the court and in its immediate neighbourhood æsthetic and literary interests were represented by Major von Knebel, the chamberlains von Seckendorf and von Einsiedel, and the private secretary Bertuch, who were all distinguished as original writers, translators, or musicians. Bertuch was, in addition, a clever bookseller, and as such started many useful undertakings, in particular, in 1785 the 'Jena General Literary Magazine,' an influential critical journal; in 1786 he also commenced the publication of the first German fashion-paper, the 'Journal of Luxury and Fashions.' We see that Weimar and Jena led the fashion of Germany not only in letters and art, but in all other respects.

The ripest productions of Wieland, Goethe, Herder, Schiller

Goethe's Masque for the 18th of December, 1818. were at the same time monuments of Karl August's glorious rule. Among the written testimonies which they themselves bore to the greatness of those times, Goethe's Masque for the 18th of December, 1818, stands out above the rest. It represents the great master left alone to look back on the past and mourn his lost companions; he recalls Wieland's 'Musarion' and 'Oberon,' and summons up before him the figures of Herder and Schiller along with the creations of their genius; meanwhile the Ilme, the river which flows through Weimar, sings the praises of his friends and gives a modest description of the poet himself. But to us more reality and more pathos seem to lie in the epigram in which he praises his duke, 'Klein ist unter den Fürsten Germanien's freilich der meine,' ('Venezianische Epigramme'), who was to him an Augustus and a Mæcenas, and who gave him what rulers seldom bestow, sympathy, leisure, trust, fields, and garden and house.

GOETHE.

On the 7th of November, 1775, Goethe came to Weimar, and at once created a revolution there. The doctrines of Rousseau and the programme of the 'Storm and Stress' party, the striving to follow nature in all the concerns of life, took the little court by storm. The duke's own inclinations were strengthened by Goethe. Etiquette was altogether discarded, and, instead of the usual court-dress, the Werther costume was adopted—high boots, blue coat, and yellow waistcoat. In their enthusiasm they all sought to harden themselves by living much in the open air, by long walks, venturous rides, skating parties at night, and exciting chases. They danced in the country with the peasant maidens, and gave up many a night to the magic of wine and poetry, to the grief of the young duchess and her ladies. Goethe himself in later years did not like to look back on this mad time, but it gained him the life-long friendship of the duke. In daily intercourse they opened their hearts to each other, and Karl August, who showed from early manhood great strength of will and sure discernment of character, perceived in Goethe the stuff for making a useful servant of his state.

Goethe comes to Weimar, 1775.

Goethe had only come as a guest of the duke; in this independent position he succeeded in getting Herder called to Weimar. By the 11th of July, 1776, he himself was appointed Councillor of the Legation, with a seat and vote in the Privy Council; in January, 1779, he undertook the direction of the War Commission and the Highways Commission; in June, 1782, he became provisionally Minister of Finance, the most responsible position in the administration. He put the finances into order, and insisted everywhere on economy. In his official career generally he followed the maxims of his beautiful poem: 'Edel sei der Mensch, hilfreich und gut.' He sought to raise the lower classes, and worked hard and indefatigably to render the government a truly humane and enlightened despotism, and thus to realise the liberal ideals of his youth. Though at first the old officials looked askance at him, while the duchess saw in him the evil genius of the duke, yet he ended by

Goethe's official activity in Weimar.

gaining general confidence. Moreover, this absorption in public affairs was most beneficial to him; the wide interests and activities of political life gave him that satisfaction which he could never find in the practice of the law. What was 'problematic' in his nature, to use his own expression, disappeared, and public service made him firm and consistent. Surrender to the duties of office taught him the general duty of self-surrender, and he was but giving voice to his own deepest experience when he wrote in his diary: 'None but he who quite denies himself is worthy to rule and able to rule.'

The court-life, too, exercised a good influence on him. Hitherto

Good influence of court-life upon him. he had delighted to disregard with student-like freedom all the customs of society, and in his first months at Weimar he had led with the duke a second student-life; but now, in the company of noble women, such as the Duchess Luise and Frau von Stein (wife of the Master of the Horse), he learnt to appreciate the value of social rules and morality. The established forms of refined social intercourse now seemed to him an unmixed good, and the aristocracy, who follow them from youth up, appeared to him the flower of society. He himself had been ennobled by Imperial diploma in April, 1782, and though neither Schiller nor he could possibly feel themselves raised as men by this rise in rank, yet the fact is a valuable external evidence of the increased esteem in which national poetry was beginning to be held. Now once more, as in the classical period of Middle High-German literature, poets moved as equals among equals in the highest grades of society. Now, too, Goethe experienced in himself that ennobling power of love which the Minnesingers praised so

His friendship with Frau von Stein. highly; in the noble character of Charlotte von Stein he seemed to have found everything 'that man in his earthly limits of high happiness can call by a divine name' (cf. the poems 'An Lida' and 'Für ewig'). He reverenced her with deep gratitude, and in one of his short lyrics, 'Zwischen beiden Welten,' he ranks her influence on his life by the side of that of Shakspeare. Goethe's relation to Frau von Stein developed the tenderest side of his nature. She was open and sincere, not passionate, not enthusiastic, but full of intellectual ardour; a gentle seriousness dignified her demeanour; a pure, sound judgment, united with a noble thirst for knowledge, rendered her capable of sharing all Goethe's poetic, scientific, and human interests. We possess innumerable letters and hasty notes which he addressed to her, and which contain germs for a thousand most beautiful poems. His letters to Frau von Stein are as rich in incident, as sincere and pathetic and full of charm as Werther's letters, but much more concise and free from declamation. And in their author we have something better than a Werther; not a morbid lover, but a true friend and brother. It is wonderful to watch the strange, passionate, extravagant, youthful genius developing into the mature man. The moral and religious forces of his nature were strengthened and elevated by Frau von Stein. Purity is the name he has for that nobler inward life which she awakened in him, and in which he seemed to rise more and more to the passionless wisdom of Spinoza. 'Calm and presentiment of Wisdom' is one of the entries in his diary at this time. 'Holy fate,' he prays, 'let me now, cheerful and self-possessed, know the happiness of being pure.' And further on he expresses this wish: 'May the idea of the pure, which extends even to the food which I take in my mouth, become ever clearer and brighter within me.'

His poetry, too, became at this time a mirror of purity. Court-festivities, and an amateur theatre in which the court took an active interest, made frequent demands on his poetic talents. His new life furnished new problems; public office and aristocratic society increased his knowledge of human nature, and supplied him with new characters, and the ideal, moral world in which he was now living was reproduced in figures of lasting grandeur. His deep recognition of the blessing of a strict law regulating the life of action made him more inclined again to recognise fixed forms in poetry. The sympathy with others, which he now fostered in his heart, his noble faith in an ennobled humanity, independent of the finite and accidental differences of rank and circumstance, of religion and nationality, all this had its influence on his style and poetic method; it is shown by the increased earnestness with which he sought to portray general human types rather than the individual and accidental peculiarities of men.

Improvements in his poetry.

Whereas in Werther he had drawn the portrait of a singular and exceptional personality, of one who seemed almost a freak of nature, he now tried to look at the individual as just a single example in which the great essential features of humanity are embodied. He had in former days gone so far as to help Lavater in his attempts to read men's faces, but now he turned from the individual stamp **His scientific** to study the general type of structure, the anatomy of **studies.** man. Werther's enthusiasm for nature, his imaginative absorption in the phenomena around him, in the character of the landscape, in the changes of the seasons and the weather, now assumed more and more in Goethe's mind the character of a deep scientific interest. The lover of nature, who clung with passion to reality and sought to fix it in his drawings and poetry, was transformed into the genuine naturalist. Life at Weimar, in country, wood and garden, brought natural objects more closely before his eyes. Forestry led to botany, and the Ilmenau mining works, of which he had the official superintendence, led to mineralogy and geology. In an eloquent essay on granite he justified the transition from ' the contemplation and description of the human heart—that youngest, most manifold, varying, and changeable of creations—to the observation of the oldest, firmest, deepest, most imperturbable son of Nature.' The disciple of Spinoza revelled in the contemplation of the universe, eternally changing, but changing according to unchangeable laws. The poet needed to conceive of Nature as an active and living organism, carrying out its life as a whole into its parts. He believed that Nature is steady and slow in her action, and that the earth is subject to gradual processes of transformation, for which enormous periods of time must be allowed. In the organic world also he believed that gradual changes are going on, resulting over enormous tracts of time in the transformation of vegetable and animal species. Everything sudden and revolutionary was hateful to him, both in the natural and in the moral world. Nature makes no leaps, he said with Leibniz, and he proved his faith by the discovery of the intermaxillary bone in man, by which he got rid of the asserted difference between the human skeleton and that of the ape.

. In all these studies Herder was his faithful companion, though

he was on the whole rather sympathetic than individually active
in research.   Herder's 'Ideas on the Philosophy of the   Goethe and
History of Mankind' derived much benefit from these   Herder.
common studies.   The idea which Kant in his unfavourable review
refused to recognise in Herder's book, because it was so stupendous
that reason shrunk back before it, the idea namely of a real blood-
relationship of all organic beings to one another, by means of which
men had developed from animals and animals from·plants,—this
idea those most nearly concerned in the work believed to be expressed in it.   There can be no doubt that Goethe and Herder
more or less grasped that point of view which we associate with
the name of Darwin.

Goethe's first period of public life, comprising the ten years from
1776 to 1786, is marked by important progress in all   Goethe's
directions.   Poetry and science, friendship and love re-   life from
ceived new impulses, and he himself became a better 1776 to 1786.
man.   Yet in all his circumstances there was something that could
not permanently endure.   His official labours did not leave sufficient
scope for his poetic faculties ; a·busy statesman might find time for
poetic and scientific sketches, for small essays, poems, and plays
for festal occasions, but not for greater, well worked out and perfected compositions.   Moreover, as a minister he could not get the
Duke to carry out everything that he considered necessary ; certain
differences in fundamental principles could not be smoothed away.
The relation, too, with Frau von Stein suffered from a certain un-
naturalness ; love cannot live by alms, and the most intimate friendship with the wife of another could not make up for his own want
of domestic happiness.

Goethe's Italian journey of 1786 to 1788 brought about a
thorough change in all directions.   The journey itself   Influence
removed the unnatural strain under which he had been of Goethe's
living.   In observation, creation, and enjoyment he journey to
could now entirely follow his inclinations.   Rich trea- Italy, 1786.
sures of nature and art were rendered accessible to him. . His views
became more settled and more just, and his altered conditions of
life left a deep impression on his whole development, moral as well
as artistic.   For two years he was free from official duties, and on

his return he only retained the Commissionership of mines, though he soon added to that the supervision of the University of Jena and the superintendence of the State-institutions for science and art; these duties he fulfilled till his death, and in addition he was for twenty-six years director of the Weimar Theatre. His sojourn in Italy and the time immediately following on it also gave him leisure at length to complete the first general edition of his works; this appeared from 1787 to 1790, in eight volumes, and after a silence of eleven years revealed him to the public, for the most part under a new aspect.

In this edition his youthful works were toned down as much as possible, his extravagances were modified or pruned away, and no more liberties were taken with the lan-guage. The greatest care had been bestowed on the 'Sorrows of Werther,' which stood first in the collec-tion. A riper art had stamped this work as a classic. The characters of Lotte and Albert were elevated, the connection of action with character made more pointed, and the episode was introduced of the peasant youth, who being placed in the same cir-cumstances as Werther, kills his rival. Moreover, in this second edition of the work Goethe sometimes adopts a slightly ironical tone in describing his hero's sentimentality. But besides the old well-known productions, which had already captivated the whole German reading-public, new works now ap-peared which were to win the further applause of the nation. Along with the songs to Friederike and Lili there were now poems to Frau von Stein; besides the revised operettas 'Erwin' and 'Claudine' there appeared other new ones, such as 'Jery und Bätely;' with the old farces in the style of Hans Sachs there was now the new satire of the 'Birds,' written in imita-tion of Aristophanes, and the 'dramatic freak,' as Goethe called it, entitled 'Triumph der Empfindsamkeit;' by the side of 'Clavigo' and 'Stella,' there were 'Faust' and 'Egmont,' 'Iphigenie' and 'Tasso.' 'Faust,' indeed, was still a fragment, but 'Egmont,' which had been planned in Frankfort, now appeared in its complete form.

'Egmont' was printed in prose throughout, but the later parts be-tray an iambic rhythm. The original Shakspearian manner gave

[Marginal notes:]

Revision of his early works in the edition of 1787-1790.

New works in the same edition.

place towards the conclusion to a more idealising treatment.   The
play was planned like 'Götz' in the name of Liberty,   Goethe's
and like 'Götz' written against tyrants.   But the   'Egmont.'
object of attack here was the Spanish violation of Dutch rights,
Spanish intolerance of Protestantism, and Spanish betrayal of a
noble and confiding hero; the interest of the piece is thus made
cosmopolitan rather than exclusively national.   The masses are
represented in this drama as easily led away and cowardly, like the
citizens in Shakspeare's 'Julius Cæsar;' this fact shows that even
in his youth Goethe did not understand by liberty the rule of the
majority.   By placing by the side of the zealous Catholic Regent,
Margaret of Parma, a sober-minded, worldly councillor, who bears,
not without reason, the significant name of Macchiavelli, and by
making it clear that it is Orange whose feet are set in the right
way, Goethe let it be clearly understood that his own political
views were of a very realistic and practical character.   This
play is meant to show that what delights us in poetry is by
no means what is practical in politics.   Egmont Character of
himself is a creation of poetry, reminding us, though   Egmont.
distantly, of Goethe's Fernando in 'Stella,' or even of Crugantino
in 'Claudine.'   He lives carelessly and gains all hearts.   The
magical charm of his affable nature delights the people, captivates
a simple girl like Clärchen, wins the Regent, and even overpowers
the son of his bitterest enemy.   But ruin approaches in the person
of Alba, and Egmont perishes because he yields to his innate *in-
souciance*, and despises the counsels of prudence.   He hopes to
the last, and when every hope for his own life is cut off, he still
hopes for his people, of whom he bears an ideal picture in his heart,
very different from the reality which we are allowed to see.   But the
timid burghers of Brussels, who melt away in panic before Alba's
soldiers, are not the whole of the Dutch nation ; Clärchen, too, is
one of them, Clärchen who has joined her fate indissolubly with
Egmont's, who throws the whole enthusiasm of her nature into the
attempt to save him, tries to excite the crowd in the streets to
revolt, and when all is in vain, precedes her lover in death.
By making Liberty appear in the last scene in a dream, disguised
as Clärchen, to solace the hero as he lies in the condemned cell,

the poet reconciles us to the issue, and even the introduction of music at the close softens the stern tragedy of an inexorable fate. Goethe's Egmont does not, like the historical Egmont, leave behind him a mourning wife and wailing children; he passes out of the world with a free, bold step, like a victor, and finds again in the next life those whom he loved in this.

While 'Egmont' is connected in its origin with 'Götz,' 'Iphigenie' **His** and 'Tasso' sprang directly out of the poet's life at **'Iphigenie,'** Weimar. 'Iphigenie,' in particular, which was completed **1787.** in the beginning of 1787, marks more than any other work of Goethe's the moral purification experienced by the author, and his return from the revolutionary ideas of his youth to the venerable traditions of the Renaissance. Though these traditions had not been unknown to his youth, yet he had never hitherto given himself up so entirely to them. The subject which he now chose was one which Euripides had treated, namely, Iphigenia among the Tauri; but **Differences** instead of availing himself of the outward and mechani- **from** cal solution of the problem, which the ancient drama **Euripides'** permitted, Goethe offered that inward reconciliation **drama.** which the modern spirit demands. He could not have recourse to any *Deus ex machinâ*, who should dictate the law of wisdom to the hopelessly perplexed human mind; he therefore transformed the human characters themselves, softened the contrast between Greeks and barbarians, and represented the king of the Tauri as so noble a nature that his final conciliation does not seem inconsistent with his previous attitude, and the peaceful conclusion of the play does not strike us as unnatural. Goethe also gave another interpretation to the oracle which brought Orestes and Pylades to Tauris; he made the return of Iphigenia to her native land, together with the recovery of Orestes, the central point in the play, and transformed the pursuing furies into the remorse which torments Orestes' own soul. He borrowed one fine psychological motive from Sophocles' 'Philoctetes:' Iphigenia allows herself to be persuaded into taking part in a lie, but she cannot carry out the part she has undertaken; she speaks the truth just at the most dangerous moment, and by this very act overpowers the opposition of the king. The gloomy Orestes and the pure-minded Iphigenia are alike

in being thus sincere and upright, Pylades, on the contrary, the
experienced man of the world, at once bold and prudent, a devoted
friend and full of ardour for heroic deeds, has chosen Ulysses as
his model; he accordingly prefers the path of cunning and strata-
gem, and thus supplies the foil to the characters of Orestes and
Iphigenia.

Orestes is a diseased mind like Werther. But it is not imaginary
evils that pursue him, nor wavering sentiment which   **Character of**
destroys his power; a dreadful crime weighs upon   **Orestes.**
him, and a guilt-laden family seems about to die out in him. The
horrors accumulated on the house of Tantalus are first revealed
to us in Iphigenia's conversation with King Thoas, when she tells
him of the good fortune and the arrogance of her great ancestor
Tantalus, the unrestrained passions of his son and grandson, and
her own cruel fate, her sacrifice by her father and her rescue by the
goddess Diana. Pylades and Orestes later on complete the dreadful
tale, and the latter has to acknowledge with his own lips the fearful
deed he has wrought, the murder of his mother. The tortures
of remorse and self-abhorrence seize on him again at the recital
of his crime; his mind seems quite darkened, and madness takes
possession of his faculties. The longing for impending death
gathers like the gloom of night more and more darkly round
his head. But he does not like Werther lay violent hands on himself, and the force of a tortured imagination, which transports him
into the next world, is at the same time his salvation. Death, though
only grasped in illusion, is a reconciler; Orestes thinks he sees Atreus
and Thyestes, the two hostile brothers, united again in Elysium,
and Agamemnon wandering there hand in hand with Clytemnestra.
This visionary glance into the quiet world of the departed calms
the storm which is surging in his bosom, and in his sister's arms the
guilt-laden man, torn by remorse, is restored again to his former self.
But the clouds are not yet all dispersed, and there is still reason
for fear; it is yet doubtful whether the return to Greece will be
successfully accomplished. Even Iphigenia's trust in Providence is
temporarily shaken; 'Save me,' she prays to the Olympian gods,
'save me and save your image in my soul.' But from her own
pure, childlike heart comes deliverance. Her faith in truth does not

deceive her ; in recovering her own true self she recovers her inward peace, and brings the same peace to her friends. Barbarians and Greeks, gods and men are reconciled, all discords are resolved into harmony, and men's differences forgotten in their common humanity.

Orestes returning to life through dreams of death, and cured by the touch of Iphigenia, typifies Goethe freeing himself from morbid thoughts, and finding peace for his soul in the friendship of Frau von Stein. The race of the Tantalidæ also, passing from arrogance and passion to submissiveness and self-control, from fear and hatred of the gods to trust and love, may well be taken as symbolical of Goethe himself, who now laid aside the rebellious and defiant attitude of his Prometheus and found happiness in the constant love of God as set forth in the teaching of Spinoza.

Iphigenia represents the power of ideal womanhood. Her Character of approach brings peace and reconciliation; her priest-Iphigenia. hood imparts a milder character to the religion of the barbarians, and the soft tone of her voice propitiates the harsh king. The weak woman overcomes all resistance, but she is not really weak, for she knows no fear; the pure instinct which she follows makes her bold, and she remains constant to the idea of right which she has formed. In the school of obedience and misfortune, in the separation from home and family, and in the service of the virgin goddess she has acquired that firmness of character by which she gains her purpose. Her noble character lifts her into the atmosphere of a still higher general goodness; and the maxims and reflections on the nature of man and woman, on the blessings of friendship, on sincerity and prudence, which run through the whole play, continually reveal an insight into the highest principles of the moral world.

The Hellenic style of some of Goethe's youthful poems appears Style of in this play purified, toned down and raised to an even Goethe's level of artistic perfection; this perfection was wanting 'Iphigenie' in the original prose sketches for the play, and was and only attained in the blank verse of the final version. Wieland's only attained in the blank verse of the final version. 'Alceste.' The style of Goethe's 'Iphigenie' had already been anticipated to some extent in a work which Goethe, in his

youth had unsparingly scoffed at, in Wieland's opera 'Alceste,'
which has some lines bearing a marked resemblance to passages in
Goethe's drama.   The Renaissance-drama of Italian and French
literature had, after the appearance of Lessing's 'Sara,' more and
more lost its power in Germany; the Alexandrine tragedy had
been long ago discarded, and the Opera alone remained faithful to
classical subjects, and continued the spirit and the style of the
Renaissance-drama.   Gluck composed an 'Orpheus,' an 'Alcestis,'
an 'Iphigenia in Aulis,' and an 'Iphigenia in Tauris.'   Wieland
followed the example of the Italian and French librettists ; in order
to raise the level of German opera he took up a mythological theme,
the story of Alcestis, and in his treatment of it hit upon the
tone which Goethe had only to follow out consistently in order to
make his 'Iphigenie' the noblest work which revived classicism
can show in all modern literatures.   Goethe introduced the spirit
of the opera into the spoken drama, and succeeded in gaining for
the German stage the favour of the higher classes who were still
under the traditions of French classicism. He observed the strictest
laws of form, and adhered most rigorously to unity of time, place,
and action throughout all the five acts.   In this, too, he laid great
restraint on himself, and revealed his power by the very restrictions
he laid on it.

One might say that Goethe, in his 'Iphigenie,' raised the dramatic
art of Racine to a higher level. He made it freer and *Superiority*
more original. He despised the conventional introduc- *of 'Iphigenie'*
tion of the confidante, the convenient but improbable *to Racine's*
narrations, the affected reserve in the delineation of *dramas.*
passion, and many other traditional ideas.   Racine, too, had begun
an 'Iphigenia in Tauris,' and in some features Goethe's play
resembles the fragments of Racine's piece.   Racine, too, favoured
the inner world, and tender emotions are the leading interest of his
dramas ; but with Racine love is almost always the spring which sets
in motion outward complications and passionate inward conflicts.
With Goethe, on the contrary, love plays a very subordinate part ;
Thoas, the King of the Taurians, is indeed a suitor for Iphigenia's
hand, but Pylades does not, as we might naturally expect, conceive a strong passion for her.   Selfish desire has here no place,

and it only appears in Thoas in order to yield to renunciation. Those contests of generosity too, which formerly enjoyed such favour, are banished from this piece; there is no opportunity for Orestes and Pylades each to emulate the other in readiness to die for his friend.   Outward action is almost entirely wanting, and the ordinary stage-manager does not know what to do with the

'Iphigenie,' a psychological drama.

piece. All the incident there is takes place in the souls of natural but morally noble people, and these do not struggle with outside evil or vulgarity, but only with the wishes, emotions, and convulsions of their own hearts, in order to bring out in the end the victorious power of self-denial and self-conquest. In 'Iphigenie,' Goethe created a new order of drama which might be called psychological drama, and which was peculiarly appropriate to a literary period in which lyric poetry flourished more than dramatic. Germany, which since the Reformation and Pietism had had its attention so much drawn to the inner life, now, in this epoch, turned this introspective tendency to good account in the sphere of poetic creation.

The style and technique of 'Iphigenie' are continued in 'Tasso;'

Goethe's 'Tasso.'

and in 'Tasso,' too, Goethe gives us a psychological drama, a powerful tragedy, in which the catastrophe results purely from character. Tasso was a well-known personality to Goethe from his childhood, one of the first great poets whose name he heard mentioned. Tasso's fate, as traditionally reported, furnished the clearest example of the tragedy of a poet's life, and naturally appealed strongly to Goethe's mind, since he had ex-

Reflects Goethe's own experience.

perienced in his own nature how easily a poet is led to transfer the images of his own imagination into the actual world, and how apt he is to misconstrue reality or to demand from it what it cannot grant, and thus to bring about a painful conflict. Tasso suffered from a distrustful sensitiveness, which became a mania of believing himself the special object of conspiracy and persecution; he conceived a strong passion for a princess who was entirely beyond his reach, and he had finally to be removed from the circle in which alone he found happiness. Goethe had had the opportunity of experiencing personally during his first months of Weimar the attitude of the man of the world towards the poet, and he had soon himself to play the part of the prudent, cool and even cruel man of the world, when the unfortunate Lenz came to the court of Weimar. Lenz was treated with the greatest kindness and forbearance, like a sick child, but at last, through some foolish act like Tasso's, he drew down on himself an irrevocable sentence of banishment. Lenz and Goethe are both re-presented in Tasso, and Tasso's opponent, the statesman Antonio Montecatino, has also many features drawn from Goethe himself. Goethe, the visionary and turbulent young lawyer at Frankfort, and Goethe, the Weimar Minister, are to a certain extent embodied in Tasso and Antonio, though the latter, who is wanting in the gifts of the Graces, is at the same time a reminiscence of Goethe's opponents in Weimar. In this drama again, self-denial, moderation, and re-nunciation appear as the chief requirements for a wise conduct of life, and women are again the guardians of morality and good manners. The noble, self-possessed princess, who has learnt patience and toleration in the school of suffering, and who gives the poet such delicate sympathy and understanding, who has cured him of every false impulse and has pointed out to him the truest happiness, cannot deny kinship with Iphigenia and Frau von Stein. Her lively, somewhat intriguing friend, Leonore of Sanvitale, furnishes as delicate a contrast as Pylades in 'Iphigenie,' only in quite a different direction; the slight egoism in all her sympathy with other people, her flattering friendship for Tasso, joined with the after-thought of making the distinguished man whom she wishes to benefit at the same time a pleasure and an ornament to herself, all this renders her one of the most interesting types of the modern female world, and Goethe must certainly himself have often experienced the kind of egoistic sympathy which he here depicts. Tasso's eloquent praises of Ferrara are of course an expression of Goethe's feelings for Weimar. Like Tasso, Goethe had seen the world in his Weimar friends, and had long only written for them; like Tasso, he could say: 'Man is not born to be free, and for a noble character there is no greater happiness than to serve a prince whom he can honour.' Tasso's patron, the Duke of Ferrara, in his justice, his sincerity, his chivalrous splendour, and his capability of making use of everyone in the right place, may be taken as an idealized picture of Karl August.

The whole work was not cast in one mould, and in this respect **Style of** it is inferior to 'Iphigenie;' Goethe had only taken **'Tasso.'** two acts in prose with him to Italy, and the transformation into iambic verse was only completed in 1789. His strong regret at leaving Italy, his passionate longing to return thither, and the feeling of exile with which he looked back on it, have left their stamp on this drama; but he did not find it easy to take up the subject again on his return to Weimar, and he went through a careful course of study before completing the play. Numerous events of Tasso's life are skilfully introduced, changed, combined, or alluded to, and the whole play moves in an atmosphere of aristocratic refinement, which gives unity to the work. The contrasts are toned down, and the characters have not the distinctness of portraits. The grand language which the old Greeks are made to speak in 'Iphigenie,' here gives place to a smooth, brilliant, courtier-like tone. The figurative style which was peculiar to Goethe from his youth twines itself in golden threads through the artistic web of the dialogue, and grand thoughts are united with charming ease and melody of expression. In spite of the lack of outward incident, the play ought to produce the strongest dramatic effect, if there were actors capable of revealing all the force of suppressed grief which lies hidden in the noble words, and if there were a public whose hearts could fully echo the melting tones which Goethe here drew from his lyre.

As in 'Iphigenie' and 'Tasso,' so in Goethe's poems written at **Poems** Weimar till 1786, we notice the same advance to- **written at** wards calmness and wisdom. At first he is still **Weimar** restless and troubled, and longs for peace (cf. 'Wan- **before 1786.** derer's Nachtlied'). Then he comforts himself in the evening calm of woods and mountains ('Über allen Gipfeln ist Ruh'). In one poem he still doubts whether he shall go or remain; in another he is full of hope for the work which he has begun ('Hoffnung'). At one time he compares himself to a skater, who boldly makes a path for himself, and soothes his care in these words: 'Quiet, my love, my heart! Though it cracks, it does not

break! Though it breaks, it breaks not with thee.' At another
time he compares himself to a sailor, and calms the anxiety of
his friends; he stands bravely at the helm, wind and waves
play with the vessel, but wind and waves do not disturb his
heart.   In the poem 'Ilmenau,' he makes a clear confession of the
wildness of the first months at Weimar, and at the same time shows
how different is the idea which he and the duke now have of the
function of government.   'Mieding's Tod' is a monument to the
Weimar amateur-theatre, where 'Iphigenie' was first acted, Goethe
himself taking the part of Orestes to the admiration of all be-
holders.

Like his 'Iphigenie,' his hymns, too, are now full of the pettiness
of mortals, the greatness of the gods, and the love and blessing
which they pour on mankind.   In the poem called 'Zueignung,'
he receives the veil of Poetry from the hand of Truth, and
in 'Die Geheimnisse,' a poem which was planned 'Die Geheim-
about the time that Herder began his 'Ideas,' but   nisse.'
which unfortunately remained a fragment, he purposed to reveal
to his fellow-men in a poetic form the highest form of truth yet
discovered.   He meant in melodious stanzas to proclaim humanity
as the highest essence of all religions.   He assigns personal representatives to the various religions, who live in a kind of monastic
community presided over by a specially eminent man, named
Humanus.   We recognise here an affinity with Herder's and
Lessing's views, and a connection with the deepest thoughts of the
Order of Freemasons, to which both Herder and Goethe belonged.
But these representatives of different nations and religions in
mediæval costume, half monks and half knights, also involuntarily
recall to our minds the Knights Templars, the Holy Grail, and the
ties of relationship which in Lessing's 'Nathan,' as in Wolfram's
'Parzival,' bind heathens and Christians together.   And when at the
very beginning of 'Die Geheimnisse' we are met by the words:
'From the power which binds all beings that man can free himself
who conquers himself'—we are at once reminded of Walther von
der Vogelweide's question and answer : 'Who kills the lion? Who
kills the giant? Who triumphs over this and that? That does he
who subdues himself.'

The humanity which Goethe teaches in 'Die Geheimnisse' has a Christian colouring; the arms of Luther, the rose and cross, which Valentin Andreä made the symbols of the imaginary Rosicrucian fraternity, and which were afterwards adopted in actual secret societies, appear in this poem too as the most sacred symbol; the cross signifies self-sacrifice, 'the first and last virtue, in which all others are included,' as Goethe said in later years; the rose designates the fair blossoms of life which spring from self-sacrifice, and whose blessing Goethe himself experienced in the purification of his life and the ennobling of his art.

The intercourse with his Weimar friends raised Goethe's standard

Improvements in metre and style. of outward poetic form. Whereas Wieland treated the stanza arbitrarily as it suited him best, Goethe in 'Zueignung' and in 'Die Geheimnisse' endeavoured to construct it according to stricter rules. About the year 1780 Herder began to translate from the Greek anthology, and to reveal the beauties of the Hellenic epigrams at the very time when Voss was rendering Homer into German; at the same time too Goethe, who had learnt the laws of blank verse from Herder, began to write in distichs and hexameters, though before this he had never employed purely classical metres. But it was not only in the matter of metric form that Goethe's power had increased; in poetic conception also his lyric poetry now shows signs of progress. If we compare the poem 'An den Mond' with the Strassburg song 'Wilkommen und Abschied,' we notice that there is less of outward incident, but the inward emotion affects us all the more. Outwardly it is merely a walk in a well-known valley through moon-lit fields towards the river; but the outward world which unfolds itself to the eye points to an inner world. Nature and the human soul join in a mysterious harmony. However great may be the difference, both in style and matter, between the productions of Goethe's Frankfort or Strassburg periods and 'Iphigenie,' 'Tasso,' the lyric poems we have just noticed, or indeed most of his works written at Weimar before his Italian journey, still we can also recognise a relationship between them. Werther lives on in Tasso, and though in the 'Triumph der Empfindsamkeit,' Goethe might ridicule his 'Werther' and Rousseau's 'Nouvelle Héloise' as the ideals of sentimental romance, yet he had not made an end of sentiment; but his sentiment now assumed a religious colouring, that is to say, if the mere mood of renunciation, an asceticism without dogmatic foundation, a spiritual enthusiasm based on a pantheistic philosophy, may still be called religious. And this renunciation was combined with a certain secret longing for the good things of life, a suppressed emotion, pent-up tears, which complete the peculiar character of this spiritual and finely touched poetry.

The spiritualizing tendency of those first years at Weimar asserts itself in nearly all Goethe's works of that period. External Nature is now not only loved and described for her own sake, but as symbolising and reflecting the inner life of mankind. In one poem, 'Harzreise im Winter,' all the incident is restricted to a few slight allusions, in order to give the fullest scope to ethical ideas. The Staubbach waterfall in the Lauterbrunnen valley suggested the 'Gesang der Geister über den Wassern :' *Spiritualizing tendency. Lyrics.*

> ' Soul of man, thou art like to the water.
> Fate of man, thou art like to the wind.'

The 'Letters from Switzerland' again enable us clearly to follow the development of this intellectual view of nature. They consist of two series, the first corresponding to the 'Werther period,' the second to the period which produced 'Iphigenie;' the former are a record of Goethe's Swiss journey of 1775, the latter were written on a journey which he undertook with the Duke in *' Briefe aus der Schweiz.' First and second series.* 1779, and in which they boldly triumphed over the difficulties of winter. The first series of letters are written in imitation of Sterne's ' Sentimental Journey,' and do not show any special genius; they are thoroughly subjective, and overflow with declamatory eloquence and fantastic reflections in true Wertherian style, in which the real subject, the natural scenery, is often completely lost sight of. All these faults are absent from the second series of letters, which is highly original and an admirable work of art. The tone here is much more objective, though still mingled to a great extent with subjective elements. These later letters show us the many-sided statesman and scholar, with ripened judgment and clear glance. Observation of nature is the chief interest, and supplies us with some glorious pictures; but besides the mere description, the author gives us in thoughtful observations an analysis of the impression produced by them on his mind, the comparisons which they suggest, or the inward experiences which they remind him of. In the end only, when we come to the most barren regions, does he draw for us the men who belong to them with their peculiar views of life, adding a touching legendary figure who edifies his flock near the St. Gothard, and a zealous Capuchin, who speaks to the travellers of the power, unity, and strength of the Roman Catholic Church,

While both parts of the ' Letters from Switzerland' evidently aim at a certain artistic unity in composition, in the ' Italian Journey,' on the contrary, we have little more than carelessly arranged materials, as they lay ready to the poet's hand in his letters and diaries on the journey. Here Goethe has become quite objective, living in things as they are, and interesting himself in facts as such. He piles up as much material as he can get, not everything indiscriminately that offers itself, but everything that specially attracts him. He is indifferent to the historical associations of places, for he wishes no web of fancy to interpose itself between him and the real objects; he wants to see and grasp things himself, to replace the conceptions which he had derived from books and hearsay, by direct personal acquaintance. He does not only see the landscape, but also the elements of which it is composed; as a geologist he studies the volcanoes, as a botanist he seeks to reduce to order the manifold new forms which crowd under his observation, and thus arrives at the theory of the development of all parts of the plant from the leaf, a process which he designates as metamorphosis. He enjoys the freedom of Roman life and describes the manners of the people. After he had journeyed hastily through Italy and Sicily he took up his abode for a time in Rome. He did not care about fine society, but lived with German artists and a few friends. Catholicism was repulsive to him, and even his humanitarianism, which in ' Die Geheimnisse' still wore a Christian colouring, now became anti-Christian and intolerant towards

The ' Italienische Reise.'

religious-minded people. He now rejected mediævalism together with Catholicism. He had long ago become alienated from Gothic architecture, which had once appealed so strongly to his feelings as the essentially German style, but now he went even further and returned wholly to the stand-point of Oeser, Winckelmann, and Lessing. Following the general spirit of the age, he Goethe's no longer believed in one only saving religion, but classicism. he still held to one only perfect art, the one true style which only the ancients and their followers possessed. Classical art and the Renaissance alone attracted his attention, and the somewhat cold Palladio was his model architect. In painting he almost entirely overlooks the mediæval predecessors of Raphael and Michael-Angelo, while he highly esteems their successors of the Venetian school, Caracci, Domenichino, and Guido Reni. In art, too, he does not care for history, but for the most perfect achievement, the Ideal.

After his return from Italy he developed still further the interests which he had there acquired. The 'Metamorphosis 'Metamor-of Plants' appeared as a treatise in 1790, and later on phose der as a poem; he also gave his serious attention to the Pflanzen' types of the animal world, and already a new sphere (1790). of research was attracting him, namely, the science of colour. But successful as he was in adding new ideas to zoology Studies in and botany, he quite failed in physics; he strove in physics. vain with the genius of Newton. An opposition, similar to that between Herder and Kant, separated him from the enlightened school of the eighteenth century. It was from Mathematics that that school, from Newton down to Kant, drew its chief strength, and Goethe's mathematical training had been totally neglected. It was the tendency of modern natural science, since Copernicus, to get beyond mere sensuous perception and to escape its illusions; but the poet too often took sensuous perception for direct certainty. Against the Newtonian doctrine of the composite nature of white light he cherished somewhat the same kind of hatred which Hamann felt for analysis; 'distinguishing and counting,' he himself says, 'did not lie in my nature.'

In the year 1791 Goethe first gave utterance to his opposition
Goethe's to the Newtonian theories; in 1810 he completed his
'Farben- investigations, and though they contributed nothing
lehre,' 1170. to physics, yet they gave a decided impulse to physio-
logical optics. The sensuous and moral influence of colour was
ably discussed, and the colouring of various painters submitted to
examination; the history of the science of colour was treated as
a symbol of the history of all sciences, and the whole was interwoven with beautiful and pregnant thoughts, everywhere opening
wide intellectual vistas.

Nature and Art were always connected in Goethe's mind. The
consideration of colouring, which had been forced upon him during
his sojourn in Italy, had given the impulse to his researches on the
theory of colour, and he now sought to systematise and simplify
works of art in the same manner as he had surveyed the organic
world. We have said that Goethe believed that the manifold
Goethe's forms of plant and animal life had been developed
views on from primitive forms, from original types; in the
Art. same way he thought he had reason for asserting that
the Greek sculptors proceeded after the method followed by nature,
that they set out from the general type of man and followed him
in all his differences of race, age, character, expression, and that in
their ideal gods they disregarded the accidental peculiarities of
individuals, and only retained the essential, typical features of
humanity. His anatomical knowledge and even his old physiognomical experiments were a direct advantage to him in his study
of art. The various fields of his research thus reaped mutual
benefit from each other, and he seemed at this period to feel himself 'that the sum total of his powers had been reached.' In such
a mood we find him writing from Rome, that he would henceforth only occupy himself with 'lasting conditions,' and thus,
following the doctrine of Spinoza, would give immortality to his
mind. He interwove his own deepest religious and philosophical
convictions with the types of ancient mythology; before the
highest achievements of Greek art everything arbitrary and fanciful
seemed to him to fall away: 'Here is Necessity,' he exclaimed,
'here is God.'

In his art-studies Goethe had found a companion in the Swiss painter Heinrich Meyer, whom he became acquainted Goethe and with in Rome, and with whom he soon entered into Meyer. perfect sympathy. Together with Meyer he began to study more closely the historical aspect of art. The old German school of art was to be studied in Nürnberg and Augsburg, while in a new journey to Italy in Meyer's company the mediæval Italian art, as specially exemplified in Florence, was to be carefully investigated. But in the summer and autumn of 1797 Goethe only got as far as Switzerland, where he met Meyer; the reports which he furnishes us of these months show again a marked advance on the style of the 'Italian journey.' In his earlier writings Goethe would set to work without much system; now everything was carried on methodically, and the material was arranged as in a report of a scientific journey. In describing his well-known native town of Frankfort he tries to put himself in the position of a stranger, seeing it for the first time. He uses certain tabulated forms of description in order to gauge easily and accurately peculiarities of country and people, places and individuals, circumstances and works of art. And we find him always inclined to consider all phenomena not only as existing, but as having had their existence developed in accordance with law, to trace out their causes and discover the forces which have been at work in their production. The great aim which floated before him in all these enquiries was the composition of comprehensive works on the theory and history of art, works of which only fragments were ever accomplished. The periodical entitled 'The Periodical, Propylæa' (1798–1800) was devoted almost exclusively 'Die Pro- to the same object, while prize-competitions in painting pyläen.' and art-exhibitions supplied practical suggestions in the same direction. The autobiography of Benvenuto Cellini, which Goethe translated, furnished instruction on the subject of Florentine history, art, and skilled handicraft. The work entitled ' Winck- 'Winckel- elmann and his Century,' which appeared in 1805, mann und comprised a grand account of Winckelmann by Goethe, sein Jahr- and a history of art in the eighteenth century from the hundert,' pen of Meyer. A history of colouring by Meyer was in- 1805. serted in Goethe's ' Theory of Colour.' In later years the periodical

entitled 'Art and Antiquity' became the journalistic organ of the
Weimar patrons of art, as these two allies called them-
Periodical, selves. Their views on art suffered no perturbation
'Kunst und
Alterthum,' from their historical studies, or from the new tendencies
published which were coming up around them ; they remained
by Goethe faithful followers of Winckelmann, and worshipped
and Meyer. ancient art as the only ideal. Goethe adhered faithfully
to the stand-point which he had not so much gained as confirmed
in Italy, and it was only out of friendly sympathy for others that he
occasionally returned to the mediæval tendencies of his youth.

In poetry, as in art, he had struck out in the direction of classical
antiquity even before his sojourn in Italy. This ten-
Good effect
of his Italian dency became stronger and more fruitful while he was
journey on there, though he never carried out some fine dramatic
him. projects which floated before his mind's eye during
his first days in Italy and Sicily, plans for an 'Iphigenia in Delphi,'
and a 'Nausikaa.' But in another respect also Italy marked a great
epoch in Goethe's poetry. The inner character of his poetry assumed a totally different aspect after the Italian journey, corresponding to a complete transformation in his moral character.
From his early youth Italy had always been included in his life's
programme, and the more the difficulties of his life in Weimar
weighed upon him, the stronger grew his yearning for the South ;
all his unsatisfied longings became at last concentrated in the wish
for this journey. The yearning was now fulfilled, and though the
parting from the land of promise was the cause of new grief, yet
no one could deprive him of what he had seen and enjoyed. He
rejoiced in the wealth he had acquired, and his circumstances in
Weimar were now also arranged in full accordance with his wishes.
Goethe and His need of love had also found satisfaction ; from
Christiane the summer of 1788 Christiane Vulpius possessed his
Vulpius. heart, and afterwards presided over his household ; she
was the daughter of a Weimar official, pretty, bright, good-natured,
simple-hearted, and devoted with her whole soul to her lover. It
was not till the 19th of October, 1806, that she was united to
Goethe by a church-ceremony, but from the beginning he looked
upon her as his wife, and though this connection lost him the

friendship of Frau von Stein, a rupture which pained him deeply, yet he found perfect happiness with Christiane. Poems like the 'Morgenklagen,' 'Der Besuch,' the Roman elegies and the Venetian epigrams freely reveal his feelings. 'I live,' he exclaims, 'and were hundreds of years granted to men, I should wish the morrow still to be like to-day.' The gods, he says, have given him all that man can pray for, and he describes his beloved in this beautiful simile : 'I went along the sea-shore, seeking shells; in one I found a pearl, which now remains treasured near my heart.' ('Venezianische Epigramme,' 93, 94, 28.)

This final satisfaction, this earthly happiness, estranged him from the refined and delicate sentiment which breathes in **His poetry** 'Iphigenie' and 'Tasso.' His poems are no longer full **becomes** of yearning, nor are they so spiritual in character. The **more real.** purely intellectual tone disappeared. Werther and Tasso are more closely akin to each other than Tasso and the Roman elegies. The coarser elements of Goethe's youth came again to the front; he became, to use his own expression, realistic. He was in his thirty-ninth year when he returned from Italy, and he meant henceforth to write nothing which a mature man who knew the world would not read and enjoy. As on his journeys he gazed calmly around him, observed things as they were, and reproduced them without adding to them, so in his poetry he now gave up extravagant sentiment, and sought above all to be true to reality. There is no reference now to the ideal of renunciation, no rosy gleam borrowed from the next world; his poems now treat of earthly passion and earthly enjoyment, love of the good, the useful, and the beautiful; they express reverence for what is great, gratefulness to a kind master, faithfulness to friends, and are not sparing in censuring bunglers, enthusiasts, and deceivers of the people.

In the Roman elegies, which are modelled after Propertius, the poet transfers to Rome the happiness which he had **The** found at Weimar. With the elegiac metre of the **'Römische** ancients the mythological figures appear again, which **Elegien.'** Goethe had discarded in his youth at Herder's demand; but the beauty of these poems is never disturbed by dry pedantry or piled-up allusions, as is the case sometimes with the Roman poets. Here we have either clear personifications, like Fama and Amor, or sharply-outlined figures whom the poet endows with such real, present life that their name is quite a matter of indifference, or else a revival of some myth under a new form. It is true that even thus the introduction of gods and heroes in these poems prevented their acquiring a wide popularity; but these plain-spoken love-poems are not meant to be popular; they presuppose mature manhood, ripe experience of life, and classical culture. To the classical scholar they seem to excel Propertius, for what Propertius only occasionally succeeds in is here characteristic of the whole, namely, graphic scene and action. These Roman elegies are a series of beautiful pictures, with all the added charm of life and movement. None furnishes a more brilliant example of what we mean than the short elegy (No. 11) in which Goethe lays these poems on the altar of the Graces, rejoicing that he may do so, since the high ideals of the gods surround him, amongst whom Love should not be absent; in four distichs he portrays and characterizes seven gods and goddesses, so clearly and yet with such simple words that it is evident that his art was formed more under the influence of Homer than of Propertius. Lessing's and Herder's theory of poetry founded on the study of Homer, which Goethe had imbibed in his youth, here came to reinforce his rich knowledge of classical sculpture, and enabled him to handle the worthiest subject with unsurpassable skill.

Revival of classical elements in his poetry. The highest creations of Greek religion and art had been the chief subject of Goethe's studies while in Rome, and in these elegies he shows that the classical ideals of humanity still exercised their power over his mind; the classical gods now appear again in his poetry, and the artistic conception which he had formed of them now bore the ripest poetic fruit. In reading the Roman elegies we seem indeed to feel that 'the sum total of his powers had been reached.'

Typical method in art and poetry. As in art and nature, so too in poetry he now sought after the typical. Formerly he had turned away from the human heart, the most capricious part of creation, and in order to make something permanent and immutable his object of worship had directed his attention to stones; but now he learnt also to discover and portray the unchangeable, the 'lasting relations' in the moral world, such as the family, the home, the neighbourhood, the community, the state, the contrast between the settled and unsettled, or the active and the contemplative life, or the life of selfish pleasure and the life of renunciation ('Die Wahlverwandtschaften'); and for this very reason the Greek gods assumed new importance for him, since they too denote lasting types in the moral world.   At an earlier period Goethe would at once mark the genus to which the individual belonged, as in 'Iphigenie' he only used Diana as a name for the Divine generally, and in Iphigenia herself created a type of ideal womanhood; but now, on the contrary, he sought for those typical forms which lie between the individual and the genus.   The difference between Goethe's earlier and later method is most apparent   The in the 'Natural Daughter,' a play produced about the   'Natürliche year 1800.   Here we have a duke who educates his   Tochter.' child in seclusion; the girl fulfils all his expectations, and grows up to be his chief delight, but following an impulse of pride, he shows her too early to the world, and thereby excites the envy of his son, who thinks his interests are prejudiced by her; the son secures her secret removal, and the duke is made to believe that she is dead.   We leave him lamenting over the grave of his lost happiness.   Here Goethe shows us the typical father from all sides; whatever else may characterize the man, it is the paternal nature which is made most prominent ; the incidents which are developed before us, the tragic issue which we see approaching, all this results from paternal pride.   The typical element is the chief spring of action, and it is a primitive human relation that is presented before our eyes.

The new style which Goethe had acquired through his journey to Italy first showed itself in his Roman elegies.   The love represented in 'Tasso' presupposes high culture,   Comparison moral refinement, strong outward restraints, strange   'Tasso' inward distortion, and the peculiar circumstances of   and the a court where the poet is cherished and treated with   Roman much consideration on account of his talent.   Tasso's   elegies. love and its passionate outburst is, like Tasso's whole character, a pathological phenomenon, an abnormal case, a 'rarity in natural history,' as Fritz Jacobi would have said. The poet, on the contrary, who in the Roman Elegies sings of his own feelings and experiences, reveals himself as a thoroughly healthy and natural human being; and the love which he describes is the primitive human phenomenon—two people who are attracted to each other, then devoted to each other with body and soul, who overcome all hindrances in order to possess each other, and who forget the world around them, and even defy it where they think it necessary to do so; it is the thing which repeats itself in all ages, among all nations, in all classes, and here only shines with immortal glory through the charm of art.

Schiller and Goethe.

Notwithstanding the high point of development which Goethe's powers had attained, notwithstanding the wonderful co-operation of his various intellectual interests, still, the first years after his return

Pause in Goethe's poetic activity after his return from Italy.

from Italy were not favourable to his activity as a poet. His artistic and scientific studies exercised a more powerful attraction over him, and seemed to absorb all his intellectual powers. The more he found full satisfaction in the intellectual and domestic world in which he was now living, the less did he feel the need of disclosing his inner experiences to the outside world. With the departure of those dissatisfied yearnings which had filled his soul in earlier years, his poetry had been deprived of part of the air in which it used to breathe. Yet another reason may be assigned for his poetical barrenness at this time. In the years 1792 and 1793

His military experiences.

he took part, in company with his princely master, in the campaign in Champagne and in the siege of Mainz; this still further expanded his horizon, and the reports which he compiled from his diaries of this period are models of graphic description. They contain nothing but what he has himself seen, and show the unerring accuracy of observation which he had acquired while in Italy. But these military experiences contributed further to strengthen his realism, and in fact at this period of his life all his finer and tenderer sentiments and emotions seemed benumbed, and threatened to be extinguished altogether. Then, suddenly, his intercourse with Schiller gave him a new poetic impulse, and called him, as he said, out of the charnel-house of science back into the fair garden of life.

During Goethe's absence in Italy Schiller had come to Weimar. In the spring of 1789 he was made Professor in Jena, and Goethe had to write the official report of his appointment. But no approach towards intimacy between the two men was made till the summer of 1794, so long was it before Goethe could overcome the aversion which Schiller's youthful dramas had awakened in him, and which had not been diminished by his ' Don Carlos.' Common personal interests and acquaintances, and Schiller's journalistic activity now established an outward connection which soon developed into the closest friendship.

Schiller made Professor in Jena, 1789.

While Goethe had for years observed a dignified reserve, contributing to hardly any periodicals, and in fact only writing for himself and his nearest circle of acquaintance, Schiller on the contrary was in continual contact with the public. Since 1787 he had published a succession of Year-books and Calendars, and had furnished poems, essays, or reviews for other periodicals. Now, in the year 1795, he wished to start a new monthly magazine, ' die Horen' (' the Hours '). He first gained the services of a few important collaborators, who were friends of Goethe's, and then in his and their name invited Goethe to become one of the contributors. A somewhat cool yet encouraging consent was the result of the petition ; but on Goethe's next visit to Jena an important conversation took place between him and Schiller, in the course of which it became apparent to both that there was more sympathy between them than they had supposed. After this visit Goethe wrote, expressing his hope of a further exchange of ideas, and Schiller answered with a letter summing up Goethe's character and career, and intended to show him that no German had so thoroughly understood his whole nature, and so clearly recognised his worth as Schiller. From this moment an alliance was formed between them, and that correspondence was begun which is the best monument of their friendship. Their letters contain unreserved communications on all

Schiller gains Goethe as a contributor to 'die Horen.'

Friendship between Schiller and Goethe. Their correspondence.

their æsthetic and scientific labours, reciprocal criticisms, generous
advice, frank acknowledgement of one another's merits, manifold
judgments on collaborators, opponents, and other contemporaries,
detailed discussions on matters of principle and questions of technique in poetry, and especially on the difference between the epic
and the drama. For the space of eleven years, from 1794 till
Schiller's early death in 1805, there was not a trace of a quarrel
between them, not the slightest diminution of personal affection or
of sympathy in each other's interests and labours. During these
eleven years no one stood so near to Goethe as Schiller. Herder
had become estranged from him, and in his æsthetic development
no longer advanced but rather retrogressed; Wieland had passed
his best years, while Schiller's highest powers were yet undeveloped.

Schiller incites Goethe to fresh poetic activity. Schiller's grand intellectual and imaginative achievements spurred his more deliberate friend, older than
himself by ten years, to fresh poetical activity. As
questions of art were discussed with Meyer, so now
literary matters were discussed with Schiller. Goethe
now sought as it were to conquer the field of poetry anew, both in
theory and in practice. Now for the first time he tried to practise
poetry with a conscious resort to all rules of art, with a perfect
mastery in all its styles, and with a methodical selection of his subjects.
He endeavoured to acquire once for all that perfect dominion of the
will over the creative power, which he had already manifested in
completing his ' Tasso,' when the subject no longer appealed to his
sympathy. To use his own words, he learnt to command poetry.

The supremacy of Weimar in German literature, for which Wieland and Herder had helped to lay the foundation, was now an
The 'Horen,' accomplished fact. In Weimar alone could a period-
1795-97. ical like Schiller's ' Horen ' have been started. The
plan on which it was based showed extreme boldness. The most
eminent representatives of German literature dared in this periodical
to run counter to the spirit of the times. According to Kant's
testimony, there were at that time no subjects of interest to the
general reading public beyond affairs of state and matters of religion. Since 1789 the French Revolution and its consequences
had made political discussion in Germany, as elsewhere, the order

of the day ; and religion was the great theme of the party of enlightenment, and was handled with brilliant success by the Berlin
journalists.   But these very subjects of politics and religion were
excluded from the 'Horen,' and all light entertainment was likewise
banished.   This periodical was to re-unite the politically divided
world under the banner of truth and beauty.   It was to look beyond
the confined interests of the present, and to turn its attention to
the purely human elements which are raised above the influence
of the age.

The new periodical was to be edited from Jena, and was to establish itself there as a magazine for original production by the side
of the Jena Literary Newspaper, which was a purely critical organ.
Schiller enlisted a brilliant force of collaborators ; every department
was represented by the highest talents, and yet he over-estimated
their power ; in part he credited his readers with a greater capacity
for severe thought than they really possessed, in part the articles pre-
supposed a higher æsthetic culture than had yet found its way into
wider circles.   And thus the spirit of the times proved the stronger,
and the existence of the 'Horen' could not be prolonged beyond
three years, 1795, 1796, and 1797.   The fame of the editor and his
colleagues had been exceedingly great, and the first success surpassed all expectations.   But disillusionment soon set in ; the discontent of the public was nourished and turned to account by the critics,
and the fate of the 'Horen' clearly showed that in dismembered
Germany the culture of single individuals and small circles might
attain a high level without the whole nation having any share in it.

Besides the 'Horen' Schiller published annually, from the years
1796–1800, a 'Musenalmanach,' which contained the   The
best productions of contemporary lyric poetry.   The   'Musen-
'Musenalmanach' for 1797, published in September   almanach,'
1796, contained Goethe and Schiller's famous 'Xenien,'   1796–1800.
four hundred and fourteen distichs, mostly of a satirical nature,
in which the contrast between the allies of Weimar   Goethe and
and their literary contemporaries found drastic ex-   Schiller's
pression.   These productions of mingled wit and   'Xenien,'
rudeness contained poisonous arrows which were sure   1796.
to wound, annihilating criticisms, finest traits of characterization,

pregnant judgments, all arranged in groups with powerful dramatic effect, and concluded by a grand scene in the lower world. The chastising answers to the critics of the 'Horen' were here expanded into a satirical picture of the whole of German contemporary literature. Older poets whose power was gone, the lights of the day who pandered to the common taste, the shallow apostles of enlightenment, the insignificant journals were all shrivelled up and consumed in the fire of the criticism of these two great writers. Lessing had occasionally given utterance to scathing judgments of the same kind, and in fact, such sweeping criticism was essayed by many during the so-called period of genius, being fostered by the rapid development of German literature, in which even men of great merits were soon superannuated.

The 'Musenalmanach' for 1797 created an indescribable sensation; two thousand copies were immediately bought up, and many rejoinders and innumerable criticisms soon made their appearance. But few of the retorts on the authors of the cruel distichs rose above tame wit and low sentiment. The justice of the attack was clearly proved by the miserable weakness of the defence, and a continuation of the warfare was unnecessary. The fame of Goethe and Schiller increased unchecked. Goethe had compared the state of German literature about 1790 to an aristocratic anarchy, in which Klopstock, Wieland, Gleim, Herder, and Goethe each ruled his own little kingdom; but now, this anarchy had to yield completely to a duumvirate, a continuous Consulate. The struggle with the spirit of the times steeled the powers of the two allies. What the 'Horen' had failed in was accomplished by the terrible system of the 'Xenien,' by the publication of new poetic works of art, and by a systematic activity in connection with the Weimar stage.

From 1791 to 1817 Goethe was the director of the newly-founded Weimar Court Theatre, which under his guidance passed through its greatest epoch. Karl August, in erecting this theatre, was following an example already set by several other German princes. After the failure of the Hamburg attempt under Lessing's auspices to establish a national theatre, German princes had taken up the cause of the German drama. In Vienna the long patronised French actors were dismissed, and Joseph II, in 1776, gave to the Burg-Theater the title of Court and National Theatre. The Court Theatre at Gotha, founded in 1775, had, it is true, but a short-lived existence, but its best members were transferred to the new Mannheim National Theatre, started in 1779. After the death of Frederick the Great the former French play-house, on the Gendarme-market in Berlin, was given up to the German drama, and opened as the Royal National Theatre on the 5th of December, 1786. Actors and A considerable number of eminent actors and a few play-writers. real geniuses exercised their powers on these and other stages. Ekhof, who died in Gotha, satisfied even Lessing's demands, while Schröder, the step-son of Ackermann (see p. 468), embodied the tendencies of the 'Storm and Stress' movement. Schröder was director of the Hamburg theatre from 1771 to 1780, and then again from 1786 to 1798; between these two periods he acted in Mannheim and Vienna, and everywhere incited people to emulate him. He produced the master-pieces of Shakspeare on the German stage, he attracted remarkable disciples, and personally he passed through the whole scale of theatrical achievements, from the ballet-dancer and clown to the first-rate tragedian. Both Ekhof and Schröder considered truth to nature as the highest law for the dramatist and the actor. Iffland, Ekhof's pupil and an admirer of Schröder, was for long the chief ornament of the Mannheim theatre, and afterwards, from 1796 to 1814, Director of the Berlin theatre ; he surpassed both Ekhof and Schröder in refinement and delicacy of feeling, but being less strong in natural genius, had to replace this want by careful study and skilful calculation of effect.

Schröder and Iffland, like many other actors at this time, tried their hand at dramatic authorship, and became most Schröder fertile writers. Both sought chiefly to reproduce in and Iffland's their dramas the private life of the middle-classes, and dramas. thereby to supplant the chivalrous dramas which had sprung up like mushrooms in the footsteps of Goethe's 'Götz.' Schröder borrowed much from English comedies; he seldom pandered to the fashionable sentimentality, but on the contrary turned it to ridicule on several occasions. Iffland on the other hand was for the most part an original author, and his chief strength lay in drawing affecting pictures of real life. None of Schröder's pieces are now acted, while Iffland's 'Hagestolzen' (Bachelors) and 'Jäger' are still always witnessed with pleasure. Contemporary with these two dramatists, **Kotzebue's** and after them, August von Kotzebue ruled the German **plays.** stage till about the end of the eighteenth century. His play entitled 'Menschenhass und Reue,' with which he began his career in 1789, at once produced a great sensation, reaching even beyond Germany. No one entered so thoroughly into the ordinary instincts of the masses, no one could flatter them so cleverly, and no one arranged dramatic effects so conveniently for the actor as Kotzebue. He cultivated not only the middle-class drama, but also the chivalrous drama, comedy, and farce. In him as in Iffland the tendencies of the period of the literary Revolution lived on. They were both followers of Rousseau, taking up the party of nature as against civilization, and offering a somewhat tame opposition to the established order of government. But Iffland's decided moral tendency gives place in Kotzebue to an apotheosis of licentiousness draped in the guise of virtue. In his plays sentimental toleration and cheap emotion are allowed to overthrow the traditional ideas of morality, and generally recognised rules of conduct are ridiculed as European prejudice. His caricature of humanity renders all great tragic conflicts impossible, and his chief idea seems to be to force vice and misery upon us in all their nudity.

. Lessing's 'Minna' and 'Emilia,' Goethe's 'Götz,' 'Clavigo,' and 'Stella,' and Schiller's youthful dramas emerge as single points of light among the productions of Schröder, Iffland, and Kotzebue, and the other still more insignificant plays which satisfied the shallow taste of this period. 'Nathan,' 'Iphigenie,' and 'Tasso' could not be put upon the stage. Hardly any attempt was made to take up the Iambic tragedy, and prose still asserted its predominance. Under the plea of naturalness common-place reality reigned supreme both in matter and form during the whole second half of the last century. But as the drama had already freed itself from the bombastic Alexandrine, so now it was gradually to adopt the nobler iambic metre.

Meanwhile the Opera, with German, French, or Italian words, and

music by German composers, attained its highest perfection.   The
drama had still to compete with the Opera, and could
not free itself or the public from its influence.   Composers of slight, popular talent, such as Dittersdorf
and Wenzel Müller, followed in Hiller's steps in the cultivation
of the operetta.   Gluck separated himself from the Italian virtuoso school, and succeeded in endowing the serious opera with the
truth of the drama, giving it expressive declamation and characteristic music.   Mozart avoided the faults of the Italian school,
though he did not entirely separate himself from it; he learnt
much from Gluck, and surpassed all his predecessors in his immortal series of musical dramas, ranging from the ' Entführung aus
dem Serail ' to the ' Zauberflöte.'

The Opera. Gluck and Mozart.

It was in 1791, the year of the production of the ' Zauberflöte,'
and of Mozart's death, that Goethe undertook the
direction of the Weimar Court Theatre.   He too took
an interest in the opera, and provided good German
text-books for it, but by the side of the opera he also
gradually formed a *répertoire* of good plays.   His own
theories and practice in art and Heinrich Meyer's counsel and aid
were turned to advantage in providing decorations and costumes.
Goethe took the best actor as his standard, and sought to train the
others up to his level.   He extended the warmest personal sympathy to willing talents, as, for instance, to the actress Christiane
Neumann, whom he trained in the part of Arthur in Shakspeare's
' King John,' and whose memory he celebrated after her early death
in the beautiful elegy, ' Euphrosyne.'   But at first Goethe avoided
difficult or hazardous enterprises.   The talents which he had at his
command were not of first-class order, and his theatre was but little
above the average of German theatres, although it produced upon
its boards Schiller's ' Don Carlos,' ' Egmont ' (in Schiller's arrangement), and also a few plays of Shakspeare in a sim-
plified form, as acted, for instance, by Schröder.   But
with Schiller's newly-awakened dramatic activity the
Weimar theatre rose to a much higher level.   Between
October, 1798, and March, 1804, 'Wallenstein's Lager,'
' The Piccolomini,' ' Wallenstein's Death,' ' Mary Stuart,' ' The

Goethe director of the Weimar Theatre, 1791-1817.

High level of the stage under his manage- ment.

Bride of Messina,' the 'Maid of Orleans,' and 'Wilhelm Tell,' were all produced at Weimar. Schiller, who since December 1799 no longer lived in Jena but in Weimar, shared with Goethe the labours of rehearsals and of providing scenery. Goethe now became yet more zealous in his exertions, and his ideas of dramatic art rose still higher. He resolved to introduce upon his stage the most ideal form of drama, the drama in blank verse. After most careful training of the actors, Lessing's 'Nathan' and Goethe's iambic plays were produced for the first time on the stage, and soon even Terence, Plautus, and Sophocles were revived by the bold managers of the Weimar Theatre. Shakspeare's plays were revised with a view of bringing them more into harmony with the demands of the classical drama, and Calderon also was turned to account. Goethe's 'Götz' underwent several alterations. Masques were first introduced in Terence's 'Brothers,' and were after that often made use of; and Schiller made a German version of an Italian Masque, Gozzi's 'Turandot.' The desire to extend the *répertoire* of the ideal drama, and at the same time to meet the taste of the duke, led Goethe and Schiller to resort to French tragedy. Goethe changed Voltaire's 'Mahomet' and 'Tancred' from Alexandrines into ordinary iambics, and Schiller did the same for Racine's 'Phèdre;' new versions were also made by other hands of Racine's 'Mithridate' and Corneille's 'Cid.'

In the outside world no one followed the progress of the Weimar

Influence of the Weimar Theatre on others.

Theatre with greater interest than Iffland. He was the same age as Schiller and had begun his literary career about the same time, and Schiller's first triumphs on the Mannheim stage had been due in part to Iffland's co-operation. He acted frequently in Weimar, and this brought him into personal contact with Goethe. At first his example influenced the young theatre, but later on he himself received suggestions from it. As theatrical manager in Berlin he endeavoured to produce Schiller's new plays on his stage as soon as possible after their representation in Weimar; the 'Maid of Orleans' was performed in Berlin and in a few other places before it appeared on the Weimar stage. After Iffland's death Count Brühl assumed the management of his theatre; he too was a worshipper of Goethe, and endeavoured to work in Goethe's spirit, but he had not the power or the taste to exclude from his stage the miserable French melodramas which were then the fashion everywhere. It was one of these wretched melodramas, the performance of which Karl August commanded and Goethe strenuously opposed, which put an end to the classical period of the Weimar stage, for Goethe lost his appointment of manager in consequence of his opposition to the duke's wishes. Goethe's dismissal.

Goethe's own dramatic writings reaped little advantage from his official connection with the stage. His position offered him, it is true, frequent opportunities, which he always gladly availed himself of, for composing stage-speeches, prologues and short pieces for special occasions; but though much that was beautiful thus came to light, still, after 'Tasso,' Goethe did not for several decades achieve any truly great dramatic work. About the end of the century 'Faust' was advanced a few important steps; and, after his own works, there is perhaps nothing that we owe Schiller greater gratitude for than his incentive energy in reviving Goethe's old interest in 'Faust.' But this unique poem was not concluded till long after this, and what Goethe further accomplished at this time consisted of trifles like the 'Bürgergeneral,' or unsatisfactory productions, wanting in inward or outward completeness, like the 'Grosscophta' and the 'Natürliche Tochter.' The five act comedy entitled the 'Grosscophta' (i. e. Cagliostro), was acted for the first time in Weimar on the 17th of December, 1791. It was intended at first to be an opera, and it would have been an advantage to the piece if this original plan had been adhered to; as we have it, it is a dramatisation of the well-known Diamond Necklace story, giving a horrible picture of the depravity of the upper classes. The characters are superficial sketches, the dialogue and the development of the plot are very carelessly handled, and there is an utter want of interest in the character of the arch-swindler.

The 'Natural Daughter' stands on a far higher level than this transformed Opera. It was performed at Weimar on the second of April, 1803, and, like the 'Grosscophta,' it bears on the French Revolution and the state of things which led to it. Till the present day, this play has not succeeded in winning the favour of the German public, though it is one of Goethe's most refined and original works. It introduces us to a state of society in which the royal prerogative enjoys an exaggerated veneration, while in reality it is powerless and exposed to

The 'Natürliche Tochter,' 1803.

the most shameless abuse on the part of ambitious intriguants. Eugénie, the heroine, an ardent Royalist, and in reality an offshoot of the royal family, though not yet publicly recognized as such, falls a victim to a base intrigue, and is torn away from her father's home. In the place of concealment to which she has been taken she gives her hand to a man of the bourgeois class, and thereby, presumably, renounces the rights of her birth. With this incident the fifth act of the drama closes. The work, as we now have it, was to have formed the first part of a trilogy, and in its fragmentary condition it

Incompleteness of the work.

cannot produce its full effect, notwithstanding the masterly characterization, the powerful situations, and the grand, though occasionally somewhat vague language. The sequel was to have shown how the weakness of the government and the ruler's incapacity to remove inherited abuses left the way open for all selfish interests, and how a prince, who believed he was ruling, was really himself but a tool in the hands of designing persons; further, Goethe meant to have depicted the triumph of the lower elements in society, and after party had followed on party, and government on government, Eugénie would have re-appeared on the scene of political action with her loyalty towards the king and his family unchanged, and would have remained by their side as a ministering angel in their hour of greatest need; finally, according to Goethe's plan, after much bloodshed in the conflict of classes the military power was to have at length triumphed. This play was suggested by a French Mémoire, of very doubtful historical and artistic value, but which in Eugénie's experiences offered a convenient thread of connection for the chief events of the French Revolution. France, it is true, is never named throughout, but the French Revolution is represented as a typical phenomenon and traced to what Goethe considered to be its causes. He lays bare with an unsparing hand the sins of those in power, but at the same time he does not flatter the people, and he suspects selfish motives behind their enthusiastic words. It is the greatest pity that we only possess the beginning of this grandly-planned poetic work.

But though Goethe's dramatic activity was stagnating at the very time when Schiller's skill as a dramatist was developing itself to the utmost, it was not till now that he developed his highest power in the sphere of epic poetry. After 'Werther' he had written no novel or tale, and the period of his life immediately preceding his Italian journey has nothing to show in the way of epic beyond a few ballads, such as the 'Fisher' and the 'Erlking.' But, meanwhile, 'Wilhelm Meister's Lehrjahre' was quietly taking shape, 'Wilhelm Meister's Lehrjahre.' and the first good effect of Schiller's sympathy was to persuade Goethe to complete this comprehensive romance; a work which contributed more than any other to spread the fame of its author, and, especially in Berlin, to establish his literary authority for ever. While the readers of 'Werther's Sorrows' had been made to contemplate the world through the eyes of a romantic youth, in 'Wilhelm Meister,' on the contrary, the world was represented as it is, and as unprejudiced men are wont to regard it. The work is divided into eight books, of which the first five appear to have been planned under the influence of the views of Goethe's Frankfort period. Wilhelm is a warm-hearted hero, like Fernando in 'Stella.' He has a susceptible nature, and is a favourite among First five women, but his will is weak and he is too hasty in books. entering into binding relations. He shows a decided Wilhelm's striving after the harmonious development of his mind, character. taste, and even personal appearance, and he has most exalted ideas of a possible reform of the German stage. He looks more into his own soul than into the outer world, and is constantly pouring out his views and feelings to others. His knowledge is derived more from the poets than from experience or observation, and in consequence he is inclined to self-deception. Sometimes, however, there comes over him a recognition of his schoolboy-like nature, and in Shakspeare he finds a leader and a friend who at least stimulates him to get to know the world around him better, and to use this knowledge for the advantage of the German stage. For

Wilhelm is wavering between business and the stage; his father
wishes to keep him to the former, while his own inclinations impel
him to the latter. Throughout we recognize in this character young
Goethe himself, the son of the Frankfort citizen, the Shakspearian
enthusiast; only that Goethe's business was law, while Wilhelm,
like Goethe's friend, Fritz Jacobi, is a merchant, and secondly,
that Goethe benefited the stage solely as a poet, not as an actor,
while Wilhelm, though he does also write poetry, feels himself
specially attracted by the theatrical career. He is constantly associating with actors and actresses, such as Marianne, a character rather
resembling Clärchen, the calculating Melina and his emotional
wife, the misogynist Laertes, the frivolous but altogether charming
Philine, the stage-manager Serlo and his passionate, deeply injured
sister Aurelia, who has been forsaken by an aristocratic lover.
Delicious and animated scenes are brought before us, alternating
with serious discussions on art, little intrigues, exciting events, and
tragic situations. In the fifth book Wilhelm's father dies, and then
he really goes on the stage; his first part is Hamlet, in which he
pleases the public, and thus his career in life seems decided.

But at this very point the author leads us into another world,
Last three and takes up a different stand-point. Wilhelm's act-
books. ing, we are told, was a failure; we are assured that he
had no talent for it, and an aristocratic circle, with which he has
till then only come into occasional and slight contact, now takes
possession of him. In the first five books the aristocracy does not
play a very noble part, being represented by a Baron who dabbles
in the drama, a Baroness whose coquetry goes beyond all limits,
a somewhat crazy Count and his beautiful but not scrupulously
faithful wife. But now in Lothario we are introduced to the noblest
type of an aristocrat and German gentleman, a character bearing
an indubitable resemblance to Karl August. This Lothario is surrounded by a circle of devoted friends: the cold, sensible Jarno,
whose prototype may have been Merck of Darmstadt, an Abbé,
who was perhaps suggested by Herder, Lothario's sister Natalie, a
gentle, sympathetic soul, pure and noble-hearted, who might be
compared to Frau von Stein, and the practical Theresa, a kindred
nature to the active Lothario, whom she afterwards marries. Wil-

helm's position with regard to these people is much the same as
that of Goethe at the Court of Weimar. A life of action now
seems to him the only kind of life worth living; he considers it a
privilege to serve Lothario, and his love-troubles find a happy ending in the love of Natalie. Caste prejudices do not appear among
these excellent people, and the novel finishes with several *més-
alliances.* The male members of this aristocratic circle are united
in a secret society which had long had its attention directed to the
hero, and which at length receives him as one of its members;
here we are again reminded of the Order of Freemasons, to which
the Duke, Herder, and Goethe belonged.

The 'Confessions of a beautiful Soul,' inserted at the end of the
fifth book, are really a biography of Fräulein von
Klettenberg, that Frankfort friend of Goethe's who con-   Inserted
verted him for a time to Moravian Pietism, and whom   'Bekennt-
                                                        nisse einer
he now represented as an aunt of Lothario and Na-   schönen
talie. These 'Confessions' complete the picture   Seele.'
of morals to which Goethe introduces us in this book. Wilhelm
and the actors, as well as Lothario, Jarno and their associates are
children of the world, entirely occupied with the present life, finding
full satisfaction in their æsthetic calling or in useful activity, and
almost all equally ready to take the pleasures of life and love without scruple wherever they may find them. Wilhelm, it is true, has
higher principles, but without any religious basis. The aunt on
the contrary, and her niece Natalie, who is spiritually akin to her,
belong to quite a different sphere; the aunt is the picture of a
Moravian Pietist, while Natalie belongs to the humane family of
Iphigenia. Two tragic figures are added to these,   Characters
wandering in a twilight of mystery over the earth—   of Mignon
Mignon and the harper; they are daughter and father,   and the
unknown to each other, exiles from their native coun-   harper.
try, and united to Wilhelm Meister by ties of love and gratitude.
None of Goethe's creations appeal more strongly to the depths of
the human soul than these two characters, with their touching
songs. Solemn echoes of old mysticism seem revived in these
songs full of earthly misery and longing for heaven; the laments
of the loving but unloved maiden, the homeless, friendless child,

who may not reveal her inmost soul because her lips are sealed by
a vow, alternate with the tears of the guilty, God-forsaken, lonely
and remorseful old man. A deep gloom rests on the head of each,
and the future seems to have no dawn of brightness for them.

Mignon and the harper are creations of Goethe's earlier and tenderer period. Knowledge derived from observation of real life,
for which the court offered such rich opportunity, was combined in
'Wilhelm Meister' with material accumulated some time before, and

'Wilhelm Meister' begun 1777, finished 1796. the free morals which reigned around Goethe at Weimar are reflected in the book. We have evidence that
he began to work at it in February, 1777, and it was not
finished till almost twenty years later; the work began
to appear in January, 1795, and was completed in October, 1796.
The story is supposed to take place about the time of the Bavarian
War of Succession. Lothario has fought in the War of American
Independence, and is now actively occupied in improving his peasantry. His liberal reforms seem to realise all Werther's demands;
the aristocracy no longer oppress and scorn the aspiring son of the
people, but receive him into their society. Among the various
ranks of society special prominence is given to the aristocracy and
the trading middle-classes; the former appear in the best light,

The theatrical interest. while the latter are almost caricatured in the person
of Wilhelm's friend and brother-in-law. But the chief
interest centres round the actors, who appear now as
vagabonds, now in high honour; they have manifold points of
contact with those above and below them in the social scale, but
they form a society by themselves, and have their own peculiar laws
and customs. The theatrical life, and everything connected with it,
is unfolded before us with almost systematic completeness, and we
are all the more astonished when we find this supposed theatrical
romance taking quite another direction, and notice at the same time
that the new and presumably higher region into which the hero
has entered is treated with much less care than the early part of

Want of unity in the work. the work. The long discussion on Hamlet, and the
space and interest devoted to all matters connected
with the drama and the stage in the first part of the
book, seem out of place, if all this is only to illustrate a false ten-

dency of the hero's, and if we are not even to perceive the effect on his future life of the experiences which he had gathered among the players. Then, too, the aims and objects of Wilhelm's new life are at first so vague. His early life was ruled by a dominating propensity, by a conscious purpose; but in the circle of Lothario he becomes the tool of other people, and we have no idea what part he will play.

Here we light on the defect of the work. The truth is that Goethe hurried the conclusion in order to get the book off his hands. Hence, complete unity of composition is wanting; motives are let drop, inconsistencies may be pointed out, and the style becomes inferior towards the close. But the descriptive power shown in the whole work, and especially in the earlier parts, is so great, the appeal to the imagination and understanding so powerful, the style so animated and graphic, the speeches and actions so well calculated, the suspense *Excellences of style and method.* so skilfully excited, protracted or diminished, that neither the slow development of events, nor the theoretical discussions, nor the many purely circumstantial episodes excite the reader's impatience, that on the contrary our interest remains assured both to the hero and to the circumstances which develop themselves around him. Inanimate nature, which plays such an important part in 'Werther,' here quite retires into the background; it is humanity alone that excites the interest of the poet. He does not directly describe the long and varied series of characters which he passes before our eyes, but imparts life to them by the often marvellously skilful invention of characteristic speeches and actions. He treats all his characters with sympathetic toleration, and, like nature herself, produces in equal perfection, one might *Tolerant views.* almost say with equal love, bad and good, mean and noble characters. He was not the first to employ this manner, but he brought to its culmination the movement which was started in protest against Richardson's unnaturally virtuous heroes.

Much in the plan of 'Wilhelm Meister' is derived from Wieland's 'Agathon.' In its general scheme, as a romance tracing the gradual education and development of the hero, as well as in many peculiarities of technique, 'Agathon' was its prototype; even the hero's transition from extravagant enthusiasm to common-sense views and

'Wilhelm Meister' and Wieland's 'Agathon.'

practical activity was a feature transferred from the older work to the newer and more perfect one. Both these novels are faithful pictures of real life; both bring before us erring men, lenient in their views, and needing to be judged leniently, and but few elect ones who have attained to virtue and purity. The ideal is not embodied in any one striking personality, and no attempt is made at directly inculcating moral lessons; but the picture of a circle of talented people, open to all higher interests and exercising a peculiar charm on all who come in contact with them, the revelation of the inexhaustible richness of human nature, and the varied motives influencing its will and action,—all this exercises not only an æsthetic but also a moral influence on our higher nature.

The author did not consider this work as terminated; certain passages point to a sequel, which was later on somewhat poorly

'Unterhalt- ungen deut- scher Ausge- wanderten.'

supplied in 'Wilhelm Meister's Wanderjahre.' During the interim between these two works, Goethe's activity in the way of prose-narrative is represented by the 'Conversations of German Emigrants' which appeared in Schiller's 'Horen,' consisting of a few tales and an allegory narrated by a company of emigrants; who have retreated before the French invasion from the left to the right bank of the Rhine. While gaining an acquaintance with the characters and fortunes of these people, we are at the same time enabled to observe the disturbing and deteriorating influence exercised on human relations and forms of social intercourse by that political party-strife which the Revolution had transplanted to Germany. Boccaccio had already employed a similar frame-work, with a public calamity in the background, to hold his tales together; and, like Boccaccio, Goethe has here given a new form to traditional matter as well as to experience and fiction, and has transfused the whole with the charm of his art.

In the year 1800, Goethe published 'The good Wives,' a little

'Die guten Weiber.'

masterpiece, written as the text to some pictures in a small publication. Here again we find dialogue alternating with short stories, which can hardly be called tales, but only germs for tales. Thus Goethe tried his hand at all kinds of prose

narrative, from the novel to the tale and to a dialogue furnishing
suggestions for a tale; and at the same time, as we shall see, he
exhausted all the forms of narrative poetry from the epic to the ballad
with its cognate half-dramatic or half-lyric forms.

With the Roman elegies should be classed 'Alexis and Dora,'
also written in elegiac metre, and the dialogue entitled
'The new Pausias and his flower-girl,' both artistic
masterpieces of inexhaustible beauty. In the first we
have the story of a bond of love entered into at the
moment of separation, in the same way as Herder
had found his bride; one short, hurried moment, big
with fateful issues, a sudden expansion of the heart,
mute wooing and consent, a vow of eternal constancy while the
companions of the departing lover are impatiently calling him to
the ship, and then the picture of the past, present, and future, wishes,
hopes, and doubts passing through the mind of the voyager. The
second poem shows us a lover sitting at the feet of his beloved one;
she is twining a wreath and he is handing her the flowers, and their
conversation reveals to us, in dramatic and passionate language, the
circumstances of their first acquaintance and the subsequent short
history of their love. Both these poems are clothed in classical
garb, but Goethe had in his mind at the same time a story of
national interest, namely, 'Hermann und Dorothea.'
He began to work at it immediately after the completion of 'Wilhelm Meister's Lehrjahre,' in the September of 1796, and by June, 1797, he had already
completed it; it is his highest achievement in epic poetry, the most
perfect product of his cultured realism, the noblest fruit of that style
which he had acquired during his sojourn in Italy. He had practised his hand in hexameters by transposing the old
Low-German 'Reinecke Fuchs' into this metre, in
1793, and he now employed the same metre as Voss had used in
his 'Luise' and other idylls, in relating a story of
German middle-class life. But Voss kept his readers
confined within a circle of narrow and petty interests,
and entertained them with occurrences of trivial import and conversations of no consequence; a mere dry reproduction of every-

Poems. 'Alexis und Dora,' and 'Der neue Pausias und sein Blumen-mädchen.'

'Hermann und Dorothea,' 1797.

Reinecke Fuchs, 1793.

Goethe and Voss compared.

day life without any idealizing touch; at the same time he never
succeeded in presenting a clear picture to his readers, and was thus
the exact opposite of Homer. Goethe, on the contrary, taught the
Germans to see their own domestic life with the eyes of Homer;
he made his characters express their deepest experience, and gave
them a wide moral, social, and political background; he made all
the incidental matter bear some relation to the leading idea; in
fact he followed out the strict epic method, which Lessing had
deduced from Homer.

In 'Werther,' Goethe had already furnished a poetically idealized
picture of middle-class family life, but with much sentimental adornment. In 'Faust' and 'Egmont' he drew
a succession of appreciative pictures of small civic life,
and not very different from these is the description of
the interior of a knightly castle in 'Götz.' In his operetta, 'Jery
und Bätely,' which in Scribe's version and with Adam's music still
nowadays finds favour on the French and German stage, he replaced the conventional operetta rustics of the school of Weisse,
by real Swiss peasants, such as he had become acquainted with
on his Swiss journey in 1779. In 'Wilhelm Meister,' it is true, he
made the middle classes contrast unfavourably with the aristocracy;
but immediately after he had concluded this novel, he produced
in 'Hermann and Dorothea' a truthful and beautiful picture of the
people and family events in a small German town. The great
movements in the outside world, which in 'Wilhelm Meister' only
incidentally exercise their influence on the narrative, appear in
'Hermann and Dorothea' as an essential element in the story, and
the fortunes of the characters introduced are made dependent on
them.

In the year 1731, the Archbishop of Salzburg, Graf Firmian,
expelled some few hundred Protestants from his
territory, and the fugitives passed through South
Germany; there was a story that a maiden of the
company found favour in the eyes of a rich burgher's
son, who had long been in vain pressed to marry, but who now, with
sudden resolution, after having with some difficulty won the approval
of his father, his father's friends and the village clergyman, wooed

[Side notes: "Goethe's treatment of middle-class life." and "Basis of fact in 'Hermann und Doro-thea.'"]

the maiden and brought her happily home. Goethe took up this story and transformed the burgher's son into his Hermann, while the fugitive Salzburg maiden became his Dorothea. Besides the father, he introduced Hermann's mother ; he kept the character of the clergyman and made an apothecary represent the friends. But he transferred the incident itself to present times, and in place of the homeless Protestants he introduced German emigrants from the left bank of the Rhine, who had been driven from their homes by the plundering French soldiers and the numerous troubles of war. He changed the religious into a political hostility, and viewed the disturbing events of the time from a pre-eminently national stand-point.

Both Goethe and his princely master were hostile to the French Revolution, which was everywhere asserting its power, and troubling men's minds in Germany as elsewhere. *Goethe's attitude* To uphold the national literature in despite of revolu- *towards the* tionary influences, and to retain the public sympathy *French* for it, was a matter of vital interest for Goethe, Schiller *Revolution.* and many like-minded friends. The publication of the ' Horen,' as we have seen, was meant to serve this purpose. But the gigantic phenomenon of the Revolution also forced itself on Goethe's mind in the light of poetic material for his hand to shape. In the ' Venetian epigrams' of 1790, he gave bold utterance to his views, addressing both upper and lower classes in terse, plain-spoken language. In the ' Conversations of Emigrants,' the new opinions afloat form the central interest of the work. ' Reinecke Fuchs ' is full of allusions to contemporary events, and Goethe meant to draw a picture of society disorganized in this profane Bible, this low-toned narrative of the triumph of impudence amid the strife of selfish interests. He also planned a political novel after the style of Rabelais. Several of his dramas directly treat of the French Revolution; such are the ' Grosscophta,' the ' Bürgergeneral,' the unfinished play 'Die Aufgeregten,' and later on, ' Die natürliche Tochter.' But all these attempts gained but slight popularity, while the patriotic spirit of his ' Hermann and Dorothea ' kindled enthusiasm in all patriotic hearts.

Hermann, despairing of winning the girl he loves, turns his thoughts to the distress of his Fatherland, and thinks of entering

military service, to defend his native soil against the foreigner.
And when he has won Dorothea, in exchanging rings
with her, he utters a solemn vow to live after the
example of those nations who fought for God and law,
for parents, wives, and children, and offered a firm
and united resistance to the enemy.

Patriotism
and con-
temporary
interest in
'Hermann
und
Dorothea.'

Though Goethe thus laid the scene of his poem
in the immediate past—for the time of the story is
supposed to be about August 1796—though he carefully interwove in
the narrative the passing peculiarities of the age in manners and
taste, though he introduced allusions to new fashions in dress,
house-decoration, and horticulture, to the rise of prices, to Mozart's
'Zauberflöte,' and other similar contemporary interests, yet in
this work too, his main endeavour was to depict permanent conditions of human existence, and to contrast these conditions with the
disquieting vicissitudes in public and private affairs. While the
characters in 'Wilhelm Meister' are still for the most part, as in
'Werther,' so individualised as to produce the impression of portraits, and only a few are made ideal figures, in 'Hermann and
Dorothea,' on the contrary, Goethe makes use of the typical method
throughout, and thereby produces his best effects. The story was
peculiarly adapted for this treatment; from the first, the
strong and important contrast is forced upon us between
settled and unsettled or wandering life, the one being
represented by the established existence of a small town,
the other by the homeless condition of the fugitives.

All the misery of an uprooted existence is represented in Dorothea;
she is poor, an orphan, with no brother or sister, and her lover has
fallen under the guillotine in Paris. But her isolation
makes her self-reliant, and the distress of her neighbours calls forth all the loving-kindness of her heart. She becomes
an Amazon in a moment of danger, and she gives thoughtful
succour to the sick and the weak.

In contrast to Dorothea, Hermann represents settled conditions
of life; he has all that Dorothea lacks, wealth, parents, and a home.
Around him he sees developed the regular relations of life: the
intimacy of married couples, their care for their children, inter-

course with neighbours and with the kind counsellor, the clergyman. The people of the little town, so far as we be-   Other
come acquainted with them personally or by report, characters in
seem to be divided into two groups—a progressive party   the poem.
and a conservative party. Hermann's father, landlord of the Golden
Lion, and the apothecary are votaries of fashion and think much of
the good things of this life. The apothecary contemplates the great
events of the time as a selfish old bachelor, and rejoices in his isolation.   The landlord of the Golden Lion, too, is selfish, hates
all care and trouble and takes life easily; he loves show, aims at
rising higher in the social scale, wishes his son to be greater than
he has been, and, as a first step towards this, to find a rich bride.
He and the apothecary gaze in admiration at the greatest tradesman in the place, who always has the latest thing in fashion at his
command, and they endeavour as far as possible to imitate him. In
contrast to these three, the inn-keeper, the apothecary, and the big
tradesman who does not personally appear on the scene, we have
as a *pendant* the clergyman, the mother, and Hermann. Hermann
gives his father but little satisfaction, for he does not wish to rise
above his station. He has little culture or social talent and does
not dress by the fashion; but he is strong and loves work which
gives vigour to his body. He understands horses and agriculture;
he hates wrong and protects the weak, and is a thoroughly good,
strong, simple nature, though somewhat distrustful of himself, as is
seen in his wooing. He is filled with patriotic feeling, with the
instinct of defence against foreigners, but at home he wishes for
nothing more than to fill well the sphere allotted to him. On his
side stand the mother and the clergyman; the latter an educated
man, of wide, practical views, who rules his flock by judicious discernment; the form era simple woman, who with wise persistence
waits for the right season, and skilfully attains her object. Both
recognise Hermann's true worth while the father depreciates him,
and both countenance his love for Dorothea.

This love, as it appears in him and in the girl, is the primitive
phenomenon of instinctive mutual liking, wherein there lies at the
same time a mysterious, unfathomable power, a kind of fate. Rapid
decision is necessary here as in 'Alexis,' for the opportunity

will pass, and if the girl is not secured now, her lover will probably quite lose sight of her in the troublous times.
Notwithstanding the haste with which Hermann forms
and carries out his resolution, no doubt arises in our
minds as to whether the two will suit each other, so far

Love of Hermann and Dorothea.

has the poet permitted us to look into their souls. We feel that no
lasting opposition can arise between these two strongly marked
characters; she knows how to serve, and he will not be stern in
commanding; she will respect, and he will worship. Both have
already shown themselves persistent in the pursuit of good, and
trustworthy in their own peculiar sphere of life, she in the troubles
of war, he in a life of comfort and peace. But Goethe preserves
the typical contrast to the last, and keeps the deepest and most
significant words for the end. Dorothea has gained a firm footing
in a disturbed world, but her past experience makes her distrustful
of her happiness even when it seems so certain. As she says, she
is like a sailor who, having landed safe at last, still seems to feel
the firm ground rocking beneath his feet. Hermann, on the other
hand, from his experience draws confidence in the permanent and
unchanging conditions of life. ' All the firmer, Dorothea,' he says,
' let our alliance be in the general convulsion. Our love shall keep
strong and last; we will hold fast to each other and to our fair
possessions.'

The typical contrast, which is the basis of the whole poem, is
further brought out in the reference at the close to
Dorothea's first lover, a man of weak character who
had been swallowed up in the chaos of the French

Condem-nation of the Revolution.

Revolution. In striking contrast to the enthusiasm which led him
to Paris, we have Hermann's sober reflection : ' The man who in
a tottering age is unsteady in character, only increases the evil and
spreads it further and further ; but the man of firm principles shapes
the world to his will. It is not for the Germans to carry on the
terrible revolution, and to waver hither and thither.'

Goethe preserves a strictly impartial attitude towards the condition of things which he brings before us. He throws no strong
shadows on any of his characters ; but he portrays with unrivalled
humour the novelty-loving Philistines of the little town, the irascible

landlord and the talkative apothecary, and his sympathy is quite
unmistakably on the side of the permanent and con-   Objective
servative forces, by means of which a new home and   character
a new happiness are founded in the midst of the out-   of the
ward confusion. Though sometimes the initiated reader   poem.
may recognise the author himself behind his characters, yet the
treatment is perfectly objective throughout, and on the whole we
may say that none of his dramatis personæ are made to utter anything which is not in harmony with their character and their level
of culture.

In the story of the Salzburg emigrants, as Goethe received it, it
turns out at the last that Dorothea, who is supposed to be so poor,
has really a considerable portion to offer with herself; this seemed
to Goethe an ignoble element in the story, and he consequently
omitted it in his poem ; but otherwise he had little to alter, only
making the subject more connected and complete. Excellences
He has succeeded in arranging the events so well, of style and
that he raises us, as the poem goes on, from a   method.
somewhat prosaic level to the highest regions of poetry. He
runs through almost the whole scale of human feelings; even
the subject of death is discussed among the friends of the landlord, who are anxiously awaiting the arrival of Hermann with his
bride.

The poem is divided into nine cantos which, like the books of
Herodotus' history, bear the names of the nine Muses. The tone
of each canto is in appropriate relation to the name which it bears,
and thus all the various branches of poetry are brought before us.
The easy breadth of the epic is here combined with dramatic
concentration. Unity of time is adhered to, the whole story taking
place in the course of an afternoon. The poet seldom comes forward with his own comments, but like a skilful dramatist acquaints
us with the nature of the chief actors through the medium of the
conversation of secondary characters. Hermann is introduced as a
speaker in the second canto, Dorothea not till the seventh ; but
Goethe manages that we should know the whole time what all the
characters have been doing. The somewhat narrow landscape is
incidentally described, so that, notwithstanding frequent change of

scene, a clear and connected picture is presented to our eyes. The whole story is graphic in the highest degree, yet quiet in tone throughout. Goethe has expressly abstained from exciting any artificial suspense; when Hermann is filled with anxious concern on seeing the ring on Dorothea's finger, the reader, on the other hand, has long ago been fully informed as to its history. The style and manner are of the school of Homer, but never betray mere slavish imitation. The simple subject would not bear the splendour of the Homeric diction; but notwithstanding its simplicity and truth, an inexhaustible charm breathes through the whole poem. Instead of outward splendour, there is a depth of spiritual insight, which appeals to simple hearts with irresistible power.

The way in which Hermann is misjudged by his father, while his mother thoroughly understands him, seems a reminiscence of Goethe's own youth. Hermann's mother bears many points of resemblance to the active Elisabeth von Berlichingen, and Goethe's mother may have supplied the model for both. German family life had a special attraction for Goethe as a subject for poetic treatment, since he himself had become the possessor of home, and wife, and child. This immortal poem was a fruit of that domestic happiness which he now enjoyed. He himself has pointed out this connection in the beautiful elegy entitled 'Hermann und Dorothea,' where he asks of the muse, not laurels, but roses for the domestic wreath, and calls on his friends to listen to his completed work, inviting them to the domestic hearth, where the wife stirs the fire, while the boy, in busy play, throws twigs upon the flames.

Reflections of Goethe's own life in the poem.

The spirit of the modern classical period of German literature, the wished for and accomplished harmony with Greek antiquity, is clearly perceptible throughout this epic of Goethe's. The Homeric tone is immortally linked with the best elements of German middle class life. But Goethe did not stop at this homely subject. Once master of the Homeric style, he longed to apply it to Homer's own world; he commenced an 'Achilleis,' beginning where the Iliad ends, and intended to relate the death of Achilles. He only wrote the beginning of it, and even after about five hundred lines we feel somewhat

Goethe's 'Achilleis.'

wearied; but those five hundred lines rank among the best work that he ever produced. The poem opens with a splendid scene,— Achilles gazing over Troy, where Hector's funeral pile is slowly burning down, watching it through the night hours, and rising in the morning with his heart filled with unmitigated hatred of the dead. After this, the Greek gods and goddesses are brought before us in an Olympian assembly. Goethe could here indulge in the miraculous elements which he had had to banish from his *bourgeois* epic; those mythological types of the ancient world, which Italy had brought so near to him, and which he had sought to interpret as an archæologist, could here be turned to poetic account. He did not, however, simply adopt the gods of Homer, but developed them, and here again surpassed the Greeks in soul, in moral depth, in the inner life. His Zeus is a cheerful, comforting Divinity; Ares is the thorough type of the stern soldier, and the presentment of Hephæstos, who finds pleasure only in labour, but whose works have to receive their charm from the Graces, is equally characteristic. Thetis is the ideal mother, Venus gentle and feminine, Here hard and ungracious, and only in her jealousy a true woman. The ideal Pallas Athene, in her friendship with Achilles, is a picture of those women who benefit men of genius by their sympathetic friendship and their enthusiastic appreciation.

Goethe's genius was still, as in his youth, flexible enough to be occupied at one and the same time with the clear cut figures of Greek mythology, and with the shadowy beings of Northern mists and gloom. As he had given poetic embodiment to the cheerful types of German middle class life, so now in his ballads he turned to artistic account the creations of popular superstition. In the year 1797 he and Schiller emulated each other in **Goethe's** ballad-writing, and Goethe developed a wonderful **ballads.** variety in this province of poetry. In most of his ballads human beings are brought into contact with supernatural powers, and are destroyed or exalted, put to shame or warned. Among his best productions of this kind we may mention, 'Der Erlkönig,' 'Der Fischer,' 'Der Todtentanz,' 'Der Zauberlehrling,' 'Hochzeitlied,' 'Der Schatzgräber,' 'Die Braut von Korinth,' 'Der Gott und die Bajadere.' Sometimes the effect is produced by the mere fact of the intervention of miraculous powers in human destinies; sometimes such intervention bears a deeper, symbolical meaning, and the events narrated are of a typical character. Thus the 'Bride of Corinth' symbolises the contrast between paganism and Christianity. Some of Goethe's ballads belong to a purely human sphere; they are serious or humorous, not always real narratives, but sometimes only significant scenes (cf. 'Das Veilchen' and 'Das Blümlein Wunderschön'). The ballads of the Miller's daughter, written in part in dialogue, form a complete cycle by themselves. In the 'First Walpurgis-Night,' choruses and single characters speak alternately, Christian watchmen are alarmed by German heathens, and the effect is almost that of a scene in an opera. On the other hand, some poems which Goethe calls ballads are only soliloquies uttered by particular characters in definite situations, such as 'Mignon,' or the 'Rattenfänger' (The pied Piper).

Goethe's lyric poetry now also took a new departure. Till then the subjects for his songs had always suggested themselves spontaneously, being furnished by outside events, or from **His lyric poetry.** his own inner life; they resulted from a strong impulse to disburden his soul in poetry. Now, however, he began also in his lyric poetry consciously to look out for subjects, and to borrow ideas from popular or other tradition, transforming them and improving them, and thus gaining the same conscious mastery over lyric poetry as he had gained over other forms of writing.

A large collection of lyrics written under this influence appeared under the title of 'Social Songs' in a pocket-calendar for the **'Der Geselligkeit gewidmete Lieder,' 1804.** year 1804, which he published in conjunction with Wieland. This collection is full of products of the maturest art, but there is less variety of style and imagination, less of that tone of direct, self-experienced truth which affects the reader so powerfully in the earlier poems. These lyrics are in part choruses, in part songs put into the mouth of fictitious characters; all kinds of situations are described at length, under the most various disguises, but amusement and mere fancy always preponderate. Goethe now no longer chiefly embodied his own joys and sorrows in his lyrics;

in them, too, as in 'Herman and Dorothea,' he has become more objective, and practises that artistic self-forgetfulness for which he had laid the foundation during his sojourn in Italy. And here again he employs his typical method, developing a poetic idea in all directions, and seeking to discover the permanent in the transitory, the eternal in the terrestrial. 'Die glücklichen Gatten,' a picture of an elderly couple, looking back with unaltered affection and sentiment on the beginning of their married life, and proudly and joyfully reviewing in their mind their grown-up children, reminds us of 'Hermann and Dorothea;' and the poem 'Wandrer und Pächterin,' in which the daughter of a banished ruling house finds the happiness of love in rustic seclusion, recalls to us the leading idea of 'Die natürliche Tochter.' In both these poems the warlike and revolutionary convulsions of the time form the background of the picture, contrasting with the firmly-established family relations in the one poem, and with the new bond springing from old ties of friendship in the other.

An art which seeks for permanent types will easily tend towards symbolism, and will naturally be inclined to the allegorical form, which represents typical contrasts in the most concise and graphic manner to the understanding and the imagination. The 'happy couple,' whom we have noticed above, appear again as Father Märten and Mother Martha, in the prologue entitled 'Was wir bringen,' which appeared in 1802. The contrast between conservatism and progress, which we noticed in 'Hermann and Dorothea,' is renewed in   Prologue, 'Was wir bringen,' 1802. this couple; Martha clings to the old, while Märten is all for novelty. But these two characters are also meant to remind us of Philemon and Baucis, and it further becomes apparent that in conjunction with other allegorical figures, intended for Naturalism, the Opera and Tragedy, they here represent the Farce and the middle class Drama. The contrast between the old times and the new, between age and youth, is represented once more in allegorical figures in the play entitled 'Paläophron   Paläophron und Neoterpe,' written in the autumn of 1800, in   und celebration of the birthday of the Dowager Duchess   Neoterpe.' Anna Amalia, and also of the dawn of the new century. Paläophron, the old man, sends away his comrades *Griesgram* (Grumbler), and *Haberecht* (Arguer); Neoterpe, the young girl, also dismisses her companions *Gerngross* (Brag), and *Naseweis* (Impudence); then age and youth, who were previously at feud, are reconciled. Here, too, the poet preserves his objective attitude, and shows his justice and impartiality.

The nineteenth century which Goethe thus greeted made gaps in the ranks of the German poets, and caused Goethe himself some deep griefs. In February 1803, Gleim died; in March, Klopstock; in December, Herder. 'The Prussian Grenadier' and the poet of the Messiah had outlived their powers, and their death was no sensible loss; the former was eighty-four, the latter was seventy-nine years of age. But Herder had only entered on his sixtieth year, and had just published his translation of the Spanish Romances of the 'Cid,' the work which, perhaps, most of all has preserved his fame in the memory of the German nation. His sympathy with the French Revolution and other circumstances had estranged him from Goethe; he looked with coldness, or even with aversion, on Goethe and Schiller's common labours, and, in order to depreciate their achievements, he exalted the productions of the eighteenth century far above their due. His controversy with Kant had served to isolate him still further. Kant himself died in 1804 at the age of eighty; and on May 10, 1805, Schiller, in whose mental development the Kantian philosophy had caused a real ferment, was snatched away in the midst of most successful labours, at the early age of forty-two.

Deaths among German writers at the beginning of the century.

Schiller's death, 1805.

To Goethe, Schiller's death was a terrible blow, and greater trials were yet in store for him. In Schiller he had lost the most faithful of friends and colleagues, but in the next year, by the Battle of Jena, the future of Germany, and even the very existence of the Duchy of Weimar, were hazarded. The nation for which he had lived was deeply humiliated, and the prince whom he had served was threatened with loss of his throne. But the worst apprehensions were not realised; the Duke retained his land, and

Battle of Jena (1806) and its consequences.

Goethe rallied his powers for fresh efforts. He was nearly sixty years old, but the struggle against a dreadful fate seemed to give him fresh strength ; he sought to conclude his labours, to round off his literary career, and found that this led him into new creations. He published a complete collection of his works, Goethe's including the first part of ' Faust.' He gave to the later works. world his ' Theory of Colour.' He turned with fresh zeal to his historical studies, and furnished most important contributions to the history of the human mind. He sought to give expression to the great movements of the times in symbolical and allegorical compositions. The necessity of self-renunciation was now particularly borne in upon him, and he gave expression to this truth in the ' Wahlverwandschaften ' (Elective Affinities), and in the sequel to ' Wilhelm Meister.' New generations were arising, new views were asserting themselves, or else old ones in a new form, and Goethe embraced or opposed these views with the same energy as he had shown in earlier years. It was not till after 1815 that age seemed perceptibly to grow upon him ; in 1816 his wife died, and in 1817 he gave up the management of the theatre. But he still wrote or edited various autobiographical and scientific works, and he completed ' Wilhelm Meister's Wanderjahre.' He was still able to write such a poem as ' die Trilogie der Leidenschaft,' and he was yet to publish the ' Westöstliche Divan,' and, above all, to complete ' Faust.'

SCHILLER.

Schiller was born in lowly circumstances, and dragged on many years in poverty. His father, an officer in the Wür- Schiller's temberg army, held an appointment as park-keeper life and at a country-seat of the Duke of Würtemberg's. character. Schiller was educated at the Duke's academy, and was destined for the bar, but his dislike of law-studies led him to renounce the legal career. After slightly studying medicine he was appointed regimental surgeon, but by this time his whole thoughts were really absorbed by literary interests. His publication of the ' Robbers ' (1781) brought down on him the displeasure of the tyrannical Duke of Würtemberg, the same who had imprisoned Schubart, (see p. 116). Schiller resolved to escape from a place so uncongenial to him as Stuttgart, and fled with a friend to Mannheim. After this he went through many vicissitudes, often finding himself in great want, till in 1787 he came in search of fortune to Weimar. Schiller's wild and turbulent youth was reflected in his early poetry. His poetic talent rushed on regardless of rules ; his first works were inspired by revolutionary zeal and delight in powerful effects. No one counselled him on his way, but the public loudly applauded him, and he found enthusiastic friends. He long strove in vain to gain a firm footing anywhere, nor did he ever attain a large share of the world's good things. The Duke of Weimar gave him a small professorship in Jena, and later on he led a meagre existence in Weimar. To add to his troubles, soon after his migration to Weimar his health began to fail. But fate granted him three great gifts : the friendship of Goethe, the unfailing love of his noble wife Charlotte von Lengenfeld, and, what was still more than happiness in friendship and marriage,—inextinguishable nobility of soul. Though he had to wait long and pass through many trials and struggles before a ray of happiness brightened his lot, yet there remained something in his soul untouched by all his troubles, something which could soar above them. The turbulent youth became a man of firm and noble character.

Schiller watched with interest the steps in Goethe's development, and was much influenced by his writings before he became acquainted with him. Like other young poets, Schiller was carried away by the literary revolution inaugurated by ' Götz.' But from the beginning his fundamental attitude of mind was different from Goethe's. While Goethe found his ideals again in reality, Schiller measured reality by the ideal, and found it wanting. Reality, the world of sense, the prose of everyday life, what Goethe called ' the common' (*das Gemeine*)—all this Schiller sought from the first to transcend, and transcended.

His youthful plays were satirical. In ' Die Räuber,' in ' Fiesco,'

His youthful plays and poems. in ' Kabale und Liebe,' he painted republican ideals as a contrast to the condition of Germany at that time, to the despotism and oppression which he saw immediately around him. His youthful poems, written for the most par

in pompous trochees, show all the glaring colours and effective
rhetorical devices of the satirist, strong contrasts, exaggerated
pictures, and a rich use of high-sounding words. Among them
we may mention : 'Eine Leichenphantasie,' 'Die Schlacht,' 'Die
Kindesmörderin,' 'Hector's Abschied,' 'Rousseau,' the poems to
Laura, 'Die Freundschaft,' and 'Triumph der Liebe.' A Würtemberg war-song, 'Graf Eberhard der Greiner,' reminds us of that
patriotic poetry which the Prussian Grenadier brought into vogue.
In his earlier poems Schiller seldom struck any gentler tones.
Haller, Klopstock, and Bürger were his poetic models, and
Rousseau was the philosopher who most strongly appealed to
him. He sought to express sublime ideas in grand pictures, but
he was held fast by a gloomy pessimism. The desires of his heart
rose up in rebellion against the commands of duty. 'I too was
born in Arcadia,' he exclaims, 'but my short spring only brought
me tears.'

But just as Goethe rose from the pessimism of Werther to the
optimistic humanity of 'Iphigenie,' so too for Schiller there came
a time of liberation and purification.   The happiness of friendship
made the world look brighter to him. From the depth of his rejoicing
heart he sang that wonderful hymn to Joy : 'Freude,   Hymn,
schöner Götterfunken.' General love of humanity,   'An die
tolerance, and reconciliation, a kind Father above the   Freude.'
stars—these thoughts came to him like a grand revelation. He
formed for himself a mystical philosophy, entirely built on the idea
of love. Without faith in unselfish love, he says, there could be no
hope of God, of immortality, or of virtue. Love was God's motive
in creating the world of spirits. Love is the ladder by which we
attain resemblance to the Divinity. To die for a friend, to die for
humanity, these seem the highest proofs of love which the poet can
conceive of.

At this time his 'Don Carlos' received that form in which it was
presented complete to the public. The titular hero 'Don Carlos.'
of the piece, and his passion for his stepmother, lost
favour in Schiller's eyes, and Marquis Posa, the representative of
liberal ideas, who sacrifices himself for his friend Carlos, was
brought into the foreground of the play. This change affected

the whole character of the tragedy. In the earlier version Philip and his son Carlos are inimical to each other, and base intriguers try to widen the breach between them and to hinder a reconciliation ; but Schiller now gave the play a more refined and spiritual character ; a friend with the best possible intention warns Carlos, who thus becomes suspicious of the Marquis, and this suspicion results in the destruction of both. In the earlier version the naturalism of the satirist predominated, but now Schiller sought to ennoble his subject, to raise individual and local elements to a universal level, and to give expression to his own ideal of perfection. In ' Don Carlos ' he made the same transition to idealistic art which Goethe had made in his ' Iphigenie.' He struck out the wild and bombastic tirades against the priests, which he had at first put in the mouth of his Don Carlos, and replaced them by an indirect but all the more effective warfare. He abandoned the rhetorical style, and, following Lessing's example, made the play generally more concise.

Lessing's ' Nathan,' Goethe's ' Iphigenie,' and Schiller's ' Don Carlos ' are the first important examples of German iambic tragedy. All three are devoted to the ideals of humanity and toleration. In each of them there is one prominent scene, in which a despotic sovereign is made to hear the voice of truth, and is unable to resist its force. There is a striking resemblance even in detail between the scene in ' Nathan,' where the wise Jew puts the Sultan to shame, and the scene in ' Don Carlos,' where the Marquis Posa touches the heart of the Spanish despot. Only we must remember that when Lessing published ' Nathan ' he was fifty years old, and that when Schiller published ' Don Carlos ' he was twenty-eight. There is certainly more probability in the course of things represented in Lessing's drama, and there is no doubt that the sober Nathan ranks as a poetic creation above the enthusiastic youth Posa. Both plays are a protest against religious intolerance. But while Nathan moves the heart of Saladin by appealing to his better nature, to the ideals which are alive also in his breast, Posa looks for freedom of thought from the pupil of the Great Inquisitor, and demands from the son of Charles V a state in which the law should not be dictated by the will of one individual, and in which the

Marginal note: ' Nathan,' ' Iphigenie,' and ' Don Carlos.'

sovereign's chief aim should be the happiness of his people. Schiller wished to portray that 'manly pride before king's thrones,' which he had demanded in his 'Hymn to Joy.' And it was just the immaturity of such a character as Posa's that appealed to men's hearts; in its very psycho- logical and poetic faults there lay an irresistible power. Two years before the outbreak of the French Revolution Schiller painted one of those enthusiasts who then appeared in real life, and in part determined the destinies of Europe. In Posa he created a political ideal, which, even in the nineteenth century, inspired many popular leaders, and which played its part in revolutions and constitutional struggles.

Character of Marquis Posa.

Lessing had used the stage as a pulpit, Schiller made it into an orator's tribune. But changes in his own views led him gradually further and further from the tendencies of his early dramas. The French Revolution filled him with horror; the former worshipper of Brutus wished to take up his pen in defence of Louis XVI, and felt that he could no more seek the majesty of human nature among the masses; the events of the times robbed him of all political hopes 'for centuries,' as he said. He now recognised that the ennobling of human character must precede all attempts at the reform of government.

Schiller's horror at the French Revolution.

Schiller now sought to master Goethe's new poems critically, and to learn from them. He made a thorough study of 'Egmont,' and wrote a detailed criticism of 'Iphigenie,' and this latter drama directed him to Euripides. He now first learnt to appreciate the Greeks, and thought they would help him to acquire true simplicity. He translated two plays of Euripides and he read Voss's Homer. In a grand, thoughtful poem, he mourned for the Greek deities, and in another he praised the glorious vocation of the artist. He had a very high ideal of what a poet should be. He says, that since a poet can only give his individuality in his poetry, his first and greatest task should be to ennoble that individuality, to raise it to the level of the purest and grandest humanity. Ripe and perfect productions can only flow from a ripe and perfect mind.

'Die Götter Griechen- land's,' and 'Die Künst- ler.'

Schiller resolved to raise his own mind to this lofty level, but the consequence was that his poetic activity slumbered for a long period. Between the appearance of 'Don Carlos' and the com-

Novel, pletion of 'Wallenstein' a period of twelve years
'Der Geist- elapsed. A novel entitled 'The Ghost-seer' remained
erseher.' unfinished. Plans for an epic poem on Frederick the Great or Gustavus Adolphus never got beyond the preliminary metrical exercises. For Schiller, the period from 1787 to 1799 was similar to that which Goethe passed through after his Italian

Period of journey; it was a time of distaste for poetry, a time
preparation of preparation, research, and reflection, from which
and research, he returned with his mind enriched and ripened to
1787-1799. the cultivation of the drama. Not only was Goethe stirred up through Schiller to fresh poetic creation, but Schiller too was through Goethe's friendship led back from science to poetry. Their friendship was for each the beginning of a new era of productiveness. While Goethe extended his knowledge by observation, Schiller devoted himself to speculation, and made himself at home in the world of ideas. While Goethe looked around in nature and art, and thereby won for himself a new ideal of cultured poetry, Schiller, during this interval of rest from poetic production, studied history and philosophy and gained thereby new æsthetic principles.

Histories, Two larger historical works and several small essays
'Abfall der bear brilliant testimony to his talent as a historian.
Nieder- 'Don Carlos' led him on to write the history of the
lande,' and 'Revolt of the Netherlands,' and the 'History of the
'Dreissig- 'Revolt of the Netherlands,' and the 'History of the
jähriger Thirty Years' War' suggested to him the writing of
Krieg.' 'Wallenstein.' The Kantian philosophy produced a powerful impression on him, and he felt moved to develop it and

Schiller's also to oppose it. He not only learnt to bear cheer-
philosophy. fully a suffering life full of disappointments and privations, but, with a peculiar kind of asceticism, he rose with sublime heroism above all earthly suffering into the calm regions of art. He learnt to contemplate without envy the happiness of others which was denied to him, the happiness of such an Olympian nature as he saw before him in Goethe. His philosophy was conditioned by the circumstances of his own life. He

depreciated the sensuous world as much as any mediæval opponent of Lady World, and he exalted all the higher that divine art
which raises men above earthly things. Beauty, according'to Schiller,
is supersensuous, as everything good and great is with Kant. But
whereas Kant would only recognise as good what was done against
the natural inclinations, Schiller, on the contrary, praised that condition of man where duty and inclination coincide, where the
supersensuous and the sensuous worlds are in harmony. Art produces this condition, and to Schiller it seemed realised in the Greek
divinities. Schiller, like Goethe, returned to the old mythological
ideals. The Greeks, he said, transferred to Olympus what ought
to be carried out upon earth ; they banished from the faces of
their glorious gods the traces of care and labour which furrow
the brow of mortals, as well as the worthless enjoyment which
smooths the vacant countenance, and they liberated the eternally
placid Olympians from the chains of any duty or high purpose
in life.

As with Goethe the study of nature and of art each reaped benefit
from the other, so history and philosophy did with Schiller. The
philosophical ideas in which he found rest furnished him the means
for surveying in large outlines the development of the human race,
and for detecting the greatest contrasts of style in the history of
literature. To him as to Herder the fullest glory in this respect
seemed to rest on the Greeks. But the disciple of   Schiller, a
Rousseau still believed in a lost ideal state of humanity,   disciple of
which he calls nature, and which stands in contrast to   Rousseau.
civilisation. (See ' Die vier Weltalter,' and ' Das Eleusische Fest.')
Plants, minerals, animals, and landscapes, the peculiar conduct of
children, the ways of rustics and of primitive man, all seem to him
to belong to the same order. They are what we were, and what
we ought to become again ; our civilisation is meant to lead us by
the paths of reason and freedom back again to nature. They are
pictures of our lost childhood, and at the same time of our highest
ideal perfection. ' *Naïveté*' is their common characteristic; the
naïveté which the child possesses is to be found also in the most
perfect women and in the mode of thought of a genius. The
Greeks had this *naïveté*, and Schiller calls Goethe a ' naive ' poet,

while he designates himself and kindred spirits as 'sentimental.'

'Naive' and 'sentimental' poets. The naive poet is natural; the sentimental poet seeks to be so. The former reproduces reality; the latter represents the ideal. The poetry of the former has the advantage in its sensuous reality, that of the latter in its loftier subject. The former exercises a calming influence, the latter an agitating one. The former gives us pleasure in the living present, while the latter makes us discontented with real life.

Schiller's philosophy frequently supplied him with material for his poetry. Numbers of his poems have art for their subject, the poetic art in particular. ('Die Theilung der Erde,' 'Dithyrambe,'

Poems on Art, and on the Beautiful. 'Die Macht des Gesanges,' 'Pegasus im Joche.') The beautiful, says Schiller, lives not in the real world, but only in the heart and the soul. In vain the pilgrim sets out to find the heavenly and imperishable anywhere on earth. ('Der Pilgrim.') The way to the ideal leads away from real life. ('Das Ideal und das Leben.') Sometimes, it is true, beauty appears on earth; 'in a vale among poor shepherds,' poetry may find a home. ('Das Mädchen aus der Fremde.') Arcadia lies around the child playing in its mother's lap. ('Der Spielende Knabe.') Women and children reveal the perfection, the original destiny of man. The plants too are symbols of this perfection :—

'Suchst du das Höchste, das Grösste? Die Pflanze kann es dich lehren.
Was sie willenlos ist, sei du es wollend—das ist's!'

Schiller also likes to linger over the great stages in the development of the human race, to trace how the darkness of primitive barbarism was gradually lightened, how the savages became men, how men first lived in harmony with nature and dominated her, how they went astray from nature, and finally returned to her by their own free will. ('Das Eleusische Fest.')

There is little of deep speculation in all this, but many fruitful

General character of Schiller's poetry. ideas, to which the poet returns again and again, reproducing them under a hundred different aspects. No other literature possesses a poetry of thought surpassing this in spiritual significance, in wealth of imagination, in power of form. Schiller's vocabulary is not rich,

but he turns it to the best advantage. Where he makes use of
rhyme he inclines to become rhetorical; but his distichs rank
equal with Goethe's, and he surpasses Goethe in his power of
coining aphorisms and giving them epigrammatic force. The
' Votivtafeln ' are specially remarkable in this respect;   The
in their comprehensive treatment of the typical rela-   'Votiv-
tions and typical contrasts of life, they almost come up   tafeln.'
to the cultured realism of Goethe. The poet imparts a charm even
to subjects whose fitness for poetic treatment one would at first be
inclined to doubt, such as the various poetic metres. He shows
marvellous power of graphic representation in such poems as ' Der
Tanz' or ' Herculaneum und Pompeji.' A poem like 'Der Abend'
stands quite by itself; it is a short ode in Klopstockian metre,
describing the evening scene in mythological pictures. The symbolism by which Schiller sometimes gives to lifeless things a human
signification, is quite in Goethe's style; the ' Song of   'Lied von
the Bell' rises to the highest level possible in this   der Glocke.'
class of poetry. The realistic description of the casting of the bell
which runs throughout the poem, and the constantly recurring
pictures of life which are connected with it, the extraordinary skill
with which all the important human relations are treated,—childhood,
youth, love, marriage, the happy household, the fire which destroys
it from without, death which destroys it from within, the splendid
pictures of order and peace, of war and revolution, all contribute to render this poem quite unrivalled in literature.

Though Schiller's particular views are constantly recurring in
these poems, yet his own personality is kept in the background.
He wishes to teach universal truths, and even where he represents
feelings, it is by means of imaginary situations and fictitious
characters. He endeavours wholly to forget himself in his subject.
Classical mythology and hero-legends often supplied   Poems on
him with materials ('Klage der Ceres,' 'Das Sieges-   classical
fest,' 'Kassandra,' &c.). The Trojan cycle of legends subjects and
possessed from early years the greatest fascination for   others.
Schiller; but now he drove self-renunciation so far as to transport himself into the feelings of North-American savages, and
to sing their lament for the dead. ('Nadowessier's Todtenlied.')

Not only classical, but also mediæval subjects transformed themselves quickly and easily under his hand into a series
Ballads. of ballads, expressive of the most various moods, and
often most powerful in depicting a chain of destiny. ('Ritter
Toggenburg,' 'Der Kampf mit dem Drachen.') The Greek idea
of the envy of the gods is as graphically brought before us in 'Der
Ring des Polycrates,' as mediæval piety is in 'Der Gang nach
dem Eisenhammer,' or the connection between guilt and punishment in 'Die Kraniche des Ibycus.' Schiller repeatedly gives to
these narratives the unity of a dramatic scene, but at the same
time he affords brilliant evidence of his epic power in the Homeric
fulness of detail of his descriptions. He was able to make up for a
somewhat narrow field of natural observation by study, and power
of imagination. For the splendid description of Charybdis in 'Der
Taucher,' the utmost which he had at his command was a few verses
of the Odyssey, which he realised by his acquaintance with the
rushing and roaring of a mill-stream. Most graphic, too, is his
description of the wild animals in 'Der Handschuh,' and of the
horrible dragon slain by the Maltese knight in 'Der Kampf mit
dem Drachen.'

These poems of Schiller's show that he had learnt to appreciate
the complex variety of life, instead of contenting himself with mere
startling contrasts. He had grasped the history of various periods,
Schiller's and really entered into its spirit. His study and
treatment his philosophy were of constant benefit to his poe-
becomes try, and he had acquired that power of objective
objective. treatment, of self-renunciation, which is the hardest
demand of art. This power is particularly apparent in the
'**Wallen-** dramas which he now produced, and especially in
stein.' 'Wallenstein,' where the chief characters, with the exception of Max and Thekla, appealed so little to his personal feelings, that he was able to be completely objective in his treatment
of them. In his 'History of the Thirty Years' War,' Schiller had
pictured the mysterious general as free from the religious prejudices
of his time, and hence falling a victim to the power of the Church ;
it was no great step from this view to making him the representative of Liberalism, and letting him succumb to the Jesuits, just as

Don Carlos and Marquis Posa succumbed to the Inquisition. But
Schiller did not make this the chief motive of his drama, but subordinated it to another point of view. He conceived his hero as
the type of the practical realist, such as he had described him in
one of his scientific treatises. Wallenstein's desires Character of
draw him down to earth; power and greatness are to   the hero.
him the highest good, without which life would not be worth living.
Such a character as this was totally out of sympathy with Schiller's
personal feelings, and he felt that in so far as his audience was
possessed with his own idealistic views, in so far such a character
would be repugnant to them. It seemed, therefore, all the more
necessary to him to make the 'romantic son of fortune,' whom he
placed in the centre of his dramatic poem, appeal to the human
sympathies in the hearts of his audience. He sought to give him
all the moral dignity which he could possibly attribute to a realist,
and formed him in part after such models as Karl August and
Goethe. He not only endowed him with extraordinary strength of
will, an unusual talent for ruling, a generous disposition, which
bound noble characters to him and idealized his picture in their
souls, but he also attributed to him a mind which recognised in
all that happened a lofty necessity, and which desired to subordinate itself to nature as a whole. In the peculiar circumstances of the Thirty Years' War, Wallenstein's object is not to
serve the interests of the Emperor, or the interests of the Jesuits,
but to seek the welfare of the German Empire and to bring
about a European peace. He only enters into alliance with the
Swedes in order to carry out his lofty aims, and careless about
differences of creed, he even favours Protestantism where it
might promote his objects. Moreover, Schiller brings his hero
into pathetic situations, where those whom he loves turn from
him, and those whom he trusts forsake him. He also lays
bare to us the source of his actions, the thoughts and struggles
which precede them. Besides the outer and inner world, he, like
Goethe, introduces us to the sphere of fancies, forebodings, visions,
superstitions and divine dispensations, and seeks to replace as far
as possible by these means the supernatural phenomena of ancient
tragedy. He showed a true view of the world in representing

'man in the midst of life's turmoil,' not separated from the general
course of the world, but intimately involved in it.   He followed his
own contemptuous view of life and reality in representing the
realist as drawn to destruction by those material advantages to
which he clings so strongly, and as attaining himself to the perception that : ' The earth belongs to the evil spirit, not to the good.'
By these various means Schiller attained deep and powerful effects,
and diminished the guilt of his hero by explaining as completely as
possible his mode of action.

Wallenstein, as Schiller represents him, was as a youth serious
beyond his years, solitary and reserved, but sometimes
roused to strong feeling.   A fall from a high win-
dow and his wonderful escape from death deepened
his seriousness ; he became a Roman Catholic, and after that considered himself a being favoured by Providence.   In the war he
rose quickly to importance ; the Emperor loved him and trusted
him, and he was successful in all that he undertook.   But horrible
deeds were done in the Imperial service.   Wallenstein became the
scourge of all lands, and drew down a thousand curses on his head.
At the Diet of Regensburg the storm which had been gathering
burst upon him, and the Emperor sacrificed him to his enemies.
From the time of his fall he was a different man, wavering and un-
sociable, suspicious, gloomy, and restless.   He sought to replace
by an outward support the inward reliance which he had lost ; he
devoted himself to astrology, and sought counsel from the stars when
his own mind wavered.   His recall to the supreme command of the
troops did not make things better ; it did not result from favour or
good will, but from the Emperor's need of him, and Wallenstein
himself made no secret of his intention to be his own master, and
no longer to allow the decrees of the court to be imposed upon
him.   He used the Imperial authority as an instrument for carrying
out his own policy.   He negociates with the Swedes, at first only
purposing to strengthen his power thereby, to keep all paths open
to his ambition, and so finally, in one way or another, to gain a
monarch's crown when the peace comes.   He dallies with the
thought of a tremendous deed, without the serious intention of
carrying it out.   But the mere evil thought produces strained re-

*Wallen-
stein's
career.*

lations which react on him and interfere with his freedom of choice. He is too proud to conceal his bold, ambitious schemes. Such men as Illo and Terzky urge him on to revolt, because they see that they will reap their own base advantage from the step. In obedience to a false dream-oracle, he puts implicit trust in Octavio Piccolomini, and it is this very Octavio who reports to Vienna every rebellious utterance and every daring step of the General's. He has also other spies around him, and the court thinks him guilty of high-treason long before he really is. His enemies try to draw away his army from him, and thus to prepare the way for a second deposition; they stir up his anger and provoke him afresh to disobedience. But he still shrinks from treason, and feels the force of duty. He has an evil genius by his side in his sister-in-law, Countess Terzky, and a good one in young Max Piccolomini. His sister-in-law forestalls his good counsellor by a few minutes, and these few minutes decide his fate. He concludes the alliance with the Swedes, and breaks the chains of duty. Wallenstein's whole conduct only becomes intelligible to us when we recognise what enormous power he held in his hands, how much this power was due to his own personal efforts, and how strong the temptation must therefore have been to him. (Cf. Prologue to ' Wallenstein.')

Schiller has made us intimately acquainted with the lower as well as with the upper strata of Wallenstein's army. Eleven acts did not seem to him too much in order to attain his object, and the first of these acts, ' Wallenstein's camp,' shows us the First part, poet at the summit of his art, while it also shows how ' Das Lager.' much he had learnt from Goethe. Instead of the naturalism of his youthful dramas he here adopts Goethe's generalising and typical method. All the possible types of military life are embodied in individuals, who are cleverly contrasted with each other. They are characterized by their various conduct towards civilians and peasants, by their different estimates of Wallenstein, and by their different views of the military profession, as well as by more individual traits. We are led up from the lower to the higher types of military life, and are introduced to an idealist among all the realists, in the person of the Walloon Cuirassier serving under Max Piccolomini. A most varied picture of life is unfolded before us, and the

climax is attained in the splendid soldier's song at the end of the
act : ' Frisch auf, Kameraden, auf's Pferd, auf's Pferd !'

The various types of soldier somewhat prepare us for the
various types among their leaders, as they are brought
Second and
third parts,
'Die Piccolo-
mini,' and
'Wallen-
stein's Tod.' before us in the ' Piccolomini' and in the closing
tragedy : ' Wallenstein's death.' The generals are
not only outwardly classified as those who remain
throughout devoted to Wallenstein, such as Illo and
Terzky, those who from the beginning are decidedly
against him, such as Octavio Piccolomini, and those who go over
from Wallenstein to the Emperor, such as Isolani, Buttler, and
Max Piccolomini, but they also furnish among themselves typical
contrasts, though less accentuated than in the characters of the
'Camp.' Here again the scale rises from the base to the noble,
from egoism to self-sacrifice, and again an idealist, Max Piccolomini, stands out prominently amid the ranks of the realists and
materialists. However different the motives of action may be in the
different individuals, yet the poet has throughout taken care that
Wallenstein's departure from his duty should appear as the real
cause of the army's defection from him. In ' Don Carlos ' even
the ideal characters are not over-scrupulous about faithfulness and
honesty, when it is a question of advancing the good cause ; but in
' Wallenstein ' Schiller ranges himself sternly on the side of duty,
loyalty, and law, on the side of the conservative virtues and the old
institutions which offer resistance to arbitrary power. He attacks
revolution like Goethe, and he also attacks it, like him, by æsthetic
means. He maintains an impartial attitude towards his characters,
and does not throw all the light on the one side and all the shadow
on the other. Only Gordon, commander of Eger, a friend of
Wallenstein's youth, unites full sympathy for the general with
thorough loyalty to the emperor. Of those who remain faithful
to law against arbitrary power, some do so out of purely ignoble
motives, some out of a mixture of base and noble inducements.
Characters of
Max and
Thekla. The pair of lovers in the tragedy, Max Piccolomini,
Octavio's son, and Thekla, Wallenstein's daughter, are
the most consistent idealists in the piece ; they are
both ruined by the conflict of their own characters with those of

their respective fathers. When they tear themselves from Wallen-stein's side and flee from the malicious powers of life, his good angels seem to have departed from him. But even these good angels are not quite faultless. Max says he would pardon forcible resistance and even open rebellion in the great hero, when threatened at his post, but he cannot forgive treason, he cannot forgive his allying himself with the enemy. And Thekla is wanting in strength of character, for after Max's death she gives way to the selfish longing of an overwhelming grief, and forsakes her duty, forsakes her mother in the moments of her deepest distress.

The realist is one-sided and so is the idealist, and only both in conjunction furnish a complete picture of humanity. This is Schiller's teaching in 'Wallenstein.' Max and Thekla form the necessary supplement to the other characters. The idealist, Max, stands in striking contrast with the realist, Wallenstein, a contrast destined to be one of the most momentous features in the tragedy. We might consider Max the real hero of the second part of the trilogy, and Wallenstein only the hero of the third part. Max is very much younger than Wallenstein; he has received many kindnesses from him, and carries an idealized picture of him in his soul. Where the realist loves, says Schiller, he will seek to make happy; where the idealist loves he will seek to ennoble. The realist can even forgive baseness in thought and action, only not arbitrariness and eccentricity; thus Wallenstein suffers such men as Illo and Terzky about him, and does not reckon upon gratitude from an Isolani, but Octavio's unsuspected falseness overwhelms him. 'That,' he exclaims, 'has happened contrary to the course of the stars and to destiny.' The idealist, on the other hand, will reconcile himself to the extravagant and tremendous, if only it testifies to force of character, to great capabilities; thus Max would even understand and pardon Wallenstein's open rebellion, but not his treachery. Where the realist would ask what anything is good for, the idealist asks whether it is good in itself. Where Wallenstein follows expediency, Max follows right. Max sets reason, Wallenstein natural necessity, against established tradition. Max tells his general he need enquire of no other oracle but the

Margin note: Contrast between idealist in Max, and realist in Wallenstein.

one in his own conscience; he himself follows the voice of his
heart, and his heart decides for duty.   Human nature, Schiller
teaches, is not capable of a consistent idealism; even the
idealist, in order to act morally, must be fired by enthusiasm,
and can do nothing except he be inspired.   Then indeed he is
able to accomplish great things, and his conduct will be characterized by a loftiness and nobleness which will be sought in vain in
the actions of the realist.   But even Max's soul is not so constituted
as to wander in cold serenity along the path of duty; he too has
an inward struggle to go through.   His inclinations draw him to
Wallenstein whom his duty commands him to leave; Thekla
must assure him that he has chosen the right.   Then there flashes
on his mind a thought in which he sees salvation; he will fight
against the Swedes, and will fall in battle.   Acting under the influence of this enthusiasm, he leads his followers to death.   ' He
is the happy one,' Wallenstein says of him, ' his life is complete
and perfected;' and he feels how much he will miss his noble
character :—

> 'The bloom has now departed from my life,
> And cold and colourless it lies before me.
> He stood beside me like my vanished youth,
> He made reality seem like a dream, .
> And round the common show of earthly things
> He threw the golden halo of the dawn.'

The rising scale of characters, the systematic representation of
Unreality of contrasts, the typical conception of the individuals,
'Wallen-   all this removes ' Wallenstein ' as a work of art from
stein.'   the sphere of reality.   Schiller strongly insisted that
art should furnish only a semblance, a show of things as they
are, that the audience should never be allowed to forget this, should
never be reminded forcibly in the drama of common-place reality.
This idea is here realised in the first instance by the rhymed doggrel in which all the characters in the ' Camp ' are made to speak.
The iambics of the two following tragedies serve the same purpose,
which is still further strengthened by the traditional dramatic
fiction that all the characters should be able to give a detailed and
well-expressed exposition of their views and opinions.   Schiller did

not mind letting the hero and his generals speak with most un-
military verbosity.   Throughout he effects his characterization
more by means of what his *dramatis personæ* say about themselves,
and what others say of them, than by actions which should reveal
their character to the audience.   He only occasion-   The charac-
ally attempts to make the language characteristic of teristic and
the speaker, as for instance in the 'Camp,' and in the idealized
the colloquy between Buttler and Wallenstein's mur-   dramatic
derers; in the latter scene we are made acquainted   style.
with the wild, ruffianly soldier of the 'Thirty Years' War,' and the
brutality of the murderers serves to enhance the grandeur of their
victim.   Perhaps this mixture of the two styles, the characteristic
and the idealized, is a mistake in the drama.   It might have been
better if one or the other had been adhered to consistently throughout.   The motley life and the many small though somewhat disconnected actions in the 'Camp,' serve by their brightness and
vivacity to dim the interest of the long-sustained speeches in the
'Piccolomini' and 'Wallenstein's Death.'

With the conclusion of this tragedy Schiller had discovered
the new and classical form for his dramas in general.   Though
he always modified the treatment in each play, in accordance with
its subject, yet on the whole we may say that henceforward he
only applied with full freedom the art which he had, so to speak,
newly acquired in writing 'Wallenstein.' · Unfortunately he was only
able to complete four more original plays : 'Mary Stuart,' 'The Maid
of Orleans,' 'The Bride of Messina,' and 'Wilhelm Tell.'

'Mary Stuart' was one of his older projects, and perhaps
originally planned like 'Don Carlos' as an attack   'Maria
on Catholic policy.   But in his actual execution   Stuart.'
of the drama Schiller abstained from giving it any such one-
sided tendency.   He had now become tolerant   Schiller's
enough to look at Catholicism from a purely artistic   impartial
point of view, and to subordinate his own religious   attitude
opinions to the artistic ends of the drama.   He   towards
is perfectly impartial in his representation of the   Catholicism.
effects of the Jesuit Propaganda upon Mortimer, and equally
impartial in his presentment of a Catholic religious function.

His only object is to exalt his heroine and to gain for her the sympathy of the audience. He does not attempt to conceal the fact that she is supported by the League and the Jesuits, but he does not bring it prominently before us, so as not to detract from her merits in the eyes of a Protestant audience. In other ways too, everything is done, as in 'Wallenstein,' to make the heroine appeal to our human sympathies. Her

Character of errors are represented as the result of youthful
Mary. inexperience, and she lives to repent them bitterly. Of that which condemns her to death before the law she is really innocent, being only incriminated by the false witness of a former servant. She exercises a magical influence on all who approach her, and there is nothing more touching than the scene in the fifth act, where the love and devotion of her faithful servants makes them throw themselves at her feet in the face of death. Mortimer, too, is fascinated by her, and dares for her sake an attempt on Elizabeth's life; Leicester also falls under the charm, and leaves Elizabeth for her, and many others, whom we only just hear mentioned, have succumbed to her wonderful attraction. Love and hatred, earthly passion and earthly desires have not been banished from her soul by misfortune. Her meeting with Elizabeth in the garden at Fotheringay reveals her true character. She is transported with delight at being allowed to enjoy the beauties of nature again, and her sanguine character makes her take this favour as an earnest of complete liberty soon to be given her. In her exalted frame of mind she feels she cannot humble herself before Elizabeth as she ought, and when she stands face to face with the Queen, the woman and the demon break out in her; she annihilates her victim with words, but in so doing weaves her own destruction, and yet counts herself blessed, since she has tasted revenge. In the face of death, however, all earthly desires forsake her. She forgives those who have done her wrong, and hopes by her innocent death to atone for her old crime, her complicity in the murder of her husband and her marriage with the murderer. In this chastened mood she goes to the scaffold.

The more Mary's character was exalted, the more her rival had to be degraded. Everything in the outward course of the play turns on the incident of the signing of the death-warrant by Elizabeth. It is not human sympathy that makes her hesitate to sign it, but only fear of the reproach of tyranny. The group of statesmen around her is excellently drawn ; Burleigh is hard and unfeeling, desiring Mary's death for reasons of state policy ; Leicester is miserably weak and faithless, loving Mary and wishing to save her, yet without sufficient courage for the deed, and at the last, only concerned about his own safety. Elizabeth indirectly incites first Paulet, Mary's keeper at the time, and then Mortimer, his nephew, to the murder of her enemy; but the former is too upright, and the latter is a secret disciple of the Jesuits and ardently devoted to Mary. Jealousy and wounded pride finally persuade Elizabeth to the fatal step. In the scene with Mary in the garden at Fotheringay she feels herself lowered in Leicester's eyes, and this determines her. Under the pretence of yielding to the importunities of the people, and under the impression that Mortimer is going himself to make an attempt on Mary's life, she signs .the death-warrant, but even then in a form which shall shield herself and throw the blame on her secretary. She purposely leaves him with the signed warrant in his hands, refusing to give him definite instructions. Burleigh, finding him in perplexity and despair, snatches the paper from him and causes the sentence to be put into execution. And Elizabeth then actually disowns the action of the secretary! Talbot, the honest man at court, cannot stand this and resigns his office ; Leicester, overwhelmed by Mary's death, goes to France.

Schiller has sketched the contrast between the two rivals with great power, but has not carried it very deep. Mary, who has a bad name, is better than her reputation ; Elizabeth, who is generally respected, is worse than her reputation. Mary is generous and open-hearted, and ready to acknowledge her sins; Elizabeth is cautious and underhand in action, and a hypocrite. While Mary is chastened and raised to a level where she no longer feels the want of earthly delights, Elizabeth sinks in the eyes of her most faithful servants and loses those earthly good things which she thinks so much of. The lower side of feminine nature is made the chief lever of action in

[marginal notes:] Character of Elizabeth.

Contrast between the two.

the drama, and brings about the catastrophe. Jealousy turns the balance; Mary Stuart finds satisfaction in pouring out insulting speeches on her rival's head, and it is this that incites Elizabeth to vengeance.

To a certain extent this tragedy may be considered as a practical example of Schiller's theoretical dictum, that in the ancient classical **Excellences** drama, which he endeavoured to follow, more importance **of composi-** was attached to the chain of events than to the present- **tion and** ation of character. The exposition in the first act of **style.** 'Mary Stuart' is a masterpiece of technique ; it gives us interesting action and dialogue, the dialogue resulting from the action and also characterizing the speakers, while at the same time it communicates to the audience what is essential for them to know.

In 'Mary Stuart' Schiller gave new evidence of that impartiality and objectivity which he had acquired in writing his ballads and 'Wallenstein.' There is no character in the piece which is entirely after the poet's own heart. The idealism of Max Piccolomini is not to be found here, and Mortimer, who plays very much the same kind of part, is one of those enthusiasts whom Schiller in his mature years judged so hardly, one of those self-willed natures who know no restraint for their turbulent desires, and think that liberty consists in the abrogation of all moral laws.

With the same tolerance as he has shown in 'Mary Stuart,' **Die 'Jung-** Schiller in the 'Maid of Orleans' again chose a **frau von** Catholic heroine, one of the miraculous figures of the **Orleans.'** Middle Ages. But his Joan of Arc is also a represent- ative of ideal womanhood, a champion in a good cause, consecrated by religion and by her own pure nature. Schiller throws his whole sympathies into the scale on her side. He meant her to be an embodiment of that *naïveté* which he esteemed so highly, and at the same time to picture once more the sad fate of the beautiful upon this earth. (See 'Das Ideal und das Leben.') Her peace of soul is destroyed as soon as earthly love lays hold on her heart. Schiller's Johanna is no Amazon of heroic bearing and manly **Character of** disposition, but a simple, pathetic character with a **Johanna.** childlike imagination, childlike language, and a holy childlike faith, which is the source of her power. She comes from that idyllic, pastoral region where poetry and beauty have their home. In her the angel and the child are united, and as soon as she ceases to be a child, as soon as the woman makes itself felt in her, the charm is broken. The supernatural world is made almost as prominent and material in this play as in Goethe's 'Faust.' Johanna herself possesses miraculous power and wisdom, and has visions. After her heart has been touched by human love, she feels that she has fallen from her high vocation, and she receives the accusation condemning her in silence, as a chastening from heaven. At length she overcomes her human passion and finds peace once more. In her imprisonment her heroic strength returns again, and a new miracle comes to her aid; her heavy chains fall from off her, she liberates the king, triumphs and dies, and the gates of heaven open to receive her.

Schiller was not quite equal to the task which he set himself in writing the 'Maid of Orleans.' He meant to represent in his Johanna the charm of naturalness, but he has not been successful in this. When the Duke of Burgundy is overpowered by the child-like simplicity of her words we can only marvel, for what she says does not affect us in the same way. Schiller is unable to express the charm of *naïveté*, and he replaces it by declamatory lyric strains.

In many respects the 'Maid of Orleans' resembles an opera. Even the prelude has an operatic ring about it, and Johanna often gives utterance to what might be called arias — lyrical, declamatory soliloquies, sometimes *Operatic character of the play.* written in the recognised aria form of rhymed stanzas. The chief characters, too, are rather types than individuals, and Johanna, the Dauphin and Agnes Sorel together form a lyrical trio, more suited to the opera than the drama. The knights are all cast in the same mould, and are arranged, like a chorus, in two groups, the English and the French, with Burgundy in their midst, who goes over from the former to the latter; and in the English, as in the French group, those who are for the Maid are distinguished from those who are against her. Doubt is gradually introduced into the French group, while into the English group love gradually makes its way. The evil principle is represented by Queen Isabeau, the implacable enemy of the Maid, and at the same time the moral opposite of all that is good and beautiful.

The characters of Talbot, the English general, and Thibaut, Johanna's father, are also meant to stand in contrast to the Maid. Talbot is a sceptical man of the world, Thibaut a selfish realist, who has no faith in the power of God upon earth, and only fears the power of devils. Johanna herself wanders through the play like the spirit of liberty, and succeeds in doing what Goethe's Clärchen failed to do. She stirs up her nation against the foreign intruders, and the armies which she leads are victorious. She, too, has a Brackenburg by her side in her faithful peasant-lover, Raimond, who remains absolutely devoted to her, and stands by her when all forsake her.

The 'Maid of Orleans' is a chivalrous drama, and in it Schiller **General** has not wholly scorned the usual apparatus of this **features of** class of drama, such as it developed itself subsequently **the play.** to the appearance of Goethe's 'Götz.' But Schiller's play rises far above the level of the ordinary chivalrous drama, in the first place because it deals with occurrences of public importance, not with private outrages and feuds. The technical difficulties arising from the constant fighting are surmounted with masterly skill. Fights between large numbers are reported, single conflicts are directly represented, but are always interwoven with human and personal interests. There are some things in this play that remind us strongly of the Iliad, such as the constant fighting, the interference of the supernatural, the equal rank of all the nobles, and their attitude towards their king. The language, the similes, the situations, even the metre itself, sometimes point to Greek models, and something of the Homeric glory seems shed over the whole drama.

In his 'Bride of Messina' Schiller approached more nearly than **'Die Braut** in any other of his dramas to the classical model, **von Messina.'** departing, however, from one rule of the ancients (as he had already done in his 'Maid of Orleans,' though not in 'Mary Stuart' or 'Wallenstein'), in representing death upon the stage. This play is not based on fact or tradition, as most of Schiller's dramas are. Schiller fully recognised that his special strength lay

in dramatising historical events, in spiritualising reality, and preferred to make use of some existing story rather than create a new
one.   He had long been seeking for a subject which should offer
all the advantages of Sophocles' ' Œdipus Tyrannus ;'   Resem-
but since he could not find one which would fulfil   blance to
these requirements, he invented the story of the ' Bride   Sophocles'
of Messina,' forming it after the model of Sophocles'   ' Œdipus.'
play.   In the ' Bride of Messina,' as in ' Œdipus,' we have a home
lying under a curse, an oracle which a man seeks to flee from and
just thereby fulfils, a child which was meant to be killed but
which remains alive, unnatural love and murder of a near relation,
a hidden deed which in the course of the play comes to light, and
a guilty man who punishes himself, only that his guilty deed
does not, as in the Greek drama, lie in the far past, but is quickly
done, and quickly discovered and expiated in the course of the
same day.

    Numerous details in the style and matter of this drama remind
us of ancient tragedy, but the play is also marked by   Excellences
original talent throughout.   In none of Schiller's   of the play.
dramas is the language so carefully moulded and raised to such an
even level of perfection as here.   He has nowhere else displayed
such unity in character-drawing, or lifted us into such a pure sphere
of poetry.   He ventured to make freer use than usual of the
creations of classical mythology, since his scene was laid on
Sicilian soil, where Hellenism lived on in its monuments, and
where the superstitious fancy of the Middle Ages could nourish
itself, both from classical and Arabian sources.   The Sicilians
had always been noted for great vigour, heroism and stoicism,
but also for jealousy and revengefulness, and Schiller in his
play adhered to what history recorded of them.   Don Cæsar's
heart burns with jealousy against his brother ; thirsting for
revenge he slays him, and with stoical heroism afterwards kills
himself.

    The ' Bride of Messina,' like Schiller's first play, ' The Robbers,'
introduces two brothers at enmity with each other.   The idea of
tragical conflicts between relations was one which had a deep hold
on Schiller's imagination, and indeed, in the eighteenth century

particularly, there were many instances of such conflicts in real life.

Quarrel between two brothers its leading idea. There was an increasing feeling in favour of more intimacy and tenderness in family relations, but in many cases the old, hard relationship had not yet given way to the improved state of opinion. The conflict between Frederick the Great and his father furnishes a notable example of how strained the paternal and filial relation might become; and Schiller himself, in that age of paternal government, must on his flight from Stuttgart have felt that he was rebelling against his sovereign like a son against his father. It seemed to him a fruitful idea, to transfer the strongest personal tension into that very family circle which was more and more growing to be considered as the abode of peace and tenderness. We find the incident of conflicts between near relations playing some part in every one of his plays. The two hostile brothers in the 'Bride of Messina,' as in 'The Robbers,' are in love with the same woman; but this woman is, without their knowing it, their own sister, and the father of these three had robbed his father of his bride, and thereby drawn down his curses on his head, which are now fulfilled in his grandchildren. In the past we have a conflict like that between King Philip and Don Carlos; in the present a conflict like that between Karl and Franz Moor, or between Eteocles and Polynices in Euripides.

Characters of the play. The actors in the 'Bride of Messina' seem to arrange themselves in a symmetrical group :—Isabella, the mother, in the midst, on either side her sons, the two hostile brothers, each of whom is surrounded by his followers. The mother unites the two sons, but there is yet another point of union for all three: Beatrice, the daughter and sister, unknown at first to all three as such, and whose emerging from seclusion conjures up all the misfortune. The two brothers are strongly contrasted, Don Cæsar being hasty and wrathful, Don Manuel melancholy and reserved. The whole tragic issue really results from this contrast, for without the hastiness of the younger and without the brooding melancholy of the elder brother, the catastrophe would not have taken place. Their former quarrel, which rose to deadly enmity, may also be attributed to this contrast of their characters. Their father, a gloomy despot, only suppressed this quarrel by force, and never tried to heal it by love. In their relation to their mother both show themselves loving sons; both fall in love with Beatrice equally suddenly, and both in the same manner. Beatrice and Isabella are not individualised but treated typically. The unnatural separation from her parents poisons Beatrice's young life. She has been secretly saved from death and brought up in seclusion, is secretly loved, and secretly carried off by order of her lover. She succumbs to feminine weakness, is twice disobedient and follows her own fancy, and her curiosity brings about the fatal *dénouement.* Isabella is the type of motherhood. Her maternal affection makes her reconcile her two sons, and save her daughter's life by concealing her. But gloomy superstition dominates her as it dominated her husband. She leaves her daughter in concealment, after all danger to her life has been removed through her father's death, simply because she is afraid that a dream of many years ago, of which a monk gave her a terrible interpretation, may be realised in this daughter. Gloomy superstition, unbridled desires, haste in action, are the characteristics which Schiller attributes to the ruling family in Messina. They are of northern descent and rule tyrannically over a Southern people. The subject-people bear the oppression with gloomy hatred; they fan the quarrel between the brothers, and wish misfortune to their foreign rulers. Schiller has expressed the feelings of the Sicilian people through the mouths of the prince's followers. He attributes to them the passions of a subject race, but at the same time a wide-ranging reflection, such as would beseem impartial spectators. He united them in a chorus, or rather in two semi-choruses, one of old and one of young men, and thus completed the resemblance to the classical drama.

The chorus here occupies a middle position between the chorus of Greek tragedy and the organized masses or uniform Introduction groups which Schiller had introduced in his earlier plays. of a chorus. Tragedies with few actors, such as 'Iphigenie' or 'Tasso,' were not in his line. He liked to set masses in motion. In his first play the robbers are grouped like a chorus around their leader. The conspirators in 'Fiesco' likewise form a homogeneous multitude.

In 'Don Carlos' Philip the Second's Court affords us, at least in one scene, a picture rich in figures. Wallenstein's camp and Wallenstein's generals present a grandly organized chorus. The domestics of Mary Stuart and the *suite* of Queen Elizabeth contain the germs for choruses. In the 'Maid of Orleans' we have two hostile armies in juxta-position. So, too, in the 'Bride of Messina' the semi-choruses represent two hostile armies, the retinue of two princes. They take part in the action, in accordance with Schiller's view of the function of a chorus (see Schiller's preface to this play: 'On the use of the chorus in tragedy'); but they also utter general reflections, and sometimes speak all together as a whole, thus approximating to the classical tradition, and this for the first time in the history of the modern German stage. They surround the central action with a glorious web of lyric poetry. All the most important facts and conditions of life are touched upon as in the 'Song of the Bell,' and the whole sensuous power of rhythm and rhyme is united with the loftiest thoughts and with an entrancing melody of language.

The 'Bride of Messina' is the highest work of pure art that Schiller has produced. He maintains a perfectly objective attitude towards the characters, but still, a certain political significance may even here be detected. There is an echo in this play of his **Schiller the** old favourite theme, the struggle against tyranny. **poet of** Schiller's hatred of despotism finds expression in **Liberty.** every one of his plays. In 'Wallenstein' the emperor and his servants are not painted in the best light; in 'Mary Stuart,' Elizabeth's tyranny is unsparingly laid bare; the 'Maid of Orleans' treats directly of a revolt against the oppression of a foreign conqueror; and so, too, the 'Bride of Messina' pictures the destruction of a powerful race which could not take root in a conquered land. The French Revolution and the events which followed it may very likely have influenced Schiller in the choice of these subjects, and also of the story of 'Wilhelm Tell.'

'Wilhelm Tell' represents a conspiracy like 'Fiesco,' and, like **Wilhelm** the 'Maid of Orleans,' gives the history of a successful **Tell.'** struggle against foreign tyranny. The poet's attitude is not impartial here; his whole heart is clearly on the side of the

oppressed Swiss. In the 'Maid of Orleans' Schiller had represented a peasant-girl leaving the world of idyll to enter the great
political world, so as to restore her fatherland to independence.
In 'Wilhelm Tell' he shows us a whole nation living in the world
of idyll till the oppression of tyranny breaks in upon them; in
the end they throw off the hated yoke, and violated nature re-asserts
her sway. In the Swiss people, as in Joan of Arc, Schiller wished
to portray *naïveté* of character, and he has succeeded better here
than in the 'Maid of Orleans.'

In 'Wilhelm Tell' the Swiss people form at once the chorus
and the centre of interest of the drama. The Swiss   Characters
nation itself is the hero of the play, only split up   of the play.
into individuals, and represented in typical characters. In the
first place aristocracy and peasantry are distinguished. The
peasantry is represented by an old man, a man in the prime of
life, and a youth: Walther Fürst, Werner Stauffacher, and Arnold
Melchthal. In introducing them together on the stage, whenever
he requires them, Schiller boldly disregards all considerations of
dramatic probability. These three men are at the same time representatives of the three Swiss cantons concerned in the struggle,
and are all united in their resistance to tyranny and arbitrary force.
The old man, Walther Fürst, is friendly towards the nobility, while
the youth is opposed to them. Among the representatives of the
aristocracy, too, there is a split between age and youth, the old times
and the new; the old Baron of Attinghausen holds with the peasantry and with liberty; his nephew Rudenz has joined the foreigners. But it is only love of the noble Bertha von Bruneck that
has thus led him astray, and the maiden whom he worships directs
him herself to the right path, and points out to him his duty to
stand by his countrymen. Rudenz and Melchthal, the aristocratic
and the peasant youth, are at first hostile to each other, but in the
course of the drama they draw nearer and nearer together, and
their final reconciliation, their mutual co-operation, their bond of
friendship, signify the reconciliation of classes.

Wilhelm Tell stands apart in the midst of all these people, in
the same manner as Max Piccolomini is isolated from the chorus
of Wallenstein's followers. He is not represented as an idealist,

in contrast with realists, for here all live in the state of harmonious

Character ideal nature. Tell is the combative sportsman in con-
of Tell. trast with the peaceful shepherd; he represents the
self-reliant strong men in contrast with more ordinary men who
believe themselves stronger when allied with others. Tell acts
where others only talk, deliberate, or hesitate. He knows no fear,
and does not reflect long where it is a question of immediate action;
at the same time he is humane and benevolent, and trusts God's
help in time of need. He is strong and active in body and expert
in all manly exercise, a sure shot, a bold sailor, a skilful carpenter,
and always ready to help on occasion. He is scanty of words,
but on his solitary paths he thinks all kinds of thoughts, and is
looked upon as a dreamer. Simple-hearted and unpretending,
respectful to those set over him, and less inflamed than the rest
against the tyranny of the imperial governors, he is willing to suffer
and be silent, to wait and hope, though he will not stand aloof
from his friends in case they really want his aid. Then suddenly,
tyranny brutally intervenes in his own life. The governor Gessler,
the true cold-blooded tyrant of fiction, totally destitute of humane
feelings, and resolved to subdue the Swiss people by force, this
man compels Tell, on pain of death, to shoot an apple from the
head of his own child. Afterwards he treacherously draws a
dangerous confession from him, and then causes him to be bound,
meaning to imprison him. Tell is almost miraculously delivered
from the hand of his oppressor, and at once forms the firm resolve
to kill this terrible tyrant. Gessler has sinned against nature in
arming the father's hand against his son, and from that moment he
is a lawful prey in the natural world, and the outraged father
'avenges holy nature,' by killing the tyrant as he would have killed
a wild animal which threatened danger to his house. Not the
slightest moral doubt rises in his mind. He is firmly convinced
of the justice of his deed; and though his gentle wife is horrified,
and though John Parricida dares to put himself on a level with
him, still his clear conviction remains unshaken. 'I lift up my
pure hands to Heaven,' he exclaims to Parricida, 'and curse thee
and thy deed.'

The story of Wilhelm Tell has its real origin in an old myth

which was adorned with all the elements of primitive German poetry.
The story was related in the sixteenth century, with a **Story of Tell.**
simplicity worthy of Herodotus, by the Swiss chronicler,
Aegidius Tschudi.   Wilhelm Tell was one of the traditional heroes
of the Revolution.   Rousseau had mentioned him with honour, and
the Göttingen band of poets had sung of him.   While in Switzerland, immediately after the completion of ' Hermann and Dorothea,'
Goethe turned his attention to the story, meaning to make an epic
out of it; but he relinquished the plan in Schiller's favour.   Schiller
endeavoured to free his hero from all connection with the regicides
of the French Republic.   He endowed him with that naive conviction of right which is to be found in a primitive age, and thus by
implication established the principle that in less primitive times a
similar mode of action must be judged differently.   All the Swiss
conspirators only wish to defend their wives and children.   They
all approve Tell's conduct, especially as he killed the tyrant
at the very moment when he was cruelly hardening his heart
against the pathetic entreaties of a poor woman whose husband
he had unjustly imprisoned, and was threatening to employ new
measures of violence against the unhappy land.

Schiller's ' Wilhelm Tell' bears some points of resemblance to
Goethe's ' Hermann and Dorothea.'   Both these **'Wilhelm**
works defend the good old customs and the liberty **Tell' and**
and sacredness of hearth and home.   The spirit of **'Hermann**
Homeric poetry breathes in both, and both arose from **und Doro-**
a worship of humanity in a state of nature and innocence.   **thea.'**

' Wilhelm Tell' is the first of Schiller's plays which has a happy
ending.   The hero does not succumb or die, but rises with fresh
strength and frees himself from his oppressors.   We **Leading**
still recognise in this play the old fundamental thoughts **ideas of**
of Schiller's poetry, the Rousseauian glorification of **'Wilhelm**
an ideal primitive state of humanity.   In his other **Tell.'**
dramas he had introduced his audience to a world which had grown
beyond the state of nature.   The world of reality which he depicts
will not tolerate what is beautiful and noble, and drags down the
man who follows his earthly instincts.   The good are in harmony
with nature and with heaven, and good oracles lead them in the

path to glory. The bad accept evil oracles, and a race which sins
against nature is destroyed from the face of the earth. In ' Wilhelm Tell' we are surrounded, for the first time, by pure nature,
and introduced to glorious human beings in a glorious country;
the unnatural element, which destroys idyllic life, comes from without, and disappears before the breath of liberty ; nature asserts her
eternal rights, and the beautiful is not destroyed, but survives.

After the completion of ' Tell' Schiller had begun a new tragedy,
Fragment, 'Demetrius,' taking his subject this time from Rus-
'Demetrius.' sian history. Again he brings before us a homogeneous mass of people, skilfully individualised, and a Polish diet is
presented with incomparable power. The general drift of the play
is similar to that of the ' Maid of Orleans'—a victorious advance
in the consciousness of a good cause, fortune favouring the hero,
then sudden doubt, inward conflict and outward defeat. The pre-
tender, who believes himself to be the rightful ruler, learns that he
is not, but nevertheless continues to play his part as such ; he thus
succumbs to the malicious powers of the world, and falls pierced
through at the feet of his reputed mother, who repudiates him.

Schiller had only begun the second act of ' Demetrius ' when he
Schiller dies, was cut off by death at the early age of thirty-five.
1805. Glorious as are his achievements, we feel that if he
had been spared he might have presented us with still richer and
greater works.

CHAPTER XIII.

ROMANTICISM.

GOETHE died on the 22nd of March, 1832, a hundred years after the appearance of Haller's poems, Bodmer's translation of Milton, and Gottsched's 'Cato,'—works which must have been considered at the time as important literary events. Goethe died, March 22, 1832.

Our survey of German literature will only extend to this point. The figure of Goethe, which has towered above all others since the revolutionary year 1773, will thus still remain the central point of interest in this last period. Goethe lived to see at least two generations of German poets. When he Poet-families. came to Leipzig to study, Elias Schlegel was still in great fame; when he formed his alliance with Schiller, men were already beginning to speak of Elias Schlegel's two nephews under whose leadership the Romantic school gradually developed itself. Shortly before Goethe planned his 'Götz,' Madame Sophie de la Roche, the youthful friend of Wieland (see vol. ii. p. 40) published her first novel; shortly before he finished his 'Werther,' the daughter of Sophie Laroche married an Italian merchant Brentano, in Frankfort, and Goethe's mother used to tell the Brentano children just as beautiful fairy stories as she had told to her own son in his childhood. Two of these Brentanos attained literary fame: Clemens joined the Romantic school; Bettina, afterwards the wife of another Romanticist, Achim von Arnim, had an enthusiastic devotion for Goethe, and after his death wrote a highly idealised description of himself and his mother.

Goethe's long life enabled him to witness several important phases in the intellectual life of Germany. In his youth a love

for the historical past of Germany had seized on the minds of
many. Imaginative writers filled the old Teutonic
Three phases in German intellectual life witnessed by Goethe. forests with Bards and Druids, and cherished an
enthusiastic admiration for Gothic cathedrals, and for
the knights of the Middle Ages and of the sixteenth
century. Herder's interest in the past had the widest
range, and he sought out poetry in all forms, in all
literatures, among all nations. Classical antiquity was not neglected
at this time, but it did not exclusively dominate the general taste.

In Goethe's mature years, on the contrary, the interest in
classical antiquity dwarfed all other æsthetic interests, and Germany and Europe were flooded by the classical fashion for which
Winckelmann had given the first strong impulse. The churches
became ancient temples, the mechanical arts strove after classical
forms, and ladies affected the dress and manners of Greek women.
The leaders of German poetry, Goethe and Schiller, both attained
the summit of their art in the imitation of classical models.

But in Goethe's advancing years, with the beginning of the nineteenth century, a counter-current again set in. Schiller's ' Maid of
Orleans' and his ' Wilhelm Tell' marked a return to mediæval themes.
The tendencies of 1770 to 1780, which had never quite disappeared, asserted themselves with new and increased force, and
the love of classical antiquity became once more but one
among many influences. The nations which were groaning under
Napoleon's oppression sought comfort in the contemplation of a
fairer and grander past. Patriotism and mediævalism became for
a long time the watchwords and the dominating fashion of the day;
not that catholic literary sympathies disappeared altogether, any more
than an increased piety suppressed the freer religious movements.
But Herder's spirit now replaced that of Winckelmann, and the
literary movement, which had been started some thirty years before
against the school of Enlightenment, was now called Romanticism.

Roman- ticism. All foreign literatures, but especially the old German
and popular branches of poetry, were drawn upon for
suggestions; while the grand achievements of the modern classical
period of German literature were of the greatest benefit to the
succeeding age. The scientific activity to which Herder had given

such encouragement was continued. New efforts were made in all the sciences, new points of view gained, and new forces acquired. But the division of labour now became greater, and what had been united in Herder now separated itself into various currents. The single branches of art, science and learning acquired more representatives, and appealed to wider circles, and parties were now divided by sharper lines.

SCIENCE.

German science and poetry in the eighteenth and nineteenth centuries were sometimes ranged in opposition to one another, sometimes united in an alliance most beneficial to each, though not without its dangers, if carried too far. *Relation of science and poetry in Germany in the 18th and 19th centuries.*

It cannot be denied that the growth of science gave a strong impulse to the rising school of poetry, but feeling and imagination had to free themselves from the almighty sway of common sense, ere German literature could attain its highest development. This improvement of taste again reacted beneficially on science. The ponderous accumulations of learning which had been not uncommon in the previous century, disappeared, or gave place to convenient, encyclopædic works of reference. The German genius lost that heaviness which sometimes clings to it, and became lighter, easier and more lively. The improvement of language produced all the good effects which Leibniz had expected of it; greater choiceness of expression went hand in hand with greater subtlety of thought, and this improvement gradually spread to all branches of literature, increasing their clearness, and in consequence strengthening their influence on the nation.

German prose now assumed a more artistic form. Journalism, as it rapidly developed, launched out into all styles, from the fiery, metaphorical periods of a Görres, to the short, biting sentences of a Börne. The Austrian State-papers exhibited the harmonious periods of Friedrich Gentz, whose dazzling wealth of language sometimes poured itself forth with all too great fluency. Savigny handled *Development of German prose-writing.*

juristic subjects with a clearness equal to Goethe's. With less success, Varnhagen sought to imitate Goethe's style in his numerous biographical sketches. A farmer, Johann Schwerz, wrote elegantly and gracefully on farming matters. General von Clausewitz in his book ' On War,' produced a scientific and literary work of the highest order; it combines the strict logical analysis of the eighteenth century with the careful criticism and historical learning of the nineteenth; it unites deductive theory with respect for facts of experience, and shows an enchanting originality, together with great clearness of method and a vigorous and picturesque style.

Among the writers of this time we recognise sometimes the influence of Schiller, sometimes that of Goethe. A really cultivated style of writing now arose, though at the same time there were not wanting those who followed Klopstock's example in experimenting with the language, and attained a certain uncouth originality. But side by side with these bunglers there were a few writers, like Jacob Grimm for example, who had a natural instinct for language, and who, by appreciative study of their native dialect and thorough understanding of the hidden laws and forces of speech, developed a truly creative power of language.

The women of this period were not behind the men in literary activity. Schiller's sister-in-law, Caroline von Wolzogen, produced a novel, ' Agnes von Lilien,' which was taken by professional **Literary** critics for a work of Goethe's, and poetesses like **women.** Sophie Mereau and Amalie von Imhoff were thought worthy to contribute to Schiller's ' Musenalmanach.' But the letters or memoirs or diaries from the pen of women of this period are still more worthy of notice, revealing to us, as they do, the level of feminine conversation at that time. Bettina von Arnim surrounds all objects with her fairy-like fancy, and transfers us from reality into a world of poetry, where truth and fiction are indistinguishably merged in each other. Rachel Levin, later on Madame Varnhagen, parades her extravagant wit somewhat too ostentatiously, combining, after the true manner of the humorist, things most remote from each other, and affecting a kind of prophetic insight. Henriette Herz, on the contrary, spreads a serene purity around her, and reminds us more than any other of the type of woman which Lessing favoured. Caroline Schelling ranks first among all the literary women of the time ; her graceful chatty letters are full of good sense and imagination, of refined malice and charming raillery, and their clear yet thoughtful descriptions, their charming language, and their hidden poetry raise them to the level of true works of art.

Rachel Levin, Henriette Herz, Caroline Schelling, and other women of the same stamp, ruled society in Berlin and Jena, which were the centres of the rising literature. Their circle of friends included the scientific men and poets, who were about twenty or thirty years younger than Goethe, who from the first were under his influence, and continued to work on the foundation which he had laid. They strove to give to their works an artistic value, but they also allowed themselves to be led astray into adopting an oracular tone, transferring the pleasing parodoxes of conversation to the realm of science, and substituting a happy fancy or a telling expression for the solution of the problem itself.

Such a method was chiefly prejudicial to philosophy and less directly to natural science. Philosophers like Lambert and Kant were indeed true successors of Leibniz, in **Philosophy.** that they had acquired a complete training in mathematics and physical science, and had themselves rendered services to the advancement of the exact sciences. But Kant's disciples could not boast of any such training. The master's philosophy thus became a mere fashion, chiefly rife in the University of Jena, and having the Jena Literary Journal for its newspaper organ. In the hands of these apostles Kant's teaching was transformed ; his theory of knowledge and the critical side of his philosophy generally were neglected, and his warning against all attempts to know the unknowable was disregarded. A system was elaborated which could be easily taught, and which might **Followers** serve in need as a substitute for religion. Among **of Kant,** these neo-Kantians, Fichte, Schelling and Hegel **Fichte,** were the most remarkable. All these three laboured **Schelling** at first in Jena. Fichte shared Kant's stern morality, **and Hegel.** and despised the sensuous world to such a degree as to deny it all reality. His bold idealism wished to derive the whole world from reason, and really approximated more and more to the pantheism of Spinoza. Spinoza became, about the middle of the nineteenth century, the leading spirit of German philosophy. Schelling went from Fichte to Spinoza, and from Spinoza even back to Jacob Böhme. Like the older German Spinozists, such as Herder and Goethe, he was inspired by an intense enthusiasm for nature conceived of as an organic whole. Hegel started from Schelling, but worked out a system at once more consistent and more comprehensive than his; a system which embraced in its compass not only nature but all spiritual life, and sought to enrich and strengthen all the sciences by reconstructing them *a priori* out of pure thought.

Schelling's and Hegel's writings produced a tremendous effect. Schleiermacher, on the other hand, one of the most powerful and learned minds that Germany has ever produced, and whose influence among theologians was quite unequalled, was not duly honoured as a philosopher till long after his death. Schopenhauer remained unnoticed for many decades, though as a stylist he stood highest among the German philosophers. While Schelling's language, at its best, shows a graceful obscurity, and Hegel's is purely barbarous, Schopenhauer was a true master of speech. At the same time he was a man of really deep and original thought, who stood in much closer relation to Kant than other writers, and successfully developed the Kantian philosophy in certain directions. Herbart, a calm methodical thinker, obtained only late in life a limited recognition of his merits. All other thinkers were eclipsed by Schelling and Hegel, whose daring idealism most appealed to the age, and led natural science astray.

As early as the eighteenth century science had suffered from the growing power of poetic imagination. Goethe, in despising mere analysis and mathematical calculation, was only realising and strengthening the predominant tendency of the age. Towards the end of the last century, mathematics, physics and chemistry were almost at a standstill in Germany. The few men who distinguished themselves in these sciences stood quite alone. The genius of Gauss, who by his 'Disquisitiones Arithmeticae' proved himself the connecting link between an earlier and a later period of exact science, was but slowly appreciated in the province of mathematics. Men's excited imagination scorned colourless abstractions, and demanded glowing life in everything.   Nature's secrets were now no longer to be wrung from her by the forcible method of experiments.   Even in anatomy and physiology no one comparable to Albrecht von Haller arose for some time in Germany.   But the starry heaven never lost its charms for these enthusiasts, and the teleological observation of the minute details in nature led to the most glorious botanical discoveries.   The sensuous perception, which had been quickened and trained by the contemplation of the most sublime works of art, proved of great use in mineralogy.   To distinguish and establish the characters of nations and countries was a poetical as much as a geographical task, and the thorough scholarly habits of the eighteenth century, the delight in amassing vast and universal knowledge, the careful accumulation of facts, furnished valuable material for scientific generalization, either in statistics, zoology, or geography.

In the first decades of this century it seemed as if the true scientific attitude was in jeopardy in Germany.   Men's imagination, influenced by art, impatiently demanded of science a complete whole with no gaps in it, and metaphysics were ready to construct such a whole.   Philosophers dreamed of an intuitive method, which should easily solve the problems that baffled patient investigation.   Most provinces of research in natural science were invaded by those pernicious metaphysical theories which have become so notorious under the name of 'Naturphilosophie.'   The capacity for observing in an unprejudiced manner and for rightly estimating the value of an experiment diminished to an alarming degree, while systems hastily and carelessly evolved found a willing acceptance even in the domain of practical medicine.   The believers in animal magnetism entered into alliance with the believers in ghosts and in other 'occult powers of nature.'   A few romantic and ardent spirits sought the cause of disease in the sinful soul, and recommended the expulsion of the devil as the most effectual medicine.

[sidenote: Exact methods discredited.]

[sidenote: 'Natural philosophy,' circa 1800–1820.]

But in spite of all this, 'Natural Philosophy' did really strengthen the general interest for natural science, and extend German national culture in this direction. By promising to reveal the secrets of the universe, it attracted many intellectual young men who, when they did not find their hopes fulfilled, sought for sounder knowledge in other paths, and eventually rivalled foreigners, because in their modest devotion to science they were content with firmly establishing some few facts instead of grasping at the whole of knowledge.

The reaction against 'Natural Philosophy' began about 1820, simultaneously with a great stirring of new life in all the provinces of exact science. Germany suddenly produced a whole series of mathematicians, scientists and doctors of the first order, and Germans now took the lead in many departments where a short time ago they had been mere learners.

Reaction against Natural Philosophy, circa 1820.

Geography alone had remained untouched by the pernicious influences of Natural Philosophy, and Alexander von Humboldt, the most brilliant representative of this science, threw the whole weight of his influence into the scale against the dreams of metaphysics. Geography rose together with the rise of German poetry, but did not sink with its decline. Active spirits explored distant regions of the earth with the same joy of discovery with which poets penetrated into the world of the soul. Engelbert Kämpfer reported about Japan. German explorers, from Messerschmidt, Gmelin and Pallas down to Alexander von Humboldt, Ehrenberg, Rose and their successors, contributed to the scientific knowledge of Russian Asia. Carsten Niebuhr made us more intimately acquainted with Arabia, Babylonia, and Persia. Hornemann penetrated into the interior of Africa. The two Forsters, father and son, accompanied James Cook on his second journey round the world. In 1799 Alexander von Humboldt went on his own responsibility to America, and his example was followed by many Germans in this century. German explorers were the first to rise above the level of isolated geographical facts, to geographical comparisons and generalisations. The comparative method, of which we

Geography.

Explorers.

only occasionally find traces in Gmelin and Pallas, became in
Reinhold Forster the pervading tendency. His son   The
Georg adopted the same method and handed it on comparative
to his friend Alexander von Humboldt, who in his   method.
turn exercised a decisive influence on Karl Ritter. The comparative science of the earth, including both comprehensive
physical generalisation, and investigation of the connection between the earth and human life, between geography and history,
is a creation of German origin.

Georg Forster, who left Mainz in order to take an active part
in the French Revolution, and who died in misery in Paris, was
endowed with a rare versatility of mind and readiness of pen.
His powers of observation and reflection were quite marvellous.
He first practised the art of description on nature,   Georg
but afterwards extended it to buildings and pictures, Forster's
to the aspect of towns and of public life. His 'Ansichten
'Views on the Lower Rhine,' the memorial of a short vom Nieder-
journey taken in company with Alexander von Hum-   - rhein.'
boldt in the year 1790, bear eloquent testimony to his talent in
this direction.

Alexander von Humboldt was superior to Georg Forster in
universal learning, in clear system and method, and in activity as
an explorer and organizer. Humboldt added an in- Alexander
credible number of new facts to science, and used   von
them all for one end—the comprehensive study of the Humboldt,
earth. Comparison was the very soul of his method. 1769-1859.
He did not entirely confine himself to physical geography; his
descriptions of countries from the standpoint of political economy
are models of what such writings should be, and his interest in
America led him to make historical investigations about Columbus.
Nor were æsthetic interests quite neglected by him; Georg
Forster's descriptions of the tropical world had fired his imagination and awakened his longing, and after he had   His
himself seen and enjoyed its wonders, he rivalled 'Ansichten
Bernardin de St. Pierre in his glowing pictures,   der
'Views of Nature,' as he called them. His style, rich   Natur.'
in epithets and introducing many technical names, does not attain

to Goethe's graphic power, but it became the model for most
German writers of travels.   Here, too, Humboldt did not content
himself with the mere picture of things, but penetrated beneath
them to the underlying law.

Alexander von Humboldt was not at all, or only quite transi-
torily, affected by the Natural Philosophy movement.   The mythical idea of a vital force, which he glorified in almost poetic
language, was at that time held by many investigators, who were
far from being natural philosophers.   But he too, like Schelling,
Oken or Hegel strove to represent natural phenomena as a
complete whole.   Buffon and Herder had already exhibited the
relations in which the earth stands to the universe.   Georg Forster
conceived a similar plan and Humboldt carried it out.   In his celebrated Berlin lectures, given in the winter of 1827–28, and which

His   form the foundation of his 'Kosmos,' he drew a picture
'Kosmos.'   of the universe which nowhere went beyond the limits of
fact or justifiable hypothesis; these lectures formed the truest and
most effective retort to the rubbish of the Natural Philosophers.

In the same large and comprehensive spirit in which Alexander
von Humboldt investigated the nature of the earth, his brother
Wilhelm sought to fathom the nature of man.   Both brothers
moved in the highest ranks of society.   Wilhelm was repeatedly

Wilhelm von   minister and ambassador; Alexander was repeatedly
Humboldt,   entrusted with diplomatic missions, and was on inti-
1767–1835.   mate terms with two Prussian kings.   Both were
personally attached to Goethe, and Wilhelm was besides a devoted
friend of Schiller.   When the friendship between the two great
poets was formed, Wilhelm von Humboldt was living in Jena, and
he no doubt did his best to bring Schiller and Goethe closer to

His   each other.   'Hermann and Dorothea' furnished him
'Aesthe-   with the text for his 'Æsthetic Essays,' in which
tische   he preached Goethe's theory of the epic, and also did
Versuche.'   much to acquaint people with the poet's real character.   A criticism of Schiller, which he wrote a quarter of a
century after Schiller's death, was equally successful in revealing to
the world the deepest nature of his great friend.   Like Schiller and
Goethe, he found ideal humanity in the Greek race.   He declared

that in the most solemn and the most cheerful moments, in
the happiest and saddest events of life, and even in His love of
the hour of death, a few lines of Homer, though the classics.
they were only those cataloguing the Greek ships, would make
him feel the divine element in human nature more than any other
literary work.   But his studies of the Greek and other literatures,
his careful estimates of modern German poets, his investigation
of the contrasts of sex in humanity and in nature, his study of
the peculiarities of the French stage in Paris, his visit to the
Spanish hermits of Montserrat—all these labours were only ad-
juncts to a comprehensive science of man ; and the study of
language, indispensable for this purpose, ended by absorbing his
whole interest.   He pursued this study with the catholic sympathy
characteristic of the eighteenth century, and sought out the various
types of grammatical construction, from the admired forms of
Greek and Sanskrit literature to the American, Malay, His study of
and Polynesian idioms.   His posthumous work on language.
' The Kawi language in the island of Java,' and especially the introduction ' On the variety of construction in language, and its
influence on the intellectual development of the human race,' is
looked upon as his scientific masterpiece.

He retired, when still young, from official life, in order to devote
himself to study.   In an essay written in 1791, and referring to the
new French constitution, he protested against the attempt to build
up a state-fabric according to mere principles of reason. His views on
In his paper, entitled ' An endeavour to determine the the functions
limits of the functions of the State,' he protested against of the State.
the all-powerful bureaucracy of the preceding century, and limited
the interference of the State to securing its citizens against inward
and outward enemies.   Public education and all matters of religion
seemed to him to lie outside the sphere of the State's functions.
Though in this he rather overshot the mark, yet his opposition to
the spirit of the eighteenth century was eminently practical and
opportune.   The historical and conservative views of Justus Möser
now first attained real power.   Statesmen like Baron von Stein
sought to repel the encroachments of the bureaucracy, and to increase
the participation of the citizens in public affairs.   But Humboldt

himself could not retain that contemplative leisure in which he found his happiness.   The needs of his Fatherland forced him into political activity, and he, who had been the enemy of all State-directed education, was compelled in January 1809 to assume the direction of the education department in the Prussian government. His splendid administration, which lasted a year and a half, formed the culminating point of his public activity, and was a brilliant era in the history of German education generally.

'The State must replace by intellectual force what it has lost in physical force,' said King Frederick William III on the 10th of August, 1807, in proposing the foundation of a new university; and Queen Louise remarked to a distinguished official: ' Frederick II conquered provinces for Germany; the present king will make conquests for Germany in the intellectual kingdom.'   No Prussian

W. von Hum-
boldt as
Prussian
Minister of
Education,
1809-1810.

official did more to fulfil these words than Wilhelm von Humboldt. He secured the foundation of the University of Berlin under the most difficult circumstances, and in so doing also gave a new lease of life to the Berlin Academy of Sciences.   The Prussian gymnasia had been progressing satisfactorily since the time of Frederick the Great, and with a Hellenist like Humboldt at the head of educational matters, classical studies would naturally receive still greater attention.   But Humboldt also favoured the increased wish for physical development and exercise by introducing gymnastics into the school curriculum.   At the same time he took an interest in the cultivation of music in schools, and directed elementary instruction into new paths.

We have noticed how in Basedow's mind the principles laid down by Rousseau with regard to a natural education were combined with the demands of the Illuminati; the same views operated in Pestalozzi, who based the earliest instruction on sensuous perception, at the same time assigning more importance to religion and family influences in education than Rousseau had done.   From the beginning of the century his method of instruction spread more and more, and when, after the humiliation of Prussia, a better education for the coming generation seemed the highest immediate duty and the only present source of hope, Pestalozzi's method, recommended by Fichte and taken up by Humboldt, attained predominant influence in the elementary schools of Germany.

In the autumn of 1810, when Humboldt had already resigned office, the University of Berlin was opened, and the Prussian capital became henceforth the chief centre of intellectual life in Germany and the scene of the greatest advancement in science. It was chiefly at Berlin that after 1820 the representatives of a new and exact school of natural science were gathered together. From the very beginning Berlin possessed a few of the chiefs of that new philosophical and scientific movement which had sprung up in the train of German poetry. Fichte was the second rector of the University, and Hegel settled in Berlin and founded an influential school of philosophy. The University and the Academy counted among their members at different times theologians like Schleiermacher, Marheinecke, De Wette and Neander, jurists like Savigny and Eichhorn, historians like Niebuhr, Rühs, Wilken, Friedrich von Raumer, Pertz and Ranke, philologists like Bopp and Pott, classical scholars like Friedrich August Wolf, Böckh, Immanuel Bekker, Lachmann and the brothers Grimm.

Opening of the University of Berlin, 1810.

Men of science and letters in Berlin.

The development of religious life in the nineteenth century was directly opposed to the tendencies of the eighteenth century. The revolt against the school of enlightenment, which had been begun by Herder in 1774, became more and more marked, till Schleiermacher's 'Addresses on Religion' in 1799 formed the turning-point of the movement in Germany. In Schleiermacher, as in young Goethe, Moravian and Pantheistic elements were mingled. He described the union of the soul with God in the poetic language of a mystic, and he did homage at the same time to the spirit of the 'holy, rejected Spinoza.' He transferred religion into the sphere of feeling, and avoided the name of God, preferring to replace it by World or Universe. He addressed himself especially to the cultured among the despisers of religion, and sought to convince the enlightened Berlinese that religion was an essential element of intellectual life. When he printed the third edition

German theology in the 19th century.

Schleiermacher's 'Reden über die Religion,' 1799.

of these addresses twenty-two years later, it seemed to him more
necessary to direct his words of exhortation to canting Christians and
slaves of the letter, to those who ignorantly and uncharitably gave their
brethren over to damnation, to the superstitious and over-credulous
among the educated classes; so great was the revolution which
had accomplished itself in the religious life of Germany during that
period.   Germany's humiliation, struggle and liberation revived
piety in her midst.   Even Wilhelm von Humboldt took an interest
in the rise of the religious spirit.   Contemporary with and after
him, Ludwig Nicolovius, who had married Goethe's niece, made his
influence felt as Prussian minister of education and public worship.
He was personally intimate with Hamann and Fritz Jacobi, and shared
their religious views.   Schleiermacher's sermons kindled a glow of
piety in many hearts.   In his religious utterances as in his scientific
ethics, he sought to appeal to all the various sides of human life.
In his most complete work, on 'Dogma' (Glaubenslehre), he

His   sought to bring the fundamental views of his 'Addresses
'Glaubens- on Religion' into closer harmony with the traditional
lehre.'   Christian dogmas, to save as many as possible of these
by transforming their meaning, and yet to leave everywhere free
scope for scientific investigation.   On the occasion of the three-
hundredth anniversary of the Reformation, King Frederick William
III, consistently with the old policy of his house, actually effected a
union between the two Protestant confessions, a measure which had
often been talked of before. : Contemporaneously, however, intolerance again raised its head, and orthodoxy persecuted all liberal
tendencies as heresy. : Catholicism acquired new strength in the
nineteenth century; the Jesuit order was re-established in 1814, and
Protestantism and Catholicism attacked each other afresh, though
only with the pen.

Metaphysicians intervened in vain in this old quarrel.   In the
intellectual as in the natural sciences they could create nothing permanent, but only supplied general suggestions which did great harm
in particular cases.   For several decades metaphysic exercised a
baneful dominion over æsthetic and psychology, inasmuch as it replaced genuine observation and investigation by mere theory.
But the philological and historical schools were already arrayed in

determined opposition to metaphysic, and their influence in this
respect reacted on theology.

In spite of single errors, history and philology did make some
important advances at this time. The classical ten-
dency of German poetry was as useful to classical as **Advances in historical**
the romantic tendency was to national philology; and **and**
poetry in its turn derived benefit from philological **philological criticism.**
studies. Many hidden achievements of national and
foreign literature were now brought to light. In the arrangement
of literary material, in collecting and publishing, the Germans
showed themselves superior to all other nations, and the improved
methods of treating such material have mostly proceeded from
them.

In the intellectual, as in the natural sciences, a strong critical
spirit now prevailed. The students of the eighteenth century made
short work both in ecclesiastical and in profane history with anything which seemed in contradiction to the recognised nature
of things. They everywhere scented untruth and deception, and
sometimes went too far in their scepticism, thereby evoking in
a few Romanticists a certain tendency to over-credulity. But on the
whole criticism gained steadily in boldness, prudence and acumen.
Wolf doubted the unity of authorship in Homer, and Niebuhr questioned the truth of early Roman history. Not that **Wolf,**
these new critics imputed conscious deception to pri- **Niebuhr, and**
mitive writers; they merely made allowance for the **Lachmann's**
unconscious distortion of legends, for the lower standard **theories.**
of probability in early times, for the absence of contemporary written
records and the errors which would naturally arise therefrom, for the
way the truth might have been obscured to satisfy æsthetic demands, or to meet party exigencies or other prejudices. They
conjectured, as the basis of early history, the existence of old
popular ballads, like those which Herder had first brought into
general notice. They allowed for the same mythologising element
in primitive poetry which Herder had so strongly insisted on; and,
again following Herder's example, they adopted worthier, nobler
views of the character of the priests among ancient nations.
Their criticism was not merely destructive, but also constructive.

Though unity of authorship was denied to the Iliad, the Odyssey and the Nibelungenlied, and these great epics were in a certain measure destroyed thereby, yet Lachmann restored them again by means of a process which Herder had applied to the Song of Solomon, i. e. by assuming, as their original basis, a series of ballads of less extent, but of greater artistic merit. Lachmann also discovered in the Nibelungenlied a mythical as well as a historical element, and thus, with truly constructive criticism, recovered a lost chapter of old German mythology. It is true this kind of criticism was sometimes driven too far; Niebuhr was **Mistaken** mistaken in deriving the traditional history of early **criticism.** Rome entirely from lost epic poems. The brothers Grimm and others were mistaken when they placed the origin of popular poetry in a mysterious obscurity, and drew a strong contrast between it and artificial poetry. Savigny again was entirely mistaken when he wrapped the origin of law in the same kind of mysterious obscurity, and when he refused to recognise any original creation of law in any except the early epochs of the history of nations.

We have seen how geographers sought by means of generalisation and comparison to construct a history of the earth ; similarly in philology and its kindred sciences the historical and comparative method, which had hitherto been applied with but slight skill **Science** or success, now became an important instrument of **of language** research and criticism. On the other hand, the philo- **and history.** sophy of history, which depends on comparison and generalisation, lost that favour which it had enjoyed for a time in the preceding century. The method of historical analogy was but little applied; the present was seldom invoked to aid in the interpretation of the past. The joy in the newly acquired facts rather blinded men's eyes to the necessity of explaining them if they were to be of any use. But in the science of philology the comparison of the grammatical structure of languages apparently most remote from each other led to the discovery of the primitive Aryan race, and at once suggested similar problems in other groups of languages, problems such as Wilhelm von Humboldt undertook to solve for the Polynesian and Malay races.

' The historical method was applied wherever it could throw light. Enquirers were not so eager now to define the The essence of things as to investigate their origin and historical growth. History now took the place of *a priori* method. construction. Historical right and theoretical right were clearly distinguished from one another, and all true progress in science was effected by means of adherence to the same historical method. Savigny traced the historical development of Roman law, showing how it had been gradually expanded and distorted. Historians in the same manner traced the history of the authorities on which they had to rely, and thereby learnt to estimate the true value to be assigned to their evidence. Students of literature, in publishing texts, first followed up the history of tradition, before undertaking to establish what was genuine. It was through historical research that the grammarians first gained an insight into the real life of language, and Wilhelm von Humboldt, who was the most eloquent exponent of this newly acquired knowledge, really but confirmed what Herder had surmised as early as his Strassburg period. Even the Hegelian philosophy owes its success in part to the fact that it seemed to satisfy in the shortest way the desire to understand the origin and growth of things, and also skilfully formulated and generalised a number of superficial reflections about the historical process of development.

The studies of the Romanticists were also historical in so far as they no longer cherished a bigoted contempt for whole epochs in the past; the Middle Ages especially, which had Mediæval- formerly been so depreciated, were now studied with ism. special zeal and enthusiastically admired. In religion, art and music mediævalism became fashionable, while theoretical as well as practical politics fostered the historical-conservative tendencies of the Romantic school as a useful weapon against parliamentary constitutions, and in defence of the privileged classes.

In ecclesiastical and secular history we notice the same objective and impartial attitude, strangely contrasting with the tendencies of the eighteenth century. The most distinguished History. ecclesiastical and secular historians of the older school were to be found at the University of Göttingen. Such were

Mosheim, Pütter, Gatterer, Schlözer, Spittler, Meiners, Heeren and Planck. In contrast to these Justus Möser prepared the way for the juster historical views of the nineteenth century, and at the same time brought historical style under the laws of epic art. The Swiss historian Iselin belongs to the older school, while his countryman

Iselin and Johannes Müller.

Johannes Müller represents the modern tendencies in historical writing. While Iselin painted in bold out- lines the progress of humanity, and dwelt much on the barbarism of the Middle Ages, Müller, in an artificial, senten- tious style imitated from Tacitus, drew the first appreciative picture of mediæval life, and with patriotic enthusiasm traced the history of the Swiss confederation down to the fifteenth century. The twenty-four books of his Universal History formed a triumph of the objective school of historical study. In the art of narration,

Archenholz and Schiller.

Archenholz and Schiller were far superior to Müller. Archenholz described the Seven Years' War from the standpoint of an enthusiastic admirer of Frederick the Great, without any trouble of research or verification, but in a lively and popular style. Schiller, with a slight amount of learning, showed a rare talent for penetrating criticism, a sure discernment of the inner relation of events, and a power of graphic description such as one would expect from so great a dramatist. In historical writing, as in other departments of knowledge, we find the spirit of the eighteenth century continued on into the beginning of the nineteenth, and only gradually losing its power. Rotteck wrote a universal history from the standpoint of a vulgar liberalism, and achieved a great success among the general reading public. But it was only the appreciative objective treatment which really met the

Schlosser, Wilken, Stenzel, Voigt, Neander.

demands of the time and satisfied more critical minds. Friedrich Christoph Schlosser, a stern moral censor and strictly bourgeois in his manner of looking at things, succeeded in appreciating the greatness of the Middle Ages even from the religious side. Wilken wrote the history of the Crusades, Friedrich von Raumer the history of the Hohenstaufen, and Harald Stenzel that of the Franconian emperors. Johannes Voigt presented Pope Gregory VII in a more pleasing light. Neander gave himself up to the task of delineating the individuality of such men as Julian the Apostate, Bernard of Clairvaux, Chrysostom, and Tertullian. And in the third decade of this century there arose in Germany a truly great and universal historian, Leopold Ranke, a critic and narrator of the first order, a master of characterization, **Ranke.** endowed with a marvellous power of sympathy, and possessing a thorough knowledge of politics and literature. His style at first resembled that of Johannes Müller, but was always more graphic and brilliant, and soon became thoroughly individual.

It was the endeavour of the eighteenth century to discover the peculiar tendencies, the 'genius' of nations. Winckelmann adhered faithfully to this point of view in his studies of antique art, and Christian Gottlob Heyne later on transplanted Winckelmann's ideas · into the classical teaching of the Universities. Herder gathered together all the different phases of national character in a whole, not even omitting language in his observations and comparisons. In the nineteenth century this class of studies was continued by Wilhelm von Humboldt; and his 'Sketch of the Greeks,' which he sent to his friend Wolf, furnished the latter with a **Study of** basis for a science of antiquity, and thereby for a **nationalities.** new view of philology generally. Philology in Humboldt's sense is the science of nationality; it investigates all the various phases of life in a nation, and points out the distinguishing peculiarity in each. Humboldt's lofty aims in the pursuit of this method have not yet been really attained in the study of any nation, and perhaps are unattainable as he intended them. But comprehensive research into all the aspects of national life became now an object of serious study. It was undertaken with regard to the Greeks by Welcker, Böckh and others, and was extended from poetry, art, mythology and science to material interests, to finance and navigation, weights and measures.

But their own nationality as well as the Greek now forced itself on the attention of German scholars. The German **Strong** nationality and its distinguishing features was the **patriotic** problem which Fichte treated in his 'Addresses,' and **tendency.** which also occupied Ernst Moriz Arndt and the men of action. It is true they idealized without sufficient investigation, and took the existing condition of things for permanent truth; but the glorified picture of the nation which they held up to their compatriots was an enormous moral force, and inspired hope and courage in times of need. Cosmopolitanism everywhere retired, and the national standpoint asserted itself not only in history, but **Study of** also in politics and political economy. Literary **German** research in this period was superior to historical; **literature.** the study of German literature was represented by men like Jacob Grimm and Georg Gottfried Gervinus, whose ' History of German poetry' began to appear three years after Goethe's death (1835), and formed, so to speak, the epilogue of the modern classical period of German poetry.

Herder gave the initiative in all directions, in history, philology **Strong** and literary criticism. He furnished many utterances **influence of** on German mediæval poetry, and was peculiarly **Herder.** successful in discerning the really great minds of the seventeenth century. His idea of Hellenism influenced Schiller. The sceptre of æsthetic criticism passed from Gottsched to Lessing, from Lessing to Herder, and from him to the brothers Schlegel. The combination in Herder of the study of literary history with the art of the translator, his enthusiastic appreciation of other writers, which sometimes led him into mere slavish imitation, all this lived on in the two Schlegels, while the general plan which they laid down as the basis of literary history was derived from Schiller. They put ' classical' and ' romantic' in the place of Schiller's contrast of ' naive' and ' sentimental' poetry, and they counted Goethe's ' Hermann and Dorothea,' for instance, as belonging to the classical school of poetry.

August Wilhelm Schlegel, Friedrich Schlegel, Ludwig Tieck, Friedrich von Hardenberg, who wrote under the name of Novalis, **The older** Johann Dietrich Gries, and a few others, form the **Romantic** inner circle of the so-called older Romantic school. **school.** They were friends of Fichte and Schleiermacher at Berlin and Jena, and began to come prominently into notice about the time when Schiller and Goethe commenced their friendship, and when Goethe published his ' Wilhelm Meister' (1795). They attacked the Berlin school of enlightenment, and satirised the shallow society-literature, as Schiller and Goethe did in the 'Xenien.' But they went too far in their hostility towards the eighteenth century. In their extreme horror of the fashionable cry for 'nature' in everything, they departed altogether from nature and reality in their writings, and demanded, in accordance with Fichte's views, that a work of art should be a free product of the inner consciousness. They freed imagination from all restraints, repudiated all established forms, and confused the various kinds of poetry. They set up the finest principles of objective criticism, and ruthlessly disregarded them in practice. They loudly proclaimed the praises of Goethe, but they misunderstood Wieland, depreciated Lessing, and did not even recognise Schiller's genius. Nicolai, Kotzebue and their party, the representatives of the school of enlightenment, did not take these attacks in silence. Pasquinades, criticisms, manifestos and satirical dramas, continuing to a certain extent the warfare of the 'Xenien,' were launched by each side against the other. But the political events of 1805 and 1806, the defeats of Austria and Prussia, put an end to all literary feuds; the Romanticists, like Fichte, returned to reality and national life, and the two Schlegels now gathered their forces together for important achievements in the province of literary history. In the school of the older Romanticists generally the history of literature and the art of translation made great progress.

Tieck was a man whose views and education were essentially those of the 'Storm and Stress' period; he was an enthusiastic admirer of 'Götz' and the 'Robbers,' and he himself never got beyond the formless literary productions of Goethe's youthful companions. He had early become acquainted with the German popular stories, and revived them under various forms. His interest in Shakspeare led him on to the study of the English and German drama in the sixteenth and seventeenth centuries. He made Siegfried's youth the subject of some early romances; he translated 'Don Quixote' (1799); he produced a modern version of old German Minnesongs (1803), and published the love-memoirs of Ulrich von Lichtenstein (1812). He uttered, so to speak, the manifesto of Romanticism in the following lines:—

Tieck.

His translations.

' Magical moonlit-night,
 Holding the senses fettered,
 Wonderful fairy-world,
 Arise in thy olden glory.'

Wilhelm Schlegel, the elder of the two brothers, acquired pure
Wilhelm poetic form through his personal acquaintance with
Schlegel. Bürger. He gradually freed himself from Bürger's
travestying method of translation, and rather adopted Herder's
principles, uniting the most careful imitation of the original with a
truly German character, with fluency of language, unity of style,
and pure poetic effect. Wieland's translation of Shakspeare had
been made more complete and accurate by Eschenburg, but a
prose version of Shakspeare could never hope to find general
acceptance. Wilhelm Schlegel was the first to apply those newly
developed forces of German language and metrical art, which
dated from the appearance of Goethe's first Iambic plays, to
making a noble German version of the great English dramatist.

Between 1797 and 1801 he translated sixteen of Shakspeare's
plays, and in 1810 there followed yet a further instalment. Schlegel's
Shakspeare certainly surpassed Voss' Homer. It did not conceal
the wide difference between creative and imitative art, but it
showed the close kinship between one perfect work and another,
His and for this reason it may rank directly by the side of
Shakspeare the works which Goethe and Schiller produced in the
and other period of their common labours. Wilhelm Schlegel
translations. showed almost the same perfection in his renderings
of Italian, Spanish and Portuguese poetry, and called forth many
Translators. imitators in this field, such as Gries for Tasso, Ariosto
and Calderon, Kannegiesser, Streckfuss, and King
John of Saxony for Dante, Witte and Soltau for Boccaccio and
Cervantes; at the same time many writers rivalled each other
in completing the translation of Shakspeare, while new German
versions of the classics were continually appearing. These translators did not all proceed according to Schlegel's principles; only
a few hit on the right mean between faithfulness to the original and
faithfulness to the German laws of language and form. Wilhelm
von Humboldt's version of Æschylus' 'Agamemnon,' and Schleiermacher's ' Plato,' for instance, possess the former in the highest

degree, but are often deficient in the latter. Wilhelm Schlegel's art
of translation was based as much on the devoted study of language
as on independent poetic power, as much on wide literary interests
as on the highest conceptions of German poetry. He was the
critic *par excellence* among the allies of the Romantic school. His
'Lectures on dramatic art and literature,' which ap-   His
peared from 1809 to 1811, show him from his best   'Vorles-
side. The chief place is here rightly assigned to the   ungen über
Greeks and the English; but patriotic prejudice   dramatische
blinded him in his criticism of the French, and even   Litteratur'
led him to condemn Molière.   (1809–1811).

Friedrich Schlegel was pre-eminently the theorist of the older
Romantic school, bold and paradoxical to the point of   Friedrich
absurdity and bad taste, but also a man of many-sided   Schlegel.
interests, who exercised a strong influence over other minds.   In
his first studies of Greek poetry, he took Winckel-   His 'Sprache
mann as his example, while he was in part also   und Weis-
influenced by Humboldt's principles. He gave a new   heit der
impulse to the study of mediæval art. His essay   Indier,' 1808.
on the 'Language and wisdom of the Indians,' which appeared
in the year 1808, paved the way for Indian studies in Germany,
and with its bold but suggestive hypotheses was the pioneer for
the surer conclusions of comparative philology.   In the same year,
1808, Friedrich Schlegel became a Roman Catholic, and there is
clear evidence of his change of opinion in his 'Lectures   His Lectures
on the history of old and modern literature' (1815),   on German
a work of great excellence in many respects.   In   literature.
these lectures Friedrich Schlegel only gave a bare outline of old
German poetry. With greater power and enthusiasm Wilhelm
Schlegel had addressed the Berlin public on the same subject in
the winter of 1803 to 1804. He compared the Nibel-   Revived
ungenlied, as Bodmer's school had already done, with   interest in
the Iliad. He called it a miracle of nature and a   old German
sublime work of art, which had never since been   literature.
equalled in German poetry. He himself thought of publishing a
new edition of it, and Tieck cherished a similar plan. Both were
anticipated by Friedrich Heinrich von der Hagen, who had attended

Schlegel's lectures, and who published successfully four editions
of the Nibelungenlied, and also a modernised version
of the poem; but his labours in this department were
afterwards eclipsed by Lachmann.

F. H. von der Hagen and Lachmann.

In the winter of 1807 to 1808 old German poetry became fashionable among the educated classes in Berlin, and in 1808 a new
generation of romantic poets who from the first directed
their attention chiefly to the older and popular German
literature, gathered round a small and short-lived newspaper, the 'Zeitung für Einsiedler' (Journal for Hermits), published
in Heidelberg. This band of poets consisted of Achim von Arnim
from Berlin, Joseph Görres from Coblenz, Clemens Brentano from
Frankfort, the brothers Grimm from Hanau, and Ludwig Uhland
from Tübingen. Arnim, the editor of the journal above mentioned,
and Brentano were at that time living in Heidelberg; Görres too
was teaching there at the University, which was springing up into
new life and vigour under the government of the Elector of Baden.
The other authors contributed from a distance.

Later Romantic school.

Achim von Arnim planned a comprehensive revival of the old
and the popular literature. From 1806 Arnim and Brentano published conjointly a collection of German songs, under
the peculiar title of 'The Boy's Wonder-Horn.' These
songs are patriotic in character, in contrast to the
cosmopolitan tone of Herder's people's songs. Arnim
revived with more or less freedom narratives and dramas of the
fifteenth to the seventeenth century. Brentano revived a tale
of Jörg Wickram, and in his light jocose treatise on the 'Philistine' he declares it to be the clearest proof of Philistinism not to
understand and admire the marvellous inventive genius and extraordinary artistic power displayed in 'Schelmuffsky.'

Arnim and Brentano, 'Des Knaben Wunder-horn.'

In 1807 Görres wrote a work on 'The German people's books,'
and furnished an appreciative survey of that whole
class of literature which was sold at fairs, and which
is still esteemed among the lower ranks of the nation.
The 'People's Books' comprised dream-books,
medicine-books, and riddle-books, weather-prophecies, craftsmen's
proverbs, fabulous travels, legends and romances like those of

Görres, 'Die deutschen Volks-bücher.'

Genovefa, Magelone, Melusine, the Emperor Octavian, the invulnerable Siegfried, Duke Ernst, Henry the Lion, Eulenspiegel, Doctor Faustus, and the wandering Jew.

The brothers Grimm, Jacob and Wilhelm (the former born in 1785, the latter in 1786), frequently appeared before the public as joint-authors. In 1812 and 1815 they published their 'Fairy-tales' in common, in 1816 the 'German Legends,' and from 1852 they both laboured in producing a 'German Dictionary.' From their childhood to the death of Wilhelm, they lived almost continually together. Wilhelm was married, Jacob unmarried, but beloved in his brother's family like a second father. Their common labours embraced all departments of German philology in the wide sense given to it by Wilhelm von Humboldt. The power of great discovery was strongest in the elder brother, the power of quiet development in the younger.

Jacob and Wilhelm Grimm's 'Kinder und Hausmärchen,' 'Deutsche Sagen,' 'Deutsches Wörterbuch.'

Jacob seemed at first to wish to attempt a history of German poetry and legends, a comprehensive survey of poetic material. But in his 'German Grammar,' which he began to publish in 1819, he furnished a history of all the Teutonic languages, and by his method as well as by his discoveries became one of the founders of the modern science of language. He felt, as no one had felt before, the natural poetry hidden in language. In 1816 he wrote an essay on the poetry in law, and expanded it in 1828 into the work entitled 'Antiquities of German Law.' In 1835 he published his 'German Mythology,' in which he traced the vestiges of heathenism in the older poetry and in popular superstition. He brought to light many noble customs of early German times, and enabled men to enter more thoroughly into the spirit and style of the old Germanic epics. He made a wide study of the productions of popular poetry, and himself translated a few Servian songs. He frequently rose to the highest level of general observations, full of natural philosophy and unadorned wisdom. Even his errors are attractive; one would rather believe them than repudiate them.

Jacob Grimm's 'Deutsche Grammatik,' 'Deutsche Rechtsalterthümer,' and 'Deutsche Mythologie.'

Wilhelm Grimm directed his researches in particular to the
Wilhelm old German hero-legends; he translated old Danish
Grimm's hero-songs, ballads and fairy-tales, published many
literary monuments of German poetry and language from the
studies. eighth to the thirteenth century, and did the chief
work in the collection of German fairy-tales made by him and
his brother Jacob. He knew what children liked to hear, and
His created the homogeneous style of these stories, with-
fairy-tales. out exactly inventing it; he adopted the best, most
naive and most charming traits in the oral narratives current
among the people, arranging them according to the measure of his
own refined taste. He accomplished for the German fairy-tales
what Arnim, Brentano, Tieck and others only attempted for the
popular songs and romances. He gave back to the whole nation
those innocent children's stories which had taken refuge with the
lower classes, and produced a work of art perfect of its kind, and
which found favour and imitation even outside Germany. His
'Märchen' made him rank among the best German popular
writers and children's authors, such as Peter Hebel, Christoph
Schmid and Ludwig Aurbacher; yet at the same time he always
remained a scholar, adhering faithfully to his authorities, while the
other writers whom we have mentioned refashioned with poetic
licence Biblical stories, or legends, tales, and farces of the older literature, and did not even mind introducing inventions of their own.

Genuine devotion to poetry distinguishes the brothers Grimm
Characteris- from many other scholars. We can clearly observe
tics of the in them how the high excellence of German poetry
brothers led to a science of German poetry. Like Goethe
Grimm. they were specially attracted by the idyll, which
educated the men of the previous century to appreciate the simple
charms of natural everyday life. They were animated by a
pathetic optimism, and they possessed that sober imagination
which delights in small things and narrow interests, lingering
over them with strong affection. They transferred the old
philologists' virtue of exactness to the things which lay immediately around them. They descended to the most insignificant facts, and approached a nonsensical sounding nursery-

rhyme as seriously as though it might contain the deepest revelations of primitive times. Their 'meditation on the insignificant,' as Wilhelm Schlegel mockingly termed it, was really the basis of their scientific greatness and the source of their popularity. They, more than any other writers, reaped what Herder had sown, and of the whole multitude of Romanticists, none, except Uhland, was so dear to the German people as the brothers Grimm.

Uhland's learned works became known, for the most part, only after his death. He was born in April 1787, and already at the University he began to turn his attention to the Nibelungenlied. It was not merely as a scholar that he approached Old-German poetry; it inspired him in his own poetic creation, and early determined his taste. His poetic talent was of advantage to him in his literary researches, as, for instance, when in his ' Walther von der Vogelweide ' he drew the first complete picture of an old German singer, or when, in the spirit of Herder, he explained the northern myths of the Thunder-God as being originally a personifying poetry of nature. He soon extended his studies to mediæval French, and he and Wilhelm Schlegel were the founders of Romance philology in Germany. What he did for the old French epics was afterward done by Friedrich Diez for the poetry and life of the Troubadours.

Study of literature. Uhland and Diez.

With Uhland and Diez also the study of literature went hand in hand with the art of translation, and Karl Simrock of Bonn, from 1827 on, did more than any other man to render Middle High-German poetry accessible to the general public through modern German versions. Philological and poetical research was pushing forward in all directions. Friedrich Schlegel had already directed his attention to India, and his brother Wilhelm and others carried on his work in this direction. Joseph von Hammer, continuing what Herder had begun, made the Germans acquainted with Persian, Arabic, and Turkish poetry; Friedrich Rückert followed in his steps and enjoyed his personal direction, but he also included Indian, Hebrew, and even Chinese literature, in the sphere of his labours, and made wonderful translations from all of them. A literary conquest seemed to

Karl Simrock.

The Schlegels, Hammer, and Rückert.

have been made both of the East and the West, and the most difficult metrical forms, rhythms and rhymes did not refuse to adapt themselves to a language which a hundred years before this was hardly able to stammer Alexandrines, and which was fain to greet a Gottsched as a welcome law-giver.

No one followed all these efforts with greater interest than Goethe ; he stood in the midst of the whole scientific movement of the nineteenth century, and at the same time retained his allegiance to the school of Herder. He was certainly not altogether free from the tendencies of the school of natural philosophy. His theory of colours was influenced by those tendencies, and gave them further encouragement. His theory of the metamorphosis of plants now first began to find general recognition. Many of the movements then stirring in Germany and elsewhere were in harmony with early ideas of Goethe's to which he had not given public utterance. The brilliant achievements of Alexander von Humboldt filled him with sympathetic admiration, and he repeatedly extended favour and tolerance to the Romanticists. The two unsuccessful dramatic productions of the brothers Schlegel, the 'Ion' of the elder brother and the 'Alarcos' of the younger, were, through Goethe's recommendation, performed on the Weimar stage even in the lifetime of Schiller. He was much gratified by the dedication of the 'Wunderhorn' to himself, and gave his full approval to the work. He read extracts from the Nibelungenlied in his own circle of friends. In his Masque entitled 'Romantic poetry,' produced in 1810, he introduced characters drawn from old German poetry. He showed his sympathy with the Romanticist enthusiasm for old German stories by publishing at this time the first part of 'Faust,'—a work which he had begun in early years in an outburst of national enthusiasm, and whose appearance now threw into the shade all other attempts at modernising or · reshaping old German legends. But there is one point which caused him serious anxiety. He could not bear to see Mediævalism acquiring ever greater power not only in historical interests, but in art, religion and life. The faithful Meyer was compelled, in 1807, to declare war in the name of the joint-firm of the Weimar

Goethe's sympathy with the tendencies of this period.

friends of art against the modern German school of religious
patriotic art, and against all canting piety. Goethe himself celebrated
the Reformation tercentenary by some warning anti-papistical
verses, appealing to all Germans to take care that the old enemy
should gain no advantage, and ending with the assurance :

> 'Auch ich soll gottgegebne Kraft nicht ungenützt verlieren
> Und will in Kunst und Wissenschaft wie immer protestiren.'

His scientific activity had in this century taken a perceptibly historical and critical direction. Political history, indeed, he
hardly touched upon, except in a few isolated instances.
But he now followed up his book on Winckelmann with
his 'History of the Theory of Colour,' and with several
writings on the history of literature. His translation of
Diderot's dialogue, 'Rameau's Nephew,' was accompanied by an
excellent analysis of the French spirit in the eighteenth century.
He now began to concern himself more with his own history and
past productions. Between the years 1806 and 1808 he published
an edition of his works in twelve volumes ; between 1815 and 1819
one in twenty volumes, and between 1827 and 1830 one in forty
volumes, each time making fresh additions. In connection with the
first edition he began writing 'Wahrheit und Dichtung,' in which he
made the history of literature in the eighteenth century a background
for the history of his own youth. While such a thoughtful investigator
of human nature as Wilhelm von Humboldt considered
genius to be inexplicable, Goethe undertook in this book
to trace the connection of cause and effect, and to explain how he had come to be what he was. This autobiography was a scientific achievement of the highest
order, and, at least in the three first volumes of 1811,
1812, and 1814, a masterpiece of historical art. It is charmingly told,
and the composition is most successful, with its apparently fortuitous,
but in reality cleverly contrived transitions and divisions. It is rich
in characters and events, and the interest never flags for a moment.
The fourth volume, published from Goethe's literary remains, contains in part disconnected materials, not yet artistically worked up.
Further records of his life are furnished in his reports of his Italian

His scientific and literary studies.

'Wahrheit und Dichtung' and other autobiographical works.

journey, in the war reports of 1792 and 1793, in the 'History of
my Botanical Studies,' in the 'Day and Year-books,' in his pub-
Essays on lished correspondence with Schiller, and elsewhere.
Oriental He gave an account of his oriental studies in the pre-
literature. fatory essays to his 'West-eastern Divan,' which contain valuable contributions to the knowledge of the oriental literatures, reports on oriental research in general, besides æsthetic and
Maxims. philosophic opinions. In later life he was fond of
putting down in short maxims and reflections the sum
of his thoughts on various subjects, and to this habit we owe many
precious sayings, highly suggestive and full of the deepest wisdom
and loftiest ideas.

In 1804 a chance occurrence made him return to criticism, which
Goethe's he had really given up since 1772, in which year he
journalistic contributed with Merck and Herder to the 'Frankfurter
work, 1804. gelehrten Anzeigen.' The editors of the 'Allgemeine
Litteraturzeitung' left Jena, and took their journal with them.
Goethe at once wished to replace it, and called a new critical review
into existence, in connection with which he developed marvellous
journalistic skill, and showed the greatest energy and talent for
organization. In articles of his own he furnished some splendid
models of objective literary criticism; he did justice equally to
'Über Kunst Voss' poems and to the 'Wunderhorn.' Later on he
und used his publications on 'Art and Antiquity,' which he
Alterthum,' began in 1816 and continued to his death, as a vehicle
1816-1832. for encouraging young talents, attacking false tendencies,
and showing his sympathy with German and foreign literary productions by means of reviews, notices, quotations and translations.
In these papers he welcomed Rückert and Platen, Manzoni and
Byron, Tegnér and the French Romanticists. In these he expressed his delight with the historical works of Niebuhr, Schlosser,
and Friedrich von Raumer; in these he published some of Jacob
Grimm's translations from the Serbian, and repeatedly manifested his
deep interest in the popular poetry of all nations. In these he
uttered the hope that Germany might through its zealous activity in
translation become, in a measure, the market of universal literature,
and that foreign nations would learn German in order to gain

access to the intellectual achievements of so many ancient and modern nations.

The sympathy which he extended on all sides was richly requited. He was in regular correspondence with Berlin ; friends of his took care that no important work which appeared in the Prussian capital should escape his notice, and that his words of approbation should not fail to reach and delight the authors. French, English, Italian, and Polish poets paid him their homage in person and from afar. He was, as it were, the president of the European republic of letters, and he placed his nation at the head of the intellectual movement of the century.

Goethe's large correspondence.

Lyric Poetry.

We can hardly doubt that the advance of science and learning which we have noticed, together with the increase of religiosity and the strong development of political activity, gradually undermined the power of German poetry in the nineteenth century as in the thirteenth and weakened the nation's sympathy for serious poetic efforts. But in the first decades of this century, lyrical poetry at least developed a wealth of individuality and style, of subject and form, a depth of feeling and variety of expression far above anything achieved by the Minnesingers, and unparalleled in any other literature.

German lyric poetry in the beginning of this century.

The leading contrasts of the older German lyric poetry were almost typically expressed in Hagedorn and Haller. The bright light poetry of the former was continued by the Anacreontic poets, the serious and weighty poetry of the latter by Klopstock and his school. The Anacreontic poets remained in sympathy with the witty, trivial French poetry, and specially favoured the idyll and the burlesque satire; Klopstock and his followers were admirers of Young's melancholy 'Night Thoughts,' and of the misty world of Ossian, and inclined to elegy and biting satire. The former praised in their didactic poems the earthly paradise of moderation; the latter dwelt on the sublime awfulness of death, and opened out vistas of eternity. These

The Anacreontic poets, and the school of Klopstock.

contrasts were not strictly marked in every poet, and they were sometimes united in the same person. Goethe began as an Anacreontic poet, and Schiller followed in the steps of Haller; but each of these poets drew suggestions from many different sources and each developed his own individual style. They were both able to do justice to various metres and various styles, without ever sinking to the level of mere imitators.

Anacreontic poetry really decayed in the eighteenth century, even though many of its representatives lived on into the nineteenth. Georg Jacobi produced a few very beautiful songs, pure in form and sentiment. Klamer Schmidt, of Halberstadt, acquired some fame about 1770 as an imitator of Petrarch and Catullus and as the author of rather trivial versified epistles, chiefly remarkable for the ingenuity of their rhyming.

Anacreontic poetry. G. Jacobi, Schmidt, G. von Göckingk, Gotter, Tiedge.

Günther von Göckingk wrote some poetic epistles somewhat richer in matter and thought than Schmidt's; his songs between two lovers form a complete romance, often showing great dramatic power. Friedrich Wilhelm Gotter of Gotha was a thorough disciple of the French school, and one of the last representatives of the Alexandrine tragedy; he also distinguished himself by writing epistles, in which clever rhyming takes the place of creative power. August Tiedge was a writer of epistles like Gleim and his friends, to whose band he belonged; in his language he rather reminds us of Schiller, and in his elegies and his 'Urania,' (1801) a lyrico-didactic poem on God, Immortality and Liberty, he takes us back to Klopstock and Haller.

Friedrich Matthison was decidedly of the school of Klopstock, Hölty, and Ossian; he became known about 1780, and was esteemed as a sentimental poetical landscape-painter, and even praised by Schiller. In his 'Elegy written in the ruins of an old castle,' he paints the life of chivalry and revels in the thought of the past. His 'Lake of Geneva' is written in praise of the district which was the cradle of the modern romantic feeling for nature, and in a truly Klopstockian manner introduces allusions to distant times and things. His 'Distichs from Italy' are

School of Klopstock. Matthison, Salis, Friederike Brun, Baggesen.

more graphic and animated, and may be compared with Goethe's
Roman Elegies and Venetian Epigrams. Baron von Salis and
Friederike Brun were connected with Matthison by personal
friendship, and their poetic productions also are akin to his. The
Dane Jens Baggesen, through his idyllic epic 'Parthenais' (1802),
joined in the worship of Switzerland; he transferred the Greek
gods to the mountains of the Bernese Oberland, and importuned
them with the little journeys and love-experiences of contemporary
people. Schiller's Swabian countrymen too, Conz, Neuffer and Hölderlin, cultivated natural description and classical forms. Neuffer tried his hand at the idyll after Voss'
model, and the unhappy Hölderlin, who ended in madness, sang
a few most affecting songs.

Hölderlin was born in 1770, and in Tübingen, as a fellow-student with Hegel and Schelling, he became an
ardent pantheist and at the same time an enthusiastic
admirer of the old Greek world. His romance 'Hyperion' and
his unfinished tragedy 'Empedocles' are only the expression of
his personal sentiments; epic and dramatic poetry are with him
only masks for lyric poetry. He is as unwilling as Klopstock to
touch the earth. Schiller had the greatest influence on him, and
his earliest rhymed stanzas do homage, in rhetoric very similar to
Schiller's, to the usual ideals of enthusiastic youth. But his rhyme-less odes and free rhythms, his distichs and hexameters which were
written between 1796 and 1801, show us an original genius of high
power, inspired by the Hellenic spirit. His art ripened into a calm
beauty. His disappointment in love found expression in his poetry,
and his songs were short, like his happiness. Deep sorrow quivers
beneath his quiet words; inward and outward incidents, psychological
experiences and natural description are united in harmony; his
exact observation of outward nature acquires, like Goethe's, a sym-bolical character. Definite outlines are not wanting in his land-scapes; he has given us a clear and faithful picture of Heidelberg
in a poem which also contains a most exquisite description of the
approach of the starry night. But he prefers to revel in vague
feelings and emotions. He worships the grandeur of nature with
the piety of a Greek, and mentions the names of the gods with

Conz and Neuffer.

Hölderlin.

awe. 'Hyperion's Song of Fate' pictures with bitterness the contrast between the blessed spirits up on high in light, and suffering men below, falling blindly from one hour to another, like water hurled from cliff to cliff, for years and years down into uncertainty. But Hölderlin is also much impressed by the life and character of Jesus, the friend of man; the thought of him recalls remembrances of home and childhood, and, as in days gone by, he finds tears of comfort dropping from his eyes.

Hölderlin, Voss, and Claudius, were all three religious-minded men, though the first was a pantheist, the second a rationalist, and the third orthodox. Voss was really a disciple of Klopstock, but the poetry of domestic life, which he shared with Claudius, quite brought him down to the earth, and his popular songs place him by the side of an Anacreontic poet, like Christian Felix Weisse. Hebel's 'Alemannic poems' (1803) may be classed together with Voss'

Hebel's 'Alemannische' Gedichte. Low-German idylls, while his prose-writings, his 'Tales of the Rhenish Family Friend' and his 'Biblical stories for young people,' belong to the same group as Claudius' popular works. Hebel was a clergyman and schoolmaster in Karlsruhe, but his birthplace was a village in the highlands of Baden; the 'Alemannic poems' are written in the dialect of that district, and the characters are also drawn from the life which the poet had known there. We have noticed how Goethe drew suggestions for his idyllic descriptions from the Old Testament; Hebel proceeded in an exactly opposite manner. For instance, he transferred the story of David's adventure with Nabal and Abigail into contemporary peasant life, and made out of it his 'Stadthalter von Schopfheim.' While the poetic landscape-painters too often gave a mere lifeless description of nature with a few slightly connected incidents, Hebel succeeded in animating nature by naively humanising it in the manner which Herder had conjecturally attributed to primitive times, and thus created a peculiar mythology of his own, introducing all the features of peasant life. He drew little scenes from real life with a sure hand and with bright humour. He is fond of putting songs in the mouth of some special character, such as a contented peasant, a youth in love, a beggar or a nightwatchman, and he likes to reproduce a conversation between a

mother and her children, or a father and his sons.   Herein also
he continued the style of Claudius, and the poets of the Göttingen
'Hain,' but he surpassed them all by his deep sympathy with the
thoughts and interests of the people.

Hebel's example exercised an influence on the thoughtful artist
soul of Martin Usteri, the author of a song which was   Usteri's
formerly very popular in Germany, 'Freut euch des Swiss poems.
Lebens.' Usteri used his native Zurich dialect in songs and hexametric idylls, and also wrote ballads and historical romances in the
old Swiss German.   He was a moderate romanticist, who knew
how to touch and amuse his readers better than many a pretentious
poet of greater fame.

Poetry in dialect became a general fashion about the beginning
of the century.   Some time before this, the tin-mer- Other poems
chant Konrad Grübel of Nürnberg had published in dialect.
a collection of poems describing the Philistinism of   Grübel
small towns in a style which reminds one of the Nürn- and Sailer.
berg shoemaker, Hans Sachs; and still earlier the Catholic priest
Sebastian Sailer had written his delightful dramas in the Swabian
dialect which were now for the first time collected and printed.
Professor Arnold of Strassburg wrote a dramatic idyll in the Alsatian dialect entitled 'Whit-Monday,' and his example   Arnold,
was followed by Castelli in Vienna, and by Holtei in Castelli, and
Silesia.   Most of these attempts were introduced to   Holtei.
the German public through Goethe's recommendation.   Thus there
arose a new kind of popular poetry, rather different, it is true, from
the old traditional popular poetry which Romanticism had brought
into new honour.

The older romantic school produced little of lasting merit in
lyric poetry.   Novalis was their best lyric poet, and   Lyric poets
he died in 1801, at the early age of 29.   Over the   of the
grave of his bride he sang from the depths of his   romantic
sorrow his marvellous 'Hymns to Night;' they are   school.
not written in strict metre, but in melodious prose   Novalis.
which reminds us of the rendering of Ossian in Goethe's 'Werther.'
Novalis' religious hymns show us a basis of Moravian piety influenced by Schleiermacher's addresses on religion; they are a noble

expression of a childlike love of Christ, a simple faith in the real presence of the Saviour, independent of any fixed creed. Here we find thoughts from Goethe christianised, and secular things treated in a religious spirit, in a manner akin to Paul Gerhardt's. These hymns are all written in rhymed verse, except one hymn in rhymeless metre, which reminds us of some of the Pindaric poetry of Goethe's youth, or of Faust's words to Gretchen about the all-embracing, all-sustaining deity.

Tieck threw off his productions with a light hand, and was content with the first draught. He had great talent, but was wanting in seriousness and thoroughness. His poems are full of obscurities and incorrectnesses, empty jingling rhymes and trivial thoughts; there is a lavish display of figurative language and poetic ideas, and all to illustrate passing moods, for from the depth of the heart he has little to tell us. He seems to care more about sound than sense in his poetry, and this often leads him into mere absurdity. The poems written during his travels in 1805 and 1806 are on a somewhat higher level than the rest. The free unrhymed metres in these poems sometimes approach hexameters, and the sculpture-like descriptions occasionally remind us of Goethe. But Tieck's enthusiasm for art and antiquity is less successful than his observation of the life going on immediately around him, street-scenes, beggars, pilgrims and such-like; in his descriptions of these we find what we miss so much in most of his poetry, i. e. a connected course of action, an attempt at dramatic plot.

While Tieck mostly excites mere vague emotions, Wilhelm Schlegel, on the contrary, is wanting in all force of emotion; he is always correct, but often cold and dull. His love-poems are full of high-sounding words and graceful thoughts, but are woefully deficient in spontaneity and dramatic power. His knowledge of Italy profited him nothing; his poems in distichs are pure Renaissance-poetry, and do not rise above the level of the better Latin elegies of the sixteenth century. His romances, on the contrary, derived great benefit from Schiller's influence, and really show some original power. He was equally successful in composing sonnets full of reflections, while he accomplished his best in a few humorous satirical poems. In this class of

poetry Friedrich Schlegel is, if we except a few clever parodies, on
the whole inferior to his brother.   But in his rhymed poems he
unites melody with feeling and correct form, and   Friedrich
sometimes gives us a definite dramatic situation.   Schlegel.

   Patriotic thoughts and imitations of older German poetry are to
be found both in Tieck and in the two Schlegels, most   Patriotic
of all in Friedrich Schlegel; but others were destined   poetry.
to greater and more lasting success in this sphere.   Wilhelm
Schlegel fully recognised the want of an energetic, sincere and
patriotic German poetry, especially at that time, when German independence seemed threatened by the conquests of Napoleon.
Schlegel's wish was to be fulfilled; Germany's need raised up a
band of patriot poets, who sang songs more powerful than any yet
produced in German literature, songs which inspired the German
people in their struggle for liberty.   ·

   Goethe did not possess the great gift of patriotic song.   He was
one of those faint-hearted ones who believed the power of the
great Napoleon to be invincible.   Younger poets attempted what
he neglected.   Patriotic poetry was produced without interruption
from 1806 to 1815, and reached its zenith in 1813 and 1814.
Achim von Arnim lamented in angry tones the Prussian defeats.   Henry Joseph von Collin published in 1809   Arnim
his Austrian 'Wehrmannslieder;' Heinrich von   and
Kleist expressed in stormy language his unbounded   Collin.
hatred of the foreigner.   Friedrich Baron de la Motte Fouqué
wrote in 1813 a war-song for the Volunteers:—
                                                   H. v. Kleist,
'Frisch auf zum fröhlichen Jagen.'   Max von Schenk-   Fouqué,
endorf was by nature a gentle lyrist with great power   Schenken-
of melodious language.   He had formed his style on   dorf,
Goethe, the popular songs and the Minnesingers, and   Stägemann.
was filled with enthusiasm for emperor and empire, for chivalry
and the Middle Ages, for the Rhine and its castles.   He followed the
course of the struggle in enthusiastic but occasionally somewhat
empty verses.   Friedrich August von Stägemann, a Prussian, like
Arnim, Kleist, Fouqué and Schenkendorf, but more vigorous than
Schenkendorf and more moderate in tone than Kleist, reminds us
sometimes of Ramler, sometimes of Schiller.   The solemn ode-

style which he adopted prevented his poems from becoming popular. Friedrich Rückert, in his 'Geharnischte Sonnete,' did not even triumph over the difficulties of rhyme. In

Rückert.

his war-songs and in his satirical and eulogistic songs he tried in vain to strike the tone of popular poetry. The intellectual element would effect an entrance where only force and passion were needed, and glorious poetic touches were often spoilt by imperfections of thought and form. Theodor Körner, 'singer and hero,' as Uhland called him, sealed with his death the

Körner.

sentiments expressed in his songs. These songs, half-lyrical, half-rhetorical in tone and set to beautiful melodies, exercised a most inspiring influence. There is no backward glance on past times here, no sentimental dreaming, but youthful energy and ardent enthusiasm in a great cause. Körner came from Dresden, but fought and fell in the Lützow Volunteer Corps. His father was Schiller's friend, and Theodor grew up in the worship of Schiller, and imbibed his lofty spirit. He became an idealist like Max

Arndt.

Piccolomini, and his patriotic views were those expressed by Schiller's Joan of Arc.

Ernst Moriz Arndt surpassed Körner and all his brother-poets both in immediate and in lasting influence. His prose and verse went straight to the German heart and conscience. He was a popular orator through his pen, and held a position in the struggle with Napoleon similar to that held by Walther von der Vogelweide in the struggle with Rome. He was spiritually akin to Luther, especially in his trust in God. Arndt was born in 1769, studied in 1793 and 1794 during Fichte's time at Jena, and watched in his early youth the dawn of Romanticism. But he was unaffected himself by the movement, for all his powers were devoted to one object from

His patriotic pamphlets.

which he never swerved—to free his country from the foreign yoke. In 1803, under the title of 'Germany and Europe,' he gave a description of the state of things in 1802. Three years later he began his 'Spirit of the Times,' and in 1812, together with Baron von Stein, he joined the European movement against Napoleon. He then sent forth a number of pamphlets, the 'Catechism for the German warrior and defender,' 'What means Landsturm and

Landwehr?' 'The Rhine Germany's stream, but not Germany's
boundary,' 'Prussia's Rhenish Mark,' and many others, all full of
life and ardour, of faith and hope.   The first in particular is most
grand, with its Biblical style and prophetic tone.   They all express
enthusiasm for Prussia, though their author was really a native of
Rügen, which was at that time still Swedish.   At the same time
Arndt wrote his most beautiful songs.   In celebrating the German
heroes, Schill, Dörnberg, Gneisenan, Chasot, he
adopted the graphic style of the older historical   His songs.
popular songs, and was fond of beginning with a question (cf. in
particular his songs: 'Was ist des Deutschen Vaterland?' and
'Was blasen die Trompeten?')   He describes the battle of Leipzig
after the manner of some old German gleeman's songs, in the form
of alternate question and answer between those who have been
waiting for news and the messenger from the battle-field.   Besides
his war-songs, Arndt also wrote popular love-songs, parting-songs
and cradle-songs, and lifted up his soul with simple piety to God
in prayer.   He produced splendid social and drinking-songs, and
as a riper successor of the Göttingen tyrant-haters, he gave utterance to the grand chorus:

> 'Der Gott der Eisen wachsen liess
> Der wollte keine Knechte.'

After the peace he was made professor of modern history in
Bonn.   But before long he became implicated in the   Arndt
wretched political persecutions; his papers were   Professor
taken possession of and he was deprived of his office.   in Bonn.
It was not till after the accession of King Frederick   Died 1860.
William IV that this wrong was repaired; in 1840 the old man
was allowed to resume his professorial duties, and he continued to
fulfil them till 1854.   He lived on till 1860, bright and happy to
the last.   In his delightful autobiography he remarks: 'Man is
happy according to the measure of his most powerful feelings, that
is to say, if his feeling is of such a nature as not to overpower
his reason.'   Arndt's breast was dominated by powerful emotion in
the days of trouble, but his clear reason was never led astray.   He
was a sterling man in heart and brain, like the brothers Grimm,
not a scholar by nature, and not like the Grimms sprung from the

educated classes, but a peasant by birth and in constant sympathy with the peasants.

The tone given to poetry by the Wars of Liberation lived on The 'Bur- among the youth of the Universities and among the schenschaft.' gymnastic societies. The revolutionary extravagances of the Göttingen band of poets revived again in a more serious form in the students' associations (*Burschenschaft*). Karl Follenius composed his ' great song,' in which he gave utterance to the following vow : ' This sword shall know no rest till all those princes and fathers, taskmasters, slaves, and traitors are covered by earth and night.' But these students' associations were soon suppressed, and their elegy was sung by August Binzer in his poem :—' Wir hatten gebauet ein stattliches Haus.'

About the same time the name of Uhland became famous. His Uhland's poems which he had begun to publish in 1806 did not early poems appear in a complete collection till 1815. The and his two ' Fatherland poems,' which were called forth by the dramas. Würtemberg constitutional struggle, appeared in 1816, and in an enlarged edition in 1817. In 1818 and 1819 he published his two dramas : ' Ernst, Duke of Swabia,' and ' Louis the Bavarian ; ' they were both beautiful poems, but never achieved a success on the stage, nor indeed deserved to achieve it.

Uhland, Justinus Kerner and a few others formed the so-called The new Swabian school. They were on an average about romantic or thirty years younger than their countryman Schiller, Swabian and about twenty years younger than their countryman school. Hölderlin, who lived on among them for a long time with a mind shrouded in darkness. Uhland and Kerner appeared before the public together; they both contributed to the ' Hermit's Newspaper,' and they form one group with Arnim and Brentano.

Arnim and The love of popular songs was the bond which united Brentano. these poets. But Arnim and Brentano rendered greater service to German literature through the publication of the ' Wunderhorn ' than through their own original productions. Brentano was a master in all the technique of popular song, though he was deficient in real sympathy with the public, so that few of his songs penetrated into wider circles. In Arnim's poems we seldom find one that is not spoilt by some obscurity or caprice, a pun in the wrong place, a prosaic expression, or forced rhymes.

Justinus Kerner sang his songs as naturally and artlessly as Arnim, but he was most successful in hitting the true tone of popular song. Poetry was part of his being; he possessed in the highest degree the talent of poeticising his own experiences. The letters to his affianced bride are particularly charming in their *abandon* and their wild fancy. Life and death, humour and madness meet us in close connection in Kerner's writings. His doctor's vocation did not blunt his sympathy for the sufferings of humanity. Though there is often an echo of sadness in his songs, yet he can also rise to a level of sublime grandeur. In reading some of his descriptions of nature, we seem to stand again on the primitive soil from which in past times mythology grew up.

Justinus
Kerner.

In contrast to Kerner, his friend Uhland was silent and repellant, and entirely wanting in all charm of poetic personality. Little of his personal experience seems to have found expression in his poetry. But he had the advantage over Kerner in sure taste, and in that stern industry which does not rest till all the demands of good taste are fulfilled. Kerner declared that neither art nor learning had helped him in writing his songs, but only his own feelings. Uhland, on the contrary, possessed both learning and art, and these two gifts made him, with lesser poetic talent, the greater poet of the two. He had little originality and his songs are confined to a limited number of subjects; we find comparatively little about love in them, more about scenery, times and seasons, wanderings and various stereotyped ideas. He cannot strike passionate but only gentle tones, and he too is constantly recurring to thoughts of death, and is fond of giving his poems a melancholy ending. He was most successful in his development of the ballad, for which his extensive learning supplied him with the best subjects. He began to write ballads in 1803, and in his earliest attempts in this branch of poetry we can clearly trace the influence of Klopstock, Matthison and Ossian, while the Northern Sagas also supplied him with some of his first subjects. He next gave himself up to a

Uhland
(1787-1862).

His ballads.

trivial kind of romanticism, full of sadness and renunciation, and wrote ballads in which kings and queens with crimson mantles and golden crowns, king's daughters and beautiful shepherds, harpers, monks and nuns play a great part. But he was already beginning to feel the influence of Goethe, and after 1807 the 'Wunderhorn' furnished him with poetic ideas, while the popular songs, the Nibelungenlied and the Spanish Romances determined his style and language. His sentimentality now disappeared and his poems assumed a more cheerful character. Most of his ballads of this period are full of chivalrous adventure and strong passions, while a few introduce some truly popular characters ('Des Goldschmied's Töchterlein,' 'Der gute Kamerad'). In 1810 Uhland went to Paris, and there acquired a comprehensive knowledge of the Middle Ages, which found expression in his poems. The German and French heroic legends, Norman traditions, the biographies of the Troubadours were now all made to yield him subjects for poetic treatment. He could represent with graphic power both the gallant and the coarse type of chivalry ; he was even successful in the humorous vein, and the summit of his powers was reached in his poem 'Taillefer,' which

His 'Taillefer,' patriotic poetry, and 'Schwä-bische Kunde.'
appeared in 1812. From 1813 to 1817 his poetry was almost entirely patriotic in character, being chiefly called forth by the battle for right against arbitrary power in the Würtemberg constitutional struggle. Even his ballads assumed at this time a local and patriotic colouring, and this tendency resulted in such splendid productions as his dryly humorous 'Swabian News.' In later years his poetic inspiration seemed to dry up entirely, and though he wrote a few poems in 1829 and 1834, yet when he died in 1862, his death could hardly be felt as a loss to German poetry, but only to German learning.

Uhland's method and style.
Uhland's method of treatment in all his poems deserves great praise. The easy volubility of his early poems soon gave place to emphatic conciseness. Many of his songs, it is true, are too much taken up with detailed description, but others show us real progress of action, and a few at least present a definite situation. In his ballads he shows a

complete mastery of all metres and styles, and is equally successful in suggestive brevity and in epic minuteness of detail.   He gives to every subject its suitable form, is seldom obscure or stilted, and always attains the purpose he has in view.   No one can deny his complete mastery of the poetic art.   The Romantic movement, like the earlier 'Storm and Stress' movement, again called in question the standard of correctness already attained.   But Uhland re-established the old correctness of form, and became thereby a model for younger and older contemporary poets, such as Chamisso, Eichendorff, Wilhelm Müller and others.

Chamisso (1781–1838) was a French nobleman by birth, who found a new home in Berlin.   He described in a truly   **Chamisso,** German spirit the love and life of woman and home-   **1781-1838.** joys and sorrows.   His poems comprise popular songs, legends and fairy-tales, but the great movements of the time have also left some impression on them.   Such a picture from the life of the people as his 'Old Washerwoman' may have been suggested by the example of his compatriot Béranger.   He found his greatest happiness in the observation of nature ; among the semi-barbarous people with whom he was brought into contact in a journey round the world, he felt himself quite at home, and their poetry incited him to imitation.

Eichendorff came from Silesia, Wilhelm Müller from Dessau. Both fought in the wars of Liberation against France.   **Eichendorff,** Both were much influenced by the popular songs, and   **1788-1857,** wandering was a favourite subject with both, so that in   **and** them the unsettled minstrel of the Middle Ages was   **W. Müller,** revived, at least in poetic fiction.   They both liked   **1794-1827.** to write poems from the standpoint of some particular character, as Goethe, Uhland, Hebel and others sometimes did, and thus their lyric poetry introduces us to musicians, peasants, soldiers, students, sailors, huntsmen, apprentices, shepherds, or fishermen.   In 'Die Schöne Müllerin,' Müller assumed the disguise of a miller, to sing his own love-joys and love-sorrows.   But in their disposition, as well as in their religious and political views, Eichendorff and Müller were quite different.   Eichendorff was a Roman Catholic, Müller a Protestant ; the former wrote several religious poems, the latter gave but occasional expression to his deep religious sentiments. Eichendorff had a strong admiration for the Middle Ages, and placed his ideal in the past; Müller had only a literary appreciation of old German poetry, lived with enthusiasm in the present, belonged, like Chamisso, to the Liberal party, and accompanied the Greek struggle for freedom with sympathetic songs. Eichendorff affects us more powerfully than Müller, touching our imagination as with a magic wand. Müller's poems, whether joyful or sorrowful, have a ring of freshness and vivacity about them. He greeted the spring with songs of ardent rejoicing, and the style of the Anacreontic school was revived in his songs of wine and love.

Chamisso produced some glorious ballads; Eichendorff and Müller paid less attention to this branch of poetry.

Imitators of Uhland. Schwab, Ebert, Simrock. Uhland's example, however, made the ballad very popular, in fact, all too popular with some other writers. He found imitators in the Swabian Gustav Schwab, the Bohemian Egon Ebert, and the Rhenish writer, Karl Simrock. Every district of Germany sooner or later had its Uhland, who clothed its local history and legends in more or less fluent verses.

Uhland's political poetry also called forth many imitations. Graf **Political poetry.** Auersperg, who wrote under the name of Anastasius Grün, lifted up his voice on behalf of Austrian liberty. Wilhelm Müller's Greek songs found successors in Count Platen's Polish songs. The old cosmopolitan interest in foreign nations took not only a literary but also a political turn. This same interest had already led poets to lands of the distant East, far away from the tumults of modern Europe, to Persia as it was in the Middle Ages, when Hafis sang of wine and love. Rückert's 'Eastern Roses' were an offshoot from Goethe's 'West-eastern Divan.' But though Goethe might call himself Hatem, the turban was but a masque, and though he spoke of Timur, the reader might easily recognise Napoleon. As for the Suleika who answers Hatem in melodious verses, we know now that she lived in Frankfurt, that her name was Marianne von Willemer, and that two of the tenderest and most beautiful among the 'Divan' songs proceeded from her pen.

In later years Goethe was fond of having recourse to forms which impose a definite restraint on the poet. His social songs of 1803 had already shown how he welcomed external incitements to poetic creation. In the first decade of this century the sonnet-form which Bürger had so strongly favoured came into fashion with the Romantic school, and immediately the anti-Romanticists vigorously attacked it. Voss raved against it, and Baggesen published his 'Klingklingel-almanach' turning it and other Southern forms of poetry into ridicule. When the controversy was at its height Goethe began to use the same form in a cycle of sonnets, filling it with that wealth of outward action or inward emotion which came so easily to him, and which all other poets found so difficult. In 1812 and 1813 Joseph von Hammer published a translation of Hafis' 'Divan' or Collection of poems. This gave Goethe the idea for his 'Divan' which he began in 1814 and published in 1819. The poems are arranged according- Goethe's ing to a definite order in twelve books, and soar from ' West- earthly love, hatred and enjoyment to the heights of östlicher Paradise. At the end there are some short elucida- Divan.' tory essays, embracing a wide field of reflection. The whole work is, one might almost say, phenomenal, so deep and suggestive are the poet's thoughts. The Biblical writings which were the first foundation of his culture drew him to the East, and the sacred figures which he used to approach half with awe-struck reverence, half with the unhesitating familiarity of Hans Sachs, rose up before him in this work in gigantic proportions. Goethe here ventures to link the most sublime conceptions directly with matters of love, with the sadness of parting and the joy of meeting again. The songs exchanged with Suleika and the dialogues with the cup-bearer, introduce an element of dramatic life into the midst of those wide, silent spaces into which the poet leads us. Goethe pretends to be taking refuge in the East from a world in which 'thrones are falling, kingdoms trembling;' but in this eastern world it is the analogies with the West which attract him, and while calling himself a fugitive he really never leaves home. The celebrated wine of 1811 refreshes him. He introduces Napoleon's Russian campaign in a significant connection. He does homage to his duke who was one of the commanders in the allied army, and to a certain lady, by whom he probably means his own wife. He tells his nation the truth in plain-spoken terms, and distinctly declares that his business is not politics, but the moral and literary culture of the people. He reproaches the Germans for their attachment to the fashions of the day, and tells them that Teutomania is as bad as Gallomania. He stigmatises their meagre capacity for recognizing true merit, their envy, their grudging approval, all that he had himself experienced. He calls the attention of the critics to the one thing needful: Respect for the man who understands his *métier*, and a thorough understand-ing of the purposes of the author before attempting to blame him. The foreign dress is throughout but a slight disguise; the style of Persian poetry is imitated, but never too slavishly, by pregnant sayings and surprising combinations; the Oriental element pene-trates the Western element like a rare perfume, without altering it in substance. Islamism is assumed to be the dominant religion, but behind it there appears the old Persian Nature-worship, just as Goethe's Pantheism appears behind Christianity; and we are re-minded of Goethe's own chastening through hard service, when we find him sympathising with the purity of the old Persians which sprang from their sun-worship, and putting these words into the mouth of a religious man on his death-bed:—

> 'Und nun sei ein heiliges Vermächtniss
> Brüderlichem Wollen und Gedächtniss:
> Schwerer Dienste tägliche Bewahrung,
> Sonst bedarf es keiner Offenbarung.'

In later years Goethe made some additions to the 'Divan,' among them, the charming dialogues between the poet and the Houri, in which he demands an entry into Paradise, and brings forward this reason for his claim: 'For I have been a man, and that means I have struggled.' In these later poems, too, he develops the thought which he had expressed in the opening poem of his 'Divan'—'That poet's words float ever round the gate of Paradise, gently knocking for entrance, and praying for eternal life.' But side by side with the 'Divan' Goethe also pro-duced at this time poems free from the Oriental masque, and which affect us with the strong thrill of reality. The relation to Suleika represented a friendship which might venture to dally with the semblance of love. But in the summer of 1823, the old man was once more the victim of a deep passion, which overpowered his

[margin note] Later additions to the 'Divan.'

whole being, and the memory of which he enshrined for pos‑ terity in the Marienbad 'Elegy,' the most complete love-poem that we have from his pen. It occupies the middle place in the so-called 'Trilogy of Passion.' There are a few rather obscure passages in it, as in the 'Divan,' but to the appreciative mind it is a priceless poem, drawing tears to the eyes, yet soothing grief. Here, too, love is linked with the highest religious and moral thoughts ; we have a characterization of the beloved one, scenes from the life of love, outward and inward incident, now memory of the past, now a picture of the present ; observation of nature and emotions of the heart, individual and typical elements are marvellously blended, and this mysterious yet lucid poem is artistically completed by two others, which raise the whole Trilogy to a more ideal level, and allow the discord to resolve itself into a final harmony.

'Trilogie der Leidenschaft.'

Reflection becomes old age better than love ; and so in later years Goethe produced numerous aphorisms like those with which the 'Divan' is so richly stored. These sayings, para- bolical, epigrammatical, or gnomic, were the last results of Goethe's thinking, and are full of deep wisdom, constituting the final outcome of his poetry just as the maxims and reflections do of his prose.

Goethe's Aphorisms.

All the authors around Goethe were more or less directly in- fluenced by and indebted to him. Thus the 'Divan' exercised a great power both over Rückert and Platen. Rückert's 'Östliche Rosen' appeared in 1822, Platen's first 'Ghaselen' in 1821. Both these writers imitated the Persian form of the Ghasel more closely than Goethe. Both brought the outward poetic form to the highest perfection, but with this difference—that Rückert improvised, while Platen filed and polished ; in Rückert, therefore, as in Tieck, we often find a want of artistic completeness, whereas with Platen this is never the case. Friedrich Rückert lived from 1788 to 1866, Count Platen from 1796 to 1835. They were both Franconians, Rückert being born at Schweinfurt, Platen at Ans- bach. Rückert's was a contented, Platen's a discontented nature, Rückert lived and died happily in his own country, which he

Rückert (1788–1866) and Platen (1796–1835).

had never left but for short journeys; fortune drove Platen to foreign parts, to the South, where he lies buried in Syracuse. Of the two Rückert was by temperament an idyllic poet, Platen a satirist.

Rückert began to write poetry in 1807. Like other poets of the time he loved to endow Nature with life and personality, but it was not the sublimer aspects of nature that attracted him so much as the trifling details of domestic life, or the fancies of **Rückert's** legend and fairy-tale. His poetry offers frequent **poetry.** parallels between nature and the inner life, supplying the germs for parables. His chief faults are : first, the somewhat doubtful taste with which he introduces into his lyric poetry witticisms, reflections, and many ideas and forms of expression only fit for prose; and secondly, his excessive accumulation of metaphors. We can understand why eastern poets were such congenial models to Rückert, for their imagination, as Goethe says, could make anything suggest anything else in heaven or earth; they are accustomed to link ideas together that have no kinship with one another, and they have no power of distinguishing the suitable from the unsuitable, in consequence of which their poems have a patchwork look, as if anything had been put down which fitted in with the rhyme.

Shortly after Rückert had published his 'Eastern Roses,' he described in 'Love's Spring' the feelings of his own time of court-**His** ship. This collection of 350 poems contains a few **'Liebes-** really touching strains full of deep emotion, and a few **frühling.'** enthusiastic and hyperbolical songs written in the strong rush of exalted feeling, and heaping all possible virtues and graces on his beloved ; but with the exception of these the book contains nothing but empty verbiage and rhymed jingle, such as we find in many of the Minnesingers of the thirteenth century. The cycle **His** of sonnets entitled 'Amaryllis' impresses us much **'Amaryllis.'** more favourably as a whole; they were written in the summer of 1812, and were inspired by a capricious innkeeper's daughter, whose real name was Marielies. Here we find what we miss so much in 'Love's Spring,' namely, dramatic scene and action, life-like characterization of the beloved one, in a word, fact and reality instead of mere lyrical effusion, artistic power as well as depth of emotion. Rückert's best poems are some of his shortest, some of the Siciliennes, Ritornelles and Quatrains appended to his 'Amaryllis;' the somewhat limited scope of these forms ensured artistic perfection.

Rückert established his poetic fancy in the Eastern land of marvels, and never tired of making translations and versions of Eastern poems, and of presenting his own philosophy in poetic form as 'The Wisdom of the Brahman.' Platen, on the contrary, made few excursions into the realms of Eastern poetry. Besides the modern rhymed stanzas he, like Klopstock, employed classical metres and completely mastered some of the most difficult of them. The smallest poems that proceeded from his pen bear, if not in their first, yet always in their last form, the stamp of perfection. He is always guided by good taste except in those passages in his poems where he speaks of himself. He was so hardy as to try to compete with Goethe in the province of lyric poetry, and indeed he is worthy to be measured by the same standard as Goethe, though he has nowhere attained to Goethe's perfection. He has nowhere touched the inmost secrets of the heart which Goethe so often reveals with such magic power. None of his poems stir our soul to its depths except perhaps the short one beginning: 'Die Liebe hat gelogen.' Platen's lyric poetry is not rich in action, and even his ballads for the most part only set forth a single situation. Pictures of country and town he has drawn with masterly skill, but he is deficient in loving sympathy with human existence as it is. He sometimes reminds us of Schiller's pessimistic satirical humour, as when we find him declaring poetry to be the counterpart of discordant reality. He shows his strength most in angry or scornful attack, whether on Napoleon or Russia, whether on the Jesuits or on the Illuminati, whether on the taste of the previous century or on Romanticism. His anti-romantic comedies (see p. 306) are full of powerful characters, creations of his hatred and contempt.

It was no wonder that Platen, as an enemy of Romanticism, counted among his opponents the railing spirit of Heinrich Heine.

Heine was born in 1799 in Düsseldorf. He studied in Bonn under

Heine.

Wilhelm Schlegel, whom he glorified in sonnets just as, at an earlier date, Wilhelm Schlegel himself had sung the praises of Bürger. Heine was a thorough Romanticist. He modelled his first poems of 1822 on the old Minnesongs, as is shown by the frequent archaisms they contain. He transported himself into mediæval times, and praised the Rhine like Schenkendorf. He wrote sentimental romances of that superficial kind which Uhland had quickly laid aside. He loved to speak of death like Justinus Kerner, and was in all respects one of those poets of ' Weltschmerz ' and moral laxity who worshipped Lord Byron as their spiritual father, and who soon became the fashion throughout Europe. In this respect, too, Heine was faithful to the traditions of the older Romanticists.

Like Brentano, Uhland, Eichendorff and Wilhelm Müller, Heine studied the popular songs, and the ' Wunderhorn ' was the basis of his poetic culture as it had been of theirs. He never tried his hand at classical, rhymeless, rhythmically strict metres; he borrowed from the popular songs the somewhat careless metrical form as well as the vivid dramatic colouring which contrasts so strongly with Platen's delicate and refined drawing. He never assumed a fictitious character in his poems as Uhland, Müller and Platen so often

Heine and Brentano compared.

did, but as a rule communicated to his readers his own feelings and experiences in his own person. He is perhaps most closely akin to Clemens Brentano, from whom he is chiefly distinguished by this, that he understands what is effective, and is deterred by no scruple of shame from producing the effect which he wishes. He always keeps in view his audience, to whose noble or low instincts, as it may be, he wishes to appeal. Brentano, on the contrary, wrote first and foremost for his own satisfaction. There is nothing which exemplifies more clearly the increased literary skill of the later Romantic School than Heine's song of the ' Loreley.' This story of the fair enchantress on the Rhine is not really a popular legend, but was created by Brentano, who first brought it before the public in 1802 in the form of a ballad inserted in a novel and beginning :—' Zu Bacherach am Rheine.' Heine took hold of the theme, and in six verses worked it up into a complete epic and lyric whole. These stanzas, set to a sentimental melody, have established themselves as a popular song, and thus Heine by a bit of skilful manipulation reaped what Brentano had sown. Like Brentano, Heine was intended to go into business, but unable to endure the life, he soon, though without having pursued any regular studies, devoted himself exclusively to poetry. With Heine as with Brentano the contrast between the prose of business-interests and the inner life of imagination, the sharp collision of the finite with the infinite, seems to have exercised a marked influence on his whole character as a man and as a poet. Like Brentano he created for himself a fabulous world out of materials partly derived from his own experience and partly invented. Brentano had already set the example of lying unscrupulously in his conversation and in letters for the sake of producing a comic effect, and Heine found in such lying a favourite and infallible method of conducting public controversy. Again, Heine loves to destroy by a jest the sentimental mood which he has excited, and seems even to mock at his own emotion ; and this feature, too, is to be found in Brentano, who, for instance, would end a solemn hymn to the gods with the confession, 'Know that I'm hungry,' or who, as Tieck narrates, loved to move women to tears by remorseful self-accusations, and would then laugh at them as ' geese ' for believing all he said. But in this Heine was only pursuing to its last results a principle of Romanticism which had originated in the previous century. Since Addison and others, Socrates had been an ideal of European authors, and Socratic irony   Irony of an object of their aspiration. Authors would treat   Heine. their heroes with a kind of smiling superiority, and loved in particular to affect the superior wisdom of the man of the world who has outgrown the extravagant ideals of youth. Friedrich Schlegel discovered irony in Goethe's ' Wilhelm Meister,' and demanded irony of every perfect poet : this irony he sometimes defined as analogous to the Socratic mingling of jest and earnest, sometimes as a ' constant self-parody,' sometimes as a ' transcendental buffoonery,' sometimes as ' the clear consciousness which abides amid the perpetual flux of ever-brimming chaos.' This ideal of self-parody was realised by the Romanticists and established itself firmly in the humorous literature of the time; but by no one was it so consistently pursued as by Heinrich Heine. Even to his most serious poems he will give such a sudden and exaggerated turn, that innocent souls, who take him seriously, will be all the more deeply affected, while the less innocent think they hear an aside of superior intelligence whispering : ' stupid geese to believe all I say.'

The humanistic poets of the sixteenth century were fond of writing poetical descriptions of travels. In the eigh-

Accounts of travels. Goethe, G. Jacobi. teenth century Laurence Sterne's 'Sentimental Journey' was much admired and imitated, and furnished German lyric poets in particular with a convenient device for connecting their personal feelings with outward objects and trivial incidents. Between these narratives after the manner of Sterne, and the scientific accounts of travels penned by an Alexander von Humboldt and his predecessors and successors, there are many grades, and German writers ranged up and down the whole scale, from the most extreme subjectivity to the strictest objectivity. In Goethe's records of his two Swiss journeys taken, the one in 1775, the other in 1779 (see p. 161), we have both extremes conjoined. The lyric poet, Georg Jacobi, copied Sterne in a ' Summer Journey' and a ' Winter Journey.' Fritz Stolberg published ' Travels in Germany, Switzerland, Italy, and Sicily.' Moritz August

F. Stolberg, Thümmel, Arndt, Seume, Kerner, Chamisso, etc. von Thümmel, the author of ' Wilhelmine,' wrote a very entertaining and enlightened account of a 'Journey in the southern provinces of France.' Ernst Moriz Arndt repeatedly published narratives of his many journeys and wanderings. In the beginning of the century Gottfried Seume described his 'Tour to Syracuse.' Justinus Kerner delighted his friends by his highly original ' Reiseschatten von dem Schattenspieler Luchs.' Adalbert von Chamisso described his journey round the world from the point of view of the man of science and of the poet. Matthison, Baggesen, Tieck, Wilhelm Müller and Platen, all produced memorials in

Heine's ' Reisebilder.' poetry or prose of various journeys to Switzerland and Italy. Heine followed with his ' Reisebilder,' which appeared from 1826 to 1831, and had an extraordinary success. In this book the genuine descriptions of scenery, and above all the North Sea pictures sometimes reveal a real power of observation and expression, at other times a grotesque mythologising fancy. In the rest of the book, however, and particularly in the much admired section on Italy, we have not much more than an imitation of Sterne's 'Sentimental Journey.' There is the same cobweb of individualism spun over external objects, the same political gossip of the emptiest nature, along with a poetic conception of the world almost as meagre as Klopstock's, and reiterated till we are tired of it. The real is tricked out with or supplanted by the unreal, lifeless things are represented as animated, living things imagined as dead, while dreams and reality are indistinguishably mingled; the poet and nature reflect each other; a spirit of melancholy pervades all things, and is revealed particularly in black eyes. These flowers have no fragrance for us; they are, as it were, faded after a night of revelry. The filth alone, of which there is enough in the 'Pictures of Travel,' is as filthy as ever it was. What a contrast have we in this book of Heine's with the calm, pure outlook maintained by Goethe as he journeyed through Italy !

Still the names of Goethe and Heine must always be mentioned together in connection with German lyric poetry. Heine is one of the most fruitful among German song-writers, and among those who came after Goethe he may **Heine's Lyrics.** perhaps claim the first place as the poet who bears, as no other ever bore, a laughing tear in his scutcheon. His peculiar power lay in the blending of elegy with jest and satire, and his influence on the whole of Europe is not yet exhausted. Much that he produced till 1856, the year of his death, lies outside the range of the present work. It should be remarked, however, that the wonderful fertility and variety of modern German lyric poetry were not yet exhausted even with him; but with later poets, dead as well as living, we are not now concerned.

The song develops its full power only when set to music. Modern German lyric poetry, from its first beginnings in the previous century, had been accompanied and fostered by music. Beethoven, and **Songs set to music. Beethoven and Schubert.** still more Schubert, have done much to immortalise by their melodies the best German songs. Schubert, in his brief life, displayed an unequalled gift of sympathy with all the moods and emotions which ever stirred either Goethe or any other song-writer. Yet even he was far from exhausting the whole treasure of German lyric poetry; contemporary with him and after him there arose a great number of song-composers, and the lesser masters were often successful in creating the most popular songs.

NARRATIVE WRITING.

The development of the epic and the drama down to the date of Goethe's death is not so striking as that of lyric poetry. In both these provinces comparatively few great works of art were produced, though both furnished characteristic and important creations. In the province of romance we have Jean Paul, in that of the drama Heinrich von Kleist and Grillparzer.

The art of narrative rose in the course of the eighteenth century, both in matter and form, from the level of prose to that of poetry; in the nineteenth it sank for the time again into prose. Subsequently to Hagedorn and Gellert, German poets had learned how to narrate by writing fables and short tales in verse. These smaller essays in narrative poetry prepared the way for the true epic; Klopstock introduced the religious, Wieland the purely imaginative epic. Klopstock's sonorous hexameters found many imitators, and the example of Voss and Goethe turned the attention of many to the fruitful field of the idyll, to the trivial incidents of everyday life among the people. Wieland's stanzas likewise called forth imitations; the chivalrous romances of the Middle-Ages supplied both him and his followers with suitable materials, and in the somewhat effeminate years of the second decade of this century the smooth verses of Ernst Schulze's 'Bezauberte Rose' won great though not lasting fame. In Aloys Blumauer's 'Adventures of the pious Aeneas' (1784), the humorous and popular romance of the previous century, which preceded the rise of the ballad, appears raised to the level of the mock-heroic poem. About the same time appeared

Marginal notes:
Development of narrative writing from the end of 18th century.

Blumauer's travestied Aeneid, and Kortum's 'Jobsiad.'

Kortum's celebrated 'Jobsiad,' which with its doggerel verses, its intentionally wooden style and rude woodcuts, was meant as a parody of the popular literature and the style of Hans Sachs, which Goethe and Wieland had tried to revive in a more serious spirit. Herder in his 'popular songs' had introduced into German literature a few most beautiful serious Spanish romances, and in his romances of the 'Cid' he passed on to an epic in detached songs. Clemens Brentano meant to pro- *Brentano's* duce a work of the same kind in his grandly con- *'Rosen-* ceived but unfinished romances, entitled the 'Wreath *kranz.'* of Roses.' The happy thought struck Arnim of applying the grandiloquent tone of the Spanish Romances to comic subjects, and Immermann followed his example in *Arnim.* his 'Tulifäntchen.' Platen's legendary epic of the *Immer-* 'Abassides' revived the five-footed trochees of the *mann's* Servian popular songs which Goethe had transplanted *'Tulifänt-* into German poetry, and also the influence of Ariosto, *chen.'* to whom Wieland owed so much. Rückert's 'Nal *Platen's* *'Abassides.'* und Damajanti' is written in short freely-rhymed couplets. It is a small episode from the great Indian Epic, just as his 'Rostem und Suhrab' was an episode from the Persian epic of Firdusi. *Rückert* Simrock treated the old German hero-legend of *and* Wieland the smith in a poem written in the Nibe- *Simrock.* lungen stanza, which Tieck and Uhland had applied to the ballad. The life of Christ, which in Klopstock's 'Messiah' had formed the beginning of the modern German epic, was worked up by Rückert into a rhymed harmony of the Gospels, a monotonous and lifeless work, which can only be compared to the rhymed Bible para- phrases of the sixteenth century. Almost all forms of the epic were thus gradually worked out; but there was nothing that came up to Wieland's 'Oberon,' to 'Goethe's 'Hermann und Dorothea,' or to Herder's 'Cid;' only Homer and the newly-revived Niben- lungenlied could be compared with these master-pieces.

The favour of the general reading public was bestowed now as previously on novels, which as a rule met with imme- *Novel-* diate but ephemeral success. They appeared before *writing.* the modern epic, and continued to exist side by side with it, till its

decline in popularity still more strengthened their hold on the public
mind.   But the novels of this period were entirely dominated by
fashion, and their authors could seldom adapt themselves to more
than one style of writing.   Many-sided epic creation such as we find
in Wieland or Goethe, is unparalleled among the other authors of
this time ; even Wieland returned in later years to the class of
half-historical, half-didactic novel, of which his ' Agathon ' had been
so successful an example, but he did not repeat his early triumphs.
Most of the novel-writers were the slaves of a single manner and
style which they followed more or less mechanically in all their
works.   Hence, after first successes their popularity died away.

Wieland's ' Agathon,' with its mixture of philosophic and epic, of
Influence of historical and fictitious elements, was quite a new phe-
Wieland's nomenon in modern literature.   Xenophon's Romance
' Agathon.' about Cyrus was the only thing like it in the whole of
literature.   Through ' Agathon ' the novel generally was raised
from the sphere of mere light literature, and in a measure ennobled.   ' This is,' said Lessing, ' the first and only novel for the
thinking mind of classical taste.'   Goethe's ' Wilhelm Meister,' which
was written under the influence of ' Agathon,' brought back the
philosophical romance into the domain of German life.   Both
' Agathon ' and ' Meister ' deal more with the history of a human
soul than with varied outward incident, and thus testify to the importance assigned to the inner life in modern German literature.
Not but what even in the earlier romance of ' Simplicissimus,' full as
it is of incident, the inward development of the hero was quite left
out of sight.   ' Simplicissimus,' ' Agathon,' and ' Wilhelm Meister,'
have likewise in common the semi-autobiographical character.
Many of these feigned autobiographies were produced in the last
Moritz's century;   we will only mention ' Anton Reiser,' by
' Anton Karl Philipp Moritz, which came out between 1785
Reiser' and 1790; it is entitled a psychological romance,
(1785-1790). and it affords us a most interesting glimpse into the
labyrinth of a German mind during the Storm and Stress period.

If we leave out of consideration the romances of the seventeenth
century, Wieland's ' Agathon ' was really the foundation of the
historical novel in Germany.   Novel-writers at the first confined

themselves to classical antiquity, but soon the Middle Ages were also drawn upon, and chivalrous romances were produced such as had been started some time before in France, and had come into favour in Germany through Goethe's 'Götz.' In the nineteenth century Fouqué gave to this class of writing a specifically northern and pious colouring. Yet there was always something arbitrary about this foreign costume; the manners of older times were painted from very slight knowledge, and truth was entirely sacrificed to effect. Achim von Arnim alone, in his unfinished novel, 'The Guardians of the Crown' (1817), combined real knowledge of the Reformation period with graphic power, and, it must be added, with his usual formlessness and exuberant fancy. It was Walter Scott's great example which in the second decade of this century first made conscientious faithfulness and study of details the rule in historical novel-writing, and rendered this class of literature capable of rivalling and even anticipating the history of civilisation. Wilhelm Hauff's 'Lichtenstein,' like Uhland's Swabian ballads, reflected the local patriotism of Würtemberg, and showed a sympathetic appreciation of the national past. A few years later Willibald Alexis, of Breslau, devoted his attention with great success to the history of Brandenburg and Prussia, and even revealed certain modest charms in the uninteresting scenery of that province.

Classical and chivalrous romances.

Arnim's 'Kronenwächter' (1817).

Ulrich Hegner of Winterthur had, as early as 1814, drawn his materials from contemporary life, and in his novel, 'Salys' days of Revolution,' had described the first beginnings of the Swiss Revolution; the plan of the book was excellent, but he showed little skill in development, though on the whole the narrative is interesting and pleasing. In Hölderlin's 'Hyperion,' a master-piece of German prose produced between 1797 and 1799, the scene is likewise laid in the immediate past, in modern Greece; the individual tendencies of the author preponderate over the historical elements, and the Greece here described is really, as in 'Agathon,' the ideal land of German longing and the home of classical culture.

Hegner's 'Salys' Revolutionstage' (1814).

Hölderlin's 'Hyperion,' 1797-99.

Goethe's 'Wilhelm Meister,' owing to the long period devoted to the writing of it, had become a semi-historical romance. When it finally appeared before the world it was no longer a picture of present circumstances, but of an age which was already passing away, and moreover it touched very little on events of public interest. The best writers could hardly hope to rival this work, however much the most highly cultured of them, who scorned to appeal to the mere instincts of the masses, might feel tempted to try and imitate it. The older Romanticists were soon in the field, but

Imitations of 'Wilhelm Meister.' Tieck, Schlegel, Novalis, Grimm, Eichendorff, Immermann.

were none of them successful. In 'Franz Sternbald's Wanderings,' by Tieck, the author's intention was to accompany a pupil of Albert Dürer's to Rome and back again; Friedrich Schlegel's 'Lucinde' was the audacious production of a *dilettante* philosopher devoid of all epic talent; Novalis, in his 'Heinrich von Ofterdingen,' returned to the Middle Ages and chose a legendary poet as his hero. With Tieck the leading theme was to be painting, with Schlegel it was to be the art of life, with Novalis poetry, just as the stage had been the chief interest for a considerable portion of 'Wilhelm Meister.' Arnim's 'Gräfin Dolores,' which appeared in 1810, belongs in another sense to the same class as 'Wilhelm Meister,' for it gave a typical picture of fashionable society, and set up a new ideal of the true nobleman. 'Ahnung und Gegenwart,' by Joseph von Eichendorff (1815), reflects the spirit of general depression which prevailed during the period preceding the wars of Liberation; the hero, a nobleman after Arnim's pattern, who has taken part in all the struggles of the Tyrolese, ends by going into a monastery, while his dearest friend emigrates to America. For this work, too, 'Wilhelm Meister' evidently furnished the model, and the same influence is equally apparent in Karl Immermann's 'Epigoni,' a picture of the author's own times, which appeared in 1836, four years after Goethe's death. It was not till he wrote 'Münchhausen,' (1838-1839), that Immermann developed his free and original powers as an author.

Many of the above-mentioned novels, 'Wilhelm Meister' not excepted, embodied a distinct purpose; they were meant to teach something, to prove something, to impress on the public in a popular shape some general moral truth or doctrine. Even the chivalrous romances were at first marked by a somewhat low and narrow ideal of Germanism, a spirit of rebellion against princes and clergy, which owed its origin to the time of the literary Revolution, to ' Götz' and the 'Robbers.' Side by side with the chivalrous romances the robber-romances came into vogue, and about the **Ghost-** same time Schiller's ' Ghost-seer' called forth the **stories.** ghost-stories and stories of marvels. All powers working in secret, the *Vehmgerichte*, which had already appeared in ' Götz,' the secret societies which had played a part in ' Meister,' became favourite themes with the novel writers of the time, and new glory was now shed on the time-honoured creations of popular super-stition, the ghosts who haunted old castles, and the favourite giants and dwarfs, nixies and water-maidens. Generally speaking, these fabulous creations just tickled the fancy without conveying any moral. Haller and Wieland, however, laid the scene of their specifically didactic novels in the Eastern land of marvels, and others followed their example. The didactic novel which had flourished so luxuriantly in the seventeenth century, was yet more congenial to the spirit of the age of enlightenment. **Didactic** But this class of writing soon devoted itself to **novels.** national, local, and domestic interests. **Pestalozzi's 'Lienhard und**

In 1781 Pestalozzi began to write his ' Lienhard und **und** Gertrud,' in which his own noble, loving, and pious **Gertrud.'** nature is clearly reflected. The book is pathetic and sincere in tone, a true people's book, derived from faithful observation of the life of the peasantry, surpassing Rousseau's ' Emile' on the one hand, and preparing the way for Peter Hebel and the later village stories on the other.

The didactic novel was less popular in the nineteenth century than it had been in the eighteenth. The artificial form and the lengthy discussions no longer pleased the general public, and **Novel-** only a few readers preferred to learn history from novel **writing be-** writers rather than from the professional historians. **comes more** Limits were set to sentimentality and humour, nor were **objective.** the individual tendencies of the author allowed to dominate his whole

narrative. More importance was now attached to the creation of
lifelike figures than to revealing the personality, however interesting, of a highly gifted and sensitive author. Self-analysis was
free to reveal itself in other forms of literature, but it was resolved
to banish it from the novel. In the interval between Richardson
to Jean Paul, however, this newer view of the scope of the novel
Influence of had yet to establish itself. The English led the
English fashion in novel-writing, and the success of ' Robinson
novelists. Crusoe ' was but the first of a long series of successes. Richardson started the sentimental domestic novel. Fielding brought down Richardson's heroic characters to a more human
level. Goldsmith discovered new materials and motives for the idyll.
Sterne carried the humorous novel to its furthest extreme. All these
writers found imitators in Germany, and only the immortal greatness
of 'Don Quixote' could hold its own against them.

The domestic novel occupied the same place in the epic sphere as
Novels of the middle-class tragedy did in the drama. It made a
domestic study of every-day reality, of its noble feelings, its good
life. deeds, its fair humanity, but also of its misery, vice and
vulgarity. It breathed the very atmosphere which Schiller ab-
horred. Its purpose was not to elevate but to be affecting, and it
awakened pity even for the rogue. There was one sentimental
novel which established itself as a classic, and that was Goethe's
' Werther.' No others, so far as German literature is concerned,
are worth mentioning. Müller's ' Siegwart' repels us now-a-days in
its sentimental parts, and such interest as it still has
Müller, is due to the coarse naturalism which alternates with
Lafontaine. the sentimentality. From about 1790 August Lafon-
Engel's taine was the great producer of works of this kind,
' Herr but far above his somewhat mechanical productions
Lorenz we must rank Engel's ' Herr Lorenz Stark,' which
Stark.'
appeared in 1801 ; we seem to discern in it a faint breath of Les-
sing's spirit, and the desired pathos is produced by simple means.

The idyllic novel, under which heading we may also class
Clauren's ' Lienhard und Gertrude,' reached its lowest level in
'Mimili.' Clauren's repulsive work ' Mimili.' In this novel,
written at the time of impending peace, the wars of Liberation,

Prussian patriotism, Swiss scenery, High German interlarded with Swiss German, coquettish naturalism, culture and sensuality, are mixed up into a disgusting compound which the public of that day, however, swallowed with delight.

The satirical and humorous romances began with Musäus' 'Grandison the Second' (1760), and Wieland's 'Don Sylvio' (1764). Both these works were imitations of 'Don Quixote,' as was also Gottwerth Müller's 'Siegfried von Lindenberg,' which appeared in 1769. The novels of Richardson play the same part in Musäus' stories as the Romances of chivalry do in Cervantes' 'Don Quixote.' Literary satire often took the form of continuations or exaggerated imitations of the works it meant to ridicule. Thus Nicolai ventured to pro- duce the 'Joys of young Werther' as a pendant to the 'Sorrows of young Werther.' In the same way Wilhelm Hauff published his 'Man in the Moon' under the name of Clauren, and as a parody of that author's manner. The humorous novel, in its narrowest sense, stood chiefly under the influence of Sterne's 'Tristram Shandy.' Sterne's want of form, his endless digressions, his witty, learned and fascinating reflections crammed full of allusions and quotations, his mixture of the pathetic and the comic,—all this attracted writers like Hippel and Jean Paul, and incited them to imitation. This whole class of writing reminds one of Rabelais, and still more of Fischart, giving full vent as it does to the author's individuality. Montaigne's Essays, uniting a highly personal character with great breadth of view, set an example which Hamann in Germany followed and even exaggerated.

Theodor Gottlieb von Hippel was a countryman of Hamann's; his 'Lebens-läufe nach aufsteigender Linie' (Careers of life in ascending order) appeared between 1778 and 1781, and his less important 'Kreuz-und Querzüge des Ritters A bis Z' ('Zigzag journeys of the knight A to Z') were published between 1793 and 1799. His characters are wonderfully original creations, though sometimes painted in rather glaring colours; each one of them has his hobby as in Sterne, and his favourite characters

Margin notes: Satirical and humorous romances. Musäus, Wieland, Müller.　Nicolai and Hauff.　Hippel.

like to manifest themselves in witty sayings.   But this humorist, like Justinus Kerner, always has death before his eyes.   He even pictures a count who has arranged his whole castle for people to die there, and who thus pursues the burial of the dead on a large scale, much as other men pursue sport.   The 'Careers of Life' is a grand though somewhat unreadable work.   There is something imperishable about it; it seems to breathe the same air in which Kant and Hamann lived.   Its genius and depth of thought are most apparent if we compare it with the products of the Berlin school, such as Nicolai's 'Sebaldus Nothanker.'

Jean Paul Friedrich Richter was born in 1763 at Wunsiedel

Jean Paul compared with Hippel. in the Fichtel Mountains, and he died in 1825 in Bayreuth.   He was twenty-two years younger than Hippel, and much more versatile, owing to the general increase of culture during that period.   Like Hippel he came of a schoolmaster's and clergyman's family.   But while Hippel, in spite of the subjectivity of his style, manages to preserve a fairly impartial attitude towards the characters and circumstances which he describes, Jean Paul is a true 'sentimental' writer, in Schiller's sense of the word (see p. 206).   He shows a yearning for nature in his love of scenery and of children. He is satirical, idyllic and elegiac, and thus reveals all the features of the sentimental author.   Hippel was a good Prussian, and cherished an enthusiastic admiration for Frederick the Great and Catharine the Second.   In his 'Careers of Life' he attacked an effete oligarchy, such as then existed in Kurland, contrasting it with a genuine state like Prussia.   Jean Paul, on the contrary, could only indulge in polemics against German provincialism through the medium of burlesque satire, and as though the state of things he described were prevalent throughout Germany.   The hero of Hippel's 'Careers of Life' comes of a clergyman's family, and Hippel pictures the parish clergy with all their comical peculiarities, and yet at the same time makes them out to be thoroughly worthy of respect; at the same time he gives us, from the interior of his parsonage, numerous glimpses into the outside world. Jean Paul, on the other hand, buries himself in the idyllic sphere in order to forget the imperfections of the outside world, and photographs with laughing tenderness narrow and trivial conditions of life. Hippel never wearies of urging upon his readers the early Christian precept, *Memento Mori*, and he assigns a good deal of space to pietistic, emotional and lachrymose religiosity, though it never dims his eyes to the true facts of human existence ; but Jean Paul dreams himself away into a future life of blessedness in order to escape from the rude reality. Hippel only brings before us fully developed and consistent characters, men of a pre-Wertherian period; but in Jean Paul we meet with those 'problematic' characters, who are not happy in themselves and do not make others happy, who neither present a picture of idyllic contentment in their narrow provincial life, nor attempt to rise above it by honestly working at a profession, but try to make up for their loss by satirical humour or indulgence in fantastic dreams.

Jean Paul began his literary career in 1783 with the 'Grönländische Processe,' a work of a satirical character. In his 'Schulmeisterlein Wuz' (1790) he entered the field of the idyll. His first novels, 'Die unsichtbare Loge' (1793), and 'Hesperus' (1795), were fictitious biographies, histories of the development of a character, like 'Agathon' and 'Wilhelm Meister,' in which youthful ideals come into collision with reality. In 'Quintus Fixlein' he furnished a more fully developed idyll of a schoolmaster's life, while 'Siebenkäs' (1796 and 1797) traces the fortunes of a 'problematic' nature of the order described above. Jean Paul reached the summit of his powers in 'Titan' (1800–1803) and the 'Flegeljahre' (1804–1805). 'Titan' takes up the problem of his first two novels, only giving it wider scope; it traces the inner history of a German prince who grows up ignorant of his origin, and who ends by ascending the throne. He is meant to impress us as an enlightened and humane sovereign, under whose rule the country will rejoice. By the side of this healthy and sane man stand sickly characters who are ruined; such are the ethereal and spiritual Liane, his first love, Hinda, his second love, an exaggerated, truly Titanic nature, the Titanic voluptuary Roquairol, the prince's friend and rival, the genial humorist Schoppe, who conducted

Jean Paul's works.

His 'Titan.'

part of his education, and who ends in madness. The book ought to have been called ' Anti-Titan,' for it is written against the ideals of the ' Storm and Stress' movement, against ' Titanism' and impetuous genius, sentimentality and misanthropic humour. But Jean Paul has not attained his object in this work; the delineation of the sickly characters, in spite of its power, is exaggerated, and the picture of the healthy-minded man excites our incredulity. The author strove in vain to get out of his own peculiar world, and to produce in ' Titan' a serious ideal romance with Southern scenery. Like a Dutch genre-painter, he was more

His 'Flegel- jahre.'

at home in depicting the details of common life, and he returned to this province in the ' Flegeljahre,' which is his best work, though unfortunately he never completed it. The twin brothers, Walt and Vult, whom this story tells of—the former uncouth and shy, of a childlike, dreamy and unpractical nature, the latter clever, bold, energetic and satirical—are both reflections of Richter's own nature, and repre- sent the two sides of his character, as a poet and as a man. They are more objective, however, and show greater skill in development of character than any of his many earlier creations reflecting himself.

Soon after the ' Flegeljahre' appeared, Jean Paul embodied his experiences as a writer and a schoolmaster in two

His 'Vorschule der Aesthetik,' 'Levana,' and pamphlets.

works, the ' Preparatory Course of Aesthetic' (1804), and 'Levana, or the theory of Education' (1807). At the same time he was actively engaged in writing political pamphlets, which won him considerable fame. He was an enthusiastic adherent of the French revolution, struggled for freedom of the press, and sought to inspire his countrymen with hope and courage in the

His humorous tales.

years of the foreign dominion. His last series of tales are for the most part of a purely humorous nature, and picture queer characters in a realistic and delightful manner.

Jean Paul had a great gift of humour, a rich imagination and a strong faculty for catching the poetical aspect of everything. His narrative is broad and animated, full of life and action, but he seldom fuses his materials together into an artistic whole, and his writing shows the same want of form as Sterne's. His style is Jean Paul's overladen with encyclopædic knowledge, far-fetched manner and metaphors, parentheses, and digressions; his sentences style. are awkward, and he does not even shrink from violations of good taste; subjects the most wide apart jostle each other, and the author seems to delight in jumping from one extreme of feeling to another. All this from the first prevented Jean Paul's works from appealing to the general public, and it is owing to these faults of style that the circle of his readers has gradually become smaller and smaller. But for all that, he deeply influenced the humour of the Romanticists, the younger of whom sometimes adopted his ideas, and still oftener his style and striking metaphors. His wide Even Goethe occasionally affected Jean Paul's style, influence. though with great discretion. With Ludwig Börne and the journalists who followed in his steps, intellectual display was considered indispensable. The high-flown Oriental fashion in poetry was from first to last, as regards style, a mere continuation of Jean Paul's manner, reinforced from fresh sources.

Jean Paul has left his mark on German prose and German style in general; it is all the more to be regretted that he did not succeed in moulding his grand creations into perfect works of art. But the same was the case with almost all the novels of this period. In this respect they were surpassed by the novelette or tale, which has more limited means at its disposal, and is obliged to be more sparing in its use of imagery. The narratives and Short tales. fables in verse, which Hagedorn and Gellert had brought again into favour, and which had been continued by Gleim, Lessing, Wieland, Lichtwer, Pfeffel, Langbein and others, went out of fashion in the nineteenth century, and we find but a very few fable-witers following with halting steps in the traces of their celebrated and popular predecessors. In the place of these versified tales the short prose narrative considerably increased in circulation and influence. It gradually descended from fantastic regions to the level of reality, and was in other respects also subject to the same tendencies as the novel.

Gottlieb Meissner, a disciple of Wieland's, began to write his

'Sketches' in 1778, and it was these that brought the tale specially

Meissner into vogue. In 1782 Musäus began his 'German

and Popular Stories,' in which he went back to the old

Musäus. German legends; and in 1787 he started the collection
which he called 'Straussfedern,' consisting of reproductions of
French tales. This last series was continued by Gottwerth Müller
and later on by Ludwig Tieck. Tieck tried his hand in all the

Tieck. various departments of the prose epic, and rose from
imitation to original production. His 'Popular
Tales' of 1797 contain a simple reproduction of the story of the
'Haimonskinder' (p. 297), a sentimental adaptation of the 'Schöne
Magelone,' a modernised version of the 'Schildbürger' (p. 298),
satirising shallow enlightenment, and the original story of the
fair-haired Ekbert, in which we at first believe ourselves in the
world of reality, but are gradually drawn deeper and deeper into a
legend of horrors. Down to 1812 we find him continuing these
revivals of old-German legends and at the same time producing
stories of his own, such as the Rune-mountain, Love-magic, the
Elves, the Goblet, some of which are gruesome in the extreme.
But between 1821 and 1840 he produced a long series of tales,
the materials for which were generally derived from real life, and
for the most part from modern life; they are free from all traces
of the fabulous element, yet they almost all miss the true epic tone
and are too improbable to affect us strongly.

During the second decade of this century romantic narrative was at its best. In 1810 and 1811 appeared Heinrich
von Kleist's tales; in 1841 Fouqué's 'Undine,' and Achim von
Arnim's first independent collection of tales; in 1812 Grimm's
'Fairy Stories;' in 1814 Chamisso's 'Schlemihl;' from 1814 to

Clemens 1822 Amadeus Hoffmann's numerous ghost stories;

Brentano. in 1817 Clemens Brentano's powerful but strangely
told 'Geschichte vom braven Kasperl und der schönen Annerl,'
as well as his mad tale, 'Die mehreren Wehmüller und ungari-
schen Nationalgesichter.'

Heinrich von Kleist displayed in his tales the same thrilling
power as in his dramas. A story such as 'The Earthquake in
Chili' stands out as a masterpiece among all prose narrative.

A guilty young man and maiden are saved by the earthquake at the very moment when she is going to suffer the penalty **H. v. Kleist's** of death and he is about to destroy himself. Filled with **tales.** joy at this unexpected deliverance and reunion, they return to the town to offer thanks to God; but they hereby expose themselves to the fanaticism of the mob, and fall victims to its fury. Kleist's style of narration is highly objective; with the greatest conciseness, he manages to communicate a large mass of details and even casual accessories; he takes the greatest pains to ensure clearness in his writing, and does not shrink even from disagreeable facts where the narrative entails them. Long discourses he reports indirectly and as summarily as possible, but in important moments he makes his characters themselves speak in a laconic and interjectional style. The greater part of the story is written in long, involved periods, overladen with relative and conditional clauses and bristling with particles. The author narrates with calm deliberation, repressing all personal sympathy beyond some occasional epithets, until the final catastrophe is reached, when his emotion seems to overpower him and he utters, apparently against his will, his horror of the fanatical murderers and his admiration of the one courageous defender of the unfortunate pair.

Achim von Arnim chose as his models the story-tellers of the seventeenth century, and made free use, like Grim- **Achim von** melshausen for instance, of the creations of popular **Arnim.** superstition, endowing them, however, with an independent and well-defined life of their own. His style of narrative is sometimes quite excellent, free from all artificial excitement, deliberate, clear and healthy in tone, though always marked by a strong predilection for the marvellous.

Fouqué made his happiest stroke in 'Undine,' a revival of an old German legend, the outline of which he had found in **Fouqué.** Theophrastus Paracelsus; his conception of the water-spirits is very prettily carried out, but the problem of human interest is superficially treated, and the simple popular tone adopted at the outset is repeatedly departed from, to suit the author's convenience.

Chamisso's 'Peter Schlemihl,' on the contrary, is a faultless
work of art and one of deep import. There, too,
Chamisso. a popular superstition forms the leading motive,
namely, the idea that a man might lose his shadow, the devil
carrying it off when he could not get the man himself into his
power. This tale deserves its universal renown. The poet has
made the hero a symbolical portrait of himself; 'Schlemihl' means
an unlucky wight, and Chamisso has attributed to this poor devil the
same incapacity of coping with the world, which in his own case
had disposed him to solitude, to intercourse with nature and with
children of nature. But it is not necessary to be acquainted with
this fact in order to follow with interest the clear and simple narratives, and even to discover some symbolical signification in it.

While Fouqué's 'Undine' pictured a conventional age of
chivalry, Chamisso laid the scene of his story in the present, and
thereby achieved an effect similar to that which Arnim produced,
when he introduced an enchantress and other magical beings side
by side with definite historical characters. This mixture of the
real and the imaginary was carried to its furthest extreme by
Hoffmann. Ernst Theodor Amadeus Hoffmann, who borrowed
motives from Jean Paul, Tieck, Chamisso, Arnim,
Heinrich von Kleist, and often even drew his inspiration from
pictures alone. He followed in the steps of Cervantes. In emulation
of Novalis' 'Ofterdingen' he narrated the minstrel-war on the
Wartburg in the style of an old German popular romance, and in
other cases, too, he made use of older materials. But he impressed
the stamp of his own individuality on all that he handled, working
carefully and methodically, and holding his readers' imagination spell-
bound. He relates with perfect composure horrors which make our
hair stand on end as in a fearful dream. But he produces his effects
more by what happens and appears to the outer senses than by
characters and inward experiences, and perhaps it was for this
very reason that he reaped a great success. He at once became
popular in France, like Solomon Gessner in the previous century,
and found zealous imitators among the French romanticists. Like
Tieck and Brentano he attacked Philistinism, which he represented
as a creature of darkness, while, according to him, the ghosts

of Romanticism embody true and natural life. Science too is, in his eyes, a work of the Philistines, and he makes a romantic student declare that the way in which a professor speaks about nature offends all his tenderest feelings. In such utterances as these we recognise the kind of mind to which the so-called Natural Philosophy appealed. But experimental science proved in the end to be a match for Romanticism.

The strong wine of the older Romanticists was meanwhile being watered, sugared and perfumed in Berlin and Dresden by men like Clauren, Theodor Hell and Friedrich Kind, Clauren, and, thus diluted, was administered in harmless doses Hell, Kind. even to Philistines, and taken everywhere with great relish in the third decade of this century. Nevertheless Eichendorff still continued the literary war against the Philistines. His Eichendorff. 'Taugenichts' (1826) is written in the most delightful vein; it is an improbable story full of misunderstanding, error and strange occurrences, and the reader is almost infected with the lighthearted mood of the hero, who triumphs over all obstacles, sings the most beautiful songs, never knows what is happening around him, but is always dreaming and loving.

About this time, in 1829, Goethe brought his 'Wilhelm Meister' to a hurried termination in a sequel entitled 'Wilhelm 'Wilhelm Meister's Wanderjahre, oder die Entsagenden.' This Meister's latter part of the work bears marks of carelessness, Wander- and is noticeably deficient in artistic unity. The jahre.' old secret society into which Wilhelm had been received now has a new object in view, namely, emigration to America. Each member remains in the service of the society, but seeks to develop his capabilities in that direction in which he can most benefit the whole brotherhood. Each submits to be separated from his nearest and dearest. Wilhelm parts from Natalie, takes a journey into Italy, finds his vocation as a surgeon, and ends by practising his skill on his own son. The education of this son forms one of the chief points of interest in the 'Wanderjahre.' He is sent to an institution, spoken of as the 'Pædagogical province,' the idea of which was probably suggested to Goethe by Fellenberg's Institution at Hofwyl in Switzerland. He soon finds a partner of his affections. His years of apprenticeship are the very opposite to what Wilhelm's had been; where the former had erred, the latter is guided in the right way; whereas Wilhelm was wanting in self-control, his son is to learn to exercise it; whereas the father was undisciplined, the son is to grow up under rule and discipline.

The whole seems rather a collection of materials for a book than a complete work. Much about which the reader would like to be informed remains obscure. Strange and off-hand assumptions are made without the slightest hesitation; a wealth of practical experience and wisdom drawn from nature and history is spread out before us, but the narrative sometimes comes to a standstill, and the chief charm of the book lies in the episodical novelettes. Some of the heroes of these episodes become acquainted with Wilhelm and are thereby brought into relation with his fate or with the 'self-denying brotherhood.' The tales themselves, which form to a certain extent a continuation of the 'Conversations of the Emigrants,' are of unequal merit; the story of the 'man of fifty years' can alone be ranked among the highest achievements of Goethe's art. If we survey the whole group of Goethe's tales, we find that he too passed from ghost-stories and fairy-tales to representation of real life.

Of the number of tales destined to be inserted in the 'Wander-jahre' and dealing with the theme of renunciation, the story of the 'Elective Affinities' was separated from the rest and published in an expanded form as a novel. It appeared in 1809 and is the epic masterpiece of the whole period from Schiller's death to Goethe's; it is executed with Goethe's full poetic power, and is the supreme prose-utterance, just as 'Hermann and Dorothea' is the supreme poetic utterance of his cultured realism. The novel falls into two parts, each of eighteen chapters, and the symmetry and parallelism are also carried out in other respects. It is true that there are some defects in its construction; a detached story is inserted in the middle of the novel, extracts from a journal are introduced, and the second part is perhaps too obviously spun out to an equal length with the first; but in other respects the work is without a rival. Nowhere do we meet with such subtleties of

composition, with such fine adjustment of motives, with such consistency in the development of action from character, and of
character from surrounding circumstances. It is in no wise in
contradiction with this that the 'third world,' as Goethe called it,
the world of forebodings, portents, superstition and evil chances,
is also made to play a part in the development of the story. In
the plan of his narrative Goethe displays the whole of his rare
talent for the invention of characteristic actions, but he also does
not avoid direct psychological analysis when requisite. He has
adhered to unity of scene as far as possible; whoever is not living
on the country-estate where the whole interest of the plot is concentrated, escapes our close observation. Goethe in no wise
shrinks from prosaic details; money-matters, questions of agriculture, the financial circumstances of the characters introduced,
and various little anxieties and interests of country life are the
subject of detailed discussion. Continued systematic labour for
the property and its embellishment forms the background to the
play of emotion which occupies the first part. Across this background move the four characters who are gliding from a smooth,
easy path of life deeper and deeper into the abysses of a tragical
fate.

A 'permanent relation,' a typical institution of human society,
such as Goethe had sought out for poetic treatment Marriage its
since his Italian journey, forms the problem of this leading
work also; marriage is here the leading theme. In theme.
'Wilhelm Meister' Goethe had treated marriage according to the
frivolous views of the eighteenth century; in the 'Wahlverwandschaften' it is considered from the more serious point of view of a
more serious age. It was at this time, too, that Goethe's 'Stella'
received its tragic termination. Marriage is looked on from all
sides in the 'Wahlverwandschaften;' we listen to the tale of, or
actually witness various marriages, and the whole work centres
round one such union. Eduard and Charlotte had loved each
other in early youth, but married late, it being the second marriage
with each of them. The Captain, a friend of Eduard's, and Ottilie,
a niece of Charlotte's, come to their country-seat on a visit;
Eduard feels himself drawn to Ottilie, Charlotte to the Captain,

and in both cases the affection is returned. Charlotte and
the Captain have moral strength, and restrain themselves, while
Eduard and Ottilie give themselves up to their passion; but
Ottilie, too, learns renunciation and dies, and Eduard follows her
in death.

The typical contrast between self-denial and renunciation is carried
Characters out in the individual characters. Eduard stands in
in the work. contrast to the Captain; the former can deny himself
nothing, and obstinately persists in following his wishes; the latter is
in all things trained as a soldier, and accustomed to self-control.
Eduard is unsystematic and of a dilettante nature; the Captain is
methodical and precise, and thoroughly master of all that he under-
takes. The character of Ottilie, the central figure of the romance,
is made thoroughly individual in many respects, though the merely
typical aspects of her character ultimately predominate. She is contrasted with two different characters, with Charlotte, and with
Luciane, Charlotte's daughter by her first marriage. In the one case
we have the contrast between the unformed girl and the married
woman, in the other between one girl and another. Charlotte acts
calmly from high principle, while Ottilie's actions are entirely
dictated by instinct and personal feeling. Charlotte has had experience of life, and looks on the world with calm self-possession,
while Ottilie wanders on blindly, and allows herself to be led by
others, especially by the man she loves, till suddenly there comes
a horrible awakening from her dream, and she learns through bitter
sufferings the truth about life, love, and duty. Luciane, for her
part, possesses all the qualities for getting on well in the world,
Ottilie all the qualities for making others happy. The former is
brilliant but selfish; the latter modest and self-sacrificing. Luciane
is not introduced to us till the second part, in which we are also
made more closely acquainted with two of Ottilie's suitors, who
again stand in contrast to each other, namely, the architect and
the master at the school where Ottilie and Luciane were educated.
The architect is of an artistic and romantic nature, the teacher a
practical man and a rationalist. The artist paints his beloved as
an angel in the canopy of his Gothic chapel, and persuades her to
represent the Virgin Mary in some *tableaux vivants*; the teacher

thinks he would be introducing her to a suitable sphere of action in making her mistress of a boarding-school.

The architect expresses the author's own view. Ottilie has unresistingly yielded to passion, but she comes round to the view that she must practise utter self-denial. She is of a pious nature, entirely penetrated by a sense of the divine; the author himself calls her 'the heavenly one.' She takes a vow, and lays a penance upon herself of fasting and silence, under which she gradually fades away. After death the people attribute to her body wonderful healing powers, and the faithful and sin-laden make pilgrimages to the Gothic chapel in which she lies buried. The writer wishes that his readers no less than the simple folk should enshrine in their hearts the memory of his suffering heroine as of a glorified saint, and should remember her quiet virtues, whose gentle influence this poor world ever welcomes with eager joy, and mourns their loss with tears and yearnings.

It is in the 'Elective Affinities' that Goethe shows most strongly his artistic appreciation of the mediæval and Catholic tendencies of Romanticism. He hardly displays such sympathy in any other work, unless it be in a dramatic sketch of the same period, which he never completed, and in a few parts of 'Faust.'

THE DRAMA.

The German stage suffered an irreparable loss in Schiller's early death. In point of time Heinrich von Kleist and Franz Grillparzer were his successors, but as a matter of fact Kleist's merit was not adequately recognised till long after his death. Grillparzer's fame during his life-time spread little beyond his native land of Austria, and even with the Austrian public he did not always find due recognition.

Goethe entertained the idea of completing Schiller's 'Demetrius,' but he never carried it out; nor did his plan for a drama which should present a story of Christian martyrdom of the time of the conversion of the Saxons ever get beyond a mere sketch. After Schiller's death Goethe only wrote slight pieces for special occasions.

Goethe's later dramatic works.

Thus he wrote a Prelude to celebrate 'the happy reunion' of
the Royal Family in Weimar after the troubled times of 1806
'Pandora.' and 1807. 'Pandora,' produced about the same
time, was, it seems, meant to celebrate the general
return of peace; while 'Epimenides' Awakening' was performed
at Berlin in commemoration of the victory over Napoleon. It
is much to be regretted that 'Pandora' remained unfinished, for
what we have of it is glorious both in idea and execution. The
poet here re-introduces us to the mythical favourite of his earlier
years—Prometheus. He and his brother Epimetheus are at strife
at the commencement of the drama, and they were probably to be
reconciled during the course of it by the return of Pandora. They
represent in a typical manner a contrast found in the moral world:
Prometheus is active, Epimetheus contemplative; the former is a
realist, the latter an idealist. Both are one-sided, and have to learn
to triumph over their one-sidedness, and to appreciate each other's
merits.

Finer spirits like Platen perceived the value of this remarkable
German fragment. But the mass of the public passed it by in
Drama after indifference, and learnt nothing from the great master
Schiller. who still continued to bring to light new capabilities
of his inexhaustible genius. Extravagance, experiments, and lifeless routine marred the German drama after Schiller's death.
Stage-managers cared for nothing but the success of the moment.
The most gifted writers were either incapable of gauging the
requirements of the actual stage, or else they systematically set
at nought the laws of dramatic technique. The influence of the
literary revolution of 1773 is still clearly perceptible, especially in
the carelessness of form which it brought into fashion. With the
exception of Wilhelm Schlegel's translation of Shakspeare, the
extreme section of the Romantic school accomplished but little in
the province of the drama. The two brothers Schlegel made
Tieck's each but a single essay in dramatic authorship, and
'Drama- neither with success. Tieck, Brentano and Arnim,
turgische only produced dramas for reading, some of which
Blätter.' were very extravagant, while all of them lacked
sustained beauty. Tieck's 'Dramaturgische Blätter,' theatrical

criticisms published in the years 1823 and 1827, appeared in
Dresden, where Tieck had some connection with the theatre.
They have been compared with Lessing's 'Hamburgische Dramaturgie,' but in reality they only demonstrate the author's caprice
and superficiality, his blind admiration of Shakspeare, and his
hostility towards Lessing and Schiller. Far more valuable was
another production of this period which likewise emanated from
Dresden, Karl Maria von Weber's 'Freischütz,' the   Weber's
masterpiece of romantic opera, and a priceless con- 'Freischütz.'
tribution both to dramatic art and to popular music. The magic
powers, which Tieck conjured up in vain, were here introduced
with the greatest effect, and proclaimed to all people the glory
of German romanticism.

The jealous depreciation of Schiller's genius on the part of the
Romanticists doubtless deterred many of the younger dramatists
from entering the only school where they could have learnt the
true principles of dramatic art. But the power of his genius
triumphantly asserted itself both at that time and later, in spite
of all its detractors. Theodor Körner unfortunately   Theodor
never got beyond mere imitation of Schiller, before   Körner.
his untimely death in the war against Napoleon. The   Adam
Dane, Adam Oehlenschläger, was one of Schiller's   Oehlen-
warmest admirers, and did not refrain from ridiculing   schläger.
the Romantic movement. He was a great literary leader in his
own fatherland, but in Germany his fame was more transitory.
He enriched the German drama with subjects drawn from the
Scandinavian heroic period, breathing into them virtue, gentle
sentiment and a humane idealism; he painted the contrast between
an innocent and pious Christianity and a rude and cruel heathenism, but he also depicted brave and noble heathendom in conflict
with monkish deceit and cunning. He described the constancy
and early love characteristic of the heroic North. His 'Cor-
reggio' is a more expanded and sentimental treatment of the
theme which Goethe had handled powerfully, but less fully, in his
'Artist's earthly Pilgrimage and Apotheosis.'

Zacharias Werner was another writer more or less connected
with Schiller, whose daring, however, he absurdly exaggerated

The operatic effects and the supernatural elements in the 'Maid
    Zacharias of Orleans' were what suited Werner's taste best.
    Werner. But, in spite of all his pretensions to depth and
culture, he only came up to the level of Kotzebue, who could
also adopt the manner of Schiller when he chose. His delineation
of character is always superficial, often arbitrary and full of
exaggeration; instead of pictures of real human beings he gives
us scenic effects, songs, visions, secret societies, spirits who wander
on earth in the guise of harp-players and talk mysterious nonsense.
He waters down marked historical characters such as Luther or
Attila, throwing around them a rose-pink theatrical light, which
       makes them appear smaller and more trivial. His
       His 'Twenty-Fourth of February' began that series of
  'Vierund-
  zwanzigster so-called 'Fate-tragedies,' in which the most horrible
  Februar,' crimes are made to result from improbable coin-
    first of cidences or trivial motives. It is a favourite device
  the 'fate-
  tragedies.' with these Fate-tragedians to make the instrument of
       murder a sword or a knife which has already once
been used in the family for a similar purpose, and which is
generally to be seen in a conspicuous position on the stage
at the very first drawing-up of the curtain. Werner's play is a
miserable production, totally destitute of dramatic skill. The
author's chief object seems to be to pile up the horrors as thick
as possible.

    Adopting this play of Werner's as his model, Müllner, a lawyer
    Müllner's in Weissenfels, gave to the German stage in 1812 a
    plays. play called 'The Twenty-Ninth of February,' and in
1813 he produced his notorious drama 'Die Schuld' (Guilt),
under the influence of which Grillparzer's 'Ahnfrau' (Ancestress),
and a number of other tragedies of a similar sort, were written.
'Die Schuld' and 'Die Ahnfrau' are written in rhymed trochees
of four feet, a metre which the romantic worship of Calderon had
brought into fashion; it easily degenerated into an exaggerated
rhetorical style, which enhances the horror of the prophecies,
curses, portents, dreams and wild passions, of which these plays
are full.

    By the side of worshippers of Calderon worshippers of Shak-

speare were not wanting, who characteristically affiliated themselves to the German Shakspeare of the seventeenth century,
Andreas Gryphius. Achim von Arnim and Karl Im-   Arnim and
mermann each wrote a play on the story of 'Cardenio   Karl
and Celinde' (see p. 283). In his drama, 'Friedrich Immermann.
der Zweite,' Immermann appealed to the increased interest taken
by his contemporaries in German mediæval history, and more
particularly in the house of Hohenstaufen. This drama is a well-
planned history-play in the manner of Shakspeare; the poetic
diction is fresh and original, and the fifth act really excellent, but
still the play had no striking success. Christian Christian
Grabbe immediately followed in Immermann's steps,   Grabbe.
and began a cycle of Hohenstaufen-tragedies. In 1829 he produced 'Friedrich Barbarossa,' in 1830 'Heinrich der Sechste;'
these, like all his other plays, are full of the most absurd declamation,
and are utterly deficient in dramatic sequence. In   Ernst
1830 Ernst Raupach had begun his Hohenstaufen- Raupach's
cycle, which was completed in 1837, and embraced Hohenstau-
no less than sixteen dramas; Raupach boasted that   fen-cycle.
these were 'strictly historical dramas,' which means that in them
we are spared nothing of what the author knows, or thinks he
knows, of history. These plays reckon on such patience or such
thirst for knowledge on the part of the audience as seems to us
almost incredible; not but what it actually did exist, for ten of
them were once performed in Berlin in chronological succession,
and all the seats were subscribed for. Raupach understood his
audience. From the year 1825 he retained a firm footing in
Berlin, producing tragedies, comedies and opera-texts, His great
one or more new ones every year, with the same skill fertility.
as Kotzebue, and guided by no other artistic principle than that of
pleasing the public. He adopted the classical or the romantic
style as need required, sometimes using prose, sometimes iambics,
sometimes both in turn, sometimes other rhythms. In 'Tasso's
Tod' he tried to write like Goethe, and with his trilogy of
'Cromwell' he trenched on Shakspeare's special province. He
borrowed from Calderon and he also revived the style which Lessing
had adopted in 'Miss Sara Sampson.' In 'Der Müller und sein Kind'

he furnished the public with a popular piece akin to the Fate-tragedies, and teeming with superstitions, portents and ghosts. He put the story of Genovefa on the stage, a task which had been vainly attempted by Maler Müller and Tieck. Following the example of Fouqué, F. R. Hermann, J. W. Müller and Chr. F. Eichhorn, he dramatised the legend of Siegfried and Kriemhild, retaining to a great extent the words of the Nibelungenlied, but at the same time putting in so much padding, that the whole produces on us the same kind of impression as Gounod's 'Faust,' when Goethe's own lines are dimly discerned through the double trans-lation. The reward for all these *tours de force* of Raupach's was oblivion.

Against the German stage as it was between 1820 and 1830 Platen wrote his Aristophanic comedies, 'Die verhängnissvolle **Platen's** Gabel' (The Fatal Fork) ridiculing the Fate-**satirical** tragedies and more especially Grillparzer's 'Ahnfrau,' **comedies.** and 'Der romantische Oedipus' directed against the Shakspearian imitations, particularly against Immermann or 'Nim-mermann' as Platen called him. Immermann did not abstain from replying, and was seconded by Heine. We are struck with the unfairness on both sides, but we can also enjoy these polemical productions purely for their artistic merits. These comedies of Platen's must be reckoned among the most original that we possess; they contain verses of wonderful harmony along with effective carica-tures and brilliant wit, while at the same time we find serious thoughts and the highest ideal of the value of art expressed in fascinating language. Platen's original plays do not show the same talent and were never popular.

In 1821 Tieck published Heinrich von Kleist's posthumous works, and in 1826 his collected works. From that time on Kleist has become ever dearer to the hearts of the German people, and a closer acquaintance with his works has ever raised his fame higher. He was a tragic poet and had a tragic fate; he com-mitted suicide at the early age of thirty-four. He did not begin **Kleist's life.** his studies till his twenty-second year, and then the Kantian philosophy, from which Schiller derived strength and support, drove him to despair. Alternately buoyed

up by the brighest hopes and despondent almost to madness, he
at length resigned himself to the obscurity of a small government
office; but this could not satisfy him permanently. He was in
Königsberg at the time of the humiliation of Prussia by Napoleon;
in July, 1807, he went to Dresden, where he soon became intimate
with Tieck and other authors, and worked as editor of a newspaper.
But in 1809 he migrated to Austria, which at that time was fighting
against Napoleon. Thither he took with him political pamphlets
breathing the same spirit as Arndt's, in which he reproached the
Germans for their want of patriotism and poured out on Napoleon
all the vials of his wrath. But the battle of Wagram crushed all
hopes of deliverance, and Kleist returned to Berlin and resumed
his work as a journalist. His poetic efforts meeting with no
encouragement or applause, and his family refusing to help him
· any longer, he lost all hope for himself, his art and his fatherland.
After the alliance of Prussia with France he cared to live no
longer. The thought of suicide had for years been familiar
. to him, and now, when a morbid-minded lady-friend of his
besought him in a moment of excitement to kill her, he promised
to do so, and shot her first and then himself on the twenty-first of
November, 1811.

Kleist wrote a few lyric poems, a number of tales and seven
dramas. The first of these, 'Die Familie Schroffen-   **Kleist's**
stein,' appeared in 1803; it treated the same   **plays.**
theme as 'Romeo and Juliet,' and produced a great sensation in
certain circles. His 'Amphitryon' (1807), suggested by Molière,
is not very successful in its attempt to give a serious turn to a
frivolous farce. In his 'Penthesilea' (1808) an Amazon-Queen
tears to pieces with her own teeth the hero Achilles, whom she
passionately loves. 'Käthchen von Heilbronn' (1810), a chivalrous
drama bearing many points of resemblance to the 'Maid of
Orleans,' is a story of devoted love. 'Der zerbrochene Krug'
(1811) is a comedy of rustic life, and represents a trial at law
in which the judge himself turns out to be the culprit. Kleist's
two last plays were 'Die Hermannsschlacht' and 'Der Prinz
von Homburg,' both of which were first made known after his
death, by Tieck. The first of these dramas is full of passionate

hatred of the French, and gives a picture of the struggle against the oppressor Napoleon, such as Kleist imagined him, cunning, cruel, inhuman, unscrupulous. 'Der Prinz von Homburg,' on the contrary, breathes a spirit of love and humanity, of devotion to Prussia and respect for the house of Hohenzollern. Prussia had not been thus glorified in German poetry since the time of the Grenadier-songs and 'Minna von Barnhelm.'

Kleist showed remarkable talent in more than one respect. His language possesses a peculiar charm, though he had not a sure command of the elements of German grammar.

His excellences as a dramatist.

His presentment of reality is very powerful, yet he can also transport us by one single stroke into a completely ideal sphere. His style is emphatic, without ever degenerating into rhetorical declamation. His was a manly nature like Lessing's and Schiller's, but much more rugged, more decided, more resolved not to yield anything to the degeneracy of the time. He does not wish to touch our hearts, but to storm them by tragic force. He develops his characters to the furthest extreme, stopping short at no horror or crime. He does not mind wounding the feelings of the public; he only takes care to place the pleasing by the side of the horrible, so as to produce an æsthetic balance. Kleist was in many respects a son of the eighteenth century; he, too, had been filled with enthusiasm for Rousseau, and was thoroughly tolerant and humane. In his attacks on heroic stoicism he goes further than any other man of his time. 'Equanimity,' he says, 'is only the virtue of athletes.' Lessing had already drawn attention to the Greek heroes who do not suppress their anguish, but cry and weep like children, and in his 'Prince of Homburg' Kleist did not shrink from representing a man who is otherwise impetuous, brave and victorious, as panic-stricken by the dread of death.

Like the poets of the 'period of genius,' Kleist places the heart

His manner and style.

above the understanding. But the heart does not always speak clearly, and sometimes counsels wrong. A man may have acted on the impulse of his heart and yet, when confronted by his deed, may be terrified to despair. Kleist must have had such experiences himself, for he often describes them. (See 'Amphitryon' and 'Penthesilea.')

As an artist, too, Kleist shows kinship with the poets of the 'Storm and Stress' movement. He is far removed, it is true, from that negligence of form which was continued in so many of the romanticists, far removed from that illusion which even Achim von Arnim shared, that genius could write by the light of its own nature and need not trouble about rules. In this respect Kleist is rather a follower of the ancients and of Shakspeare, Lessing, Schiller, and, to a less degree, of Goethe. His dialogue sometimes reminds us of Lessing. In his glorious fragment 'Robert Guiscard' he attempted, like Schiller, to revive the classical chorus, and in his 'Penthesilea' he depicted a female warrior as Schiller had done in his 'Maid of Orleans.' In spite of these points of resemblance, however, Kleist stands on different ground to Schiller; he is a realist, that is to say, he delineates living individuals, while Schiller was an idealist and pourtrayed abstract types of character. Kleist aimed at copying the great phenomena of human life as he saw it in his own experience, or fancied it in his powerful imagination. His plays continued, in some respects, the naturalism started by Goethe's 'Götz.' He comes nearer to Shakspeare than any other modern dramatist, but his dissonances are harsher and his harmonies softer. He is not so objective as Shakspeare, and has read less in the book of human nature, and in consequence draws his characters more from his own heart; but for him they acquire quite an objective existence and confront him like ghosts, whose features stamp themselves with startling clearness on a timid imagination, to be revived again and again in the memory. There are few lyrical passages or soliloquies in Kleist's dramas, especially in the later ones; his plays are the opposite extreme of psychological dramas like Goethe's 'Iphigenie' and 'Tasso.'

It was a fatal misfortune both for the German drama and for Kleist that Goethe could not interest himself in his favour. On the 2nd of March, 1808, 'Der Zerbrochene Krug' was performed at Weimar, but it was an entire failure, and the author only excited horror and disgust in

Goethe's antipathy to Kleist.

Goethe's mind. Goethe's antipathy is easily to be accounted for.
The literary revolution, which he had himself ushered in with
'Götz,' still continued to exercise its influence, and Kleist was
moulded by its tendencies; but Goethe had long since returned
to those classical traditions with which his youthful temerity had
led him to break, and accordingly he now rejected whatever in
the least violated the standards of classicism. Zacharias Werner
obeyed Goethe; Kleist did not, and hence he was doomed.

Another young dramatist of this period produced a far more
favourable impression on Goethe: this was Franz
Grillparzer. Grillparzer of Vienna, who was deeply touched by the
warm reception which he met with from the great poet in the
autumn of 1826. In the person of Grillparzer, Austria, which had
for a long time been unrepresented in German literature, came
once more to the front. Since the sixteenth century the Austrian
Court had only favoured Italians; even Abraham a Sancta Clara
was not an Austrian by birth, and men like Michael Denis
(vol. ii, p. 57), Aloysius Blumauer (vol. ii, p. 282), or Johann
Alxinger, the latter a writer of epics in Wieland's style, were not
authors of any great reputation. The only form of literature that
had much life in Austria was the drama.

Franz
Grillparzer.

Vienna was one of the places where the German popular drama
flourished most, and the Viennese public remained
loyally attached to Harlequin and his improvised buffoonery. Gottsched's reforms were slow in making
their way there. The first so-called regular drama
was performed there in 1747, and in 1748 the most
eminent actors of Neuber's scattered troop came to Vienna, where-
upon a lengthy conflict began against the farce and against the
clown, who wished to assert his position even in the regular drama.
As late as 1763 we find the clown taking the place of the servant
Norton in the performance of 'Miss Sara Sampson,'
and not till 1770 was the victory of the reforming
party complete. After that the Viennese stage still
retained for some time the French character which
Gottsched's reforms had given it. From 1752 to 1772 a permanent troop of French actors occupied the present Burg-Theater,

Popular
character
of the
drama in
Vienna.

French
influence
after 1770.
Ayrenhoff.

and when they were dismissed, the nobility, who had been the chief patrons of the French plays, had to be propitiated by the production of German plays written entirely in the French style. From the very ranks of the Austrian nobility there appeared a dramatist who was a thorough-going adherent of French classicism, Cornelius Hermann von Ayrenhoff. His comedy, 'Die Post-kutsche,' had the honour of winning the praise of Frederick the Great. Ayrenhoff produced tragedies and comedies after the style of Corneille, and died in 1819 as Lieutenant-Fieldmarshal. But the Burg-Theater soon triumphed over these French prejudices, and impartially aimed at the best. When in 1776 it became the Court and National Theatre, one of its actors, Müller by name, travelled, under the commission of Prince Kaunitz, through Germany, making engagements with actors ; he visited Lessing, took counsel with him, and carried some of his advice into effect on his return. Various Viennese actors proved themselves fertile playwrights. Outside the theatre also there was great activity in dramatic production, and though nothing of first-class merit was produced, yet the average of writing was fair, and the necessities of the real stage were always kept in view. Shakspeare, Lessing, Goethe, and Schiller were soon represented in the repertoire of the Court Theatre, and most of Mozart's operas were put on the stage for the first time. The directors were very cautious about admitting plays of what they considered doubtful taste, or dangerous political views ; all Schiller's plays except 'Fiesco' were for a long time excluded. The 'Maid of Orleans' was only countenanced with some careful alterations and suppression of the author's name, and 'Wilhelm Tell' was not allowed to be acted till 1827.

Rise of the Court and National Theatre.

An Austrian dramatist of high aspirations, Heinrich Joseph von Collin, produced a play, 'Regulus' (1801), which won great applause, but he never improved upon this first production. Joseph Schreyvogel, on the contrary, produced nothing of his own worth noticing, though his taste and powers of criticism secured him lasting and powerful influence. The years from 1814 to 1832, in which he took part in the manage-

Schreyvogel.

ment of the Burg-Theater, were a halcyon period in the career
of that institution. His general views were those of Lessing;
he was an enemy of romanticism, and despised popular and
old German poetry. He freely criticised Goethe and Schiller,
and the classical dramas of the latter alone met with his entire
approval.

Schreyvogel's influence determined the artistic development of

Character of Grillparzer's dramas. Franz Grillparzer, and raised him from the first above
the one-sided tendencies of the literary revolution and
of Romanticism. Though a disciple of the German
classicists, Grillparzer would never have ventured to
produce a play with so little action as Goethe's 'Iphigenie' or
'Tasso.' His language seldom reaches a high level of perfection,
though it is always in keeping with the dramatic situation. In
moments of the deepest emotion his characters are either dumb or
else utter themselves with the utmost brevity, and his dialogue is
throughout more natural than Kleist's. Like Kleist he was a perfect
master of dramatic technique, but, being a man of gentler mould
than Kleist, he was more accommodating to the likings of the public.
Though perhaps inferior to that writer in originality and power, he
had a healthy mind which kept him free from all exaggeration. He
lived from 1791 to 1872, and made a modest career as an official;
it was only late in life that he enjoyed, with some feeling of bitterness, the reward of assured fame. He felt himself cramped in a
variety of ways in his much-loved native land. Vienna had an
enervating effect on his mind, and in addition to this an arbitrary
censorship of the press had always to be taken into account.

His chief plays. Seven of his plays were performed between the years
1817 and 1834; these were 'Die Ahnfrau,' 'Sappho,'
the trilogy 'Das goldene Vliess' (the story of Jason and
Medea), 'König Ottokar's Glück und Ende,' 'Ein treuer Diener
seines Herrn,' 'Des Meeres und der Liebe Wellen' (the story of
Hero and Leander), and 'Der Traum ein Leben.' There followed
in 1840 a comedy drawn from Merovingian history entitled, 'Weh
dem der lügt,' which was a failure, and three tragedies which were
not made known till after his death. The above titles show that in
the choice of his subjects he partly adhered to the old traditions of

the Renaissance-drama, and partly met the new interest taken by
his contemporaries in the national past, devoting his attention, however, entirely to Austrian history. ' Die Ahnfrau' and 'Der Traum
ein Leben' form a special group in which the action hurries on
tumultuously; the four-footed trochaic metre in which they are
written connects them with the Spanish dramatic form, which
Müllner's 'Schuld' and the translations of Calderon had brought
into fashion. When well acted the 'Ahnfrau' produces even now
a great effect, and Grillparzer has written nothing else of the same
tragic power as the scene in which the robber Jaromir is maddened
by the thought that he has unwittingly killed his own father.
In his later plays Grillparzer concentrated his powers   His
more and more on the careful drawing of character,   character-
but his figures were always narrowly individual, for   drawing.
he tried to make them true to life by copying them from the types
of Viennese society.   While Schiller aimed at making his tragic
heroes appeal to the human sympathies of his audience, Grillparzer preferred to lower them a little, and sometimes even set them
in an unattractive light, as though he wished to make it less painful to his audience to see them in distress.   Their misfortunes are
frequently the result of external circumstances, of chance, misunderstanding, intrigue, of the vices of others, or the weakness of those
whose strength had been relied upon, or finally of well-devised
measures taken by those who have to guard the law.   If Grillparzer
had written a 'Mary Stuart,' Mary's character would have been
lowered and Elizabeth's raised; at least this is the way in
which he treated a similar contrast between Ottokar of Bohemia
and Rudolph von Hapsburg.   While with Schiller ruin is the fate
of the beautiful upon earth, with Grillparzer we find ourselves in a
very well-arranged world, in which evil·is sure to be punished and
good rewarded.   But good means with him the domestic virtues,
the simple mind, the honest heart which he specially praises in the
Austrians; evil, on the other hand, means for him self-assertion,
thirst for fame, inordinate ambition, which is sure to lead to sin and
misery.   In his play, 'Der Traum ein Leben,' the moral of which
is as usual not to be over-ambitious, Grillparzer produces a weird
effect by so arranging his plot that the spectator does not know

where waking life ends and dream-life begins, and so mistakes as real all the horrors of the dream. This play and the 'Ahnfrau' most remind us of the Romanticists. Grillparzer learned how to create such thrilling effects as they contain partly from E. T. A. Hoffman and partly in the Leopoldstadt theatre, which as a boy he frequented.

As we have seen, the regular drama triumphed in Vienna about 1770. But though Harlequin had died out, yet burlesque lived on. Philip Hafner's comedies were quite a continuation of the old popular drama, only that they did not trust for the dialogue to the actors' powers of extemporising. These plays were printed again and again, and continually revived on the stage. In 1780 Karl von Marinelli founded the Leopold-stadt theatre, which became the favourite home of farce. The farces acted on its boards reflected the harmless gaiety of Viennese life, ridiculed the Hungarians and Bohemians, revived the favourite old flying machines, and teemed with transformations, ghosts and marvels. In them Harlequin came to life again, under the name of Kasperl, as an Austrian peasant boy, awkward and stupid, but with a certain natural cunning, who was generally, like Harlequin, made the servant of the hero.

Farce in Vienna.

In the nineteenth century farce-writing received a great impulse. The popular stage found its classical author, shortly after the appearance of Grillparzer, in the person of Ferdinand Raimund. He was himself an actor like Shakspeare and Molière, and was perhaps not much inferior to them in natural talent, but his very defective education prevented his ever rising to the highest work. He began by altering to his requirements parts which he was going to act, inserting new scenes, and writing a few new songs. Then for one of his benefits, finding no piece that quite met his approval, he wrote the entirely original play entitled 'Der Barometermacher auf der Zauberinsel.' This was in 1823, and between that year and 1834 he wrote seven more pieces, among which 'Der Diamant des Geisterkönigs,' 'Das Mädchen aus der Feenwelt,' 'Der Alpenkönig und der Menschenfeind,' and 'Der Verschwender,' are the most worthy of notice. Raimund was a year older than Grillparzer. In 1836,

Ferdinand Raimund's plays.

in a fit of melancholy, he committed suicide. He was excitable, sensitive, and filled with burning ambition. He was a virtuoso in his mastery of the Austrian dialect, and showed great originality in the dialect-farces which he wrote; but he aspired higher than this, and accordingly took to writing a high-flown style of German in iambic rhythm, which sounds very stilted and unnatural. He was thoroughly at home in the world of the   His bourgeoisie and of the peasantry, and created from   character- it wonderfully real and life-like characters; when,   drawing. however, he tried to quit this sphere and draw ideal figures, he was generally unsuccessful. He was excellent in farce, but he did not care to be a mere jester, and his recoil from the character sometimes carried him into tragedy, to the great offence of the particular audiences for whom he wrote. He succeeded in making the magical farce really interesting by humanising his magicians, ghosts, and fairies as thoroughly and as unhesitatingly as Hans Sachs did sacred personages; in fact he simply transplanted into supernatural regions the society of the Viennese bourgeoisie, with all their manners and customs, their standing witticisms and conventionalities, their musical *soirées*, and their hackney coaches. But in his heart he despised this bourgeois world of which and for which he wrote with such brilliant imagination, and in his 'Alpen-könig' he finally soared above it. The Alp-king is a sublimation of human nature, something like an ancient god. The delineation of the misanthrope whom the Alp-king converts from his errors, rivals Shakspeare's Timon and Molière's Misanthrope; here Raimund was writing from his own personal experience, and he showed great genius and skill in overcoming the difficulties which beset the conception and development of a character who is at once to excite our pity and ridicule. The magic element retreats still further into the background in ' Der Verschwender' (The Spendthrift), in which the hero's fate depends entirely on his own character. This play is Raimund's masterpiece; it is full of exciting action, and at the same time everything is made subservient to the development of a character; the other figures are many and various, some of them only sketched, but all parts out of which a capable actor could make something. The character of Valentine, the spendthrift's faithful servant, is a sort of idealised Hanswurst.

While the popular drama with its old characters was thus experiencing a revival of prosperity, Goethe was busy in completing one of his oldest theatrical projects, which the popular

Goethe's
'Faust.'

stage had first suggested to him, and was finally recasting a subject at which many of his contemporaries had tried their hand without marked success, namely, the legend of Dr. Faustus.

Periods of great literary activity, but of crude taste, have frequently created the rough material out of which more cultured periods have formed their most beautiful works of art. The epoch of the migration bequeathed to after ages the German heroic legends. The rule of Charlemagne and his successors was the source of the French national epics, and furnished both Old French and Middle High-German poetry with welcome subjects. It was the Germany of the sixteenth century which produced the living Dr. Faustus, the original of that legendary character who was finally immortalised by the greatest poet of the

History
of the
Faust
legend.

eighteenth and nineteenth centuries. The character of Faust is a connecting link between two periods of German literature, and its gradual progress can be traced through both periods, from the lowest depths of mere popular buffoonery to the loftiest heights of poetic art.

This mysterious personage was first introduced into literature through the 'History of Dr. Faustus, the notorious magician and master of the Black Art,' which appeared at Frankfurt-on-the Main in the year 1587, and was the work of a very orthodox Protestant. This work is a confused compilation of the various anecdotes current about Dr. Faustus, and also probably of a few written records concerning him. Georg Rudolph Widmann of Schwäbisch Hall, a fanatical Lutheran, recast the 'History' in 1599, adding words of warning and exhortation along with several notes on magic, which were further added to in 1674 by the Nürnberg Doctor, Johann Nicolaus Pfitzer. In 1728 an author, who concealed his real personality under the name of 'A Christian Believer' (Ein Christlich Meynender), struck out all the appended learned matter, and published an abridgment of the 'History,' which was repeatedly printed and modernised, and extensively sold at the book-fairs as a 'People's Book.' But meanwhile the story had naturalised itself under another form in the minds of the German public.

Soon after its first appearance in Germany, the 'History' had become known in England, and Christopher Marlowe made it the basis of a tragedy, which was brought to Germany by English comedians not later than the beginning of the seventeenth century; there, after passing through the various phases which marked the development of the popular drama, it was finally banished from the real stage, and became a puppet-play, which it continues to be to the present day. The Faust of the popular drama is a Professor in Wittenberg, who, being discontented with science, declares he will turn his attention to magic; his good genius warns him against it, his bad genius spurs him on; at this very moment his servant Wagner announces the arrival of two students who hand him a long wished-for book of magic. With the help of this book he conjures up the spirits, the fleetest of which he is willing to take into his service; at length Mephistopheles, who is as swift as thought, satisfies his demands. Then this spirit fetches up the conditions of the contract from the Prince of Hell; he is to serve Faust for twenty-four years, at the end of which period the doctor is to fall a prey to the powers of hell. The contract being signed, Faust wishes to visit a prince's court, and Mephistopheles conducts him through the air to the court of Parma, where Faust delights the prince by his magic art, and conjures up before him figures of bygone ages, amongst them the Greek Helena. He then returns to Wittenberg, where he finds his servant Wagner again, and puts to Mephistopheles embarrassing questions about hell and the state of the damned. He also asks for information about heavenly bliss; this Mephisto refuses to give, and when Faust insists upon it he flees. Thereupon Faust resolves to seek mercy from heaven, and curses magic. Hell hears the curse, and Mephisto again approaches while Faust is praying,

[Side notes: Marlowe's 'Faust' and the German popular drama. / Sketch of the popular drama of 'Faust.']

and offers him, though in vain, a sceptre and a crown. But
Helena, whom Mephisto summons up from the lower world, wins
the heart of Faust, and draws him away from penance; when he
tries to embrace her, however, she disappears. At last, at a
time when he is entertaining some students, Faust feels his
end approaching; the twenty-one years are now over, and he falls
into the power of the devil.

Hanswurst stands as a foil by Faust's side, and parodies him
throughout the whole piece. Like Faust he conjures up the spirits,
but they have no power over him. The contrast between the two
figures culminates in the last scene; Hanswurst, formerly Faust's
servant, has now become a night-watchman, and while Faust's last
hours are striking, while a heavenly voice is announcing to him the
last judgment, while the anguish of death is upon him, Hanswurst
is composedly singing the night-watchman's song and enjoying
himself as only a snug Philistine can. The moral is the ordinary
one: do not indulge in too lofty aspirations, for they lead to
damnation, and he alone is happy who is contented with little.

It was in this form that Lessing became acquainted with the
Lessing's popular tragedy, and resolved to adapt it to the
fragment of regular stage. He could not let Faust fall a prey to
a drama the powers of darkness, for that was to openly con-
on Faust. demn the passion for truth as devilish. In the
seventeenth of his 'Litteraturbriefe,' dated the sixteenth of February, 1759, he published one scene of the play as he planned it,
and thereby doubtless incited younger poets to deal with the same
subject. The leaders of the literary revolution found in Faust a
kindred spirit, a strong genius with high aspirations, who forsook
the beaten track, and rose, like a Titan in revolt, against the
ordinary limits of humanity. It was soon announced in the papers
that besides Lessing, both Goethe and Maler Müller were at work
on a 'Faust,' and some anxiety was expressed lest rationalism
should suffer in consequence of the introduction on the stage by
poets of genius of the devil and a magician. But an insignificant
Viennese writer named Paul Weidmann forestalled both these
works in 1775 with an 'allegorical drama,' as he called it, a miserable production in which the unities of time and place were care-

fully observed, and a few motives tediously spun out. In 1776 and 1778 Maler Müller published two fragments of his dramatised life of Faust; and in 1790 a fragment of the first part of Goethe's 'Faust' was given to the world. The former of these two publications excited no curiosity as to what the whole might be, the latter made its readers entertain the greatest expectations of the completed work. A third dramatist of the 'genius-period,' Klinger, had treated the same subject, not in a drama but in a novel, which appeared in 1791; it represented Faust as the inventor of printing, and conducted him through a maze of evil doings, some conscious and some unconscious, some of his own and some of others' doing, to hell. Count Julius Soden followed in Weidmann's and Klinger's steps with his 'popular drama,' published in 1797; here Faust appears as an enemy of tyrants and a patriot, who displays great bravery in conflict with the rebellious peasantry, but is for all that carried off at the last by the devil. Johann Friedrich Schink, too, a violent opponent of Romanticism, adhered to Paul Weidmann's conception in his 'Johann Faust' completed in 1804, only that he raised his hero to a higher moral level, and made him stronger in resisting temptation.

Treatment of the Faust-legend by other writers.

At length in 1808 the first part of Goethe's 'Faust' appeared in its completed form. This did not deter a miserable poet, Karl Schöne by name, from composing in 1809 a new 'Romantic Tragedy of Faust' on the basis of Klinger's novel. August Klingemann's 'Faust' of 1815, a skilfully constructed play, also reminds us more of Klinger and the popular drama than of Goethe. Klingemann represented Faust as the inventor of printing, as did also the fertile writer Julius von Voss, who wrote a drama on the same subject somewhat later (1823). Contemporary with this drama of Voss, C. C. L. Schöne attempted to continue Goethe's Faust in Goethe's own style, and his miserable production was even surpassed in worthlessness by a similar essay on the part of J. D. Hoffmann in 1833. Grabbe was foolish enough to think he would produce a great effect by introducing Faust and Don Juan in the same drama, and by making them rivals in love (1829); and in

First part of Goethe's 'Faust' appears complete in 1808.

1832 Karl von Holtei worked up the story of Faust into a weak melodrama. Meanwhile, in 1827 and 1828 fragments

Second part of Goethe's 'Faust' appears complete in 1832. of the second part of Goethe's 'Faust' had been published, and after his death, towards the end of 1832, the second part appeared complete. Forty-two years thus elapsed between the publication of the first instalment and that of the complete work, and Goethe's work at the book extended over a still longer period.

Goethe was acquainted with the popular drama, and with the

History of the writing of 'Faust.' 'People's Book' of Faust. He took up the story about the same time that he began to work at 'Götz,' when Shakspeare's history-plays were his models, and he thought of dramatising the story of Cæsar's life. At this time he used to express contempt for the traditional rules of dramatic art, and his 'Faust' bears clearly the stamp of this period of his development, in so far as it shows a disregard of all theatrical conventions, and needs alteration and re-arrangement before it can be done justice to upon the stage.

Goethe began with a rough sketch of the drama, only working out a bit here and there, and that in prose. But when he came to know and admire Hans Sachs, he resolved to clothe this old German story in an old German garb, and chose doggrel verse for the purpose. In the autumn of 1775 a number of scenes were already completed, but in Weimar he let the work lie. After his Italian journey he again took it up, and gave the 'Fragment' of 1790 its provisional conclusion. After this he devoted no further attention to the drama, until Schiller urged him to complete it. In the summer of 1797 he sketched out a plan for the whole work, both first and second part, and took it up afresh, only to give it up in April, 1801. It was not till April, 1806, that it was so far advanced that the first part could be published. Much later, in 1824, he resolved to complete the second part, and by July, 1831, this too had been done.

The whole plan was not carried out. Important scenes which Goethe had had in view are wanting, and unevennesses were not smoothed away. It is when taken as a whole, and seen, so to speak, from a distance, that the poem discloses the same unity as the Homeric epics or the Nibelungenlied or Gudrun. The period of sixty years over which the work was extended, the frequent interruptions to which it was subjected, and the variety of moods under which it was written, have prevented 'Faust' from attaining any closer unity than this. In most of the first part we admire the sure, bold hand of the young or mature artist; in the second part, along with marvellously effective scenes, we find weaker portions, in which the hand of the now aged master seems to tremble.

Neither the Hans-Wurst of the popular drama nor the Philistine condemnation of the aspiring human mind could answer Goethe's purpose. He could not any more than Lessing deliver over his hero to the devil in accordance with the old legend and the popular drama, and he therefore from the beginning prepares us for a final reconciliation. The popular play, following the Renaissance-style of the seventeenth century, contained a prelude in hell, in which Charon accuses the furies, i. e. the devils, before Pluto, who thereupon exhorts them to be more diligent, or even specially charges them with the task of leading Faust astray. Goethe, on the contrary, prefaces his work with a prologue in Heaven, in which, with the boldness of Hans Sachs, he introduces God Almighty Himself and the heavenly hosts, among whom the devil Mephisto mingles. We learn from God's own lips that Faust's high aspirations are pleasing to Him, and that He will soon lead him from the darkness in which he gropes into light; and when Mephisto receives permission to tempt Dr. Faust, we know that he will not succeed in drawing him away from the primal Source of his being, that the devil may indeed disquiet an aspiring soul, but cannot entice him permanently into the path of sin and error.

Differences from the popular drama.

Sketch of the first part of 'Faust.'

Faust is next introduced to us as a scholar among his books, and as in Marlowe and the popular drama, he reveals in a monologue his dissatisfaction with all knowledge and his expectations of magic. He has in his possession the mysterious book which tells him how to conjure up the spirits. He pronounces an incantation; the earth-spirit appears, gigantic in its proportions; Faust cannot at first endure his look, but he nerves himself to do so, and then the spirit repels him. His first attempt has failed; his powerlessness becomes clear to him, and despair takes hold of his soul. He seizes the poison-cup, and is in the very act of raising it to his lips, when the neighbouring church-bells chime out and he hears the tones of the Easter hymn : ' Christ is arisen ! ' The remembrance of his childhood's faith and happiness deters him from taking the fatal step. He bursts into tears, exclaiming: ' Earth has won me back again ! ' On the evening of Easter Sunday, during a walk, Mephisto joins him in the shape of a poodle, which molests him at his work when he gets home; Faust, soon perceiving the real nature of the animal, pronounces an incantation over him as in the old ' People's Book,' and compels him to appear in human form. He then expresses a wish to make a compact with him, but Mephisto wishes to get away, and knows how to escape. A great University function, a public disputation in which Mephisto should again appear, was planned by Goethe, but never carried out, and as the play stands, Mephisto's next appearance is in Faust's study. A compact is then concluded by which Mephisto enters the doctor's service; as long as the latter remains discontented the compact is to last, but if ever in calm contentment he shall say to the moment: ' Tarry a while, thou art so fair,' he is at once to fall into Mephisto's power.

Mephisto then drives him forth; he is to leave the study and see something of real life. They first enter a tavern and join a company of carousers on whom Mephisto plays magical tricks. They go on to a witches' kitchen, where Faust drinks a draught of reju-venescence. With the renewal of youth, love asserts its power over him, and, as in the ' People's Book,' he is consumed by a passion for a girl of the burgher class; Gretchen's innocence purifies his heart, but the devil entices him to sin; he succumbs and ruins Gretchen. Goethe hardly mentions the remorse and despair which we must imagine his hero to feel on account of the wrong he has done to an innocent girl; his repentance falls between the first and second parts of the book.

In the opening scene of the second part Faust is reposing on a flowery lawn, while elves float around his guilty head and try to

quiet with dew of Lethe his bitter qualms of self-reproach. We
soon find him with Mephisto at the court of an em-   Sketch of
peror, whom they assist in his financial difficulties, the second
and amuse with magic arts. Faust conjures up the   part.
vision of Helena before the emperor's eyes, but the sight of her
exercises a magical power on Faust himself. He wishes to gain
possession of her, and lays hold of her; there follows a sudden
explosion, and Faust drops stunned to the ground, while Helena
is dissolved in mist. Here the first act closes.

Mephisto brings the fainting Faust back to his old study.
There, meanwhile, Faust's old servant Wagner has been at work,
and has made a great discovery; he has succeeded, namely, in
fashioning by artificial means a human being, Homunculus, who
turns out to be a precocious spirit of a peculiar kind; he calls
the Northern devil Mephisto, his cousin, but he outstrips him
in insight into things. He guesses Faust's thoughts, which are
still dwelling on Helena, and recommends that he should be taken
to classic soil; in Pharsalus, he says, it is now the time of the
classical Walpurgisnight, when there will be a great gathering of
the ghosts of Greek antiquity; there alone can Faust be cured
of his passion. It is done; Mephisto and Homunculus journey
with Faust through the air, and alight on the Pharsalian fields on
the banks of the river Peneios. As soon as Faust touches the
ground he asks: 'Where is she?' and he wanders among the
mythological beings asking of all : ' Has one of you seen Helena?'
The Centaur Chiron takes him on his back and carries him to the
prophetess Manto, the daughter of Æsculapius, as a madman for
her to heal. But she exclaims: ' I love him who desires the
impossible,' and promises to admit him through a dark way to the
presence of Persephone, with whom he may plead for Helena.
The scene in which he thus pleads was never written. In the
third act, however, after the marvels of the classical Walpurgis-
night have vanished, after Homunculus has been shattered at
the feet of beauty, against Galatea's shell-throne, and Mephisto
has donned antique costume and has transformed himself into
Phorkyas, we see Faust's wishes fulfilled. Helena is in the upper
world, in the Peloponnesus at Sparta. She has forgotten every-

thing since the fall of Troy and the return of the Greeks, and imagines that she has just landed and has been sent on before by Menelaus to prepare a sacrifice. She is met on the threshold by Mephistopheles in the guise of Phorkyas, who announces to her that she herself is the victim destined to fall beneath the sacrificial axe. But Mephisto offers her deliverance; he says that during Menelaus' absence a tribe of warriors from the north have settled in the mountains behind Sparta, and that their chief would grant her protection. Helena agrees, and forthwith Mephisto folds her in a magic mist, and transports her and her women to a castle, where Faust, surrounded by a retinue of spirits, receives her with all the state of a sovereign, quickly wins her love and retires with her to Arcadia. The boy Euphorion, the firstfruits of their union, is a wild child, who defies all restraints; he ultimately throws himself, hoping to fly, from a pinnacle of rock, and falls dead at his parents' feet. His vanished spirit calls from the depths below to his mother, and draws her after him. Faust is thus left alone with Helena's garments, which in a little time melt into clouds, and carry him away.

In the fourth act Faust steps out of the cloud on to the top of a high mountain. Mephisto comes to him and asks him whether on his wide flight over all lands he has seen nothing that attracted him, nothing he would wish to possess. Faust has framed one such wish; he would like to recover land from the sea, to make the barren fruitful, to conquer the unruly element. He soon obtains the means for fulfilling his wish. A rebellion has broken out against the emperor whom he had already succoured once in his time of need; Faust and Mephisto now again come to his aid with magic powers, and overthrow his enemies. As a token of gratitude for this service, Faust is to receive the sea-shore in fief; but the actual scene in which this takes place is again wanting.

In the fifth act the new creation has already succeeded, and Faust rules as sovereign over the land won from the ocean. Where the waves formerly raged, meadows, gardens, woods and villages now meet the eye. Mephisto and the spirits have to help in the great work, but where they can they mingle evil with it in their devilish malice. Instead of commerce and navigation they carry

on piracy, and where their sovereign bids them enforce obedience
by pacific means they burn and slaughter. Faust begins to feel
that he will not really attain to liberty until he banishes magic
from his path. Then Care approaches him; he restrains himself
from exercising his magic power on her, but neither does he need
to do so, for Care cannot overcome him, and in vain tries to terrify
him with words; even though he is stricken blind by her breath,
there is still daylight in his soul, and unrestingly as before he urges
on his people in their work. A canal is to be made, and he
rejoices to hear the sound of the spades at work; but they are not
digging what he ordered, they are digging his grave. Faust
meanwhile is painting in his mind the picture of the happy future,
when active people will flourish on the newly-won soil. He would
like to stand on free land with a free people; if this wish were
attained he might indeed say to the moment: ' Tarry a while, thou
art so fair;' and in anticipation of this happiness he dies. But
Mephisto has lost, for he has failed to draw Faust permanently away
from the right path; to his last moment he was full of restless aspirations, active for the common welfare, looking for contentment
only in the distant future. In vain Mephisto summons his hosts
together; in the conflict between angels and devils the latter succumb. The heavenly messengers bear what of Faust is immortal
to heaven. Mary, surrounded by penitent women, meets him in the
air; Gretchen receives him and lifts him to higher spheres.

The episode of Gretchen and what leads up to it can only be
partially traced to the ' People's Book' of Faust. If
we keep this episode out of sight, and thus bring   Similarity
the second part into close proximity with the scene   to and
in which the compact is made between Faust and   differences
Mephisto, the similarity with the popular drama be-   from the
comes most apparent; the similarity, and at the same   popular
time the contrast, for whereas in the old play, love and enjoyment
bring the hero to ruin, in the modern drama love and activity are
his salvation. But all the essential elements of the composition
were provided by the popular drama; the chief difference made by
Goethe is that he represents Faust as being at once inflamed by
the sight of Helena at the Imperial Court, for the whole episode of

Helena needed to be more compressed ; and secondly that Helena, instead of being put forward as a temptation of the devil, is rather represented by Goethe as one of the objects which Faust, in his restless desires, demands from his evil companion. Mephisto only shows himself as a tempter in the fourth act, when, as in the popular drama, he offers the doctor a crown. In the popular drama Faust refuses it ; with Goethe he accepts it, but this incident is in Goethe charged with a fine moral import ; Faust accepts the crown, not for the mere sake of possessing it, but to provide himself with a sphere of activity, and in the end his kingdom is his salvation.

No doubt the inner connection in the second part is not always quite clear, but we do not notice this when we see all the marvels spread before us. The effect of this second part of Faust is that of a phantasmagoria, and in it, as in an opera or a fairy-tale, the incredible and magic elements make us less strict in our demands for careful connection and development of the various parts. Each act and scene is most dramatically conceived, and it only needs abridgment to meet the requirements of the real stage. While the first part is not divided into acts and scenes, in the second, on the contrary, each act has its peculiar tone and its definite close. We here see the hand of the stage-manager who knows how the multitude must be satisfied, charmed and held in suspense. The poet here moves in a motley, fantastic world, in which figures of classical and Christian religion, creatures of southern and northern superstition are all mingled together, in a manner which reminds us of Raimund.

Characteristics of the second part.

Goethe's 'Faust' savours all through of the popular sphere in which the story first originated. Still, in the third act, when Helena appears, the poet realises somewhat of the grandeur of Greek tragedy. Far from adhering throughout to the doggrel metre of Hans Sachs, he softens down its free rough rhythm in the later parts of the poem. Alexandrines are introduced as well as blank-verse ; Spanish trochees are occasionally admitted, and Helena speaks in the iambic trimeters of the Greek drama, until contact with the northern world leads her to use rhyme, as is described in a graceful scene

Metre and style in first and second parts.

full of delicate touches. Not only the metre but the style also alters, and the great changes which Goethe's dramatic talent under-went are reflected in this his life-work.

A prose-scene in the first part, in which Faust has just heard of Gretchen's misery, and breaks into bitter execrations of Mephisto, shows the same forcible style as a Shakspearian drama, and sounds as though it might be from Schiller's ' Robbers.' Passion is arrayed against passion, and the anger of the one side and the scorn of the other wax intense, with no sparing of coarse and strong language. The same overwhelming effect is produced by the scene in the cathedral, where Gretchen succumbs under the feeling of her guilt, amid the horrible babel which stuns her. We should notice the contrast offered by this scene to the earlier and more tender one in which she prays to the Mater Dolorosa!

The beginning of Faust's opening monologue is a close imita-tion of Hans Sachs. But the poet soon rises above the naturalism of ' Götz' to the sublime level of sentiment which we find in ' Werther.' A few scenes of the first part are marked by a truly Dutch attention to detail, by coarseness, comicality, hostility towards clergy and church ; in others we are reminded of poems like ' Prometheus' or ' Ganymed,' and are transported to higher spheres, above the level of earthly joys and earthly struggles. In one part a gentle naturalism holds sway, in another we breathe the idealism of 'Iphigenie.' Sometimes naturalism and idealism are mingled, or represented in the same scene in different persons. The two elements are mingled in the pathetic character of Gretchen, which is essentially a creation of Goethe's earlier manner, dating from the Frankfurt period of his life. He has never created anything sublimer than this ideal picture of innocence, simplicity, warmth and depth of affection ; her maidenly reserve at the outset, the spirit of noble purity which breathes around her, her little world of domestic duties, the truly feminine instinct with which she tends her little sister, the natural grace with which she reveals her feelings, the naive love of ornament natural to the girl of the people ; then the first shadows which fall on this transparent soul, the misgivings roused by Faust's bold address, the presentiment of danger and involuntary shudder felt

Character of Gretchen.

at Mephisto's presence, her pious anxiety about the spiritual welfare of her lover, her devotion and utter self-surrender to him, her
inability to refuse him anything, and then all the fell consequences
of her weakness, madness, prison and death—a fearful transition
this from the idyllic to the tragical.   Yet the charm of innocence
clings to Gretchen in the midst of her guilt ; and herein the poet
shows his wonderful skill, for he does not try to veil or excuse her
offence, and yet he fills us with that love of the heroine which purity
alone can inspire.   The halo of human forgiveness rests on the
head of this ' good soul,' as she is called in the second part, ' who
only once erred, and hardly knew that she was erring.'   In Shakspeare's Ophelia we have the germ of Gretchen's character, only
Gretchen rises high above Ophelia.   Most of the Gretchen scenes
are somewhat naturalistic in treatment, not so forcible as the scene
in the cathedral, but neither so tender and affecting as her mono-
logues.   The mad-scene in the prison is based upon an extravagant
youthful sketch, which was toned down by the poet's maturer art
in 1798.

Gretchen's female companions, her neighbour Frau Marthe and
her contemporary Lieschen are creations of Goethe's
naturalistic period.   So too is the famulus Wagner,
the Philistine counterpart of Faust, and so far akin to
the old Hanswurst.   But the first part was completed as far as
possible in the style of Goethe's cultured realism, and in accordance with the typical method of his ripest art, as we find it in
' Hermann and Dorothea.'   The ' Prelude at the Theatre ' contrasts in a typical manner the poet's vocation and the actor's.   The
songs of the three archangels which open the 'Prologue in Heaven '
are an attempt to picture to us the world under its eternal aspects.
The suicide-scene and the walk on Easter Sunday afford us typical
pictures of human life as a whole.   The fit of industry which
follows, and the disturbances of the poodle are almost symbolically
treated, and Mephisto's character is further developed in accordance with the first outlines of it given in the ' Prologue in Heaven.'
The poet now aims at closer connection, more exact determination
of time, and greater conciseness.   Thus the scene in which
Gretchen's brother appears and falls by Faust's hand is made to

*Typical
realism in
'Faust.'*

link directly with the Walpurgis-night. The Walpurgis-night was not completed, and the continuations of it afterwards suggested by literary satire somewhat lowered this scene in the public estimation.

In the second part of 'Faust' typical realism predominates exclusively, only that the realism disappears more and more, and the typical element alone remains along with a wealth of allegory and personification. The emperor's court contains nothing but typical characters. Three strong men represent the army of spirits in the fourth act. Three penitent sinners from the New Testament stand by Gretchen's side, in order to *Predominance of typical treatment and allegory in second part.* give a typical aspect to an otherwise completely individualised picture of sinning innocence. The figures drawn either from ancient mythology, or, as in the Walpurgis scene, from the storehouse of Goethe's own imagination, are made extraordinarily characteristic, and a free, fine spirit of romanticism breathes through the scenes in the rocky caves of the Ægean sea, where the sirens repose on the cliffs in the moonshine, while Galatea appears in her shell-chariot, inflames the passion of Homunculus and draws him on to his death. There is, however, a good deal of spurious symbolism in the second part, which Goethe should not have allowed himself; I refer to utterances which would be appropriate if they came from Goethe's own lips, but which are little consonant with the characters in whose mouths he puts them, and in which he either remains obscure or offends if his meaning is understood. The latter is the case with the character of Euphorion, who is not only Faust and Helena's son, but is also meant as an impersonation of Lord Byron. Nevertheless, when placed on the stage, Euphorion's graceful youth charms us, and his death affects us deeply. The master's poetical power triumphs over all symbolism and mystification.

There is a certain parallelism between the first and second parts. Notes struck in the one are repeated higher up the scale, as it were, in the other, as we should expect from a writer who sets himself to delineate types rather than particular people. Thus in the first part *Parallelism between the first and second parts.* we have a German Walpurgis-night, in the second a classical one;

Wagner, Faust's former servant, appears afterwards as an independent scholar; an inquisitive student of the first part becomes an arrogant bachelor of arts in the second; Gretchen's prayer of despair is changed into a prayer of joy. This parallelism is most observable in the case of Helena, who occupies the same leading position in the second part which Gretchen does in the first. It is not quite clearly brought out in the drama, but must have been part of the poet's original plan, that the two sinning women should be Faust's good geniuses, who purify and save him from the power of the evil one. Only in the second part we are left to divine for ourselves that the passion with which Helena, like Gretchen, inspires him at first sight, gives way ultimately, like his passion for Gretchen, to nobler feelings. In the drama as it stands there is also considerable abruptness in the sudden transition from Faust as Helena's lover to Faust as the aspiring sovereign of lands wrested from the sea.

The beginning of the third act is a supreme example of Goethe's 'cultured realism.' We detect both in the conception and development of the situation the same fulness and force of imagination which characterized his youthful poems and the ballads written subsequently. It is a grand yet terrible thought that Helena should return to her home doomed to be sacrificed on the domestic altar. The chorus of Trojan women has been marvellously treated by Goethe. He lets them retain the traditional changeableness of the chorus, but represents their rapid changes of mood as the result of the lower feminine nature. 'Precipitate and foolish, true picture of woman's nature!' the leader of the chorus exclaims to them.

Third Act of Second Part.

Helena stands in two-fold contrast, first to the chorus and then to Phorkyas. Helena is the mistress, dignified in her bearing, self-possessed and calm even in the presence of death; the chorus, on the other hand, is composed of serving women, whose demeanour is the exact opposite to Helena's in everything. But though Helena can suffer death with calm dignity, the appearance of Phorkyas fills her with horror, for he represents the extreme of ugliness, as she of beauty. The two, in their opposition, are typical of the great contrast between the beautiful

The Chorus, Phorkyas and Helena.

and the hideous which pervades creation. Beauty is everything with Helena; her beauty is her character and her fate. Phorkyas Mephisto, on the contrary, is physically and morally hideous, and delights in all malice and wickedness.

A third contrast may be noticed, namely that between Helena and Gretchen. The German burgher-maiden is all unconscious; the Greek Goddess is throughout self-conscious ; she knows her heart, and feels what is coming, and she acts not from impulse but with full reflection. We cannot believe that Goethe intended in Helena to show us beauty only from its evil side ; he must have meant also to show us beauty as a good, Helena proving a blessing to Faust. We may venture to surmise that the rousing of his creative activity was the legacy which Helena bequeathed to her northern friend.

Among the manifold figures which Goethe has created we notice four classes of male characters which often recur, retaining the same general features: the active, the negative, the emotional, and those who begin with sentiment and end with action. The emotional characters follow the promptings of their hearts, and heed not the warning voice of reflection or conscience. They break down and ruin themselves and others from stress of their own feelings, or because they yield to evil counsel. Such characters are Weislingen, Clavigo, Werther, Crugantino, Fernando, Tasso, Eduard; they are all selfish and vacillating, either gloomy like Orestes, or careless like Egmont, or despondent in grief like Epimetheus.

Four classes among Goethe's male characters. The emotional type.

The working and struggling characters, who act from reflection and not from blind impulse, are Götz, Prometheus, Pylades, William of Orange, Antonio, Lothario, Hermann, Achilles, and the captain in the 'Wahlverwandschaften.' These characters are never represented as selfish by Goethe ; they work for the welfare of friends, country, or humanity, and are at once generous and self-denying.

The active type.

The negative characters are swindlers like Satyros, Pater Brey, the Great Cophta, Reinecke Fuchs, intriguants like the duke's secretary in the 'Natural Daughter,' besoms of destruction like the demons of war, cunning and

The negative type.

oppression in 'Epimenides,' with whom we may compare tools
of despotism like Alba, or instruments of revolution like the
peasant-leaders in 'Götz;' shortsighted men of the world like Carlos,
Clavigo's friend, who balances worldly gain against duty and
honour; supercilious scoffers like Jarno in 'Wilhelm Meister,' who
by very repulsion rouse others to goodness. Mephisto has something in common with each of these types, and is a conjuror to
boot. He delights in harming, and glories in sin and ruin. He
excites all the lower human impulses, and makes Faust a seducer
and a murderer. He is a scoffer, a coarse jester, and revels in all
that is senseless, filthy, ugly, or barbarous. Goethe has most
felicitously comprehended in one formula the manifold characters
in which Mephisto appears, when he makes him say that he is:
'Part of that power that would still do evil, but still does good.'
This nowhere proves itself truer than in the temptation of the
fourth act, which turns out to be for Faust's salvation. The love
for Gretchen, also, which Mephisto does his best to strengthen,
leads neither in the beginning nor in the end to the result which
he wished for; Faust does not become worse through it, but
better.

Wilhelm Meister and Faust are the two characters, who, from
the emotional, speculative, critical, or æsthetic life,
pass under the inciting influence of denying spirits
and ideal examples, to the life of useful labour. Both
these figures accompanied the poet during a good period of his
life, and both are comparatively true pictures of himself. He was
not able to give the last touch of art to either of them, but Faust
came nearer to perfection than Wilhelm Meister. The former represents the scientific, the latter the æsthetic tendency
of Goethe's youth. Like Faust, Goethe had in vain
sought satisfaction in all departments of knowledge.
Like Faust he hoped for a short time to find a clue to
the mysterious power which binds nature into one whole, in sciences
which were then still of evil fame, in the writings of old chemists
and alchemists. Like Faust he harboured thoughts of suicide.
Like Faust he was not devoid of religious feeling, especially when
engaged in contemplating nature as a whole. Like Faust he had

(margin) Wilhelm Meister and Faust.

(margin) Parallel between Faust and Goethe.

Mephistophelian friends, Merck and Herder for instance, who made him conscious of his littleness, and thereby gave a stimulus to his efforts. Like Faust he fell in love with a simple burgher-maiden, and as Gretchen was made miserable by Faust, so Friederike Brion was made miserable by Goethe, though not at all to the same extent. Like Faust he remained always conscious of the right path, and though he often went astray, yet he always returned to it. Like Faust he came to a court, had a voice in affairs of state, and was chastened in hard service for the common good. Like Faust he imbibed in the south, on classical soil, fresh strength and purer aspirations, along with a clearer insight into his own future. Like Faust he drew nigh to the Greek gods, and in communion with the immortal creations of Hellenic art and religion found the highest truths dawn upon him, and the various tendencies of his nature gather themselves up into one. Like Faust he returned to his northern fatherland, to a life of activity among his own people. His contact with the ancient world bore fruit in Germany, though in another sense than with Faust; he no longer found his vocation in political and social activity, but in science and poetry alone. Then, when a friend of equal intellectual rank with himself inspired him with new joy in creation, 'Faust' was among the first tasks that engrossed him. The classical Walpurgis-night, Helena, and the final studies which underlay the last developments of the poem, date from the period in which he practised his hand in Greek rhythms and revived the Greek gods in poetry, the period of the Roman elegies and the 'Achilleis.'

Faust was not meant to resemble Goethe in all points, but he represents Goethe's views in all great questions—in the idea that man is meant to struggle, in the conviction of the salvation to be found in hard service, in the maxim which Faust utters when dying as the last conclusion of wisdom : 'He alone deserves liberty, like life, who daily must conquer it.' Herein he was also in harmony with Schiller, whose Tell declares: 'I only really enjoy my life, when I win it every day afresh.' Both in 'Wilhelm Meister' and in 'Faust,' Goethe prizes activity for the common good more highly than æsthetic and literary interests. Neither the poet, nor

the actor, nor the speculative scholar, he seems to think, can attain
in their own spheres to such lofty discernment and to such peace
of conviction as the man of action. Thus Goethe recommended
in poetry what he himself neglected to do in real life.

Goethe's 'Faust' contained a deep moral lesson for the German nation in particular. It expressed a longing for
action in an age which was poor in deeds. Many
writers of the time echo this spirit; for example,
we find the Baron von Stein continually deploring the predominance in Germany of metaphysics and speculative science. The
Germans, he wrote, owing to their exclusion from all share in
public affairs, had lost all power of initiative and had taken to
idle broodings. And in fact since the Reformation, the German
character had become more and more introspective, and modern
German poetry has but seldom glorified the strong, indomitable
will which belongs to men of action. But under the guidance of
this same Baron von Stein a change set in. What Goethe
demanded began to be fulfilled even in his life-time, and our
times have seen this fulfilment carried further, perhaps even too
far. The brief harvest of poetic vigour, which was sown by the
deeds of Frederick the Great, was but an earnest of what was
to come, and the delight in its poets gave to a divided nation
the single common possession in which it felt pride and strength.
The poets themselves in their works directly reminded their
countrymen of past days of political greatness. The national
consciousness was quickened, and what seemed a short time before
to be a mere dream became a welcome reality. In the nineteenth
century as in the thirteenth a period of literary glory was followed
by a period of national expansion and economic prosperity. Now,
as then, poetry has suffered thereby. If in 1800 the nation was
over-intellectual, it now begins to be over-material, and threatens
to fall under the sway of those tendencies which beset the German
world of the fourteenth and fifteenth centuries, to the prejudice
both of its culture and character.

A survey of all the successive epochs of German literary history
will alone serve to reveal to us the latent capacities of the nation,
in the harmonious development of all of which lies its real

(marginal note: 'Faust' and the German nation.)

perfection. This perfection may be attained if the fatal one-
sidedness, which so easily lays hold of the German character, can
be overcome ; or, if men will restrain their natural inclinations by
conscious labour, and so carry over into the present and future
the spirit of the age which is expiring.   Many Germans of to-day
need no spurring in order to take to the life of generally useful
activity, which Faust only embraces after often going astray; everything now seems in favour of these practical men.   Meanwhile
those who live after Goethe's example, and look on poetry as a
sacred and national task, have to struggle against wind and
weather and to work doubly hard.   Let them too find encouragement in the words which the angels sing as they bear aloft the
soul of Faust :—

> ' Wer immer strebend sich bemüht,
> Den können wir erlösen.'

APPENDIX.

CHRONOLOGICAL TABLE.

Roman Period.

116 (*circa*). Tacitus, Annals ii. 88, mentions Arminius, killed A.D. 21: 'Septem et triginta annos vitae, duodecim potentiae explevit, caniturque adhuc barbaras apud gentes.'

Gothic and Merovingian Period.

250 (*circa*). Ostrogotha, King of the Goths ; celebrated in the heroic poetry.
341. Ulfilas consecrated Bishop of the Visigoths.
374 (*circa*). Ermanarich kills himself.
381. Death of Ulfilas.
437. The Burgundians defeated by the Huns, King Gundicarius killed.
453. Death of Attila.
476. Odoacer dethrones the last Western emperor.
488. Theodoric the Great leads the Ostrogoths into Italy.
530 (*circa*). The sons of Clovis destroy the Thuringian empire.
568. Alboin the Longobard in Italy.
600 (*circa*). Gradual separation of High German from Low German.

Old High-German Period.

772 (*after*). Christian Missions begin in Saxony. Saxon baptismal vow (Denkm. No. 51).
789. Decrees of Charlemagne on preaching and Christian teaching, which called forth German translations of the Lord's Prayer and the Creed, and German confessions and penances.
804. Rabanus Maurus at the head of the school at Fulda (822, Abbot of Fulda; 847, Archbishop of Mainz). In his time Tatian's Life of Christ was translated into German at Fulda.
830 (*circa*). The Heljand.

842. The Oath of Strassburg (p. 36).

870 (*circa*). Otfried's Gospels.

887. Siegfried, the leader of the Northmen, who appears in the Middle High-German 'Gudrun' as King of the Moors, falls in an attack on the Frisians.

930 (*circa*). 'Waltharius manu fortis.'

962 (*after*). Latin German song on the reconciliation of Otto the Great with his brother Henry (Denkm. No. 18).

965 (*circa*). The Latin Comedies of the nun Roswitha.

968. Roswitha's Latin poem on the life of Otto the Great.

1022. Notker the German, monk of St. Gall, dies.

Middle High-German Period.

1057–1065. Bishop Gunther of Bamberg, who ordered Ezzo's song on the Life of Christ.

1064. Gunther and others lead a great pilgrimage to Palestine.

1065 (*circa*). Williram's paraphrase of the Song of Solomon. About this time, or rather later, the 'Wiener Genesis,' probably of Carinthian origin.

1075. Death of Archbishop Anno of Cologne, celebrated afterwards in the 'Annolied.'

1100 (*before*). A poem on Gudrun, known or composed in Bavaria.

1120 (*circa*). The 'Alexanderlied' by priest Lambrecht.

1127. Death of the nun (inclusa) Ava.

1130 (*circa*). The Rolandslied by priest Konrad, dedicated to Henry the Proud.

1135. Peace in Germany under Lothair the Saxon: 1137, victory over the Normans in South Italy; this period nearly corresponds with 'König Rother,' and the conception of the 'Kaiserchronik.'

1139. Count Louis of Arnstein turns his castle into a monastery, and enters it himself, whilst his wife, Countess Guda, lives in a cloister in the neighbourhood. The Arnstein 'Song of Mary' (Denkm. No. 38). (?)

1143 and 1146 (*between*). The Universal History, by Otto von Freising.

1154 (*after*). German strophe on the Queen of England, Eleanor of Poitou (Minnesangs Frühling, 3. 7).

1155 and 1157 (*between*). The Latin drama of Antichrist. (?)

1157. Life of Frederick Barbarossa, by Otto von Freising.

1160 (*circa*). The Satirist Heinrich von Mölk.

1162. The destruction of Milan, related by the Arch-poet.

1162. Charlemagne canonized.

1170 (*circa*). 'Reinhart Fuchs,' by Heinrich dem Glichezare; 'Count Rudolf;' 'Floris;' 'Tristrant,' by Eilhard von Oberge. Kürenberg's stanza. (?)

1172. Poems on the Virgin, by priest Wernher (see IV. 2, in Bibliography).

1172 (*after*). 'Herzog Ernst.'

1173 (*after*). The 'Anegenge' (see IV. 2, in Bibliography).

1175. Friedrich von Hausen, the Minnesinger, in Italy. An old gleeman (Anonymous Spervogel) sings (when ?) the death of Hausen's father, still alive in 1173.

1176-1181. Burggraf Friedrich von Regensburg, Minnesinger.

1180-1190 (*circa*). Dietmar von Aist, Minnesinger.

1184. Festival of Mainz. The Æneid of Heinrich von Veldeke first known. (?)

1187 (*circa*). Walther von der Vogelweide begins to compose.

1187 (*after*). 'Orendel.'

1189. 'Rupertus ioculator regis' mentioned in documents.

1190 (*circa*). The oldest Nibelungen songs.

1190 (*May* 6). Death of Friedrich von Hausen.

1192. The 'Ereck' of Hartmann von Aue. (?)

1194. The elder Reinmar sings the death of Leopold V of Babenberg. Hartmann's 'Gregorius.' (?)

1195. Hartmann's first Büchlein. (?)

1197. Hartmann joins the Crusade.

1198. Hartmann's 'Armer Heinrich.'(?) Walther leaves Vienna.

1199. Hartmann's second Büchlein. (?)

1202. Hartmann's 'Iwein.' (?)

1203 (*Nov.* 12). Walther von der Vogelweide in Zeisselmauer.

1205 (*circa*). Wolfram's 'Parzival' begun.

1210. Albrecht von Halberstadt begins to translate Ovid's Metamorphoses. Conclusion of the 'Nibelungenlied,' (?) 'Gudrun,' (?) Wolfram's 'Titurel,' Gottfried's 'Tristan,' (?) the 'Wigalois' of Wirent von Grafenberg. (?)

1215 (*circa*). Neidhart von Reuenthal appears.

1215 and 1216. Thomasin composes 'Der Welsche Gast.'

1216 (*before*). Wolfram's 'Willehalm' begun.

1216 (*end of*). Hermann the Landgrave of Thuringia dies.

1220 (*circa*). Wolfram von Eschenbach dies. 'Sachsenspiegel.' (?)

1225 (*circa*). Rudolf of Ems probably began his poems.

1225 (*circa*). 'Ortnit.'

1227. Walther von der Vogelweide encourages the Crusade.

1229 (*March* 18). Frederick II crowns himself King of Jerusalem. Freidank in Palestine.

1230 (*circa*). Burkard von Hohenfels and Gottfried von Neifen at Prince Henry's Court in Swabia.

1250. The Franciscan monk, Berthold of Regensburg, begins to preach.

1250 and 1254 (*between*). The 'Weltchronik' of Rudolf of Ems.

1260. Albertus Magnus, Bishop of Regensburg.

1260 and 1270 (*between*). Albrecht's 'Titurel.'

1266-1308. Reign of Otto IV of Brandenburg, the Minnesinger.

1268 (*Oct.* 29). Conradine beheaded. Love songs composed by him are extant.

1270-1290. Reign of Heinrich of Breslau, the Minnesinger.

1272 (*Dec.* 13). Death of Berthold of Regensburg.

1275. The 'Schwabenspiegel.'

1276. Rudolf of Hapsburg besieges Vienna. Steimar and other Minnesingers in his army. Bruno von Schönebeck (near Magdeburg) translates the Song of Solomon.

1277. (*circa*). Death of Mathilde of Magdeburg.

1278. Frauenlob in the army of Rudolf of Hapsburg.

1280. Death of Albertus Magnus, at Cologne.

1286. Frauenlob at Prague, when Wenzel of Bohemia, the Minnesinger, was knighted.

1287. (*Aug.* 31). Death of Conrad of Würzburg.

1290. (*before*). 'Lohengrin.'

1293. Legend of St. Martina, by Hugo von Langenstein.

1300. Hugo von Trimberg's 'Renner' (added to, till 1318).

1302 to 1325. Reign of Wizlaw, Duke of Rügen, Minnesinger.

1314. Johannes von Würzburg (near Esslingen), 'Wilhelm von Oesterreich.'

1318. (*Nov.* 29). Death of Frauenlob at Mayence.

1322. Play of the wise and foolish virgins at Eisenach. (?)

1327. Death of Master Eckhart, the Mystic, at Cologne.

1330 (*circa*). Boner's 'Edelstein.'

1336. Claus Wisse and Philipp Colin of Strassburg, by commission of Ulrich von Rappolstein, continue Wolfram's 'Parzival.'

1340 (*circa*). 'Die Jagd' of Hadamar von Laber.

Early New High-German, or the Transition Period.

1348. University of Prague. The Black Death. Flagellants. Persecution of the Jews.

1352. Rulmann Merswin's 'Buch von den neun Felsen.'

1360 (*circa*). Short songs of three strophes became fashionable, according to the Limburg Chronicle.

1365. University of Vienna.

1370 (*circa*). 'There lived on the Main a barefooted friar who became a Leper, and who in word and melody made the best songs and rhymes, so that nobody at that time could compare with him, and everybody gladly sang his poems' (Limburg Chronicle).

1383. Heinrich of Langenstein in Vienna.

1386. University of Heidelberg.

1388. University of Cologne.

1392. University of Erfurt.

1399. Ackermann aus Böhmen.

1409. University of Leipzic.

1414–1418. Council of Constance. 'Des Teufel's Netz.'

1419. University of Rostock.

1433. Eberhard Windeck's History of the Emperor Sigismund.

1443. Æneas Sylvius, Secretary to the Imperial Chancery (–1455).

1447. Rosenblüt's panegyric on the city of Nuremberg.

1450. Printing discovered by John Gutenberg.

1453. Hermann von Sachsenheim's 'Die Mohrin.'

1454. Peuerbach begins humanistic lectures in Vienna.
1456. University of Greifswald.
1457. University of Freiburg.
1460. University of Basle.
1461. Regiomontanus gives humanistic lectures in Vienna.
1472. Albrecht von Eyb, 'Ob einem Manne sei zu nehmen ein ehlichs Weib oder nicht.' University of Ingolstadt (later Landshut, 1802; Munich, 1826).
1474. Niklas von Wyle writes in praise of women.
1477. 'Parzival' and 'Titurel' printed. University of Tübingen.
1480 (*circa*). Ulrich Fütrer's 'Buch der Abenteuer.'
1480. Theodorich Schemberg's Play 'Frau Jutte.'
1483. 'Eulenspiegel.'
1485. Konrad Celtis began his active work.
1494. Sebastian Brand's 'Narrenschiff.'
1497. Reuchlin's 'Henno,' played. The 'Narrenschiff' in Latin, by Jacob Locher.
1498. 'Reinke de vos.'
1501. Celtis publishes Roswitha's works.
1502. University of Wittenberg. Celtis' 'Amores.'
1503. Adam Wernher, of Themar, translates Roswitha's '[Abraham,' and dedicates it to the Count Palatine Philipp (Heidelberg).
1505. Augsburg newspaper on Brazil. Wimpfeling's German History.
1506. University of Frankfurt on the Oder.
1507. First evidence of the historical Faust.
1508. Luther called to Wittenberg.
1509. Erasmus, 'Encomium Moriae.'
1510. Reuchlin's dispute with the theologians of Cologne.
1511. Albrecht von Eyb's 'Spiegel der Sitten' printed.
1512. Murner, 'Narrenbeschwörung.'
1515. 'Epistolae obscurorum virorum.'
1517. Luther's Theses against Indulgences. 'Epistolae obscurorum virorum,' second part. 'Theuerdank.' Hans Sachs' first Carnival play.
1519. 'Volksbüchlein' of the Emperor Frederick.
1520. Ulrich von Hutten. 'Dialogi;' 'Clag und Vormanung;' Pirckheimer, 'Eccius dedolatus.'
1521. Luther, 'Passional Christi und Antichristi.' Hutten, 'Ich habs gewagt mit Sinnen.' 'Gesprächbüchlin.' 'Dialogi Huttenici novi.' Eberlin von Günzburg, 'Fünfzehn Bundsgenossen.'
1522 (*Sept.*). Luther's New Testament in German. Niklaus Manuel, 'Todtenfresser.' 'Unterschied zwischen Papst und Jesus Christus.' Murner, 'Grosser Lutherischer Narr.' Pauli, 'Schimpf und Ernst.'
1523. Luther's Song on the burning of the martyrs in Brussels. Hans Sachs' 'Wittenbergisch Nachtigall.' Death of Hutten.
1524. Luther's first Hymn-book; the Psalms in German. Hans Sachs' Dialogues.
1525. Manuel, 'Ablasskrämer.'

1527. Hieronymus Emser's New Testament. Hans Sachs' 'Lucretia.' Burkard Waldis, 'Verlorner Sohn.' University of Marburg.
1528. Luther's 'Ein veste Burg ist unser Gott,' in the Wittenberg Hymn-book of this year. Manuel, 'Krankheit der Mess.' Agricola's Proverbs.
1529. Hutten's posthumous Dialogue 'Arminius.' Gnapheus, 'Acolastus' (the prodigal son).
1530. Luther's Fables. Hans Sachs' 'Virginia.'
1531. Sebastian Franck, 'Chronica, Zeitbuch und Geschichtbibel.'
1532. Sixt Birck, 'Susanna.' Sebastian Franck's first anonymous collection of Proverbs.
1533. 'Fierabras.' Hans Sachs' first biblical dramas.
1534. Luther's Bible finished. Dietenberg's Bible (Roman Catholic). Sebastian Franck, 'Teutscher Nation, aller Teutschen Völcker Herkommen.' 'Jacob und seine Söhne,' Magdeburg Drama, by Greff and Major. The Fables of Erasmus Alberus.
1535. 'Die vier Haimonskinder;' 'Octavianus;' Crocus, 'Joseph;' Rebhun, 'Susanna.'
1536. 'Magelone.'
1537. Johann Eck's Translation of the Bible. Agricola's tragedy, 'Johann Hus.'
1538. Naogeorg, 'Pammachius.'
1539. 'Ritter Galmy.'
1540. Jörg Wickram, 'Verlorner Sohn.' Naogeorg, 'Mercator.'
1541. Luther's Bible revised. Naogeorg, 'Incendia.'
1543. Copernicus, 'De revolutionibus.' Naogeorg, 'Hamanus.'
1544. University of Königsberg. Chryseus, 'Hofteufel.' Beuther's High-German translation of Reineke Fuchs.
1545. Hans Sachs begins to dramatise tragic stories.
1546. Council of Trent. Luther's death.
1547. Charles V takes Wittenberg.
1548. Burkard Waldis' 'Esop.'
1549. Dedekind, 'Grobianus.'
1550. Wickram, 'Tobias.'
1551. Scheid, 'Grobianus.' Wickram, 'Gabriotto und Reinhard.' Naogeorg, 'Hieremias.'
1552. Naogeorg, 'Judas Iscariotes.'
1554. Wickram, 'Knabenspiegel,' 'Goldfaden.'
1555. Religious Truce. Sleidanus, 'De statu religionis et reipublicae Carolo V caesare.' Wickram, 'Rollwagenbüchlein.'
1556. Wickram, 'Gute und böse Nachbarn.' Jacob Frey, 'Gartengesellschaft.'
1557. Montanus, 'Wegkürzer.' Hans Sachs' Tragedy 'Hürnen Seufrid.'
1558. University of Jena. Hans Sachs' collected works, Vol. I. Lindener, 'Katzipori.'
1559. Valentin Schumann, 'Nachtbüchlein.'
1560. Hans Sachs, Vol. II.
1561. Hans Sachs, Vol. III. (Scaliger's 'Poetica.')

1563. Kirchhof, 'Wendunmuth.'
1566. Mathesius' Life of Luther. Schopper, 'Speculum vitae aulicae' (Reineke Fuchs).
1569. 'Amadis' begins to appear (-1594). Buchanan's 'Jephthes' acted in Strassburg.
1570. Fischart comes forward as a Protestant champion.
1572. Fischart, 'Eulenspiegel' rhymed. 'Aller Praktik Grossmutter,' 'Claus Narr.'
1573. Lobwasser's Psalms. Fischart, 'Flöhhatz.'
1575. Fischart, 'Gargantua.'
1576. Fischart, 'Glückhaft Schiff.' Frischlin, 'Rebecca.' Death of Hans Sachs. University of Helmstädt.
1577. Fischart, 'Podagrammisch Trostbüchlein.' Frischlin, 'Susanna.'
1578. Johannes Clajus, 'Grammatica Germanicae linguae.' Fischart, 'Ehezuchtbüchlein.' Frischlin, 'Priscianus vapulans.' Hans Sachs, Vol. IV.
1579. Fischart, 'Bienenkorb.' Frischlin, 'Hildegardis magna,' 'Frau Wendelgard.' Hans Sachs, Vol. V.
1580. Fischart, 'Jesuiterhütlein.' Frischlin, 'Phasma.'
1581. University of Altorf.
1584. Frischlin, 'Julius redivivus.'
1587. Popular books, 'Faust,' 'Hans Clauert.'
1588. Fischart on the destruction of the Armada.
1593-4. The Dramas of Duke Henry Julius of Brunswick.
1595. Rollenhagen, 'Froschmäuseler.'
1596. Kepler, 'Prodomus dissertationum cosmographicarum, continens: Mysterium cosmographicum.'
1597. 'Die Schildbürger.'
1599. Widmann's Faust-book.
1605. Johann Arndt, 'Wahres Christenthum' (-1610).
1606. The tragedy of Saul acted in Strassburg.
1607. The 'Conflagratio Sodomae' of Saurius acted in Strassburg. Wolfhart Spangenberg, 'Ganskönig.'
1608. The Ajax of Sophocles, recast in Latin, and acted at Strassburg.
1609. Hirtzwig, 'Belsazar' acted in Strassburg. Kepler, 'Astronomia Nova.'
1612. Brülow, 'Andromeda.' Johann Arndt, 'Paradiesgärtlein.' Jacob Böhme, 'Morgenröthe im Aufgang.'
1613. Brülow, 'Elias.'
1614. Brülow, 'Chariclia.'
1615. Brülow, 'Nebucadnezar.'
1616. Brülow, 'Julius Caesar.' Cluverius, 'Germania antiqua.'
1617. Hirtzwig, 'Lutherus.' Kielmann, 'Tetzelocramia.' Opitz, 'Aristarchus.' August 24, The 'Fruchtbringende' Society.
1618. Beginning of the Thirty Years' War. Weckherlin, 'Oden und Gesänge' (2nd Book, 1619).
1619. Kepler, 'Harmonice mundi.'
1620. 'Englische Comödien und Tragödien.'
1621. Last Low German Bible.

1624. 'Opicii Teutsche Poemata' (Zincgref's collection). Opitz, 'Buch von der deutschen Poeterei.'

1627 (*April* 13). First German Opera. Kepler, 'Tabulae Rudolphinae.'

1630. 'Liebeskampf oder ander Theil der Englischen Comödien und Tragödien.'

1633. 'Aufrichtige Tannengesellschaft' of Strassburg.

1634. Johann Rist, 'Musa teutonica.'

1638. Philipp von Zesen, 'Melpomene.' Jacob Balde, 'De vanitate mundi.'

1640 (*circa*). Moscherosch, 'Gesichte Philanders von Sittewalt.'

1643. Zesen's 'Deutschgesinnte' Society. Jacob Balde, 'Carmina lyrica.' Hagelgans' 'Arminius.'

1644. 'Pegnitzschäfer.'

1645. Zesen, 'Adriatische Rosemund.'

1646. Paul Fleming, 'Teutsche Poemata.'

New High-German Period.

1648. The Peace of Westphalia. Paul Gerhardt's first Church Hymns published.

1649. Frederick Spee, 'Güldnes Tugendbuch,' 'Trutz Nachtigall.'

1650. Andreas Gryphius, 'Leo Arminius' (composed 1646).

1652. Lauremberg's Scherzgedichte.

1654. Logau's Epigrams. Schwieger's 'Liebesgrillen.'

1657. Angelus Silesius, 'Cherubinischer Wandersmann,' 'Heilige Seelenlust.' Andreas Gryphius, 'Katharina von Georgien,' 'Cardenio und Celinde,' 'Carolus Stuardus' (written 1649). 'Peter Squenz' (written between 1647 and 1650).

1658. Rist's Elb Swan Order.

1659. Andreas Gryphius, 'Papinianus.'

1660 (*Oct.* 10). The 'Dornrose' of Andreas Gryphius first acted.

1663. Scriver, 'Gotthods zufällige Andachten.' Schottelius, 'Ausführliche Arbeit von der deutschen Hauptsprache.' Andreas Gryphius, 'Horribilicribrifax' (written between 1647 and 1650).

1664. Joachim Rachel, 'Satirische Gedichte.'

1665. Franciscus Junius publishes the Gothic Gospels. University of Kiel.

1667. Paul Gerhardt ; first complete edition.

1668. 'Simplicissimus.' Christian Weise, 'Überflüssige Gedanken der grünenden Jugend.'

1670. Schaubühne Englischer und Französischer Comödianten. (Among these, plays of Molière.)

1671. Christian Weise, 'Die drei Hauptverderber.'

1672. Christian Weise, 'Die drei ärgsten Erznarren.'

1673. Christian Weise, 'Die drei klügsten Leute.'

1674. Pfitzer's Faust-book. (Boileau, Art poétique).

1675. Angelus Silesius, 'Sinnliche Betrachtung der vier letzten Dinge.' Spener, 'Pia desideria.' Scriver, 'Seelenschatz' (-1691).

1678. Christian Weise, Rector in Zittau. German Opera in Hamburg (-1738).

1679. Christian Weise's first Tragedies. Joachim Neander, 'Bundeslieder und Dankpsalmen.' Abraham a Sancta Clara, 'Merks Wien.'

1682. 'Leipzig Acta Eruditorum.'

1685. Dresden Court comedy actors (–1692).

1687 to 1688. Thomasius delivers the first course of German Lectures. Cochem, 'History-book.'

1688. Thomasius, 'Monatsgespräche' (–1689). Pufendorf in Berlin. Ziegler, 'Asiatische Banise.'

1689. Lohenstein, 'Arminius and Thusnelda' (–1690).

1690. Thomasius lectures at the Ritterakademie in Halle.

1691. Spener in Berlin. Cochem, 'Leben Christi.' (!) French Tragedies translated and played in Brunswick (–1699).

1692. Francke in Halle.

1694. University of Halle.

1696. Christian Reuter, 'Schelmuffsky.'

1697. Christian Wernicke's Epigrams.

1700. Berlin Academy. Freiherr von Canitz, 'Nebenstunden unterschiedener Gedichte.'

1705. Neumeister, 'Geistliche Cantaten.' Christian Weise's last Plays.

1706. Wolff, professor in Halle.

1708. Permanent German Theatre in Vienna.

1709. (Beginning of the English Weekly Newspapers.)

1710. Leibniz, 'Théodicée.'

1711. Johann von Besser, 'Works.'

1712. Brockes' Oratorio of the Passion.

1713. Frederick William I of Prussia ascends the throne.

1714. First German weekly newspaper, 'Der Vernünftler' (Hamburg).

1716. Death of Leibniz.

1719. (Robinson Crusoe).

1721. 'Discourse der Maler' (Zurich). Brockes 'Irdisches Vergnügen in Gott.' Vol. I (9 vols. to 1748).

1723. Christian Wolff banished from Prussia. Christian Günther, 'Gedichte.'

1724. Gottsched in Leipzic. Hamburg weekly paper 'Der Patriot.'

1725. Gottsched's 'Vernünftige Tadlerinnen.' Pradon's 'Regulus,' played in Leipzic.

1727. Gottsched's 'Biedermann.' The Neuber troop of actors.

1728. The Faust-book by the author calling himself der Christlich Meinende.

1729. Hagedorn, 'Versuch einiger Gedichte.' Bach's Passion Music, according to St. Matthew.

1730. Gottsched, 'Critische Dichtkunst.'

1731. 'Insel Felsenburg' (–1743).

1732. Haller, 'Versuch schweizerischer Gedichte.' Bodmer's prose translation of Paradise Lost. Gottsched, 'Cato;' 'Beiträge zur critischen Historie der deutschen Sprache, Poesie und Beredsamkeit' (–1744).

1733. University of Göttingen.

1734. Bodmer, 'Charakter der deutschen Gedichte.'

1736. Gottsched's Poems.

1737. Pyra, 'Tempel der wahren Dichtkunst.'

1738. Hagedorn, 'Fabeln und Erzählungen.' Frederick the Great, 'Con sidérations sur l'état présent du corps politique de l'Europe.'

1739. Liscow, Collection of satirical and serious writings.

1740. Frederick the Great ascends the throne. Christian Wolff recalled to Halle. 'L'Antimachiavel.' Gottsched, 'Deutsche Schaubühne' (–1745). Breitinger, 'Critische Dichtkunst;' 'Critische Abhandlung von den Gleichnissen.' Bodmer, 'Critische Abhandlung von den Wunderbaren.'

1741. Händel's Messiah. Shakespeare's Julius Caesar translated by C. W. von Borck. Schwabe, 'Belustigungen des Verstandes und Witzes (contains Zachariä's 'Der Renommist').

1742. Uz, 'Frühling.'

1743. The Operetta, 'Der Teufel ist los.'

1744. The 'Bremer Beiträge' (–1748). Gleim, 'Scherzhafte Lieder.' Frederick the Great revives the Berlin Academy.

1745. Thyrsis and Damon's (Pyra and Lange) friendly Songs. Gottsched, 'Neuer Büchersaal' (–1754).

1746. Gellert, 'Fabeln und Erzählungen;' 'Leben der schwedischen Gräfin.' Anacreon translated by Uz and Götz.

1747. Hagedorn, 'Oden und Lieder.' Elias Schlegel, 'Theatrical Works.' The first regular play performed in Vienna.

1748 (*Jan.*). Lessing's 'Junge Gelehrte' acted. Klopstock's 'Messiah' (the first three books). Brockes' 'Irdisches Vergnügen in Gott.' Vol. ix. Specimens of the Minnesingers (published by Bodmer). Gottsched, 'Deutsche Sprachkunst.' The Neuber troop of actors at Vienna. Lessing goes to Berlin.

1749. Kleist, 'Frühling.'

1750. Baumgarten, 'Æsthetica.' Voltaire in Berlin. Hagedorn, 'Moralische Gedichte.' Frederick the Great, 'Œuvres du Philosophe de Sans Souci.'

1751. Frederick the Great, 'Mémoires de Brandebourg.' Rabener, 'Sammlung satirischer Schriften' (–1755). Gottsched, 'Das Neueste aus der anmuthigen Gelehrsamkeit' (–1762).

1752. 'Der Teufel ist los' revised by Christian Felix Weise, and performed at Leipzic.

1753. Enlarged edition of Hagedorn's 'Moralische Gedichte.' Lessing's Works, Parts I, II.

1754. Gessner, 'Daphnis.' Lessing's Works, Parts III, IV.

1755. Lessing's Works, Parts V, VI: 'Miss Sara Sampson.' Winckelmann, 'Gedanken über die Nachahmung der griechischen Werke in der Malerei, und Bildhauerkunst.' Kant, 'Allgemeine Naturgeschichte und Theorie des Himmels.'

1756. Seven Years' War begins. Gessner, 'Idyllen.'

1757. Gleim's first 'Kriegslieder.' Gellert, 'Geistliche Oden und Lieder;' 'Chriemhilden Rache' (the Nibelungenlied, partly published by Bodmer). Bibliothek der schönen Wissenschaften und freien Künste (–1806).

1758. Gleim's 'Kriegslieder,' collected in one work. Klopstock, 'Geistliche Lieder.' 'Sammlung von Minnesingern aus dem schwäbischen Zeitpunkte,' by Bodmer (–1759).

1759. Letters on Literature (-1765). Lessing, Scenes from 'Faust,' 'Philotas,' 'Fabeln.' Christian Felix Weise, 'Beitrag zum deutschen Theater' (-1768). Hamann, 'Sokratische Denkwürdigkeiten.'
1760. Musäus, 'Grandison der Zweite' (-1762).
1761. Abt, 'Vom Tode fürs Vaterland.' Wieland, 'Araspes und Panthea.'
1762. Wieland's Shakespeare (-1766).
1763. Peace of Hubertsburg.
1764. Winckelmann, 'Geschichte der Kunst des Alterthums.' Kant, 'Beobachtungen über das Gefühl des Schönen und Erhabenen.' Wieland, 'Don Sylvio von Rosalva.' Thümmel, 'Wilhelmine.'
1765. Nicolai, 'Allgemeine deutsche Bibliothek' (-1806). Leibniz, 'Œuvres philosophiques' (contains the 'Nouveaux essais sur l'entendement humain').
1766. Lessing, 'Laokoon.' Kant, 'Träume eines Geistersehers.' Wieland, 'Komische Erzählungen;' 'Agathon' (-1767). Gerstenberg, 'Gedicht eines Skalden.'
1767. Lessing, 'Minna von Barnhelm;' 'Hamburgische Dramaturgie (-1769). Herder, 'Fragmente.' Mendelssohn, 'Phädon.' Chr. F. Weisse, 'Komische Opern' (-1771).
1768. Wieland, 'Musarion;' 'Idris.' Gerstenberg, 'Ugolino.' 'Ossian,' by Denis (-1769). Sterne's 'Sentimental Journey,' translated by Bode (-1769).
1769. Lessing, 'Wie die Alten den Tod gebildet.' Herder, 'Kritische Wälder.' Klopstock, 'Hermann's Schlacht.' Möser begins his 'Osnabrückische Geschichte.' Göttingen and Leipzic 'Musenalmanach' for 1770. Hermes, 'Sophiens Reise.' Ayrenhoff, 'Der Postzug.'
1770. Wieland, 'Die Grazien.' Johann Georg Jacobi, Collected Works (-1774). Goethe and Herder in Strassburg.
1771. Klopstock, 'Oden.' Claudius, 'Der Wandsbecker Bote.' Schröder, director of the Theatre in Hamburg, first time (-1780). Haller, 'Usong.' Wieland, 'Amadis.' Sulzer, 'Allgemeine Theorie der schönen Künste' (-1774). Freiherr von Zedlitz made Superintendent of Public Instruction in Prussia.
1772. Lessing's 'Emilia Galotti.' The 'Frankfurter gelehrten Anzeigen,' edited by Merck; with the assistance of Herder and Goethe. Herder, 'Ursprung der Sprache.' The Göttingen 'Hain.' Gleim, 'Lieder für das Volk.' Wieland, 'Goldner Spiegel.' Wieland in Weimar.
1773. Fly-leaves, 'von deutscher Art und Kunst.' Goethe's 'Götz.' Bürger, 'Lenore.' Gleim, 'Gedichte nach den Minnesingern.' Klopstock finishes his Messiah. Wieland, 'Deutscher Merkur' (-1810); 'Alceste.' Lessing's contributions 'Zur Geschichte und Litteratur' (-1781). Nicolai, 'Sebaldus Nothanker' (-1776). The Order of the Jesuits suppressed by the Pope.
1774. The First Fragment of the Anonymous Wolfenbütteler. Möser, 'Patriotische Phantasien.' Herder, 'Älteste Urkunde;' and other 'Storm and Stress' writings. Goethe, 'Clavigo;' 'Werther.' Lenz, 'Hofmeister.' Wieland's 'Abderiten' begun. Bode translates Sterne's 'Tristram Shandy.' Jacobi, 'Iris.' Klopstock, 'Gelehrtenrepublik.' Basedow, 'Elementarwerk.'

1775. Karl August, Duke of Weimar. Goethe in Weimar. Lavater, 'Physiognomik' (-1778). Klinger, 'Otto.' Paul Weidmann, 'Johann Faust.' Court Theatre in Gotha. The 'Weisskunig' is printed.

1776. The Burgtheater in Vienna; 'Court and National Theatre.' Goethe, 'Stella.' Lenz, 'Soldaten.' Klinger, 'Zwillinge;' 'Sturm und Drang.' Maler Müller, 'Situation aus Fausts Leben.' H. L. Wagner, 'Kindermörderin.'—Wieland, 'Gandelin.' Miller, 'Siegwart;'—'Deutsches Museum' (-1791).

1777. The further Fragments of the Anonymous Wolfenbütteler (-1778). Wieland, 'Geron der Adelich.' Jung, 'Heinrich Stilling's Jugend.'

1778. Lessing, 'Anti-Goeze;' 'Ernst und Falk, Gespräche für Freimäurer.' Herder, 'Volkslieder' (-1779). Bürger, 'Gedichte.' Maler Müller, 'Faust's Leben dramatisirt,' First Part. Hippel, 'Lebensläufe' (-1781). Meissner, The 'Skizzen,' begin.

1779. Lessing, 'Nathan der Weise.' Mannheim National Theatre.—Gleim, 'Gedichte nach Walther von der Vogelweide.' Poems by the brothers Stolberg. Gottwerth Müller, 'Siegfried von Lindenberg.'

1780. Lessing, 'Erziehung des Menschengeschlechts.' Wieland, 'Oberon.' Johannes Müller, 'Geschichten der schweizerischen Eidgenossenschaft' (-1795). Schlözer's 'Briefwechsel' begins. Frederick the Great, 'De la littérature allemande.'

1781. (*Feb.* 15). Death of Lessing. Kant, 'Kritik der reinen Vernunft.' Dohm, On improving the civil position of the Jews. Pestalozzi, 'Lienhard und Gertrud' (-1785). Schiller, 'Räuber.' Voss, Translation of the Odyssey.

1782. Musäus, 'Volksmärchen' (-1786).

1783. Schiller, 'Fiesco.' Hölty's Poems, published by Stolberg and Voss. Jean Paul, 'Grönländische Prozesse.' The Berlin 'Monatschrift' begins.

1784. Schiller, 'Kabale und Liebe.' Voss, 'Luise.' Kortum, 'Jobsiade.' Blumauer's Travesty of the Æneid. Myller, 'Sammlung Deutscher Gedichte aus dem 12, 13, und 14 Jahrhunderte' (-1785). Herder, 'Ideen' (-1791). Kant, 'Was ist Aufklärung?' Mendelssohn, 'Jerusalem.'

1785. Goethe's Poems, 'Edel sei der Mensch' and 'Prometheus,' become known through Fritz Jacobi. Voss, 'Gedichte.' K. Ph. Moritz, 'Anton Reiser' (-1790). Iffland, 'Die Jäger.' Mendelssohn, 'Morgenstunden;' 'Allgemeine Litteraturzeitung,' Jena.

1786. Death of Frederick the Great. The Royal National Theatre in Berlin. Schröder director of the Theatre in Hamburg—second time (-1790). Goethe goes to Italy.

1787. Herder, 'Gott.' Goethe's 'Works' (-1790); 'Iphigenie.' Schiller, 'Don Carlos.' Heinse, 'Ardinghello.' Matthison, 'Gedichte.' Johannes Müller, 'Darstellung des Fürstenbundes.'

1788. Frederick the Great, 'Histoire de mon temps,' with the continuation, Archenholz, 'Geschichte des siebenjährigen Kriegs.' Schiller, 'Abfall der Niederlande.' Kant, 'Kritik der praktischen Vernunft.' Goethe, 'Egmont.' Goethe returns to Weimar.

1789. Schiller, Professor in Jena. 'Geisterseher;' 'Die Künstler.' Kotzebue, 'Menschenhass und Reue.'

1790. Kant, 'Kritik der Urtheilskraft.' Goethe, 'Metamorphose der Pflanzen;' Fragment, 'Faust;' 'Tasso.' Schiller begins his history of the Thirty Years' War. Forster, 'Ansichten vom Niederrhein.' Jean Paul, 'Schulmeisterlein Wuz.'

1791. Goethe director of the Weimar Theatre (–1817). Klinger, 'Faust.'

1792. Fichte, 'Kritik aller Offenbarung.'

1793. Voss, 'Homer' (the Iliad new, the Odyssey revised). Schiller, 'Über Anmuth und Würde.' Herder's 'Humanitätsbriefe.' Jean Paul, 'Unsichtbare Loge.'

1794. Goethe, 'Reineke Fuchs.' Friendship of Schiller and Goethe. Fichte, 'Wissenschaftslehre.'

1795. 'Horen' (–97). Schiller's Musenalmanach for 1796 (continued to 1800). Goethe, 'Wilhelm Meister's Lehrjahre' (–1796). 'Unterhaltungen deutscher Ausgewanderten.' Roman 'Elegien.' 'Schweizerreise von 1779.' Schiller, 'Briefe über ästhetische Erziehung;' 'Über das Naïve;' 'Die sentimentalischen Dichter.' Friedrich August Wolf, 'Prolegomena ad Homerum.'—Jean Paul, 'Hesperus.' Heinrich Zschokke, 'Abellino der grosse Bandit.'

1796. 'Xenien.' Goethe, 'Alexis und Dora.' Schiller, 'Beschluss der Abhandlung über naïve und sentimentalische Dichter.' Iffland, director of the Berlin Theatre (–1814). Jean Paul, 'Quintus Fixlein.'

1797. Goethe, 'Hermann und Dorothea;' 'Der neue Pausias.' Balladen-almanach (Schiller's Musenalmanach for 1798). Hölderlin, 'Hyperion' (–1799). Tieck, 'Volksmärchen.' Schlegel's Shakespeare (–1801, and 1810). Count Soden, 'Faust.' Schelling, 'Ideen zu einer Philosophie der Natur.'

1798 (*Oct.* 12). 'Wallenstein's Lager,' acted at Weimar. Goethe, 'Propyläen (–1800). Tieck, 'Franz Sternbald.' Schelling, 'Weltseele.'

1799 (*Jan.* 30), 'Die Piccolomini'; (April 20), 'Wallenstein's Tod,' acted at Weimar. (Dec.); Schiller moves to Weimar. W. von Humboldt, 'Ästhetische Versuche.' Schleiermacher's Discourses, 'Über die Religion.' Schelling, 'Erster Entwurf eines Systems der Naturphilosophie.' Friedrich Schlegel, 'Lucinde.'

1800 (*June* 14). 'Maria Stuart,' acted at Weimar. Jean Paul, 'Titan' (–1803).

1801. Schiller, 'Jungfrau von Orleans.' Collin, 'Regulus.' Tiedge, 'Urania.' Engel, 'Herr Lorenz Stark.' Gauss, 'Disquisitiones arithmeticae.'

1802. Novalis' Works. University of Landshut.

1803 (*March* 19). 'Braut von Messina' acted in Weimar. Heinrich von Kleist, 'Familie Schroffenstein.' Goethe, 'Der Geselligkeit gewidmete Lieder.' Tieck, 'Minnelieder.' Hebel, 'Alemannische Gedichte.' E. M. Arndt, 'Gedichte;' 'Germanien und Europa.' The University of Heidelberg reconstituted by Karl Friedrich of Baden.

1804 (*March* 17). 'Wilhelm Tell' acted in Weimar. 'Jenaische Allgemeine Litteraturzeitung.' Jean Paul, 'Flegeljahre.' Schink, 'Faust.'

1805 (*May* 10). Death of Schiller. Goethe, 'Winckelmann und sein Jahrhundert ;' 'Rameau's Neffe' of Diderot. Herder, 'Cid,'—(Oct. 17). Capitulation of Ulm. E. M. Arndt begins his 'Geist der Zeit.' Daub and Creuzer, 'Studien' (Heidelberg). (In the autumn) Arnim and Brentano 'Des Knaben Wunderhorn' (1806-1808).

1806 (*Oct.* 14). Battle of Jena. Goethe's Works in 12 vols. (-1808). Hegel, 'Phänomenologie des Geistes.'

1807 (*Jan.* 29). Johannes Müller's academical Lecture, 'De la gloire de Frédéric II' translated by Goethe.—(Winter, 1807-8). Fichte delivers his addresses to the German nation. Görres', 'Volksbücher.' F. H. von der Hagen, 'Erneuung des Nibelungenlieds.' Wilken begins his 'Geschichte der Kreuzzüge.'

1808. The first part of Goethe's 'Faust' published. Fouqué, 'Sigurd der Schlangentödter.' H. von Kleist, 'Penthesilea.' 'Die Einsiedlerzeitung.' 'Heidelbergische Jahrbücher.' K. Fr. Eichhorn begins his 'Deutsche Staats-und Rechtsgeschichte.' Fr. Schlegel, 'Sprache und Weisheit der Indier.' A. von Humboldt, 'Ansichten der Natur.'

1809. Goethe, 'Wahlverwandtschaften,' 'Pandora.' Zacharias Werner, 'Februar 24.' Fr. Schlegel, 'Gedichte.' A. W. Schlegel, 'Vorlesungen über dramatische Kunst und Litteratur' (-1811). (Jan.) W. von Humboldt is made Superintendent of Public Instruction in Prussia.

1810. Goethe, Masque, 'Romantische Poesie;' 'Farbenlehre.' University of Berlin opened. Arnim, 'Gräfin Dolores.' H. von Kleist, 'Erzählungen' (-1811); Käthchen von Heilbronn.' Jahn, 'Deutsches Volksthum.'

1811. Goethe, 'Dichtung und Wahrheit,' vol. i. Fouqué, 'Undine.' Arnim, 'Halle und Jerusalem;' 'Isabella von Ägypten.' Kleist, 'Der zerbrochene Krug.' Justinus Kerner, 'Reiseschatten.' Niebuhr begins his Roman History. Johannes Müller, '24 Bücher allgemeiner Geschichte.' University of Frankfort moved to Breslau.

1812. Goethe, 'Dichtung und Wahrheit,' vol. ii. Works in 20 vols. (-1819). Tieck, 'Phantasus' (-1817). Grimm, 'Kinder und Hausmärchen.' Joseph von Hammer, 'Divan des Hafis.'

1813. E. M. Arndt, 'Lieder für Deutsche;' 'Der Rhein Deutschlands Strom, nicht Deutschlands Grenze.' Müllner, 'Schuld.'

1814. Theodor Körner, 'Leier und Schwert.' Rückert, 'Deutsche Gedichte von Freimund Raimar.' Chamisso, 'Schlemihl.' E. T. A. Hoffmann's Tales (-1822). Hegner, 'Saly's Revolutionstage.' Goethe, 'Dichtung und Wahrheit,' vol. iii. Savigny, 'Vom Beruf unsrer Zeit für Gesetzgebung und Rechtswissenschaft.' Görres, 'Rheinischer Merkur' (-1816). The Order of Jesuits restored.

1815. Goethe, 'Des Epimenides Erwachen.' Schenkendorf, 'Gedichte.' Uhland, 'Gedichte.' Klingemann, 'Faust.' Eichendorff, 'Ahnung und Gegenwart.' Fr. Schlegel, 'Vorlesungen über Geschichte der alten und neuen Litteratur.'

1816. Goethe, 'Italienische Reise,' vol. i. 'Kunst und Alterthum (-1832). Uhland, 'Vaterländische Gedichte.' Öhlenschläger, 'Corregio.' Clauren, 'Mimili.'—Jacob Grimm, 'Poesie im Recht.' Karl Lachmann, 'Über die ursprüngliche Gestalt des Gedichts von der Nibelungen Noth.' Franz Bopp, 'Über das Conjugationssystem der Sanskritsprache in Vergleichung mit jenem der griechischen, lateinischen, persischen und germanischen Sprache.' Schlosser begins his 'Weltgeschichte.'

1817. Goethe retires from the direction of the Theatre ; 'Neu-deutsche religios-patriotische Kunst;' 'Italienische Reise,' vol. ii. Böckh, 'Staatshaushaltung der Athener.' The University of Wittenberg united with Halle. Hegel, 'Encyclopädie.' The Evangelical Union. Arnim, 'Kronenwächter.' Brentano, 'Wehmüller,' 'Kasperl und Annerl.' Grillparzer, 'Ahnfrau.'

1818. Grillparzer, 'Sappho.' Ernst Schulze, 'Bezauberte Rose.' Wilhelm Müller, 'Müllerlieder'; Translation of Marlowe's 'Faust.'—University of Bonn.

1819. Goethe, 'Westöstlicher Divan.' Schopenhauer, 'Die Welt als Wille und Vorstellung.' Jacob Grimm begins his 'Deutsche Grammatik.'

1821. Platen, 'Chaselen,' 'Lyrische Blätter.' Wilhelm Müller, 'Lieder der Griechen.' Tieck, 'Gedichte'; his 'Novellen' begun. Goethe, 'Wilhelm Meister's Wanderjahre,' Part I. H. von Kleist's posthumous works : 'Hermannsschlacht,' 'Prinz von Homburg.' Grillparzer, 'Goldnes Vliess.' Schleiermacher, 'Der christliche Glaube' (–1822).

1822. Rückert, 'Östliche Rosen,' 'Liebesfrühling.' H. Heine, 'Gedichte.' Uhland, 'Walther von der Vogelweide.'

1823. Raimund, 'Barometermacher.' Wilibald Alexis, 'Walladmor,' purporting to be a free translation from the English of Sir Walter Scott. Raumer, 'Hohenstaufen' (–1825). Schlosser, 'Geschichte des 18ⁿ Jahrhunderts.'

1824. Ranke, 'Zur Kritik neuerer Geschichtschreiber,' 'Geschichten der romanischen und germanischen Völker von 1494 bis 1535.' Böckh begins his 'Corpus Inscriptionum Graecarum.' F. G. Welcker, 'Die Æschylische Trilogie Prometheus.' Heinrich Zschokke, 'Sämmtliche ausgewählte Schriften,' 40 vols. (–1828). Eichendorff, 'Krieg den Philistern, dramatisirtes Märchen.' Raimund, 'Diamant des Geisterkönigs.'

1825. Grillparzer, 'König Ottokars Glück und Ende.' Rückert, 'Amaryllis, ein ländliches Gedicht' (written 1812).

1826. H. Heine, 'Reisebilder' (–1831). Immermann, 'Cardenio und Celinde.' Platen, 'Verhängnisvolle Gabel.' Raimund, 'Mädchen aus der Feenwelt.' Hölderlin, 'Gedichte.' Justinus Kerner, 'Gedichte.' Eichendorff, 'Taugenichts.' Hauff, 'Lichtenstein.' 'Monumenta Germaniae historica,' vol. i. Lachmann's edition of the 'Nibelungenlied.' The University of Munich.

1827. Simrock's Translation of the 'Nibelungenlied.' Spindler, 'Der Jude' (historical Novel). Goethe's Works in 40 vols. (–1830). (Winter of 1827–28) Humboldt's Cosmos Lectures.

1828. Jacob Grimm, 'Rechtsalterthümer.' Raupach, 'Der Nibelungen Hort.' Immermann, 'Friedrich der Zweite.' Grillparzer, 'Ein treuer Diener seines Herrn.' Raimund, 'Alpenkönig und Menschenfeind.' Platen, 'Gedichte.' Goethe publishes his Correspondence with Schiller (–1829).

1829. Goethe, 'Wilhelm Meister's Wanderjahre.' Platen, 'Romantischer

Œdipus.' Grabbe, 'Don Juan und Faust.' Ludwig Börne's Collected
Works (–1834). Lachmann's 'Critik der Sage von den Nibelungen.'
1830. Raupach's Hohenstaufen-Dramas (–1837).
1831. Grillparzer, 'Des Meeres und der Liebe Wellen.' Usteri, 'Dichtungen.'
1832 (*March* 22). Death of Goethe. The second part of 'Faust' published.

1835. Gervinus, 'Geschichte der poetischen Nationallitteratur der Deutschen'
    (–1842), since 1853 called 'Geschichte der deutschen Dichtung.' Jacob
    Grimm's 'Deutsche Mythologie' leads us back to the original sources of
    German Poetry.

BIBLIOGRAPHICAL APPENDIX.

ABBREVIATIONS USED IN THE FOLLOWING NOTES.

A. D. B. = Allgemeine Deutsche Biographie. Leipzic, 1875.

Anz. and Zs. Anz. = Anzeiger für deutsches Alterthum und deutsche Litteratur. Berlin, 1876.

Beitr. = Beiträge zur Geschichte der deutschen Sprache und Litteratur. H. Paul und W. Braune. Halle, 1874.

Denkm. = Denkmäler deutscher Poesie und Prosa. Müllenhoff und Scherer. Berlin, 1873.

Ed. = Edition or edited by.

Erl. = Erläuterungen zu den deutschen Classikern. Leipzic.

Germ. = Germania. Vierteljahrschrift für deutsche Alterthumskunde. Stuttgart, 1856. Vienna, 1859.

Gödeke = Grundriss zur Geschichte der deutschen Dichtung. Hanover, 1859. Dresden, 1881.

Koberstein = Koberstein's Grundriss der Geschichte der deutschen National-litteratur. Leipzic, 1872-73.

Progr. = Programme, a small treatise.

Q. F. = Quellen und Forschungen zur Sprach- und Culturgeschichte der germanischen Völker. B. ten Brink und Scherer. Strassburg, 1874.

Sch. = Scherer.

Schnorr's Archiv = Archiv für Litteraturgeschichte. Leipzic, 1870.

Wackernagel = Geschichte der deutschen Litteratur. Basle, 1879.

Weim. Jahrb. = Weimarisches Jahrbuch für deutsche Sprache, Litteratur und Kunst. Hanover, 1854-57.

Zs. = Zeitschrift für deutsches Alterthum. Leipzic, 1841. Berlin, 1856.

Zs. f. d. Phil. = Zeitschrift für deutsche Philologie. Halle, 1869.

I. THE ANCIENT GERMANS, i. pp. 1–15.

For *Pytheas*; Müllenhoff's Deutsche Alterthumskunde i. 211 seq., and Scherer's Vorträge und Aufsätze, p. 21 seq. The explanation of the word ' *Germans* ' is from Zeuss, Grammatica Celtica, p. 735 (2nd ed. 773). The statement as to the origin of Tacitus' Germania is based on an hypothesis of Müllenhoff. On the interest taken by the Romans in the Germans, see A. Riese, ' Die Idealisirung der Naturvölker des Nordens in der griechischen und römischen Litteratur.' (Heidelberg, 1875.)

1. *The Aryans*, pp. 3–6.

On the name of *Aryan*, H. Zimmer in Bezzenberger's Beiträge iii. 137. On the primitive Aryans, Kuhn, Zur ältesten Geschichte indogermanischer Völker (Weber, Indische Studien i. 321); the first chapters of Grimm's Geschichte der deutschen Sprache (1848); Pictet, Les origines Indo-Européennes ou les Aryas primitifs (Paris, 1859); Schleicher, in Hildebrand's Jahrbücher für Nationalökonomie und Statistik, vol. i.; Justi in Raumer's Historisches Taschenbuch, 1862, p. 301; Fick, Die ehemalige Spracheinheit der Indogermanen Europa's, p. 266 (Göttingen, 1873); O. Schrader, Sprachvergleichung und Urgeschichte, (Jena, 1883).—On the character of *Aryan poetry*, Heinzel Q. F. x. 49. On the origin of *mythology*, Scherer's Vorträge und Aufsätze, 385. On *stories of animals*, Zeitschrift für österreichische Gymnasien, 1870, p. 47 seq. On *anecdotes, fairy stories and short tales*, Zs. Anz. iii. 185. On *charms in verse*, Kuhn, in the Zeitschrift für vergleichende Sprachforschung, xiii. 49 seq. and 113 seq.—On the origin of *Aryan metre*, Scherer, Zur Geschichte der deutschen Sprache, 2nd ed. p. 624.

2. *Germanic Religion*, pp. 6–9.

This section is chiefly based on Müllenhoff in Schmidt's Zeitschrift für Geschichtswissenschaft, viii. 209. See also Müllenhoff, Deutsche Alterthumskunde. On *Dyaus*, the Aryan Heaven-God, see Max Müller's Lectures on the Science of Language ii. 468 (8th ed.). On *proper names*, Müllenhoff, Nordalbingische Studien, i. 210; Zur Runenlehre, p. 42 seq. (Halle, 1852).

3. *Oldest remains of Poetry*, pp. 10–15.

The *Wessobrunner Gebet*, Denkm. No. i. The *Germanic Accent*, Sch. Zur Geschichte der deutschen Sprache, p. 86 seq. On the character of the *Old High-German Poetry*, Heinzel, Q. F. x. On *choral poetry*, Müllenhoff, De antiquissima germanorum poesi chorica (Kiliae, 1847). The explanation of the ' *barditus* ' is also from Müllenhoff. The *Mecklenburg* verses to Wodan, Grimm's Mythologie, 4th ed., p. 129. *Summer and Winter*, ibid. p. 638. The *Love-greeting*, Denkm. No. 28. *Riddles*, Denkm. No. 7. The *Merseburg charms*, Denkm. No. iv. 1, 2.—On the priests as proclaimers of the law, Sch. Zs. Anz., iv. 101. *The three needs*, taken from Richthofen's Friesische Rechtsquellen, pp. 44–49. The sentence of banishment, Grimm's Deutsche Rechtsalterthümer p. 39. *Alliterative formulas*; ibid. p. 6 seq.

II. Goths and Franks, pp. 16–37.

On the division into periods compare Scherer's Geschichte der deutschen Dichtung im elften und zwölften Jahrhundert, Q. F. xii. pp. 1–10; Zur Geschichte der deutschen Sprache, pp. 11–15.

1. *The Heroic Songs*, pp. 19–27.

For authorities on the history of the heroic legends, see IV.—Employment of *Runes*, Liliencron and Müllenhoff, Zur Runenlehre (Halle, 1852).—The epic bard, Priscus, p. 205, 11, Bonn; compare Müllenhoff, Zur Geschichte der Nibelunge Not (Brunswick, 1855), p. 11.—The song of Hildebrand, Denkm. No. 2.

2. *Ulfilas*, pp. 28–32.

See Waitz, Über das Leben und die Lehre des Ulfilas, (Hanover, 1840). Bessell, Über das Leben des Ulfilas, (Göttingen, 1860). Kaufmann Zs. xxvii. pp. 193 seq.—The last and best editions of Gothic literary documents are: Bernhardt, Vulfila (Halle, 1875); Stamm's Ulfilas, published by Heyne, 7th ed. (Paderborn, 1878). The Gothic toast, correctly explained by Dietrich in his Aussprache des Gothischen, p. 26 (Marburg, 1862). The word *vulthrs* in the Codex Brixianus of the Gospels: see Haupt, Opuscula ii. 407; Bernhardt Zs. f. d. Phil. ii. 24. The formula *froia armes* (i.e. frauja armais) in Augustine, Epistola 178; Holtzmann Germ. ii. 448. 'Fit etiam de hordeo opus bonum, quod nos graece dicimus alfita, latine vero polentam, Gothi vero barbarice *fenea*, magnum remedium cum vino calido temperatum'; Anthimi de observatione ciborum epistula ad Theudericum regem Francorum, 64 ed. Rose. On the *Salzburg MS.*, Wilhelm Grimm, Kleine Schriften iii. 85 seq., 95 seq. On the historical connection of Gothic with Old High-German Christianity, R. von Raumer Zs. vi. 401.

3. *The Merovingians*, pp. 32–37.

The *Irish*: see Hauréau, Singularités historiques et littéraires, pp. 1–36 (Paris, 1861). It is doubtful whether the Latin hymns made use of really belong to Columban.—On *Rhyme*: Wilhelm Grimm, Zur Geschichte des Reims, Abhandlungen der Berliner Akademie 1850 (Berlin 1852); Uhland, Schriften, i, 366 seq.; W. Masing, Über Ursprung und Verbreitung des Reims (Dorpat, 1866).—The explanation of *Grimm's Law*, Sch. Zur Geschichte der deutschen Sprache, p. 168. The *language of Charlemagne*: Müllenhoff, Denkm. p. x. xxiii. The *Strassburg Oath*: Denkm. No. 67. The expression '*deutsch*': Jacob Grimm, Grammatik, 3rd Ed. 1. 12.

III. The Old High-German Period, pp. 38–59.

The *Anglo-Saxons* and their poetry: ten Brink, Geschichte der englischen Litteratur i. 12–84 (Berlin, 1877). On *Charlemagne's* influence on German literature: Sch. Vorträge und Aufsätze, p. 71–100, the fuller proofs in the Denkm.—The fragments of the translation of *St. Matthew's Gospel* in the *Fragmenta theotisca*, 2nd ed., by Massmann (Vienna, 1841), and Zs. f. d. Phil. v. 381.—Muspilli: Denkm. No. 3.

1. *The First Messianic Poems*, pp. 40–46.

Fulda: Rettberg, Kirchengeschichte Deutschlands, i. 370 seq.; Wattenbach, Deutschlands Geschichtsquellen im Mittelalter, ch. ii. § 13. *Rabanus Maurus*: Ebert, Allegemeine Geschichte der Litteratur des Mittelalters im Abendlande ii. 120; A Latin Life of Christ, the so-called *Tatian*, edited, with the German translation, by Sievers, (Paderborn, 1872).—*The Heljand*: editions by Schmeller, (Munich, 1830, 40); M. Heyne, (Paderborn, 1866 and later editions); H. Rückert (Leipzic, 1876); Sievers (Halle, 1878); Behaghel (Halle, 1882). Translations by Simrock, Grein. Vilmar, Deutsche Alterthümer im Heljand, 2nd ed. (Marburg, 1882). Windisch, Der Heljand und seine Quellen (Leipzic, 1868). Other works on the subject in Sievers.—*Otfried*, newest edition by Kelle (with grammar and glossary, 3 vols., Regensburg, 1856–81); Piper (Paderborn, 1878); Erdmann (Halle, 1882), and others. Translation by Kelle. Other works in Piper.—*Christ and the Woman of Samaria*, Denkm. No. 10.— Prologue of the *Lex Salica*: see the edition by Merkel (Berlin, 1850), p. 93; Waitz, Das alte Rechte der salischen Franken (Kiel, 1846), p. 37.

2. *The Mediæval Renaissance*, pp. 46–53.

For Otto's visit to the tomb of Charlemagne: Thietmar von Merseburg, iv. 29, Monumenta Germaniæ, S.S. (i.e. Scriptores) iii. 781.

Charlemagne and his learned friends: Hauréau, Charlemagne et sa cour (Paris, 1854); Wattenbach, ch. ii. §§ 4–8; Ebert, ii. 3–112. See too, Schnaase, Geschichte der bildenden Künste, 2nd ed., iii. 499 seq., 526 seq., 621 seq. The Latin poems in Dümmler, Poetae latini aevi Carolini (Berlin, 1881).

St. Gall. The sources for the history of St. Gall are given by G. Meyer of Knonau, in the Mittheilungen des historischen Vereins von St. Gallen, part 12–17 (1870–1879): see also the Translation of *Ekkehard iv*, Casus sancti Galli, in the Geschichtschreiber der deutschen Vorzeit, zehntes Jahrhundert, vol. xi. (Leipz. 1878).—*Psalms* in German rhymed verse, Denkm. no. 13.—*Waltharius manu fortis*, published by J. Grimm in Grimm und Schmeller's Lateinische Gedichte (Göttingen, 1838); R. Peiper (Berlin, 1873); J. V. Scheffel und Holder (Stuttgart, 1874), with Scheffel's translation. See also W. Meyer of Speyer, Philologische Bemerkungen zum Waltharius (Münchner Sitzungsberichte, 1873. 3). For the Legend, Müllenhoff, Zs. xii. 273–279. Further accounts in Scheffel und Holder.—*Notker*: the works attributed to him are published by Hattemer, St. Gallens altteutsche Sprachschätze, vols. ii. iii. and more recently by Piper. See also Denkm. Nos. 26, 79, 80.

Roswitha: Editions by Barack (Nürnberg, 1858), Bendixen (Lübeck, 1858); an excellent translation by Bendixen (Altona, 1850, 1853). Compare Köpke,

Ottonische Studien, ii. (Berlin, 1869), Köpke, Die älteste deutsche Dichterin (Berlin, 1869). Older works are mentioned in Barack.

3. *The Wandering Journalists,* pp. 53-59.

For the *Gleemen,* see Q.F. xii. 11.—The *Ludwigslied,* Denkm. No. 11. The satiric poem on a broken-off betrothal, Denkm. No. 28b. Description of the boar, ibid. No. 26. On political minstrel poetry, see Uhland, Schriften, i. 472; Wackernagel, i. 96; Denkm. No. 8; Henning, Q.F., xxxi. 16. *Otto* with the Beard, see VI, 4. *Herzog Ernst,* see IV. 3. For the mixed Latin and German poetry in the Song of Otho the Great, and Henry, Denkm. No. 18. Latin songs, Denkm. Nos. 20-25. The *Song of St. George,* Denkm. No. 17. On the moral characteristics of the period, Q. F. xii. 4.

IV. CHIVALRY AND THE CHURCH, pp. 60-91.

Chivalry: see Weinhold, Die deutschen Frauen in dem Mittelalter, 2nd ed., 2 vols. (Vienna, 1882); Alwin Schultz, Das höfische Leben zur Zeit der Minnesänger, 2 vols. (Leipz., 1879, 1880). This deals chiefly with the eleventh and twelfth centuries. Q. F., xii. 22.

1. *Latin Literature,* pp. 62-71.

Rudlieb: published by Schmeller, in Grimm-Schmeller Lateinische Gedichte (1838); Seiler (Halle, 1882). See Zs. Anz., ix. 70. Zs. xxvii. 332. The legend joined on to Rudlieb (J. Grimm, Lat. Ged., p. 220) is derived from the Eckenlied, Strophe 82 seq., and from the Biterolf, lines 6451 seq. (compare the Klage, 1108); the Thidrekssaga ch. 233-239 contains a more recent form of the same. Grimm recognised its connection with the legend of Walther and Hildegund, l. c. 384 seq.—*Otto von Freising,* published in the Monumenta Germaniæ, S.S. xx. 83: (also separately, 1867). See further Wattenbach, Geschichtsquellen, chap. v. § 4.—The *Vagant* or *Goliard* and the *Arch-Poet*: J. Grimm, Kleinere Schriften, iii. 1; Giesebrecht, Allgemeine Monatschrift, 1853 (p. 10 seq., 344 seq.); O. Hubatsch, Die Lateinischen Vagantenlieder des Mittelalters (Görlitz, 1870); Barloti, I precursori del Rinascimento (Florence, 1877). Kuno Francke, Zur Geschichte der lateinischen Schulpoesie des 12ⁿ and 13ⁿ Jahrhunderts (München, 1879). The principal collection of their poems is the Carmina Burana, Schmeller's edition (Stuttgart, 1847); a selection, Gaudeamus I Carmina vagorum selecta, several editions (Leipz., 1879). Translation by L. Laistner; Golias (Stuttg., 1879). Older *Latin Lyrics* of the middle ages in Haupt, Exempla poesis latinae medii aevi (Vienna, 1834), and Jaffé, Cambridger Lieder, Zs., xiv, 491 seq.—The *Drama of Antichrist,* published by Zetzschwitz (Leipz., 1877); W. Meyer of Speyer, (Munich, 1882, Sitzungsberichte). Translations, Zetzschwitz, Wedde. See Sch. Zs., xxiv. 450.

2. *Lady World,* pp. 71-79.

On *Wirent of Grafenberg* and *Conrad of Würzburg* see VI. 4. The description of Lady World, Wackernagel, Zs. vi. 161. See for fuller details Scherer, Geschichte der deutschen Dichtung im 11ⁿ und 12ⁿ Jahrhundert (Strasb., 1875) Q. F. xii., and compare Sch. Geistliche Poeten der deutschen Kaiserzeit, 2nd. part (Strasb., 1874-75), Q. F. i. vii.

Sermons: Denkm. No. 86. Description of Heaven and Hell, ibid. No. 30.— *Poems on Old Testament subjects*: The Wiener Genesis (ed. Hoffmann's Fundgruben, ii. 9; Massmann, Deutsche Gedichte des 12ⁿ Jahrhunderts, p. 235; in modernised style: Genesis and Exodus from the Millstätter MS., by Diemer; Vienna, 1862): the Vorauer Genesis (pub. by Diemer, Deutsche Gedichte des 11ⁿ und 12ⁿ Jahrhunderts, Vienna, 1849, p. 1); The Wiener Exodus (pub. after the Wiener Genesis); Moses, Diemer, 32. 1-69. 6; Bileam, Diemer, 72. 8-85. 3; Lob Salamos, Denkm. No. 35; Die drei Jünglinge im Feuerofen, ibid. 36; Judith, ibid. 37; a later Judith, Diemer, 127, 1-180, 29.—*Poems on New Testament subjects*: Johannes, Hoffmann's Fundgruben, i. p. 130, 1-140, 10; Adelbrecht's Johannes, Mones Anz., viii. (1839) 47-53; 'The Friedberg Christ und Anti-Christ,' Denkm. No. 83; 'Leben Jesu,' (Diemer, 229. 1-276. 4; Hoffmann's Fundgruben, 140, 11-190, 28, this contains the description of the crucifixion mentioned on p. 74.); the poem of the nun Ava, Diemer 276-4 seq. Fundgruben, i. p. 190, 29 seq. 'Hamburger jüngstes Gericht,' Hoffmanns Fundgruben, 2. 135. 'Gleinker Entecrist,' Fundgruben, 2. 106 seq.; 'Anegenge,' Hahn, Gedichte des 12ⁿ und 13ⁿ Jahrhunderts (Quedlinburg, 1840) pp. 1-40, see Schröder, Q. F. 44.—*Legends*. Mittelfränkisches Legendar, pub. by Hugo Busch (Halle, 1879); also German rhymed legends of Silvester, Ægidius, Andreas, Paulus, Veronica, Vespasianus, Margaretha, Juliana, Veit Servatius, Albanus, Tungdalus.—'*Annolied*,' ed. Opitz, 1639, republished by Roth 1847, Bezzenberger 1848.—'*Kaiserchronik*,' ed. Massmann, 3 vols. (Quedlinburg, 1849, 1854); Diemer, (Vienna, 1849).

Didactic poems: Meregarto, Denkm. No. 32; Summa theologiae, ibid. 34 'Von der Siebenzahl, ibid. 44; Priest Arnold's Poem, Diemer, 333. 1.— *Priestly demagogues*: 'Memento mori,' pub. by Barack, Zs. xxiii. 209, compare Zs. xxiv. 426, xxv. 188. 'Vom Recht,' Karajan, Deutsche Sprachdenkmale des 12ⁿ Jahrhundert's (Vienna, 1846), pp. 3-16.

Forms of penance, Confessions of faith, Litanies, Prayers; 'Vorauer Sünden-klage,' Diemer, 295-316; 'Millstätter Sündenklage,' pub. by Rödiger, Zs. xx. 255; Hartmann's 'Credo,' Massmann, Deutsche Gedichte des 12ⁿ Jahrhunderts, p. 1; Heinrich's 'Litanei,' ibid. 43, Hoffmann's Fundgruben, ii. 216; a woman's poetical prayer, Diemer, 375-378.

Heinrich von Mölk, ed. Heinzel (Berlin, 1867), compare Zs. xix, 241.

Worship of the Virgin. Hymns to Mary, Denkm. 38-42. 'Frauenlob,' ed. W. Grimm, Zs. x. 1-142. Wernher's poems on the Virgin, ed. Hoffmann, Fundgruben, ii. 145; Feifalik (Vienna, 1860).

Fragment, ' *Comfort in despair*,' Sch. Zs. xx. 346.

3. *The Crusades*, pp. 79-91.

For the *pilgrimages*, Röhricht in Raumer's Historiches Taschenbuch, 5th Series, 5. 321.—*Ezzo's Song*, Denkm. No. 31.—*Williram's* Paraphrase of the Song of Solomon, edited by Hoffmann (Breslau, 1827) ; Seemüller, Q. F. 28 (Strassb., 1878). 'Lob Salomos,' Denkm. No. 35. 'Salomo und der Drache,' ibid., see also Sch. Zs. xxii. 19. The German poems of Solomon and Marcolfus, published by F. Vogt, vol. i. (Halle, 1880).

Lambrecht's Alexander, ed. Diemer, Deutsche Gedichte, 183, 1 ; Massmann, Deutsche Gedichte, p. 64 ; Weismann (Frankfort, 1850).—*Konrad's* Rolandslied, ed. W. Grimm (Göttingen, 1838) ; Bartsch (Leipz., 1874) ; see Weiss, Historiches Jahrbuch der Görres-Gesellschaft, i. 107 ; Schröder, Zs. xxvii. 70. The *Karlmeinet* was edited by Keller (Stuttgart, 1858), and explained by Bartsch (Nürnberg, 1861).

Shorter Epics. '*König Rother*,' ed. by H. Rückert (Leipz., 1872) ; von Bahder (Halle, 1884). '*Herzog Ernst*,' ed. by Bartsch (Vienna, 1869). See too, Zs. vii. 193, xiv. 265. '*St. Brandan*,' ed. Schröder (Erlangen, 1871). '*Orendel*,' ed. von der Hagen (Berl., 1844). Ettmüller (Zürich, 1858) ; see Meyer, Zs. xii. 387 ; Harkensee, Untersuchungen über das Spielmannsgedicht Orendel (Kiel, 1879) ; and for the Myth, Müllenhoff, Alterthumskunde, i. 32. '*St. Oswald*,' ed. Ettmüller (Zurich, 1835), Zs. ii. 92 ; see Strobl, Wiener Sitzungsberichte, 64, 457 ; Edzardi, Untersuchungen über das Gedicht von St. Oswald, (Hanover, 1876) ; Rödiger, Zs. xx. Anz. 245.

Graf Rudolf, ed. W. Grimm, 1828, 2nd ed. 1854. See von Sybel, Zs. ii. 235.

On mediæval tolerance, see Renan, Averroès et l'Averroïsme, 2nd ed. (Paris, 1865) ; H. Reuter, Geschichte der religiösen Aufklärung im Mittelalter, 2 vols. (Berlin, 1875-77).—On the legend of the sleeping emperor and its application to Frederick II, see George Voigt, in Sybel's Historische Zeitschrift xxvi. 139 ; also his Essay 'Die Kiffhäusersage' (Leipz., 1871).

V. Middle High-German Popular Epics, pp. 92-134.

National Epics, Wilhelm Grimm, Deutsche Heldensage, 2nd ed. Berlin, 1867 ; Müllenhoff, Zeugnisse und Excurse, Zs. xii. 253, 413 ; see Zs. xv. 310. On the influence of various German districts on the literature, see Q. F., xii. 20 seq.

1. *The Revival of Heroic Poetry*, pp. 93-101.

See chap. ii. of Henning's Nibelungenstudien, Q. F. xxxi, also Q. F., xii. 92, note.—*Saxon popular songs* ; Saga Ðiðriks konungs af Bern udgivet af C. R. Unger (Christiania, 1853) ; this Thidreks-saga, formerly called the Wilkinasaga, is translated by Rassmann, Deutsche Heldensage, No. 12 (Hanover, 1858). The clerical reaction has not been fully studied, see Q. F., xii. 19 seq.—For the *recitation* of the Heroic poems, Lachmann, Über Singen und Sagen, Kleine Schriften, i. 461.—For pp. 97-101, see especially Uhland, Schriften zur Geschichte der Dichtung und Sage, vol. i. (Stuttg., 1865).

2. *The Nibelungenlied,* pp. 101–115.

See Lachmann, Anmerkungen zu den Nibelungen, p. 333 seq. ' Kritik der Sage von den Nibelungen '; Müllenhoff, Zs. x. 146, xxiii. 113. Max Rieger, Germ. iii. 163. Scherer, Vorträge and Aufsätze p. 101.

The MSS. of the Nibelungen form three classes, represented by the Hohenems-Munich MS. (A) which stands alone, the St. Gall MS. (B) and the Hohenems-Lassberg MS. (C). Lachmann considers A as representing the original text, B as a revision of a MS. of class A, C as a revision of a MS. of class B. He took A for the foundation of his edition (' Der Nibelungen Noth und die Klage,' pub. by Lachmann, 3rd ed. Berlin, 1851, also a vol. of notes, Berlin, 1836). Holtzmann, (Untersuchungen über das Nibelungenlied, 1854), and Zarncke (Zur Nibelungenfrage, 1854) declared class C to be the oldest, and took MS. C as their authority. That C is the latest rendering has however been proved by R. von Liliencron (Über die Nibelungenhandschrift C, Weimar, 1856). See too, Rieger, Zur Kritik der Nibelunge (Giessen, 1855); C. Hofmann, Zur Textkritik der Nibelungen (München, 1872).—One of the Minnesinger MSS. ascribes a number of ancient songs with uncertain rhymes to a Knight of Kürenberg. Franz Pfeiffer (Der Dichter des Nibelungenlieds, 1862,) considers this knight to be the author of the Nibelungenlied. Bartsch (Untersuchungen über das Nibelungenlied, Vienna, 1865,) agrees with him, whilst trying to establish a lost original form of the poem in uncertain rhymes; B, cited as the oldest text, is the foundation of Bartsch's edition. In opposition to this, see Zupitza, Über Franz Pfeiffer's Versuch (Oppeln, 1867); Vollmöller, Kürnberg und die Nibelungen (Stuttgart, 1874); Sch. Zs. xvii. 561, xviii. 150, also Paul, Zur Nibelungenfrage (Halle, 1877). Hermann Fischer, Die Forschungen über das Nibelungenlied seit Karl Lachmann (Leipzic, 1874), supports the theory of Bartsch.

The distinction of the genuine from the spurious, and the real songs from the continuations, which Lachmann undertook in his edition, he established in the ' Anmerkungen.' His views on the origin of the poem are partly confirmed, partly modified by Müllenhoff, Zur Geschichte der Nibelunge Not (Brunswick, 1855, intended also to disprove the views of Holtzmann and Zarncke, 1854), also by R. Henning, Nibelungen Studien, Q.F. xxxi. (Strassb., 1883), and Rödiger, Kritische Bemerkungen (Berl., 1884); see also Sch. Zs. 24, 274. Heinrich Fischer, Nibelungenlied, oder Nibelungenlieder? (Hanover, 1859), tries to refute these opinions. One particular point of view, in accordance with Lachmann's arguments, is represented in Wilmanns' Beiträge zur Erklärung und Geschichte des Nibelungenliedes (Halle, 1877). See, too, Hugo Busch, Die ursprünglichen Lieder vom Ende der Nibelungen (Halle, 1882).

Translations by Simrock and others. Zarncke gives a convenient list of the works on the subject in the introduction to his edition. See too, R. von Muth, Einleitung in das Nibelungenlied (Paderborn, 1877).

' *A song about Kriemhild's disloyalty to her brothers,*' for this see Grimm's Heldensage, p. 49. A Saxon bard sings it as a warning to a man who is in danger; speciosissimi carminis contextu notissimam Grimildae erga fratres perfidiam de industria memorare adorsus, famosae fraudis exemplo similium ei metum ingenerare tentabat.—The account of a Latin Nibelungenlied composed by order of Bishop Piligrim, of Passau, in the tenth century, starts with the assertion that this Piligrim was uncle to the Burgundian Kings murdered by the Huns, and has not therefore the least guarantee of probability.

3. *Dietrich von Bern*, pp. 115-120.

The ' *Klage*,' pub. by Lachmann after the Nibelungenlied ; separate editions by Holtzmann, Edzardi, Bartsch.—The ' Saxon legends ' follow the Thidrekssaga (see V. i). The various Middle High-German poems, pp. 116, seq., are collected in ' Das Deutsche Heldenbuch ' (started by Müllenhoff), vols. 1, 2, 3 (Berlin, 1866, 1870). Vol. 6 will contain the *Rosengarten* and other poems mentioned p. 118. For the present Wilhelm Grimm's edition of the Rosengarten (Gottingen, 1836) is sufficient authority. Now, for the ' very late tradition,' p. 119, see Das Deutsche Heldenbuch, A. von Keller (Stuttgart, 1867), p. 10. The ' *Hürnen Seifried*,' Von der Hagen's Deutsches Heldenbuch, in 4°, vol. 2 (Berlin, 1825). The later ' *Hildebrandslied*,' in Uhland's Volkslieder, No. 132. ' *Ermenrichs Tod*,' pub. by K. Gödeke (Hanover, 1851); also in Von der Hagen's Heldenbuch, in 8°, vol. ii, 537 (Leipzic, 1855).

4. *Ortnit and Wolfdietrich*, pp. 120-123.

On myth and legend, see Müllenhoff, Zs. vi, 435; xii, 346 seq. The historical element, compare text with Gregory of Tours, 3, 23-25.—' *Ortnit*,' Müllenhoff, Zs. xiii, 185. Deutsches Heldenbuch, vol. iii (Berl. 1871).—' *Wolfdietrich*,' Müllenhoff, Zur Geschichte der Nibelungen Not, p. 23. Deutsches Heldenbuch, vols. 3, 4 (Berl. 1871-73).

5. *Hilde and Gudrun*, pp. 124-134.

The legend, cf. Klee, Zur Hildesage (Leipzic, 1873). The myth is connected with that on which the legend of Walther and Hildegunde is based. On the Norman leader Siegfried, see Dümmler, Ostfränkisches Reich, ii, 271, 274 seq. Proofs that the story was known in Bavaria about 1100, Müllenhoff, Zs. xii, 314. On the lost poem of the twelfth century, Sch., Q. F. vii, 63, as also on the probable home of the ' Gudrun.' This has been preserved to us only in the famous Ambras MS. of Maximilian I (see p. 258). Ed. by Vollmer (Leipzic, 1845), Bartsch (Leipzic, 1865, see Germ. x, 41, 148), Martin (Halle, 1872, with explanation and commentary: small edition 1883), Symons (Halle, 1883, see too, Beitr. ix, 1). Separation of the unauthentic portions : Ettmüller, Gudrun Lieder (Leipzic, 1841) ; Müllenhoff, Kudrun, die echten Theile des Gedichtes, with a critical introduction (Kiel, 1841); Plönnies (Leipzic, 1853). Martin agrees generally with Müllenhoff as to the interpolations. Translations : Simrock, A. v. Keller, Niendorf, Koch (only the authentic portions, according to Müllenhoff), Klee, &c. Gervinus began an edition in hexameters (Leipzic, 1836). The author of Gudrun belonged certainly to the Austro-Bavarian tribe, and is therefore, as a countryman, nearly connected with Wolfram and Walther.

VI. The Epics of Chivalry, pp. 135-186.

The ' *Flore* ' of a poet of the lower Rhineland is called by him ' Floyris.' Fragments of the poem are published by Steinmeyer, Zs. xxi, 320. The ' Tristan,' or rather ' Tristrant,' of *Eilhard von Oberge* is edited by F. Lichtenstein, Q.F. 19 (Strassburg, 1877). See Zs. xxvi, 1.

1. *Heinrich von Veldeke*, pp. 137-145.

For *Heinrich VI, and his Love Songs*, see Scherer's Deutsche Studien ii, 10 seq.

Heinrich von Veldeke. For the Counts of Looz and Rineck, Hegel, Forschungen zur deutschen Geschichte xix, 569. Veldeke's dialect, Braune, Zs. f. d. Phil. iv, 249. Veldeke's St. Servatius, Bormann's edition (Maestricht, 1858), see Bartsch, Germ. v, 410. Meyer, Zs. xxvii, 146.—'*Æneide*,' ed. Ettmüller (Leipz. 1852), Behaghel (Heilbronn, 1882). For his sources—Pey, in Ebert's Jahrbuch für romanische und englische Litteratur ii, 1 ; see too Wörner, Zs. f. d. Phil. iii, 106. Virgil in the Middle Ages, see a work by Comparetti (in German, Leipzic. 1875). Veldeke's Songs, ed. Lachmann und Haupt, Minnesangs Frühling, No. 9, see Sch., Deutsche Studien ii, 71.

Veldeke's followers. In and around Mainz (?) ' *Moriz von Craon*,' edit. by Haupt in the Festgaben für Homeyer (Berlin, 1871), p. 27 ; see Bech, Germ. xvii, 170.—' *Pilatus*,' ed. Massmann, Deutsche Gedichte, p. 145 ; Weinhold, Zs. f. d. Phil. viii, 253 ; for the legend, see Creizenach, Beitr. i, 89 ; Schönbach, Zs. Anz. ii, 166.—In Thuringia, *Heinrich von Morungen*, see the Minnesangs Frühling, No. 18, comp. Michel, Q.F. 38, Gottschau, Beitr. vii, 335. *Herbort von Fritzlar*, pub. by Frommann (Quedlinburg, 1837), comp. Germ. ii, 49, 177, 307, also H. Dunger, Die Sage vom trojanischen Kriege (Leipz. 1869), Körting, Dictys und Dares (Halle, 1874). Herbort's original ' Benoît de St. More et le roman de Troie,' A. Joly (Paris, 1870).—*Albrecht von Halberstadt.* Fragments of his poems, Zs. xi, 358, Germ. x, 237. The whole is preserved only in Jörg Wickram's revised edition (Mainz, 1545); from this Haupt restored the Prologue, Zs. iii, 289; further attempts at restoration by Bartsch, Albrecht von Halberstadt (Quedlinburg, 1861); see J. Grimm, Zs. viii, 10, 397, 464.—Here belong ' their disciples,' p. 143 ; *Otte*, author of ' Eraclius,' (published by Graef, Q. F. 50), the unknown author of ' *Athis und Prophilias*,' (the fragments pub. by W. Grimm, in the Abhandlungen der Berliner Akademie, 1846, 1852 ; comp. Zs. xii, 185, and Grimm's Kleine Schriften ii, 212 seq.)

2. *Hartmann von Aue and Gottfried von Strassburg*, pp. 145-161.

For the importance of the Upper Rhine in literary development, see Nitzsch, Deutsche Studien (Berl. 1879), p. 125.—*Heinrich der Glichezare*, fragments of his poems in J. Grimm, Sendschreiben an Lachmann (Leipz. 1840), the whole in more modern rendering in J. Grimm, Reinhart Fuchs (Berlin, 1834), p. 25.

Friedrich von Hausen. Minnesangs Frühling, No. 8. See Müllenhoff, Zs. xiv, 133 ; Lehfeld, Beitr. ii, 345. Baumgarten, Zs. xxvi, 105.—*Reinmar von*

Hagenau. Minnesangs Frühling, No. 20 ; see Erich Schmidt, Q. F. 4, (Strassburg, 1874) ; Regel, Germ. xix, 149. Becker, ibid. xxii, 70, 195. Burdach, Reinmar der Alte, und Walther von der Vogelweide (Leipz. 1880).

Hartmann von Aue. Schreyer, Das Leben und die Dichtungen H. v. A. (Program. Schulpforte, 1874); Bauer, Germ. xvi, 155. Von Ow, ibid. 162 ; Schmidt, H. v. A. Stand, Heimat und Geschlecht (Tübingen, 1875); see Martin, Zs. Anz. i, 126. On the sequence of his writings, Naumann, Zs. xxii, 25. Collected works, published by Bech, 3 vols (Leipz. 1867-69, &c). For characteristics, see Wackernagel, pp. 209, 245, 254. The Songs, Minnesangs Frühling, No. 21 ; see Zs. xiv, 144 ; xv, 125. The ' Büchlein,' with ' Der armer Heinrich,' published by Haupt. See O. Jacob, Das zweite Büchlein ein Hartmannisches (Naumburg, 1879).—' *Gregorius*,' ed. Lachmann (Berl. 1838, see Zs. v, 32) ; Paul (Halle, 1873, 1882). See Lippold, Über die Quelle des Gregorius, Hartmann's von Aue (Leipz. 1869). The original (?), Vie du Pape Grégoire le Grand, edited by Luzarche (Tours, 1857).—' *Der arme Heinrich*,' ed. by the brothers Grimm, 1815 ; Lachmann, Auswahl, 1820 ; W. Müller, 1842 ; Haupt (Leipz. 1842, 2nd ed. 1881) ; Paul (Halle, 1882). Translated by Simrock. See P. Cassel, Die Symbolik des Blutes, und der arme Heinrich des H. v. A. (Berlin, 1882).—' *Ereck*,' edited by Haupt (Leipzic, 1839, 2nd edit. 1871). Translated by Fistes. For the original, Bekker, Zs. x, 373. See Bartsch, Germ. vii, 141.—' *Iwein*,' edited by Benecke und Lachmann (Berl. 1827, 2nd edit. 1843, &c). Translated by Count Baudissin. Original (?), Li romans dou chevalier au lyon, edited by Holland (Hanover, 1862). See Rauch, Die wälische, französische, and deutsche Bearbeitung der Iweinsage (Berl. 1869) ; Güth, Herrigs Archiv 46 (1870), 251. Settegast, Hartmann's Iwein verglichen mit seiner altfranzösichen Quelle (Marburg, 1873) ; Gärtner, Der Iwein Hartmanns von Aue, und der Chevalier au lion des Chrestien de Troies (Breslau, 1875); Blume, Über den Iwein (Vienna, 1879). Heinzel, Österreichische Wochenschrift, new series ii, 385, 427, 460, 469 seq.

For the characteristics of the *Arthur romances*, see Uhland, Schriften ii, 112-127. Edition of Geoffrey of Monmouth, by Giles (London, 1844), by San-Marte (Halle, 1854).

For the development of the epic style from the tenth to the thirteenth century, see W. Grimm, Kleine Schriften iii, 241 seq. Lichtenstein, Q. F. xix, 150 seq.

Gottfried von Strassburg. Pub. by E. von Groote (Berlin, 1821), v. d. Hagen (Breslau, 1823), Massmann (Leipz. 1843), Bechstein (Leipz. 1869). Translated by Simrock, Kurtz, but best by Wilhelm Hertz (Stuttg. 1877). On the originals, Bossert, Tristan et Iseult (Paris, 1865); Heinzel, Zs. xiv, 272 ; compare Zs. xxvi. Anz. 211 seq. It was nearly connected with the English Sir Tristrem, and a northern Saga, both published by E. Kölbing, Die nordische und die englische Version der Tristan-Saga, 2 vols. (Heilbronn, 1878, 1883).— Gottfried's characteristics; Heinzel, Zs. für österreichische Gymnasien, 1868, p. 533 : Preuss, Strassburger Studien i, 1-75. For his life, K. Schmidt, Ist G. v. S. Strassburger Stadtschreiber gewesen ? (Strassb. 1876).—Bergemann, Das höfische Leben nach G. v. S. (Berl. 1876); Lobedanz, Das französische Element in G. v. S.'s Tristan (Schwerin, 1878).

3. *Wolfram von Eschenbach*, pp. 161–176.

IIis works were published by Lachmann (Berl. 1883). *Parzival and Titurel*, Bartsch, 3 vols. (Leipz. 1870–71). Parzival translated by Simrock and San-Marte. See too, San-Marte ' Leben und Dichten W. von E.' (Magdeburg, 1836, 41), and his ' Parzival-Studien,' 3 parts (Halle, 1860, 62). Domanig, ' Parzival-Studien,' 2 parts (Paderborn, 1878, 80).—Biographical : Schmeller, Abhandlungen der Münchener Akademie, 1837 ; Frommann, Anzeiger für Kunde der deutschen Vorzeit, 1861, p. 355 ; Haupt, Zs. vi, 187 ; xi, 42. For the date of the works, Herforth, Zs. xviii, 281. Wolfram's Style : Jänicke, De dicendi usu Wolframi de E. (Halle, 1860) ; Kinzel, Zs. f. d. Phil. v, 1 ; Förster, Zur Sprache and Poesie W. von E. (Leipzic, 1874) : Bötticher, Germ. xxi, 257. Kant, Scherz und Humor in W. von E. Dichtungen (Heilbronn, 1878). Stein-meyer in the A. D. B. vi, 340.—Karl Reichel, Studien zu Wolfram's Parzival (Vienna, 1858). On the Legend of the *Graal*, and Wolfram's authorities : Bartsch, Germanische Studien ii, 214 ; Zarncke, Beitr. iii, 304 ; Birch-Hirschfeld, Die Sage vom Gral (Leipz. 1877) ; Martin, Zur Gralsage, Q.F. 42 (Strass. 1880) ; W. Hertz, Die Sage vom Parzival und dem Gral (Breslau, 1882). For *Willehalm* ; Jonckbloet, Guillaume d'Orange (Amsterdam, 1867). Compared with Wolfram by San-Marte, Über W. von E. Rittergedicht Wilhelm von Orange (Quedlinburg, 1871).

On the *Tagelied* see Bartsch, Gesammelte Vorträge und Aufsätze (Frei-burg, 1883), p. 250 seq. Sch., Deutsche Studien ii, 51–60. Johannes Schmidt, Zs. f. d. Phil. xii, 333.

4. *Successors of the Great Chivalrous Poets*, pp. 176–186.

Epics after a foreign original. The ' *Lanzelet*,' of *Ulrich von Zetzikon*, edited by Hahn (Franf. 1845) ; original proofs, Bächtold, Germania, xix, 424 ; see Schilling De dicendi usu U. de Z. (Halle, 1866).—*Konrad von Fusses-brunnen*, edited by Kochendörffer, Q.F. 43.—*Wirent von Grafenberg* (comp. p. 71), edited by Benecke (Berl. 1819), Peiffer (Leipz. 1847) ; Bethge, W. von G. (Berl. 1881), where the other authorities are given.—*Stricker*, ' *Daniel*,' see Stricker's Charlemagne, edited by Bartsch, Preface.—*Konrad Fleck*, ed. Som-mer (Quedlinburg, 1846) ; see Sundmacher, Die altfranzösische and mittelhoch-deutsche Bearbeitung der Sage von Flore und Blancheflur (Göttingen, 1872) ; Herzog, Germ. 29, 137.—*Heinrich von dem Türlin*, edited by Scholl (Stuttg. 1852), see Reissenberger, Zur Krone (Gratz, 1879) ; Warnatsch, Der Mantel (Breslau, 1883 ; Weinholds Germanist. Abh. 2).

Freshly invented Epics : the ' Garel vom blühenden Thal,' by *Pleier* ex-amined by Waltz (Vienna, 1881). Characteristics of the poet ; E. H. Meyer, Zs. xii, 470.—*Wigamur*, the Knight with the Eagle ; Sarrazin, Q.F. 35.— ' *Gauriel von Montavel*,' the Knight with the Goat, by Konrad von Stoffeln ; Jeitteles, Germania, vi, 385.—*Apollonius of Tyre*, see Strobl, Heinrich von Neustadt (Vienna, 1875).

Realistic Epics : see *Rudolf von Ems*, ' Wilhelm von Orlens.'

Rhymed Chronicles : The *Styrian of Ottokar*, as yet only published in Pez,

Scriptores rerum austriacarum, iii. See Schacht, Aus und über Ottokars von Horneck Reimchronik (Mainz, 1821); Theod. Jacobi, De Ottokar chronico austriaco (Breslau, 1839); Lorenz, Deutschlands Geschichtsquellen, 2nd edit. i, 200.

Continuations of Wolfram's and Gottfried's works: Ulrich von Türheim (1233-66), continued Gottfried's ' Tristan,' (see von der Hagen und Massmann's edition), and Wolfram's ' Willehalm ' (for the sources of the latter see Suchier, Über die Quelle U. v. d. T. p. 32).—*Ulrich von dem Türlin* added the introductory history of ' Willehalm ' between 1261 and 1275; Suchier, Über die Quelle U. v. d. T. (Paderborn, 1873).—*Heinrich von Freiberg* (Toischer, Mittheilungen des Vereins für Geschichte der Deutschen in Böhmen, xv, 149) continued ' Tristan ' about 1300, ed. Bechstein (Leipz. 1877).

Rudolf von Ems : ' Der gute Gerhard,' ed. Haupt (Leipzic, 1840). ' Barlaam and Josaphat,' ed. Pfeiffer (Leipz., 1843); on the subject-matter, see Liebrecht in Eberts Jahrbuch ii. 314—*Wilhelm von Orlens*, table of Contents, Mones' Anz. 1835, p. 27. '*Alexander*' never printed. '*Universal Chronicle*': Vilmar, Die zwei Recensionen und die Handschriftenfamilien der Weltchronik R. von E. (Marburg, 1839).

Konrad von Würzburg. ' Der Welt Lohn' (p. 72), ed. Roth (Frankf., 1843). ' Otto mit dem Bart,' ed. Hahn (Quedlinburg, 1838); ' Schwanritter,' ed. Roth (Frankf., 1861); ' Engelhard,' ed. Haupt (Leipz. 1844). French legend, Herzmäre, ed. Roth (Frankf. 1846).—*Legends* : ' Alexius,' ed. Haupt, Zs. iii. 534; ' Pantaleon,' ed. Haupt, Zs. vi. 193; ' Silvester,' ed. W. Grimm (Göttingen, 1841)—' Goldene Schmiede,' ed. W. Grimm (Berl. 1840); ' Partonopier und Meliur,' ed. Bartsch (Vienna, 1871)—'Trojanerkrieg,' ed. Roth, Keller, Bartsch (Stuttg. Litter.-Verein, 1858, 77).—' Klage der Kunst ' ed. Eugen Joseph Q. F. liii. (Strassburg, 1855).

The disciples of Wolfram von Eschenbach : a M.S. of the later Titurel was printed in 1477, and another by Hahn (Quedlinburg, 1842), the description of the Grail-castle was published by Zarncke (Der Graltempel, Leipz., 1876). The author is not *Albrecht von Scharfenberg*: from a later poet of this name we possess a ' Merlin ' and a ' Seifrid de Ardemont ' in Ulrich Fütrers Epitome; see Spiller, Zs. xxvii. 158. ' Lohengrin,' ed. H. Rückert (Quedlinburg, 1858): 'Lorengel,' ed. Steinmeyer, Zs. xv. 181—*Hadamar von Laber*, ed. Stejskal (Vienna, 1880).—' Der heilige Georg,' written by *Reinbot von Durne*, by wish of Otto II. of Bavaria (1231-53), ed. v. d. Hagen und Büsching, Deutsche Gedichte des Mittelalters (1808).

Clerical Poetry. Hugo von Langenstein 'Martina,' ed. Keller (Stuttg., 1856); see Köhler, Germ. viii. 15.—Collections of *Legends* :—' Passional ' (ed. Hahn, Frankf., 1845: 'Marienlegenden,' by Pfeiffer, Stuttg., 1846., the third part, ed. Köpke, Quedlinburg, 1852, and ' Der Väter Buch ' (ed. Franke, Paderborn, begun 1880, see Zs. 25. Anz. 164; J. Haupt, Sitzungsberichte der Wiener Akad. 69, 71).—' Elizabeth,' ed. Rieger, (Stuttg. 1868), and ' Erlösung ' ed. Bartsch, (Quedlinburg, 1858).—' Marien Himmelfahrt,' Zs. v, 515—Legendary poetry in Cologne. *Brother Herman's* ' Iolante' (specimens in Pfeiffers Übungsbuch, p. 103).—*Bruno von Schönebeck*, see Chroniken der deutschen Städte, viii, 168 ; Gräters Bragur, ii. 324—Literary activity of the Knights of the German

Orders in Prussia; see Pfeiffer, Jeroschin p. xxiv. et seq.; Zacher, Zs. xiii. 504.
Middle High-German Artistic Epics: *Nicolas von Jeroschin*, ed. Pfeiffer (Stuttg. 1854, only extracts); Strehlke in the Scriptores rerum prussicarum, i. 291—*Henry of Munich*: see Wackernagel, p. 223—*Seifried's* 'Alexandreis' finished 1352: Ferd. Wolf, Wiener Jahrbücher 57, Anzeigeblatt pp. 19–24 Karajan Zs. iv. 248.

VII. POETS AND PREACHERS, pp. 187–234.

The '*Wartburgkrieg*,' ed. Simrock (Stuttgart, 1858.)
Rise of the Minnesang: Lachmann and Haupt, Des Minnesangs Frühling (Leipz. 1857 and later); see Sch., Deutsche Studien ii. (Vienna, 1874). We must distinguish between three groups: 1. *The Austro-Bavarian*, nearly connected with the popular German Lyrics, mentioned on pp. 194–196, see Minnesangs Frühling Nos. 1, 2, 4, and p. 37, 4–29. *Dietmar von Aist*, ibid. No 7. See Burdach, Zs. xxvii. 343; Anz. x 13; Becker, Germ. xxix. 360.—2 *The Lower Rhenish*, chiefly influenced by northern French models: *Veldeke*, who founded a school in Thuringia.—3. *The Upper Rhenish*, connected with the Troubadours: *Hausen* and *Reinmar*; the latter came to Austria, and propagated there his own mode of composition.

1. *Walther von der Vogelweide*, pp. 189–201.

Ed. Lachmann (Berl. 1827 and later); Wackernagel and Rieger (Giessen,1862); Pfeiffer (Leipz. 1854 and later); Wilmanns (Halle, 1869, 1883); Simrock (Bonn, 1870). Translated by Simrock (Berl. 1833 and later), Koch, Weiske, and Pannier. See Uhland, Walther v. d. V. (Stuttg., 1822, also Schriften, v. 1); Rieger, Leben W. v. d. V. (Giessen, 1863); Menzel, Leben W. v. d. V. (Leipz., 1865); Lucae, Leben und Dichten W. v. d. V. (Halle, 1867); Lexer, Über W. v. d. V. (Würzburg, 1873); Burdach, Reinmar der Alte und W. v. d. V. (Leipz., 1880); Wilmanns. Leben und Dichten W. v. d. V. (Bonn, 1882)—For p. 189, see Ignaz V. Zingerle, Reiserechnungen Wolfgers von Ellenbrechtskirchen, Bischofs von Passau, Patriarchen von Aquileja (Heilbronn, 1877). p. 9, 14; and also Kalkoff, Wolfger von Passau, 1191-1204 (Weimar, 1882).—Further accounts in Leo, Die gesammte Litteratur W. v. d. V. (Vienna, 1880).
The older poet of unknown name, mentioned p. 191, and again p. 217, goes by the name of *Anonymous Spervogel*; some think his name was *Heriger*; Minnesangs Frühling, No. 6; Sch., Deutsche Studien i. (Vienna, 1870).

2. *Minnesang and Meistersang*, pp. 201–212.

Jacob Grimm has proved that the *Meistersang* is only a continuation, though in the end a very lifeless one, of the Minnesang; Über den altdeutschen Meistergesang (Göttingen, 1811)—The MS. C (p. 201) is the one erroneously called 'Manessische' and it is the authority used by von der Hagen for his 'Minnesinger,' Part iv. (Leipz., 1838). Another illuminated MS. is the Weingartner, B, printed by Pfeiffer (Stuttg., 1843). B and C, are founded on an illuminated MS. of the thirteenth century. The Heidelberg MS. A, printed (Stuttg. 1844).—Selection: Bartsch, Deutsche Liederdichter, 2nd ed. Stuttg., 1879). Translation, Simrock, Lieder der Minnesinger (Elberfeld, 1857). See Uhland, Der Minnesang. Schriften v. 111-282. *Ulrich von Lichtenstein*, ed. Lachmann (Berl. 1841); see Knorr Q. F. ix. Sch., Zs. Anz. i. 248: Schönbach, Zs. xxvi. 307.—*Reinmar von Zweter*, ed. Röthe (Leipz., 1883), see Wilmanns Zs. xiii. 434.—*Neidhart von Reuenthal*, ed. M. Haupt (Leipz., 1858). see Liliencron, Zs. vi. 69; Tischer, Über Neidhart von Reuenthal (Leipz., 1872): Schmolke, Leben und Dichten N. von R. (Potsdam, 1875); Richard Meyer, Chronologie der Gedichte N. von R. (Berl, 1883)—*Tannhäuser* in v. d. Hagen, No. 90.—*Burkard von Hohenfels* v. d. Hagen, No. 38.—*Gottfried von Neifen*, ed. M. Haupt (Leipz. 1851), see Knod, G. von N. und seine Lieder (Tübingen, 1877).—*Steimar*, v. d. Hagen, No. 103; *Werner von Homberg*, ibid. No. 19; *Kiug Wenzel, Otto of Brandenburg, Henry of Breslau*, ibid, Nos. 4-6: on Henry of Breslau, see H. Rückert, Kleine Schriften i. 211; *Wizlau*, ed. Ettmüller (Quedlinburg, 1852)

For the culture of the *Meistersingers*, see Liliencron, Über den Inhal der allgemeinen Bildung in der Zeit der Scholastik (Munich, 1876); Jacobsthal, Die musikalische Bildung der Meistersinger, Zs. xx. 69.—*Marner*, ed. Strauch, Q. F. xiv.—*Frauenlob*, ed., Ettmüller (Quedlinburg, 1843). *Regenbogen*, see v. d. Hagen, No. 126. *The wild Alexander*, ibid. No. 135.—*Johann Hadlaub*, ed. Ettmüller (Zurich, 1841).

3. *Didactic Poetry, Satire and Tales*, pp. 212-222.

Didactic poetry; the *Winsbeke*, ed. M. Haupt (Leipz., 1845); see too, Zs. xv. 261.—' *Mässigung*;' diu Mâze, ed. Bartsch, Germ. viii. 97.—The *Wild Man*: *Wernher von Niederrhein*, pub. by W. Grimm (Göttingen, 1839): see too, Pfeiffer, Germ. i. 223. *Werner von Elmendorf*, Zs. iv. 284, see xxvi. 87, Q. F. xii. 124—*Thomasin of Zirclaria*, ed. H. Rückert (Quedlinburg, 1852): see Zs. f. d. Phil. ii. 431.—*Freidank*, ed. W. Grimm (Göttingen, 1834, 1860); Bezzenberger (Halle, 1872). See W. Grimm, Kleine Schriften, iv.; Paul, Über die ursprüngliche Anordnung von Freidank's Bescheidenheit, (Leipz. 1870).—*Hugo von Trimberg*. Bamberg, 1833, Zs. xxviii. 145.—*Jacobus a Cessolis*: the original, ed. Köpke (Brandenburg, 1879 Progr.). For the translations, see Zimmermann, Das Schachgedicht Heinrichs von Berngen (Wolfenbüttel, 1875), p. 7.—*Ulrich Boner*, ed. Benecke (Berl., 1816), Pfeiffer, (Leipz., 1844); see Zs. f. d. Phil. xi. 324.

Tales and Satires. Collections of Middle High German Tales: v. d. Hagen, Gesammtabenteuer, 3 vols. (Stuttg., 1850): Mailath und Köffinger, Koloczaer Codex altdeutscher Gedichte, (Pesth, 1817); Lassberg, Liedersaal, 3 vols. (St. Gall and Constance, 1846); Keller, Altdeutsche Gedichte (Tübingen, 1846); Erzählungen aus altdeutschen Handschriften (Stuttg., 1855). ˙ A selection: Lambel, Erzählungen and Schwänke (Leipz., 1872). On the Eastern origin of many of the European Tales and Fables, see Loiseleur Delongchamps, Essai sur les fables indiennes et leur introduction en Europe, (Paris, 1838). Benfey, Panchatantra (Leipz., 1859).

Stricker. Smaller poems published by Hahn (Quedlinburg, 1839); on the
decline of poetry in Austria, Hagen's Germania, ii, 82; on the Gauhühner
(Pfeiffer, Germ. vi, 457); the 'Priest Amis' in Lambel, No. 1.—The so-called
Seifried Helbling, Ed. Karajan (Zs. iv, 1); see Martin, Zs. xiii, 464: Seemüller,
Wiener Sitzungsberichte, 102, 567.—'Meier Helmbrecht,' by *Werner der Gärt-
ner* in Lambel, No. 3.—'*The bad wife,*' ed. M. Haupt (Leipz. 1871).—*Enen-
kel,* really hern Jansen enkel (see Sch. in Litterarisches Centralblatt, 1868,
Sp. 978). His 'Fürstenbuch,' ed. Megiser, 1618 (new ed. 1740), from the
'Weltchronik,' extracts in v. d. Hagen, Gesammtabenteuer.—The '*Wiener
Meerfahrt*' in Lambel, No. 5.—The '*Weinschwelg,*' Grimm, Altdeutsche
Wälder, iii, 13; Germ. iii, 210.

4. *The Mendicant Orders,* pp. 222–234.

The date given for the '*Sachsenspiegel*' is only approximate. Eike is mentioned in documents of 1209 to 1233. Ed. Homeyer; First Part (3rd ed.,
Berlin, 1861); Second Part, 2 vols. (Berl. 1842–44). The date of the '*Schwabenspiegel*' is given by Ficker, Wiener Sitzungsberichte, 77, 795. Ed. Wackernagel (Zürich, 1840); von Lassberg (Tübingen, 1840); one in preparation by
Rockinger.

On the economic revolution in the thirteenth century, see Schmoller, Q.F. 6
(Strasb. 1874).

On the *Heretics.* Zs. ix. 63, 65. Preger, Der Tractat des David von Augsburg
über die Waldesier (Munich, 1878, Abh. der bayr. Akad.), p. 7, 39.—The story
of the abbot, who woke his monks by naming King Arthur, is told by Cäsarius
von Heisterbach, iv, 36. See A. Kaufmann, Cäsarius von Heisterbach (Cologne,
1850). On *St. Gall,* see Wackernagel, Verdienste der Schweizer um die
deutsche Litteratur (Basle, 1833), p. 14. The hostility of the *Mendicant
Orders* to Chivalry, Br. Berthold, ii, 670. Ulrich von Lichtenstein complains,
601, 10 et seq. of the increasing bigotry amongst women.

Brother Berthold of Regensburg: Ed. Pfeiffer und Strobl, 2 vols. (Vienna,
1862, 80); see J. Grimm, Kleine Schriften, iv, 296: K. Schmidt, Theo-
logische Studien and Kritiken, 1864, i, 1–82; Strobl, Wiener Sitzungsberichte,
84; Jacob, Die lateinischen Reden des seligen Berthold von R. (Regensburg,
1880); Germ. xxvi, 316; Unkel, Berthold von R. (Cologne, 1882).

The Dominicans. Albertus Magnus; see Pouchet, Histoire des Sciences
naturelles au M.A. ou Albert le Grand et son époque (Paris, 1853); Sighart,
Albertus Magnus (Regensburg, 1857); d'Assailly, Albert le Grand (Paris,
1870); also Prantl, Geschichte der Logik, iii, 89; Jessen, Deutsche Viertel-
jahrsschrift, 121, p. 269; Carus, Geschichte der Zoologie, p. 223.—*Konrad von
Megenberg,* ed. Pfeiffer (Stuttgart, 1861).—*Mystics,* Preger, Geschichte der
deutschen Mystik im Mittelalter, i (Leipz. 1874), ii (1881). *Meister Eckhart,*
ed. Pfeiffer (Deutsche Mystiker, vol. 2, Leipz. 1857). *Tauler,* ed. Hamberger
(Frankfort, 1864). *Suso,* ed. Diepenbrock (3rd ed., Augsburg, 1854). Denifle,
vol. 1 (Munich, 1880).—*Mathilde of Magdeburg*: Offenbarungen der Schwester
Mechthild von M., ed. P. Gall Morel (Regensburg, 1869). Her followers, see
Strauch, Q.F. 26; also by Strauch, Margaretha Ebner und Heinrich von Nördlingen (Freiburg, 1882).

Opposition to the Papal power: see Riezler, Die litterarischen Widersacher der Päpste (Leipz. 1874); C. Müller, Der Kampf Ludwigs des Baiern mit der römischen Curie, 2 vols. (Tübingen, 1879–80).—German Version of the Sunday Epistles and Gospels, see I. Haupt, Wiener Sitzungsberichte, 76, 53.—On *Rulmann,* i.e. Hieronymus, Merswin, see 'Buch von den neun Felsen,' ed, K. Schmidt (Leipz. 1859); Schmidt, Nicolaus von Basel (Vienna, 1866); Nicolaus von Basel, Bericht von der Bekehrung Taulers', ed. Schmidt (Strasb. 1875); Denifle Q.F. 36, and Zs. xxiv, 200, 280, 463; xxv, 101.

VIII. THE CLOSE OF THE MIDDLE AGES, pp. 235-270.

See R. Höniger, Der schwarze Tod in Deutschland (Berlin, 1881); Lechner, Das grosse Sterben (Innsbruck, 1884). Zacher, Article on the Flagellants, in Ersch and Gruber's Encyclopädie.—The expression 'Aristophanic centuries' is adopted from Gervinus.—On the discovery of printing, see van der Linde, Gutenberg (Stuttg. 1878). The German printed works before 1500 are given by Panzer, Annalen der älteren deutschen Litteratur (Nuremberg, 1788); continued in the ' Zusätze,' reaching to 1520 (Leipz. 1802) and a second vol., which gives the German works published between 1521 and 1526 (Nuremberg, 1805).

1. *The Drama,* pp. 238-246.

See Wackernagel, p. 390 et seq., and his Geschichte des deutschen Dramas bis zum Anfange des siebzehnten Jahrhunderts, Kleine Schriften, ii, 69. Hase, Das geistliche Schauspiel (Leipz. 1858). Reidt, Das geistliche Schauspiel des Mittelalters in Deutschland (Frankf. 1868). Wilken, Geschichte der geistlichen Spiele in Deutschland (Göttingen, 1872). On the comic element in the old German plays, see Weinhold in Gosches Jahrbuch für Litteratur-Geschichte (Berlin, 1865), 1 et seq.—Collections: Hoffmann, Fundgruben ii, 260; Mone, Altteütche Schauspiele (Quedlinburg, 1841); Schauspiele des Mittelalters, 2 vols. (Karlsruhe, 1846); Pichler, Über das Drama des Mittelalters in Tirol (Innsbruck, 1850); Kummer, Erlauer Spiele (Vienna, 1882). Chiefly, but not entirely comic plays: Keller, Fastnachtspiele aus dem fünfzehnten Jahrhundert, 3 vols. (Stuttg. 1853), with a continuation, 'Nachlese' (Stuttg. 1858). We may at once mention here: Rein, Vier geistliche Spiele des 17 Jahrhunderts für Charfreitag und Fronleichnamsfest (Crefeld, 1853); A. Hartmann, Volksschauspiele in Bayern und Österreich-Ungarn gesammelt (Leipz. 1880).

Stage and Scenery: Leibing, Die Iuscenirung des zweitägigen Luzerner Osterspieles vom Jahre 1583, durch Renwart Cysat (Elberfeld, 1869); Lepsius und Traube, Schauspiel und Bühne, i (Munich, 1880), 49 (comp. ii, 15).

Dramatic varieties: For the French terminology which I have applied to German plays see Ebert, Zur Entwickelungsgeschichte der französischen Tragödie (Gotha, 1856). Mone has drawn attention to the influence of the French Drama (see Schauspiele des Mittelalters, ' Französisches Schauspiel,' in the Index); Martin, Zs. xxvi, Anz. 311, gives a striking proof. See too, Keller, p. 1516, 1517,

1. *Mysteries, or Miracle Plays.* Besides the plays for Church Festivals

from the New Test. we have Old Test. stories, Legends, and Tales. (*a*) *Christmas Plays*: R. Weinhold, Weihnacht-Spiele und -Lieder aus Süddeutschland und Schlesien (Grätz, 1853); Lexer, Kärntisches Wörterbuch (Leipz. 1862), p. 269 et seq. ; Schröer, Deutsche Weihnachtspiele aus Ungarn (Vienna, 1858); A. Hartmann, Weihnachtlied und Weihnachtspiel in Oberbayern (Munich, 1875, Oberbayerisches Archiv, vol. 34); Pailler, Weihnachtlieder und Krippenspiele aus Oberösterreich und Tirol, vol. 1 (Innspruck, 1881). Carmina Burana, p. 81; Hagen's Germ. vii, 349; Piderit, Ein Weihnachtspiel (Parchim, 1869).—(*b*) *Passion and Easter plays*: Carm. Bur. p. 95; Germ. viii, 273; Wagner's Archiv für die Geschichte deutscher Sprache und Dichtung, i, 355; Fichard, Frankfurtisches Archiv. iii, 131; Alsfelder Passionsspiel, ed. Grein (Cassel, 1874); Friedberger, Zs. vii, 545; The Augsburg play in A. Hartmann, Das Oberammergauer Passionspiel in seiner ältesten Gestalt (Leipz. 1880); the Heidelberg play, ed. Milchsack (Tübingen, 1880); the Freiburg play, ed. Martin (Freiburg, 1872, Zeitschrift der histor. Gesellsch. zu Freiburg, vol. 3); the Redentin play, ed. Ettmüller, ' Dat spil fan der upstandinge, gedichtet 1464' (Quedlinburg, 1851). The Passion play in St. Stephen's in Vienna, ed. Camesina, Mittheilungen über die ältere Feier des Charfreitags in der St. Stephanskirche (Vienna, 1869). See Grieshaber, Über die Ostersequenz Victimae paschali und deren Beziehung zu den religiösen Schauspielen des Mittelalters (Carlsruhe, 1844); Milchsack, Die Oster und Passionsspiele, i (Wolfenbüttel, 1880); Zs. xxv, 251.—Schönbach, Über die Marienklagen (Gratz, 1874).—(*c*) *Corpus Christi plays.* The Eger Fronleichnamspiel, ed. Milchsack (Tübingen, 1881); The Künzelsau Germ. iv, 338.—(*d*) *Old Testament plays.* The Fall, by Arnold von Immessen, ed. Schönemann, Der Sündenfall und Marienklage (Hanover, 1855); Joseph in Egypt (about A.D. 1265; Fundgruben ii, 242); Judgment of Solomon, Schnorr's Archiv iii, 13; Susanna, Keller, Fastn. Nachl. No. 129; Germ. xxii, 342.—(*e*) *Legends.* Assumption of the Virgin, Mone, Altt. Schausp. 21; Invention of the Cross, Keller's Nachlese, No. 125; St. Dorothea, Fundgruben, ii, 284: St. Catharine, in Stephan, Neue Stofflieferungen für die deutsche Geschichte (Mühlhausen, 1847), ii, 149; St. George (Germ. i, 171; Keller, Nachlese, No. 126); Theophilus, ed. Ettmüller (Quedlinburg, 1849). Hoffmann (from a Treves MS., Hanover, 1853, from a Stockholm and Helmstadt MS., Hanover, 1854); see too, Sass, Über das Verhältnis der Recensionen des niederdeutschen Spiels von Theophilus (Elmshorn, 1879); see too, Sommer De Theophili cum diabolo foedere (Halle, 1844).—(*f*) *History and Myths.* The Judgment of Paris, Schnorr's Archiv iii, 5, 17. Pope Joan, ' Spiel von Frau Jutten,' Keller, No. 111.

2. *Moralties and Didactic plays.*—(*a*) *New Testament Parables.* The play of the Wise and Foolish Virgins, ed. Stephan, Stofflieferungen, ii, 173. (L. Bechstein, Wartburgbibliothek, i, Halle, 1855); Rieger, Germ. x, 311; translation by Freybe (Leipz. 1870); see R. Beckstein, Das Spiel von den zehn Jungfrauen (Rostock, 1872). The fragments of a play of the rich man and Lazarus, in the Spiegelbuch, ed. Rieger, Germ. xvi, 173. (*b*) *Disputations.* Keller, No. 1, 121; comp. 106. (*c*) *Allegorical Plays*, namely, those in which allegories and personifications appear, as Shrovetide, Keller, No. 51; the time after Easter ('Meister Reuaus,' Wagner's Archiv i, 13, 95, 227); colours, Keller,

No. 103; an illness, No. 54; or death. *Dances of Death*: see Wackernagel, Kleine Schriften, i, 302; Massmann, Baseler Todtentänze (Stuttg. 1847); Rieger, Germ. xix, 257; Schröer, Germ. xii, 204. Lübeck Dance of Death, ed. Mantells (Lübeck, 1866), Bäthcke (Berl. 1873, Tüb. 1876); Berlin (Lübke), Der Todtentanz in der Marienkirche zu Berlin (Berl. 1861); Jahrbuch des Vereins für niederdeutsche Sprachforschung, 1877, p. 178; 1878, p. 105).

(*d*) *Dramatic examples.* I know no better name for those moralities where figures appear, which, like the Sinner in the Spiegelbuch (Germ. xvi, 173: Keller, No. 131), are representatives of their class; sometimes they may be compared with the Satires on all classes, and have been derived from them: see below, ' Great towns,' Reval and Basle.

3. *Farces, or burlesques.* The documents are easily found in Keller's Fastnachtspielen; see too, Schnorr's Archiv iii, 2; Germ. xxii, 420. Compare Kurz, Geschichte der deutschen Litteratur, 5th Ed. i, 711, 730.

4. *Sotties, or clown-plays.* Here too, Keller's collection is the best authority.

Great Towns as fostering places. Lübeck, Jahrbuch für niederdeutsche Sprachforschungen, 1880–1, 31 (eine Moralität, Jahrbuch, 1877, p. 9; see 1879, p. 173; shorter form in Germ. xviii, 460). *Reval*, Wagner's Archiv i, 494; *Basle*, Pamphilus Gengenbach, pub. by Gödeke (Hanover, 1856), see Wagner's Archiv i, 494.—*Nuremberg*, for Rosenblüt see Wendeler, Wagner's Archiv. i, 97, 385; for Folz, Gödeke, Germ. xv, 197; Lochner, Schnorr's Archiv iii, 324.

Roman drama revived. See Gödeke, § 113, 1–16, Schnorr's Archiv vii, 157; xi. 328. *Macropedius* (Gödeke, § 113, 21) confesses himself influenced by Reuchlin. Chilianus Eques (Reuter) Mellerstatinus (ibid. 6) appeals to the example of ' Rosphita;' which confirms Wackernagel's remark, Litteraturgeschichte, p. 405, Anm. 22. For *Reuchlin's* ' Henno,' see Hermann Grimm's Essays (Hanover, 1859), p. 119. For *Albrecht von Eyb*, Kurz und Paldamus, Deutsche Dichter und Prosaisten, i, 26–33; a specimen of his translations is given by Cholevius, Geschichte der deutschen Poesie nach ihren antiken Elementen, i, 285.

2. *Songs and Ballads*, pp. 246-253.

Meistersong: Bartsch, Meisterlieder der Kolmarer Handschrift (Stutt. 1862); Holtzmann, Germ. iii. 307. v. 210; Zingerle, Wiltener Handschrift, Wiener Sitzungsberichte, xxxvii. 331; Wackernagel, Litteraturgeschichte, p. 325, Anm. 16; Martin, Die Meistersänger von Strassburg (Strassb. 1882), Strassb. Studien, i. 76. On the conservative tendency of the Rhenish Meistergesang, Gödeke, Germ. xv. 200. On the influence of the Nuremberg Meistersingers in preserving the Heroic Legends see Steinmeyer, Zs. f. d. Phil. iii. 241.

Volkslied. *Ballads:* Uhland, Alte hoch- und niederdeutsche Volkslieder, (Stuttg., 1844, 45) Schriften, vols. iii, iv; Liliencron, Die historischen Volkslieder der Deutschen, 5 vols. (Leipz. 1865-69); Böhme, Altdeutsches Liederbuch (Leipz. 1877); L. Tobler, Schweizerische Volkslieder (Frauenfeld, 1822). See Müllenhoff, Preface to the Schleswigholsteinische Sagen (Kiel, 1845); Ferd. Wolf, Preface to Warrens Schwedische Volkslieder (Leipz. 1857). The evidence afforded by the *Limburg Chronicle* is given by Chrysander,

Jahrbuch für musikalische Wissenschaft, i. 115. More information in Böhme.
The *noble Moringers* Journey to the East seems to be derived from the
assocition of the name of Heinrich von Morungen with the Moors, and his
rival is called the young lord of Neifen because *Gottfried von Neifen* once sang
of a falsely disguised Pilgrim (Haupt., 45., 8). *Tannhäuser's* Farewell to Lady
.Venus, Keller, Fastnachtspiel Nachl. No. 124; see Walther, 100. 24.

3. *Rhymed Couplets,* pp. 253-259.

Reineke Fuchs. J. Grimm, Reinhart Fuchs (comp. VI. 2). ˙Müllenhoff,
Zs. xviii. 1. Voigt, Q. F. vii. 25. Le roman de Renart, Martin i. (Strassburg,
1882). Reinaert, pub. by Martin (Paderborn, 1874). Reinke de Vos, ed.
Lübben (Oldenburg, 1867). Schröder (Leipz. 1872) ; comp. Prien, Beitr. viii. 1.
Ranke, Deutsche Geschichte im Zeitalter der Reformation, i. 199 (3rd ed.).
—*Wittenweiler's Ring,* ed. Bechstein (Stuttg. 1851). ' *Des Teufels Netz,*' ed.
Barack (Stuttg. 1863).—*Hermann von Sachsenheim,* ed. Martin (Tübingen,
1878).

Sebastian Brand, Narrenschiff, ed. Zarncke (Leipz. 1854) ; Gödeke (Leipz.
1872). Translation, Simrock (Berl. 1872). See Zarncke, Zur Vorgeschichte
des Narrenschiffes (from the Serapeum 29, Leipz. 1868 ; second communication,
Leipz. 1871); Schmidt, Histoire littéraire de l'Alsace, i. 189.—*Thomas Murner,*
see Lappenberg, Dr. Thomas Murner's Ulenspiegel (Leipz. 1854), p. 384 et seq.
Gödeke in the Introduction to his edition of the ' Narrenbeschwörung' (Leipz.
1879). Short account in Lorenz and Scherer, Geschichte des Elsasses, 2nd ed.
Berl. 1872), p. 167. Schmidt, ii. 209.

Püterich von Reicherzhausen, Zs. vi. 31 ; Q. F. xxi. 16. *Ulrich Fütrer ;*
Hamburger, Untersuchungen über U. F. (Strassb. 1882) ; Spiller, Zs. xxvii.
262. *Maximilian I,* ' Theuerdank,' ed. Haltaus (Quedlinburg, 1836); Gödeke
(Leipz. 1878). For the ' *Weisskunig,*' Liliencron in Raumer's Historisches
Taschenbuch, v. Folge, 3. 321.—The prose of *Herzog Ernst,*' see Bartsch,
Herzog Ernst (Vienna, 1869), p. 227 ; *Tristrant and Isalde,* ed. Pfaff (Tübin-
gen, 1881).

4. *Prose,* pp. 259-264.

Prose Romances. A convenient sketch is given by Gödeke, §§ 105-108.
Reproductions in Simrock's Deutsche Volksbüchern. See Bobertag, Geschichte
des Romans i. (Breslau, 1877) and Scherer's critique, Q. F. xxi. (Strassb. 1877).
On the *Lanzelot romances,* see Peter, Germ. xxviii. 129. ' Parables of the old
Sages ' ed. Holland (Stuttg. 1860)· ' *Decamerone,*' of which the translation is
not by Steinhöwel, ed. Keller (Stuttg. 1860). For *Dr. Johannes Hartlieb,* see
Öfele, A. D. B. 670. On *Thüring von Ringoltingen* and *Wilhelm Ziely,* see
Bächtold in the Berner Taschenbuch, 1878. *Eulenspiegel,* ed. Lappenberg
(Leipz. 1854), Q. F. xxi. 26. 78.

Other prose writings : Sermons. Wackernagel, Altdeutsche Predigten und
Gebete (Basle, 1876), with an Essay by M. Rieger on old German preaching ;
Cruel, Geschichte der deutschen Predigt im Mittelalter (Detmold, 1879).
Juristic prose : Stobbe, Geschichte der deutschen Rechtsquellen, 2 vols. (Berl.
1860, 1864). *Scientific prose works* : see Albertus Magnus, in text p. 229. Pre-

scriptions : Denkm. 62. *Medicinal books* : Hoffmann, Fundgruben, i. 317 ; Pfeiffer, Wiener Sitzungsberichte, 42, 110 ; Joseph Haupt, ibid. 71, 451 ; Häser, Geschichte der Medicin (3rd ed.), i. 697, 818. *History* : see O. Lorenz, Deutschlands Geschichtsquellen im Mittelalter (2nd ed.), 2 vols. (Berl. 1876–77) ; *The Saxon Universal Chronicle*, ed. Weiland, in the Mon. Germ. Deutsche Chroniken, ii. (Hanover, 1877). On *Windeck*, Droysen (Leipz. 1853) ; Kern, in the Zs. für Culturgeschichte, 1875, p. 349. On the German versions of Latin histories for the laity, see Waitz on Hermann Korner (Göttingen, 1851), p. 16. *Dialogues.* ' *Ackermann aus Böhmen*,' ed. Knieschek (Prague, 1877). *Niclas von Wyle*, ed. Keller (Stuttg. 1861).

Mathilda of Austria. Martin, Erzherzogin Mechthild (Freiburg, 1871) ; Strauch, Pfalzgräfin Mechthild (Tübingen, 1883). For *Heidelberg*, see Wilken, Geschichte der Heidelb. Büchersammlungen (Heidelberg, 1817), pp. 308, 351, 394.

5. *Humanism*, pp. 264-270.

There is no good history of the German Universities. For the characteristics of the German Universities in the Middle Ages, see Paulsen in von Sybel's Historische Zs. N. F. vol. ix. For *Prague*, see Friedjung, Kaiser Karl iv. (Vienna, 1876), p. 127. On the *Humanists* in general : Meiners' Lebensbeschreibungen berühmter Männer aus den Zeiten der Wiederherstellung der Wissenschaften, 3 vols. (Zurich, 1795–97) ; H. A. Erhard, Geschichte des Wiederaufblühens wissenschaftlicher Bildung, 3 vols. (Magdeburg, 1827–32) ; Karl Hagen, Deutschlands religiöse und litterarische Verhältnisse im Zeitalter der Reformation, 3 vols. (Erlangen, 1841-44) ; G. Voigt, Die Wiederbelebung des classischen Alterthums (2nd ed.), 2 vols. (Berl. 1880-1) ; J. Burckhardt, Die Cultur der Renaissance in Italien (3rd ed. by L. Geiger), 2 vols. (Leipz. 1877-78 ; L. Geiger, Renaissance und Humanismus in Italien und Deutschland (Berl. 1882).

Heinrich von Langenstein : O. Hartwig, H. v. L. (Marburg, 1858). On *Gutenberg*, v. d. Linde, Gutenberg (Stuttg. 1878). On *Peuerbach and Regiomontanus*, Wolf, Geschichte der Astronomie (Munich, 1877) ; on their Lectures in Vienna, Kink, Gesch. der kais. Univ. Wien, i. (Vienna, 1854), 182 ; Aschbach, Gesch. der Wiener Univ. i. (Vienna, 1865), 480, 353 ; *Peter Luder*, Wattenbach P. L. (Karlsruh, 1869) p. 11. *Æneas Sylvius* in Vienna, Voigt, Enea Silvio de' Piccolomini, ii. (Berlin, 1862), 342. *Celtis*, Aschbach, Gesch. der Wiener Univ. ii. 189-270 ; *Hartfelder*, Sybel's Hist. Zs. 47. 15.

Gerhard Groote : K. v. Raumer, Gesch. der Pädagogik (4th ed.) i. 54 ; A. D. B. ix. 730. *Erasmus*, A. D. B. vi. 160, where other works are mentioned ; Horawitz, Wiener Sitzungsberichte, 90, 387. 95, 575. 100, 665. 102, 755. *Reuchlin :* L. Geiger, Johann Reuchlin (Leipz. 1871) ; Reuchlin, Briefwechsel (Tübingen, 1875). *Bebel :* Zapf, Heinrich Bebel (Augsburg, 1802) ; see H. B. Proverbia Germanica, ed. Suringar (Leyden, 1879).

On the *Erfurt circle :* Kampschulte, Universität Erfurt, 2 parts (Treves, 1858-60). Also Kampschulte ' *De Joanne Croto Rubiano* (Bonne, 1862) ; C. Krause, *Helius Eobanus Hessus*, 2 vols. (Gotha, 1879) ; C. Krause, *Euricius Cordus* (Hanau, 1863) ; Strauss, *Ulrich von Hutten*, 2 vols. (Leipz. 1858,

2nd ed. 1871). Hutten's works were published by Eduard Böcking in 5 vols. with 2 vols. Appendix (Leipz. 1859-1870) ; the Appendix contains the Epistolae obscurorum virorum.

IX. THE REFORMATION AND THE RENAISSANCE, pp. 271-330.

For the effect of the Peace of 1551 see Ranke, Sämmtliche Werke, vii. 1. Gödeke's Grundriss gives the fullest material for this and for all the following chapters. See too, E. Weller, Annalen der poetischen Nationallitteratur der Deutschen im 16 and 17 Jahrhunderte, 2 vols. (Freiburg, 1862-64) ; Repertorium typographicum (Nördlingen, 1864), with a Supplement (1874).

1. *Martin Luther,* pp. 272-282.

For Luther's connection with German literature, besides this section see further on, IX. 2 and 3 (Fables, Proverbs, Secular songs, Novels), and 4, The Drama. I have given no list of the numerous Lives of Luther. Julius Köstlin's work (Elberfeld, 1872, 2 vols.) has proved of great use. W. Maurenbrecher, Geschichte der Katholischen Reformation, vol. i. (Nördlingen, 1880), is a good guide to the newest literature on the subject, and for vexed questions. Our knowledge of Luther's correspondence (ed. de Witte, 5 vols. Berl. 1825-28, with a 6th vol. by Seidemann, Berl. 1856 ; also Seidemann, Lutherbriefe, Dresden, 1859 ; Burkhardt, Dr. M. L. Briefwechsel, Leipz. 1866) has been lately increased by Kolde, Analecta Lutherana (Gotha, 1883). For the *Table Talk :* M. Anton, Lauterbachs Tagebuch, 1538, the principal source of Luther's Table Talk, published by Seidemann (Dresden, 1872). On Mathesius, see Plitt, Die vier ersten Lutherbiographen (Erlangen, 1876), p. 17.

His position with regard to the New Learning. O. G. Schmidt, Luther's Bekanntschaft mit den alten Classikern (Leipz. 1883).

Translation of the Bible. See in Text, p. 30. Old High-German Gospel of St. Matthew, p. 40. Middle High-German Gospels, Germ. xiv. 440 ; Zs. ix. 264 ; Matthias von Beheim, Book of the Gospels in Middle German, Ed. R. Bechstein (Leipz. 1867). Compare in text, p. 233. The Codex Teplensis, containing Die Schrift des newen Gezeuges (Munich, 1881). Psalms (except Notker's, see p. 51), Deutsche Interlinearversion der Psalmen, ed. Graff (Quedlinburg, 1839), and others. Versions of the historical books of the Old Testament (comp. Rudolf von Ems, Universal Chronicle, p. 180) ; Die deutschen Historienbibeln des Mittelalters, ed. Merzdorf (Tübingen, 1870). Luther's Translation, critical edition, Bindseil und Niemeyer, 7 Parts (Halle, 1850-55). Facsimile of the so-called September Bible, (the New Testament of Sept. 1522), (Berl. 1883). See I. G. Palm, Historie der deutschen Bibelübersetzung D. Martini Lutheri von 1517 bis 1534 (Halle, 1772) ; J. M. Goeze, Verzeichnis seiner Sammlung seltener und merkwürdiger Bibeln (Halle, 1777). Fortsetzung des Verzeichnisses (Hamburg and Halberstadt, 1778). Neue für die Kritik und Historie der Bibelübersetzung Lutheri wichtige Entdeckungen (Hamburg and Leipzig, 1777) ; Panzer, Entwurf einer vollständigen Geschichte der deutschen Bibelübersetzung M. L. (Nuremberg, 1783 ; 2nd ed. 1791) ;

Schott, Geschichte der deutschen Bibelübersetzung M. L. (Leipzic, 1835); Hopf, Würdigung der Lutherischen Bibelübersetzung (Nuremberg, 1847); Kehrein, Zur Geschichte der deutschen Bibelübers. von Luther (Stuttg. 1851); J. M. Goeze, Historie der gedruckten niedersächsischen Bibeln von 1470 to 1621 (Halle, 1775); Mezger, Geschichte der deutschen Bibelübersetzungen in der schweizerisch-reformirten Kirche (Basle, 1876).

Language. Müllenhoff's Preface to the Denkmäler; Sch., Vorträge und Aufsätze, p. 45; H. Rückert, Geschichte der neuhochdeutschen Schriftsprache, 2 vols. (Leipz. 1875). For *Luther's language* especially: Mönckeberg, Beiträge zur würdigen Herstellung des Textes der Lutherischen Bibelübersetzung (Hamburg, 1855). Wetzel, Die Sprache Luthers (Stuttg. 1859); Frommann, Vorschläge zur Revision von M. L. Bibelübers. sprachlicher Theil (Halle, 1862); Opitz, Über die Sprache Luthers .(Halle, 1869); Dietz, Wörterbuch zu M. L. deutschen Schriften, vol. i. (Leipz. 1870, not finished); Lehmann, Luther's Sprache (Halle, 1873); Wülcker Germ. xxviii. 191. On *modernized forms:* Gödeke Grundriss, § 143. I. On *Grammars,* see Joh. Müller, Quellenschriften und Geschichte des deutschsprachlichen Unterrichtes bis zur Mitte des 16 Jahrh. (Gotha, 1882). Of *Fabian Frangk,* the most distinguished of all the old Grammarians, Müller (p. 393), says, ' He is the father of the newer classical language, the German of Luther.' For *Ölinger* and *Clajus* see R. v. Raumer, Unterricht im Deutschen (4th ed. Gütersloh, 1873), p. 20.

Sermons. See Cruel's work named above, VIII. 4; Jonas, Die Kanzelberedsamkeit Luther's (Berlin, 1852). On *Geiler von Kaisersberg.* see Lorenz und Sch., Geschichte des Elsasses, p. 150, and Martin A. D. B. viii. 509; Schmidt, Hist. litt. i. 335.

Church Song. Hoffmann von Fallersleben, Geschichte des deutschen Kirchenliedes bis auf Luthers Zeit, 2nd ed. (Hanover, 1854); E. E. Koch, Geschichte des Kirchenliedes und Kirchengesangs der christlichen inbesonders der deutschen evangel. Kirche, 3rd ed. 8 vols. (Stuttg. 1866–76); Phil. Wackernagel, Bibliographie zur Gesch. des deutschen Kirchenliedes im 16 Jahrh. (Frankfort, 1855). Das deutsche Kirchenlied von der ältesten Zeit bis zu Anfang des 17 Jahrh. 5 vols. (Leipz. 1864–77).

' *Ein Feste Burg.*' See Schneider; M. L. geistliche Lieder, 2nd ed. (Berl. 1856), p. xlii; Knaake Luthardts Zs. für kirchliche Wissenschaft und kirchl. Leben i. (1881), p. 39.

2. *Luther's Associates and Successors,* pp. 282–290.

Luther's opponents. For the *Anabaptists,* see Cornelius, Gesch. des Münsterischen Aufruhrs, Book II (Leipz. 1860), 1–98. Hase, *Sebastian Franck von Wörd* (Leipz. 1869). Schneider, Zur Litteratur der Schwenckfeldischen Liederdichter bis Daniel Sudermann (Berlin, 1857). *Murner's* ' Grosser Lutherischer Narr,' Ed. Kurz (Zürich, 1848).

Ulrich von Hutten (see above, VIII. 5, Erfurt circle). Strauss has translated and explained the ' Gespräche von U. v. H.' (Leipz. 1860). *Pirkheimer's* Eccius dedolatus is in Böcking's Hutten iv. 515. *Hans Sachs'* Dialogues have been published by Reinhold Köhler (Weimar, 1858). There is a monograph on *Eberlin von Günzburg*, by B. Riggenbach (Tübingen, 1874). On *Niclas Manuel*, see below, IX. 4. On Utz Eckstein, see Sch. A. D. B. v. 636. '*Karsthaus*' in Böcking iv. 615. Consult O. Schade, Satiren und Pasquille aus der Reformationszeit, 2nd ed. 3 vols. (Hanover, 1863). A. Baur, Deutschland in den Jahren 1517–1525 (Ulm, 1872).

Newspapers. Th. Sickel, Weimar Jahrbuch i. 344. E. Weller, Die ersten deutschen Zeitungen (Tübiugen, 1872); R. Grasshoff, Die briefliche Zeitung des 16 Jahrh. (Leipz. 1877). See Liliencron, Mittheilungen aus dem Gebiete der öffentlichen Meinung in Deutschland während der zweiten Hälfte des 16 Jahrh. (Munich, 1874, 75. Abhandlungen der bayer.-Akademie).

Meistersong. Schnorr von Carolsfeld, Zur Geschichte des deutschen Meistergesangs (Berl. 1872). Luther's Hymn-book of 1528 was discovered by Knaake in a later reprint. *Bartholomäus Ringwald*, ses Hoffmann, Spenden zur deutschen Litteraturgeschichte, ii. 17.

Marot's Psalms. See Höpfner Reformbestrebungen auf dem Gebiete der deutschen Dichtung des 16 and 17 Jahrh. (Berl. 1866), pp. 24–29. *Kasper Scheid:* his '*Grobianus*' was lately printed (Halle, 1882), with an Introduction by Milchsack. On *Dedekind* see Sch. A. D. B. v. 12. *Johann Fischart*, Erich Schmidt, A. D. B. vii. 31, where earlier works are given. See Wendeler, Die Fischartstudien des Freiherrn von Meusebach (Halle, 1879); Johann Fischart sämmtliche Dichtungen, ed. Kurz, 3 vols. (Leipz. 1866–67); Dichtungen von J. F. ed. Gödeke (Leipz. 1880). For the '*Glückhaftes Schiff*,' see Bächtold in the Mittheilungen der Antiquarischen Gesellschaft in Zürich 44 (Zurich, 1880).

3. *Secular Literature,* pp. 290–300.

Melanchthon: Monograph, by C. Schmidt (Elberfeld, 1861). See K. von Raumer, Gesch. der Pädagogik, I, 145: Paur, Zur Litteratur und Kulturgeschichte (Leipzic, 1876) p. 169. '*Melanchthons Naturauffassung:*' Stintzing, Gesch. der deutschen Rechtswissenschaft i. 283.—*Gesner*; Carus, Gesch. der Zoologie p. 274.—*Theophrastus Paracelsus*; Kopp, Entwickelung der Chemie (Munich, 1873) p. 22; Häser ii. 71.—*Flacius*; Preger, Mathias Flacius Illyricus und seine Zeit, 2 vols. (Leipzic, 1859, 61); Schulte, Beitrag zur Entstehungsgeschichte der Magdeburger Centurien (Neisse, 1877); Baur, Epochen der kirchlichen Geschichtschreibung (Tübingen 1852).—Dahlmann in his Quellenkunde (Göttingen, 1830) p. 19, was the first to see that Wimpfelings Epitome rerum Germanicarum was the first German History. On *Wimpfeling* see Lorenz und Sch. Gesch. des Elsasses, p. 160, Schmidt, Hist. Litt. i. 1, and the monographs by Wiskowatoff (Berl. 1867), and by Schwartz (Gotha, 1875). —For *Sleidanus* see Kampschulte in the Forschungen zur deutschen Gesch. iv. 57.—For *Biographies*, the best authority is Melch. Adam, Vitae Theologorum, Jure-consultorum et Politicorum, Medicorum, atque Philosophorum, maximam partem Germanorum. Ed. tertia (Francof. 1706). *Adam* was a Silesian, and died in 1622. The first ed. of his Biographies was published at Heidelberg, 1615–20, in 5 vols.—*German Autobiographies: Götz von Berlichingen*, ed.

Franck von Steigerwald (Nuremberg, 1731): *Hans von Schweinichen*, ed. Österley (Breslau, 1878); *Sebastian Schertlin von Burtenbach*, ed. Holzschuher und Hummel (Frankfort, 1777), Schönhuth (Münster, 1858)! *Thomas and Felix Plater*, ed. Boos (Leipzic, 1878): *Barthol Sastrow*, ed. Mohnicke, 3 vols. (Greifswald, 1824).

The Latin Poets are noticed by hardly any one except Wolfgang Menzel in his Deutsche Dichtung (3 vols. Stuttgart, 1858, 59), but his accounts are very inaccurate. A small work by a certain *Gerard Faust*, of Coblentz, Poetae historici item Germani aliquot celebres singulis Distichis descripti (Argentor. 1546) mentions no less than ninety-two names of Latin poets in Germany. Bylovius (Amores, Francof. 1597) mentions the poets, and the women whose praises they sang, together, and thus passes in review the German love-poetry written in Latin: and one sees how the number of these poems had increased towards 1600. For religious polemical works, in which the opponent is ridiculed as an animal, see *Johann Major* (1533–1600): comp. G. Frank, Johann Major, der Wittenberger Poet (Halle, 1863). We may further refer to Classen, Jacobus Micyllus (Frankf., 1859, Progr. 1861): Henkel Petrus Lotichius Secundus (Bremae, 1873): comp. Des P. L. S. Elegien, translated by Köstlin, (Halle, 1826); for *George Sabinus*, Melanchthons profligate son-in-law, see Töppen, Gründung der Universität Königsberg (Königsb. 1844), and Muther, Aus dem Universitäts-und Gelehrtenleben im Zeitalter der Reformation (Erlangen, 1866) p. 329–367.

Translations. For a general view, see Gödeke §§ 114, 143, ii. The best works are still those by J. F. Degen: Litteratur der deutschen Übersetzungen der Griechen, 2 vols. (Altenburg, 1797, 98) with an Appendix (Erlangen, 1801): Versuch einen vollständigen Litteratur der deutschen Übersetzungen der Römer, 2 parts (Altenburg, 1794–97) with Appendix (Erlangen, 1799). See also Schummel, Übersetzer-Bibliothek (Wittenberg und Zerbst, 1774).

Fables. Steinhöwels Æsop. ed. Österley (Tübingen, 1873). *Luthers* Fables, Gödeke p. 155 and 364, No. 7. *Erasmus Alberus*, ibid. p. 359: see Schnorrs Archiv. vi. 1., x. 273, xi. 177, 628, xii. 26. *Burkard Waldis*, 'Esopus,' ed. Kurz, 2 vols. (Leip. 1862): *Tittmann*, 2 vols. (Leipz. 1882): see Milchsack, B. W. (Halle, 1881). ' *Georg Rollenhagen*,' 'Froschmeuseler,' ed. Gödeke, 2 Parts (Leipz. 1876): *Fischarts Flöhhatz*, has been republished by Wendeler (Halle, 1877). For *Spangenberg* see Lorenz and Sch. Geschichte des Elsasses, p. 303.

Proverbs. Hoffman von Fallersleben in the Weimar Jahrbuch II. 173: in the Horae belgicae ix. 3. Tunnicius, ed. Hoffmann von Fallersleben (Berlin, 1870), also Germ. xv. 195. Latendorf, *Agricola's* Sprichwörter, ihr hochdeutscher Ursprung (Schwerin, 1862): L. v. Passavant against Agricola's Sprichwörter, ed. Latendorf (Berl., 1873). *Sebastian Francks* first anonymous collection of Proverbs of the year 1532, ed. Latendorf (Pösneck, 1876).

Farcical Anecdotes. Gödeke, Schwänke des 16 Jahrh. (Leipz., 1879), with an introduction giving the characteristics of the separate collections. There are new editions of *Pauli* (Stuttg., 1866), *Kirchhoff* (Stuttg., 1869) by Österley; of the *Rollwagenbüchlein* (Leipz., 1865) by Kurz, and of *Lindener* (Tübingen, 1883) by Lichtenstein.

Secular Songs. The utterances of Luther and other Reformers in Gödeke, p. 122: Zs. xv. 325: Deutsche Studien, iii. 59.—See, in general, Hoffmann von Fallersleben, Die Deutschen Gesellschaftslieder des 16 and 17 Jahrh. 2 ed. (Leipz., 1860).

Novels. See above, VIII. 4. Against the prose novel, see Marbach of Strassburg, in Raumur, Gesch. der Pädagogik 4th ed. i. 245, notes ; compare Reifferscheid, Zs. für Kulturgeschichte 1875, p. 703.—The People's Book ' *Kaiser Friedrich*,' Zs. v, 253; see Q. F. xxi. 93.—*Jörg. Wickram* ; Lorenz und Sch. Gesch. des Elsasses, p. 267: Sch. Q. F. xxi. 35. E. Schmidt, Schnorr's Archiv viii, 317.—For the ' *Finkenritter* ' see Müller-Fraureuth, Die deutschen Lügendichtungen bis auf Münchhausen (Halle, 1881) p. 24.—*Claus Narr*, see Schnorr Archiv vi. 277. *Hans Clauert*, see Sch. A. D. B. 17, 226, reprint (Halle, 1882).—On Faust, see below, XIII. 4.

4. *The Drama from* 1517–1620, pp. 300–314.

See in Gottsched, Nöthiger Vorrath zur Gesch. der deutschen dramatischen Dichtkunst (Leipz., 1757: 2nd part, with Freieslebens Nachlese, 1765): see Gödeke Grundr. §§ 113, 145–155, 170–172. Compare Prutz, Vorlesungen über die Geschichte des deutschen Theaters (Berl., 1847): Genée, Lehr- und Wanderjahre des deutschen Schauspiels (Berlin, 1882): also Devrient, Geschichte der deutschen Schauspielkunst, 5 vols. (Leipz., 1848–74).—Texts in Tittmann, Schauspiele aus dem 16 Jahrh. 2 parts (Leipz., 1862).

Luther and the Drama. Gödeke Grundr. p. 306; Sch. Deutsche Studien, iii. 13. Luther's Sermon on the Contemplation of Christ's Sufferings, Werke, Altenb. i. 296.

Various sorts of Drama. The Prodigal Son, Sch. Q. F. xxi. 50 ; Holstein Progr. (Geestemünde, 1880): E. Schmidt, Komödien vom Studentenleben (Leipz., 1880).—For *Joseph in Egypt*, see Sch. Deutsche Studien, iii. 29: Thiebold Garts Joseph, ed. E. Schmidt (Strassb. 1880).—For *Susanna*, Herm. Grimm, 15 Essays, New Series (Berlin, 1875), p. 147 : R. Pilger, Die Dramatisirung der Susanna im 16 Jahrh. (Halle, 1879).

Switzerland and Alsace: E. Weller, Das alte Volkstheater der Schweiz (Frauenfeld, 1863). *Niklas Manuel*, ed. Grüneisen (Stuttg., 1837): Bächtold (Frauenfeld, 1878, Bibliothek alterer Schriftwerke der deutschen Schweiz, vol. 2). *Dasypodius*, Sch. Wagners Archiv i. 487. *Sixtus Birk*: Sch. A. D. B. ii. 656.—Lorenz und Sch. Gesch. des Elsasses, p. 263, 295. A. Jundt, Die dramatischen Aufführungen im Gymnasium zu Strassburg (Strassb. 1881).

Hans Sachs. Keller and Götze began a new edition (Tübingen, 1870); a Collection of the Carnival Plays by Götze (Halle, 1880; the chronology is wrong): a Selection by Gödeke und Tittmann, 3 vols. (Leipzic, 1870, 71) with Introduction. The books on Hans Sachs do not teach us much.

Luther's circle. Joachim Greff: Sch. Deutsche Studien, iii. 11; Holstein, Schnorr's Archiv x. 154.—*Johann Agricola*, Monograph Kordes (Altona, 1817); Kawerau (Berlin, 1881); see Schnorr's Archiv x. 6, 273.—*Paul Rebhun*, ed. Palm (Stuttg., 1859).—*Thomas Naogeorg;* Sch. Zs. xxiii. 190.—*Johannes Chryseus*, Sch. A. D. B. iv. 253.

Nicodemus Frischlin: his German poems were published by Strauss (Stuttg.

1857). See Strauss, N. F. (Frankf. 1856); Sch. A. D. B. viii. 96, also vii. 106, Flayderus.

English actors. A. Cohn, Shakespeare in Germany (London and Berl. 1865), Tittmann, Die Schauspiele der engl. Com. in Deutschland (Leipz. 1880); compare Sch. Zs. xxiii. 197.—*Jacob Ayrer*; ed. Keller, 5 vols. (Stuttg. 1865); see Tittmann, Schauspiele aus dem 16 Jahrh. ii. 123.—Duke *Heinrich Julius of Brunswick*, ed. Holland (Stuttg. 1855); Tittmann, (Leipz. 1880); see Hermann Grimm, Fünfzehn Essays, New Series, p. 142. For *Bertesius* see Sch. A. D. B. ii. 512.—*Landgrave Maurice* of Hesse; see Rommel, Gesch. von Hessen, vi. 399-403; Lynker, Gesch. des Theaters und der Musik in Cassel (Cassel, 1865), p. 224, 247.

5. *The Thirty Years' War*, pp. 314-330.

Kepler. Reuschle, K. und die Astronomie (Frankf. 1871); *Valentine Andreä,* Hossbach, V. A. und seine Zeit (Berl. 1819): E. Schmidt in the Goethe Jahrbuch, iv. 127: other works on the subject A. D. B. i. 446.—*Johann Arndt,* A. D. B. i. 548.—*Jacob Böhme,* ed. Schiebler, 6 vols. (Leipz. 1831-46). Hamberger, Die Lehre J. B. (Munich, 1844); Huber, Kleine Schriften, p. 34 (Leipz. 1871).—Book trade, Q. F. xxi. 62, notes.

Weckherlin, Poems published by Gödeke (Leipz. 1873); see Höpfner, ·G. R. Weckherlins Oden and Gesänge (Berl. 1865).—*Julius Wilhelm Zincgref,* Schnorr Archiv viii. 1. 446. The best memorial of the Heidelberg poetic circle is the Appendix to Zincgref's edition of Opitz's poems (Strassburg, 1624), a reprint (Halle, 1879). See Höpfner, Reformbestrebungen, (Berl. 1866). Otto Schulz, Die Sprachgesellschaften des 17 Jahrh. (Berl. 1824); Barthold, Gesch. der fruchtbringenden Gesellschaft (Berl. 1848); Krause, Der fruchtbringenden Gesellschaft ältester Ertzschrein (Leipz. 1855).—Compare Lemcke, Gesch. der deutschen Dichtung neuerer Zeit, vol. i. (from Opitz to Klopstock, Leipz., 1871).

Martin Opitz. See Palm, Beitr. zur Gesch. der deutschen Litteratur des 16 and 17 Jahrh. (Breslau, 1877), p. 129. Guttmann, Über die Ausgaben der Gesammtwerke von Opitz, Progr. (Ratibor, 1850): Strehlke, M. O. (Leipz. 1856); Weinhold, M. O. von Boberfeld (Kiel, 1862); Zöllner in the Deutsches Museum, 1865; Bernh. Muth, Über das Verhältnis von M. O. zu Dan. Heinsius (Leipz. 1872); L. Geiger, Mittheilungen aus Handschriften i. (Leipz., 1876). Selected Poems of Opitz, ed. Tittmann (Leipz., 1869). New edition of the 'Deutsche Poeterei' (Halle, 1876).—Review of German Poetics in Blankenburg, continuation of Sulzer, i. 402. Gödeke, Grundriss ii. 438: Koberstein ii, 44-55.

August Buchner. Hoffmann von Fallersleben, Weim. Jahrb. ii. 1; W. Buchner, August Buchner (Hanover, 1863). *Paul Fleming,* P. F. Lateinische Gedichte, ed. Lappenberg (Stuttg., 1865); P. F. Deutsche Gedichte, ed. Lappenberg (Stuttg., 1865); Tittmann, Selection (Leipz., 1870). *Simon Dach.* Ed. Österley (Tübingen, 1876); Selection, Österley (Leipz., 1876): see Friedrich S. D. Progr. (Dresden, 1862); Henneberger's Jahrbuch für deutsche Litteraturgeschichte I (Meiningen, 1855), 42.

The Nuremberg Poets. Tittmann, Die Nürnberger Dichterschule (Göttingen,

1847). *Johann Rist,* Hansen, J. R. und seine Zeit. (Halle, 1872); J. R. 'Das friedewünschende Teutschland' and 'Das friedejauchzende Teutschland' published by Schletterer (Augsburg, 1864). *Philipp von Zesen,* Lemcke, p. 268.

Andreas Gryphius. Edition of his Comedies and Tragedies by Palm (Tübingen, 1878 and 1882); Dramatic poems, pub. by Tittmann (Leipz., 1870); Lyric poems, ed. Tittmann (Leipz., 1880); Sunday and Holiday Sonnets pub. by Welti (Halle, 1883) in Braune's Neudrucke, in Nos. 3 and 6, of which 'Horribilicribrifax' and 'Peter Squence' are printed; 'Olivetum,' translated by Strehlke (Weimar, 1862). See Strehlke in Herrigs Archiv, xxii, 81. J. Hermann on A. G. (Leipz., 1851); O. Klopp, A. G. als Dramatiker (Hanover, 1852); Klix, A. G. (a Speech, Glogau, 1864); Th. Paur, Zur Litteratur und Kulturgeschichte, p. 263; Kollewijn, Über den Einfluss des holländischen Dramas auf A. G. (Amsterdam and Heilbronn); also Schnorrs Archiv ix, 56, 445; xii. 219; Zs. xxv, 130; xxvi, 244; Aug. vii, 315.

X. The Dawn of Modern Literature, pp. 331–401.

Hettner's History of German Literature in the 18th century (4 vols., Brunswick, 1862–1870) begins at the Peace of Westphalia; as does Julian Schmidt, Geschichte des geistigen Lebens in Deutschland (2 vols., Leipz., 1862–63).

1. *Religion and Science,* pp. 335–359.

Joachim Jungius. Monograph by Guhrauer (Stuttg., 1850). *Balthasar Schuppius,* Monograph by Vial (Mainz, 1857); Oelze (Hamburg, 1863); Bloch (Berl. 1863, Progr.); see Weicker, Schuppius in seinem Verhältnis zur Pädagogik des 17n Jh. (Weissenfels, 1874, Progr.). Reprint of 'Der Freund in der Noth' (Halle, 1878). *Georg Calixtus*; Henke, G. C. and seine Zeit, 2 vols. (Halle, 1853–60); see Henke, G. C. Briefwechsel (Halle, 1883). *Hermann Conring,* H. C. der Begründer der deutschen Rechtsgeschichte (Berlin, 1870); Bresslau, A. D. B. iv., 446. *Justus Georg Schottelius*; Schmarsow, Q. F. 23; R. v. Raumer, Geschichte der germanischen Philologie, p. 72; Lemcke, p. 259.

Roman Catholics. Jacob Balde; Herder's Terpsichore, Sämmtliche Werke, ed. Suphan, vol. 27; Westermayer, J. B. sein Leben und seine Werke (Munich, 1868). *Friedrich Spee,* Trutz-Nachtigall von Friedrich Spee, ed. Balke (Leipz., 1879); see p. liv. for more works on the subject. *Johann Scheffler,* ed. Rosenthal, 2 vols. (Regensburg, 1862); see Weimar Jahrb. i, 267; Schrader, Angelus Silesius und seine Mystik (Erfurt, 1853, Progr.); Kahlert, A. S. (Breslau, 1853); Kern, Johann Scheffler's Cherubinischer Wandersmann (Leipz. 1866). *Martin von Cochem.* He died, according to Bern. a Bononia Bibl. Scriptorum ordinis minorum S. Francisci Capuccinorum (Venet., 1747), on Sept. 10, 1712; and, according to the same book, his Life of Christ appeared at Frankfort in 1691; 2nd ed. at Frankfort and Augsburg 1708 and 1710, &c. *Abraham a Sancta Clara,* Monograph Karajan (Vienna, 1867): Sch. Vorträge und Aufsätze, p. 147; Zs. für die österr. Gymn.,

1867, p. 49 ; Zs. xxi, Anz. 279.   Reprint of 'Auf, auf, ihr Christen' in the ' Wiener Neudrucke,' ed. A. Sauer, Heft i (Vienna, 1883).
Protestants. Paul Gerhardt.   Historical and critical edition by J. F. Bachmann (Berlin, 1866) ; an edition arranged chronologically according to the oldest editions, by Gödeke (Leipz., 1877).   See Bachmann, P. G. (Berl., 1863).   *Philip Jacob Spener* ; Hossbach, Ph. J. S. und seine Zeit, 2 parts, 3rd ed. (Berl., 1861).   *Joachim Neander.*   Iken, J. N., sein Leben und seine Lieder (Bremen, 1880).   *Gottfried Arnold.*   Ed. Ehmann (Stuttg., 1856), in two separate volumes, ' Sämmtliche geistliche Lieder,' and ' Geistliche Minne-Lieder,' comp. Dibelius, G. A. (Berlin, 1873). *Gerhard Tersteegen.*   Collected writings, 8 vols. (Stuttg., 1844) ; Selection Kapp (Essen, 1841).   The ' Geistliche Lieder,' ed. Barthel (Bielefeld, 1853) ; compare Barthel, Leben G. T., (Bielefeld, 1852) ; Kerlen, G. T. (Mülheim a. d. Ruhr, 1853).   *Zinzendorf.*   His poems ed. by Knapp (Stuttg., 1845) ; see Varnhagen, Biographische Denkmäler, vol. v. (2nd ed. Berl., 1846).   *Benjamin Schmolck.*   Hoffmann, Spenden zur Deutschen Litteraturgeschichte ii, 73 *Barthold Heinrich Brockes* ; Monograph, A. Brandl (Innsbruck, 1878).   For the Passion Oratorio, see Chrysander, Händel i, 433 ; also Chrysander in the A. D. B. xii, 777, and Gervinus, Händel und Shakespeare (Leipz., 1868), p. 373, 472.   *Secular learning.*   How the various authors follow each other, and which, from the date of their birth, or the influences which affected them, are the most nearly connected with one another, can be conveniently seen in Guden's ' Chronologische Tabellen zur Geschichte der deutschen Sprache und National Litteratur ' (3 parts, Leipz., 1831).   For *Pufendorf,* see von Treitschke, Preuss. Jahrb. 35, 614 ; 36, 61.   For *Stieler, Schilter, Morhof,* see R. v. Raumur, Geschichte der germ. Phil.   For *Leibniz* and *Wolff,* and later on for *Kant, Fichte, Schelling,* and *Hegel,* Überwegs Grundriss der Gesch. der Philosophie ; Zeller's Geschichte der deutschen Philosophie seit Leibniz (Munich, 1873).   Schmarsow has republished the ' unvorgreiflichen Gedanken,' with explanations.   Q. F. xxiii. *Thomasius,* see Windelband, Gesch. der neueren Philosophie i, 490 ; Bluntschli, Gesch. des allgem. Staatsrechts und der Politik, p. 181 ; Biedermann, Deutschland im 18 Jh. ii, 348 ; Roscher, Gesch. der Nationalökonomik, p. 340 ; Prutz, Gesch. der deutschen Journalismus i, 286 ; B. A. Wagner, Christian Thomasius (Berl., 1872).   *August Hermann Francke,* Kramer, Biographie, 2 vols. (Halle, 1880-82) ; see Kramer, Beitr. zur Geschichte A. H. F. (Halle, 1861), with additions (Halle, 1875).

2. *The Refinement of Popular Taste,* pp. 359-382.

Idyllic Poetry ; comp. X, 3.
Bombast.   There is no monograph on *Hoffmannswaldau* ; on *Lohenstein* more than he deserves ; see Passaw, Daniel Caspar von L. (Meiningen, 1852) ; Kerckhoffs, Daniel Casper von L. Tragedies (Paderborn, 1877) ; Conrad Müller, Beitr. zum Leben und Dichten D. C. von L. (Breslau, 1882 ; Weinhold's Germanist Abh. i).
Patriots and Satirists.   See Creizenach ' Armin in Poesie und Litteraturgeschichte' Preuss. Jahrb. 36, 332 ; *Spalatinus* published a book in 1535, ' Von

dem thewern Deutschen Fürsten Arminio ; Ein kurtzer auszug aus glaubwir-
digen latinischen Historien.' *Hans Michael Moscherosch.* Ed. Dittmar
(Berl., 1830); Bobertag (Berl. and Stuttg.); see E. Schmidt Zs. xxiii, 71 ; R.
Köhler, Schnorr's Archiv i, 291 ; Lorenz and Sch., Gesch. des Elsasses, p. 309.
Johann Lauremberg. Ed. Lappenberg (Stuttg., 1861); Braune (Halle, 1879).
Joachim Rachel; see Aug. Sach, J. R. (Schleswig, 1869). *Friedrich von Logan.*
Ed. G. Eitner (Tübingen, 1872); Selections (Leipz., 1870). See Erich Schmidt,
Der Kampf gegen die Mode in der deutschen Litt. der 17 Jh. (Im Neuen Reich,
1880, No. 39).

Popular Songs. Collection ' Venus-gärtlein' (1659) ; ' Gesechste Tugend- und
Laster-Rose,' by Holdlieb (Nuremberg, 1665) ; ' Tugendhafter Jungfrauen und
Junggesellen Zeit-Vertreiber' (see Serapeum, 1870, p. 145) ; 'Hans Guck in
die Welt' and others. The poets mentioned on page 370 are treated of by Lemcke,
p. 238 in connection with Fleming ; the Bibliothek deutscher Dichter des 17.
Jh. of Wilhelm Müller and Karl Förster only gives a selection from Schwieger
(vol. xi, Leipz., 1828). For *Finckelthaus*, see Pröhle, Schnorr's Archiv iii, 66,
and vi, 127. For *Greflinger*, see Gruppe, Leben und Werke deutscher Dichter
i, 264 ; von Öttingen Q. F. 49 (Strassburg, 1882); Walther Anz. x. 73.

Christian Weise. See Palm, Beitr. zur Gesch. der deutschen Litt. (Breslau,
1877)), p. 1—83 ; comp. Erich Schmidt, Zs. xxiii, Anz. 141.

French influence, and the opposition to it in Prussia. (Frederick I, and
Frederick William I). For *Frederick I*, see Ranke, Zwölf Bücher preussischer
Geschichte i, 451. For Frederick William I.'s tutor, *Joh. Fried. Cramer*, see
A. D. B. iv, 548.

Leipzic literature. On the ' *Acta Eruditorum*,' see Prutz, Journalismus, p. 275.
Burkard Menke, Monograph by Treitschke (1742). *Johann Christian Günther.*
Selection by Tittmann (Leipz., 1874); Litzmann (Leipz., Reclamsche Universalbibliothek, No. 1295, 96); see Hoffmann, Spenden ii, 115 ; O. Roquette, Leben
und Dichten J. Chr. G. (Stuttg., 1860); Kalbeck, Neue Beitr. zur Biographie, J.
Chr. G. (Leipz., 1879); Litzmann, Im Neuen Reich, 1879'; ii, 517 ; Zur Textkritik und Biographie J. Chr. G. (Frankfort, 1880). For *Gottsched*, see XI, 1.

English influence. See Kawczynski Studien zur Litteraturgeschichte des 18
Jh. Moralische Zeitschriften (Leipz., 1880) ; Milberg, Die moralischen Wochen-
schriften des 18 Jh. (Meissen). Brandl Zs. xxvi, Anz. p. 26.

Albrecht von Haller. A. v. H., a Memoir published by an appointed com-
mittee (Bern, 1877) ; Adolf Frey, A. v. H. und seine Bedeutung für die deutsche
Litteratur (Leipz., 1879); A. v. H. Poems, published by Ludwig Hirzel
(Frauenfeld, 1882) ; A. v. H. Journals of his Journey to Germany, Holland,
and England, 1723-1727, pub. by L. Hirzel (Leipz., 1883). On Haller's
scientific knowledge, see Henle in the ' Göttinger Professoren' (Gotha, 1872), p.
29. *Friedrich von Hagedorn.* Ed. Eschenburg. 5 parts (Hamburg, 1800);
Reprint of the ' Versuch einiger Gedichte of 1729, by Sauer, in Seuffert's
Deutsche Litteraturdenkmale des 18 Jh. (Heilbronn, 1883) ; Characteristic
letters in Helbig's Liscow, p. 44. See Schmitt, in Henneberger's Jahrb. i, 62.
Christian Ludwig Liscow. K. G. Helbig, Chr. L. L. (Dresden, 1844); Lisch,
Liscows Leben (Schwerin, 1845); Classen, Über Chr. L. L. Leben and
Schriften (Lübeck, 1846); Litzmann, Chr. L. L. (Hamburg and Leipz. 1883).

3. *The Novel*, pp. 382–393.

See John Dunlop, History of Fiction (Edinburgh, 1814); Cholevius, Die bedeutendsten deutschen Romane des 17 Jh. (Leipz., 1866); Bobertag, Gesch. des Romans, ii, 1 (Breslau, 1879); comp. E. Schmidt, Schnorr's Archiv ix, 405. *Pastoral Romances.* Cholevius, p. 64; where extracts are given of Zesen's ‘Adriatische Rosemunde.’ *Hero and love romances.* For Bucholtz, see Cholevius, p. 117. *Duke Anton Ulrich of Brunswick*, Cholevius, p. 176. *H. A. von Ziegler und Klipphausen*, Cholevius, p. 152; Lohenstein, Cholevius, p. 311. For the characteristics of the historical novels of this time, see Gosche in his (afterwards Schnorr's) Archiv i, 101. *Allegorical Tales.* Johann Ludwig Prasch; a German translation of his ‘Psyche cretica’ was published in 1705. *Popular Tales.* On *Martin von Cochem* as the author of Griseldis, Genovefa und Hirlanda, Reinhold Köhler's article on Griseldis in Ersch und Gruber's Encyclopädie, and in the Zs. f. deutsche Phil. v. 59; Seuffert, Die Legende von der Pfalzgräfin Genovefa (Würtzburg, 1877), p. 69. On the popular story of the *invulnerable Siegfried*, see Jacob Grimm, Zs. viii, 1. *Spanish Influence. Hans Michael Moscherosch*, see X, 2. *Grimmelshausen*, see Duncker, Zs. des Vereins f. hess. Gesch., new series, ix, 389. Zs. xxvi, 287. Ed. Keller, 4 vols. (Stuttg., 1854, 62); Kurz, 4 vols. (Leipz., 1863–64); Reprint of ‘Simplicissimus’ by Kögel (Halle, 1880). School of Moscherosch and Grimmelshausen; *Christian Weise*; Reprint of the Erznarren (Halle, 1878). *Schelmuffsky.* There are several reprints; see Zarncke, Christian Reuter (Leipzic, 1884). *Robinson Crusoe.* Hettner, Robinson and the Robinsonaden (Berl. 1854). The Island of Felsenburg has been reproduced by Tieck, 6 vols. (Breslau, 1827). On the author see Stern, Histor. Tashenb. 5. Folge 10, 317.

4. *The Drama*, pp. 393–401.

The Opera. Arrey v. Dommer, Handbuch der Musik-Geschichte (Leipzig 1868), p. 263; on the German Opera in Hamburg, p. 404: see Lindner, Die erste stehende deutsche Oper (Berl. 1855.) *Artistic and School Drama.* For J. Chr. Hallmann, see E. Schmidt, A.D.B. x. 444.—*Christian Weise,* see X. 2. His peasant comedy of Tobias und Schwalbe has been reproduced by R. Genée (Berlin 1882). *Gottscheds* Nöthiger Vorrath goes to 1760, the Chronologie des deutschen Theaters (1775, by Chr. Heinr. Schmidt) to 1775. See W. Creizenach, Zur Entstehungsgeschichte des neueren deutschen Lustspiels (Halle 1879). J. Bayer, Von Gottsched bis Schiller, 3 vols. (Prague 1863). *Popular Drama.* See ‘Liebeskampf, oder ander Theil der Englischen Comödien und Tragödien’ (1630), and Schau-Bühne Englischer und Französischer Comödianten (Frankf. 1670). Gödeke, Grund. 410. Also Lindner, Karl XII vor Friedrichshall, eine Haupt und Staats-Action (Dessau 1845). K. Weiss, Die Wiener Haupt und Staats-Actionen (Vienna 1854): E. Schmidt,

Zs. xxv.234.—On *Magister Velthen* see Fürstenau, Zur Geschichte der Musik und des Theaters am Hofe zu Dresden, I. (Dresden 1861). 269.

XI. THE AGE OF FREDERICK THE GREAT, ii. pp. 1–141.

See Koberstein's remarks on the great influence of Prussia on German literature since the beginning of the seventeenth century (Vermischte Aufsätze zur Litteraturgeschichte und Ästhetik, Leipz. 1858, p. 249); K. Biedermann, Friedrich der Gr. und sein Verhältnis zur Entwicklung des deutschen Geisteslebens (Brunswick, 1859); Julian Schmidt, Der Einfluss des preussischen Staats auf die deutsche Litteratur (1869; Bilder aus dem geistigen Leben unserer Zeit, Leipz. 1870, p. 42); H. Pröhle, Friedrich d. Gr. und die deutsche Litteratur (Berl. 1872); see Suphan Zs. f. d. Phil. v. 238; D. Jacoby, F. d. Gr. und die deutsche Litt. (Basle, 1875); Krause, F. d. Gr. und die deutsche Poesie (Halle, 1884).

1. *Leipzic,* ii. pp. 2–19.

Gottsched's *Conversations with Frederick the Great.* Neuestes aus der anmuthigen Gelehrsamkeit, viii. 122, 389, 552. Jul. Schmidt, Gesch. des geistigen Lebens, ii. 137.—Gellert's *Conversations;* Gellert's Sämmt. Schriften ix. (Berl. 1867), 13 et seq.

Johann Christoph Gottsched. Danzel, Gottsched und seine Zeit (Leipz. 1848); For his writings see Jördens, Lexicon deutscher Dichter und Prosaisten ii. 212. See, too, M. Bernays A.D.B. ix. 497.

Christian Fürchtegott Gellert: ed. Klee, 10 vols. (Leipz. 1839). Briefe an Fräulein Erdmuth von Schönfeld (Leipz. 1861); Tagebuch aus dem J. 1761. (Leipz. 1862). See E. Schmidt, A.D.B. viii. 544. On Fables, E. Schmidt, Zs, xx. Anz. 38 (compare p. 380 in text). On the *Bremer Beiträger* see the various articles in the A.D.B., and also Schiller, Braunschweigs schöne Litteratur in den Jahren 1745-1800. (Wolfenbüttel, 1845). Also the Leipzic weekly journal, ' Der Jüngling,' communication by Erich Schmidt, Q. F. 39, 50-73. Letters of Giseke and J. A. Schlegel, Schnorrs Archiv. v. 41, 575. Gellert's followers: *Johann Friedrich von Cronegk*; see H. Feuerbach, Uz und Cronegk (Leipz. 1866). *Joachim Wilhelm von Brawe,* Monograph by A. Sauer, Q. F. 30 (Strassb. 1878).—*Christian Felix Weisse*: Monograph by J. Minor (Innspruch, 1880).

Revival of German Popular Song: see Hoffmann von Fallersleben, Unsere volksthümlichen Lieder. 3rd ed. (Leipz. 1869).

2. *Zurich and Berlin,* ii. pp. 19–47.

For *Swiss literature* in general consult Mörikofer, Die Schweizerische Litt. des 18 Jh. (Leipz. 1861): A. Frey, in the Neue Zürcher Zeitung, 1882, Nos. 207-212.

For *Bodmer* and his circle, Zehnder, Pestalozzi (Gotha 1875): see too Stäudlin, Briefe berühmter und edler Deutschen an Bodmer (Stuttg., 1794).

Chapter XI.

385

Reprint of Bodmer's writings in Seuffert's Deutsche Litteraturdenkm. des 18 Jh. Nos. 9. 12.

Frederick the Great. The works on Frederick the Great as a writer are given by Wiegand, Q.F.v. (Strassb. 1874). See, too, Posner, Zur litterarischen Thätigheit F.d.G. in the Miscellaneen zur Geschichte König F.d.G. (Berl., 1878), p. 205-490. It contains a list of all the editions and translations of his books. For his poems, Haupt, Opuscula III. 137. Herder's Humanitätsbriefe, and the extracts he gives (Herder's Sämmtl. Werke. ed. Suphan xvii. 28 et seq.) are worth reading. For the *Academy*, see Bartholmess, Histoire philosophique de l'Académie de Prusse, 2 vols. (Paris, 1850-51).

Halle. See Waniek, Immanuel Pyra, und sein Einfluss auf die deutsche Litteratur des 18 Jh. (Leipz. 1882). For *Uz* see H. Feuerbach, Uz und Cronegk (Leipz. 1866).

Gleim. Collected Works, ed. Körte, 7 vols. (Halberstadt, 1811-1813), vol. 8 (Leipz. 1841); also Körte, Gleims Leben (Halberst. 1811). He also edited from Gleim's papers, Briefe der Schweizer Bodmer, Sulzer, Gessner (Zurich 1804); Briefe zwischen Gleim, Wm. Heinse und Joh. v. Müller, 2 vols. (Zurich 1806). Pröhle, Aus dem Briefwechsel zwischen Gleim und Jacobi (Zs. f. preuss. Geschichte 1881, Heft 11, 12). See Schnorr's Archiv iv. 9, v. 191. Reprint of the Kriegslieder by Sauer, in Seuffert No. 4 (Heilbronn, 1882).

Ewald Christian von Kleist: Critical edition by A. Sauer, 3 vols. (Berlin) with Biography and letters. See Schnorr's Archiv. xi. 457.

Sulzer: Hirzel an Gleim über Sulzer den Weltweisen, 2 parts (Zurich and Winterthur 1779). Isis; Monatschrift von deutschen und schweizerischen Gelehrten, vols. v. vi. (Zurich, 1807). See Weim. Jahrb. iv. 164.

Klopstock. For the editions of his works see Gödeke, p. 601. Bosse, Klopstockische Studien (Cöthen, 1866 Progr). Hamel, Klopstock-Studien, 3 parts (Rostock 1879, 80); see Anz. ix. 46; Pawel, Klopstocks Oden, Leipziger Periode (Vienna, 1880). Erich Schmidt, Beiträge zur Kenntnis der Klopstockschen Jugendlyrik, Q.F. 39. Reprint of the first three Cantos of the *Messiah* in their original form, by Muncker, in Seuffert, No. 11. (Heilbr. 1883). A Commentary on the Odes exists, by H. Düntzer, 6 parts (Leipz. and Wenigen-Jena, 1861). Collections of letters; Klamer Schmidt, Klopstock und seine Freunde, 2 vols. (Halberstadt, 1810); (Clodius) Auswahl aus Klopstocks nachgelassenem Briefwechsel, part 1 (Leipz. 1821); Schmidlin, Klopstocks sämmtliche Werke, 3 vols. (Stuttg. 1839) vol. 1; Lappenberg, Briefe von und an Klopstock (Brunswick, 1867). See Cropp in the Hamburg Schriftsteller-lexikon iv. 4-61; Strauss, Kleine Schriften, new series pp. 1-230. Klopstocks Jugendgeschichte: Erich Schmidt, Über Klopstock (Im neuen Reich, 1881, Nos. 2, 3). Ein Höfling über Klopstock (ibid. 1878, ii.. p. 741, comp. Strauss, Kleine Schriften, p. 23); Loise, Études sur l'Allemagne moderne (Brussels, 1878), p. 85-193; Muncker, Lessings persönliches und litt. Verhältnis zu Klopstock (Frankfort, 1880).

Wieland. There is no critical edition. Wieland himself prepared mal collections of his prose works, or of selected and newest poems, and in 1794-1802 he published his collected works in 39 vols. with 6 supplements. After his

death,Gruber edited the collected works in 53 vols. (Leipz. 1818–28). Wieland's
' *Hermann*' first became known through Muncker (Seufferts Litteraturdenkm.
No. vi., Heilbronn, 1882). For ' *Oberon*,' there are explanations by Düntzer,
and a criticism by Max Koch, Das Quellenverhältnis von Wielands Oberon
(Marburg 1880). For the motives of other poems see R. Köhler in Schnorrs
Archiv iii. 416, v. 78. For the ' *Abderites*' see Seuffert's Discourse, Wieland's
Abderiten (Berlin, 1878). *Letters.* Auswahl denkwürdiger Briefe, ed. Ludwig
Wieland, 2 vols. (Vienna 1815); Ausgewählte Briefe, 4 vols. (Zurich, 1815, 16);
Briefe an Sophie von La Roche (Berl., 1820). Buchner, Wieland und die
Weidmannsche Buchhandlung (Berl. 1871); Wieland und Georg Joachim Gö-
schen (Stuttg. 1874). Funck, Beiträge zur Wieland-Biographie (Freib. 1882).
List of other letters in Döring, Chr. M. Wieland ein biogr. Denkmal.
(Sangerhausen, 1840) p. 439; Zs. xx. 358. See Gruber, C.M W. geschildert, 2
vols. (Leipz. 1819); Wieland's Leben, 4 parts (Leipz. 1827); consult R. A.
Böttiger, Litt. Zuständen und Zeitgenossen, 2 vols. (Leipz. 1838); and Raumer's
Hist. Taschenbuch, x. 359. Löbell, Entwickelung der deutschen Poesie, vol.
ii. (Brunswick, 1858) is devoted to Wieland; Hallberg, Wieland (Paris. 1869).
For Wieland's youth, Sch. Zs. Anz. i. 25, Zs. xx. 355; Hoche, Ein Schulheft
Wielands, Jahns Jahrbücher, 88 (1863), 253–259. Pröhle, Lessing, Wieland,
Heinse (Berl. 1877). *Julie Bondeli*, Schädelin, J.B. die Freundin Rousseaus
und Wielands (Bern, 1838); E. Bodemann, J. v. B. and ihr Freundeskreis
(Hanover, 1874).

3. *Lessing*, ii. pp. 47–82.

Collected Editions. G. E. Lessings Schriften, 6 parts, (Berl. 1753-55);
Lustspiele von G.E.L., 2 parts (Berl. 1767); Trauerspiele (Berl. 1772); G.E.L.
Vermischte Schriften, part i. (Berl. 1771), parts 2-4 (Berl. 1784-85); parts
5-30 (Berl. 1791-94) part 31 (Lessings Leben, von Schink, Berl. 1825). Ed.
Schink, 32 vols. (Berl. 1825-28); K. Lachmann, 13 vols. (Berl. 1838-40); W.
von Maltzahn, 12 vols. (Leipz. 1853-57; Lachmann's edition revised, omitting
all letters to Lessing); Hempel's edition, so named from the publisher, a very
valuable one, 20 vols. (Berl., no date). Consult vol. 19, 673. Redlich,
Lessing-Bibliothek. B. A. Wagner gave supplements: Lessing Forschungen
Berlin 1881); Zu Lessings spanischen Studien (Berl., 1883 Progr). Lessing's
correspondence is given most fully in Hempel's edition; see, too, Schnorr's
Archiv xi. 517. A. Schöne published Lessing's letters to his wife (Leipz.1870);
Wattenbach published letters from his circle of friends, Neues Lausitzisches
Magazin 38. 193.

Biographies and Criticisms. K. G. Lessing, G. F. L.'s Leben, 3 Parts (Berl.
1793, 95); Fr. Schlegel, Lessing's Geist aus seinen Schriften, 3 vols. (Leipz.
1804); Schink, Charakteristik L. (Leipz.1817); L. Leben (Berl. 1825); Danzel
und Guhrauer, G. E. L. sein Leben und seine Werke, 2 vols. (Leipz. 1850, 54.
2nd ed. by v. Maltzahn and Boxberger, Berl. 1880-81); Löbell, Entwickelung
der deutschen Poesie, vol. 3, (1865), pub. by Koberstein; Sch. in the Deutsche
Rundschau, Feb. 1881, by Erich Schmidt, Lessing i. (Berlin, 1884); Popular
accounts, by A. Stahr (Berl. 1859); Crouslé (Paris, 1863); Sime (London,
1877); Zimmern (London, 1878); Fischer (Stuttg. 1881); Düntzer (Leipz.
1882). Consult Cherbuliez, Études de littérature (Paris, 1873), pp. 1-119;

Loise, Études, p. 194.—Hebler, Lessing-Studien (Bern, 1862); Philosophische
Aufsätze (Leipz. 1869), p. 79. Peter, Lessing and S. Afra (Deutsche Rundschau,
March 1881 ; see Schnorr's Archiv x. 285); Uhde, Lessing und die Komödi-
anten der Neuberin, (Hammann und Henzen Dramaturgische Blätter, Parts 7,
8); O. v. Heinemann, Zur Erinnerung an G. E. L. (Leipz. 1870); Pröhle,
Lessing, Wieland, Heinse (Berl. 1877).—Lehmann, Forschungen über Lessing's
Sprache (Brunswick, 1875); see E. Schmidt, Anz. ii, 38; M. v. Waldberg,
Studien zu Lessing's Stil (Berl. 1882).

Philosophy and Theology. Guhrauer, Lessing's Erziehung des Menschengeschlechts (Berl. 1841); H. Ritter, Über Lessing's philosophische und
religiöse Grundsätze (Gött. 1847); Schwarz, L. als Theolog (Halle, 1854);
Dilthey in the Preuss. Jahrb. 19, 117, 271 (comp. 20, 268, 439); Zeller, L. als
Theolog, Vorträge und Abhandlungen, 2, 283-327; Rehorn, Lessing's Stellung
zur Philosophie des Spinoza (Frankf. 1877); Witte, die Philosophie unserer
Dichterheroen I (Bonn, 1880), 25-234; Mönckeberg, L. als Freimaurer (Hamb.
1880). *Reimarus*, D. F. Strauss, H. S. Reimarus und seine Schutzschrift für
die vernünftigen Verehrer Gottes (Leipz. 1862).—*Goeze*, G. R. Röpe, J. M.
Goeze, eine Rettung (Hamburg, 1860); Boden, Lessing und Goeze (Leipz. and
Heildeberg, 1862).

Æsthetic. Lessing's Laokoon, ed. H. Blümner, 2nd. ed. (Berl. 1880); see
Sch., Zs. xx, Anz. 85.— *Winckelmann*. K. J. Winckelmann, sein Leben, seine
Werke und seine Zeitgenossen, 2 vols. (Leipz. 1866-72). Cosack, Materialien zu
G. E. L. Hamburgischer Dramaturgie (Paderb. 1876); Schröter und Thiele, L.
Hamb. Dramat. erläutert (Halle, 1877); see Bollman, Anmerkungen zu L.
Hamb. Dram. (Berl. 1874); Gotschlich, L.'s Aristotelische Studien (Berl.
1876); Baumgart, Aristoteles, Lessing und Goethe (Leipz. 1877); E. Schmidt,
Anz. v. 133.

Dramas. Nodnagel, L's. Dramen erläutert (Darmstadt, 1842); Düntzer, L.
als Dramatiker und Dramaturg (Wenigen-Jena,1862); Sierke, L. als angehender
Dramatiker (Königsberg, 1869 Diss.); Motz, L.'s Bedeutung für das deutsche
Drama (Basle, 1872).—On the influence of *Miss Sara Sampson*, see Sauer,
Q. F. xxx. 80.—*Minna von Barmhelm*, Düntzer Erl.—*Emilia Galotti*, Hebler,
Lessingiana (Bern, 1877); B. Arnold, Lessing's Em. Gal. in ihrem Verhältnis
zur Poetik des Aristoteles und zur Hamb. Dramat. (Chemnitz, 1880 Progr.); see Zs.
xxv. 241, Düntzer Erl.—*Nathan der Weise*, see Naumann Litteratur über Lessing's Nathan (Dresden, 1867 Progr.); Bohtz, Lessing's Protestantismus und Nathan der Weise (Göttingen, 1854); Wackernagel, Kl. Schriften, ii. 452; Strauss,
Lessings N. d. W. (Berl. 1864); Caro, Lessing und Swift (Jena, 1869); Sch.,
Vorträge und Aufsätze, p. 328; Pabst, Vorlesungen über Nathan (Bern,
1881); Düntzer Erl. For Boccaccio's tale, see Landau, Quellen des Decamerone (Vienna, 1869), pp. 62, 142; for the similar story, Wackernagel,
p. 471 (Gosche Jahrb. f. Litteraturgesch. i. 199). There is a fine reprint of
the first edition of Nathan (Berl. 1881). Schiller's edition, Schiller's sämmtl.
Schriften, 15 b, 85 Gödeke.

For *Nicolai* and *Mendelssohn* see below, XI. 5. *Gleim* and *Kleist* have been
mentioned above, XI. 2. For *Denis*, see von Hofmann-Wellenhof, Michael
Denis (Innsbruck, 1881). For *Abbt*, Thomas Abbts vermischte Werke, 6 vols.

(Berl. 1772–81); Nicolai, Ehrengedächtnis Th. Abbts (Berl. 1767); Herder, ii. 249; Prutz, Litterar. Histor. Taschenb. 1846, p. 371. For *Johann Timotheus Hermes*, Prutz, Menschen and Bücher (Leipz. 1862), ii, 1. et seq.

4. *Herder and Goethe*, ii. pp. 82–114.

Justus Möser: Sämmtliche Werke, ed. Abeken, 10 Vols. (Berl. 1842, 43), compare Kreyssig, J. M. (Berl. 1857).

Hamann: Schriften, ed. Friedrich Roth, 8 Parts (Berl. 1821–43); see Gildemeister, Hamann's Leben und Schriften, 6 vols. (Gotha, 1857–73); Minor, J. G. Hamann in seiner Bedeutung für die Sturm und Drangperiode (Frankf. 1881).

Herder. Sämmtliche Werke, 45 vols. (Stuttg. 1805–20), 60 vols. (Stuttg. 1827–30), not good; an excellent edition is coming out by Bernhard Suphan (Berl. 1877). Separate works, '*Denkmal Johann Winckelmanns*,' by Herder, written 1778, publ. by Albert Duncker (Cassel, 1882). '*Cid*,' with notes by Düntzer (1860); Reinhold Köhler, Herders Cid und seine französische Quelle (Leipz. 1867); Herders Cid, die französische und spanische Quelle, zusammengestellt von Vögelin, (Heilbr. 1879). '*Legenden*,' Düntzer, Erl.—*Letters*. Aus Herder's Nachlass, 3 vols. (Frankf. 1856, 57). Herder's Reise nach Italien (Giessen, 1859). Von und an Herder, 3 vols. (Leipz. 1861, 62); all published by H. Düntzer and F. G. von Herder; see too Grenzboten, 1867, I. 289. Im neuen Reich, 1879, No. 26, 1880, I. 685.—Biographical and literary authorities, Danz and Gruber, Characteristik J. G. von Herders (Leipz. 1805); Caroline von Herder, Erinnerungen aus dem Leben, J. G. v. H., 2 vols. (Stuttg. 1820); Weimarisches Herder Album (Jena, 1845); J. G. v. H. Lebensbild *Herder's early Correspondence and writings*, 6 vols. (Erlangen, 1846); Julian Schmidt, on *Herder* in the Bibliothek der deutschen Nationallitteratur des 18 und 19 Jh. (Leipz., Brockhaus); and in the Preuss. Jahrb. 44, 536; Ch. Joret, Herder et la renaissance littéraire en Allemagne au 18° siècle (Paris, 1875). R. Haym, Herder nach seinem Leben und seinen Werken, vol. i (Berl. 1880); Suphan, Zs. f. d. Phil. iii. 365, 458, 490, iv. 225, vi. 45, 165; Preuss. Jahrb 43, 85, 142, 411; 50, 593. See too Bächtold, Aus dem Herderschen Hause (Berl. 1881); A. Werner, Herder als Theologe (Berl. 1871); Renner, Herder's Verhältnis zur Schule (Gött. 1871 Progr.); Morres, H. als Pädagog (Eisenach); Lehmann, H. in seiner Bedeutung für die Geographie (Berl. 1883 Progr.); R. Lindemann, Beiträge zur Charakteristik K. A. Böttigers und seiner Stellung zu Herder (Görlitz, 1883).

Goethe's Youth. In general, see XII. 1. Goethe's Works and letters before he settled at Weimar: (S. Hirzel), Der junge Goethe, 3 vols. (Leipz. 1875). See too, Schöll, Briefe und Aufsätze von Goethe aus den Jahren 1766 bis 1786 (2nd ed. Weimar, 1857); see Sch. Aus Goethe's Frühzeit, Q. F. 34 (Strassb. 1879); Minor and Sauer, Studien zur Goethe-Philologie (Vienna, 1880). Goethe's Autobiography, 'Dichtung und Wahrheit,' comes down to 1775; it is well to consult Löpers' remarks in his edition (Berl. Hempel).—For Goethe's family, and some of his youthful friends, consult Kriegk, Die Brüder Senckenberg (Frankf. 1869), p. 313; O. Volger, Goethes Vaterhaus (Frankf. 1863); Weismann,

Aus Goethe's Knabenzeit (Frankf. 1846). *Goethe's Mother, Frau Rath,* Briefwechsel von Katharina Elisabeth Goethe, ed. R. Keil (Leipz. 1871), see v. Biedermann, Goethe Forschungen (Frankf. 1879), p. 385. Schnorr's Archiv iii. 109.—The '*Mitschuldigen,*' Sch. Zs. xxiv. 231.—Goethe's work as a lawyer, Kriegk, Deutsche Kulturbilder aus dem 18 Jh. (Leipz. 1874), p. 263, Goethe als Rechtsanwalt.—The Frankfurter gelehrte Anzeigen of 1772 are reprinted in Seuffert's Litteraturdenkm. (Heilbronn, 1883); a valuable authority for Goethe's development.—*Götz,* ed. Bächtold (Freib. 1882); the two oldest editions of Götz are compared in Minor and Sauer, p. 117; see Düntzer, Götz und Egmont (Brunswick, 1854), Erl. For the historical Götz, Wegele, Zs. f. Culturgesch. 1874, p. 129. For chivalrous Dramas, see O. Brahm, Das deutsche Ritterdrama des 18 Jh. Q. F. 40 (Strassb. 1880). For Shakespeare's influence, see Koberstein, Vermischte Aufsätze, p. 163; R. Genée, Geschichte der Shakespeareschen Dramen in Deutschland (Leipz. 1870).— *Prometheus,* Düntzer, Goethe's Prometheus und Pandora (Leipz. 1874); the original text publ. by Erich Schmidt, in the Goethe-Jahrbuch, i. 290.—*Clavigo* and *Stella,* Düntzer Erl. For Stella, see Sch. in the Deutsche Rundschau, vi. 66; for Clavigo, Danzel, Gesammelte Aufsätze (Leipz. 1855), p. 152. *Werther,* Düntzer, Erl.; Erich Schmidt, Richardson, Rousseau, Goethe (Jena, 1875); Appell, Werther und seine Zeit, 3rd ed. (Oldenburg, 1882).

5. *The Literary Revolution and the Illuminati,* ii. pp. 114-141.

J. M. R. Lenz. Gesammelte Schriften, ed. Tieck, 3 vols. (Berl. 1828): 'Der Waldbruder,' reprint by M. v. Waldberg (Berl. 1882); Drei Gedichte, prepared for Christmas, 1882, by K. Weinhold; see A. Stöber, Der Dichter Lenz und Friedericke von Sesenheim (Basle, 1842); E. Dorer-Egloff, J. M. R. Lenz und seine Schriften (Baden, 1857); O. F. Gruppe, R. Lenz, Leben und Werke (Berl. 1861); P. T. Falck, Der Dichter J. M. R. Lenz in Livland (Winterthur, 1878); E. Schmidt, Lenz und Klinger, zwei Dichter der Geniezeit (Berl. 1878).

F. M. Klinger. Theater, 4 Parts (Riga, 1786-87); Neues Theater (Leipz. 1790); Werke, 12 vols. (Konigsb. 1809-15; Sämmtl. Werke, 12 vols. (Stuttg. 1842); see M. Rieger, Klinger in der Sturm and Drangperiode (Darmstadt, 1880); E. Schmidt, Lenz und Klinger (Berl. 1878); O. Erdmann, Über Klingers dramatische Dichtungen (Königsb. 1877); on the attitude of Klinger towards Kant's philosophy, see Altpreuss. Monatschrift, 15, 37. There is a reprint of the play 'Sturm und Drang,' in the Reclamsche Universalbibliothek, No. 248, and of the tragedy 'Otto' in Seuffert's Litteraturdenkm. Part 1. (Heilbronn, 1881).

H. L. Wagner. E. Schmidt, H. L. W. Goethe's Jugendgenosse, 2nd ed. (Jena, 1879). Reprint of his 'Kindermörderin,' by August Sauer, J. M. R. Lenz und H. L. Wagner (Berl. and Stuttg.), p. 283, and ibid, p. 359, the Satire 'Prometheus Deukalion and seine Recensenten,' once attributed to Goethe. Seuffert, No. 13 (Heilbroun, 1883).

Maler Müller. Werke, 3 vols. (Heidelb. 1825), see B. Seuffert. M. M. (Berl. 1877). Reprint of 'Fausts Leben,' Seuffert's Litteraturdenkm. No. 3 (Heilb. 1881).

Graf Törring. O. Brahm, Das deutsche Ritterdrama des 18 Jh.; Studien über J. A. v. Törring, seine Vorgänger und Nachfolger, Q. F. 40 (Strassb. 1880). *Schiller.* See below, XII. 3. For his political background, Adolf Wohlwill, Weltbürgerthum und Vaterlandsliebe der Schwaben (Hamburg, 1875). *C. F. D. Schubart.* Gesammelte Schriften, 8 vols. (Stuttg. 1839, 40); D. F. Strauss, Schubart's Leben in seinen Briefen, 2 vols. (Berl. 1849); A. Wohlwill, Schnorr's Archiv vi. 343; ix. 172; x. 188, 282. *H. C. Boie.* Weinhold, H. C. B. (Halle, 1868); Zs. f. d. Phil. i. 378.— *Martin Miller,* E. Schmidt, Deutsche Rundschau, 28, 450; Kamprath, Das Siegwartfieber (Wiener Neustadt, 1877 Progr.).—*L. H. C. Hölty;* Ed. Karl Halm (Leipz. 1869); Schnorr's Archiv. 7. 187.—*Stolberg,* Der Brüder C. and F. L. Grafen zu Stolberg gesammelte Werke, 20 vols. (Hamburg, 1820, 25); Alfred Nicolovius, F. L. Graf zu S. (Mainz, 1846); W. v. Bippen, Eutiner Skizzen (Weimar, 1859), pp. 52, 185. T. Menge, Der Graf F. L. S. and seine Zeitgenossen, 2 vols. (Gotha, 1862); Hennes, F. L. Graf zu S. und Herzog Peter F. L. von Oldenburg (Mainz, 1870). Stolberg in den zwei letzten Jahrzehnten seines Lebens (Mainz, 1875); aus F. L. von S. Jugendjahren (Frankf. 1876); J. Jansen, F. L. Graf zu S. 2 vols. (Freib. 1877); 2nd ed. in 1 vol. (Freib. 1882).—*J. H. Voss.* Sämmtl. poet. Werke, ed. Abraham Voss (Leipz. 1835); Reprint of the Odyssee of 1781, by M. Bernays (Stuttg. 1881; also E. Schmidt, Zs. 26, Anz. 52; also Schröter, Gesch. der deutschen Homer-Übersetzung, Jena, 1882); see the letters with notes, pub. by A. Voss, 4 vols. (Halberstadt, 1829-33, containing the beautiful notice of Ernestine Voss); Wilhelm Herbst, J. H. V., 3 vols (Leipz. 1872-76); Julian Schmidt, Preuss. Jahrb. 38. 628. On the Homer, A. W. Schlegel, 10, 115. See Prutz, Der Göttinger Dichterbund (Leipz. 1841).

G. A. Bürger. His poems were published first at Göttingen, 1778. Best edition by A. Sauer (Berlin and Stuttgart, s. a.) Sämmtl. Schriften, 4 vols. (Gött. 1796-98); Selection by Grisebach (Berl. 1872); see Daniel Bürger on the school (Halle, 1845 Progr.); Pröhle, G. A. B. (Leipz. 1856); Ebeling, G. A. B. und Elise Hahn (Leipz. 1868); Gödeke, G. A. B. in Göttingen und Gelliehausen (Hanover, 1873); A. Strodtmann, Briefe von und an G. A. B., 4 vols. (Berl. 1874).—For ' Lenore,' Wackernagel, Kleine Schriften, ii, 399.

J. K. Lavater. Gesner, Lavaters Lebensbeschreibung, 3 vols. (Winterthur, 1802, 3); Hegner, Beiträge zur näheren Kenntnis und wahren Darstellung J. K. L. (Leipz. 1836). Bodemann, J. K. L. (Gotha, 1856); Ehmann, Briefwechsel zwischen Lavater und Hasenkamp (Basle, 1870); E. Schmidt, Im neuen Reich, 1873, i. p. 368.

M. Claudius. Ed. Redlich (Gotha, 1871); Ungedruckte Jugendbriefe des Wandsbecker Boten, ed. Redlich (Hamb. 1881); cf. Herbst, M. C. der Wandsb. B. (Gotha, 1857); Mönckeberg, (Hamb. 1869).

F. H. Jacobi. Werke, 6 vols. (Leipz. 1812-24; Auserlesener Briefwechsel, 2 vols. (Leipz. 1825-27; Zöppritz, Aus F. H. J. Nachlass, 2 vols. (Leipz. 1869); Briefe an Bouterwek, pub. by Meyer (Gött. 1868); Deycks, F. H. J. im Verhältnis zu seiner Zeitgenossen (Frank. 1848); Zirngiebl, F. H. J. Leben, Dichten und Denken (Vienna, 1867); Harms, Über die Lehre von F. H. J. (Berl. 1876 Abh. der Akad.). A. Holtzmann, Über Eduard Allwills Brief-sammlung (Jena, 1878).—*J. G. Jacobi.* E. Martin, Ungedruckte Briefe von und an J. G. J.,Q. F. 2 (Strassb. 1874), see Zs. xx, 324; Daniel Jacoby in the A. D. B. 13, 587.

Wilhelm Heinse. W. H. sämmtliche Schriften, ed. H. Laube, 10 vols. (Leipz. 1838); Pröhle, Lessing, Wieland, Heinse, (Berl. 1877); J. Schober, W. H. (Leipz. 1882); Schnorr's Archiv x. 39, 372, 479.

Berlin. Berlin not only possessed a Public, but the word first arose there, as is shown in Gottsched's Neuestes aus der anmuth. Gelehrsamkeit, x, 751, in the year 1760: ' that portion of the German world (in Berlin it is now called Public) which has hitherto admired him.'—*C. F. Nicolai.* v. Göckingk, Nicolais Leben und litterar. Nachl. (Berl. 1820) ; Foss, in Schnorr's Archiv ii. 374 ; J. Minor, Lessing's Jugendfreunde (Berl. and Stuttg.), p. 275. On the *Berliner Monatschrift,* see Meyen, in Prutz Litterarhistor. Taschenb. 1847, p. 151. *Moses Mendelssohn.* Gesammelte Schriften, 7 vols. (Leipz. 1843–45).

XII. WEIMAR, ii. pp. 142–228.

Anna Amalia. Carl Freiherr v. Beaulieu-Marconnay, Anna Amalia, Carl August and der Minister von Fritsch (Weimar, 1874).—*Karl August* : Wegele, K. A. (Leipz. 1850); A. D. B., 15, 338. Schöll, Carl-August-Büchlein (Weimar, 1857): specially Droysen, C. A. und die deutsche Politik (Jena, 1857.)

1. Goethe, ii. pp. 145-170.

Collected Editions. S. Hirzel gives a chronological table of all Goethe's writings, Verzeichnis einer Goethe-Bibliothek, ed. by Ludwig Hirzel (Leipz. 1884); see too, W. v. Biedermann from time to time in Schnorrs Archiv. The first attempt at a collected edition of Goethe's works was made by the Berlin bookseller, Himburg (vols. I, II, 1775; III, 1776; a 3rd ed. in 4 vols. 1779). Goethe's own editions, ' Schriften,' 8 vols. (Leipz. by Göschen, 1787-90): ' Neue Schriften,' 7 vols. (Berl., by Unger, 1792-1800): the three editions, by Cotta, of the ' Werke' (Tübingen or Stuttg. and Tübingen): 12 vols. 1806-8, with 1810, the ' Wahlverwandschaften' (which had appeared alone in 1809) as vol. 13; 20 vols. 1815-19; 40 vols. ('Vollständige Ausgabe letzter Hand,' 1827-31). Lastly, ' Goethe's Nachgelassene Werke,' 15 vols. 1832-34; with 5 further vols. 1842. ' Goethe's poetische und prosaische Werke (Stuttg. and Tübingen, Cotta,) 2 vols., and Hempels ed. (Berl.) in 36 vols., with notes and explanations by W. v. Biedermann, H. Düntzer, S. Kalischer, G. v. Löper, and F. Strehlke. A new ed. is in progress, 3 vols. published.

Biographies, Characteristics, etc. Abeken, Ein Stück aus G. Leben (Berl. 1845): G. in den Jahren 1771-75 (2 ed. Hanover,1865); Albrecht, Zum Sprachgebrauch Goethes (Crimmitschau, 1876 Progr.); Bernays, Über Kritik und Geschichte des Goetheschen Textes (Berl. 1866); A. D. B. ix 413-438, (separately printed Leipz. 1880); W. v. Biedermann, Goethe-Forschungen (Frankf. 1879); H. Blaze de Bury, Les Maîtresses de Goethe (Paris, 1873); Bossert, Goethe (Paris, 1872); G. et Schiller (Paris, 1873); Bratranek, Zwei Polen in Weimar (Vienna, 1870); Braun, G. im Urtheile seiner Zeitgenossen

(Berl. 1883); C. A. H. Burkhardt, Das Tiefurter Journal (Grenzboten, 1871, ii. 281); Das herzogl. Liebhabertheater (ibid. 1873, iii. 1); Classische Findlinge (ibid. 1873, iii. 293, iv. 79, 91, 1874, i. 201); Carus, Goethe (Vienna, 1863); Diezmann, Aus Weimars Glanzzeit (Leipz. 1855); G. und die lustige Zeit in Weimar (Leip. 1857); Goethe-Schiller Museum (Leipz. 1858); Weimar Album (Leipz. 1860); Düntzer, Studien zu Goethes Werken (Elberfeld, 1849); Neue Goethestudien (Nuremberg, 1861); Frauenbilder aus G.'s Jugendzeit (Stuttg. 1852); Freundesbilder aus G.'s Leben (Leipz. 1853); Aus G.'s Freundeskreise (Brunswick, 1868); G.'s Leben (Leipz. 1880); Fielitz, G. studien (Wittenberg, 1881, Progr.); L. Geiger, G. Jahrbuch (Frankfort, each year since 1880); G. Gerland, Über G.'s historiche Stellung (Nordhausen, 1865); Gödeke, G.'s Leben und Schriften (Stuttg. 1874); H. Grimm, Goethe (Berl. 3d ed. 1882); Grosse, G. und das deutsche Alterthum (Dramburg, 1875, Diss.); Henkel, Das Goethesche Gleichniss (Stendal, 1883, Progr.); Keil, Vor hundert Jahren, 2 vols. (Leipz. 1875); Goethe, Weimar und Jena in 1806 (Leipz. 1882); Lehmann, G.'s Sprache und ihr Geist (Berl. 1852); Lewes, Life and Works of G. (London, 1855); Mézières, W. Goethe, 2d ed. 2 vols. (Paris, 1874); Minor and Sauer, Studien zur G. Philologie (Vienna, 1880); K. W. Müller, G.'s letzte litterarische Thätigkeit (Jena, 1832); Fr. v. Müller, G. in seiner praktischen Wirksamkeit (Weimar, 1832); Nicolovius, Über Goethe (Leipz. 1828); Pietsch, G. als Freimaurer (Leipz. 1880); Ein Engländer (Henry Crabb Robinson) über deutsches Geistesleben, von K. Eitner (Weimar, 1871); H. Rollett, Die G. Bildnisse (Vienna, 1883); Rosenkranz, G. und seine Werke (Königsb. 1847); J. W. Schäfer, G.'s Leben, 2 vols. (3rd ed. Leipz. 1877); Schöll, G. in Hauptzügen seines Lebens und Wirkens (Berl. 1882); A. Stahr, Weimar und Jena, 2 vols. (Oldenb. 1852); G.'s Frauengestalten (5th ed. Berl. 1875); Kl. Schriften, vol. 3 (Berl. 1875); Varnhagen, G. in den Zeugnissen der Mitlebenden (Berl. 1823); H. Viehoff, G.'s Leben, Geistesentwicklung und Werke, 4 vols. (4th ed. Stuttg. 1877); O. Vilmar, Zum Verständnisse G's., 4th ed. (Marburg, 1879); Vogel, G. in amtlichen Verhältnissen (Jena, 1834); W. Wachsmuth, Weimars Musenhof in den Jahren 1772 bis 1807 (Berl. 1844); Winter, G.'s deutsche Gesinnung (Leipz. 1880).—Schäfer and Herman Grimm's books are very useful.

Letters and Conversations, connection with persons and places. General collections of Letters.—Döring, G.'s Briefe 1768 bis 1832 (Leipz. 1837); Riemer, Briefe von und an G. (Leipz. 1846); G.'s Briefe, 4 vols. (Berl., no date); Strehlke, G's. Briefe (Berl. 1881). See Gervinus, Über den Goetheschen Briefwechsel (Leipz. 1836).—*Bettina von Arnim,* née Brentano, G.'s Briefwechsel mit einem Kinde, 3 vols. (3rd ed. Berl. 1881); G. in Berlin (Berl. 1849); O. Brahm, G. und Berlin (Berl. 1880); Sulpiz, *Boisserée* (Stuttg. 1862); Lucius, Frederick *Brion* von Sessenheim (Strass. 1877); see too, E. Schmidt, Im neuen Reich, 1877, ii. 441; also Näke, Wallfahrt nach Sesenheim (Berl. 1840); Kruse, Deutsche Rundschau, 17, 218; Kraus, ibid. 20, 158; A. Baier, Das Heidenröslein (Heidelberg, 1877); Briefe von Karl August und G. an *Döbereiner,* pub. by O. Schade (Weimar, 1856); *Dornburg,* R. A. C. Schell, G. in Dornburg (Jena and Leipzig, 1864); L. Geiger in the Goethe-Jahrbuch, ii. 316; *Dresden,* W. v. Biedermann, G. und Dresden (Berl. 1875); *Eckermann,*

Gespräche mit Goethe, 3 vols. (3rd. ed. Leipz. 1868): G.'s letters to *Eichstädt*, pub. by W. v. Biedermann (Berl. 1875); G. und das sächsische *Erzgebürge*, by W. v. Biedermann (Stutt. 1877); Letters from G. to *Johanna Fahlmer*, pub. by Urlichs (Leipz. 1875, see Sch. Im n. Reich, 1875, No. 48); Joh. *Falk*, G. aus näherem persönlichen Umgange dargestellt (3rd ed. Leipz. 1856); F. J. Frommann, Das *Frommansche* Haus und seine Freunde (2nd ed. Jena, 1872); Letters from G. to *Göttling*, pub. by K. Fischer (Munich, 1880); Letters from G. to Rath *Grüner* (Leipz. 1833); Aus *Herders* Nachlass, i. 1–177; G.'s letters to the brothers *Humboldt*, pub. by Bratranek (Leipz. 1876); Letters from G. to *F. H. Jacobi*, pub. by Max Jacobi (Leipz. 1846); Briefwechsel des Grossherzogs *Karl August* mit G. 2 vols. (Weimar, 1863: see Düntzer, G. und K. August, 2 vols. Leipz. 1861, 65); Hlawaczek, G. in *Karlshad* (Karlsbad, 1877); G. and the composer, P. C. *Kayser*, pub. by Burkhardt (Leipz. 1879); *Kestner*, G. und Werther, pub. by A. Kestner (2nd ed. Stutt. 1855); Lappenberg, Reliquien des Frl. v. *Klettenberg* (Hamburg, 1849: see F. Delitzsch, Philemon, 3rd ed. Gotha, 1878); Short letters from G. to *Klopstock* in 1776 (Leipz. 1833; see Lyon, G.'s Verhältnis zu Klopstock, Döbeln, Diss.); Letters from G. to *Knebel*, pub. by G. E. Guhrauer 2 vols. (Leipz. 1851: see Knebel's Litt. Nachlass, pub. by Varnhagen and Mundt, 3 vols. Leipzig, 1840); Knebel's letters to his Sister, pub. by Düntzer, Jena, 1858; Zur deutschen Litteratur und Geschichte, Briefe aus Knebels Nachlass, pub. by Düntzer, 2 vols. (Nuremberg, 1858); Letters of G. to S. von *La Roche*, and Bettina Brentano, pub. by G. von Löper (Berl. 1879: see Schnorrs Archiv. 10, 83); Letters from G. to *Lavater*, ed. by H. Hirzel (Leipz. 1833); *Leipzig*, O. Jahn, G.'s Briefe an Leipziger Freunde (2 ed. Leipz. 1867); W. v. Biedermann, G. und Leipzig, 2 Parts (Leipz. 1865); Tomaschek, G. als Student in Leipzig (Zs. f. österr. Gymn. 1873, p. 1181); *Lili*, E. Jügel, Das Puppenhaus (Frankf. 1857), p. 323; Graf Dürckheim, Lillis Bild (Nördlingen, 1879): H. *Luden*, Rückblicke in mein Leben (Jena, 1847), pp. 1–132; G. and *F. Mendelssohn-Bartholdy*, by K. Mendelssohn-B. (Leipz. 1871); *Merck* (Letters to J. H. Merck, Darmstadt, 1835 and 1838; Briefe aus dem Freundeskreise von Goethe, Herder, Höpfner und Merck, Leipz. 1847, all pub. by K. Wagner); Freundschaftliche Briefe von G. und seiner Frau an Nicolaus *Meyer* (Leipz. 1856); G.'s Unterhaltungen mit *F. von Müller* by Burkhardt (Stuttg. 1870); *Nicolovius*, Denkschrift auf G. H. L. Nicolovius, by Alfred Nicolovius (Bonn. 1841); Goethe, *J. G. von Quandt*, und der Sächsische Kunstverein, by H. Uhde (Stutt. 1878); E. W. Neumann, G. in *Regensburg* (Schnorr's Arch. iv. 185); Letters from G. to *Reinhard* (Stutt. 1850); *Riemer*, Mittheilungen über G. 2 vols. (Berlin, 1841); A. Stöber, Der Actuar *Salzmann* (Mühlhausen, 1855); Aus *Schellings* Leben, 3 vols. (Leipz. 1869, 70); Letters from *Schiller* to G. (4th ed. Stutt. 1881; see Düntzer, Sch. und G., Stutt. 1859); Schiller's and Goethe's letters to A. W. *Schlegel* (Leipz. 1846); H. Wenzel, G. in *Schlesien* (Oppeln, 1867); Schönborn und seine Zeitgenossen (Hamburg, 1836; see Weinhold, Schönborn's Aufzeichnungen über Erlebtes, Zs. der Gesellsch. für die Gesch. der Herzogth. Schleswig-Holstein und Lauenburg, 1870, vol. i. Redlich, Zum 29 Januar 1878, Hamb. 1878); G. and Ph. *Seidel* (Im neuen Reich, 1871); Goethe-Briefe aus F. *Schlossers* Nachlass, pub. by J. Frese (Stutt. 1877); Briefw. zwischen G. und

Staatsrath *Schulz*, pub. by Düntzer (Leipz. 1853); Leben der Malerin Louise *Seidler*, by H. Uhde (2nd ed. Berl. 1875: see H. Grimm, Fünfzehn Essays, p. 288); G.'s letters to *Soret*, pub. by H. Uhde (Stutt. 1877); G.'s letters to *Frau von Stein*, pub. by A. Schöll, 3 vols. (Weimar, 1848, 51, 2nd ed. by W. Fielitz, vol. i, Frankf. 1883: see Düntzer, Charlotte von Stein, 2 vols. Stutt. 1874; Düntzer, C. v. Stein, und Corona Schröter, Stutt. 1876); Letters from G. and his Mother to Freiherr v. *Stein*, ed. by Ebers and Kahlert (Leipz. 1846); Letters from G. to K. Graf v. *Sternberg*, pub. by Bratranek (Vienna, 1866); Goethe's letters to Gräfin A. zu *Stolberg* (2nd ed. by W. Arndt. Leipz. 1881); *Strassburg*, Leyser, G. zu Strassbusg (Neustadt a d. H. 1871); for G.'s journey to Lorraine, see Gödeke, in the 'Gegenwart,' 13, 5; v. Löper in Schnorr's Archiv. 7. 529, 8, 225; G.'s letters to C. G. *v. Voigt*, ed. by O. Jahn (Leipz. 1868); W. Herbst, G. in *Wetzlar* (Gotha, 1881); Seuffert, Der junge G. und *Wieland*, Zs. 26, 252; Letters from G. to M. v. *Willemer* (Suleika), pub. by Th. Creizenach (2nd ed. Stuttg. 1878; see H. Grimm, Fünfzehn Essays, p. 258); G.'s letters to F. A. *Wolf*, pub. by M. Bernays (Berl. 1868); letters from G. to *Zelter*, pub. by Riemer, 6 vols. (Berlin, 1833-34.

Religion and Science. L. v. Lancizolle, Über G.'s Verhältnis zu Religion und Christenthum (Berlin, 1855); van Oosterzee, G.'s Stellung zum Christenthum (Bielefeld, 1858); J. Bayer, G.'s Verhältnis zu religiösen Fragen, (Prague, 1869); R. Jobst, G.'s religiöse Entwickelung bis 1775 (Stettin, 1877, Progr.); E. Filtsch, G.'s Stellung zur Religion (Langensalza, 1879, Diss.); Steck, G.'s religiöser Entwicklungsgang (Protestantische Kirchenzeitung, 1880, Nos. 22, 23); J. Schmidt, G.'s Stellung zum Christenthum (G. Jahrbuch, 1881, p. 49); O. Pfleiderer, G.'s religiöse Weltanschauung (Protest. Kirchenz. 1883, No. 15); F. K. J. Schütz, G.'s Philosophie, 7 Vols. (Hamburg, 1825, 26); E. Caro, La Philosophie de Goethe (Paris, 1866); A. Harpf, G.'s Erkenntnisprincip (Philosoph. Monatshefte, 1883); Danzel, Über G.'s Spinozismus, (Hamb. 1850); Jellinek, Die Beziehungen G.'s zu Spinoza (Vienna, 1878); Heyder, Über das Verhältnis G.'s zu Spinoza (Zs. f. die Lutherische Theologie und Kirche, 27, 261); Suphan, G. und Spinoza in der Festschrift zur zweiten Säcularfeier des Friedrichs-Werderschen Gymn. zu Berlin (Berl. 1881).—Oscar Schmidt, G's. Verhältnis zu den organischen Naturwissenschaften (Berl. 1853); Virchow, G. als Naturforscher (Berl. 1861); Helmholtz, Über G.'s naturwissenschaftliche Arbeiten (Populäre wissenschaftliche Vorträge, i. 31); Häckel, Natürliche Schöpfungsgeschichte; O. Schmidt, War G. ein Darwinianer? (1871); F. Cohn, G. als Botaniker (Deutsche Rundschau, 28, 26); S. Kalischer, Einleitungen zu Bd. 33-36 der Hempelschen Ausgabe; Du Bois-Reymond, G. und kein Ende (Leipz. 1883); S. Kalischer, G. als Naturforscher (Berl. 1883). G.'s letters on Natural Science were pub. by Bratranek, in 2 vols. (Leipz. 1874).—Wegele, G. als Historiker (Würzb. 1876).

Poems. G.'s lyric poems, explained by Düntzer, 2nd ed. 3 vols. (Leipz. 1875-77); G.'s poems explained by H. Viehoff, 2nd ed. 2 vols. (Stutt. 1869-70); G.'s Werke, Vol. i: Poems, Part i, with notes by G. v. Löper (Berl. 1882). See Kannegiesser, Vorträge über eine Auswahl von G.'s lyrischen Gedichten (Breslau, 1835); Bergk, Acht Lieder von G. (Wetzlar, 1857); W. v. Biedermann, Zu G.'s Gedichten (Leipz. 1870); Masing, Über ein Goethesches Lied. (Leipz. 1872); Miklosich (Über G.'s Klaggesang von der edlen Frauen des Asan Aga. (Vienna, 1883, Sitzungsberichte); E. Lichtenberger, Étude sur les poésies lyriques de Goethe, 2nd ed. (Paris, 1882). *Egmont.* See Düntzer, Götz und Egmont, Erl.; Bratranek, G.'s Egmont und Schiller's Wallenstein (Stuttg. 1862); Schiller's Critique, 6. 80. G.; Schiller's Edition, 15 b, 1 G.

Iphigenie. The fourfold text published by J. Bächtold, (Freib. 1883); see Schiller 6. 239 G.; Düntzer, Die drei ältesten Bearbeitungen von G.'s Iphigenie (Stutt. 1854), Erl.; Danzel, Gesammelte Aufsätze, p. 146; O. Jahn, Aus der Alterthumswissenschaft (Bonn, 1868), p. 353; W. v. Biedermann was the first to observe the connection with Sophocles' Philoctetes; see Imelmann, Anmerkungen zu deutschen Dichtern (out of the Symbolae Joachimicae), p. 27. On the origin of the Iphigenie, Grimm, p. 269.

Tasso. Fully explained by Düntzer (Leip. 1854), Erl.; Lewitz, Über G's. Torquato Tasso (Königsb. 1839); Hasper, Über G.'s T. T. (Mühlhausen i. Th. 1862, Progr.); A. F. C. Vilmar, Über G.'s Tasso (Frankf. 1869); J. Schmidt, Preuss. Jahrb. 46, 174. See Th. Jacobi, Tasso und Leonore (Prutz, Litterarhistor. Taschenb. 1848, p. 1). For Lenz see Gruppe's Leben und Werke deutscher Dichter, iv. 256. For Leonore Sanvitale, Schnorrs Archiv iv. 215.

Italian Journey. Grimm, Fünfzehn Essays, p. 137; L. Hirzel, G.'s Italienische Reise (Basle, 1871); Th. Cart, G. en Italie (Paris, 1881).—*Art Studies.* Danzel, G. und die Weimarischen Kunstfreunde in ihrem Verhältnis zu Winckelmann (Gesammelte Aufsätze p. 118); Grimm, G.'s Verhältnis zur bildenden Kunst (Zehn Essays, p. 192). See also Stichling, G. und die freie Zeichenschule zu Weimar (Weimarische Beiträge, Weimar, 1865, p. 33).—*Iphigenie in Delphi,* Sch. in Westermanns Monatshefte, 46, 73.—*Nausikaa,* ibid. 46, 726.—*Roman Elegies.* H. J. Heller, Neue Jahrbücher für Philol. und Pädagogik, 1863, ii. Part 8-11; Düntzer, ibid. 1864, Part 4.

2. *Schiller and Goethe,* ii. pp. 170-199.

Xenien. E. Boas, S. and G. im Xenienkampf, 2 Parts (Stuttg. 1851); die S. and G. Xenien, erläutert von E. J. Saupe (Leipz. 1852); see S. and G.'s Xenien Manuscript, published by W. v. Maltzahn (Berl. 1856).

The Theatre. Theatre Letters of G., and friendly letters of Jean Paul, by Dietmar (Berlin, 1835); Scholl, Goethe, p. 280, 'Goethes Verhältnis zum Theater'; E. Genast, Aus dem Tagebuche eines alten Schauspielers, Vol. i. (Leipz. 1862); H. Schmidt, Erinnerungen eines Weimarischen Veteranen (Leipz. 1856); E. Pasqué, G.'s Theaterleitung in Weimar, 2 vols. (Leipz. 1863); W. G. Gotthardi, Weimarische Theaterbilder aus G.'s Zeit. 2 vols. (1865); E. W. Weber, Zur Geschichte des Weimarischen Theaters (Weimar, 1865).—*Ekhof,* Uhde in Neuer Plutarch, iv. 121.—*Schröder,* F. L. W. Meyer, F. L. Schröder, 2 Parts (Hamb. 1819); see letters of Iffland and Schröder to the actor Werdy, pub. by O. Devrient (Frankf. 1881).—*Iffland:* Iffland, Meine theatralische Laufbahn (Leipz. 1798); Z. Funck, Aus dem Leben

zweier Schauspieler, Iffllands und Devrients (Leipz. 1838).—*Kotzebue:* Leben
A. v. Kotzebues (Leipz. 1820); A. v. Kotzebue, Urtheile der Zeitgenossen und
der Gegenwart, by W. v. Kotzebue (Dresden, 1881); other works in Gödeke,
p. 1064.—*P. A. Wolff:* Monogr. Martersteig (Leipz. 1879).
The Natural Daughter. Düntzer, Erl.; for the authority: Mémoires his-
toriques de Stéphanie-Louise de Bourbon-Conti, 2 vols. (Paris, Floréal, an. vi.)
Wilhelm Meister. See Schiller and Goethe's letters; Körner, Gesamm.
Schr. p. 107; Fried. Schlegel, 2. 165. M. Jenisch, Über die hervorstechend-
sten Eigenthümlichkeiten von Meisters Lehrjahren (Berl. 1797); Düntzer, Erl.
Conversations of German Emigrants. Düntzer, G.'s Reise der Söhne Mega-
prazons und Unterh. d. Ausg. (Leipz. 1873) in the Erl.
Hermann und Dorothea. W. von Humboldt's ästhetische Versuche, 1st
Part. Über G.'s H. und D. (Brunswick, 1799); A. W. Schlegel, 11. 183,
Cholevius, Ästhet. und histor. Einleitung zu G.'s H. und D. (2nd ed. Leipz.
1877); Düntzer, Erl. See too, Rümelin, Reden und Aufsätze, p. 382.
Achilleis. Strehlke, Über G.'s Elpenor und Achilleis (Marienburg, 1870,
Progr.).

3. *Schiller,* ii. pp. 199–228.

Editions. An historical and critical ed. under Gödeke's direction, 15
Parts, in 17 Vols. (Stuttg. 1867–1876); R. Boxberger's ed. (2nd ed. Berl.
1882, 8 vols.); Schiller's Calendar, July 18, 1795–1805, pub. by Emilie v.
Gleichen-Russwurm (Stuttg. 1865); Notes to the poems by Düntzer and
Viehoff, and to the Dramas by Düntzer and Eckardt, in the Erl.—*Letters.*
S.'s Letters, with historical notes, 2 vols. (Berlin); letters to his wife, S. and
Lotte, 1788–1805, 3rd ed. corrected by, W. Fielitz, 3 Books (Stuttg. 1879);
See Charlotte von S. und ihre Freunde (pub. by L. Urlichs), 3 vols. (Stuttg.
1860); Briefe von S.'s Gattin an einen vertrauten Freund (von Knebel), pub.
by Düntzer (Leipz. 1856); Hennes Fischenich und C. von S. (Frankf. 1875);
W. Toischer, Lotte S. (Vienna, 1881). Other letters: S.'s Beziehungen zu
Eltern, Geschwistern, und der Familie von Wolzogen (Stuttg. 1859); S.'s
Briefwechsel mit seiner Schwester Christophine und seinem Schwager Rein-
wald (Leipz. 1875); S.'s Geschäftsbriefe, ed. by K. Gödeke (Leipz. 1875);
Briefw. zwischen S. und Cotta, ed. by W. Vollmer (Stutt. 1876); Briefe an S.,
ed. by L. Urlichs (Stutt. 1877). Many letters to S. are in the Neue freie
Presse, No. 4220. The most important are S.'s Briefwechsel mit Körner, 2nd
ed. pub. by K. Gödeke, 2 Parts (Leipz. 1874; comp. C. G. Körner's Gesam-
melte Schriften, pub. by A. Stern Leipz. 1881; F. Jonas, C. G. Körner, Berl.
1882); Briefw. zwischen S. und W. von Humboldt, 2nd ed. (Stuttg. 1876);
Briefw. mit Goethe (see XII. 1); S.'s Briefw. mit dem Herzog von Schleswig-
Holstein-Augustenburg, pub. by F. Max Müller (Berlin, 1875, see Deutsche
Rundschau, Oct. 1881, p. 156); Briefe von S. an Herzog F. C. von Schleswig-
Holstein-Augustenburg, pub. by A. L. J. Michelsen (Berlin, 1876). See Breul,
Zs. xxviii. 358.
Biographies, Characteristics, etc. Belling, Metrik S.'s (Breslau, 1883);
E. Boas, S.'s Jugendjahre, 2 vols. (Hanover, 1856); Boxberger, S. und
Haller (Erfurt, 1869, Progr.); also Schnorrs Archiv 2. 198; 4. 252, 494;

Braun, S. im Urtheile seiner Zeitgenossen, 2 vols. (Leipz. 1882); Brosin, S.'s Verhältnis zu dem Publicum seiner Zeit (Leipz. 1875); S.'s Vater (Leipz. 1879); E. L. Bulwer, S.'s Life and Works; Th. Carlyle, The Life of S. (1825, Supplement, 1872, London, 1873); W. Deecke, Über S.'s Auffassung des Künstlerberufs (Lübeck, 1862); Düntzer, S.'s Leben (Leipz. 1881); Egger, S. in Marbach (Vienna, 1868); Fielitz, Studien zu S.'s Dramen (Leipz. 1876); Kuno Fischer, S. Festival Speech (Leipz. 1860); S. Three Lectures (Leipz. 1868); 'Jacob Grimm, Rede auf S. (Berl. 1859); G. Hauff, S. Studien (Stuttg. 1880); L. Hirzel, Über S.'s Beziehungen zum Alterthume (Aarau, 1872); K. Hofmeister, S.'s Leben, Geistesentwickelung und Werke im Zusammenhange, 5 Parts (Stuttg. 1838–42); D. Jacoby, S. und Garve, Schnorr's Archiv 7. 95; A. v. Keller, Beiträge zur Schillerlitteratur (Tüb. 1859, 1860); E. Palleske, S.'s Leben und Werke, 2 vols. (Berlin, 1858, 1859); J. Reuper, S.'s Dramen im Lichte der zeitgenössichen Kritik (Bielitz, 1874, Progr.); Rümelin, Rede über S.'s politische Ansichten (Heilbronn, 1850); Schlossberger, Archivalische Nachlese zur Schillerlitteratur (Stuttg. 1877); G. Schwab, S.'s Leben (Stuttg. 1840); Streicher, S.'s Flucht von Stuttgart und Aufenthalt in Mannheim (Stutt. 1836); K. Tomaschek, S. in seinem Verhältnisse zur Wissenschaft (Vienna, 1862); K. Twesten, S. in seinem Verhältnis zur Wissenschaft dargestellt (Berl. 1863); H. Viehoff, S.'s Leben, Geistesentwickelung und Werke, 3 Parts (Stuttg. 1875); Fr. Vischer, Fest Rede (Zurich, 1859); K. Weinhold, Festrede auf S. (Grätz, 1859); C. v. Wolzogen, S.'s Leben (see Schnorr's Archiv 1. 452, 4. 482), 2 Parts (Stuttg. 1830). The best work is Hoffmeister's.

The Dramas. The Robbers. A sheet of the first suppressed Edition is pub. by A. Cohn in Schnorrs Archiv 9. 277; Boxberger, ibid. 3. 283, 4. 496; Minor, ibid. 10. 97; Boxberger, Die Sprache der Bibel in S.'s Räubern (Erfurt, 1867, Progr.); K. Richter, S. und seine Räuber in der französischen Revolution (Grünberg, 1865).—*Fiesco:* J. Franck, Zs. 20. 366.—*Don Carlos:* Reprint of 1st ed. by W. Vollmer (Stuttg. 1880); see Levy, Zs. 21. 277.— *Wallenstein:* Süvern, Über S.'s W. in Hinsicht auf griechische Tragödie (Berl. 1800); K. Tomaschek, S.'s W. (Vienna, 1858); Fielitz, Studien, p. 7; Schnorr's Archiv ii. 159, 402, viii. 544, ix. 560.—*Maria Stuart:* Fielitz, p. 44. *Maid of Orleans:* Fielitz, p. 71; Peppmüller in Schnorr's Archiv 2. 179; Römpler, Bermerkungen zur Schiller's J. v. O. (Plauen, 1872, Progr.); E. F. Kummer, Die J. v. O. in der Dichtung (Vienna, 1874).—*Bride of Messina:* Gerlinger, Die griechischen Elemente in S.'s B. v. M. (Augsb. 1858); Gevers, Über S.'s B. v. M. und den König Œdipus des Sophokles (Verden, 1873, Progr.); Liebrecht, Zur Volkskunde (Heilbronn, 1879), p. 471; Imelmann, Anm. zu deutschen Dichtern, p. 16.—*Wilhelm Tell:* notes by W. E. Weber (1839, 2nd ed. Bremen, 1852); see Joachim Meyer, S.'s W. T. auf seine Quellen zurückgeführt (Nuremberg, 1840); Schnorr's Archiv 1. 461, 2. 539, 544; Imelmann, Anmerkungen p. 19. For the legend, W. Fischer, Die Sage von der Befreiung der Waldstädte nach ihrer allmäligen Ausbildung (Leipzig, 1867); E. L. Rochholz, Tell und Gessler in Sage und Geschichte (Heilbronn, 1877).

XIII. ROMANTICISM, ii. pp. 229–335.

R. Haym's work, Die romantische Schule (Berl., 1870) only gives the older
Romanticism, and does not extend much beyond the beginning of the
19th century. The same applies to Dilthey's Leben Schleiermachers (Berl.,
1870). I have extended the term Romanticism so as to include Heinrich
Heine, and have named the whole period between Schiller's death and the death
of Goethe after the prevailing tone of ideas. For the connection between the
'Period of Genius,' and Romanticism, see Deutsche Litteraturrevolution, Sch.'s
Vorträge und Aufsätze, p. 337. The great example of this connection is
Goethe's Faust. For divisions 2 to 4, see J. v. Eichendorff, Gesch. der poet.
Litt. Deutschlands, vol. 2 (Paderb. 1866). H. Hettner, Die romantische Schule
(Brunswick, 1850).

1. *Science,* ii. pp. 231–259.

For the persons here mentioned, see Gödeke 3, 81–124.

The improvement of the language. With the exception of Andersen's Über
die Sprache Jacob Grimm's (Leipz., 1869), little has been written on this subject, and indeed, the history of German prose writing is very imperfect. For
Fr. L. Jahn, see the Monograph by Euler (Stuttg., 1881), p. 441.

Women. Schiller's sister-in-law, Caroline v. Wolzogen, the authoress of the
novel Agnes von Lilien, see Litterarischer Nachlass der Frau C. v. W., 2 vols.,
2d ed. (Leipz., 1867). For Bettina, see G. v. Löper, A. D. B. ii. 578, and
Hermann Grimm (above, XII. 1). Rahel v. Varnhagen. 'Rahel, ein Buch
des Andenkens für ihre Freunde' (Berl., 1833, in 3 vols; Berl., 1834). Letters
to David Veit, 2 vols. (Leipz., 1861); to Varnhagen, 6 vols. (Leipz., 1874,
75); Aus Rahels Herzensleben (Leipz., 1877); see Gödeke iii., 79. Henriette
Herz, J. Fürst, H. H. ihr Leben und ihr Erinnerungen, 2d ed. (Berl., 1858);
Briefe des jungen Börne an H. H. (Leipz., 1861). Caroline Schelling, née
Michaëlis, G. Waitz, Caroline, 2 vols. (Leipz., 1871). Caroline und ihre Freunde
(Leipz., 1882). See R. Haym, Preuss. Jahrb. vol. 28, 356; Sch. Vorträge und
Aufsätze, p. 356.

Philosophy. Among the philosophers the history of literature is most
occupied with Schopenhauer for style, and Schelling for poetry. For Schelling,
besides the well-known terza rima, 'Die letzten Worte des Pfarrers zu Drottning
auf Seeland' (Aus Schellings Leben i. 293), and some other poems in Schlegel
and Tieck's Musenalmanach for 1802, see also the 'Epikurisch Glaubensbe-
kenntnis Heinz Widerporstens' (aus Schelling's Leben i. 182, where, however, it
is not noted that H. W. is a character from Hans Sachs, Keller v, 321); and
'Nachtwachen von Bonaventura' (Reprint, Lindau and Leipz., 1877; see Zs.
xxiii. 203).

Mathematics and Natural Sciences. I have gathered my information chiefly
from Whewell's Inductive Sciences, from Häser's Geschichte der Medicin,
from Articles in the A. D. B., and especially from the Geschichte der Wissenschaften in Deutschland, brought out by the Munich Historical Commission.

Cosmology and A. v. Humboldt. O. Peschel, Geschichte der Erdkunde
(Munich, 1865). G. Forster's Sämmtliche Schriften, 9 vols. (Leipz., 1843);

Briefwechsel mit Sömmerring, pub. by Hettner (Bruns, 1877); on A. v. Humboldt, the Monograph ediied by Bruhns, 3 vols. (Leipz., 1872); H. W. Dove, Gedächtnisrede auf A. v. H. (Berl., 1869); see A. v. H. Letters to Varnhagen (Leipz., 1860); to Bunsen, (Leipz., 1869); to Gauss (Leipz, 1877); to his brother Wilhelm (Stuttg., 1880); on A. v. H. and the two *Forsters*, A. Dove, A. D. B, vii. 166, 172; xiii., 338. On *Karl Ritter*, the Monograph by Kramer, 2 parts (Halle, 1875).

Wilhelm von Humboldt. W. v. H. Gesammelte Werke, 7 vols. (Berl., 1841-52); Über die Verschiedenheit des menschlichen Sprachbaues (reprint by Pott, 2 vols., Berl., 1876). Die sprachphilosophischen Werke W. v. H., ed. H. Steinthal (Berl., 1883, also Zs. f. Völkerpsychologie, xiii. 201); Briefe an F. G. Welcker, ed. R. Haym (Berl., 1859); Ansichten über Ästhetik und Litteratur von W. v. H., ed. F. Jonas (Berl., 1880); Briefe an eine Freundin (Leipz., 1847); Briefe an Henriette Herz (Varnhagen, Br von Chamisso, Gneisenau, &c, i. 1-132). See G. Schlesier, Erinnerungen an W. v. H., 2 vols. (Stuttg., 1843, 45). R. Haym, W. v. H. Lebensbild und Charakteristik (Berl., 1856); H. Steinthal, Gedächtnisrede auf W. v. H. (Berl., 1867); A. Dove, A. D. B. xiii. 338.

Moral Science. For *Schleiermacher*, besides Dilthey's Life, see Sigwart, Kleine Schriften, i, 221.—For *History*, see Baur, Die Epochen der kirchlichen Geschichtschreibung (Tüb., 1852); Waitz, Göttinger Historiker von Köhler bis Dahlmann (Göttinger Professoren, p. 231). Gervinus, F. C. Schlosser (Leipz., 1861); especially p. 53, Geschichte des neunzehnten Jh. viii. 65.

Ludwig Tieck. Phantasus, 3 vols. (Berl., 1812-17); Works, 20 vols (Berl., 1828-46); Poems, 3 vols. (Dresden, 1821-23; 2d ed. 1834; new ed. Berl., 1841). Kritische Schriften (Leipz., 1848-52); Gesammelte Novellen, 12 vols. (Berl. 1852-54); Nachgelassene Schriften, 2 vols. (Leipz., 1855); see R. Köpke, L. T., 2 parts (Leipz., 1855); von Friesen, L. T., 2 vols. (Vienna, 1871). A. Stern, Zur Litteratur der Gegenwart (Leipz., 1880), p. 1-44; Briefe an Tieck, ed. K. v. Holtei, 4 vols. (Breslau, 1864). *A. W. Schlegel.* Ed. E. Böcking, Sämmt. Werke, 12 vols. (Leipz., 1846-47); Œuvres écrites en français, 3 vols. (Leipz., 1846); Opuscula latina (Leipz., 1848); Vorlesungen über schöne Litteratur und Kunst, ed. by J. Minor, in Seuffert, No. 17, 19 (Heilbr. 1854). See M. Bernays, Zur Entstehungsgeschichte des Schlegelschen Shakespeare (Leipz., 1872); Schnorr's Archiv, x. 236: Strauss, Kleine Schriften, p. 122.—*Fr. Schlegel.* Sämmtl. Werke, 10 vols. (Vienna, 1822-25, larger ed., 15 vols., 1846); his youthful prose works from 1794-1802, pub. by J. Minor, 2 vols. (Vienna, 1882). See Dorothea von Schlegel, née Mendelssohn, und deren Söhne, Briefwechsel, ed. by Raich, 2 vols. (Mainz, 1881).

Later Romantic School. See K. v. Raumer, Geschichte der Germanischen Philologie (Munich, 1870); and Sch., Jacob Grimm (Berl. 1865, 2d ed. 1885); also Eichendorff, Litt. Nachlass (Paderb. 1866), p. 290.—*Arnim.* Sämmtl. Werke (Berl., 1839; new ed., 22 vols., 1853-56). Reprint of Hollins' Liebeleben by J. Minor (Freib., 1883). The Wunderhorn has been reprinted several times.—*Brentano.* Gesammelte Schriften, 9 vols. (Frankf., 1851-55). See Diel, S. J. Clemens Brentano, ein Lebensbild, 2 vols. (Freib., 1877, 78); J. B. Heinrich. Cl. B. (Cologne, 1878); Grisebach, Die Deutsche Litteratur (Vienna, 1876), p. 218; Varnhagen, Biogr. Portr. (Leipz., 1871), p. 59.—*Görres.* Monograph by Sepp; Gesammelte Briefe, 3 vols. (Munich, 1858–1874).—*The Brothers Grimm.* Sch. A. D. B., ix. 678, 690. Correspondence between Jacob and Wilhelm Grimm in youth, ed. by H. Grimm and G. Hinrichs (Weimar, 1881). Briefw. des Freiherrn K. H. G. v. Meusebach mit J. und W. Grimm, ed. by C. Wendeler (Heilbronn, 1880); see H. Grimm's, Fünfzehn Essays, 3rd series (Berl., 1882), p. 287.—*Uhland,* see XIII. 2.

Translations. See Gödeke iii. 215–225, 1281–1403. He mentions 532 Translators. See too the letters of H. Voss to Fr. Diez, pub. by A. Tobler in the Preuss. Jahrb. 51, 9.

2. *Lyric Poetry,* ii. 259–282.

Fr. v. Matthisson. Gedichte (Mannheim, 1787); Schriften, 8 vols. (Zurich, 1825–29).

Fr. Hölderlin. Gedichte (Stuttg., 1826): collected works, 2 vols., (Stuttg., 1846). See Gödeke ii, 1124. A. Jung, F. H. und seine Werke (Stuttg., 1848). Hallensleben, Beitr. zur Charakteristik Hölderlins (Arnstadt, 1849, Progr.); W. Hoffner, H. und die Ursachen seines Wahnsinns (Westermann's deutsche Monatshefte Mai, 1867, p. 155). J. Volkelt, F. H. (Im neuen Reich, 1880, No. 37); Sch. Vortr. und Aufs. p. 346. J. Klaiber, Hölderlin, Hegel und Schelling in ihren schwäbischen Jugendjahren (Stuttg., 1877); Wilbrandt Hist. Taschenb., v. Folge 1, 371.

Joh. Peter Hebel. Works, 8 vols. (Karls., 1832–34). Briefe von J. P. H. an einen Freund (Mann., 1860, Appendix 1862). Aus Hebels Briefwechsel (Freib., 1860); Fr. Becker, J. P. Hebel (Basel, 1860); see Längin, J. P. H. (Karls., 1875).—*Joh. Martin Usteri.* Poems, ed. Dav. Hess., 3 vols. (Berl. 1831). For poetry in local dialects, see Gödeke, §§ 308, 346.

Novalis. (Fr. v. Hardenberg). Works, ed. by Fr. Schlegel and Tieck, 2 vols. (Berl., 1802; 5th ed., 1837); 3rd vol., ed. by Tieck and E. v. Bülow (Berl., 1846); F. v. H. eine Nachlese (Gotha, 1873). Novalis, Briefwechsel mit F. und A. W., Charlotte und Caroline Schlegel, ed. by Raich (Mainz, 1880). See Dilthey, Preuss. Jahrb., xv. 596.

Patriotic Poetry. Gödeke, § 311 (iii, 225–240); The songs of the Burschenschaft, ibid. § 316 (iii, 258–266).—*E. M. Arndt.* See R. Haym, Preuss. Jahrb. v. G. Freytag, A. D. B., i. 541; Monogr. E. Langenberg (Bonn, 1865); v. Löper in Schnorr's Archiv ii. 546; Arndt's Briefe, Preuss. Jahrb. 34, 589. E. M. A. Briefe an eine Freundin, pub. by E. Langenberg (Berl., 1878).

Justinus Kerner. See Strauss, Kl. Schriften, new series, p. 298; Marie Niethammer, J. K. Jugendliebe (Stuttg., 1877).—*Ludwig Uhland.* There are various editions of his poems and dramas, that of 1876 (3 vols., pub. by W. L. Holland) contains a chronological table of the poems (ii. 316). A. v. Keller, U. als Dramatiker (Stuttg., 1877); Uhland's Schriften zur Geschichte der Dichtung und Sage, 8 vols. (Stuttg., 1865–73), See L. U. Leben von seiner Wittwe (Stuttg., 1874); Fr. Fischer, Kritische Gänge, new series, iv, 97 (and for the Würtemberg authors in general, Krit. Gänge, i. 4–78); H. v. Treitschke, Histor. und polit. Aufsätze (Leipz., 1865), p. 278; G. Liebert, L. U. (Hamburg, 1857); O. Jahn, L. U. (Bonn, 1863); F. Notter, L. U. (Stuttg., 1863); Gihr.

U. Leben (Stuttg., 1864); K. Mayer, L. U. seine Freunde und Zeitgenossen, 2 vols. (Stuttg., 1867). For the ballads and romances, Düntzer Erl. (Stuttg., 1876); H. Eichholz Quellenstudien zu Uhlands Balladen (Berl., 1879). *A. v. Chamisso.* Works, 6 vols. (Leipzig, 1836-49); see Varnhagen, Briefe von Chamisso, Gneisenau, &c., i. 135 : Fulda, Ch. und seine Zeit. (Leipz., 1881): —*I. v. Eichendorff.* Sämmtliche poetische Werke, 4 vols. (3rd ed., Leipz., 1883): Vermischte Schriften, 5 vols. (Paderborn, 1866).—*Wilhelm Müller.* Vermischte Schriften, ed. G. Schwab, 5 vols. (Leipz., 1830): Gedichte von W. M. with introduction by F. Max Müller, 2 parts (Leipz., 1868).

Goethe's Westöstlicher Divan. Commentary by C. Wurm (Nuremberg, 1834); von Löper's annotated edition (Berl., Hempel); ed. Simrock, with extracts from the book of Kabus (Heilbronn, 1875); Düntzer in the Erl. (Leipz., 1878).—*Friedrich Rückert.* Gesammelte poetische Werke, 12 vols. (Frankf., 1867, 69; last ed., 1882). See Fortlage, F. R. und seine Werke (Frankf., 1867); C. Beyer, F. R. ein biographisches Denkmal (Frank., 1868); Nachgelassene Gedichte, F. R. und neue Beiträge zu dessen Leben und Schriften (Vienna, 1877); G. Voigt, F. R. Gedankenlyrik nach ihrem philosophischen Inhalte dargestellt (Annaberg, 1881); see too A. Sohr, Heinrich Rückert (Weimar, 1880).—*August Graf von Platen-Hallermünde.* Ed., 2 vols. (Stuttg., 1876); 3 vols. (Berl., Hempel); see Platen's Tagebuch (Stuttg., 1860), and the works mentioned in Gödeke (3, 571).

Heinrich Heine. Sämmtl. Werke, 21 vols. (Hamb., 1861-63); see A. Strodtmann, H. H.'s Leben und Werke, 2 vols. (Berl., 1867, 69).

3. *Narrative Writing,* ii. pp. 282-301.

See the passage on narrative poetry in Koberstein, vol. 5, p. 3-155. On romances, Eichendorff, Der deutsche Roman des 18ⁿ Jh. in seinem Verhältnis zum Christenthum (Paderb. 1866).

Epics. Ernst Schulze (Sämmtl. poet. Werke, 3rd ed., 5 parts, Leipz. 1855, with life by R. Marggraff). *A. Blumauer* (Die travestirte Æneide, ed. by E. Grisebach, Leipz. 1872). *Karl A. Kortum* (Jobsiade, 13th ed., by Ebeling, Leipz. 1868). *Arnim,* Gedichte, p. 212. 'Geschichte des Mohrenjungen,' from the Dolores i. 233, (ed. 1840).

Novels. 'Anton Reiser,' see W. Alexis in Prutz, Litterarhist. Taschenb. 1847, p. 1-71; E. Schmidt, Richardson, Rousseau, und Goethe, p. 289; ' *Siegwart,*' see E. Schmidt, 302. ' *Siegfried von Lindenberg,*' (latest ed. Leipz., 1867). *Jean Paul Friedrich Richter,* Sämmliche Werke, 60 vols. (Berl. 1826-28), 33 vols. (Berl. 1840-42): see R. O. Spazier, J. P. F. R. ein biographischer Commentar zu dessen Werken, 5 vols. (Leipz. 1833), and besides the books mentioned by Gödeke, ii. 1121, E. Förster, Denkwürdigkeiten aus dem Leben von J. P. F. R., 4 vols. (Munich, 1863); P. Nerrlich, J. P. und seine Zeitgenossen (Berl. 1876): Briefe von Charlotte von Kalb an J. P. und dessen Gattin, ed. P. Nerrlich (Berl. 1882): K. C. Planck, J. P.'s Dichtung im Lichte unserer nationalen Entwicklung (Berl. 1867): Fr. Vischer, Kritische Gänge, new series vi. 133.

Tales. Gottlieb Meissner, (see A. Meissner, Rococobilder, 2nd ed., Lindau and Leipz., 1876).—' *Undine,*' on its origin, Fouqué in his ' Musen,' 1812, Part

iv. p. 198 ; Theophrastus alluded to the Knight of Staufenberg, so that the poem written in rhymed couplets about 1300 by Eckenolt, a follower of Konrad of Würzburg, and printed at Strassburg in 1480, and modernised by Fischart in 1588 (ed. Jänicke, Altdeutsche Studien, Berl. 1871), still exercised an influence.—'*Schemihl*,' for its origin see Chamisso, vi. 117, Fulda, p. 125-136. For the superstition see Grimm, Myth. 976 ; Müllenhoff, Schleswig-holsteinische Sagen, p. 554: Rochholz, Germ. v. 69, 175—*Hoffmann*, Gesammelte Schriften, 12 vols. (Berl., latest 1871-73), see Hitzig, Aus H.'s Leben und Nachlass, 2 vols. (Berl. 1823): Z. Funck, Aus dem Leben zweier Dichter (Bamberg, 1836).

Goethe. '*Wilhelm Meister* ;' see F. Gregorovius, Goethe's W. M. in seinen socialistischen Elementen entwickelt (Königsb. 1849): A. Jung, G. Wanderjahre und die wichtigsten Fragen des 19^n Jh. (Mainz, 1854): Düntzer, Erl. For the astronomical Episode, W. Förster in Westermann's Monatshefte 46, 330, see 47, 130. '*Die Wahlverwandschaften*,' see Rötscher Abh zur Philosophie der Kunst, Part 2, (Berl, 1838): Düntzer, Erl. ; H. Grimm, Fünfzehn Essays, p. 239 ; Brahm, Zs. xxvi. 194. A letter by Minchen Herzlieb, the supposed original of Ottilie, has been published by Martin, Zs. xxvi. 376.

4. *The Drama*, ii. pp. 301-335.

Goethe. '*A Christian martyr, in early Saxon times*,' see v. Biedermann, Goethe = Forschungen, p. 154—'Pandora,' Düntzer, G. Prometheus und Pandora (Leipz. 1850). Erl. (1874). Schöll, G. (p. 418); Sch., Deutsche Rundschau, April, 1879.

Theodor Körner. Sämmtl. Werke, ed. K. Streckfuss, (Berl. 1834)—*A. Öhlenschläger.* Schriften, 18 vols. (Breslau, 1829, 30): Werke, 21 vols. (Breslau, 1839)—*Zacharias Werner.* Ausgew. Schriften, 13 vols. (Grimma, 1841): see Hitzig, Lebensabriss F. L. Z. Werners (Berl. 1823): H. Düntzer, Zwei Bekehrte (Leipz. 1873): E. Schmidt, Schnorrs Archiv vi. 233: A. Hagen, Altpreuss. Monatsschrift xi. 8. p. 625.—The *fate-tragedies*, see O. Brahm, Schnorrs Archiv ix. 207 ; J. Minor, Die Schicksals tragödie (Frankf. 1883).

Karl Immermann. K. I. 2 vols. (Berl. 1870) ; Werke, (Berl., Hempel). On the 'Frederick II,' see Raupach to Immermann in Holtei, Dreihundert Briefe aus 2 Jahrhunderten (Hanover, 1872), iii. 60. *Christian Grabbe.* Gottschall, 2 vols. (Leipz., 1869) ; Blumenthal, 4 vols. (Detmold, 1874). *Raupach.* Gödeke, iii. 531-553. For the *Nibelungen* in modern poetry see G. R. Röpe, Die moderne Nibelungendichtung, (Hamb. 1869) ; H. von Wolzogen, Der Nibelungenmythos in Sage und Litteratur (Berl. 1876) ; K. Rehorn, Die deutsche Sage von den Nibelungen in der deutschen Poesie (Frankf. 1877): J. Stammhammer, Die Nibelungen-Dramen seit 1850 (Leipz. 1878).

Heinrich von Kleist. Gesammelte Schriften, ed. Tieck, revised by Julian Schmidt (Berl. 1859) ; Werke (Berl. Hempel): see R. Köhler, Zu H. von K. Werken (Weimar, 1862) ; H. v. K. Politische Schriften, ed. R. Köpke (Berl. 1862); E. von Bülow, H. von K. Leben and Briefe (Berl. 1848) ; H. von K. Briefe an seine Schwester Ulrike, ed. A. Koberstein (1860): H. von K. Briefe an seine Braut, ed. K. Biedermann (Breslau, 1884) ; see A. Wilbrandt H. von K. (Nördlingen, 1863) ; Th. Zolling, H. v. K. in der Schweiz (Stuttg., 1882) ;

E. Schmidt, in the Österr. Rundschau, Part 2 (Vienna, 1883), p. 127. Julian Schmidt Preuss. Jahrb. 37, 593; O. Brahm, H. v. K. E. (Berlin, 1884); also Lloyd and Newton, Prussia's representative man (London, 1875). *Drama in Vienna.* See H. M. Richter, Geistesströmungen (Berl., 1875). Wlassak, Chronik des K. K. Hof Burgtheaters (Vienna, 1876). Gödeke has done good service in the history of the popular Theatre (iii. 796–845). Sauer in the 'Wiener Neudrucke' gives in Nos. 2 and 4 pieces by Kurz, and C. G. Klemm.—*J. Schreyvogel* (adopted name, West); see A. Schönbach, J. Schrey-vogel-West (Appendix to the Wiener Abendpost 1879, Nos. 52–56). *Grillparzer.* Sämmtliche Werke, 10 vols. (Stuttg. 1872): (Theob. v. Rizy.) Wiener Grillparzer-Album (Stuttg., 1877): see Sch., Vortr. und Aufs. p. 193–307, and the works there mentioned, p. 196; Fäulhammer, F. G. (Gratz, 1884); G. Wolf, Grillp. als Archivdirector (Vienna, 1874): L. A. Frankl, Zur Biographie F. G. (Vienna, 1883). *Raimund.* Sämmtliche Werke, ed. Glossy and Sauer, 3 vols. (Vienna, 1881). A characteristic letter of Raimund on the 'Verschwender' is given in Schnorrs Archiv v. 279.

Faust. On the historical Faust: (Text, vol. i. 299) W. Creizenach, in the A. D. B. vi. 583. There is a reprint (Halle, 1878) of the first ed. of the 'Historie,' and a photographic facsimile in Sch., Deutsche Drucke älterer Zeit, ii. (Berl. 1884), Faust's Leben by G. R. *Widmann*, pub. by A. v. Keller (Tüb. 1880) is in fact the Faust-book of Dr. *Pfitzer*. On the origin of the popular book see Hermann Grimm, Fünfzehn Essays, 3rd Series, p. 192—The Faust of *Marlowe* was introduced to the German public by Wilhelm Müller, in a translation (Berl. 1818, with a Preface by A. v. Arnim). On its history in Germany see W. Creizenach, Versuch einer Geschichte des Volksschauspiels vom Dr. Faust (Halle, 1878); also F. Lichtenstein, in the Zs. für österr. Gymn. 1879, p. 918. There was a performance at Berlin which was perhaps attended by Lessing, June 14, 1754 (Schnorrs Archiv xi. 175): another at Strassburg, where Goethe may have been present, in 1770 (ibid. viii. 360)—On *Lessing's Faust.* E. Schmidt in the Goethe Jahrbuch ii. 65 (also iii. 77, iv. 127, as an introduction to Goethe's Faust). The *Johann Faust of Weidmann* exists in a reprint by E. Engel (Oldenburg, 1877). For the *Faust of Julius v. Voss* see W. Menzel's Deutsche Dichtung, iii. 219. *Goethe's Faust.* Annotated editions by Löper (2nd ed. Berl. 1879), Schröer (Heilbr. 1881); Düntzer (Berl. and Stuttg.). Commentaries: Schubarth (Berl. 1830); Deycks, (Frankf. 1855); W. E. Weber (Halle, 1836); C. H. Weisse (Leipz., 1837); Leutbecher (Nuremberg, 1838); E. Meyer (Altona, 1847); H. Düntzer (Leipz., 1850, also Erl.); Hartung (Leipz., 1855); Köstlin (Tüb. 1860); Kreyssig (Berl., 1866); Sengler (Berl., 1873); K. Fischer (Stuttg., 1877); Marbach (Leipz., 1881); Schreyer (Halle, 1881). See Julian Schmidt (Preuss. Jahrb. 39, 361) and Fr. Vischer, Krit. Gänge, ii. 49: new series, iii. 135; Krit. Bemerkungen über G.'s Faust, Part 1 (Zürich, 1857); G 's Faust, neue Beiträge zur Kritik des Gedichts (Stuttg., 1875); Altes und Neues, ii. (Stuttg., 1881), p. 1. See Sch., Aus G.'s Frühzeit, Q. F. xxxiv. 76, 94; Max Rieger, G.'s Faust nach seinem religiösen Gehalte (Heidelberg, 1181), p. 37; and also Sch., in Deutsche Rundschau, 1884, May

INDEX.

Neidhart von Reuenthal, i. 204–206, 218, 249, 259, 363; ii. 339, 367.
Neifen, Gottfr. von, i. 207, 251; ii. 339, 367.
Netherlands, i. 35 (Language); i. 125, original home of 'Gudrun;' i. 253 (Animal epics); i. 261 (Till Eulenspiegel in the Literature of the Netherlands); i. 267 (Brothers of common Life); i. 301 (Latin Drama); i. 326 (Dramatic writings of the Renaissance).
Neuber, Caroline, and her troop of actors, i. 400; ii. 310, 345.
Neuffer, Chr. Ludw., ii. 261.
Neukirch, Benj., i. 372, 373, 381.
Neumark, Georg, i. 359.
Neumeister, Erdmann, composer of Cantatas, i. 351, 373; ii. 345.
Newspapers and Periodicals, i. 285, 375; ii. 345, 349, 376.
Newton, ii. 25, 163.
'Nibelungenlied,' i. 16, 17, 22, 95, 97, 101–115, 118, 125, 127, 130, 132, 139, 200, 252; ii. 339, 360.
Nicolai, Friedr., ii. 51, 249, 391; 'Sebaldus Nothanker,' ii. 61, 290, 347; 'Freuden des jungen Werther,' ii. 132, 289; 'Allgemeine Deutsche Bibliothek,' ii. 134, 347; 'Berlinische Monatschrift,' ii. 134.
Nicolaus, see Jeroschin, Wyle.
Nicolovius, Ludw., ii. 242, 393.
Niebuhr, Carsten, ii. 236.
Niebuhr, Barth. Georg, ii. 241, 243, 350.
Nisami, Persian poet, i. 135.
Normans and Normandy, i. 54, 60, 61, 126; ii. 338.
Norwegian Language, i. 35; 'Saga,' 95 (= 'Saxon legends,' see ii. 361), 116; ii. 359.
Notker, Labeo or Teutonicus, i. 49, 51; 'Psalms,' i. 51, 273; ii. 338.
Novalis, see Hardenberg.
Novels, Tales and Stories, i. 4 (comp. ii. 354), 217, 220, 253, 263; Poetical Novels since Hagedorn and Gellert, ii. 282; Novels in the 19th Century, ii. 294; Collections, ii. 367.
Nuremberg, i. 244–246, 304, 323; ii. 371, 379.

Oberge, Eilhard von, i. 136, 144, 155, 158, 161, 259; ii. 338, 362.
Odoacer, in history, i. 21; ii. 337: in legend, i. 22, 116.

Oehlinschläger, Adam, ii. 303, 350, 402.
Oelinger, Albert, Grammarian, i. 275; ii. 375.
Ofterdingen, Heinr. von, i. 188.
Opera, i. 351; Influence of Italian Opera on German Church Music and the German Theatre—German Opera, ii. 344: (First German O.) i. 394; ii. 155: its culminating point, ii. 177, 383.
Opitz, Martin, i. 316, 319–322, 323, 364 ('Hercynia,' see i. 321), 366, 370, 394 ('Dafne'); ii. 38, 344, 379.
'Orendel,' i. 22, 84, 87, 177; ii. 339, 359.
'Ortnit,' i. 120–123, 259; ii. 339, 361.
Ostrogotha, King of the Goths, i. 21, 22; ii. 337.
Oswald, St., i. 84, 87, 128, 177; ii. 359.
Oswald of Wolkenstein, see Wolkenstein.
Otfried von Weissenburg, i. 40, 42, 44–46, 296; ii. 33, 338, 356.
Otte, 'Eraclius,' ii. 362.
Otto, Bishop of Freising, i. 66; ii. 338, 357.
Otto, the Great, i. 46, 53, 56, 57, 85, 86; ii. 357.
Otto II., i. 53, 57.
Otto III., i. 46, 53; ii. 357.
Otto IV., Margrave of Brandenburg, Minnesinger, i. 208; ii. 339, 367.
Ottokar of Styria, i. 178.

Pamphlet Literature, i. 263.
'Pantschatantra,' collection of Indian Tales, translated into German, i. 260.
Parables, see Fables.
Paracelsus, see Theophrastus.
Passion Music, see Metre and Opera.
Patrick, St., i. 33.
Pauli, Joh. 'Schimpf und Ernst,' i. 295; ii. 341, 377.
Paulinus of Pisa, i. 47.
Paulus Diaconus, i. 47.
'People's Books,' i. 260; ii. 341, 378. 'Volksbüchlein vom Kaiser Friedrich,' ii. 290, 386: 'Volksbüchlein vom Gehörnten Siegfried,' ii. 383.
People's Songs, see Poetry.
Percy, Bishop, Collection of Ballads, ii. 56.
Pestalozzi, ii. 240, 287, 288, 348.
Petrarch, i. 200, 263, 320, 363.

4 (1

END OF VOL. II.